GONDOLIN PRESS

Fr. Paul L. Kramer, B.Ph., S.T.B., M. Div., S.T.L. (Cand.)

TO DECEIVE THE ELECT

VOLUME ONE

Defection from the Faith & the Church – Faith, Heresy, and Loss of Office:

THE CATHOLIC DOCTRINE ON THE QUESTION OF A HERETICAL POPE

gondolin press

TO DECEIVE THE ELECT. VOLUME ONE – *Paul Kramer*

All the literary and artistic rights are reserved. The rights for translation, electronic storage, copy and total or partial adaptation, by any equipment, (including microfilm and photostats) are reserved for all countries. The publisher is at any of the untraceable entitles disposal.

© **Gondolin Institute**
Fort Collins CO

www.todeceivetheelect.com

2019 © Gondolin Institute LLC

ISBN 978-1-945658-13-6 *(soft cover)*
ISBN 978-1-945658-11-2 *(hard cover)*

First Edition: September 2019
Printed in U.S.A.

INTRODUCTION

"The Saint Prophecies great Schisms and Tribulations in the Church."

"The time is fast approaching in which there will be great trials and afflictions; perplexities and dissensions, both spiritual and temporal, will abound… **there will be very few Christians who will obey the true Sovereign Pontiff and the Roman Church** with loyal hearts and perfect charity. At the time of this tribulation a man not canonically elected will be raised to the Pontificate, who, by his cunning, will endeavour to draw many into error and death. [...] except those days were shortened, according to the words of the Gospel, **even the elect would be led into error**, were they not specially guided, amid such great confusion… Sanctity of life will be held in derision even by those who outwardly profess it, for in those days **Our Lord Jesus Christ will send them not a true Pastor, but a destroyer.**"[1]

"What I have dreamed is never to come, it is too painful and I hope that the Lord will not allow the Pope to deny all truths of faith and to put himself in place of God. How much pain I felt in the night, my legs became paralyzed and I could not move any more, for the pain I felt when I saw the Church reduced to a cluster of ruins"[2]

Bruno Cornacchiola
(Seer of the Apparition of Our Lady of Revelation)

On March 17, 2015, I spent the day with Fr. Nicholas Gruner in Slane, Ireland, not knowing that it would be the last time we would ever meet on this earth. One of the last things he said to me was to ask me again to systematically present in book form the argumentation and evidence proving that Pope Benedict XVI did not validly resign from the office of the papacy, and demonstrate that he is still the only

---

[1] *Works of the Seraphic Father St. Francis of Assisi*; R. Washbourne, 18 Patterson Row, London, 1882.

[2] *Il Veggente: Il segreto delle Tre Fontane*; Saverio Gaeta, p. 218 – *'Quello che ho sognato non si avveri mai, è troppo doloroso e spero che il Signore non permetta che il Papa neghi ogni verità di fede e si metta al posto di Dio. Quanto dolore ho provato nella notte, mi si paralizzavano le gambe e non potevo più muovermi, per quel dolore provato nel vedere la Chiesa ridotta ad un ammasso di rovine."*

legitimate Pontiff of the Roman Church. He had been asking me to write on this matter for more than a year, but due to other commitments, I had been unable to make any sustained effort to complete this task.

As his unexpected death approached, Fr. Gruner became ever more convinced of the urgency to prove with a mass of evidence and sound argumentation that Benedict XVI remains in office as the sole Vicar of Christ on earth; and that Francis is a manifest heretic who cannot validly occupy the papal throne. Unfortunately, I was not able to really occupy myself with this work until more than a year after Fr. Gruner's death, when circumstances compelled me to devote my time and energy to finally move toward getting this work done.

When I say circumstances compelled me to get to work on writing the book, I refer to the publication of books and articles that heretically argue that a manifest heretic pope would remain in office until he is judged to be a heretic by the Church – a judgment that neither would ever take place in an ecclesial organization that is occupied in its highest offices by heretics; nor in the Catholic Church which professes as a matter of faith that the pope is the supreme judge in all cases who is judged by no one. I say they "heretically argue" because the idea that any manifest heretic could validly hold office is, as I prove in Volume One of this work, contrary to the doctrine of the universal magisterium of the Church, and also rests on the heretical premise that a manifest heretic (i.e. one who is manifestly a formal heretic) would still be a member of the Church until he is judged a heretic by juridically competent ecclesiastical authority. In my earlier series of articles which I have amplified and revised, and which comprised in embryonic form what eventually became the main body of this volume, I have demonstrated that the Church teaches *de fide*, that the manifest sin of public formal heresy constitutes a defection from the Catholic faith, which by its very nature separates the heretic from the body of the Church; and as a consequence, any officeholder in the Church (including the pope if that were possible), who would publicly defect from the faith into heresy, would automatically lose office *ipso jure*, as is set forth in Canon 194 §1. 2°.

Another heresy I deal with in the first volume, is the newly resurrected opinion which had been defunct for more than a century, that a manifestly heretical pope must first be judged by the Church before losing office. The opinion was generally abandoned after the dogmatic definition of the universal primacy of jurisdiction of the Roman Pontiff explicitly set forth the absolute injudicability of the pope, making it doctrinally untenable and inadmissible to hold that opinion; since *Pastor Æternus* defines *simpliciter*, and therefore without exception, that the pope is the supreme judge for *all cases that pertain to ecclesiastical jurisdiction*; and therefore, as the popes have repeatedly taught in their *ordinary magisterium*, while he is in office, the pope cannot be judged by anyone. Since the solemn definition of the primacy of the Roman Pontiff gave definitive dogmatic force to the doctrine of papal *injudicability*, the proposition that a pope, while holding office, can ever be juridically judged by his subjects for any offense whatsoever was clearly seen to be heretical insofar as it directly opposes the absolute judicial supremacy and immunity of the inherent in the primacy, and therefore was generally abandoned by theologians and canonists after the First Vatican Council. The opinion that a reigning pontiff, by way of exception, could be judged and deposed for heresy had its origin among medieval canonists and remained popular among theologians and canonists for about a century after the Counter-Reformation period, even though it could already have been seen to oppose pronouncements of several popes, of the Fifth Lateran Council, and the Council of Trent. *Pastor Æternus* was the *coup de grâce* that finally put this errant theory out of its heretical misery, and as a consequence, was generally abandoned by theologians. That a true and valid pope while in office can ever be judged by anyone is heresy. The doctrine that a pope while validly holding office can never be judged by anyone for heresy or any other crime is explained in this volume and demonstrated beyond all shadow of doubt to be a *de fide* dogma of the Catholic Church. That a pope can be judged for heresy may only be understood in a qualified sense; namely, that if he were to fall into heresy, he "can be shown to be already judged", (i.e. shown to have already fallen from office), as Pope Innocent III taught in *Sermo IV De Diversis*. This doctrine, already taught in the twelfth century by some early Decretists was adopted and explained theologically by St. Robert Bellarmine and others after him, (notably Ballerini and Gregory XVI), and became the magisterial teaching of the Church beyond legitimate dispute after the codification of Canon Law in 1917. According to can. 188.4° of the 1917 Code, any holder of **whatsoever office** who publicly defects from the Catholic faith into heresy loses office automatically, even before any judgment is pronounced by the competent authority. The opinion that an obstinate public heretic retains office, or remains a member of the Church until he is judged, is contrary to the Catholic faith.

Mons. Nicola Bux[3], a consultor of the Sacred Congregation for the Canonization of the Saints and a former consultor of the Sacred Congregation for the Doctrine of the Faith, explains in the same vein how a manifestly heretical pope falls from office and is judged:

> «In the Decree of Gratian (pars I, paragraph 40, chapter VI) there is this canon: "*No mortal will presume to speak of the pope's guilt, since, appointed to judge everyone, he must not be judged by anyone, unless he deviate from faith*". The distancing and deviation from the faith is called heresy, a word that comes from the Greek 'airesis' and means the choice and absolutization of a truth, minimizing or denying the others that are in the category of Catholic truths… Obviously the deviation must be manifest and public. And in the case of manifest heresy, according to St. Robert Bellarmine, the Pope can be judged.»[4]

Mons. Bux explained, in answer to the question by Aldo Maria Valli, "Don Nicola, are you saying that in case of heresy, just as a heretical Christian ceases to be a member of the Church, does the pope cease to be pope and head of the ecclesial body, and he loses all jurisdiction?":

> Yes, heresy affects the faith and the status of a member of the Church, which are the root and foundation of jurisdiction. This is the thought of the fathers of the Church, especially Cyprian, who dealt with Novatian, antipope during the pontificate of Pope Cornelius (cf. Lib 4, ep 2). Every faithful, including the Pope, with heresy separates himself from the unity of the Church. It is well known that the Pope is at the same time a member and part of the Church, because the hierarchy is within and not above the Church, as stated in Lumen Gentium (n.18). Faced with this eventuality, so serious for the faith, some cardinals, or even the Roman clergy or the Roman synod, could admonish the pope with fraternal correction, could

---

[3] https://www.aldomariavalli.it/2018/10/13/monsignor-nicola-bux-lunita-si-fa-nella-verita/

[4] «Nel Decreto di Graziano (pars I, dist. 40, cap.VI) vi è questo canone: "Nessun mortale avrà la presunzione di parlare di colpa del papa, poiché, incaricato di giudicare tutti, egli non dev'essere giudicato da alcuno, a meno che non devii dalla fede". L'allontanamento e la deviazione dalla fede si chiama *eresia*, parola che viene dal greco *"airesis"* e vuol dire scelta e assolutizzazione di una verità, minimizzando o negando le altre che sono nel novero delle verità cattoliche (ricordo a questo proposito che von Balthasar scrisse un saggio intitolato *La verità è sinfonica*). Ovviamente *la* deviazione deve essere manifesta e pubblica. E in caso di eresia manifesta, secondo san Roberto Bellarmino, il papa può essere giudicato.»

"resist him in the face" as Paul did with Peter at Antioch; they could refute him and, if necessary, call him in order to make him repent. Should the pope be pertinacious in error, we must distance ourselves from him, in accordance with what the Apostle says (see Titus 3: 10-11). Furthermore, his heresy and his pertinacity should be declared publicly, so that he does not cause harm to others and everyone can protect themselves. At a time when heresy was well-known and made public, the pope would ipso facto lose his pontificate. For theology and canon law, pertinacious is the heretic who calls into doubt a truth of faith consciously and voluntarily, that is, with the full awareness that this truth is a dogma and with the full adherence of the will. I remember that one can have obstinacy or pertinacity in a sin of heresy committed even by weakness. Moreover, if the pope did not want to maintain union and communion with the whole body of the Church, as when he tried to excommunicate the whole Church or to subvert the liturgical rites based on the apostolic tradition, he could be schismatic. If the pope does not behave like a pope and head of the Church, neither is the Church in him nor is he in the Church. By disobeying the law of Christ, or by ordering what is contrary to natural or divine law, what has been universally ordained by the councils or the Apostolic See, the pope separates himself from Christ, who is the chief head of the Church and in relation to whom the ecclesial unity is constituted. Pope Innocent III says that the pope must be obeyed in everything, until he turns against the universal order of the Church: in this case, unless there is a reasonable cause, it should not be followed, because, behaving thus, he is no longer subject to Christ and therefore separates from the body of the Church.[5]

---

[5] «**Scusi don Nicola, sta dicendo che in caso di eresia, proprio come un cristiano eretico cessa di essere membro della Chiesa, anche il papa cessa di essere papa e capo del corpo ecclesiale, e perde ogni giurisdizione?**

Sì, l'eresia intacca la fede e la condizione di membro della Chiesa, che sono la radice e il fondamento della giurisdizione. Questo è il pensiero dei padri della Chiesa, in specie di Cipriano, che ebbe a che fare con Novaziano, antipapa durante il pontificato di papa Cornelio (cfr *Lib. 4, ep. 2*). Ogni fedele, compreso il papa, con l'eresia si separa dall'unità della Chiesa. È noto che il papa è nello stesso tempo membro e parte della Chiesa, perché la gerarchia è all'interno e non sopra la Chiesa, come affermato in *Lumen gentium (n.18)*. Di fronte a questa eventualità, così grave per la fede, alcuni cardinali, o anche il clero romano o il sinodo romano, potrebbero ammonire il papa con la correzione fraterna, potrebbero "resistergli in faccia" come fece Paolo con Pietro ad Antiochia; potrebbero confutarlo e, se necessario, interpellarlo al fine di spingerlo a ravvedersi. In caso di pertinacia del papa nell'errore, bisogna prendere le distanze da lui, in conformità con ciò che dice l'Apostolo (cfr. *Tito 3,10-11*). Inoltre la sua eresia e la sua contumacia andrebbero dichiarate pubblicamente,

In the first volume, I examine and explain the theology of defection from the faith and the Church; and refute primarily the erroneous and heretical arguments of the legalist-fundamentalist propagandists of Conciliarism, John Salza and Robert Siscoe, who heretically profess that a Church council possesses the authority to juridically pass judgment on a reigning Pontiff for the delict of heresy; and who heretically defend the thesis that a manifest heretic pope would, even as a manifest heretic who has publicly defected from the faith into formal heresy, remains in office as pope until judged guilty by his inferiors in the Church.

In the second volume I will systematically present the case against Jorge Mario "Francis" Bergoglio, and prove that Benedict XVI is still the only legitimate claimant to the papal throne at this time. This is very easy to prove, and the arguments are so cut and dry that they are easily grasped and readily seen to be conclusive, correct and irrefutable. As always, the more clear, convincing and to the point is my argument, the more Salza & Siscoe reply with obfuscation, distortion, misrepresentation, and even deliberately falsify the text and invert the meaning of my words in order to make my reasoning appear logically incoherent, contradictory, and the product of an unsound mind. The fraud that Salza & Siscoe deliberately employ to obfuscate, falsify and

---

perché egli non provochi danno agli altri e tutti possano premunirsi. Nel momento in cui l'eresia fosse notoria e resa pubblica, il papa perderebbe *ipso facto* il pontificato. Per la teologia e il diritto canonico, pertinace è l'eretico che mette in dubbio una verità di fede coscientemente e volontariamente, cioè con la piena coscienza che tale verità sia un dogma e con la piena adesione della volontà. Ricordo che si può avere ostinazione o pertinacia in un peccato d'eresia commesso anche solo per debolezza. Inoltre, se il papa non volesse mantenere l'unione e la comunione con l'intero corpo della Chiesa, come quando tentasse di scomunicare tutta la Chiesa o di sovvertire i riti liturgici fondati sulla tradizione apostolica, potrebbe essere scismatico. Se il papa non si comporta da papa e capo della Chiesa, né la Chiesa è in lui né lui è nella Chiesa. Disobbedendo alla legge di Cristo, oppure ordinando ciò che è contrario al diritto naturale o divino, ciò che è stato ordinato universalmente dai concili o dalla Sede apostolica, il papa si separa da Cristo, che è il capo principale della Chiesa e in rapporto al quale si costituisce l'unità ecclesiale. Papa Innocenzo III dice che si deve obbedire al papa in tutto, fino a che egli non si rivolti contro l'ordine universale della Chiesa: in tal caso, a meno che non sussista una ragionevole causa, non va seguito, perché, comportandosi così, non è più soggetto a Cristo e quindi si separa dal corpo della Chiesa. Non nascondo, però, che quanto indicato, sebbene sia limpido e liscio nella teoria, nella pratica incontra non poche difficoltà; inconvenienti anche di carattere canonistico».

distort is so systematically applied and systemically pervasive throughout their writings, that I have had to devote an entire chapter of this book to expose just some small portion of their fraud and sophistry. Volume III will focus on the false religion of the counterfeit *conciliar* "Antichurch" (and its Masonic ecclesiology) that was foretold in the Secret of Fatima, in Scripture, and by the ancient Fathers; and which came into being more than half a century ago, and has existed as a cancer growing in the body of the Catholic Church – an alien entity inhabiting the same space as the Holy Catholic Church; and since the election of Jorge Bergoglio, has been in the process of visibly separating itself from the true apostolic Church founded by Our Lord Jesus Christ.

It may come as a surprise to many that Fr. Gruner believed that Benedict XVI, and not Francis, is the only valid Pope of the Catholic Church, but you can hear him explain (on 14 Nov. 2014 in Deerfield, Ill.) and state quite plainly that Benedict, "whatever he was doing, he was not resigning the papacy"; and he added, "that's the mystery which will be explained by the secret [of Fatima]." You can listen to Fr. Gruner explain the matter briefly at this link: https://vimeo.com/228833627.

Briefly, what can be said on Pope Benedict's renunciation (not properly resignation or abdiction), is that Pope Benedict XVI, knowing full well that a valid renunciation of the papacy requires a correctly expressed renunciation of the Petrine *munus*, nevertheless did not renounce the *munus Petrinum*; but very pointedly renounced only the "exercise of the *ministry*", and therefore, the renunciation suffered from a fatal and nullifying *defect of intention*. An officeholder does not renounce his office by merely renouncing the active exercise of the ministry connected with that office, because in canon law, office and ministry are not the same thing. Canon 145 §1 explains that, "An ecclesiastical office is any function (*munus*) constituted in a stable manner by divine or ecclesiastical ordinance *to be exercised* for a spiritual purpose."[6] The exercise of a ministry is not essentially the function of an office (Can. 41), so one who renounces only the exercise of a ministry does so without renouncing his office. The distinction between *munus* and *office* is a conceptual distinction of formal aspects of the same entity – accordingly, "*munus*", which is comprised of the duties pertaining to the function of the office; and the office itself (*officium*), to which that

---

[6] «Can. 145 — § 1. Officium ecclesiasticum est quodlibet munus ordinatione sive divina sive ecclesiastica stabiliter constitutum in finem spiritualem exercendum.»

function pertain. The Petrine *office* is the Supreme Pontificate itself. The *munus* consists in the function of that office, and the *ministry* consists in the execution of acts performed in conjunction with the office. Thus, a functionary to whom is entrusted the mere execution of a ministry to be carried out in conjunction with an office can exercise delegated authority of that office without actually holding that office itself.

I have systematically analysed Benedict's own words (as did even more completely Canon Law Professor Fr. Stefano Violi in his article which appeared in the *Rivista Teologica di Lugano*[7]), in which Benedict very carefully distinguishes between the ministry and the *munus*, and then states his intention to renounce only the ministry, but **not** the Petrine *munus* itself. Not only is this clearly expressed in Benedict's official *Declaratio* of 11 Feb. 2013, but Benedict stated even more explicitly on 27 Feb. 2013 that he received his commitment to serve (i.e. the *munus*) on 19 April 2005, which he said was "for always" and added, "my decision to renounce the active exercise of the ministry does not revoke this." Thus it is clear, as Fr. Violi demonstrated, that Benedict XVI did not validly resign the *office*, but only *the exercise of the ministry*. A renunciation made in this manner is clearly invalid, since to validly resign the office, the pope must **correctly express** his intention to renounce his ***munus***: Can. *"332 § 2 – Si contingat ut Romanus Pontifex* **muneri suo** *renuntiet,* **ad validitatem** *requiritur ut renuntiatio libere fiat et* **rite manifestetur***, non vero ut a quopiam acceptetur."* Not only did Benedict not correctly express any **intention** to renounce his *munus*, but he expressly stated his renunciation of the ministry does not revoke his *munus*. Therefore, his intention was defective, which thereby rendered it null and void; and on the basis of an invalid act of renunciation, he erroneously stated that the act of renunciation vacates the Chair and necessitates a conclave to elect a successor – a clear-cut case of an invalidating **substantial error**: *"Can. 188 — Renuntiatio ex metu gravi, iniuste incusso, dolo vel* **errore substantiali** *aut simoniace facta, ipso iure irrita est."* It is on the basis of this substantial error rooted in a *defect of intention*; and on the erroneous belief that the Petrine office can be shared by two men, i.e., that the pope can remain in office and parcel out the exercise of a portion of his *munus* to a successor in a shared ministry, that Benedict XVI erroneously maintains that his canonically invalid

---

[7] Stefano Violi, *Facoltà Teologica dell'Emilia Romagna — Facoltà di Teologia (Lugano);* **La rinuncia di Bernedetto XVI. Tra storia, diritto e coscienza**; in *Rivista Teologica di Lugano* [Theological Journal of Lugano] (2/2013).

renunciation was "valid". The resulting equivocation in the act, namely, that Benedict clearly stated his intention to retain his *munus*, and at the same time stated that his renunciation vacates the Chair, manifestly nullifies his renunciation; since, such a gross equivocation as this plainly renders the juridical intention of *Declaratio* **unintelligible**, and therefore incapable of having any juridical effect.

The "substantial error" has created the *appearance* that two men in papal attire and both with papal names, and who address each other (in public at least) as "Your Holiness", in some manner share the Petrine *munus*. It is, therefore, patently absurd for anyone to claim that the election and subsequent "unanimous acceptance" of Bergoglio – an acceptance which followed an election occasioned by an invalid renunciation, nullified by a defect of intention, as well as an invalidating substantial error; and therefore an acceptance which took place following an *invalid resignation* – **a "universal acceptance" which includes in some manner both men' claim on the munus**, and which is therefore **not exclusive to one or the other**, since what has been accepted is both men's claim on the Petrine *munus* – and, according to Salza & Siscoe, this "universal acceptance" is somehow supposed to prove that Jorge Mario "Francis" Bergoglio is the validly reigning pontiff, and that Benedict XVI is merely a "former pope" whose renunciation was valid! Just as in so many other questions, Salza & Siscoe apply the doctrine of *universal acceptance* in an entirely oversimplified, fundamentalistic manner, which tramples roughshod over all the critical distinctions which must be taken into account in order to properly apply the principle to the case at hand. It is declared by Paul IV in *Cum Ex Apostolates Officio,* and confirmed by St. Pius V in *Inter Multiplices,* that the election of a heretic to the papacy is invalid, even if he receives universal acceptance and obedience (*adorationem, seu ei praestitam ab omnibus obedientiam*) from the whole Church. Furthermore, the theologians who have elaborated the doctrine that "universal and peaceful acceptance" is a sign confirming the *dogmatic fact* of a valid pontificate, specify that **the one individual *canonically elected*** to the papal throne, universally and *exclusively* accepted by the Church, is indeed the valid successor of Peter; and they apply that principle to the popes of their own day, such as Van Noort, who explains in his day that it is a *dogmatic fact* that Benedict XV is the true pope of the Catholic Church; and another says the same of Pius XI, or of whichever pope happened to be reigning at the time of the publication of their works. Fr Francesco Bordoni[8], explains that it is «De fide tenendum, **quemlibet electum canonice** in Summum Pontificem, de quo constet, esse verum Papam, ac proinde talem nunc esse Innocentium decimum in Papam electrum die 15. Septembris 1644. Coronatum vero die quarta Octobris 1644 eiusdem anni.»[9] Such a *"universal acceptance"* of one man, as existed during those pontificates of men who were *canonically elected to the Supreme Pontificate* does not exist today, since there are **two men elected by the cardinals who both lay claim on the Petrine munus**. There is more than sufficient reason to posit at the very least, *positive doubt* about the canonical validity of Bergoglio's election, due to the apparent and founded doubt in the canonical validity of Pope Benedict's renunciation. Hence, it is obvious that since the applicability of the principle of "universal acceptance" as formulated and explained by theologians is premised on a canonically valid election, it is clearly not applicable to the election of such a claimant as Bergoglio, whose election is doubtfully valid; because two men, both elected by the cardinals claim the *munus* in some manner, and the claims of both on the Petrine *munus* are widely accepted; even though the precise nature of each man's claim on the *munus* is not generally understood. Thus, the inapplicability of the principle of universal acceptance to the present case ought to be obvious, yet Salsa, Siscoe, (and their fundamentalist followers) manifest an incapacity to grasp what is obvious.

Today, unlike before, we do not have one sole claimant to the Petrine *munus*, we have Benedict XVI who renounced the exercise of his active papal ministry, while clearly expressing his intention one day before he relinquished his active ministry (27 Feb. 2013), to not renounce altogether his *munus*, so that somehow, while retiring from the active

---

[8] Father Francesco Bordoni of Parma († 1671), theologian, jurist, and historian, was the most notable Franciscan friar of his time, and was described by the Franciscan historian Luke Wadding as «vir doctus varioque scientiarum genere ornatus.» He was a man of vast culture, whose writings span multiple genres – dogmatic and moral theology, canonical, historical, literary, and hagiographical. Fr. Bordoni was a theological consultor for the City of Parma and Synodal Examiner, and later Minister General of the Order (1653-1659). He was also a Marian Doctor and zealous defender of the Immaculate Conception.

[9] P. Francesco Bordoni, *Sacrum Tribunal Judicum In Causis Sanctæ Fidei Contra Hæreticos Et Hæresi Suspectos,* Romæ, MDCXLVIII, *Cap. V. De Romano Pontifice,* p. 114.

ministry, he could in some manner continue to be pope and remain in the Petrine office "in the service of prayer", retaining a passive exercise of the papal ministry while relinquishing the power of governance: "I no longer bear the power of office for the governance of the Church, but in the service of prayer I remain, so to speak, in the enclosure of Saint Peter." That he intended by these words to mean that he does not renounce the papacy *per se*, but only the *active exercise of the papal ministry*, and intends to remain permanently in the Petrine office in a passive capacity, is clear from his words at the beginning of the paragraph: "Here, allow me to go back once again to 19 April 2005. The real gravity of the decision [to accept the *munus* of the papacy] was also due to the fact that **from that moment on I was engaged always and forever by the Lord**. ... The 'always' is also a "for ever" – **there can no longer be a return to the private sphere**. My decision to **renounce the active exercise of the ministry does not revoke this**."[10] With these words Benedict XVI states explicitly that the gravity of his decision to accept the papacy consisted in the fact that he was thereby engaged (*impegnato*) in a *commitment* (A commitment, '*un impegno*' in Italian, in Latin is *munus*.), received from Christ, which is "for always", and his "decision to renounce the active exercise of the ministry does not revoke this." Thus, Benedict did not renounce the Petrine office or its ministry, but only the active exercise of the ministry. He then goes on to say that he will no longer wield the power of office, but will remain "within the enclosure of St. Peter". Marco Tosatti, quotes a passage of Antonio Socci's latest book, *The Secret of Benedict XVI*, which gets to the crux of the matter: «"So, for Benedict XVI we must ask ourselves: did he really renounce the Petrine ministry altogether? Is he no longer Pope?" Socci answers: "From the subjective point of view we can therefore say that his intention – which is decisive to define the act he did – was not to be no longer Pope... It is clear that — despite having made a renunciation of the papacy (but what kind?) he has intended to remain still pope, albeit in an enigmatic way and in an unprecedented form, which has not been explained (at least until a certain date) ". [...] And in fact we must remember that Benedict said, speaking of the Roman pontiff: "The

---

[10] «Qui permettetemi di tornare ancora una volta al 19 aprile 2005. La gravità della decisione è stata proprio anche nel fatto che da quel momento in poi ero *impegnato* sempre e per sempre dal Signore. Sempre [...] Il "sempre" è anche un "per sempre" – non c'è più un ritornare nel privato. La mia decisione di rinunciare all'esercizio attivo del ministero non revoca questo."»

"always" is also "forever" – there is no longer a return to private life. My decision to renounce the active exercise of the ministry does not revoke this.".»[11]

It was already clearly expressed in the text of his official *Declaratio* of renunciation, what was the reason why Pope Benedict decided to withdraw from the active *administration of his munus*. He states as the reason for his decision, his waning energy and consequent inability to administer the official duties of the papacy due to advanced age: *Conscientia mea iterum atque iterum coram Deo explorata ad cognitionem certam perveni vires meas ingravescente aetate non iam aptas esse ad munus Petrinum aeque administrandum*. However, he states his awareness of *the spiritual nature of the official service*, i.e. the *munus* of the Petrine office; to wit, it is not merely active and verbal, but is to be fulfilled to no lesser degree by praying and suffering: *Bene conscius sum hoc munus secundum suam essentiam spiritualem non solum agendo et loquendo exsequi debere, sed non minus patiendo et orando*. It is this *passive function of the office* that he expressly stated was the reason for his intention to retain his *munus* in his above cited discourse of 27 Feb. 2013. It was only the active service, the execution of the ministry regarding grave affairs of the Church and proclaiming the gospel, which he said he could no longer adequately perform: *Attamen in mundo nostri temporis rapidis mutationibus subiecto et quaestionibus magni ponderis pro vita fidei perturbato ad navem Sancti Petri gubernandam et ad annuntiandum Evangelium etiam vigor quidam corporis et animae necessarius est, qui ultimis mensibus in me modo tali minuitur, ut incapacitatem meam ad ministerium mihi commissum bene administrandum agnoscere debeam*. Therefore, in the next sentence he declares his intention to renounce that active ministry: *Quapropter bene*

---

[11] https://www.marcotosatti.com/2018/11/27/il-segreto-di-benedetto-xvi-il-nuovo-libro-di-antonio-socci-pone-domande-inquietanti-in-attesa-di-risposte/.

«"Così, per Benedetto XVI dobbiamo chiederci: ha davvero rinunciato del tutto al ministero petrino? Non è più papa?". Risponde Socci: "Dal punto di vista soggettivo possiamo dunque affermare che la sua intenzione – che è decisiva per definire l'atto che ha compiuto – non era quella di non essere più papa... È evidente che – pur avendo fatto una rinuncia relativa al papato (ma di che tipo?) egli ha inteso rimanere ancora papa, sia pure in un modo enigmatico e in una forma inedita, che non è stata spiegata (almeno fino a una certa data)". [...] E in effetti bisogna ricordare che Benedetto disse, parlando del pontefice romano: "Il "sempre" è anche un "per sempre" – non c'è più un ritornare nel privato. La mia decisione di rinunciare all'esercizio attivo del ministero non revoca questo".»

conscius ponderis huius actus plena libertate declaro me ministerio Episcopi Romae, Successoris Sancti Petri, mihi per manus Cardinalium die 19 aprilis MMV commisso renuntiare ita ut a die 28 februarii MMXIII, hora 20, sedes Romae, sedes Sancti Petri vacet et Conclave ad eligendum novum Summum Pontificem ab his quibus competit convocandum esse. As the Professor of Canon Law, Fr. Stefano Violi (quoted below) says, Benedict XVI did not resign the papal office, but only its administration.

Since the Petrine office is indivisible (as Domenico Gravina O.P. already explained ca. 1610, long before the solemn definition of the Primacy of the Roman Pontiff), it cannot be shared in an "expanded ministry".[12] Cardinal Manning explains,[13] «Gravina teaches as follows: "To the Pontiff, as one (person) and alone, it was given to be the head;"[14] and again, "The Roman Pontiff for the time being is one, therefore he alone has infallibility."[15]» Later in the same century that Gravina wrote on the papacy, Fr. Francesco Bordoni explained in the same vein that Vatican I defined, that it pertains to the nature of the primacy that its holder, holding highest office is *first* in rank (Tum quia, Papatus est prima

---

[12] Bordoni, *Op. cit.* p. 140 – «An duo Summi Pontifices simul, vel successive creari possint a Collegio Cardinalium, qui communiter vel divisum concorditer gubernent Ecclesiam [?] ... [num. 120] Unum caput vivens, & visibile semper fuit in Ecclesia Dei militante, ita quod plures Papas repugnant simul esse... si quandoque visi fuerunt plures Pontifices Summi, illi tales non erant, sed intrusi, illegitimi, & nullius auctoritatis, vocati Antipapæ, qui indiversis conciliis coacti fuerunt cedere, seu potius spoliati fuerunt iniqua possessione præsentæ dignitatis. Quod repugnet simultanea pluralitas Papatus probatur...Tum quia Papatus non esset suprema dignitas, si duo (p. 141) simul esse possent, siquidem unus de necessitate deberet subesse alteri. Vide dicta præcedenti *cap. sub. q:3.* (p. 96. Num. 31) Quæ faciunt ad rem. [...]: Quarto demum unitas Ecclesiæ desumitur ex unitate capitis, qui in tota Ecclesia unus est Dominus, & Christus Iesus... quam capitis dignitatem communicavit Petro, & eius successoribus... Unitas igitur Ecclesiæ salvatur in unitate capitis Romani Pontificis...» [And he concludes saying only Peter was pope, to whom only was said, *Feed my sheep.*]

[13] Cardinal Henry Edward Manning, *The Vatican Council and its Definitions*, Second Edition, New York & Montreal, 1871, p. 105.

[14] "Uni et soli Pontifici datum est esse caput." — Gravina, *de supremo Judice controv. Fidei*, quæst. i. apud Rocaberti, tom. viii. p. 392.

[15] "Nullus in terra reperitur alter, qui cæteris sit in fide firmior et constantior sciatur esse quam unus Pontifex Romanus pro tempore; ergo et ipse solus habet infallibilitatem." — Gravina, quæst. ii. apud Rocaberti, tom. viii. p. 422.

dignitas, ergo omnes alias excedere habet)[16]. Now *first* is the ordinal form of **one**, and **one** *is by definition* **an individual**. *That which is by nature individual is incapable of division, and therefore cannot be shared with a plurality in such a manner that the office of the Pope and the Bishop of Rome could be divided between two men.*[17] St. Vincent Ferrer explained in his *Treatise on the Modern Schism*:

> It is true of faith that the pope has full authority over all. As Christ said to Peter: and whatsoever thou shalt bind upon earth, it shall be bound also in heaven: and whatsoever thou shalt loose upon earth, it shall be loosed also in heaven. (Mt. XVI, 19). If there were two popes at once one would have more power than the other, or not? If one did not have more power than the other, neither would be pope because the pope has authority over all, as stated above. If the lower had it he would not be pope. So the Lord promised speaking by Ezekiel: I will save my flock, and will never be prey to the nations; I will raise up for her only one pastor, who will shepherd them (Ez. XXXIV, 28 and 31). For all these reasons it is clear that it is wrong to believe that the two chosen in question are true popes. Therefore, erring very seriously who, in an effort to obtain graces and dispensations, or achieve any kind of privileges, go to each other, revering like real popes. For being true that both cannot be popes one of them is an apostate and antipope. It is clear that those in their pleas revere both as such; they can not escape to the penalties and curses prescribed at the canon of the Decree begins in the name of the Lord... (J. Gratianus, Decretum (Concordantia discordantium canonum) 1, dist. 23, e. 1: 44 In nomine Domini).[18]

---

[16] Bordoni, *Op. cit.* p. 116 — «Dignitas Papatus a Christo soli Petro, & in eius persona omnibus successoribus, ut supra probatum fuit, non autem aliis Apostolis promissa, & tradita fuit, quia Christus loquendo de hac dignitate semper verba direxit tantum ad Petrum sive in promissione, sive in collatione eiusdem; ... sermo semper a Christo dirigitur solummodo ad Petrum, & numquam ad alios Apostolos... [p. 124] Tum quia, Papatus est prima dignitas, ergo omnes alias excedere habet, & sibi subijcere atque continere, ut Monarchia sit perfectissima in Pontificatu.»

[17] *Ibid., cap. iv.* p. 99: «Romana Ecclesia in persona Romani Pontificis est caput, mater, & magistra omnium fidelium, super quos primatum obtinuit, Est caput omnium Ecclesiarum...» [*cap. v.* p. 109-110] Eadem est dignitas Episcopatus & Papatus in Romano Pontifice, et utruamque habuit S. Petrus in urbe Roma, ubi resedit, ut Episcopus, & ut Papa. [...] coincident in Pontifice Romano Episcopatus, & Papatus.»

[18] «Sexta. Es verdad de fe que el papa tiene potestad plena sobre todos; por lo cual dijo Cristo a Pedro: Cuanto atares en la tierra será atado en los cielos, u cuanto desatares en la tierra será desatado en los cielos (Mt. XVI, 19). Si hubiera

The singularity of the Petrine primacy is clearly defined in *Pastor Æternus* with these words[19]:

> «And it was to Peter alone that Jesus, after his resurrection, confided the jurisdiction of supreme pastor and ruler of his whole fold, saying: Feed my lambs, feed my sheep. (John. XXI, 15-17) To this absolutely manifest teaching of the sacred scriptures, as it has always been understood by the Catholic Church, are clearly opposed the distorted opinions of those who misrepresent the form of government which Christ the lord established in his church and deny that Peter, in preference to the rest of the apostles, taken singly or collectively, was endowed by Christ with a true and proper primacy of jurisdiction. The same may be said of those who assert that this primacy was not conferred immediately and directly on blessed Peter himself, but rather on the church, and that it was through the church that it was transmitted to him in his capacity as her minister. Therefore, if anyone says that blessed Peter the apostle was not appointed by Christ the lord as prince of all the apostles and visible head of the whole church militant; or that it was a primacy of honour only and not one of true and proper jurisdiction that he directly and immediately received from our lord Jesus Christ himself: let him be anathema.»[20]

---

dos papas a la vez, o el uno tendría más potestad que el otro, o no. Si uno no tuviera más potestad que el otro, ninguno de los dos sería papa, porque el papa tiene potestad sobre todos, como queda dicho. Si la tuviera, el inferior no sería papa. Así prometió el Señor, hablando por Ezequiel: Yo salvaré a mi grey, y no será jamás presa de las gentes; suscitaré para ella un pastor único, que la apacentará (Ez. XXXIV, 28 y 31). Por todas estas razones aparece claro que no es lícito creer que los dos elegidos en cuestión son verdaderos papas. Por consiguiente, yerran muy gravemente quienes, con el afán de obtener gracias y dispensas, o por alcanzar cualquier clase de privilegios, acuden a uno y otro, reverenciándolos como papas auténticos. Pues siendo cierto que no pueden ser papas los dos, sino que uno de ellos es apostático y antipapa, es evidente que quienes en sus súplicas reverencian a los dos como tales, no escapan a las penas y maldiciones prescritas en aquel canon del Decreto que comienza: En el nombre del Señor... (J. Gratianus, Decretum (Concordantia discordantium canonum) 1, dist. 23, e. 1: 44 In nomine Domini"). Y nadie puede ser excusado en esto por ignorancia, como se verá en lo que sigue.» [*Tratado del cisma moderno de la Iglesia Capitulo I Sexta*]

[19] English version by *Papal Encyclicals Online*.
[20] «...uni Simoni Petro contulit Iesus post suam resurrectionem summi pastoris et rectoris iurisdictionem in totum suum ovile dicens: Pasce agnos meos: Pasce oves meas (Ioan. XXI, 15-17). Huic tam manifestae sacrarum Scripturarum doctrinae, ut ab Ecclesia catholica semper intellecta est, aperte

The singular Petrine primacy is transmitted to Peter's individual successors: «... the holy and most blessed Peter, prince and head of the apostles, the pillar of faith and the foundation of the catholic church, received the keys of the kingdom from our lord Jesus Christ, the saviour and redeemer of the human race, and that to this day and for ever he lives and presides and exercises judgment in his successors the bishops of the holy Roman see, which he founded and consecrated with his blood. (Cf. Ephesini Concilii Act. III) Therefore whoever succeeds to the chair of Peter obtains by the institution of Christ himself, the primacy of Peter over the whole Church.»[21] The key word in this text is *"he"* ("is" in Latin), the ***individual successor*** of Peter who at any given time occupies the Chair of Peter. And most definitively,

> «Wherefore we teach and declare that, by divine ordinance, the Roman church possesses a pre-eminence of ordinary power over every other church, and that this jurisdictional power of the Roman pontiff is both episcopal and immediate. Both clergy and faithful, of whatever rite and dignity, both singly and collectively, are bound to submit to this power by the duty of hierarchical subordination and true obedience, and this not only in matters concerning faith and morals, but also in those which regard the discipline and government of the church throughout the world. In this way, by unity with the Roman pontiff in communion and in profession of the

---

opponuntur pravae eorum sententiae, qui constitutam a Christo Domino in sua Ecclesia regiminis formam pervertentes negant, ***solum Petrum prae ceteris Apostolis, sive seorsum singulis sive omnibus simul, vero proprioque iurisdictionis primatu fuisse a Christo instructum***; aut qui affirmant, eundem primatum non immediate, directeque ipsi beato Petro, sed Ecclesiae, et per hanc illi ut ipsius Ecclesiae ministro delatum fuisse. Si quis igitur dixerit, beatum Petrum Apostolum non esse a Christo Domino constitutum Apostolorum omnium principem et totius Ecclesiae militantis visibile caput; vel eundem honoris tantum, non autem verae propriaeque iurisdictionis primatum ab eodem Domino nostro Iesu Christo directe et immediate accepisse; anathema sit.»

[21] «sanctus beatissimusque Petrus, Apostolorum princeps et caput, fideique columna et Ecclesiae catholicae fundamentum, a Domino nostro Iesu Christo, Salvatore humani generis ac Redemptore, claves regni accepit: qui ad hoc usque tempus et semper in suis successoribus, episcopis sanctae Romanae Sedis, ab ipso fundatae, eiusque consecratae sanguine, vivit et praesidet et iudicium exercet (Cf. Ephesini Concilii Act. III). Unde quicumque in hac Cathedra Petro succedit, *is* secundum Christi ipsius institutionem primatum Petri in universam Ecclesiam obtinet.»

same faith, the church of Christ becomes one flock under one supreme shepherd. This is the teaching of the catholic truth, and no one can depart from it without endangering his faith and salvation.» [22]

Thus the first Vatican Council solemnly declares that no one, except at the cost of their faith and salvation, can deviate from the doctrine of Catholic truth that the Church of Christ is **one flock under one supreme pastor**. The doctrine of the *singularity* of the Primacy of the Roman Pontiff, defined in *Pastor Æternus*, is the basis of the *singularity* of papal authority set forth in Canon Law: "**Can. 331 — *Ecclesiae Romanae Episcopus, in quo*** permanet *munus* a Domino *singulariter Petro, primo Apostolorum*, concessum et successoribus eius transmittendum, **Collegii Episcoporum est caput, Vicarius Christi atque universae Ecclesiae his in terris Pastor**, qui ideo vi muneris sui suprema, plena, immediata et universali in Ecclesia gaudet ordinaria potestate, quam semper libere exercere valet." From this it manifestly follows that a partial act of renunciation which would thereby make room for an expanded Petrine ministry to be shared by two or more men, is null and void due to a substantial error, as well as to defect of intention; and therefore ***does not suffice to vacate the Chair of Peter.***

It was clearly and without doubt that Pope Benedict did not intend to abandon his office. From the text of his *Declaratio* and his subsequent comments, it is also clear enough that he intended to invalidly expand the Petrine ministry with his invalid act of renunciation by which he attempted to divide the indivisible. Prof. Violi explains the rationale for Benedict's partial renunciation in his article,

---

[22] «Docemus proinde et declaramus, Ecclesiam Romanam, disponente Domino, super omnes alias ordinariae potestatis obtinere principatum, et hanc Romani Pontificis iurisdictionis potestatem, quae vere episcopalis est, immediatam esse: erga quam cuiuscumque ritus et dignitatis pastores atque fideles, tam seorsum singuli quam simul omnes, officio hierarchicae subordinationis, veraeque obedientiae obstringuntur, non solum in rebus, quae ad fidem et mores, sed etiam in iis, quae ad disciplinam et regimen ecclesiae per totum orbem diffusae pertinent; ita ut custodita cum Romano Pontifice tam communionis, quam eiusdem fidei professionis unitate, Ecclesia Christi sit **unus grex sub uno summo pastore**. Haec est catholicae veritatis doctrina, a qua deviare salva fide atque salute nemo potest.»

"Benedict XVI declared his renunciation of the Petrine ministry. Concerning the dictate of the canon, however, he declared his renunciation not of the office but of its administration. A renunciation limited to the active exercise of the *munus* constitutes the absolute novelty of the resignation of Benedict XVI [...] Benedict XVI exercised the fullness of power by depriving himself of all the power inherent to his office... without however abandoning his service to the Church; this continues through the exercise of the most eminently spiritual dimension inherent to the *munus* entrusted to him, which he did not intend to renounce."[23]

Similarly Cardinal Müller spoke in this vein, "We have the case for the first time in Church history that there are two legitimate living popes. Of course, only Francis is the pope, but Benedict is the emeritus, and yet also still to that extent in some way connected to the papacy. [...] Both exercise an office which they have not given themselves that they themselves also cannot define, which already is 'de-fined' by Christ himself, even as it has adapted to the faith-consciousness of the Church. And each experiences in the papal office, as in every other ecclesiastical office, that there is a great burden, which can be borne only by means of grace."[24] These ideas were already expressed on 21 May 2016 by

---

[23] *Between History, Law and Conscience* – Professor Stefano Violi: http://archive.fatima.org/news/newsviews/newsviews031315.pdf
— http://chiesa.espresso.repubblica.it/articolo/1350913 "Benedetto XVI dichiarava la sua rinuncia al ministero petrino. Rispetto al dettato del canone però dichiarava di rinunciare non già all'ufficio ma alla sua amministrazione. La rinuncia limitata all'esercizio attivo del munus costituisce la novità assoluta della rinuncia di Benedetto XVI. [...] Benedetto XVI ha esercitato la pienezza del potere privandosi di tutte le potestà inerenti il suo ufficio, per il bene della Chiesa, senza però abbandonare il servizio alla Chiesa; questo continua mediante l'esercizio della dimensione più eminentemente spirituale inerente al *munus* affidatogli, al quale non ha inteso rinunciare."

[24] Müller: "Wir haben zum ersten Mal in der Kirchengeschichte denn Fall, dass zwei legitime Päpste leben. Natürlich ist nur Papst Franziskus der Papst, aber Benedikt ist der emeritierte und insofern doch auch noch irgendwie verbunden mit dem Papsttum. [...] Beide üben ein Amt aus, das sie sich nicht selber gegeben haben, das sie auch nicht selber definieren können, das ja schon „de-finiert" ist, von Christus selber, auch so wie es sich ausgelegt hat im Glaubensbewusstsein der Kirche. Und jeder erfährt ja im päpstlichen Amt, so wie in jedem anderen kirchlichen Amt, dass es eine große Last ist, die man nur mithilfe der Gnade tragen kann."

Archbishop Georg Gänswein[25], but it has been largely forgotten that Gänswein said exactly the same thing very shortly after the election of Bergoglio in 2013. At that time, Gänswein stated quite explicitly that he was expressing the mind of Pope Benedict, who (he said) could not say it himself, so that he (Gänswein) had to say it for him. Thus, it is certain that Pope Benedict, without intending to abdicate the the office of the Supreme Pontificate, renounced not the *munus*, but only its administration, by renouncing the "active exercise of the ministry". However, such an act is plainly invalid, because a pope who refuses to renounce his *munus*, cannot authorize the election of a successor to whom he would hand over the exercise of the administration of the Petrine *munus*, which can only be validly exercised by the singular individual who holds the Petrine office and its Primacy.

Mons. Gänswein, who was the personal secretary of Pope Benedict and his spokesman has only restated and explained in the vernacular what Pope Benedict already stated in terse canonical Latin on 11 Feb 2013, and reiterated in his final public audience on 27 Feb 2013. Absolutely none of Salza's, Siscoe's, Paul Folbrecht's, Steve Skojek's or Matt Gaspers' comments address the essential point made by Violi, Socci, and myself (as well as a growing number of others), that Benedict XVI in his renunciation stated expressly his intention to retain a partial exercise of his Petrine *munus*, for which reason he renounced only the exercise of the "active ministry", but not the *munus* itself. This plainly stated intention renders the act of renunciation null & void, since the See is not vacated unless the pope abdicates the office, and thus, fully and unequivocally renounces the Petrine *munus*.

Furthermore, Benedict's claim made in his act of renunciation, that his renunciation of the Petrine ministry will vacate the Chair and necessitate the election of a successor is logically inconsistent; and stands in irreconcilable opposition to his statement in the same document expressing his intention to retain the passive exercise of the *munus*; and

---

[25] "Dall'elezione del suo successore, Papa Francesco – il 13 marzo 2013 – non ci sono dunque due Papi, ma di fatto un ministero allargato con un membro attivo e uno contemplativo. Per questo, Benedetto non ha rinunciato né al suo nome né alla talare bianca. Per questo, l'appellativo corretto con il quale bisogna rivolgersi a lui è ancora 'Santità'. Inoltre, egli non si è ritirato in un monastero isolato, ma all'interno del Vaticano, come se avesse fatto solo un passo di lato per fare spazio al suo Successore e a una nuova tappa della storia del Papato che egli, con quel passo, ha arricchito con la centralità della preghiera e della compassione posta nei Giardini vaticani."

his subsequent explicit affirmation that, "My decision to renounce the active ministry does not revoke this." These logically opposed statements constitute a fatal equivocation in the act of renunciation which renders the act null & void. In order that an act have juridical force, in must intelligibly state what the act intends, since that intention pertains to what essentially constitutes the act, which, in order to be valid, must include "those things which essentially constitute the act itself" (Can. 124 §1). If it makes statements that stand in logical opposition regarding the intended juridical effect of the act; its meaning becomes irremediably unintelligible, and therefore canonically invalid – exactly like a doubtful law, it is incapable of having juridical force: *Lex dubia lex nulla.*

What is absolutely certain, however, is that Pope Benedict did not resign the Petrine office. What Benedict did attempt, was the theological impossibility of dividing the exercise of the indivisible *munus Petrinum* between two men. Both Archbishop Gänswein and Prof. Violi, although not grasping the theological impossibility of dividing the exercise of the indivisible *munus Petrinum* between two men, have understood perfectly that this was actually Pope Benedict's stated intention, but hardly anyone else has attempted to gain a precise understanding of the specific nature of the act by analyzing the text of the *Declaratio*, and determining its moral object. Violi has stated it plainly in the passage quoted above:

"Benedict XVI exercised the fullness of power by depriving himself of all the power inherent to his office … without however abandoning his service to the Church; this continues through the exercise of the most eminently spiritual dimension inherent to the *munus* entrusted to him, which he did not intend to renounce."

If Pope Benedict had simply "resigned", "abdicated", or "renounced the Petrine office"; he would not be dressed in white, and not be retaining the papal name and coat of arms. He did not simply "resign". He renounced the "exercise of the ministry", and expressed the intention to continue in the passive aspect of the *munus* of office (which he said was not less important than the active aspect); and for this reason he refrained from renouncing the *munus* itself. This leaves us with two papal claimants: One who refuses to abdicate the office and totally relinquish his claim on the *munus* of office; and the other who fills the partial vacuum left by Benedict's withdrawal from the exercise of papal jurisdiction. Since such an act that would divide the papacy is patently contrary to the divine constitution of the Church, which defined the singularity of the Petrine office in *Pastor Æternus*; the renunciation of Pope Benedict can be judged invalid with absolute certitude.

Against this clearly proven fact, that Benedict XVI did not renounce his *munus*, there are many (like *OnePeter5* blogger, Steve Skojek) who leave out all mention of the important facts and arguments presented by theologians and canonists that disprove their arguments. My full exposition of the case against the validity of Benedict XVI's renunciation will be presented in Volume Two of this work. Skojek leaves out Benedict's statement of 27 Feb. 2013, in which he says he received his papal duties (i.e. the *munus*) on 19 April 2005; and his "decision to renounce the active exercise of the ministry does not revoke this." Skojek replies only to bloggers' arguments against the validity of the renunciation of the office, but studiously ignores the expert analysis of Canon Law professor Fr. Stefano Violi, and other serious and academically qualified authors who argue that Benedict did not resign the office. Skojek is silent about Professor Violi article, as well as Mons. Nicola Bux's questioning the validity of Benedict's "resignation"; and Marco Tosatti's statement saying (as Mons. Gänswein said as Pope Benedict's spokesman in 2013), that Pope Benedict still intended in some manner to remain pope. He mentions the more recent statements of Archbishop Gänswein, but leaves out all mention of Gänswein's 2013 statement, in which he said that Benedict intended to remain pope in some respect; and that Benedict could not say it himself, so he (Gänswein) had to say it for him. Skojek adamantly defends the thesis that the former Buenos Aires nite-club bouncer, who explicitly and notoriously denies such dogmas as the necessity of faith for justification & salvation, the abrogation of the Mosaic Covenant, and the mission of the Church to proselytize all nations, is a valid occupant of the papal throne – a thesis which is plainly impossible according to can. 188. 4° of the 1917 Code, and can. 196 of the 1983 Code. That's all I would have said on this point here in the *Introduction*, but at the risk of turning this *Introduction* into a whole volume by itself, I must say yet something more here, because this point is at present being hotly disputed; although, as I mentioned earlier, a full exposition on this question which will appear in Volune Two of this work.

Pope Benedict XVI did not renounce the *munus Petrinum*; and therefore, the only legitimate question is really not one of Francis or a *sede vacante*, but whether Francis or Benedict is the true pope. I have systematically analyzed Benedict's own words (as did even more thoroughly Canon Law Professor Fr. Stefano Violi), in which he very carefully states his intention to renounce only the Petrine ministry, but **not** the Petrine *munus*. Benedict stated expliciy that he received his committment to serve (i.e. the *munus*) on 19 April 2005, which he said was "for always" and added, "my decision to renounce the active exercise of the ministry does not revoke this." Thus it is clear that Benedict XVI did not validly resign the papacy, since to validly resign the office, as explained above, the pope must correctly express his intention to renounce his *munus*. Not only did Benedict not correctly express any intention to renounce his *munus*, but he expressly stated his renunciation of the ministry does not revoke his *munus*. Therefore, he erroneously stated that his renunciation vacates the chair – thus, the invalidating substantial error explained above. (Can. 188)

According to Benedict XVI, the execution of the *munus* is both the active ministerial and spiritual, and Benedict declared his renunciation not of the office, but of its administration; a limited renunciation of only the active exercise of the *munus*, which constitutes the absolute novelty of the renunciation of Benedict XVI. The Code of Canon Law is absolutely clear – for a papal renunciation of office to be valid, the pope must rightly express his renunciation of the *munus*: "Can. 332 § 2. *Si contingat ut Romanus Pontifex* **muneri suo** *renuntiet,* **ad validitatem** *requiritur* **ut renuntiatio** libere fiat et **rite manifestetur***,* non vero ut a quopiam acceptetur." Benedict XVI did not renounce the *munus*. Canon Law does not define what is a *"pope emeritus"* – that term is the invention of Pope Benedict XVI. "Former pope" is John Salza's specification of the meaning of that term according to Private Judgment, but it does not reflect what was Benedict's stated intention – he did not intend to simply become a *former pope*. If that had been his intention, he would have reverted to his former status of a *cardinal*, as did popes in previous centuries who abdicated the office. It was precisely because it was *not* his intention to renounce his *munus*, that Benedict assumed the title *Pope Emeritus*, and continued on in his execution of the spiritual duties of the Petrine *munus* as he understood them. Benedict did not state that he intended to partially renounce his *munus*, because it was his intention to exercise a shared ministry with a successor who would wield the power of governance inherent in the Petrine *munus* which he did not intend to relinquish. Hence, in his *Declaratio,* he distinguished between the active and the passive aspects of the *munus*, and stated his intention to continue in the passive exercise of the *mumus,* and therefore he conspicuously refrained from renouncing his *munus*, and renounced only the active exercise of the ministry:

> I have come to the certainty that my strengths, due to an advanced age, are no longer suited to an adequate exercise of the Petrine *munus*. I am well aware that this *munus*, due to its essential spiritual nature, must be **carried out not only with words and deeds, but no less with prayer and suffering**. However, in today's world, subject to so many rapid changes and shaken by questions of deep relevance for the life of faith, in order to govern the barque of Saint Peter and proclaim the Gospel, both strength of mind and body are necessary, strength which in the last few months, has deteriorated in me to the extent that I have had to recognize my incapacity to adequately fulfill the *ministry* entrusted to me. For this reason, and well aware of the seriousness of this act, with full freedom I declare that I renounce the *ministry* of Bishop of Rome, Successor of Saint Peter, entrusted to me by the Cardinals on 19 April 2005, in such a way, that as from 28 February 2013, at 20:00 hours, the See of Rome, the See of Saint Peter, will be vacant and a Conclave to elect the new Supreme Pontiff will have to be convoked by those whose competence it is.[26]

Two weeks later in his final public audience, he explained even more clearly his meaning:

> Here, allow me to go back once again to 19 April 2005. The real gravity of the decision was also due to the fact that from that moment on I was engaged always and forever by the Lord. Always – anyone who accepts the Petrine ministry no longer has any privacy. He belongs always and completely to everyone, to the whole Church. In a manner of speaking, the

---

26 «Conscientia mea iterum atque iterum coram Deo explorata ad cognitionem certam perveni vires meas ingravescente aetate non iam aptas esse ad **munus Petrinum aeque administrandum**. Bene conscius sum **hoc munus** secundum suam essentiam spiritualem **non solum agendo et loquendo exsequi debere, sed non minus patiendo et orando**. Attamen in mundo nostri temporis rapidis mutationibus subiecto et quaestionibus magni ponderis pro vita fidei perturbato ad navem Sancti Petri gubernandam et ad annuntiandum Evangelium etiam vigor quidam corporis et animae necessarius est, qui ultimis mensibus in me modo tali minuitur, ut **incapacitatem meam ad ministerium** mihi commissum bene **administrandum** agnoscere debeam. Quapropter bene conscius ponderis huius actus plena libertate declaro me **ministerio** Episcopi Romae, Successoris Sancti Petri, mihi per manus Cardinalium die 19 aprilis MMV commisso renuntiare ita ut a die 28 februarii MMXIII, hora 20, sedes Romae, sedes Sancti Petri vacet et Conclave ad eligendum novum Summum Pontificem ab his quibus competit convocandum esse.»

private dimension of his life is completely eliminated. I was able to experience, and I experience it even now, that one receives one's life precisely when one gives it away. Earlier I said that many people who love the Lord also love the Successor of Saint Peter and feel great affection for him; that the Pope truly has brothers and sisters, sons and daughters, throughout the world, and that he feels secure in the embrace of your communion; because he no longer belongs to himself, he belongs to all and all belong to him.

The "always" is also a "for ever" – there can no longer be a return to the private sphere. My decision to resign the active exercise of the ministry does not revoke this. I do not return to private life, to a life of travel, meetings, receptions, conferences, and so on. I am not abandoning the cross, but remaining in a new way at the side of the crucified Lord. I no longer bear the power of office for the governance of the Church, but in the service of prayer I remain, so to speak, in the enclosure of Saint Peter. Saint Benedict, whose name I bear as Pope, will be a great example for me in this. He showed us the way for a life which, whether active or passive, is completely given over to the work of God.[27]

Hence, Benedict did not renounce the *munus* of the Petrine Office. He still occupies the Petrine Office. As Canon Law Professor Fr. Stefano

---

[27] «Qui permettetemi di tornare ancora una volta al 19 aprile 2005. La gravità della decisione è stata proprio anche nel fatto che da quel momento in poi ero impegnato sempre e per sempre dal Signore. Sempre – chi assume il ministero petrino non ha più alcuna privacy. Appartiene sempre e totalmente a tutti, a tutta la Chiesa. Alla sua vita viene, per così dire, totalmente tolta la dimensione privata. Ho potuto sperimentare, e lo sperimento precisamente ora, che uno riceve la vita proprio quando la dona. Prima ho detto che molte persone che amano il Signore amano anche il Successore di san Pietro e sono affezionate a lui; che il Papa ha veramente fratelli e sorelle, figli e figlie in tutto il mondo, e che si sente al sicuro nell'abbraccio della vostra comunione; perché non appartiene più a se stesso, appartiene a tutti e tutti appartengono a lui.»

«Il "sempre" è anche un "per sempre" – non c'è più un ritornare nel privato. La mia decisione di rinunciare all'esercizio attivo del ministero non revoca questo. Non ritorno alla vita privata, a una vita di viaggi, incontri, ricevimenti, conferenze eccetera. Non abbandono la croce, ma resto in modo nuovo presso il Signore Crocifisso. Non porto più la potestà dell'officio per il governo della Chiesa, ma nel servizio della preghiera resto, per così dire, nel recinto di san Pietro. San Benedetto, il cui nome porto da Papa, mi sarà di grande esempio in questo. Egli ci ha mostrato la via per una vita, che, attiva o passiva, appartiene totalmente all'opera di Dio.» (Benedict XVI General Audience Saint Peter's Square Wednesday, 27 February 2013)

Violi points out, **Benedict did not cite the canon on renunciation of the office, and did not use the proper canonical terminology established by Boniface VIII in «Quoniam alicui»**. Benedict's *Declaratio* does not express the renunciation of the papacy, but distinguished between the *munus* and the *ministerium*, and renounces only the *ministerium*:

> Coming now to the formula used to express the resignation, two data emerge from the *declaratio*: in the first place, the lack of any reference to can. 332 § 2; in the second place a choice of vocabulary different from that of the norm *Quoniam alicui* of Boniface VIII, which speaks of resignation from the papacy (*renuntiare papatui*), rather than from the codicial dictate which regulates the *renuntiatio muneri*. The *declaratio* in fact affirms the *renuntiatio ministerio*. The novelty of Benedict XVI's formula can be grasped in all its scope by reconstructing the argumentative ligatures of the text.
>
> After having recalled the primacy of conscience, Benedict XVI affirms: «My strength, due to old age, is no longer suitable for exercising the Petrine ministry adequately» (37). His conscious awareness considers the supervening unfitness to properly administer the Petrine responsibilities (*munus*) of office. Through this formulation (*vires meas... not iam aptas esse to munus Petrinum aeque administrandum*), the official responsibilities (*munus*) are distinguished from their administration. His forces appear to him unsuitable for the administration of the *munus*, but not for the *munus* itself.[28]

---

[28] «Venendo ora alla formula utilizzata per esprimere la rinuncia, due sono i dati che emergono dalla declaratio: in primo luogo il mancato richiamo al can. 332 § 2; in secondo luogo la scelta di un lessico differente tanto dalla norma Quoniam alicui di Bonifacio VIII che parla di rinuncia al papato (renuntiare papatui), quanto dal dettato codiciale che disciplina invece la renuntiatio muneri. La declaratio infatti afferma la renuntiatio ministerio. La novità della formula di Benedetto XVI può essere colta in tutta la sua portata ricostruendo le articolazioni argomentative del testo.»

«Dopo aver richiamato il primato della coscienza, Benedetto XVI afferma: «de mie forze, per l'età avanzata, non sono più adatte per esercitare in modo adeguato il ministero petrino» (37). La consapevolezza della coscienza riguarda la sopravvenuta inidoneità ad amministrare rettamente l'incarico (munus) petrino. Attraverso questa formulazione (vires meas... non iam aptas esse ad munus Petrinum aeque administrandum), l'incarico (munus) viene distinto dalla sua amministrazione. Le forze gli appaiono inidonee all'amministrazione del munus, non al munus stesso.»

Benedict, explains Violi, distinguished also between the munus and its execution, and distinguished between the various activities that comprise the *executio muneris*:

> In the passage quoted, Benedict XVI proposes two fundamental distinctions with regard to the Petrine munus: first he distinguishes between *munus* and *executio muneris*, evoking Gratian's distinction between *potestas officii* and its *executio*, (39) and taking up the distinction between *munus* and its administration; secondly, it distinguishes between the different activities that make up the *executio*, between an administrative-ministerial execution (*agendo* and *loquendo*) and a more spiritual one (*orando* and *patiendo*).
>
> The *executio* of the Petrine *munus* is then accomplished not only by action and speech, but also, in no less a degree, by prayer and suffering. To the administrative-ministerial execution, which consists in action and teaching, a more spiritual performance is added, not inferior to the first, consisting in suffering and prayer.[29]

Violi then gets to the crux of the matter in explaining what was the alleged theological-juridical justification for Benedict's extraordinary unprecedented partial resignation: **«*The juridical theological foundation is the plenitudo potestatis sanctioned by can. 331. Precisely in the bundle of the powers inherent in the office is also the privative power or the free and unquestionable right to renounce all the powers without renouncing the munus.*»**[30] The pope cannot confer the power of his primacy on a coadjutor in the

---

[29] «Nel passo citato Benedetto XVI propone due fondamentali distinzioni in ordine al munus petrino: in primo luogo distingue tra munus e executio muneris, evocando la distinzione grazianea tra potestas officii e la sua executio (39) e riprendendo la distinzione tra munus e la sua amministrazione; in secondo luogo distingue, tra le diverse attività che compongono la executio, tra un'executio amministrativo-ministeriale (agendo e loquendo) e una più spirituale (orando e patiendo).»

«L'executio del munus petrino si compie allora non solo con l'azione e la parola, ma anche, non in grado minore, con la preghiera e il patire. All'adempimento amministrativo-ministeriale, che consiste nell'azione e nell'insegnamento, si aggiunge un adempimento più spirituale, non inferiore al primo, consistente nel patimento e nella preghiera.»

[30] «Il fondamento teologico giuridico è la *plenitudo potestatis* sancita dal can. 331. Proprio nel fascio delle potestà inerenti l'ufficio è compresa anche la potestà privativa ovvero la facoltà libera e insindacabile di rinunciare a tutte le potestà stesse senza rinunciare al *munus*.»

manner that he can deprive a bishop, who remains in office, of his power, and confer it on an apostolic delegate. The difference between the episcopal office and the Petrine office is that the bishop receives his jurisdiction not directly and immediately from God, but it is given to him mediately by a grant from the pope[31]; but the pope receives his power immediately from God. For this reason, the pope has the power to deprive a bishop of his jurisdiction; but for so long as he remains pope, he cannot deprive himself of the power of jurisdiction which was immediately conferred upon him singularly by God, and therefore inalienably and properly belongs to the holder of the Petrine office. Hence, he can only deprive himself of the power of his office by renouncing the office itself and every claim on its *munus*. A papal renunciation by which a pope would attempt to deprive himself of the power which was exclusively conferred upon himself as the sole individual who may exercise that power in virtue of his office as the successor of Peter; and which would attempt to confer on another that power which only God can confer, namely, the power to execute some aspect of the Petrine *munus*, which is exclusive to the holder of the Primacy, and therefore non-transferrable, would be certainly invalid, because it would directly violate the divine constitution of the Church decreed by Christ as *"one flock under one supreme pastor"*.

In his Catholic Family News article, *Socci's Thesis Falls Short: Review of 'The Secret of Benedict XVI'*, Prof. Roberto de Mattei fails to address the points argued by Prof. Violi, and summarized by Antonio Socci. De Mattei erroneously attributes a false premise (an indelible sacramental character) as the basis of Socci's argument; but the foundation of Socci's argument is not that at all: Socci merely summarizes the argument of Prof. Violi, whose argument De Mattei does not attempt to refute but merely says Violi and Gänswein "contribute to the confusion". De Mattei does not address the arguments presented by Violi, but gratuitously dismisses them as "bizarre". De Mattei observes, «Among the best works which refute this attempt to re-define the pontifical Primacy, there is an accurate essay by Cardinal Walter Brandmüller entitled *Renuntiatio Papae. Alcune riflessioni storico-canonistiche* ("*Archivio Giuridico*" 3-4 [2016], pp. 655- 674). The tradition and praxis of the Church affirms with clarity, affirms the cardinal, that one man and one

---

[31] «... *giurisdizione particolare*... vien loro [ai Vescovi] communicata dalla Chiesa per mezzo del papa suo capo.» [Gregorio XVI, *Op. cit. Discorso Preliminare*, §. LXVIII. p. 58.

man only is the Pope, inseparable in his unity and in his power. "The substance of the Papacy is thus clearly defined by Sacred Scripture and by the authentic Tradition, and so no Pope is authorized to redefine his office" (p. 660).» I have not read Cardinal Brandmüller's essay, since I am in no need of being convinced that "one man and one man only is the Pope, inseparable in his unity and in his power;" but the man who might greatly need convincing on this point is Pope Benedict XVI. Prof. de Mattei remarks, «If Benedict XVI believes that he is still the Pope, simultaneously with Francis, he would negate the truth of Faith by which there exists only one Vicar of Christ, and he would have to be considered a heretic or suspected of heresy.» If that is what he does in fact believe, then he would certainly have to be considered suspect of heresy; but such a belief strongly appears to be approvingly endorsed in his article, *Der Primat des Papstes und die Einheit des Gottesvolkes*, which appeared in a work which he edited, *Dienst an der Einheit*. In that article, Joseph Ratzinger wrote, "Corresponding to the triune nature of God, the Church must be led by a triumvirate, whose three occupants together are the pope. It was not lacking in resourceful speculation, which (somewhat following Solovyov's story of the Antichrist) found that, in this way, a Roman Catholic, an Orthodox and a Christian from the Reformation confessions together could form the Pope-Troika. Thus, directly from theology, the concept of God, the closing formula of ecumenism, seemed to have squared the circle, through which the papacy, the chief annoyance of non-Catholic Christendom, must become the definitive vehicle for the unity of all Christians."[32] These are the words of a man who is clearly receptive to the idea of a shared Petrine ministry, and who has no problem with it.

Matt Gaspers is also wrong on this point. Gaspers, in a group e-mail discussion, begins by assuming the conclusion in his premise (petitio

---

[32] *Dienst an der Einheit*, Patmos, Düsseldorf, 1978, p. 167: "Entsprechend der Dreipersönlichkeit Gottes müsse auch die Kirche durch ein Dreierkollegium geleitet werden, dessen drei Inhaber zusammen der Papst seien. Dabei fehlte es nicht an findigen Spekulationen, die (etwas unter Anlehnung an Solowjews Geschichte vom Antichrist) herausfanden, daß auf diese Weise ein römischer Katholik, ein Orthodoxer und ein Christ aus dem Bereich der reformatorischen Bekenntnisse zusammen die Papst-Troika bilden könnten. Damit schien, unmittelbar aus der Theo-logie, dem Gottesbegriff, die Schlußformel der Ökumene gefunden, die Quadratur des Kreises geleistet, durch die das Papsttum, Hauptärgernis der nicht-katholischen Christenheit, zum definitiven Vehikel für die Einheit aller Christen werdem müßte."

principii): Premise — «***the abdication*** of Pope Benedict XVI in February 2013 made possible the election of Pope Francis»; thus he assumes that Benedict's renunciation of the exercise of the Petrine *ministry* was an abdication of the Petrine *office*. This **fallacious assumption** is the basis of his next assertion: Conclusion —

> «Until we are explicitly told otherwise by Benedict himself, or it is proven and formally declared by proper Church authorities, **we must assume his resignation was valid** according to the conditions set forth in the current Code of Canon Law (1983): "If it happens that the Roman Pontiff resigns his office, it is required for validity that the resignation is made freely and properly manifested but not that it is accepted by anyone." (Can. 332 §2) All the same, however, it certainly seems to be a "very serious mystery," as Archbishop Negri noted – perhaps a "mystery of iniquity" (2 Thess. 2:7)»

The canon in question states:

> Can. 332 — § 2. Si contingat ut Romanus Pontifex muneri suo renuntiet, ad validitatem requiritur ut renuntiatio libere fiat et ***rite manifestetur***, non vero ut a quopiam acceptetur.

> Here is the www.vatican.va website translation: "§2. If it happens that the Roman Pontiff resigns his office, it is required for validity that the resignation is made freely and properly manifested but not that it is accepted by anyone."

For a juridic act to be valid, that which essentially constitutes the act must be properly expressed in the act, or else it is not valid: "Can. 124 §1. For the validity of a juridic act it is required that ...those things which essentially constitute the act itself, be present".[33] What essentially constitutes the *renuntiatio muneris* is the properly expressed intention to vacate the office. As mentioned above, canon law distinguishes clearly between *munus* and *ministerium*. The *office* and its *ministry* are not the same thing. The Petrine *munus*, as a *stable function* constituted by divine ordinance is an *office*, and is not merely a *ministerium*, i.e. a *ministry*, which can be exercised without a stable *munus*. Therefore, the above cited canon on papal renunciation of office refers to the renunciation of the papal *munus*, and not merely the *ministerium*. The mere execution of a

---

[33] «Can. 124 — § 1. Ad validitatem actus iuridici requiritur ut a persona habili sit positus, atque in eodem adsint quae actum ipsum essentialiter constituunt, necnon sollemnia et requisita iure ad validitatem actus imposita.»

ministry consists in the *active exercise* of that ministry, which is distinct from the office itself. According to the norm of canonical tradition which is is at present expressed in the above cited canon: for a pope to validly resign the Pontificate, he must rightly manifest, i.e. *properly express* juridically the renunciation of his *munus* (*ad validitatem requiritur ut renuntiatio* [...] *rite manifestetur*). One does not properly express the renunciation of the *munus* by renouncing the exercise of the ministry while declaring at the same time in what limited manner one intends to continue to exercise the *munus*; and consequently, the renunciation of the active exercise of the *ministry*, distinct from the office itself, does not suffice to vacate the office.

Benedict made clear his intention not to renounce the *munus*, and therefore, not to renounce the office or the Pontificate to which the *munus* pertains; but only the active exercise of the ministry, i.e. the execution of the duties of office which is exercised in virtue of the *munus Petrinum*. Gaspers admits the distinction between *munus* and *ministerium*: «The specific words in question are munus and ministerium, both of which are translated simply as "ministry," but they bear distinct connotations that warrant attention.» However, in Benedict's *Declaratio* of 11 Feb. 2013 and his allocution of 27 Feb. 2013, he carefully distinguished between *munus* and *ministerium*, distinguishing between the two, so it is inadmissible when dealing with a legal document that uses precise terminology that properly distinguishes the difference of meaning of terms, to indiscriminately interpret against the letter of canon law in such a manner that negates the proper distinctions between them. Hence, by no means can it be rightly interpreted that by declaring his renunciation of the mininstry, Benedict thereby rightly expressed a renunciation of his *munus*.

So, Gaspers is saying that on the basis of a conclusion that assumes its premise, we must assume that Benedict abdicated the Petrine office by renouncing its *munus* – that *munus* which Benedict manifested clearly was not his intention not to renounce, and which he distinguished from the exercise of the active *ministry* which he did renounce; and that therefore, on the basis of the fallacious assumption of that premise, that Benedict abdicated the Pontificate, "Until we are explicitly told otherwise by Benedict himself, or it is proven and formally declared by proper Church authorities, we must assume" – i.e. assume that Benedict's renunciation of the active exercise of the ministry but not the *munus* itself, constituted a valid renunciation of the *munus*, and therefore of the Pontificate, i.e. "we must assume his resignation was valid according to the conditions set forth in the current Code of Canon Law". Thus, according to Gaspers, on the basis of the conclusion assumed in the premise, namely, that Benedict abdicated the office; we must assume, that he validly resigned the office according to Canon Law! Non sequitur! The idea that we must wait for the Church to issue a formal declaration in order to correct one's own misconception which posits an abdication from office that was never actually expressed is patently unreasonable. Pope Benedict XVI already issued a formal declaration which renounced only the active exercise of the ministry while pointedly refraining from renouncing the *munus*. One cannot assume that he renounced what he did not properly renounce, until he declares formally that he did not renounce it, because that would presume a valid juridical effect of a wrongly expressed renunciation of something that was in fact, never renounced!

In another recent article[34], historian Roberto de Mattei commented on arguments invoking "substantial error." Professor de Mattei explained, "The Church is a visible society, and canon law does not evaluate intentions, but concerns the external behavior of the baptized. Canon 124, §2 of the Code states that: 'A juridic act placed correctly with respect to its external elements is presumed valid.' [...] Did Benedict XVI intend to resign only partially, by renouncing the *ministerium*, but keeping the *munus* for himself? It's possible, but no evidence, at least to date, makes it evident." He added, "We are in the realm of intentions, Canon 1526, § 1 states: '*Onus probandi incumbit ei qui asserit*' (The burden of proof rests upon the person who makes the assertion.) What Prof. de Mattei did not consider is that the juridic act was not "placed correctly", because the *intention to renounce was not "rightly expressed"* (Can. 332 — § 2); since it *was so equivocally stated, that it remains unclear exactly what he was intending to renounce*. The statute he cites to support his opinion is a canon in the section of the code dealing with contentious litigation in which one party accuses another of wrongdoing – a provision which has no application to the question of the validity of a papal resignation: there is no onus to prove what Benedict intended, but the invalidity of the act is demonstrated by pointing out that Benedict's renunciation suffered the fatal invalidating defect of not clearly stating what it did intend. The same article quoted a theologian who «acknowledged that it is possible that Pope Benedict thought there

---

[34] https://www.lifesitenews.com/news/did-benedict-really-resign-gaenswein-burke-and-brandmueller-weigh-in.

might be a real distinction between *munus* and *ministerium* but was unsure. In that case, he said, Benedict's abdication would be invalid only if he had in his mind the thought: "I only want to resign the *ministerium* if it is in fact distinct from the *munus*." But he said it would be equally possible that, being unsure whether there was a distinction, Benedict could have had in mind the thought: "I want to resign the *ministerium* whether or not it is distinct from the *munus*." In that case, the theologian said he believes the resignation would have been valid.» It is precisely to prevent such situations from occurring, in which it would be necessary to carefully dissect and analyse the text of a juridical act in order to get inside of the mind of the signatory and gain what would be at best a probable understanding of his intention, that Can. 332 — § 2 was worded in the manner that it is. Thus, if its intention is not clear and unequivocal, then the act is null and void. The same article also quoted Cardinal Walter Brandmüller, former president the Pontifical Committee for Historical Sciences, who stumbled in his defense of his belief that: "The resignation was valid, and the election was valid." The article relates, «In our conversation with the German Cardinal, he cited two Roman legal dictums which he said are important to keep in mind: *de internis non iudicat praetor* (a judge does not judge internal things) and *quod non est in actis, non est in mundo* (what is not in the acts [of the process], is not in the world). In judging the validity of any juridical act, Cardinal Brandmüller said we need to consider the "facts and documents" and "not what the people in question might have been thinking."» The problem is that in considering the "facts and documents", it emerges clearly that the document is defective in expressing its intention, for which reason it is plainly seen to be canonically invalid, without any need to theorize about "what the people in question might have been thinking". The article quoted Cardinal Burke, who said, of Benedict's renunciation: "I believe it would be difficult to say it's not valid." The cardinal said, "The *munus* and the *ministerium* are inseparable," he also explained. "The *munus* is a grace that's conferred, and only in virtue of that grace can one carry out the ministry." Indeed, the *munus* is given to the one who must carry out the ministry, and therefore they are inseparable. This is something that Pope Benedict needs to ponder, because his words and actions strongly suggest he is not convinced on these points. Cardinal Burke went on to say, "Once you renounce the will to be the Vicar of Christ on earth, then you return to what you were before," he said. However, if Pope Benedict had indeed renounced the will to be the Vicar of Christ on earth, he would have renounced his *munus* and returned to his former state; but this he did not do, because he intended in some manner to continue in the Petrine *munus* while handing the exercise of the ministry over to another.

The principal argument of Salza & Siscoe in their article which replies to me, and argues in favour of the validity of Benedict's "resignation", expressly assumes the premise that Benedict validly resigned the papacy! (And these are the men who are always falsely and scurrilously accusing me of *petitio principii*.) A plain and simple application of the cited canons proves beyond question that Benedict's renunciation was invalid, and consequently, he is still the only reigning pope. They also speciously (and maliciously) argue with yet another example of *petitio principii*, accusing me of preferring, in Protestant manner, my own "Private Judgment" to the "public judgment of the Church", for my having insisted that Benedict XVI remains in office as the only valid pope. For Salza & Siscoe, the election of Jorge Bergoglio constitutes a "public judgment of the Church", and their argument uncritically assumes as a premise that this "judgment of the Church" was a valid juridical act. However, for a decree, declaration, or a papal election to be validly constituted as a "public judgment of the Church", it must be a valid juridical act. If it is not a *valid juridical act*, **then it is not a "public judgment of the Church".** Neither the renunciation of Benedict XVI (and consequently) nor the election of Cardinal Bergoglio was a valid juridical act, so neither act can be considered to be a public judgment of the Church. I will provide in Volume Two a systematic exposition on the question of whether Francis or Benedict is the legitimate pope; and I will explain on the basis of undeniable, publicly known facts, that Pope Benedict XVI to this day maintains his claim on the Petrine *munus* which he never renounced.

Fr. Gruner also quite correctly explained that a heretic, because he is not Catholic, cannot validly hold the papal office; (https://www.youtube.com/watch?v=t3D6gV2sEnQ), and stated, (although in a qualified manner), that Francis is not a Catholic. Fr. Gruner wanted compelling, systematic argumentation that would conclusively argue the case against Francis, so that he could then confidently state his case against Francis openly in public, and without qualification. Privately, Fr. Gruner stated categorically to some trusted individuals that Benedict, and not Francis, is the pope. One of them was Dr. Peter Chojnowski.[35] He was also heard

---

[35] http://radtradthomist.chojnowski.me/2017/08/what-fr-gruner-actually-thought-and.html?m=1.

pronouncing the name "Benedict" in the prayer for the pope at the Canon of the Mass.

While Fr. Gruner, in the video clip, overstates St. Bernard's case of heresy against Cardinal Pierleoni (who took the papal name, Anacletus II)[36]; it will be shown in this book that his doctrinal principle, namely, that a public heretic, being not Catholic, cannot validly be pope, is entirely correct. The importance of this point cannot be exaggerated, because if a heretic intruder were to usurp the papal throne, he would not be a true and valid pope; because, as Pope Paul IV ruled, and based his ruling on the doctrine, (taught solemnly but not *ex cathedra*), in *Cum ex apostolatus officio* (and then confirmed and renewed by St. Pius V in *Inter Multiplices*[37]), that an external heretic, (even an occult one), even if canonically elected cannot validly occupy the throne of Peter. If he would be proven to have been a heretic before being elected, he would not be the pope and his election would not be valid, even if his election would have been procedurally correct; and that would be so even if he had been generally accepted as pope. This doctrine was taught by medieval canonists since the time of the early Decretists in the twelfth century, and was raised to the level of the papal ordinary magisterium by Paul IV, who made it the basis of his ruling, which he enacted as a statute for the universal Church. While many of the most eminent authors

---

[36] St. Bernard: "The life and character of our Pope Innocent are above any attack, even of his rival; while the other's are not safe even from his friends. In the second place, if you compare the elections, that of our candidate at once has the advantage over the other as being purer in motive, more regular in form, and earlier in time. The last point is out of all doubt; the other two are proved by the merit and the dignity of the electors. You will find, if I mistake not, that this election was made by the more discreet part of those to whom the election of the Supreme Pontiff belongs. There were cardinals, bishop, priests, and deacons, in sufficient number, according to the decrees of the Fathers, to make a valid election. The consecration was performed by the Bishop of Ostia, to whom that function specially belongs." (Catholic Encyclopedia)

[37] «*Et insuper*, **vestigiis felicis recordationis Pauli Papae IV**, *praedecessoris nostri, inhaerendo, constitutionem alias contra haereticos et schismaticos per eumdem Paulum praedecessorem, sub data vide licet Romaese apud Sanctum Petrum, anno incarnationis dominicae millesimo quingentesimo quinquagesimo octavo, quinto decimo kalendas martii, pontificatus sui anno IV, editam, tenore praesentium renovamus et etiam confirmamus, illamque inviolabiter et ad unguem observari volumus et mandamus, iuxta illius seriem atque tenorem.*» **(21.12.1566)**

rightly hold that God would never permit that a heretic would be elected pope, Bellarmine's argument in *De Ecclesia Militante, Cap. X* demonstrates the impossibility that there could be a heretic pope universally accepted and ruling the whole Church who would be secretly deposed by God without being judged by men; yet at the same time, Bellarmine argues in *De Romano Pontifice lib. ii cap. xxx* that it would be impossible for him as a heretic to remain pope as an incapable subject who lacks the necessary disposition to remain pope. This contradiction, which would result if an occult heretic were to be validly elected, sufficiently demonstrates the impossibility that there could ever be a validly elected heretic pope. While it is humanly impossible to ever know if a man is secretly an *internal* heretic, if he is an *external occult* heretic, evidence may be able to be brought against him to prove the invalidity of his claim; and if he is a manifestly formal heretic in a manner that is *public* or soon to become public, it is plainly evident that he is certainly not a valid pope. Heresy does not need to be actually *notorious* or *widely known* to be considered *canonically public*; hence, when it is known with certitude that a claimant is a public heretic as the term "public" is defined in *CIC 1917 Canon 2197* 1°, the Catholic has the right and even the duty to refuse submission and recognition to him. As will be explained in this work, the inconsistencies in the expositions of such eminent ecclesiastical writers as St. Robert Bellarmine, Fr. Francesco Bordoni, and others on this point, ultimately cannot really be always construed to be logical inconsistencies in their own thinking, but rather serve to underscore the problematic nature intrinsic to the logical opposition existing within the notion itself of a heretic pope. However, since the codification of canon law in 1917, the Church's canonical doctrine on the *ipso facto* loss of ecclesiastical office for public heresy is a settled point. The question of how a public heretic losses clerical office is closed.

When the question of the deposition of a heretical pope was still an open question, all the authors who admitted the removal of a manifest heretic, but who rejected an *ipso iure divino* fall from the papacy, held that the Church must first juridically judge the heretic according to ecclesiastical law for the *crime of heresy* before he could fall from the papacy. This is also the position of John Salza and Robert Siscoe. The question is now closed. Since the codification of canon law in 1917 (Canon 188. 4°), the Church's definitive canonical doctrine on this point, expressed in her ordinary magisterium, is that all ecclesiastical offices are lost by the fact alone of public defection into heresy without any declaration (*sine ulla declaratione*), apart from any considerations of penal law. By interpreting the administrative canon on *Tacit Resignation of Office* according to the prescriptions of the *penal section of the code*, Salza & Siscoe fraudulently concoct the opinion that canonical warnings are necessary for the *ipso facto* loss of office to take place. As I have explained in my articles (upon which this book is based), it is not necessary or even possible that there be ecclesiastical warnings administered to a pope; nor can there be a juridical process to judge a reigning pontiff to be a heretic, (that is, if it were possible for a validly elected pope to be a heretic). Ecclesiastical warnings can only be administered by a superior, and therefore cannot be administered to a pope. Furthermore, Cardinal de Lugo[38] (whom I quote later in this volume), considered by St. Alphonsus to rank second only to St. Thomas as a theologian, explained that the pertinacity of formal heresy can sometimes be known without warnings, and that *even the Holy Office, in some penal cases, judged them not to be necessary*. Salza & Siscoe attempt to interpret the Church's doctrine on this and other related points by conflating it with older, contrary opinions, which oppose the more recent decisions of the ecclesiastical magisterium – rather like interpreting the 1854 dogmatic definition of *Ineffabilis Deus* according to the previously formulated contrary opinions of the Dominican School. As will be shown especially in the first volume of this work, this type of fraudulent sophistry is the most frequently chosen weapon of verbal sleight of hand employed by the deceitful duo to deceive even the elect into believing that their doctrinal deviations from the orthodox teaching of Catholic truth represent the mind of the magisterium. This is exactly what Salza & Siscoe do by interpreting the administrative canons on loss of office according to the canons of penal law.

Accordingly, Salza & Siscoe speciously put forth the question on a heretical pope: *but who makes the determination that he is a manifest heretic?* And they assert that only the Church has the authority to make the determination of heresy by *establishing the **crime of heresy**.*[39] The fallacy

---

[38] Juan de Lugo y de Quiroga (1583 – 1660) was an eminent Spanish Jesuit theologian and canonist. *Wikipedia* says of him, «In moral theology he put an end, as Ballerini remarks, to several disputed questions. St. Alphonsus de Ligouri did not hesitate to rank him immediately after the Doctor of the Church St. Thomas Aquinas, "post S. Thomam facile princeps", and pope Benedict XIV called him "a light of the Church".»

[39] "A man becomes Pope when God joins the man elected (the matter) to the pontificate (the form); and he ceases to be Pope either upon death, or when God disjoins the man from the pontificate, either due to the crime of heresy

of their position consists in the failure to recognize that when the **fact** of public defection into heresy is *manifest*, and thus, *obvious to the mind or eye*, it is already *established* **per se** *as a* **manifestly evident fact** (apart from any considerations of penal law), and hence, the defection from the faith is already manifestly *"determined"* as a **patent public fact**, and therefore does not need to be *juridically determined as a* **crime** *in a penal process* before private individuals would have the right to form a judgment of conscience in the matter. As will be shown in Volume One, the Church bases its law on loss of office for public defection from the faith into heresy on the *fact* of the defection alone; and not on whether or not a crime, i.e. a *penal delict*, has been committed in the act of defection; and juridically declared. Thus, the Salza/Siscoe opinion is like saying that even if the rain is visibly falling in a torrential downpour, one may not privately judge that it is raining until a competent tribunal juridically pronounces the formal judgment of the court against the clouds for raining. The reason why it is so important to understand this point is that "Pope" Francis (unlike his Conciliar predecessors who to my mind have not been proven to be formal heretics) can be plainly shown to be a manifest heretic; and since he is therefore not a valid pope, he can solemnly pronounce heretical definitions as a counterfeit pope in even his most solemn but invalid decrees, and thereby lead a vast multitude of souls (who think he is infallible), into heresy and apostasy; since a very large portion of the hierarchy is following him in the stampede into apostasy and out of the Catholic Church. The radical legalism of Salza & Siscoe leads undiscerning Catholics inexorably into the sin of false or indiscreet obedience, because, 1) they mistakenly believe they must give religious assent to every pronouncement of his *authentic magisterium* (which in reality he does not possess), no matter how heretical it may appear to them; and 2) because they must not only resist his evil laws and precepts, but they must not be subject to him, nor recognize any authority in him, nor obey him as their superior in anything. The very act of submission to the pretended authority of an openly heretical enemy of the Catholic faith constitutes *per se* an objectively grave act not only of *indiscreet obedience*; but done in ignorance, constitutes an act of *material schism* as well. Thus, while the *Recognize and Resist* policy of Catholics towards the errant conciliar popes was morally justified from the time of the post-council up to the end of February 2013, when Pope

---

(established by the judgment of the Church) or by resignation." [Salza & Siscoe in, *Is Francis or Benedict the True Pope?*]

Benedict went into what is increasingly seen to be a coerced retirement; it is no longer morally licit to adhere to it for so long as the heretical intruder (or another like him) remains in power, because it is morally wrong and schismatic to recognize and be subject to a manifestly formal heretic.

That Jorge Bergoglio is manifestly a formal heretic is plainly demonstrated by his obstinate and explicit rejection of some of the most basic dogmas of Christian belief – notably his outright and categorical rejection of Christ's explicit teaching on evangelizing and converting all nations; his explicit rejection of the dogma of absolute necessity of faith for justification; his pagan notion of "God" which logically rejects of the dogmatic Christian notion of God as distinct from and infinitely transcending the created universe – a notion of God which he contemptuously dismisses as a "vague idea in the clouds", and a "god spray". I have already written and posted articles on this topic, and on the invalidity of Pope Benedict's "resignation", and in Volume II, I will have more to say on these points.

I can say with absolute certitude that Jorge "Francis" Bergoglio is a formal heretic on the basis of the consideration that it is impossible for him to be in any degree inculpable for denying the most basic and universally known revealed truths of our religion, such as the necessity of faith in God for justification and salvation; because that pertains to the Natural Law which is written in the heart (Rom. 2:15). St. Alphonsus writes, *"Certum est hominem teneri ex lege naturali ad Deum per Fidem, Spem et Charitatem se convertere, et ideo elicere earum virtutum actus"*[40] – and therefore there is besides the patent matter of heresy, the **pertinacity**: the inexcusable form of the sin of heresy, which puts Jorge Bergoglio visibly outside of communion with the Catholic Church:

> *"Hæresis est error intellectus, et pertinax contra Fidem, in eo qui Fidem suscepit. ... Unde patet, ad Hæresim, ut et Apostasiam, duo requiri, 1.* **Judicium erroneum**, *quod est ejus quasi* **materiale**. *2.* **Pertinaciam**; *quæ est quasi* **formale**. *Porro pertinaciter errare non est hic acriter, et mordicus suum errorem tueri; sed est eum retinere, postquam contrarium est sufficienter propositum: sive quando scit contrarium teneri a reliqua universali Christi in terris Ecclesia, cui suum iudicium præferat"* – [St. Alphonsus M. de Liguori, Lib. II. Tract. I. De præcepto Fidei. Dubium III].

---

[40] St. Alphonsus de Liguri, Opera Moralia, Lib. II, Tract. I, De Præcepto Fidei. cap. II.

Since this matter pertains to the Natural Law and is universally known by all Christians to be *de fide*, it is patent and certain that both of the conditions for matter and form are present in Bergoglio's denial of the most fundamental principle upon which all religion is based and hinges on, since in such matters of natural law, "whoever shall have sinned without the law shall perish without the law". (Rom. 2:12).

Jorge Bergoglio is absolutely and most certainly a manifest formal heretic – one who has publicly defected from the Catholic faith. In conscience one has the right to make such a judgment because it *is* a legitimate matter of conscience, and can be known with certitude. All the canons, and teachings against privately judging superiors and prelates do not refer to judgments of conscience, such as the judgment concerning the manifest heresy of one's superior, when it can be known with certitude; but rather, they prohibit judgments that require jurisdiction; and explain that private individuals do not possess the requisite jurisdiction for rendering an official judgment, and therefore they may not presume to judge their superiors juridically, and depose them with force of law. However, the right of conscience to judge privately as a matter of conscience in such cases as that of manifest heresy pertains to divine law, since such judgments of conscience are sometimes necessary for salvation; and such a right is acknowledged in Canon Law: "Can. 748 §1. *All persons are bound to seek the truth in those things which regard God and his Church and by virtue of divine law are bound by the obligation and possess the right of embracing and observing the truth which they have come to know.*" Indeed, the Salza/Siscoe objection that the making such a judgment is forbidden to the private individual who must wait for the public judgment of the Church, and that asserting this right it is an exercise of the Protestant principle of Private Judgment, is not only false, but it effectively nullifies the Rule of Faith which safeguards the conscience of the individual. In Chapter 32 of his classic work on Liberalism (which in one of its variations is precisely the religion of Jorge Bergoglio), Fr. Félix Sardá explains this point:

> Of what use would be the rule of faith and morals, if in every particular case the faithful cannot of themselves make the immediate application; if they were constantly obliged to consult the Pope or the diocesan pastor? Just as the general rule of morality is the law, in accordance with which each one squares his own conscience, dictamen practicum, in making particular applications of this general rule, subject to correction if erroneous; so the general rule of faith, which is the infallible authority of the Church, is and ought to be in consonance with every particular judgment formed in making

concrete applications, subject of course to correction and retraction in the event of mistake in so applying it. It would be rendering the superior rule of faith useless, absurd and impossible to require (168) the supreme authority of the Church to make its special and immediate application in every case upon every occasion, which calls it forth. This would be a species of brutal and satanic Jansenism like that of the followers of the unhappy Bishop of Ypres, when they exacted, for the reception of the sacraments, such dispositions as would make it impossible for men to profit by that which was plainly intended and instituted for them by Jesus Christ Himself. [41]

The opinion that only the Church authorities are able to judge in matters of heresy, and that we cannot know if someone is a heretic by the application of human reason without a pronouncement of Church authority, is patently absurd, since it is by the application of human reason to the matters of faith that ecclesiastical judges reach their conclusions in heresy cases and pronounce judgment. Fr. Sardá explains in the same work the role of reason in forming such private judgments; and explains in the same chapter that the individual is competent to render such judgments by applying human reason enlightened by faith to propositions, opinions, authors and journals of false doctrines:

> 5. The judgment of simple human reason duly enlightened.
> Yes, human reason, to speak after the manner of theologians, has a theological place in matters of religion. Faith dominates reason, which ought to be subordinated to faith in everything. But it is altogether false to pretend that reason can do nothing, that it has no function at all in matters of faith; it is false to pretend that the inferior light, illuminated by God in the human understanding, cannot shine at all, because it does not shine as powerfully or as clearly as the superior light. Yes the faithful are permitted and even (166) commanded to give a reason for their faith, to draw out its consequences, to make applications of it, to deduce parallels and analogies from it. It is thus by use of their reason that the faithful are enabled to suspect and measure the orthodoxy of any new doctrine, presented to them, by comparing it with a doctrine already defined. If it be not in accord, they can combat it as bad and justly stigmatize as bad the book or journal which sustains it. They cannot of course define it ex cathedra, but they can lawfully hold it as perverse and declare it such, warn others against it, raise the cry of alarm and strike the first blow against it. The faithful layman can do all this, and has done it at all times with the applause of the Church. Nor in so doing does he make himself the pastor of the flock, nor even its humblest attendant; he simply serves it as a watchdog who gives the alarm. Oportet

---

[41] Fr. Félix Sardá y Salvany; *Liberalism is a Sin*, p. 154.

allatrare canes. "It behooves watchdogs to bark" very opportunely said a great Spanish Bishop in reference to such occasions.

Is not perchance the part played by human reason so understood by those zealous prelates, who on a thousand occasions exhort the faithful to refrain from the reading of bad journals and works without specially pointing them out? Thus do they (167) show their conviction that this natural criterion, illuminated by faith, is sufficient to enable the faithful to apply well known doctrines to such matters.

Like the errant canon who falsely accused Don Sardá of doctrinal error for expressing such opinions including the one I have just quoted, Salza & Siscoe have accused me of asserting the Protestant doctrine of Private Judgment for my having upheld the very same teaching, to wit, the Catholic Doctrine that the faithful have the right in conscience to judge in matters of faith according to reason against heretics who masquerade as Catholics; yet, in the ruling of the Sacred Congregation of the Index, pronounced during the reign of Pope Leo XIII, the magisterial authority of the Church not only approved this opinion which I advocate, (but which Salza & Siscoe condemn), but the Sacred Congregation even singled out for praise the author who advocated the opinion.[42]

One can therefore safely judge even privately that Jorge "Francis" Bergoglio pronounces the judgment of heresy against himself by directly denying and attacking a revealed truth of the universal magisterium which is and has been universally known to all Catholics throughout the bi-millennial history of the Church; namely, the explicit and solemn command and teaching of Our Lord Jesus Christ to "make disciples of all nations" (Matt. 28:19-20). He is obstinate in his perverse denial and

---

[42] "The Sacred Congregation of the Index has received the denunciation of the little work bearing the title *"El Liberalismo es Pecado"* by Don Félix Sardá y Salvany, a priest of your diocese; the denunciation (pg. iii) was accompanied at the same time by another little work entitled *"El Proceso del Integrismo,"* that is *"a refutation of the errors contained in the little work El Liberalismo es Pecado."* The author of the second work is D. de Pazos, a canon of the diocese of Vich. Wherefore the Sacred Congregation has carefully examined both works, and decided as follows: In the first not only is nothing found contrary to sound doctrine, but its author, D. Félix Sardá merits great praise for his exposition and defense of the sound doctrine therein set forth with solidity, order and lucidity, and without personal offense to anyone. Fr. Jerome Scheri, O.P. Secretary of the Sacred Congregation of the Index." (Sardá, *Liberalism is a Sin, Preface* [by Conde B. Pallen, Ph.D., LL.D.], p. x.)

outright rejection of this dogma, professing his own opposed doctrine, which he professed previously in his interview with Eugenio Scalfari: "Proselytism is solemn nonsense." Bergoglio says Christ's teaching is "solemn nonsense":

Bergoglio on 13 October 2016 declared: "It's not right to convince someone of your faith," [...] "Proselytism is the strongest venom against the path of ecumenism."

> «"Non è lecito convincere della tua fede: il proselitismo è il veleno più forte contro il cammino ecumenico". A lanciare il grido d'allarme è stato il Papa, rivolgendosi a braccio ai luterani ricevuti in udienza oggi nell'Aula Paolo VI.» – ANSA

That Jorge Bergoglio is a manifest formal heretic is plainly demonstrated by his outright and explicit rejection of some of the most basic dogmas of Christian belief – notably, 1) his rejection of Christ's explicit teaching on evangelizing and converting all nations; 2) his rejection of the dogma of absolute necessity of faith for justification and redemption; 3) his rejection of the Catholic doctrine on marriage; 4) his rejection of the dogma of hell; 5) his rejection of the Church's teaching on capital punishment; and 6) his pagan notion of "God" which logically denies the dogmatic Christian doctrine of God as distinct from and infinitely transcending the created universe; which he contemptuously dismisses as a "vague idea in the clouds", a "god spray", and a "Catholic God"; and 7) his rejection of the dogma of the cessation of the Mosaic Covenant and its supercession by the New Covenant of Jesus Christ. These points will be fully elaborated in Volume II. However, since his first public expression after his election in March 2013 of manifestly formal heresy in an official document was his rejection of the perpetually taught dogma of the abrogation of the Mosaic Covenant, a few words on this point are in order.

"Pope" Francis in *Evangelii Gaudium* n. 247 asserts the inexcusable heresy: "We hold the Jewish people in special regard because their covenant with God has never been revoked". This text is an explicit profession of heresy, directly opposed to the solemn dogmatic definition of Pope Eugenius III and the Ecumenical Council of Florence, and the doctrine taught by the supreme magisterium of Pope Benedict XIV in *Ex Quo Primum*, set forth repeatedly and explicitly citing the definition of Florence, to wit, that the Mosaic covenant has been "revoked" and "abrogated". It is not for no reason that the Fathers unanimously teach that the Old Covenant was revoked: they simply received that doctrine straight out of the New Testament writings of St. Paul ("in Christ it is made void" – 2 Cor. 3:15). In Chapter 8 of Hebrews, the Apostle explains that the Mosaic Covenant is called the Old Covenant precisely because it it made old by the New Covenant, and is to be ended: " Now in saying a new, he hath made the former old. And that which decayeth and groweth old, is near its end." On this solid basis of Scripture and Tradition, the Catholic Church has defined (Council of Florence) that the Old Covenant is revoked, abolished, and abrogated (cf. Benedict XIV, *Ex quo primum*, 1 March 1756). It never occurred to Bergoglio that the the fulfillment of the Old Covenant not only does not logically oppose the notion of its revocation, but also contradicts the Catholic teaching that it is precisely in its fulfillment by the New Covenant of Jesus Christ that the Old Covenant is made void.

The objection that says the Old Covenant was never revoked because the promise made to Abraham is irrevocable, is a heretical *non sequirur*. The Covenant with Abraham is irrevocable, but it is not and has never been professed to be the Old Covenant. Even for Jews, "The Covenant" is the Sinai Covenant, mediated by Moses. It was that covenant of which the prophet Jeremiah spoke, saying it would be replaced by a new covenant: " Behold the days shall come, saith the Lord, and I will make a new covenant with the house of Israel, and with the house of Juda: Not according to the covenant which I made with their fathers, in the day that I took them by the hand to bring them out of the land of Egypt: the covenant which they made void, and I had dominion over them, saith the Lord." (Jer. 31: 31-2).Thus it is patent that the doctrine of the non revocation of the Old Covenant, professed by Jorge Bergoglio; (and explicitly set forth in the so-called *Catechism of the Catholic Church*), is contrary to the perpetual dogma of the Catholic faith, and is therefore heretical.

I have been saying for more than four decades that when a "pope" will officially teach explicit and clear heresy flatly contradicting the infallibly defined dogma of the Catholic faith, then you will know that he is the false pope prophecied in many Church approved prophecies and Marian apparitions. Pope Innocent III, the Council of Constance (Sess. 37), St. Robert Bellarmine, St. Alphonsus Liguori, Don Pietro Ballerini, Pope Gregory XVI, and many others, all teach that if a pope demonstrates himself to be a manifest heretic, i.e. a plainly manifested public formal heretic, he ceases by himself to be pope. Bellarmine explains that the Roman Pontiff is the visible head of the Church, and the head is a member. One who is not a member cannot be the head, and therefore the election to the supreme pontificate of a public heretic is canonically null & void. The heresy of Bergoglio in no. 247 is such a clear-cut case of manifest, public heresy, expressed in stark, unequivocal terms, that it can be said without doubt that if this proposition of no. 247 is not manifestly heretical, then hardly anything else can be said to be so. It is morally impossible that one who manifestly displays such clearly expressed contempt for a universally known and solemnly defined dogma of faith by plainly denying it, can be believed to validly hold the office of Roman Pontiff. St. Francis of Assisi foretold in the above quoted prophecy of the uncanonically elected pope who would not be "a true pastor but a destroyer". Bergoglio plainly fits the description.

Bergoglio has a long history of heresy that is well documented. He has for a long time denied the dogma of the cessation of the Mosaic Covenant and its supercession by the New Covenant of Jesus Christ. Unlike the heretical expressions of Montini, Wojtyla & Ratzinger, which are heretical but capable of a benign interpretation, or else ambiguous and convoluted, Bergoglio's denial of defined dogma in no. 247 of *Evangelii Gaudium* is explicit, direct and univocal so that his meaning can only be that which is expressed by the objective signification of the terms. It's like someone saying, "God the Son did not become incarnate", or, "There are not three persons in one God." Anyone who speaks like that, according to the canonical *indicia* of formal heresy, is most certainly a manifest heretic. The heretical assertion in Bergoglio's proposition is so direct, explicit and univocal, that he is without a shadow of doubt a manifest heretic, whereas that cannot be so easily said of Roncalli, Montini, Wojtyla, or Ratzinger. Unlike Bergoglio, when the heterodoxy of their propositions was pointed out, Wojtyla & Ratzinger modified their formulations. The dogma of the cessation of the Jewish Covenant and its supercession by the New & Everlasting Covenant of Jesus Christ is the basis for the foundation of the Catholic Church, and therefore was one of the basic dogmas taught to all children in catechism and religion classes before Vatican II, so it is morally inconceivable that Bergoglio is unaware that it is a defined article of faith. Having seen the classroom manuals used in Jesuit faculties in the middle of the last century, it is manifestly evident to me that it is not possible that he can be excused for ignorance. Not only did he receive the formal theological training for the priesthood, but Bergoglio was a professor of theology. It is also inconceivable that he would not have researched and systematically examined the point of doctrine before expressing his position on that point in no. 247 of *Evangelii Gaudium*.

Pope Innocent III teaches (*Sermo IV*) that when a pope "withers away into heresy", "he can be judged by men, or rather can be shown to be already judged" – thus it is a teaching of papal magisterium that a heretic pope is to be rejected by the faithful like "salt that has lost its savour". Similarly Bellarmine and St. Alphonsus (both quoted extensively in this volume) teach that if a pope were to fall into manifest heresy, he would fall from office straightaway. St. Alphonsus teaches that, "if God allowed a Pope to be notoriously heretical and contumacious, he would cease to be Pope, and he would vacate the Pontificate."[43] Those who say only a future pope can make such a judgment teach perversely: since an infidel who has fallen from the supreme pontificate must not be professed by the faithful to be the successor of St. Peter, since that would be professing a lie. God cannot possibly will and command that the Catholic faithful submit to obedience to a false pastor who is outside the Church, because the infinitely good God cannot command us to do evil or profess a lie. The same is equally true in the case of a reasonable and well-founded positive doubt, since one cannot be bound to profess as certain that which is positively doubtful. Yet, those who teach that we must refrain from making such a judgment and continue to acknowledge the heretic as pope until a formal ruling is made by the Church or by a future pope fall into this perverse error. It is also plainly evident from the text and context of the passages cited in this volume, of Bellarmine, Innocent III, St. Thomas, St. Alphonsus, Ballerini, and Gregory XVI, that for someone to publicly "fall into manifest heresy" or "wither away into heresy" is entirely a unilateral process; and therefore, it does not depend on any official judicial or declaratory sentence for one to be considered a public heretic, nor for one who falls into public heresy to be judged as such by private persons – and this especially in the case of one who is apparently pope, since no tribunal on earth has jurisdiction over a pope. One has the moral duty in conscience to make this kind of judgment when the question of papal heresy arises, since all Catholics are bound by their baptismal vows to be in communion only with the true successor of St. Peter, and to submit only to him in obedience as to the Vicar of Christ: hence, there is the strict moral obligation for

---

[43] «Del resto, se Dio permettesse che un Papa fosse notoriamente eretico e contumace, egli cesserebbe d'essere Papa, e vacherebbe il Pontificato.» [Alfonso M. De Liguori, *Verità della Fede*, Napoli, 1838, Part. III. Cap. VIII. p. 455]

Catholics to discern and judge in the matter of a heretic pope to the extent that it is morally possible.

JORGE BERGOGLIO IS THE SPARHEAD OF THE GREAT APOSTASY FORETOLD IN THE SECRET OF FATIMA

Another reason which emerged, and necessitates this book, is that there are pseudo-Catholic propagandists of the counterfeit Conciliar Church (most notably Kevin Symmonds[44]) who attempt to prove that the entire secret of Fatima has been revealed already, and attempt to prevent Catholics from coming to understand what specifically are the *dangers to the faith* mentioned in the Secret, which Cardinal Ratzinger spoke of in his well-known interview published in the November 1984 issue of the periodical, *Jesus*; saying that it warns of "the dangers threatening the faith and the life of the Christian"; and that what is revealed in the Secret **corresponds to what is revealed in Scripture**. In that interview, the future Pope Benedict XVI called attention to the fact that the specific content of the Secret does not merely correspond in a general way to what is revealed in Scripture; but he referred specifically to *"i novissimi"*; i.e., "the last things", which in such a scriptural context cannot refer to the four last things of Christian Doctrine (death, judgment, heaven & hell); but are a clear reference to the "last things", i.e. τα εσχατα – the *eachatological events* of the end-time scriptural prophecies – the *apocalyptic texts* of Scripture. The distinguished theologian, Fr. E. Sylvester Berry (as well as many other theologians and ecclesiastical writers), in one of the passages quoted below in his work

---

[44] Christopher A. Ferrara summed up the dubious "contibution" of Kevin Symmonds to the questions regarding the Third Secret of Fatima in one of his published articles: «Symonds has burst onto the neo-Catholic scene with elaborate claims about how his supposedly groundbreaking research into source documents has undermined the "Fatimist" case for the existence of a missing explanatory text accompanying the vision. An interviewer for Catholic World Report goes so far as to declare that Symonds has "formed a picture that offered an alternative view to that of [Father] Gruner and the Abbé [de Nantes]." Symonds' claims do not bear close scrutiny. Having read his lengthy book on the subject, which is heavy with appendices and footnotes of no great import, I found that he has contributed nothing of substance to the Third Secret controversy, although he has a knack for writing and speaking portentously even if he's not saying anything particularly important.»

on *The Apocalypse of St. John*, speaks of these events as a *judgment*: "This judgment shall be the great persecution of Antichrist and its attendant evils."

This *judgment* is not to be confused with the *General Judgment* which pertains to *the four last things*; and which is explained in the catechism: «The judgment which will be passed on all men immediately after the general resurrection is called the general judgment.»[45] [...] «The general judgment was described by Our Saviour Himself ... "For the Son of Man is to come with his angels in the glory of his Father, and then he will render to everyone according to his conduct" (*Matthew 16:27*). [...] "And he charged us to preach to the people and to testify that he it is who has been appointed by God to be judge of the living and the dead" (*Acts 10:42*)»[46] A most authoritative exposition is given in the *Catechismus Romanus*, (sometimes referred to as *The Catechism of the Council of Trent*); which explains that the General Judgment will take place at the time of the general resurrection. [47] This General Judgment, which is to take place at the end of the world (*in consummatione sæculi*); when Christ will come

---

[45] *Baltimore Catechism No. 3*.

[46] *Baltimore Catechism No. 3 – Father Connell's Confraternity Edition*, 1949, 1952; reprinted 1995, p. 104.

[47] «6 Nullus homo tunc invenietur, qui mortis et resurrectionis sit expers Explicare praeterea diligenter oportebit, ex Apostoli doctrina, quinam ad vitam suscitandi sint; nam ad Corinthios scribens, sicut in Adam, inquit, omnes moriuntur, ita et in Christo omnes vivificabuntur 18. Omni itaque malorum bonorumque discrimine remoto, omnes a mortuis, quamquam non omnium par conditio futura est, resurgent: qui bona fecerunt, in resurrectionem vitae; qui vero mala egerunt, in resurrectionem iudicii 19. Cum autem omnes dicimus, tam eos intelligimus qui, adventante iudicio, mortui iam erunt, quam eos qui morientur. Huic enim sententiae quae asserit omnes morituros esse, nemine excepto, Ecclesiam acquiescere, ipsamque sententiam magis veritati convenire, scriptum reliquit sanctus Hieronymus 20; idem sentit et sanctus Augustinus 21. Neque vero huic sententiae repugnant Apostoli verba ad Thessalonicenses scripta: Mortui qui in Christo sunt, resurgent primi; deinde nos, qui vivimus, qui relinquimur, simul rapiemur cum illis in nubibus obviam Christo in aera 22. Nam sanctus Ambrosius, cum ea explanaret, ita inquit: In ipso raptu mors praeveniet et quasi per soporem, ut egressa anima in momento reddatur; cum enim tollentur, morientur, ut pervenientes ad Dominum, praesentia Domini recipiant animos, quia cum Domino mortui esse non possunt. Eademque sententia comprobatur sancti Augustini auctoritate in libro de Civitate Dei. [17 2 Tes 1; 18 1 Cor 15; 19 Jn 5; 20 Epist. 152; 21 Lib. 20 De Civ. Dei; cap. 20; 22 1 Tes 4]»

again on the last day to judge all men (*summo illo die Christum Dominum de universo hominum genere iudicaturum esse*), is what the Church teaches in the article of the Creed which professes, "From thence he shall come to judge the living and the dead" (*Inde venturus est iudicare vivos et mortuos*).[48] This is the general judgment at the end of the world, *the judgment of the living and the dead*, revealed in Scripture by St. Paul in 1 Thessalonians 4:

> "[14] For this we say unto you in the word of the Lord, that we who are alive, who remain unto the coming of the Lord, shall not prevent them who have slept. [15] For the Lord himself shall come down from heaven with commandment, and with the voice of an archangel, and with the trumpet of God: and the dead who are in Christ, shall rise first. [16] Then we who are alive, who are left, shall be taken up together with them in the clouds to meet Christ, into the air, and so shall we be always with the Lord."

The doctrine on the judgment of the living and the dead is plainly and infallibly set forth in the Confession of Faith of the Fourth Lateran Council: "He [the only-begotten Son of God, Jesus Christ] will come at the end of time to judge the living and the dead, to render to every person according to his works, both to the reprobate and to the elect. All of them will rise with their own bodies, which they now wear, so as to receive according to their deserts, whether these be good or bad; for the latter perpetual punishment with the devil, for the former eternal glory with Christ."

The judgment, which some ecclesiastical writers refer to as a *minor judgment* in order to clearly distinguish it from the *general judgment* at the end of the world, will consist in "the great persecution of Antichrist and its attendant evils", as Fr. Berry explains; and will take place in the end times, but before the end of the world. Our Lord himself spoke of these events as the *great tribulation*: "there shall be then *great tribulation*, such as hath not been from the beginning of the world until now, neither shall be" (Matthew 24:21). Cardinal Manning, in his work quoted below, comments on the text of St. Paul to the Thessalonians, explaining that this tribulation will commence with "a revolt, which shall precede the

---

[48] «Sacrae enim Litterae duos Filii Dei adventus esse testantur: alterum, cum salutis nostrae causa carnem assumpsit, et homo in Virginis alvo effectus est; alterum, cum in consummatione saeculi ad iudicandos omnes homines veniet. Hic adventus in sacris litteris dies Domini appellatur, de quo Apostolus ait: Dies Domini, sicut fur in nocte, ita veniet 1; et Salvator ipse: De die autem illa et hora nemo scit 2. [11 Tes 5; 2Mt 24; Mc 13].»

second coming of our Lord". That revolt is the *apostasy* foretold in Scripture and in the Secret of Fatima which threatens the faith of the Christian; and is the prelude to *the great persecution of Antichrist and its attendant evils*, which will threaten not only the faith, but the life of the Christian as well.

While it is known in a general sense that the Secret of Fatima speaks of the *"apostasy"* (as the Bishop of Leiria-Fatima, Msgr. Cosme do Amaral stated in his discourse in Vienna in 1981); that term is usually understood to refer to individuals or groups who abandon the faith and leave the Church, with the greater portion of the hierarchy remaining intact. What is extraordinary about the Secret of Fatima, is that *it reveals the Great Apostasy foretold by St. Paul*; and in that apostasy it will seem (and is already beginning to seem) like almost the whole Church has defected, and will appear to be defeated, and to have disappeared from the earth, having been replaced with a counterfeit Anti-church, led by a heretic-antipope foretold in prophecy (as Fr. John O'Connor and I discussed on Fr. Gruner's radio program more than 25 years ago – (https://m.youtube.com/watch?feature=youtu.be&v=7kiu2uzZO7M) – and according to the Secret of Fatima, it will be a heretic-antipope will lead the stampede into apostasy.

The Third Secret reveals and warns against the conciliar ecumenical Anti-church, spawned by an "evil council". That council, the Secret revealed, will give rise to the movement which attempts to reform the Church into a counterfeit "church" with a false new religion. The Great Apostasy will be Vatican led, under a false and heretical "pope" – as Cardinal Ciappi said, "In the third secret it is revealed, among other things, that the great apostasy in the Church will begin at the top."[49] This is also, as is elaborated below, the conclusion of some of the most learned commentators on the Apocalypse of St. John. The footnote in the linked article documents that these words of Cardinal Ciappi were reported by Fr. Gerard Mura in *The Catholic*. Fr. Gruner showed me his actual hardcopy of the paper in which Fr. Mura's article was published, and asked me to read it. Now, the front men of Ecclesiastical Masonry are spreading the lie that I fabricated the quotation, and placed it in *The Devil's Final Battle*! However, that book was more Fr. Gruner's project than mine: he directed the work, and he appointed me to be the editor. Only one chapter was written entirely by me; the rest, I did not write, but only edited.

---

[49] http://www.fatima.org/thirdsecret/otherwitness.asp.

Cardinal Ottaviani said essentially the same thing as Cardinal Ciappi – that Satan will penetrate to the highest level in the Church. Malachi Martin, who learned the content of the Secret from Cardinal Bea, confirmed to me in a phone conversation that, according to the Secret, the apostasy will be led by an antipope who will be a heretic.

The so-called "diplomatic version" of the secret, published in 1963 in *Neues Europa*, is not really a false or bogus version of the Secret, but is a fictitious version that sets forth in more general terms the specific points of the real Secret in the authentic text of the Secret. After having been published in *Neues Europa*, it was explicitly recognized by Cardinal Ottaviani who later acknowledged privately to Fr. Luigi Villa (whom Fr. Gruner knew personally) his own authorship of it. Fr. Gruner also reported, "We have as evidence of this the testimony of Msgr. Corrado Balducci, a Vatican insider for more than forty years, who related that when Cardinal Ottaviani was asked whether the *Neues Europa* account should be published, the Cardinal, who had read the Third Secret — and who had a dry personality and was basically indifferent to most apparitions — exclaimed very emphatically: 'Publish 10,000 copies! Publish 20,000 copies! Publish 30,000 copies!' "(http://www.fatima.org/thirdsecret/neueseuropa.asp) Fr. Gruner was himself the source of this information, having heard it from the mouth of Mons. Balducci, whom he knew personally.

According to another report mentioned in the above cited article,

> «On March 17, 1990 Cardinal Oddi, who was a personal friend of Pope John XXIII and who had spoken to him regarding the Secret, gave the following testimony to Italian journalist Lucio Brunelli in the journal *Il Sabato*: "It [the Third Secret] has nothing to do with Gorbachev. The Blessed Virgin was alerting us against apostasy in the Church."»

On August 1, 1976 in Philadelphia, the future Pope John Paul II said, "We are now standing in the face of the greatest historical confrontation humanity has ever experienced. I do not think that the wide circle of the American Society, or the whole wide circle of the Christian Community realize this fully. We are now facing the final confrontation between the Church and the anti-church, between the gospel and the anti-gospel, between Christ and the antichrist. The confrontation lies within the plans of Divine Providence. It is, therefore, in God's Plan, and it must be a trial which the Church must take up, and face courageously." After he was elected pope, John Paul II briefly reiterated this point in 1981, mentioning also that it pertains to the message of Fatima. Many years ago I read the text of a prophecy of St. John Eudes, in which he says the triumph of the Heart of Mary will be the triumph over the Antichrist. This is not surprising, because it is foretold in Scripture, and most notably in the Apocalypse of St. John. In fact, when speaking on the message of Fatima on 13 May 2000 in his homily of beatification of Bl. Jacinta & Francisco of Fatima, Pope John Paul II underscored the apocalyptic character of the message of Fatima by quoting the Apocalypse in connection with the message:

> «"Another portent appeared in heaven; behold, a great red dragon" (*Rv* 12: 3). These words from the first reading of the Mass make us think of the great struggle between good and evil, showing how, when man puts God aside, he cannot achieve happiness, but ends up destroying himself. ***The message of Fatima is a call to conversion, alerting humanity to have nothing to do with the "dragon" whose "tail swept down a third of the stars of heaven**, and cast them to the earth"* (*Rv* 12: 4).»

Thus, it is this event of the Great Tribulation described in this scripture verse, that Pope John Paul II indicated as pertaining to the Third Secret of Fatima. Accordingly, the events foretold in this verse and in the surrounding texts, which reveal the great apostasy and the reign of Antichrist which the apostasy immediately precedes, constitute the substance of the apocalyptic chastisement revealed in the Third Secret of Fatima, which the triumph of Our Lady's Immaculate Heart will bring to an end.

Fr. Herman Bernard F. Leonard Kramer comments on this passage in his work, *The Book of Destiny*:

> Verse 4. The tail of the dragon draws in its coils one third of the stars of Heaven and casts them to the earth. This is one third of the clergy. In Arianism (VI. 13), there was great apostasy of bishops and priests; the stars fell from heaven in large numbers. In the Greek schism, a great star, the Patriarch, fell from heaven (VIII. 10); and a star fell from heaven who led the apostasy from the Church into Protestantism (IX. 1). Before the appearance of Antichrist, "one third" of the stars shall follow the dragon. This is a compulsory apostasy shown by the Greek word, συρει which means "to drag by force". The subsequent phrase, "and cast them to the earth", specifies this meaning with greater precision. Satan will probably through the evil world-powers of the time exercise such tyranny over the church as to leave the clergy the alternative of submission to the government or martyrdom by death or imprisonment and will enforce the acceptance of unchristian morals, false doctrines, compromise with error, or obedience to

the civil rulers in violation of conscience. St. John evidently had in mind the world-empires of ancient times, all of which were persecutors of God's people. The text suggests a use of the apostate clergy, after their own defection, in persecuting the Church. Verse nine clearly states that those who will not brave martyrdom will surrender to Satan. The dragon will have them doing his will.

According to Ven. Bede, "Tyconius more suo tertiam partem stellarum quae cecidit falsos fratres interpretatur". Though Tyconius was a Donatist, his interpretation of the Apocalypse was very popular. Origen likewise expresses this opinion (Lorn. iv. p. 306) "qui... peccatum... sequitur, trahitur a cauda draconis vadens post eum". They probably followed the lead of Methodius, who says of these stars: "And the stars, which the dragon touched with the end of his tail, and drew them down to the earth, are the bodies of heresies; for we must say that the stars, which are dark, obscure, and falling are the assemblies of the heterodox. The verse seems to allude to Isaias (IX. 15-16). The tail is a symbol of lying and hypocrisy. Through false doctrines and principles, Satan will mislead the clergy, who will have become worldly-minded, haughty, hypocritical, obsequient avaricious sycophants. It seems to forebode a long period of peace, growth and temporal prosperity for the Church, so that many will enter the priesthood from bad motives. They will look to the Church to satisfy their ambition and avarice and will think it easier to gain an honorable position in the Church than in the world. In Catholic countries pious parents often for pride or other unworthy reasons urge their sons unduly to enter the priesthood for the honor there is in it. Such have not the spirit of sacrifice or mortification in the priesthood, and when persecution shall "sift them as wheat", they shall be found to be chaff. By their lax principles they will infect the laity. They will easily welcome a mitigation or change of doctrine to sanction the lukewarm lives they want to lead. Then will Satan see a rich harvest ripening for himself. The symbolic meaning of the dragon's tail may reveal that the clergy who are ripe for apostasy will hold the influential positions in the Church having won preferment by hypocrisy, deceit and flattery.[50]

Fr. E. Sylvester Berry wrote in the second part of his commentary on Apocalypse 10:7, ("7. But in the days of the voice of the seventh angel, when he shall begin to sound the trumpet, the mystery of God shall be finished, as he hath declared by his servants, the prophets."):

---

[50] Herman Bernard F. Leonard Kramer, *The Book of Destiny* (1955), Rockford, Illinois, 1975, pp. 280 – 281.

This judgment shall be the great persecution of Antichrist and its attendant evils. Then shall be accomplished the "mystery of God" which has been announced (evangelized) by the prophets of old. To evangelize is to announce good tidings, hence this "mystery of God" is probably the plenitude of the Redemption applied to nations of earth. After the destruction of Antichrist and his kingdom all peoples shall accept the Gospel and the Church of Christ shall reign peacefully over all nations.[51]

Fr. Berry elaborates further on pp. 306-7 of the same work:

The beast is not the aggregate of infidels, heretics, enemies and persecutors of the people of God but a person. He is Antichrist, who had not yet appeared when St. John wrote his first letter (1 Jo. II. 18). St. Paul speaks of the same person, when he says: "he sits in the temple of God, showing himself as if he were God". This could not be said of a world-power or organization of any kind but only of a person. The phrase "temple of God" does not mean the ancient Temple but a Catholic Church. When this comes to pass, "the mystery of iniquity" will have reached its culmination, which mystery was already developing in apostolic times. The height of iniquity is reached when a man poses as God and demands divine honors for himself. Though this was done by rulers of kingdoms and empires, Antichrist will make the boldest pretensions to the possession of divine prerogatives. And though the rulers of the world-empires allowed temples to be built to their own divinity and demanded the worship of their statues, there is no record of their going personally to the "temple of God" to be worshipped.

On page 130 he states:

Our study of the Apocalypse thus far makes it certain that the beast cannot be identified with the Roman Empire as many interpreters have done. Others, following the opinion of St. Augustine, (St. Augustine "City of God" xx, 19.) take the beast as a symbol of all the wicked and unfaithful. This interpretation is true in a measure since Antichrist could not accomplish his nefarious work without disciples and followers. Hence the beast may be taken by extension to represent the whole empire of Antichrist. Nevertheless it is certain, in fact Suarez holds it as an article of faith, that the Antichrist is a definite individual. The words of St. Paul to the Thessalonians leave no room for doubt in this matter. (II Thessalonians ii, 3-9)

He explains on page 18:

---

[51] *The Apocalypse of St. John*, First Edition Columbus, Ohio, 1921, p. 109.

St. John uses the word "Beast" and not the word "Antichrist", because he writes a prophetical book, and by using the same term used by Daniel, he puts this book in the same category. St. John, as Daniel did, presents the world-power under a figure that would arouse the reader's resentment and would heighten his trust in God to defend His Church against its malevolent might. Had he used the word "Antichrist", he would have restricted the prophecies to the man of sin, who according to both St. John and St. Paul was a person destined to gather all the evil forces in the world and unite and co-ordinate them under his dominion for the last desperate attack on the Church of Jesus Christ. By using the word "Beast", he could unite his empire of evil and his person of evil in one single term and include under it the anti-christian world-power of his own time and unify their efforts against Christ and God by the mind and power of Satan. He thus aptly portrays the evil world-power of all times in the form of a bloodthirsty beast. And on page 19:

St. John presents Antichrist in a two-fold role, personal and political. He depicts the first in chapter XIII. and the second in chapter XVII. His idea of Antichrist is exactly that of St. Paul, that he is not on impersonal power but a man. "Little children, it is the last hour: and as you have heard that Antichrist cometh, even now there are become many antichrists" (1 Jo. II. 18, 22; IV. 3). St. Paul had expressed the same view: "unless there come a revolt first and the man of sin be revealed…etc." (2 Thess. II.), leaving no doubt of its being a man. St. John gives another view of Antichrist, that he not only "cometh" but is already in the world and his presence is in the form of a power or organization, and it manifested itself in the doctrines of the Docetae (1 Jo. IV. 3, 33; 2 Jo. 7). Irenaeus and Hippolytus apply the name to a person only not to an organization. The former identifies the "beast" with Antichrist. (Adv. Haer. V. xxvi, 1). According to St. John's view so clearly revealed in the Apocalypse, before Antichrist appears, the beast is non-existent for a time. "The beast that was and is not and yet shall be" (XVII. 8) is the anti-christian world-power. This sentence has mystified many interpreters. St. Jerome left the last clause out of his translation, probably because he considered it a contradiction. However, the beast in chapter XVII. is the empire of Antichrist though not entirely differentiated from his person. This anti-christian empire existed in former times for a long course of ages but then ceased to exist for a time.

And he continues on page 131:

It is a very general opinion that Antichrist will set himself up as the Messias. This opinion seems to be supported by the words of our Saviour:

"I am come in the name of my Father, and you receive me not: if another shall come in his own name, him you will receive." (St. John v, 43; see also I John ii, 18.) This pretension to Messiasship will make it necessary that he spring from the Jewish race.

The coming of Antichrist opens the decisive conflict between the Church and the powers of hell. It shall be the complete realization of the prophecy of Genesis: "I will put enmity between thee and the woman and thy seed and her seed." (Genesis iii, 15.) The seed of the serpent is the Antichrist and his followers; the seed of Mary, the woman, is Jesus Christ and his faithful disciples.

In the third part of the same work Fr. Berry writes:

The words of St. Paul to the Thessalonians' [II Thessalonians ii, 8] prove clearly that Antichrist must be a definite individual, and our study of the Apocalypse shows that he has not yet made his appearance in the world. But practically all interpreters who accept these conclusions take the reign of Antichrist as a prelude to the last judgment and the end of the world. Then, contrary to the plain sense of Holy Scripture, they place the universal reign of Christ before the time of Antichrist. This in turn, makes the chaining of the dragon a difficult problem. Some refer it to the time of our Saviour's death, or to the day of Pentecost. Others fix upon the date of Constantine's conversion, the reign of Charlemagne, the fall of the Western Empire, or the capture of Constantinople by the Turks, – all purely arbitrary dates as their great divergencies prove.

A careful reading of the Apocalypse shows clearly that Antichrist will appear long centuries before the last judgment and the end of the world. In fact his reign will be but the final attempt of Satan to prevent the universal reign of Christ in the world. Since the day of Pentecost the Church has been engaged in perpetual warfare. Judaism was her first enemy; then followed Arianism, Mohammedanism, the Greek Schism, the Reformation, and secret societies fostering atheism and rationalism. Today she is also battling indifferentism and a recrudescence of paganism. The reign of Antichrist shall be the final conflict in this prolonged struggle with the powers of darkness.

After the defeat of Antichrist the Gentile nations will return to the Church and the Jews will enter her fold. Then shall be fulfilled the words of Christ: "There shall be one fold and one shepherd." [St. John X, 16] Unfortunately sin and evil will not have entirely disappeared, the good and the bad will still be mingled, in the Church, although the good shall predominate. After many centuries, symbolized by a thousand years, faith will diminish and charity grow cold as a result of the long peace and security enjoyed by the Church. Then Satan, unchained for a short time, will seduce many nations (Gog and Magog) to make war on the Church and persecute the faithful. These apostate nations shall be promptly overwhelmed with a deluge of fire and the Church will come forth again triumphant. The general judgment and the end of the world will then be near at hand. Men will be living in daily expectation until Our Lord appears in the clouds with the suddenness of a lightning flash [St. Matthew xxiv, 27] Then shall all people be gathered together unto judgment.

The establishment of the Church over all nations is foretold on almost every page of Holy Scripture. "He shall rule from sea to sea and from the river unto the ends of the earth. ...And all kings of the earth shall adore him; and all nations shall serve him." [Ps. lxxi, 8, 9] "All the nations thou hast made shall come and adore before thee, o Lord." [lxxxv, 9] "His empire shall be multiplied and there shall be no end of peace" [Isaias ix, 7] "His kingdom is an everlasting kingdom, and all kings shall serve him and obey him." [Daniel vii, 27] "He shall speak peace to the Gentiles, and his power shall be from sea to sea, and from the rivers even to the ends of the earth." [Zacharias ix, 10]

The Apostles were sent forth to preach the Gospel to all nations and every creature, [St. Matthew xxviii, 16; St. Luke xvi, 15] and St Paul applies to them the words of the Psalmist: "Their sound hath gone forth into all the earth, and their words unto the end of the whole world." [Romans x, 18; Ps. Xviii, 5] Can it be supposed that these prophecies are fulfilled by the conversion of a few thousand souls in the various pagan countries of the world? Can we admit that a world steeped in paganism, and torn with schism and heresy is the only result of Christ's death upon the Cross? Such an admission is necessary if the closing of the abyss and the binding off Satan be placed at the beginning of Christianity, and the thousand years of Christ's reign, before the defeat of Antichrist.

The prophecies cited above and hundreds of others scattered through the Scriptures make it certain that the reign of Christ shall be truly universal. After the Gentile nations return to the faith, the Jews shall also submit to the yoke of the Gospel. St. Paul states this fact very plainly: "Blindness in part has happened in Israel, until the fullness of the Gentiles should come in. And so all Israel shall be saved as it is written: "There shall come out of Sion, he that shall deliver, and shall turn away ungodliness from Jacob." [Romans xi, 25, 26; Isaias lix, 20] Again he writes: "If the loss of them (the Jews) be the reconciliation of the world, what shall the receiving of them be, but life from the dead? [Romans xi, 15]

These prophecies will not be fulfilled before the time of Antichrist, since the Apocalypse clearly shows that he will come into a world harassed by paganism, apostacy, schism, and heresy. [Apocalypse ix, 20, 21] The Jews still unconverted, will accept him as Messias and assist in his warfare against the Church. Only after the defeat of Antichrist and the return of the Gentile nations to the Faith, will the Jews accept Christ as the true Messias. Then shall begin the universal reign of Christ over all peoples, and tribes, and tongues.[52]

Cardinal Henry Edward Manning, in his book, *The Present Crisis of the Holy See* (1861), expounds on the great apostasy foretold by the sacred writers of Scripture, and explained by the great theologians of the Church. He begins by quoting St. Paul's prophecy of the apostasy:

> St. Paul, writing to the Thessalonians, says: "Let no man deceive you by any means: for unless there come a revolt first, and the man of sin be revealed, the son of perdition, who opposeth, and is lifted up above all that is called God, or that is worshiped, so that he sitteth in the temple of God, showing himself as if he were God. For the mystery of iniquity already worketh: only that he who now holdeth, do hold, until he be taken out of the way, and then that wicked one shall be revealed, whom the Lord Jesus shall kill with the spirit of his mouth, and shall destroy with the brightness of his coming: him, whose coming is according to the working of Satan, in all power, and signs, and lying wonders, and in all seduction of iniquity to them that perish: because they received not the love of the truth, that they might be saved. Therefore God shall send them the operation of error, to believe lying: that all may be judged who have not believed the truth, but have consented to iniquity."

He then provides his lengthy commentary, which I present here in edited form for the sake of abbreviation:

> We have here a prophecy of four great facts: first, of a revolt, which shall precede the second coming of our Lord; secondly, of the manifestation of one who is called "the wicked one;" thirdly, of a hindrance, which restrains his manifestation; and lastly, of the period of power and persecution, of which he will be the author. First, then, what is the revolt? In the original it is called ἀποστασία, 'an apostasy;' and in the Vulgate, discessio, or 'a departure." Now a revolt implies a seditious separation from some authority, and a consequent opposition to it. If we can find the authority, we shall find perhaps also the revolt. [p. 4] The authority, then, from which the revolt is to take place is that of the kingdom of God on earth (In treating of this subject, I shall not venture upon any conjectures of my own, but shall deliver simply what I find either in the Fathers of the Church, or in such theologians as the Church has recognised) [p. 3] p. 5 Such being the authority against which the revolt is made, it cannot be difficult to ascertain its character. The inspired writers expressly describe its notes. [i.e. 1) schism, 2) heresy, 3) the denial of the Incarnation] p. 6 These, then, are the marks

---

[52] *Ibid.* p. 189-192

by which, as the Church is to be known by her notes, the antichristian revolt, or apostasy, may be distinguished.

The first point to notice is, that both St. Paul and St. Peter speak of this antichristian revolt as already begun in their own day. St. Paul says, "The mystery of iniquity already worketh [...]" [...] And St. John expressly, in the above-quoted places: [...] "This is Antichrist, of whom you have heard that he cometh, and he is now already in the world."

[p. 7] Every age has its heresy, as every article of faith by denial receives its definition; and the course of heresy is measured and periodical; various materially, but formally one, both in principle and action; so that all the heresies from the beginning are no more than the continuous development and expansion of "the mystery of iniquity," which was already at work.

[p. 8] Physiologists tell us that there is a perfect ultimate unity even in the countless diseases which devour the body; nevertheless, each disease seems to throw out its progeny by a corruption and reproduction. So in the history and development of heresy. To name no more than these, Gnosticism, Arianism, and, above all, Protestantism, have generated each a multitude of subordinate and affiliated heresies. But it is Protestantism which, above all others, bears the three notes of the inspired writers in the greatest breadth and evidence. Other heresies have opposed parts and details of the Christian faith and Church; but Protestantism, taken in its historical complex, as we now are able, with the retrospect of three [. 9] hundred years, to measure it, reaching from the religion of Luther, Calvin, and Cranmer at the one end, to the Rationalism and Pantheism of England and Germany at the other, is of all the most formal, detailed, and commensurate antagonist of Christianity. I do not mean that it has as yet attained its full development, for we shall see reasons to believe that it is still pregnant with a darker future; but even as "the mystery of iniquity has already worked," no other antagonist has as yet gone so deep in undermining the faith of the Christian world. [...]

[p. 9] All that I wish to point out is, to use a modern phrase, that the movement of heresy is one and the same from the beginning: that the Gnostics were the Protestants of their day, and the Protestants the Gnostics of ours; that the principle is identical, and the bulk of the movement unfolded to greater proportions; and its successes accumulated, and its antagonism to the Catholic Church [p. 10] changeless and essential.

[p. 10] There are two consequences or operations of this movement so strange and so full of importance, as bearing upon its relation to the Church, that I cannot pass them by. The first is, the development and worship of the principle of nationality, which has always been found in combination with heresy. Now, the Incarnation abolished all national distinctions within the sphere of grace, and the Church absorbed all nations into its supernatural unity. One Fountain of spiritual jurisdiction, and one Divine Voice, held together the wills and actions of a family of nations. Sooner or later, every heresy has identified itself with the nation in which it arose. It has lived by the support of civil powers, and they have embodied the claim of national independence. This movement, which is the key of the so-called great Western schism, is the rationale also of the Reformation; and the last three hundred years have given a development and intensity to the spirit of separate nationalism, of which we as yet see no more than the preludes. I need not point out how this nationalism is essentially schismatical, which is to be seen not only in the Anglican Reformation, but in the Gallican liberties, and the contentions of Portugal in Europe and in India, to name no more. [...] If heresy in the individual dissolves the unity of the Incarnation, heresy in a nation dissolves the unity of the Church, which is built upon [p.11] the Incarnation. And in this we see a truer and deeper meaning of the words of St. Jerome than he foresaw himself. It is not the revolt of nations from the Roman Empire, but the apostasy of nations from the kingdom of God, which was set up on its ruins. And this process of national defection, which began openly with the Protestant Reformation, is running its course, as we shall see hereafter, even in nations still nominally Catholic; and the Church is putting off its mediaeval character as the mother of nations, returning again into its primitive condition as a society of members scattered among the peoples and cities of the world.

[p.11] The other result I spoke of as the consequence of the later workings of the heretical spirit is the deification of humanity. This we have before us in two distinct forms, namely, in the Pantheistic and in the Positive philosophies; or rather in the religion of Positivism, the last aberration of Comte. I take the expression of the Pantheism of Germany from two of its modern expositors, in whom it may be said to culminate.[53] We are told that, "Before the time when creation began, we may imagine that an infinite mind, an infinite essence, or an infinite thought (for here all these are one), filled the universe of space. This, then, as the self-existent [p. 12] One, must be the only absolute reality; all else can be but a developing of the one original and eternal being. ... This primary essence is not... an infinite substance, having the two properties of extension and thought, but an infinite, acting, producing, self-unfolding mind—the living soul of the world." "If we can view all things as the development of the original and absolute principle of life, reason, or being, then it is evident conversely that we may trace the marks of the absolute in everything that exists, and consequently may scan them in the operation of our own minds, as one particular phase of its manifestation."

"In practical philosophy we have three movements: the first is, that in which the active intelligence shows itself operating within a limited circuit,

---

[53] Manning provide a reference in the footnote: "See account of the German school, Schelling, Hegel, and Hillebrand, in Morell's History of Modern Philosophy, vol. ii. pp. 126-147."

as in a single mind. This is the principle of individuality, not as though the infinite intelligence were something different from the finite, or as though there were an infinite intelligence out of and apart from the finite, but it is merely the absolute in one of its particular moments; just as an individual thought is but a single moment of the whole mind. Each finite reason, then, is but a thought of the infinite and eternal reason." The absolute essence being thus everything, all difference between God and the universe is truly lost; and Pantheism becomes complete, "as the absolute is evolved from its lowest form to the highest, in accordance with the necessary law or rhythm of its being, the whole world, material and mental, becoming one enormous [p.13] chain of necessity, to which no idea of free creation can be attached." Again: "Deity is a process ever going on but never accomplished, nay, the Divine consciousness is absolutely one with the advancing consciousness of mankind. The hope of immortality perishes; for death is but the return of the individual to the infinite, and man is annihilated, though the Deity will eternally live." Once more: "Deity is the eternal process of self-development as realised in man; the Divine and human consciousness falling absolutely together." "The knowledge of God and of his manifestations forms the subject of speculative theology. …Of these manifestations there are three great spheres of observation—nature, mind, and humanity. In nature we see the Divine idea in its lowest expression; in mind, with its powers, faculties, moral feelings, freedom, &c., we see it in its higher and more perfect form; lastly, in humanity we see God, not only as creator and sustainer, but also as a father and a guide." "The soul is a perfect mirror of the universe, and we have only to gaze into it with earnest attention to discover all truth which is accessible to humanity. What we know of God, therefore, can be only that which is originally revealed to us of Him in our own minds.".: I have given these extracts to show the [p. 47] legitimate resolution of the subjective system of private judgment into pure rationalistic Pantheism.

[p. 14] With a few words on the Positivism of Comte, I will conclude. […] "From the study of the development of human intelligence, in all directions and through all times, the discovery arises of a great fundamental law, […] The law is this: that each of our leading conceptions, each branch of our knowledge, passes successively through three different theoretical conditions—the Theological or fictitious; the Metaphysical or abstract; and the Scientific or positive. In other words, the human mind by its nature employs in its progress three methods of philosophising, the character of which is essentially different and even radically opposed, viz. the theological method, the metaphysical, and the positive. Hence arise three philosophies, or general systems of conceptions, on the aggregate of phenomena, each of which excludes the others. The first is the necessary point of departure of the human understanding, and the third is its fixed and definite state. The second is merely a state of transition. […]" [Positive Philosophy, vol. i. c. 1.]

[p. 15] From this it will be observed that the belief in God has passed into the first or fictitious period of the human reason. Nevertheless, after the completion of his Philosophy, Comte perceived the necessity of a religion. Hence the Catechism of Positive Religion, which thus begins: "In the name of the Past and of the Future, the servants of Humanity—both its philosophical and practical servants—come forward to claim as their due the general direction of this world. Their object is, to constitute at length a real Providence in all departments, moral, intellectual, and material. Consequently they exclude, once for all, from political supremacy all the different servants of God—Catholic, Protestant, or Deist— as being at once behindhand and a cause of disturbance." [Catechism of Positive Religion, Preface]

p. 16 But inasmuch as there can be no religion without worship, and no worship without a God, and inasmuch as there is no God, Comte had need to find or to create a Divinity. Now as there is no God, there can be no being higher than man, and no object of worship higher than mankind.

[p. 17] "[…] We are now able to condense the whole of our Positive conceptions in the one single idea of an immense and eternal Being, Humanity, destined by sociological laws to constant development under the preponderating influence of biological and cosmological necessities. This the real great Being, on whom all, whether individuals or societies, depend as the prime mover of their existence, becomes the centre of our affections. They rest on it by as spontaneous an impulse as do our thoughts and our actions. This Being, by its very idea, suggests at once the sacred formula of Positivism; Love as our principle, Order as our basis, and Progress as our end. […]

[p. 18] "You must define Humanity as the whole of human beings, past, present, and future. The word whole points out clearly that you must not take in all men, but those only who are really capable of assimilation, in virtue of a real coöperation on their part in furthering the common good. All are necessarily born children of Humanity, but all do not become her servants. Many remain in the parasitic state, which, excusable during their education, becomes blamable when that education is complete. Times of anarchy bring forth in swarms such creatures, nay, even enable them to flourish, though they are, in sad truth, but burdens on the true Great Being." [Catechism of Positive Religion, pp. 63, 74.]

It will be observed that both Pantheism and Positivism alike end in the deification of man; they are a boundless egotism and an apotheosis of human pride.

[p. 47] We have already seen that the third and special mark of Antichrist is the denial of the Incarnation

[p. 79] The Holy Fathers who have written upon the subject of Antichrist, and of these prophecies of Daniel, without a single exception, as far as I know, and they are the Fathers both of the East and of the West, the Greek and the Latin Church—all of them unanimously,–say that in the latter end of the world, during the reign of Antichrist, the holy sacrifice of the altar will cease * [* Malvenda, lib. viii. c. 4, &c.][54]

Don Curzio Nitoglia's comments on this theme, in his Introduction to *AUGUSTIN LEHMANN – L'ANTICRISTO – L'uomo più fatale della storia*, agree entirely with those of Cardinal Manning:

> «St. Paul, in the II Epistle to the Thessalonians, says that the end of the world must be preceded by the Antichrist and that the Antichrist will be preceded in turn by general apostasy. It will be the defection of a large number of Christians caused by indifferentism or heresy or persecution or all these causes and altered together. St. Pius X, for example, in his encyclical *E supremi apostolatus cathedra* (1904) writes:
> "When all this is considered [the general Loss of faith, ed.] there is good reason to fear lest this great perversity of minds may be as it were a foretaste, and perhaps the beginning of the evils which are reserved for the last days, and that there may be already in the world the Son of Perdition [*of whom the Apostle speaks (II Thess. ii, 3)*] (...) and in that place precisely which, according to the same apostle is the distinguishing mark of Antichrist, man has put himself in the place of God, (...) he has made the universe almost a temple unto itself to be worshiped"».[55] (p. 23)

---

[54] The celebration of the Holy Mass will not cease entirely. Don Curzio Nitoglia, in his Introduction to *AUGUSTIN LEHMANN – L'ANTICRISTO – L'uomo più fatale della storia*: quotes Fr. Arrighini: «"The Holy Sacrifice of the Mass will not fail them either. Many deny it by referring to Daniel's prophecy that 'for one thousand two hundred and ninety days the perpetual Sacrifice will cease' (12,1) From the fact that these days coincide with those already numbered in the reign of the Antichrist it was too easily believed that during this period the the Mass will not be celebrated… We therefore agree that even during the "1,290" days of the reign of the Antichrist, the Church will never cease to celebrate the divine mysteries and administer the sacraments, although not publicly, but in such a hidden manner, that the ungodly and the persecutors will not even notice it, and they will consider all of its activities to have ceased."(ARRIGHINI, P. 245-246)»

[55] Don Curzio quotes here no. 5 of the encyclical. So it can be understood in its entire context, I include here the entire paragraph: «5. When all this is considered there is good reason to fear lest this great perversity may be as it were a foretaste, and perhaps the beginning of those evils which are reserved for the last days; and that there may be already in the world the "Son of Perdition" of whom the Apostle speaks (II. *Thess*. ii., 3). Such, in truth, is the audacity and the wrath employed everywhere in persecuting religion, in

«About the universality of apostasy, St. Robert Bellarmine states that it will be the Antichrist to complete it, so if this has not reached its summit, he will have time to reach it. St. Paul also says that after the defection and apostasy the man of sin will appear *"in omni seductione iniquitatis"*; which will therefore increase the apostasy and make it universal. But, we must ask ourselves, what is left that is missing now except for the advent of the Antichrist and the physical persecution?» (p. 24)

«... the Antichrist will claim to surpass the same God to be worshiped and to serve him only [...] (p.25) The history of philosophical thought, for example: In fact it is the continuation of two contraposed principles: on the one hand the personal and transcendent God who creates the world to make man participate in his Beatitude, and on the other Lucifer who wants to grasp his end without the help of God, with his only forces: this revolt was renewed in the earthly paradise, when the serpent said to Eve *'Eritis sicut dii"*, and is renewed in the man who wants to become God with his natural forces (pantheism).»

«The realist and perennial philosophy of Aristotle and St. Thomas is the continuation of the first line, professing the adaptation of the intellect to the object and the dependence of the creature on the Creator. Gnosis follows the second, professing that the subject is to establish and create the object, and that man must create a new world – one that, unlike the present, would no longer sing out the dependence of the creature on the Creator – one in which man himself is God. Well: this false philosophy or Gnosis, which was the soul of Vatican II, penetrated inside the Church with the new theologians, whose principal representative is Teilhard de Chardin. It comes from Lucifer and leads to the Antichrist. Hence, we should not be surprised that John Paul II would write that "God is immanent to the world and vivifies it from within." All this had already been predicted by the Holy Scripture.»

«If we think of all this, the words of Paul VI to the UN cannot fail to reverberate with terror in our mind: *"We more than anyone else have the cult of man "*. The religion of the Second Vatican Council is the religion of man and prepares the way for the manifestation and the reign of the Antichrist who works in history, until he can triumph when the obstacle and the guardian are removed from the midst. The universal temple is under construction

---

combating the dogmas of the faith, in brazen effort to uproot and destroy all relations between man and the Divinity! While, on the other hand, and this according to the same apostle is the distinguishing mark of Antichrist, man has with infinite temerity put himself in the place of God, raising himself above all that is called God; in such wise that although he cannot utterly extinguish in himself all knowledge of God, he has contemned God's majesty and, as it were, made of the universe a temple wherein he himself is to be adored. "He sitteth in the temple of God, showing himself as if he were God" (II. *Thess*. ii., 2).»

(Assisi 1986) and the Universal Republic also (thanks to the New World Order, to globalization to the nefarious power of USA and Israel[56]).»[57]

---

[56] Don Curzio mentions the 'New World Order', 'globalization', 'the nefarious power of USA and Israel' – These topics are the subject matter of my previous work, *The Mystery of Iniquity*.

[57] «S. Paolo, nella II Epistola ai Tessalonicesi, dice che la fine del mondo dovrà essere preceduta dall'Anticristo e che l'Anticristo sarà preceduto a sua volta dall'apostasia generale. Si tratterà della defezione di un gran numero di cristiani provocata dall'indifferentismo o dall'eresia o dalla persecuzione o da tutte queste cause ed altre unite insieme. S. Pio X, per esempio, nella sua encliclica *E supremi apostolatus cathedra* (1904) scrive:

«Chi tutto questo considera bene [la generale Perdita della fede, *n. d. a.*] ha ragione di temere che sifaatta perversità di menti sia quasi un saggio e fose il cominciamento dei malic he agli estremi tempi son riservati, e che già sia nel mondo il figlio della perdizione (...) In quella vece ciò che appunto, secondo il dire medesimo dell'Apostolo, è il carattere proprio del'Anticristo, "l'uomo si è posto in luogo do Dio (...) ha fatto dell'universo quasi un tempio a se medesimo per esservi adorato"». (p. 23)

«Circa l'universalità dell'apostasia, s. Roberto Bellarmino afferma che sarà proprio l'Anticristo a doverla completare, per cui se questa non ha toccata il vertice, farà in tempo a toccarlo. S. Paolo dice inoltre che dopo la defezione e l'apostasia l'uomo del peccato apparirà *"in omni seductione iniquitatis"*; esso aumenterà quindi l'apostasia e la renderà universale. Ma, viene da domandarci, che cosa manca ormai più se non l'avvento stesso dell'Anticristo e la persecuziona fisica?» (p. 24)

«... l'Anticristo pretenderà di andare oltre lo stesso dio per farsi adorare e servire lui solo [...] (p. 25) La storia del pensiero filosofico, per esempio. Infatti esso è la continuazione di due princìpi contraposti: da una parte dio personale e trascendente che crea il mondo per far participare l'uomo alla sua Beatitudine, e dall' altra Lucifero che vuol cogliere il suo fine senza l'aiuto di Dio, colle sue sole forze: tale rivolta si è rinnovato nel paradiso terrestre, quando il serpent disse ad Eva *"Eritis sicut dii"*, e si rinnova nell'uomo che voul diventar Dio con le sue forze naturali (panteismo).»

«La filosofia reaalista e perenne di Aristotele e S. Tommaso è la continuazione della prima linea, professando l'adeguazione dell'intelletto all' oggetto e la dipendenza della creatura dal Creatore. La Gnosi segue la seconda, professando che il soggetto a porre e creare l'oggetto e che l'uomo deve creare un nuovo mondo – che che non canti più, come l'attuale, la dipendenza della creatura dal Creatore – in cui l'uomo stesso e dio. Ebbene: tale filosofia falsa o Gnosi, penetra all'interno della Chiesa con I n uovi teologi, il cui reppresentante principale è Teilhard de Chardin, è stata l'anima del Vaticano II; essa viena da Lucifero e conduce all'Anticristo. Perciò non dobbiamo stupirci se Giovanni

Bearing in mind these words of Don Nitoglia, "The religion of the Second Vatican Council is the religion of man and prepares the way for the manifestation and the reign of the Antichrist"; it can be seen that what was foretold in the prophecy of St. Francis quoted at the beginning of this work is being fulfilled at the present time:

> "... **there will be very few Christians who will obey the true Sovereign Pontiff and the Roman Church** with loyal hearts and perfect charity. **At the time of this tribulation a man not canonically elected will be raised to the Pontificate, who, by his cunning, will endeavour to draw many into error and death.** [...] except those days were shortened, according to the words of the Gospel, **even the elect would be led into error**, were they not specially guided, amid such great confusion..."

The first clause, "*there will be very few Christians who will obey the true Sovereign Pontiff and the Roman Church with loyal hearts and perfect charity*", has been fulfilled in the half-century that followed Vatican II. It has been an unprecedented tribulation for the Church. In his article, *La problematica della teologia contemporanea*, Fr. Cornelio Fabro indicated that the present doctrinal crisis in the Church is the greatest she has suffered in all her history. *Sœur Jeanne de la Nativité* (Jeanne le Royer, 1732 – 1798), renowned for her prophecies[58], foretold the same tribulation in greater detail: "O God! In what agitation do I see the Holy Church, when she will perceive, suddenly, the progress of these impious, their extent and the number of souls that they will have trained in their party! This heresy will extend so far that it will seem to envelop all countries and states.

Paolo II scrisse che "Dio è immanente al mondo e lo vivifica dal didentro". Tutto ci era già stato predetto dalla S. Scrittura.»

«Se pensiamo a tutto ciò non possono non rimbombare con terrore nella nostra mente le parole di Paolo VI all'ONU: "Noi più di chiunque altro abbiamo il culto dell'uomo". La religione del Concilio Vaticano II è la religione del'uomo e prepara la via alla manifestazione e al regno dell'Anticristo che opera nella storia, fino a poter trionfare quando l'ostacolo e il guardiano siano tolti di mezzo. Il tempio universale è in via di allestimento (Assisi 1986) e la Reppublica universal anche (grazie al Nuovo Ordine Mondiale, alla globalizzazione al potere nefasto di USA ed Israele).»

[58] The prophecies quoted here are taken from *Vie et Révélations de Sœur de la Nativité* (*The Life and Revelations of the Sister of the Nativity*), by Charles Genet; first published in 1817.

Never has any heresy been so fatal!"[59] She elaborates: "[There will appear] the most deadly of heresies. Faith will undergo a new expansion: some religious orders will be reborn, in small numbers; others will be founded and their fervour will be great. Most of these orders will last until the time of the Antichrist, under whose reign all communities will suffer martyrdom, be crushed and destroyed."[60] She describes in some detail: "The first assault she will have to sustain after the one that she now undergoes will come from the spirit of Satan who will stir up leagues and assemblies against her. There are also those who will hide in underground places to form their diabolical plans to attack the Church and abolish religion. They will show themselves in a device that will charm curious minds and men of little religion. By their stratagems, they will endeavour to insinuate in the minds, and to show to all that their ways are right and reasonable for the human mind. "The Holy Spirit who governs our Mother the Church will make known to her children that what wants to seduce them are the deceivers and enchanters. Then, the Church will decide by the light of the Holy Spirit that they are bad trees and saviours, that will produce only the bitter fruits and that it is necessary to cut and cut down quickly."[61] ... "Then, Satan's henchmen

---

[59] «O Dieu! Dans quelle agitation je vois la Sainte Eglise, quand elle s'apercevra, tout à coup, des progrès de ces impies, de leur étendue et du nombre d'âmes qu'ils auront entraînées dans leur parti! Cette hérésie s'étendra si loin qu'elle semblera envelopper tous les pays et tous les états. Jamais aucune hérésie n'aura été si funeste!» [Cinquième Édition, Tome II, Paris 1870, p. 213]

[60] «[Apparaîtra] la plus funeste des hérésies. La foi connaîtra une nouvelle expansion: certains ordres religieux renaîtront, en petit nombre; d'autres seront fondés et leur ferveur sera grande. La plupart de ces ordres dureront jusqu'aux temps de l'Antéchrist, sous le règne duquel toutes les communautés souffriront le martyr, seront écrasées et détruites."» [Cinquième Édition, Tome II, Paris 1870, p. 213]

[61] «Le premier assaut qu'elle aura à soutenir après celui qu'elle subit maintenant, viendra de l'esprit de Satan qui suscitera contre elle des ligues et des assemblées. Il y a en même qui se cacheront dans des lieux souterrains pour former leurs projets diaboliques pour attaquer l'Église et abolir la religion. Ils se montreront dans un appareil qui charmera les esprits curieux et les hommes de peu de religion. Par leurs stratagêmes, ils s'efforceront de insinuer dans les esprits, et de montrer à tous que leurs voies son droits et raisonables pour l'esprit humain. «Le Saint-Esprit qui gouverne notre Mère l'Église fera connaître à ses enfants que ce qui veulent les séduire sont les fourbes et des enchanteurs. Alors, l'Église décidera par la lumière du Saint-Esprit que ce sont de mauvais arbres et des sauvegeons, qui ne produiront que les fruits amers et qu'il faut

will hide in the shadows and make a lot of books appear that will do a lot of harm. Everything will happen in silence, wrapped in an inviolable secret."[62] ... "All this bad business will last a long time without appearing outside; all will pass in silence, and will be wrapped under an inviolable secret; like a fire which burns below, without noise and little by little, and which spreads without raising its flame, this evil will spread in a large space and in several countries, it will be all the more serious and dangerous for the Holy Church that she will not see so soon of these fires."[63] ... "Some priests will see fumes from this cursed fire. They will rise up against those in whom they will notice singularities of devotion that will stand out from the good customs of the Church."[64] ... "Before the Antichrist arrives, the world will be afflicted with bloody wars. Peoples will rise up against the peoples; the nations, sometimes united, sometimes divided, will fight for or against the same party. The armies will shock each other horribly and fill the earth with murder and bloodshed. These wars, internal and foreign, will cause enormous sacrileges, profanations, scandals, infinite evils. The rights of the Holy Church will be usurped; she will receive great afflictions."[65] ... "His

---

promptement couper et abattre [...]» [Cinquième Édition, Tome II, Paris 1870, p. 207]

[62] «Alors, les suppôts de Satan se cacheront dans l'ombre et feront paraître quantité d'ouvrages qui feront beaucoup de mal. Tout se passera en silence, enveloppé d'un secret inviolable."» [Cinquième Édition, Tome II, Paris 1870, p. 208]

[63] «Tout ce mauvais commerce durera longtemps sans paraître au dehors; tout se passera en silence, et sera enveloppé sous un secret inviolable; comme un feu qui brûle en-dessous, sans bruit et peu à peu, et qui s'étend sans élever sa flamme, ce mal s'etendra dans un grand espace et dans plusieurs contrées, et il sera sera d'autant plus grave et dangereux pour la Sainte Eglise qu'elle ne s'apercevra pas si tôt de ces incendies.»

[64] «Quelques prêtres apercevront des fumées de ce maudit feu. Ils s'élèveront contre ceux chez qui ils remarqueront des singularités de dévotion qui se démarqueront des bonnes coutumes de l'Église.» [Cinquième Édition, Tome II, Paris 1870, p. 208]

[65] «Avant que l'Antéchrist n'arrive, le monde sera affligé de guerres sanglantes. Les peuples s'élèveront contre les peuples; les nations, tantôt unies, tantôt divisées, combattront pour ou contre le même parti. Les armées se choqueront épouvantablement et rempliront la terre de meurtres et de carnages. Ces guerres, intestines et étrangères, occasionneront des sacrilèges énormes, des profanations, des scandales, des maux infinis. On usurpera les droits de la Sainte Eglise; elle recevra de grandes afflictions.» [Cinquième Édition, Tome II, p. 203]

followers, in order to succeed, will first of all have great respect for the Gospel and Catholicity. There will be books on spirituality which will be written by them with a warmth of devotion, and will bring souls to a point of perfection which will seem to raise them to the third heaven. Therefore, there will be no doubt of the sanctity of their authors and partisans, who will be placed above the greatest saints, who, according to them, will have only begun to sketch virtue"[66] ... "I see yet in God that the people most likely to be deceived by the artifices of the devil or by the wiles of the wicked, will be those who, faltering in faith, will have in the heart only a dead faith, it is that is to say, without vigour and without activity, and who will also be indulged in the feelings of corrupt nature, a spirit of curiosity, an itch and a certain lust, anxious to know all that is happening in these beautiful novelties of religion. As I have already said, before the judgment, there will never have been so many deceptions under the colour of religion, so much devotion and sanctity in appearance and reputation; I see these hypocrites mounted on magnificence, and filled with pride and ostentation of Lucifer, make beautiful speeches, and attract to them all the vain souls of which I have spoken, and who have almost nothing Christian except the name."[67] "When the time of the reign of Antichrist is near, a false religion will appear which will be opposed to the unity of God and His Church. **This**

---

[66] «Ses sectateurs, pour mieux réussir, affecteront d'abord un grand respect pour l'Evangile et la catholicité. Il paraîtra des livres sur la spiritualité qui seront écrits par eux avec une chaleur de dévotion, et porteront les âmes à un point de perfection qui semblera les élever jusqu'au troisième ciel. Aussi, on ne doutera point de la sainteté de leurs auteurs et partisans, qu'on mettra au-dessus des plus grands saints, qui, suivant eux, n'auront fait qu'ébaucher la vertu». [Cinquième Édition, Tome II, p. 213]

[67] «Je vois encore en Dieu que les personnes les plus sujettes à être trompées par les artifices du démon ou par les ruses des impies, seront celles qui, chancelantes dans la foi, n'auront dans le coeur qu'une foi morte, c'est-à-dire sans vigueur et sans activité, et qui d'ailleurs se laisseront aller aux sentiments de la nature corrompue, à un esprit de curiosité, à une démangeaison et comme à une certaine convoitise inquiète de savoir tout ce qui se passe dans ces belles nouveautés de religion. Comme je l'ai déjà dit, d'ici au jugement, on n'aura jamais vu tant de tromperies sous couleur de religion, tant de dévotion et de sainteté en apparence et en réputation; je vois ces hypocrites montés sur la superbe, et remplis d'orgueil et de l'ostentation de Lucifer, faire de beaux discours, et attirer à eux toutes les âmes vaines dont je viens de parler, et qui n'ont presque du chrétien que le nom.» [Cinquième Édition, Tome II, p. 213]

will cause the greatest schism the world has ever known. Errors will cause ravages as never before. The nearer the time of the end, the more the darkness of Satan will spread on earth, the greater will be the number of the children of corruption, and the number of the just will correspondingly diminish...".[68]

According to the prophecy of St. Francis, the leader of this great heresy that will immediately precede the reign of Antichrist will be a ***false pope***; one who has been ***invalidly elected***: «**At the time of this tribulation a man not canonically elected will be raised to the Pontificate, who, by his cunning, will endeavour to draw many into error and death.**» Sr. Jeanne described him in these words, "I see that when the Second Coming of Christ approaches, a bad priest will do much harm to the Church..."[69] This false pope and heretic, who will spearhead the revolt and lead the stampede into the great apostasy, is foretold in the third secret of Fatima. When I mentioned to Malachi Martin that my research into the secret of Fatima leads me to believe that the secret reveals that there will be an antipope who will be a heretic, Malachi, who knew the secret from Cardinal Bea, replied to me, "Were it only that!"

The heresy of the false pope, and the false religion he and his Sect will eventually spawn, are foretold in these prophecies. They will attack the principal dogmas of the Catholic faith, and is foretold in some detail:

> One day, a heresy will try to deny the reality of Our Lord's presence in the Blessed Sacrament. Some will deny the Divinity, others the humanity of Jesus Christ in the adorable Eucharist. Finally, the others will try to divide one from the other by separating the attributes which in the person of the Messiah become inseparable, any attribution or denomination being, in a sense, common to both natures. There will be a great number of faithful who will suffer martyrdom for the defense of the real Presence, for towards the end of the centuries this truth will be sharply attacked and victoriously defended.[70]

---

[68] Rev. Fr. R. Gerald Culleton; *The Reign of Antichrist*

[69] "Aux approches du dernier avènement de Jésus-Christ il se trouvera un mauvais prêtre qui causera bien de l'affliction à l'Église." [Cinquième Édition, Tome II, p. 235]

[70] "Un jour, une hérésie s'efforcera de nier la réalité de la présence de Notre Seigneur au Saint Sacrement. Les uns nieront la Divinité, les autres l'humanité de Jésus-Christ dans l'adorable Eucharistie. Enfin les autres tâcheront de diviser l'une de l'autre en séparant les attributs qui dans la personne du Messie

At the approach of the reign of the Antichrist, that is to say towards the last times of the Church, a false and artificial people will attack the truths of the faith the most incontestable, even the attributes of Divinity. They will pretend that God has never left to the reprobates their free will only because he foresaw the abuse they must make of it, that consequently those who lose themselves do so without their fault; that at the same time God has removed free will from the elect, whom he has filled with privileges without any correspondence or merit on their part.[71]

I see in God that from the moment they begin to announce themselves to the Church until the time when the Church will see it, it is a bad nation. I see in God that from the time they came out of their caves, until the time when the Church will recognize their malice, there will transpire a considerable time, maybe half a century, more or less, I can not not say it exactly. During all this time their diabolical profession and their pernicious hypocrisy, which will make them look like saints, will attract many souls after them; for in the beginning this heresy will have a magnificent and imposing air of goodness, and even of religion, which will be a seductive trap for many.[72]

I see in God that all these satellites of the devil will no longer wish to suffer in the Holy Church, nor priest, nor sacrifice, nor altar, nor confession,

---

deviennent inséparables, toute attribution ou dénomination étant, en un sens, commune aux deux natures. Il y aura un grand nombre de fidèles qui souffriront le martyre pour la défense de la Présence réelle, car, vers la fin des siècles, cette vérité sera rudement attaquée et victorieusement défendue." [Seconde Édition, Tome Primere, Paris 1819, p. 309]

[71] "Aux approches du règne de l'Antéchrist, c'est-à-dire vers les derniers temps de l'Église, des gens faux et artificieux attaqueront les vérités de la foi les plus incontestables, même les attributs de la Divinité. Ils prétendront que Dieu n'a jamais laissé aux réprouvés leur libre arbitre que parce qu'il prévoyait l'abus qu'ils devaient en faire, que par conséquent ceux qui se perdent, le font sans qu'il y ait de leur faute; qu'en même temps Dieu a ôté le libre arbitre aux élus, qu'il a comblé de privilèges sans aucune correspondance ni mérite de leur part." [Cinquième Édition, Tome II, p. 234]

[72] "Je vois en Dieu que, depuis le moment où ils auront commencés à s'annoncer à l'Église, jusqu'à l'époque où Église s'en apercevra, c'est une mauvais nation. Je vois en Dieu que depuis l'époque où ils sortirent de leurs cavernes, jusqu'à celle où l'Église reconnaîtra leur malice, il se passera bien du temps, peut-être un demi-siècle, plus ou moins, je ne puis pas le dire au juste. pendant tout ce temps-là leur métier diabolique et leur pernicieuse hypocrisie, qui les feront regarder comme de saints, attireront à leur suite grand nombre d'âmes; car dans les commencements cette hérésie aura un air magnifique et très imposant de bonté, et même de religion qui sera un piège séduisant pour un grand nombre." [Cinquième Édition, Tome II, p. 213]

nor communion, nor any sacrament. They will want to appear no sign of our holy religion, and they will not even be able to suffer a sign of the cross from good Christians. These impious ones will have altars and temples in which their priests will endeavor to imitate the mysteries, the ceremonies, and the sacrifice of religion, to which they will mingle many extravagant and superstitious circumstances by invoking, or rather desecrating, the holy name of God. They will counter the sacraments. First they will baptize in the name of the three Divine Persons, but soon they will change the order of the Persons, and then they will remove them, to replace them with some of their saints. Their hypocrisy will make them invent surprising austerities, and far superior to the Lent and Abstinence of the Church and to all the mortifications of the Saints. But all this will take place only in appearance, and to impose on the eyes of men. Their religion being founded only on the pleasures of the senses, they will despise inwardly the crucified life, the mortification, the suffering; and all that they will show outside will be reduced to tricks of strength, by which clever charlatans will compete to seduce the simple, and make dupes of their deceit; what will soon be manifested by the contempt they will publicly make of the faith and morals of the Gospel.[73]

---

[73] "Je vois en Dieu que tous ces satellites du démon ne voudront plus souffrir dans la sainte Eglise ni prêtre, ni sacrifice, ni autel, ni confession, ni communion, ni aucun sacrement. Ils voudront qu'il ne paraisse aucun signe de notre sainte religion, et ils ne pourront pas même souffrir un signe de croix de la part des bons chrétiens. Ces impies auront des autels et des temples où leurs prêtres tâcheront d'imiter les mystères, les cérémonies et le sacrifice de la religion, auxquels ils mêleront quantité de circonstances extravagantes et superstitieuses en invoquant, ou plutôt en profanant le saint Nom de Dieu... Ils contreferont les sacrements. D'abord ils baptiseront au nom des trois Personnes divines, mais bientôt ils changeront l'ordre des Personnes, et ensuite ils en supprimeront, pour leur substituer quelques uns de leurs saints. Leur hypocrisie leur fera inventer des austérités surprenantes, et de beaucoup supérieures au carême et aux abstinences de l'Église et à toutes les mortifications des Saints. Mais tout cela n'aura lieu qu'en apparence, et pour en imposer aux yeux des hommes. Leur religion n'étant fondée que sur les plaisirs des sens, ils mépriseront intérieurement la vie crucifiée, la mortification, la souffrance; et tout ce qu'ils en feront paraître au dehors se réduira à des tours de force, par lesquels d'habiles charlatans rivaliseront pour séduire les simples, et faire des dupes de leur fourberie; ce qui se manifestera bientôt par le mépris qu'ils feront publiquement de la foi et de la morale de l'Evangile." [Seconde Édition, Tome IV, Paris 1819, p. 428-9]

BERGOGLIO IS THE LEADER OF THE REVOLT

«Abominatio desolationis intelligi potest et omne dogma perversum: quod cum viderimus stare in loco sancto, hoc est in Ecclesia et se ostendere Deum.»

S. Hieronymus — *Liber IV, Comment. in cap. XXIV Matthei*

"The abomination of desolation can be understood to be every perverse dogma which may stand in the holy place, that is in *the Church*, and show itself as God."

St. Jerome – Commentary on Matthew Chapter 24

Jorge "Francis" Bergoglio has declared his intention to reform the Church (and is initiating those reforms) in such a manner that would transform the Church into the anti-church foretold in the secret of Fatima, as Pope John Paul II indicated – and under an apostate Vatican, as foretold by Pope Leo XIII.

Bergoglio is in the process of "reforming" the Catholic Church into a new heretical "church", with a new religion: what Freemasonry calls "dogma free Christianity". This is the long-term plan of Freemasonry to demolish Catholicism and replace it with a new, dogma-free religion (as Father Manfred Adler explained and documented in his book *Die Antichristliche Revolution der Freimaurerei*). When that reform is accomplished, (not if but when; Bergoglio says it will happen), then the visible break of the "Conciliar Church" from the true Catholic Church will be accomplished and consummated, as Pope Leo XIII foretold in the original version of his prayer to St. Michael:

> «*Behold the Church, the Spouse of the Immaculate Lamb, filled with bitterness and inebriated with gall by the most crafty enemies; who have laid impious hands on all that is most sacred. Where the See of the most blessed Peter and the Chair of the truth, was constituted as the light of the nations, there they have set up the throne of their abominable impiety, so that the shepherd being struck, the sheep may be dispersed.*»[74]

---

[74] From the 1930 Raccolta: «Questi sì astuti nemici hanno riempito ed inebriato con impudenza ed amarezza la Chiesa, la Sposa dell'immacolato Agnello, ed hanno posto empie mani sui suoi più sacri possedimenti. Nel luogo santo medesimo, nel quale è stata stabilita la Sede del beatissimo Pietro e la sedia della Verità per la luce del mondo, essi hanno innalzato il trono della loro

Thus, "where the See of the most blessed Peter and the Chair of the Truth was constituted as the light of the nations, there they [the Masonic Sankt Gallen Mafia] have raised the throne of their abominable impiety". These words actually refer to Apostate Conciliar Rome, where the "throne of abominable impiety" will be (and already is), and under Bergoglio has been "raised up", and is the visible entity that occupies the place "where the See of the most blessed Peter and the Chair of Truth" was "set up as the light of the nations", as Cardinal Henry Edward Manning also explained more than 20 years earlier in his book, *The Present Crisis of the Holy See*. Basing his conclusion on the unanimous teaching of the ancient Fathers, Cardinal Manning wrote: "I think it well to recite the text of theologians of greatest repute. First Malvenda, who writes expressly on the subject, states as the opinion of Ribera, Gaspar Melus, Biegas, Suarez, Bellarmine and Bosius that Rome shall apostatize from the Faith, drive away the Vicar of Christ and return to its ancient Paganism. ... Then the Church shall be scattered, driven into the wilderness, and shall be for a time, as it was in the beginning, invisible; hidden in catacombs, in dens, in mountains, in lurking places; for a time it shall be swept, as it were from the face of the earth. Such is the universal testimony of the Fathers of the early Church."[75] We can gather from credible prophecies when these things will take place. From the prophecy of La Salette we read, "**The Church will be eclipsed.** *At first, we will not know which is the true pope.* **Then secondly,** *the Holy Sacrifice of the Mass will cease to be offered in churches and houses; it will be such that, for a time, there will not be public services any more. But I see that the Holy Sacrifice has not really ceased: it will be offered in barns, in alcoves, in caves, and underground.*"[76] There is uncertainty in the minds of many at present, (even of high-ranking prelates who express their doubts in private), as to which is the true pope. This situation in which we find ourselves at present will be succeeded by a return to such conditions as existed during the ancient Roman persecutions, and existed during the penal times after the Reformation in Britain and Ireland, when the practice of the Catholic religion became a capital offense. It will be ushered in by a heretical "pope" whose "reforms" will gain state recognition in the apostate nations as the established religion. It will begin with a morally unacceptable concession that will be demand of all the clergy,

---

abominevole empietà, con l'iniquo piano per il quale allorché il Pastore viene colpito le pecore siano disperse.»

[75] Henry Edward Cardinal Manning, *The Present Crisis of the Holy See*, 1861, London: Burns and Lambert, pp. 88-90.

[76] Abbot Paul Combe: *The Secret of Melanie and the Actual Crisis*, 1906, Rome, p. 137.

but will be allowed either expressly or tacitly by the false pope. This has been foretold by Bl. Anna Katherine Emmerich: *April 12, 1820 "I had another vision of the great tribulation.* **It seems to me that a concession was demanded from the clergy which could not be granted.** *I saw many older priests, especially one, who wept bitterly. A few younger ones were also weeping. But others, and the lukewarm among them, readily did what was demanded.* **It was as if people were splitting into two camps..."** One can easily imagine that what will be demanded of the clergy will be a concession to the state regarding the secrecy of confession. As I write, legislation is being proposed in the State of California that would require priests to violate the seal of confession. Will Francis utter a syllable in protest against the adoption of such iniquitous perversions of law? His silence during the abortion referendum in Ireland was already a most ominous indication that he will likewise do nothing to stop such a concession from being made by the national hierarchies.

As was the case during the Arian heresy, so now also, as Fr. Linus Clovis explained in May 2016: *"The Catholic Church and the anti-church currently co-exist in the same sacramental, liturgical and juridical space".* However, the "Conciliar Church" under Jorge Bergoglio is now in the actual process of breaking away formally from the true Church, while calling itself "Catholic", and excoriating the true Catholics as belonging to fringe groups of *schismatics* fanatically attached to the past. The actual breaking-away process was started by Bergoglio with *Amoris Lætitia*, and was eerily foretold by Sr. Lucia in her well-known letter to Cardinal Caffarra: "The final battle between the Lord and the reign of Satan will be about marriage and the family. Don't be afraid ... because anyone who operates for the sanctity of marriage and the family will always be contended and opposed in every way, because this is the decisive issue ... however, Our Lady has already crushed its head."

BERGOGLIO IS A FAITHLESS APOSTATE

Jorge Bergoglio has introduced heresy into his (putative) *authentic magisterium*. While a pope's authentic magisterium is not *per se* infallible, a pope can err when exercising it, and even if he were to inadvertently teach heresy, he would still remain in office as a valid and legitimate successor of Peter. However:

1. There is yet another aspect to the argument of the authentic magisterium against the validity of the Bergoglio pontificate, which is the infallibility of the general discipline of the pope and the true Church of

Rome, which Van Noort[77] and other theologians qualify as *theologice certum*. While the pope is not personally infallible in his authentic magisterium; if he attempts to preceptively impose a moral error as a canonically normative disciplinary measure on the whole Church by imposing it as a preceptive and canonically binding universal moral directive and teaching of the authentic papal magisterium, then he would thereby demonstrate that his own binding universal moral/disciplinary precepts do not have the infallibility of the universal disciplinary precepts of the true pope and Church of Rome. That is exactly what Francis attempted to do, to wit, to impose his heretical discipline in *Amoris Lætitia* on the whole Church by raising the heretical interpretation of the bishops of the Buenos Aires region on Holy Communion for the divorced & remarried, to the level of a universally preceptive and binding moral directive and teaching of the authentic papal magisterium. That act alone proves that the Bergoglian universal moral/disciplinary precepts do not have the infallibility of the universal discipline of the true pope and Church of Rome.

2. One cannot generalize in these matters. The exact wording of each provision has to be examined with precision so it can be determined in each case exactly what is being commanded, and to what degree the legislation makes the provision obligatory; and also it must be determined if the provisions were validly enacted according to procedural law. A canonically invalid precept is simply null and void, and is "considered non-existent" (*habetur pro infecto*), and therefore is incapable of falling under the protection of the Church's infallibility. An example of this would be the canonically invalid provisions of the *General Instruction*, for the Novus Ordo Missal of Paul VI. Likewise, a provision that superficially appears to be preceptive, but actually is not, (such as the promulgation of the Montinian rite of Mass in *Missale Romanum*), would not enjoy the protection of the Church's charism of infallibility, because it does not actually impose any obligatory disciplinary norm. Most evil provisions cannot be considered properly preceptive in the sense of commanding something morally wrong, because the wording of the law is not always strictly and literally preceptive. Others must be interpreted only in a very restrictive and qualified sense; according to the canonical principle, *Odiosa sunt restringenda*. Thus, provisions which

---

[77] G. Van Noort; *De Ecclesia Christi,* Hilversum in Hollandia, 1932: "*Infallibilitas ecclesiæ se extendit ad disciplinam generalem ecclesiæ.* — Theologice certum est." (N. 90 p. 103)

appear to be of the character of general norms, insofar as they appear to generally require something that would not be morally permissible as a general norm, but only as an exception, must be strictly interpreted, and applied only as an exception. Similarly, laws granting exceptions are to be interpreted restrictively. (**Can. 18** — Leges quae poenam statuunt aut liberum iurium exercitum coarctant aut **exceptionem a lege continent, strictae subsunt interpretationi**.) Thus, exceptions that would be justified only in cases of extreme necessity would be the only legitimate exceptions allowable, even when the canons in question are worded in such a manner that would appear to intend a wider application. This would clearly be the case for such canons as "the ecumenical canon", i.e., Canon 844 of the 1983 Code. Hence, the objection that is made by so many canonical-theological semi-literates; namely, that, "If Bergoglio's heretical general disciplinary norms prove he is not a true pope, then the same principle would be applicable to Montini, Wojtyła, and Ratzinger," would not be valid.

Most important of all, infallibility does not protect mere statements of doctrinal *sententiæ*, even if they are introduced into the papal authentic magisterium, but only pronouncements of the authentic magisterium enacted into **universal law**, which preceptively impose an **obligation**, would be covered by the infallibility that protects the universal discipline of the Church. Hence, even a materially heretical assertion made by a pope exercising his *authentic magisterium* does not prove that he is deprived of the charism of Infallibility; but since it is *theologice certum* that infallibility extends to general disciplinary norms of the Church; an "authentic interpretation" of a moral teaching published in the *Acta Apostolicae Sedis* for the purpose of making that interpretation a legally binding general disciplinary norm, is protected by the charism of Infallibility, a heretical interpretation of a moral doctrine promulgated with the force of law as a general disciplinary norm would prove beyond all shadow of doubt that the putative pope who issued the directive lacks the charism of Infallibility, and thereby would plainly manifest that the form of the Supreme Pontificate is absent in that person, and that his claim to be the "Bishop of Rome" is false. Jorge Bergoglio has introduced heresy into his official *authentic magisterium* precisely in order to establish a heretical measure as an obligatory norm of the universal discipline of the Church.

At the end of the synod, Bergoglio declared in yet another interview with Eugenio Scalfari:

"This is the bottom line result, the de facto appraisals are entrusted to the confessors, but at the end of faster or slower paths, all the divorced who ask will be admitted."

These are the words of Fr. Bergoglio: "ALL THE DIVORCED WHO ASK [for Holy Communion] WILL BE ADMITTED." (http://fatima.org/perspectives/sd/perspective798.asp)

"POPE" FRANCIS HAS OFFICIALLY APPROVED OF HOLY COMMUNION FOR PEOPLE LIVING IN ADULTERY

"Pope" Francis approves the granting of sacraments to adulterers under certain circumstances:

"5) Cuando las circunstancias concretas de una pareja lo hagan factible, especialmente cuando ambos sean cristianos con un camino de fe, se puede proponer el empeño de vivir en continencia. *Amoris laetitia* no ignora las dificultades de esta opción (cf. nota 329) y deja abierta la posibilidad de acceder al sacramento de la Reconciliación cuando se falle en ese propósito (cf. nota 364, según la enseñanza de san Juan Pablo II al Cardenal W. Baum, del 22/03/1996).

6) En otras circunstancias más complejas, y cuando no se pudo obtener una declaración de nulidad, la opción mencionada puede no ser de hecho factible. No obstante, igualmente es posible un camino de discernimiento. Si se llega a reconocer que, en un caso concreto, hay limitaciones que atenúan la responsabilidad y la culpabilidad (cf. 301-302), particularmente cuando una persona considere que caería en una ulterior falta dañando a los hijos de la nueva unión, *Amoris laetitia* abre la posibilidad del acceso a los sacramentos de la Reconciliación y la Eucaristía (cf. notas 336 y 351). Estos a su vez disponen a la persona a seguir madurando y creciendo con la fuerza de la gracia.7) Pero hay que evitar entender esta posibilidad como un acceso irrestricto a los sacramentos…"

Bergoglio's explicit approval: "El escrito es muy bueno y explícita cabalmente el sentido del capitulo VIII de *Amoris lae*titia. No hay otras interpretaciones."

http://m.vatican.va/content/francescomobile/es/letters/2016/documents/papa-francesco_20160905_regione-pastorale-buenos-aires.html

What is worse, as Emmett O'Regan observes, "this papal correspondence has now been raised to the level of the authentic

Magisterium, and as such, requires *obsequium religiosum* – the submission of the will and intellect, in accordance with Lumen Gentium 25, CIC Can. 752 and CCC 892."[78] Well, it would theoretically require a religious assent if Jorge Bergoglio were really the pope of the Catholic Church, and if there could be found no positive doubt that there is error in the document. However, the doctrine approved by Francis is heresy – he is not the pope, but an antipope, who possesses *no authentic magisterium*.

What utter contempt for God's law. Bergoglio does not believe in Christ's doctrine on marriage – Jorge Bergoglio is an infidel – a faithless heretic who openly denies the most basic dogmas and moral teachings of the Church. He is not a member of the Catholic Church, nor its pope.

His recent statement claiming that monogamous cohabitation constitutes a valid marriage[79] opposes the supernatural sacramentality of Holy Matrimony and manifests the anti-supernaturalism of the radical Naturalism of his belief system. If cohabitation were to be considered a valid marriage, then there would be no need for sacramental marriage, since the cohabitation would fulfil the law of God – which is heresy. Bergoglio's idea of marriage is rooted in Masonic *naturalism* — which is no surprise, because Bergoglio's religion is identical to the Masonic religion of Naturalism.

Francis is the closer of the ecclesial revolution begun by the Protestant Reformers. If the new changes in the Mass would be ordered by Rome, it would eventually become obvious that Protestant Rome is consummating the work of the 16th Century reformers. Bergoglio, by his Motu Proprio *Magnum Principium*, has now ordered the revolution to be carried out from below:

> (Canon 383)
> «§2. It is for the Apostolic See to order the sacred liturgy of the universal Church, publish liturgical books, recognise adaptations approved by the Episcopal Conference according to the norm of law, and exercise vigilance that liturgical regulations are observed faithfully everywhere.»
>
> «§3. It pertains to the Episcopal Conferences to faithfully prepare versions of the liturgical books in vernacular languages, suitably

---

[78] *The Heretical Pope Fallacy*, 11 Dec. 2017, in Vatican Insider *La Stampa*

[79] "He said on the one hand that the "great majority" of Catholic marriages are "null", and that some cohabiting relationships "have the grace of a real marriage because of their fidelity" and in fact may be "real marriages" because of this." The Irish Catholic (http://irishcatholic.ie/article/understanding-pope%E2%80%99s-remarks-about-marriage)

accommodated within defined limits, and to approve and publish the liturgical books for the regions for which they are responsible after the confirmation of the Apostolic See.»

Thus, the last vestiges of Catholicism that Benedict XVI restored to the Conciliar liturgy must now give way to the radical Modernist liberal Protestantism of Gnostic, Neo-Pagan Rome, which is now being ushered in by His Humbleness, "Pope" Francis by means of this liturgical reform, will be carried out by the bishops' conferences. The actual engine that transformed Catholicism into Protestantism in England (and Germany, etc.), as Hillaire Belloc explained, was the liturgical reform that mutated the Catholic Mass into Cranmer's (Protestant) *Masse or Lord's Supper*, with its Protestant *lex orandi* reflecting the new *lex credendi* of the Reformation. A nearly identical reform of the liturgy was inaugurated by Pope Paul VI, with his *Ordo Missæ* (1967) and *Missale Romanum* (1969). The Novus Ordo liturgy of Paul VI does not instruct the faithful in the truths of the faith, because it was constructed in the same manner as the heretical services of the Reformers, who, as J. P. M. van der Ploeg OP explains, adapted, "existing Catholic rites, but removed from them everything which was not compatible with the particular heresies they favoured." The pattern of adaptation of the traditional rite in the making of the Novus Ordo has been shown to be substantially identical to that employed by Thomas Cranmer in the making of the Protestant Masse or Lord's Supper of 1549. Cranmer's purpose for modifying the liturgy was doctrinal, as Belloc explains: "… to get rid of the Mass was the soul of the whole affair, because he hated it, especially… its central doctrine… the Real Presence of God upon the altar. … But it would be impossible to effect so complete a revolution at one blow… it had to be done in two stages… The first new service in the place of the Mass must be of a kind that men might mistake for something like a continuance of the Mass in another form. When that pretence had done its work and the measure of popular resistance taken, they could proceed to the second step and produce a final Service Book in which no trace of the old sanctities should remain."[80]

The Conciliar reformed liturgy of Paul VI, (i.e. the "Lord's Supper or Mass" constructed by Annibale Bugnini), was the preliminary transitional liturgy – the "reformed liturgy" of the "reformed Church". It is not just I, but even the Modernist adherents of the heretical

---

[80] Hilaire Belloc, *Cranmer*, Philadelphia: Lippincott, 1931, p. 246.

'Conciliar Church' refer to it as a "reformed church". Father Richard P. McBrien, in *The Catholic Transcript* of June 21, 1996, wrote: "Opposition to this reformed liturgy and to the communal environment in which it occurs is, at root, opposition to the reformed church". It was this transitional liturgy of the transitional "Conciliar Church", or as Cardinal Ratzinger called it, "the Church of the Present", which set the stage for the consummation of the work of the sixteenth century Reformers which is at present being carried out by Bergoglian Rome.

The Conciliar Church is not a renewed Catholic Church, but rather it is a Reformed Church — a Church that has, by means of a reformed liturgy, undergone a transformistic evolution – a metamorphosis that has paved the way for the fulfilment of the Sixteenth Century Reformers' dream: *Protestant Rome*. Father Hubert Jedin, one of the premier historians of the modern era, already pointed out in 1968, that a new Protestant Reformation is taking place in the Church:

> «We know that today the inner process of schism, the formation of a "Confession" (denomination), lasted not years, but decades. Melanchton and Calvin claimed to be "Catholic" until the end of their lives while the adherents of the old faith were calumniated as "Papists." The faithful long clung to the Mass and their saints, and the church regulations introduced by Lutheran magistrates took over many Catholic customs — even processions and pilgrimages. The bulk of the simple faithful never understood that the "Reformation" was not a reform of the Church but the construction of a new Church set up on a different basis. In retrospect one must therefore maintain: the schism of the Church succeeded by nothing so much as by the illusion that it did not exist. The illusion was widespread in Rome and in the German episcopate, among many theologians, among the majority of clergymen and among the people. The parallels between now and then are obvious. ... The Church's present crisis... is in its innermost essence, as in the 16th Century, a matter of uncertainty and disorientation in the Faith.»[81]

Being transitional, the *Conciliar Church* is a "church" in transition towards something in the future – what Ratzinger termed, the "Church of the Future"; and he said we cannot really imagine what that future church will be like: «[T]he end of all ecumenical effort is to attain the true unity of the Church... For the moment, I wouldn't dare venture to suggest any concrete realisation, possible or imaginable, of this future

---

[81] Hubert Jedin, *Letter to the German Bishops*, in The Latin Mass, Nov.-Dec.1994, p. 26.

Church... We are at an intermediate stage of unity in diversity.»[82] The "unity in diversity" which Cardinal Ratzinger described in terms of existing in relation between separate denominations and the Catholic Church, cannot ever exist *within* the unity of the *one* Church founded by Christ, because that Church possesses perfect unity in the rulership of the Church by Christ through the governance of Christ's vicar on earth, the Roman Pontiff; in the one Catholic faith contained in the deposit of revelation, taught infallibly by the pope and the bishops in communion with him; and in the true worship of God consisting in the Church's sacraments and pre-eminently in the sacrifice of the New Covenant instituted by Christ, the Holy Sacrifice of the Mass.

Pope Benedict XVI does not intend for the Church the heretical unity in diversity of the interfaith communion envisaged by the Bergoglian reform. In the magisterium of Benedict, one reads:

> Christ "established here on earth" only one Church and instituted it as a "visible and spiritual community", that from its beginning and throughout the centuries has always existed and will always exist, and in which alone are found all the elements that Christ himself instituted. "This one Church of Christ, which we confess in the Creed as one, holy, catholic and apostolic [...]. This Church, constituted and organised in this world as a society, subsists in the Catholic Church, governed by the successor of Peter and the Bishops in communion with him".
>
> In number 8 of the Dogmatic Constitution *Lumen gentium* 'subsistence' means this perduring, historical continuity and the permanence of all the elements instituted by Christ in the Catholic Church, in which the Church of Christ is concretely found on this earth. [83]

Further on in the same document, concerning the Protestant churches:

> According to Catholic doctrine, these Communities do not enjoy apostolic succession in the sacrament of Orders, and are, therefore, deprived of a constitutive element of the Church. These ecclesial Communities which, specifically because of the absence of the sacramental priesthood, have not preserved the genuine and integral substance of the

---

[82] Quoted by Fr. Phillipe Marcille in *Ecumenical Leprosy*, The Angelus, March 1994, p. 24.

[83] *CONGREGATION FOR THE DOCTRINE OF THE FAITH: RESPONSES TO SOME QUESTIONS REGARDING CERTAIN ASPECTS OF THE DOCTRINE ON THE CHURCH*; June 29, 2007.

Eucharistic Mystery cannot, according to Catholic doctrine, be called "Churches" in the proper sense.

Like Cardinal Ratzinger, whose own words manifest that he could not foresee the catastrophe that Ecumenism would unleash; John Paul II also did not comprehend how ecumenism would destroy the Catholic faith down to its foundations, as Pius XI stated in *Mortalium Animos*. In *Ut Unum Sint*, John Paul II explains that the Ecumenism adopted by the Second Vatican Council is the Ecumenism that had its origin in the Protestant sects: "At the Second Vatican Council, the Catholic Church committed herself irrevocably to following the path of the ecumenical venture..." (n. 3), yet John Paul II admits that "The Ecumenical movement really began within the Churches and Ecclesial Communities of the Reform." (no. 65) What John Paul II neglects to mention is that the Ecumenical movement was condemned by Pope Pius XI on 6 January 1928, in his Encyclical Letter *Mortalium Animos*, on "Fostering True Religious Unity". The unity of the Catholic Church as is taught in Catholic doctrine is essentially incompatible with the ecumenical ecclesiology of unity in diversity, which is the heretical ecclesiology of the Reformation churches. This is obvious when one considers that the reformation was essentially a revolt against the Catholic Mass. The *Bergoglian reforms* intend to make that heretical ecclesiology the foundation of the *Reformed Church*. The result will not be a reformed Catholic Church, since the divine constitution of the indefectible Church does not allow any alteration of anything divinely instituted in the Church. The product of the reform will be a global *anti-church*.

The errors of ecumenism forcefully condemned, and the grave harm that they would inflict on the Church if that condemnation were to go unheeded were clearly explained by Pius XI in *Mortalium Animos*:

> These pan-Christians who strive for the union of the churches would appear to pursue the noblest of ideals in promoting charity among all Christians. But how should charity tend to the detriment of faith? Everyone knows that John himself, Apostle of love, who seems in his Gospel to have revealed the secrets of the Sacred Heart of Jesus, and who never ceased to impress upon the memory of his disciples the new commandment "to love one another," nevertheless strictly forbade any close social contact with those who professed a mutilated and corrupt form of Christ's teaching: "If any man come to you, and bring not this doctrine, receive him not into the house, nor say to him, God speed you." (II John 10)

This being so, it is clear that the Apostolic See can by no means take part in these assemblies, nor is it in any way lawful for Catholics to give such enterprises their encouragement or support. If they did so, they would be giving countenance to a false Christianity quite alien to the one Church of Christ... For it is indeed a question of defending revealed truth. Jesus Christ sent His Apostles into the whole world to declare the Faith of the Gospel to every nation, and to save them from error... The only-begotten Son of God not only bade His representatives to teach all nations; He also obliged all men to give credence to whatever was taught them by "witnesses pre-ordained by God" (Acts 10:41). Moreover, He enforced His command with this sanction: "He that believeth and is baptised shall be saved; he that believeth not shall be condemned" (Mark 16:16). These two commands — the one to teach, the other to believe for salvation — must be obeyed.

The energy with which this scheme is being promoted has won for it many adherents, and even many Catholics are attracted by it, since it holds out the hope of a union apparently consonant with the wishes of Holy Mother Church, whose chief desire it is to recall her erring children and bring them back to her bosom. In reality, however, these fair and alluring words cloak a most grave error, subversive to the foundations of the Catholic Faith. ... There is but one way in which the unity of Christians may be fostered, and that is by furthering the return to the one true Church of Christ of those who are separated from it; for far from that one true Church they have in the past fallen away... If, as they constantly say, they long to be united with Us and Ours, why do they not hasten to enter the Church, "the mother and mistress of all Christ's faithful"? (Conc. Lateran. IV, C. 5).

I have been saying for decades that the Church of England in particular is the prototype of the Antichurch of the Great Apostasy – that the Conciliar Church would eventually devolve into a confederation of virtually autonomous national hierarchies as St. Hildegard von Bingen foretold[84]; because, (as I pointed out in my book on *The Suicide of Altering the Faith in the Liturgy*), the Ecclesiology adopted by Vatican II Ecumenism is the Protestant Ecclesiology formulated by the Protestant sects. Here is how a Protestant Anglican explains it in his own words:

"it is a mistake to refer, as many people do, to the various branches of the Church as 'religions'. If a church is a Christian church, it is part of the

---

[84] "The time is coming when princes and people will renounce the authority of the Pope. Individual countries will prefer their own Church rulers to the Pope. The German Empire will be divided. Church property will be secularized. Priests will be persecuted. After the birth of Antichrist heretics will preach their false doctrines undisturbed, resulting in Christians having doubts about their holy Catholic faith."

Christian religion. There is one Christian religion but there are many ways of expressing it, the ways of the various branches or 'communions' or denominations of the Christian church."[85]

This notion of *unity in diversity* in the one Christian Church is the heretical foundation upon which the *Roman Protestant Conciliar Ecumenical Church* was inaugurated by Paul VI in *Unitatis Redintegratio*.

That *Roman Protestant Church*, the *reformed* "Church of the future" is here – the New Advent of Wojtyła has brought us to Bergoglio's "Great Beginning" of the "Church of the future": *Magnum Principium* is the engine of transformation, which by means of liturgical reform, will transform the "Conciliar Church" into the global confederation of autonomous national hierarchies, which will have no binding dogmas or moral absolutes – exactly like the global Anglican Communion. This is the Great Beginning of Bergoglio's new religion of the "Universal Church" of Protestant Rome, foretold by Pope St. Pius X:

> «d'établissement d'une Église universelle qui n'aura ni dogmes, ni hiérarchie, ni règle pour l'esprit, ni frein pour les passions et qui, sous prétexte de liberté et de dignité humaine, ramènerait dans le monde, si elle pouvait triompher, le règne légal de la ruse et de la force, et l'oppression des faibles, de ceux qui souffrent et qui travaillent.»[86] (*Notre charge apostolique*)

The reformed Church spawned by Vatican II realises its consummation in the *"Église universelle"* – the universal "Church" of Bergoglio's Grand Beginning, the "Dogma-free Christianity" which Freemasonry seeks to establish by means of protestantizing reforms of the Church.[87]

> **«[Satan] will set up a counter-church which will be the ape of the [Catholic] Church ... It will have all the notes and characteristics of**

---

[85] Charles W. F. Smith, *Discovering the Episcopal Church, Foreword*, Movement Publications, Cincinnati, 1989.

[86] «... the establishment of a universal Church which will have no dogmas, no hierarchy, no rule for the mind, no braking for the passions and which, under the pretext of freedom and human dignity, would bring back into the world, if it could, to triumph, the legal reign of cunning and strength, and the oppression of the weak, of those who suffer and work.»

[87] cf. "Dogmenfreies Christentum" in, Manfred Adler; *Die Antichristliche Revolution der Freimaurerei*.

the Church, but in reverse and emptied of its divine content.» – Archbishop Fulton Sheen

As I wrote earlier: «[Just after the death of Cardinal Meisner], Pope Benedict warned about the boat (of Peter), the Church: *"the boat has taken on so much water as to be on the verge of capsizing."*» Bergoglio is on record of having said that *ALL the divorced and remarried will be admitted to Holy Communion.* The Catholic discipline must be overthrown, and a new, *permissive morality* must become the basis of the new discipline, *which will be identical to the discipline of the most liberal Protestants.* This is *directly opposed to divine law; and to institutionalize it will violate the divine constitution of the Church, according to which the Church is HOLY, and teaches and legislates according to divine law. Such a reform will constitute the defection of the "Conciliar Church" from Catholicism.* Not only adulterers will be given the sacraments, but sodomites, and transgender, and all varieties of perverts as well.

Bergoglio is also on record of having stated, *that he intends to bring about union between the Catholic Church and the Protestant sects.* When that happens, *it will not be the true & visible Catholic Church, which, remaining faithful to dogma, will refuse to unite with other religions and denominations, and which will remain faithful to the Law of Christ; but it will be the APOSTATE CHURCH* – the *"Conciliar Church"*, (which as a cancer within has so corrupted the official mainstream Church, some of which at present, is at least still formally Catholic and only materially Conciliar and heretical), that will *visibly consummate its apostasy from Catholicism by visibly separating itself from the unity of true Church and join in communion with the sects. I am not speculating or theorizing about this defection which is already in progress: Jorge Bergoglio has already declared it to be the agenda of his (bogus) pontificate, which he declares he intends to make "irreversible".*[88] Bergoglio, who openly expresses his disdain for dogma, intends to "reform" the Catholic Church into a new heretical

---

[88] Austen Ivereigh reported in *Crux* on May 13, 2017: «The Spaniard who was until earlier this year Superior General of the Jesuits has written a series of reminiscences about his conversations with Pope Francis, published in two parts in the Spanish Jesuit publication *Mensajero*. Father Adolfo Nicolás, SJ, wrote them while spending some weeks in his native country before heading for the Philippines capital, Manila, where he now lives. When Nicolás – who is the same age as Francis – spoke to him of his resignation as Superior General, Francis told him: "I myself am thinking of taking seriously Benedict's challenge." But then, some months later – faced, presumably, with some resistance to his reforms – Francis told him: "I ask the good Lord to take me once the changes are irreversible."»

"church", substituting Catholicism with a new religion Catholic in name only: what Freemasonry calls "Christianity without dogmas". This is the long-term plan of Freemasonry to demolish Catholicism and replace it with a new, dogma-free religion (as Father Manfred Adler explained in his above-mentioned book). Bergoglio's concept of God and his belief system is based on the doctrines of Spinoza, Schleiermacher, and especially Pierre Teilhard de Chardin S.J. His "religion" resembles notably the pre-eminently Masonic religion of Lord Shaftesbury (Anthony Ashley Cooper, 3rd Earl of Shaftesbury, Feb. 26, 1671 – 16 Feb. 1713).

BERGOGLIO'S REFORM

On 25 May 2018, Gloria TV[89] reported Monsignor Antonio Livi's words concerning "Pope" Francis's election, who stated that Francis was elected in order to carry out a "reform in the Lutheran sense." The report stated: «Monsignor Antonio Livi … a former dean and professor at the Lateran University in Rome, told Gloria.tv in an exclusive interview that Pope Francis was elected to carry out a – quote – "reform in the Lutheran sense".» The report continues,

> «On the basis of many historical witnesses Monsignor Livi is – quote – "absolutely certain" that the election of Pope Francis was orchestrated. [...] Monsignor Livi points out that a known heretic like Cardinal Kasper was chosen by Pope Francis as the main inspirator for the Synod of the Family. For Livi this is another indication that Francis' election was a big set-up which will eventually lead to the recognition of Luther and to the creation of a Mass without consecration. According to Livi this revolution was already planned in the early sixties. The last fifty years were marked by the activity of… "evil and heretical" theologians in order to conquer power… "Now they have conquered it."»

According to another report,[90]

> «Cardinal Gerhard Müller said this week that many bishops today are involved in "a blatant process of Protestantizing" the Catholic Church, leaving many of the faithful confused and disoriented. The doctrines requiring reform encompass blessing for homosexual couples, intercommunion with Protestants, relativizing the indissolubility of

---

[89] https://www.gloria.tv/video/zhvEjGegsZhu1WVbciqaPkjFW.
[90] https://www.breitbart.com/national-security/2018/06/27/former-vatican-doctrinal-chief-many-catholics-feel-abandoned-and-betrayed-by-shepherds/.

sacramental marriage, the abolition of priestly celibacy, and approval for sexual relations before and outside of marriage, he said.»

The report quoted an interview given by the Cardinal:

> «**Cardinal Gerhard Müller:** One group of German bishops, with their president [i.e., of the German Bishops' Conference] in the lead, see themselves as trendsetters of the Catholic Church on the march into modernity. They consider the secularization and de-Christianization of Europe as an irreversible development. For this reason the New Evangelization—the program of John Paul II and Benedict XVI—is in their view a battle against the objective course of history, resembling Don Quixote's battle against the windmills. They are seeking for the Church a niche where it can survive in peace. Therefore all the doctrines of the faith that are opposed to the "mainstream," the societal consensus, must be reformed.
>
> One consequence of this is the demand for Holy Communion even for people without the Catholic faith and also for those Catholics who are not in a state of sanctifying grace. Also on the agenda are: a blessing for homosexual couples, intercommunion with Protestants, relativizing the indissolubility of sacramental marriage, the introduction of *viri probati* and with it the abolition of priestly celibacy, approval for sexual relations before and outside of marriage. These are their goals, and to reach them they are willing to accept even the division of the bishops' conference.
>
> The faithful who take Catholic doctrine seriously are branded as conservative and pushed out of the Church, and exposed to the defamation campaign of the liberal and anti-Catholic media.»[91]

When the reform will have been accomplished, then the visible break of the "Conciliar Church" from the true Catholic Church will be consummated, as Pope Leo XIII foretold in the above quoted original version of his prayer to St. Michael: "*Where the See of the most blessed Peter and the Chair of the truth, was constituted as the light of the nations, there they have set up the throne of their abominable impiety, so that the shepherd being struck, the sheep may be dispersed.*". That Conciliar *Antichurch* being set up under the rule of Bergoglio's *throne of abominable impiety* was described by Archbishop Sheen:

> «The False prophet will have **a religion without a cross. A religion without a world to come.** *A religion to destroy religions. There will be a counterfeit Church.*»

---

[91] https://www.catholicworldreport.com/2018/06/26/cdl-muller-we-are-experiencing-conversion-to-the-world-instead-of-to-god/.

«Christ's Church the Catholic Church will be one; and the false Prophet will create the other.»

«The False Church will be worldly, ecumenical, and global. It will be a loose federation of churches and religions, forming some type of global association.»

«A world parliament of Churches. **It will be emptied of all Divine content**, it will be the mystical body of the anti-christ. The Mystical Body on earth today will have its Judas Iscariot, and he will be the false prophet. Satan will recruit him from our Bishops.»

«The Antichrist will not be so called; otherwise he would have no followers. He will not wear red tights, nor vomit sulphur, nor carry a trident nor wave an arrowed tail as Mephistopheles in Faust. This masquerade has helped the Devil convince men that he does not exist. When no man recognizes, the more power he exercises. God has defined Himself as "I am Who am," and the Devil as "I am who am not." [...]»

«The pre-Communist Russian belief is that he will come disguised as the Great Humanitarian; he will talk peace, prosperity and plenty not as means to lead us to God, but as ends in themselves ...»

«The third temptation in which Satan asked Christ to adore him and all the kingdoms of the world would be His, will become the temptation to have a new religion without a Cross, a liturgy without a world to come, a religion to destroy a religion, or a politics which is a religion—one that renders unto Caesar even the things that are God's.»

«In the midst of all his seeming love for humanity and his glib talk of freedom and equality, he will have one great secret which he will tell to no one: he will not believe in God. Because his **religion will be brotherhood without the fatherhood of God**, he will deceive even the elect. He will set up a counterchurch which will be the ape of the Church, because he, the Devil, is the ape of God. It will have all the notes and characteristics of the Church, but in reverse and **emptied of its divine content**. It will be a mystical body of the Antichrist that will in all externals resemble the mystical body of Christ [...] But the twentieth century will join the counterchurch because it claims to be infallible when its visible head speaks ex cathedra...»[92]

Pope John Paul II stated that **this struggle between the Church and the *anti-church;* the Gospel and the *anti-gospel*, is revealed in the *Secret of Fatima*. As** I wrote elsewhere, "If it was so important 58 years ago that the Mother of God wanted the Secret revealed *then*, how much more urgent is it *now*, five years after the *heretical intruder* has

---

[92] Fulton J. Sheen, *Communism and the Conscience of the West* [Bobbs-Merril Company, Indianapolis, 1948], pp. 24-25.

hijacked the Vatican, and transformed it into the headquarters of his global *Reformation*, by which he intends to replace the true Catholic Church with a Masonic *counterfeit church*. **This point of the Secret must be shouted from the rooftops."**

This is pre-eminently the duty of the priests: The priest must be a guardian and watchman, who sounds the alarm when the enemy attacks. This is what **God** says on this point: «The word of the Lord came to me: "Son of man, speak to your people and say to them: 'When I bring the sword against a land, and the people of the land choose one of their men and make him their watchman, and he sees the sword coming against the land and blows the trumpet to warn the people, then if anyone hears the trumpet but does not heed the warning and the sword comes and takes their life, their blood will be on their own head. Since they heard the sound of the trumpet but did not heed the warning, their blood will be on their own head. If they had heeded the warning, they would have saved themselves. But if the watchman sees the sword coming and does not blow the trumpet to warn the people and the sword comes and takes someone's life, that person's life will be taken because of their sin, but I will hold the watchman accountable for their blood.'"» (Ezekiel 33)

Meanwhile, as the *Anti-church* makes its move to take the place of the true Church founded by Christ; so many priests and bishops uphold the supposed legitimacy of the false *"Conciliar Church"* and its counterfeit "pope". The defection of Rome has been described by Fr. Berry on page 120 – 122 of the same work:

> [120] In the foregoing chapter [12] St. John outlines the history of the Church from the coming of Antichrist until the end of the world…In this chapter he shows us the true nature of the conflict. It shall be a war unto death between the Church and the powers of darkness in a final effort to destroy the Church and thus prevent the universal reign of Christ on earth."
> [p. 121] "In this passage there is an evident allusion to some particular son of the Church whose power and influence shall be such that Satan will seek his destruction at any cost. This person can be none other than the Pope to be elected in those days. The Papacy will be attacked by all the powers of hell. In consequence the Church will suffer great trials and afflictions in securing a successor upon the throne of Peter.
> The words of St. Paul to the Thessalonians may be a reference to the Papacy as the obstacle to the coming [p. 122] of Antichrist: "You know what withholdeth, that he may be revealed in his time. For the mystery of iniquity already worketh; only that he who now holdeth, do hold until he be taken

out of the way. And then that wicked one shall be revealed." [II Thessalonians ii, 6, 7]

3. St. John now sees in heaven a red dragon with seven heads and ten horns; each head bearing a diadem. The dragon is Satan red with the blood of martyrs, which he will cause to flow. The meaning of the seven heads and ten horns must be sought in the description of the beast that represents Antichrist where they symbolize kings or worldly powers. [Apocalypse xvii, 9 – 12] Those of the dragon must have a similar meaning, and indicate that Satan's attacks against the Church will be organized and carried out by the governments and ruling powers of those days.

With the beast of Antichrist only the horns have diadems as symbols of royalty or governing power. The heads are branded with names of blasphemy. (Apocalypse, 13:1) Hence they symbolize the sins and errors that will afflict the Church. Seven, the number of universality, indicates that in in this final struggle to prevent the universal reign of Christ all forms of sin and error will be marshalled against the Church. A prelude to this may be seen in the errors of Modernism which have been rightly designated "a synthesis of all heresies." The number seven is also appropriate since all sins are included in the seven capital sins. In like manner all errors that have 9p. 123) afflicted the Church may be summed up in these seven: Judaism, paganism, Arianism, Mohammedanism, Protestantism, rationalism, and atheism.

The dragon is seen in heaven which is here a symbol of the Church, the kingdom of heaven on earth. This indicates that the first troubles of those days will be inaugurated within the Church by apostate bishops, priests, and peoples, — the stars dragged down by the tail of the dragon.

4. The tail of the dragon represents the cunning hypocrisy with which he succeeds in deceiving a large number of people and pastors – a third part of the stars. Arianism led away many bishops, priests and peoples. The pretended Reformation of the sixteenth century claimed still larger numbers but these cannot be compared to the numbers seduced by Satan in the days of Antichrist. The dragon stands before the woman, ready to devour the child that is brought forth. In other words, the powers of hell seek by all means to destroy the Pope elected in those days. [...]

It is now the hour for the powers of darkness. The new-born Son of the Church is taken "to God and to his throne." Scarcely has the newly elected Pope been enthroned when he is snatched away by martyrdom. The "mystery of iniquity" gradually developing through the centuries, cannot be fully consummated while the power of the Papacy endures, but now he that "withholdeth is taken out of the way." During the interregnum "that wicked one shall be revealed" in his fury against the Church.

It is a matter of history that the most disastrous periods for the Church were times when the Papal throne was vacant, or when anti-popes contended with the legitimate head of the Church. Thus also shall it be in those evil days to come.

6. The Church deprived of her chief pastor must seek sanctuary in solitude there to be guided by God Himself during those trying days This place of refuge prepared for the Church is probably some nation, or nations, that remain faithful to her. [See below, v. 14] In those days the Church shall also find refuge and consolation in faithful souls, especially in the seclusion of the religious life.

… Our Divine Savior has a representative on earth in the person of the Pope upon whom He has conferred full powers to teach and govern. Likewise, Antichrist will have his representative in the false prophet who will be endowed with the plenitude of satanic powers to deceive the nations. …As indicated by the resemblance to a lamb, the prophet will probably set himself up in Rome as a sort of antipope during the vacancy of the papal throne.

… The 'abomination of desolation' has been wrought in many Catholic churches by heretics and apostates who have broken altars, scattered relics of martyrs and desecrated the Blessed Sacrament. At the time of the French Revolution a lewd woman was seated upon the altar of the cathedral in Paris and worshipped as the goddess of reason. Such things but faintly foreshadow the abominations that will desecrate churches in those sorrowful days when Antichrist will seat himself at the altar to be adored as God. … Antichrist and his prophet will introduce ceremonies to imitate the Sacraments of the Church. In fact there will be a complete organization – a church of Satan set up in opposition to the Church of Christ. Satan will assume the part of God the Father; Antichrist will be honored as Savior, and his prophet will usurp the role of Pope. Their ceremonies will counterfeit the Sacraments…

And again in his following work:

«The prophecies of the Apocalypse show that Satan will imitate the Church of Christ (Catholic Church) to deceive mankind; he will set up a church of Satan in opposition to the Church of Christ. Antichrist will assume the role of Messias; his prophet will act the part of Pope, and there will be imitations of the Sacraments of the Church. There will also be lying wonders in imitation wrought in the Church.»[93]

Fr. Herman Bernard Kramer elaborates:
«The four words of the sentence, "And there was given to it authority over every tribe, and people and tongue and nation", shows the universality

---

[93] Fr. E. Sylvester Berry, *The Church of Christ: An Apologetic and Dogmatic Treatise* (1927).

of the empire and dominion of Antichrist though it need not mean the submission of every government to him. However, he will probably have followers among all peoples. All the wicked will hail him as their champion. [...] Verse seven states that Antichrist will make war against the saints and overcome them. In a war there are two opposing sides. Antichrist will be the victor in this war and become the lord of the world.»[94]

Again, Fr. Berry explains on page 133 of his above cited work on the Apocalypse: «He will be given power to wage war against the Church and to overcome it for a time. He shall rule over many nations and many peoples will adore him: his kingdom shall have the semblance of catholicity or universality. This is the great revolt of the nations foreold by St. Paul, [II Thessalonians ii, 3] but it shall not be truly universal; one nation, at least, shall remain faithful to the Church in those days, [See above, page 127.] and the elect whose names are written in the book of life will not adore Antichrist.» Fr. Kramer continues on page 320 of *The Book of Destiny*: «The Church is defeated. The papacy is abolished. St. Paul says that Antichrist "sitteth in the temple of God" to receive divine worship as if he were God (2 Thess. II. 4). This is not the ancient Temple of Jerusalem, nor a temple like it built by Antichrist, as some have thought, for then it would be his own temple. In chapter XI. 1 and 19, this temple is shown to be a Catholic Church, possibly one of the churches in Jerusalem or St. Peters in Rome, which is the largest church in the world and is in the full sense "THE temple of God".»[95] Fr. Berry comments further on the same point:

> The "mystery if Iniquity" gradually developing through the centuries, cannot be fully consummated while the power of the Papacy endures, but now he that "withstandeth is taken out of the way." During the interregnum "that wicked one shall be revealed" in his fury against the Church.
>
> It is a matter of history that the most disastrous periods for the Church were times when the Papal throne was vacant, or when anti-popes contended with the legitimate head of the Church. Thus also shall it be in those evil days to come.

---

[94] Herman Bernard F. Leonard Kramer, *Op. cit.*, pp. 315, 317.

[95] Fr. Arrighini, quoted here by Don Curzio Nitoglia, is of the same opinion: «P. Arrighini commenta; "quale poi sia il tempio dov la grande bestia si farà adorare (...) sarà sotto la cupola michelangiolesca di s. Pietro se – come è più probabile – avrà per capitale Roma ritornata pagana" (op. cit. p. 233).» [*AUGUSTIN LEHMANN – L'ANTICRISTO – L'uomo più fatale della storia, Introduzione* p. 26]

6. The Church deprived of her chief pastor must seek sanctuary in solitude there to be guided by God Himself during those trying days. This place of refuge prepared for the Church is probably some nation, or nations, that remain faithful to her. [see below v. 14] In those days the Church shall also find refuge and consolation in faithful souls, especially in the seclusion of the religious life.[96]

When the chief pastor will have been struck, the False Prophet will take his place. Fr Kramer explains on page 320 and 321 of his above cited work:

[p. 320] The influence of the False Prophet shall induce the unchristian and apostate nations to deify Antichrist. His doctrines will be enunciated in a high-sounding literary style and ornamented with an alluring mysticism, the better to fit them for fostering every degree of pride and moral abandonment. They shall then [p. 321] be enthusiastically accepted by all sinners. And these enthusiasts shall proclaim the resurrection of the Roman Empire the miracle of the ages. The Church is defeated. The papacy is abolished. St. Paul says that Antichrist "sitteth in the temple of God" to receive divine worship as if he were God (2 Thess. II. 4). This is not the ancient Temple of Jerusalem, nor a temple like it built by Antichrist, as some have thought, for then it would be his own temple. In chapter XI. 1 and 19, this temple is shown to be a Catholic Church, possibly one of the churches in Jerusalem or St. Peters in Rome, which is the largest church in the world and is in the full sense "THE temple of God".

Bergoglio is at present the leader of the revolt, the *apostasy* foretold by St. Paul. He does not believe in the transcendent God and Creator of Catholicism, but in the Teilhardian immanent 'divine principle' of Paganism, the life-giving world soul (*anima mundi*) within the universe. As mentioned above, his creed is remarkably like a synthesis of the belief systems of Lord Shaftesbury, Friedrich Schleiermacher, Benedict Spinoza, Auguste Compte, and Pierre Teilhard de Chardin. He says atheists can be saved (no need for faith in God), he has stated that the souls of the damned do not suffer eternal punishment. The damned souls, according to Bergoglio's Gnostic belief, will be annihilated. His doctrine on marriage is entirely circumscribed by Naturalism, denying the supernatural sacramentality of Holy Matrimony.

In his most recent denial of the dogma of hell, Bergoglio stated in a March 2018 conversation with Eugenio Scalfari: «"They are not

---

[96] *The Apocalypse of St. John*, p. 124.

punished, those who repent obtain the forgiveness of God and enter the rank of souls who contemplate him, but those who do not repent and cannot therefore be forgiven disappear. There is no hell, there is the disappearance of sinful souls."» Vatican spokesmen attempted to cast doubt on Bergoglio's profession of heresy; but it is well known that Bergoglio has been spouting this heresy for a long time. Three years earlier he said exactly the same thing, as Scalfari relates: «What happens to that lost soul? Will it be punished? And how? The response of Francis is distinct and clear: there is no punishment, but the annihilation of that soul. All the others will participate in the beatitude of living in the presence of the Father. The souls that are annihilated will not take part in that banquet; with the death of the body their journey is finished.»[97]

Catholics must not be fooled by Bergoglio's use of traditional Catholic theological terminology, because he, like all modernists, employs the terms according to a completely different meaning – according to the *Gnostic* sense of the Modernists and Masons, and not according to their traditional *Catholic* meaning intended by the ecclesiastical *magisterium*. Bergoglio, speaking on the mission of the Church, says, "We must avoid the loss of the good and do everything possible to save the lost" (Dobbiamo evitare che i buoni si perdano e dobbiamo fare tutto ciò che è possibile per salvare i perduti.) Bergoglio repeatedly employs such terms as "forgiveness", "repentance", and "redemption"; but he does not intend them to mean what we as *orthodox* Catholics understand them to mean (even though he willingly indulges the more conservative, "*retrograde*" Catholics to think he intends them to be understood according to their proper Catholic sense); but his meaning for these and other theological terms correspond exactly to his *Gnostic* belief system which circumscribes and specifies his understanding of the terms, as I explain briefly below. I judge it sufficient here, in this Introduction, to point out the thoroughly *Gnostic* context in which the statements of the conversation are situated[98] – a conversation

---

[97] http://www.repubblica.it/politica/2015/03/15/news/quel_che_francesco_puo_dire_all_europa_dei_non_credenti-109542750/

[98] «La misericordia cui papa Francesco dedica il prossimo Giubileo ha questo obiettivo, il figliol prodigo della parabola che il padre accoglie come la festa della vita, il perdono tra uomini e la perdonanza infinita di Dio verso le sue creature. E il pentimento che è la condizione affinché la misericordia discenda su quell'anima e la illumini con la sua luce. Papa Bergoglio non a caso ha preso il nome di Francesco, del tutto inconsueto nella Chiesa di Roma: il santo di Assisi vedeva e amava le creature di Dio, tutte le creature di Dio perché tutte portano dentro di loro una scintilla di divinità; il buon pastore è quella

reported by Scalfari which Bergoglio has never denied, and has even acknowledged by including his Scalfari conversations in his book, *Interviews with Journalists*. What is most striking there is Bergoglio's radically heretical statement on the mission of the Church, which explains why he does not believe it necessary to convert the unbelievers to the Catholic faith in order for them to attain salvation; because supernatural faith is superfluous, and all that is needed to be saved is that the soul seek the good that is already there within it: "The missionary Church does not proselytize, but seeks to awaken in people the search for the good in their souls." For one like Bergoglio, who believes in an immanent world-soul "deity", eternal redemption logically could not require anything more than that. Bergoglio professed his belief in that pagan notion of "God" on June 1, 2016.

Here is the link to the video where he says Mother Earth gave us life, and that it is she who protects us.

https://youtu.be/EOnH-NmkMv0

Francis is a PAGAN:

"A noi, a tutti, piace la madre Terra, perché è quella che ci ha dato la vita e ci custodisce; direi anche la sorella Terra, che ci accompagna nel nostro cammino dell'esistenza."

"We all like mother Earth, because it is she who gave us life and protects us" – Jorge "Francis" Bergoglio

(http://m.vatican.va/content/francescomobile/it/speeches/2016/june/documents/papa-francesco_20160601_institute-of-jainology.html)

It is **GOD** – the God who ***created all things visible and invisible*** who gave us life – NOT ***"Mother Earth"***, as Francis says. It is because **GOD** created us and gives life to us, that we profess Him *Dominum et*

---

scintilla che deve scoprire cancellando con il suo amore le scorie che la vita ha accumulato su di essa relegandola nel profondo e soffocandone la luce. Resta tuttavia il tema del peccato e del pentimento. E se il pentimento non viene? Se la scintilla si è spenta o non è mai esistita? Papa Francesco non ha mai pensato che quella scintilla possa spegnersi o addirittura che alcune nature possano esserne state private fin dalla nascita, perciò la cura delle anime non deve mai arrestarsi né essere interrotta e questo è il compito della Chiesa missionaria. Un giorno, in uno dei nostri incontri, mi parlò di quella missione che riguardava anche i non credenti. "La Chiesa missionaria – mi disse – non fa proselitismo, cerca nelle persone di suscitare la ricerca del bene nella loro anima".»

Vivificantem – *"The Lord and Giver of Life"*. "Mother Earth" does not give us life, but GOD, who created the world and all living things, and who became incarnate, so that we may "have life, and have it more abundantly" (John 10:10), gave us life. It was GOD who formed man from the lifeless slime of the earth, and breathed into him the breath of life living soul and man became a living soul: «*formavit igitur Dominus Deus hominem de limo terræ et inspiravit in faciem eius spiraculum vitæ et factus est homo in animam viventem*» — (Gen.2:7) *It is precisely our profession of the one true God, Creator of heaven and earth, that distinguishes us from the pagans*; and it was his profession of God Almighty that distinguished Melchisedech from his pagan Caananite countrymen:

> "But Melchisedech the king of Salem, bringing forth bread and wine, for he was the priest of the most high God, blessed him, and said: Blessed be Abram by the most high God, who created heaven and earth. (Genesis 14:18 – 19)

> Ps. 148:5 — "*laudent nomen Domini quia ipse dixit et facta sunt ipse mandavit et creata sunt*"

> Ps. 32:9 — "*ipse dixit et facta sunt ipse mandavit et creata sunt*"

> Judith 16:17 — "*tibi serviat omnis creatura tua quia dixisti et facta sunt misisti spiritum tuum et creata sunt et non est qui resistat voci tuæ*"

It is precisely this notion of the EARTH as the giver of life and provident protector of life which conceives of "God" not as a transcendent, infinitely and eternally perfect Supreme Being; but as a merely immanent demiurge; a "divine" life giving principle which constitutes the world as the womb that gives life to all things. In his remarkably short but concentrated work, *The Present Crisis of the Holy See* (1861), Cardinal Henry Edward Manning describes the continuous unfolding of the "mystery of iniquity", outlining the development of the spirit of Antichrist, whose revolt is characterized by its three principal marks: heresy, schism, and above all, the denial of the mystery of the Incarnation of the Son of God – thus, the Incarnation. The Word made flesh is replaced with the pantheistic *Incarnationalism* of "God" as "the living soul of the world", which culminates in the deification of man. It is this pagan *Incarnationalism* which conceives of "God" as an immanent *divine principle* – as "Mother Earth" – as the world-soul and womb which generates all life. It is this pagan and pantheistic religion, which conceives of God as "the living soul of the world", that Cardinal Manning explains is the embodiment of the spirit of Antichrist; and which Jorge Bergoglio professed on 1 June 2016. The three marks of the antichrist revolt are plainly evident in the false religion of Jorge Bergoglio.

JORGE BERGOGLIO'S RELIGION – FREEMASONIC NATURALISM

Those who doubt that "Pope" Francis is the spearhead of the apostasy foretold in Scripture and the Secret of Fatima need only consider that his agenda for reform seeks the utter demolition of the Catholic Church. Bergoglio is more radical in his revolt that Luther, Calvin, Zwingli, Melanchton, Knox and Cranmer all together. Jorge Bergoglio is the Public Enemy No. 1 of the Catholic religion. When I asked Roberto de Mattei if he agreed with the statement that Bergoglio's revolt against Christ is even more radical than the revolt of Luther and Calvin, he replied with one word: "Yes".

Bergoglio teaches that even those without faith, which is to say, infidels, can be saved – and that there is no need to obey God's commandments. Obedience to one's own faithless conscience suffices for salvation, according to Bergoglio. Divine Revelation teaches there is no justification or salvation without faith, and that the divine commandments must be obeyed: "*Tu mandasti mandata tua custodíri nimis*"; and, "*maledicti qui declinant a mandatis tuis*" (Ps. 118); "*Convertantur peccatores in infernum, omnes Gentes quæ obliviscuntur Deum*" (Ps. 9), and, "*sic viæ omnium qui obliviscuntur Deum et spes hypocritæ peribit*" (Iob. 8:13).

The dogmatic teaching of the Council of Trent, the explicit teaching of Scripture, and the universal and perpetual magisterium all teach the diametrical opposite: "When we say that faith is necessary for the remission of sins, we mean to speak of the Catholic faith, not heretical faith. Without the habit of this faith, no man is justified." [99]

---

[99] St. Alphonsus Liguori, *An Exposition and Defense of All the Points of Faith Discussed and Defined by the Council of Trent.*

BERGOGLIO DENIES THE FIRST PRINCIPLE OF CHRISTIANITY – THE NECESSITY OF FAITH FOR JUSTIFICATION & SALVATION

"First of all, you ask if the God of the Christians forgives those who do not believe and do not seek faith. Given that – and this is fundamental – God's mercy has no limits… the issue for those who do not believe in God is in obeying their own conscience. Sin, even for those who have no faith, exists when people disobey their conscience." The key words are: "those who do not believe and do not seek faith." Does God forgive them? Bergoglio says, "God's mercy has no limits…the issue for those who do not believe in God is obeying their own conscience" (!) and: "The goodness or the wickedness of our behaviour depends on this decision." Note also the moral relativism: "listening and obeying it [conscience], means deciding about what is perceived to be good or evil".

Bergoglio states with unmistakable clarity that one with no faith at all obtains forgiveness from God by obeying his conscience: "deciding about what is perceived to be good or to be evil."

For Bergoglio, the conscience is autonomous: the "Thou shalt" and "Thou shalt not" commandments are nullified – human dignity (according to Bergoglio's Masonic creed) demands that the human person decide for himself what is right or wrong, without the tyranny of "clericalism" dictating to man's conscience, "Thou shalt not!"

Bergoglio's economy of salvation dispenses entirely with any need for faith – faith is utterly superfluous. Salvation depends exclusively on following one's own autonomous conscience; and ultimately no one may dictate to that conscience by claiming to teach in God's name with divine authority.

This is Bergoglio's religion. It is as far removed from Christianity as heaven is from hell. Bergoglio's religion is not Catholicism – it is *Masonism* in its purest form. His creed is essentially identical to that of the godless Enlightenment freethinker, Lord Shaftesbury (1671-1713): "The articles of Shaftesbury's religious creed were few and simple, but these he entertained with a conviction amounting to enthusiasm. They may briefly be summed up as a belief in one God whose most characteristic attribute is universal benevolence, in the moral government of the universe, and in a future state of man making up for the imperfections and repairing the inequalities of the present life."¹⁰⁰ AH! The Fatherhood of God and the Brotherhood of Man. Shaftesbury's moral doctrine is that of the "Moral Sense", of which the two most basic principles are:

1. "1 that the distinction between right and wrong is part of the constitution of human nature;
2. that morality stands apart from theology, and the moral qualities of actions are determined apart from the arbitrary will of God."

Shaftesbury's religion was essentially Pandeism – a combination of Deism and Pantheism. (http://plato.stanford.edu/entries/shaftesbury/#8) Fr. Cornelio Fabro cites the verbatim quotations, in his *Introduzione all'ateismo moderno* – (English title, *God in Exile. Modern Atheism*) in which Shaftesbury explains that virtue does not consist in believing tenets of revelation, but in morality. In his chapter on *Theism, Deism, and Atheism in Shaftesbury*, Fabro calls particular attention to Shaftesbury's, *An Inquiry Concerning Virtue or Merit*.¹⁰¹

---

¹⁰⁰ cf. Wikipedia

¹⁰¹ Some significant quotations from that work:

«Religion and virtue seem in many respects to be so nearly related that they are generally presumed to be inseparable companions. We are so willing to think well of their union that we hardly allow it to be permissible to speak or even think of them separately. But it may be questioned whether this attitude can be theoretically justified. We certainly do sometimes encounter cases that seem to go against this general supposition. We have known people who have the appearance of great zeal in religion but have lacked even the common affections of humanity, and shown themselves extremely degenerate and corrupt. Others who have paid little regard to religion and been considered as mere atheists have been seen to practise the rules of morality and in many cases to act with such good meaning and affection towards mankind that one seems forced to admit that they are virtuous.»

«In the totality of things either everything conforms to an order that is good and the most agreeable to a general interest or there's something that is otherwise, something that could have been better constituted, designed more wisely and with more advantage to the general interest of beings as a whole. If everything that exists conforms to an order that is good and for the best, then it necessarily follows that there's no such thing as real badness in the universe, nothing that is bad with respect to the whole.»

«Anything that is in some degree superior over the world, ruling in nature with discernment and a mind, is what all men agree in calling `God'. If there

Lest anyone think Scalfari fabricated the above Bergoglio quotation, here's a parallel passage in Bergoglio's sermon:

> Francesco, il capo della Chiesa Cattolica Romana ha affermato che anche gli atei vanno in paradiso. Pochi giorni fa infatti, ha raccontato la storia di un parrocchiano Cattolico che chiese ad un prete se anche gli atei erano stati salvati da Gesù, ed ha detto:

---

are several such superior minds, they are so many gods; but if the single God or the several gods are not in their nature necessarily good, they are called `daemons'. To believe that everything is governed, ordered, or regulated for the best by a designing principle—i.e. a mind—that is necessarily good and permanent is to be a perfect theist. To have no belief in any designing principle or mind, or in any cause, measure, or rule of things other than chance, so that in nature no interests of the whole or of any particulars is in the least designed, pursued, or aimed at, is to be a perfect atheist. To believe that there are two or more designing principles or minds, all in their nature good, is to be a polytheist. To believe that the governing mind or minds are not absolutely and necessarily good—aren't conned to what is best, but are capable of acting according to mere will or fancy—is to be a daemonist.»

«We don't call any creature `worthy' or `virtuous' unless it can have the notion of a public interest, and can have organised theoretical knowledge of what is morally good or bad, admirable or blameworthy, right or wrong.»

«It doesn't seem that atheism can directly contribute to someone's having false views about right and wrong. Customs and activities favoured by atheism could lead a man to lose much of his natural moral sense; but it doesn't seem that atheism could by itself cause anyone to judge to be fair, noble, and deserving something that was the contrary. For example, atheism could never make anyone think that eating man's flesh or committing bestiality is good and excellent in itself. But corrupt religion, i.e. superstition, can cause many horribly unnatural and inhuman things to be accepted as excellent, good, and praiseworthy in themselves.»

«We have found that religion is capable of doing great good, or great harm, depending on what kind of religion it is; and that atheism does nothing positive in either way. It may indirectly lead to men's losing a good and sufficient sense of right and wrong; but atheism as such can't lead to anyone's setting up a false kind of `right and wrong'. Only false religion, or fantastical opinion produced by superstition and credulity, can do that.»

«So we can settle accurately the relation that virtue has to piety, namely: virtue is not complete unless it is accompanied by piety, because where piety is lacking there can't be the same benignity, firmness, or constancy, the same good composure of the affections, or uniformity of mind. So the perfection and height of virtue must be due to the belief in a god.»

'Il Signore ci ha creati a Sua immagine e somiglianza, e noi siamo l'immagine del Signore, ed Egli fa del bene e tutti noi abbiamo questo comandamento nel cuore: fai il bene e non fare il male. Tutti noi. 'Ma, Padre, questo non è Cattolico! Non può fare il bene'. Sì, può farlo …. 'Il Signore ha redento tutti noi, tutti noi, con il Sangue di Cristo: tutti noi, non solo Cattolici. Tutti! 'Padre, e gli atei?' Anche gli atei. Tutti!' … Dobbiamo incontrarci facendo il bene. 'Ma, Padre, io non credo, sono un ateo!' Ma fai il bene: noi ci incontreremo là' [in paradiso].

Ecco le parole in inglese così come sono state pubblicate dall'Huffington Post:

"The Lord created us in His image and likeness, and we are the image of the Lord, and He does good and all of us have this commandment at heart: do good and do not do evil. All of us. 'But, Father, this is not Catholic! He cannot do good.' Yes, he can… "The Lord has redeemed all of us, all of us, with the Blood of Christ: all of us, not just Catholics. Everyone! 'Father, the atheists?' Even the atheists. Everyone!" … We must meet one another doing good. 'But I don't believe, Father, I am an atheist!' But do good: we will meet one another there."

http://giacintobutindaro.org/2013/05/26/secondo-papa-francesco-anche-gli-atei-vanno-in-paradiso/

Bergoglio in, *Heaven and Earth*:

«As I am a believer, I know that these riches are a gift from God. I also know that the other person, the atheist, does not know that. I do not approach the relationship in order to proselytize, or convert the atheist; I respect him and I show myself as I am. Where there is knowledge, there begins to appear esteem, affection, and friendship. I do not have any type of reluctance, nor would I say that his life is condemned, because I am convinced that I do not have the right to make a judgment about the honesty of that person; even less, if he shows me those human virtues that exalt others and do me good.»

JORGE BERGOGLIO IS THE SPARHEAD OF THE GREAT APOSTASY

As I mentioned above, Cardinal Ciappi wrote on the Third Secret of Fatima, "[T]he great apostasy in the Church will begin at the top." The collect for the XVIIth Sunday After Pentecost implores God to protect His faithful from the diabolical poison (the false opinions being spewed daily by Jorge Bergoglio and his Mason occupied Vatican), so they may avoid this contagion and follow the divine truths perpetually taught by the Catholic Church with a pure mind:

> *Da, quæsumus, Domine, populo tuo diabolica vitare contagia: et te solum Deum pura mente sectari.*

Bergoglio's deadly poison, is faithlessness, which produces the death of the soul. The first Great Commandment is this: "Thou shalt love the Lord thy God with thy whole heart, and with thy whole soul, and with thy whole mind." (Mt.22:37) This commandment unconditionally demands that we believe in God, believe his revelation, and obey His precepts. "This is the greatest and the first commandment." (v. 38) This is the basis of the Second Commandment, "And the second is like to this: Thou shalt love thy neighbour as thyself." (v. 39) The Second hinges directly from the first; since, without the need to believe, love, and obey God, there cannot exist an obligation to love one's neighbour or oneself. We are bound absolutely by Divine Law to observe these commandments, because God has commanded us to obey them; and not because we are convinced in our own mind that they are correct.

To believe God and to obey Him is the basis of all religion – it is what God commands we must do in order to be saved: "On these two commandments dependeth the whole law and the prophets." (v. 40) If we refuse to believe in God, we are damned as infidels; and if we refuse to believe what He reveals, we are likewise damned as infidels: "he that believeth not shall be condemned." (Mk. 16:16)

Bergoglio says he believes in God, and in Jesus Christ, but he explicitly rejects His teaching: "You ask me if the God of the Christians forgives those who don't believe and who don't seek the faith." Bergoglio's reply: "The issue for those who do not believe in God is to obey their conscience. Sin, even for those who have no faith, exists when people disobey their conscience." (!) (Michael Day (11 September 2013)."Pope Francis assures atheists: You don't have to believe in God to go to heaven". London: The Independent.) Thus, his remark about the redemption of atheists hinges on this perverse principle – " [God] has redeemed all of us, all of us, with the Blood of Christ: all of us, not just Catholics. Everyone! ... Even the atheists, Everyone!" (David Gibson (May 22, 2013). "Pope Francis: God redeemed everyone, 'not just Catholics'". The Washington Post.)

Hence, it is manifestly evident that Jorge Bergoglio is not a Christian at all, but an apostate and an infidel. The incontrovertible proof consists in the fact that Bergoglio denies the very first principle and basis of all religion – **belief**, and he explicitly opposes, contradicts, and rejects the teaching of Christ on this most fundamental point which is the basis of all religion. Bergoglio preaches a false religion which does not require the virtue of faith or any belief in God, the blessed Trinity, or the Incarnation of Christ for redemption and salvation, but explicitly professes the opinion that men are redeemed even if they don't believe in God. Thus, when Bergoglio says that all are redeemed, "even atheists" – the clear and indisputable context of his words manifests plainly that he intends the term "redeemed" to be understood in the sense (as he says), that all who follow their conscience are without sin; and thus are on the path to *eternal redemption* (as the Church understands the term from scripture in *Hebrews 9: 12*), thus meaning "*æterna redemptio*"[102] – "eternal redemption" which is equivalent to "*salus æterna*" or "eternal salvation" – and hence, the term 'redemption' is used and understood in the cited passage by Bergoglio with the same meaning that is synonymous with 'salvation' as it is used in the Roman Canon: *pro redemptione animarum suarum, pro spe salutis et incolumitatis suæ*. Thus it is Jorge Bergoglio's plainly stated doctrine that even those without faith can be saved, and gain *eternal redemption* without even believing in God! A more explicit and inexcusable expression of the *dolus* of formal heresy is scarcely to be imagined.

Thus, Bergoglio, by rejecting the need for faith, not only denies the natural law, but flatly denies the most fundamental teaching of the entire Scripture and Tradition of both testaments, which teaches that faith in God is absolutely necessary for salvation. Infidelity is the "*maximum omnium peccatorum*", as St. Thomas explains (*II-II Q. 10 a. 3*). Hence, sin, for people who have no faith, is first and foremost the sin of unbelief, regardless of whether they obey their perverted conscience or not. One who denies the necessity to assent to the truths of divine revelation explicitly rejects the authority of the revealing God. Hence, Bergoglio is a manifest apostate and infidel – and therefore is not a member of the Catholic Church, nor its visible head on earth.

Bergoglio's religion is a different religion than the Catholic religion, because his "God" is not the transcendent Catholic God, but the immanent "god" of Teilhard de Chardin and the Freemasons: "I believe

---

[102] "Sumptis, Domine, salutaribus sacramentis: ad *redemptionis æternæ*, qu*æ*sumus, proficiamus augmentum." (Postcommunion Prayer, Monday after the Fourth Sunday in Lent.

in God – *not in a Catholic God*; **there is no Catholic God.**"[103] This is what he meant when he said, **"God does not exist; do not be shocked"** – he's saying he believes in a "god" that is not the God of Christians – he does not believe in God in the manner that God and His attributes are understood according to the perpetual doctrine of Catholic theology and dogma. It is not mere gibberish when he says, "There is the Father, the Son and the Holy Spirit, they are persons, they are not some vague idea in the clouds... This God spray does not exist! The three persons exist!"[104]

Bergoglio's notion of the Blessed Trinity denies the infinite and eternal perfection of God by denying the infinitely perfect and eternal unity of the Divine Persons: On 17 March 2017, Bergoglio declared in his discourse in St. Peter's: "dentro la santissima Trinità stanno tutti litigando a porte chiuse, mentre fuori l'immagine è di unità". ("even within the Blessed Trinity they are quarrelling behind closed doors, while on the outside the image is of unity".) Although these words were reported in the press by reputable journalists, such as Sandro Magister, none of Bergoglio's words spoken that day are posted on the Vatican website, and only for his discourses of that day is there the notification "not available" in the website's section, "Words of the Holy Father". Bergoglio's "Blessed Trinity" is not the same Trinity as the One theologically elaborated by St. Hilary, St. Augustine, and St. Thomas, but the occult "Trinity" of the esoteric *Gnosticism* of Freemasonry – a false religion which professes a doctrine of "God"—a pagan superstition systematically formulated in the philosophy of Spinoza and Hegel, elaborated in **the pantheistic religion of Lord Shaftesbury** and mystically expressed in the **pantheistic theology of Pierre Teilhard de Chardin S.J.**

Bergoglio's belief system, being based on a *Gnostic* incarnational immanentism, logically excludes the ontological possibility of the Hypostatic Union in the mystery of the Incarnation of the Son of God professed in Catholicism; (since the Christian dogma of this revealed mystery presupposes the existence of a *transcendent*, Triune God, whose eternally begotten λογος became uniquely incarnate), making "God" a *"deus sive natura"* in a proper Spinozan sense, in which it could be said with a radical ontological connotation, (such that Meister Ekhart never intended when he said), "All things are words of God." At his trial,

---

[103] Interview with Eugenio Scalfari, 1 October, 2013.
[104] Homily in the Santa Marta chapel, 9 October, 2014.

Meister Eckhart made the clarification that he spoke analogically when making such affirmations as that in his sermons; and therefore, his words were not intended to be understood according to the radical sense that would necessarily apply in the context of the Teilhadian *Incarnationalism* to which Jorge Mario Bergoglio subscribes. It was in an analogical sense that Jesus spoke when He said, "Amen I say to you, as long as you did it to one of these my least brethren, you did it to me." (Matthew 25:40) It it because of these words the Lord spoke, that Christians, down through the ages, see the face of the suffering Christ in the faces of their suffering neighbours. Bergoglio's words betray a radical meaning that goes far beyond any reasonable presumption of an analogical interpretation: "We can recognize him in the faces of our brothers, especially the poor, the sick, the imprisoned, the refugees: they are living flesh of the suffering Christ and the visible image of the invisible God." [105] This is heresy and blasphemy – Only Christ is the image of God, the *imago Dei* (Cor. 4:4; Col. 1:15). No creature is the image of God. God did not make man the image of God, but He made *him according to the image of God – ad imaginem Dei* (Genesis 1:26).[106] Even more plainly is the *incarnational naturalism* of Bergoglio's belief system manifested in his blasphemous words in the same vein spoken on another occasion, "… those persons *are* the flesh of Christ…"[107] It is due to Bergoglio's essentially pantheistic *incarnational immanentism*, that he is only able to go so far as professing a *naturalistic incarnational belief in the "incarnation" and "divinity" of Jesus Christ*, which is essentially inherent in the pantheism of his Teilhardian "Christification" of the cosmos. From this fountainhead of Naturalism springs forth the conspicuous absence of anything *supernatural* anywhere in his belief system. Hence, it is entirely consistent with his heretical theology that he referred to the Holy Eucharist, the divine and supernatural *bread from heaven having all sweetness in it* (Wis. 16:20) as a mere "piece of bread" in

---

[105] Sunday Angelus 11 Jan 2017 – "Lo possiamo riconoscere nel volto dei nostri fratelli, in particolare nei poveri, nei malati, nei carcerati, nei profughi: essi sono carne viva del Cristo sofferente e immagine visibile del Dio invisibile." 1 Jun 2013 Casa S. Marta

[106] "Let us make man to our image and likeness" – Genesis 1:26.

[107] 1 Jun 2013 Casa S. Marta – "Noi – ha continuato il Papa – possiamo fare tutte le opere sociali che vogliamo, e diranno: 'Ma che brava, la Chiesa, che buona l'opera sociale che fa la Chiesa'. Ma se noi diciamo che noi facciamo questo perché quelle persone sono la carne di Cristo, viene lo scandalo. E quella è la verità, quella è la rivelazione di Gesù: quella presenza di Gesù incarnato".

his phone conversation with Jacqui Lisbona in April, 2014. This is only one of many examples of the denial of the supernatural in Bergoglio's religion of Naturalism.

Francis cited Teilhard approvingly in footnote 53 to *Laudato Si'*, commenting on his own words, "The ultimate destiny of the universe is in the fullness of God, which has already been attained by the risen Christ, the measure of the maturity of all things. [53]" The "fullness of God" in this context is the Teilhardian 'omega point' of the immanent divine principle that animates the world. The 'omega point' symbolically conceived of in terms of a presential eschatology, and thus, as having been "already been attained by the risen Christ", i.e. in so far as its eschatological fulfillment is symbolically represented in the image of the risen Christ. Francis comments, "Against this horizon we can set the contribution of Fr Teilhard de Chardin" – which is to say, God, conceived of as an immanent *divine principle*, and therefore the incarnate Word conceived of as the *vital principle* which incarnationally animates the world; and attains the fullness of the 'omega point'— already symbolically attained in the Risen Christ, and actually realised in *the resurrection of the dead*, which is nothing other than the symbolic representation of men existing after death forever in the mode of divine ideas – existing eternally in the *omega point* of the divine mind, which is the "ultimate destiny of the universe is in the fullness of God".[108] Although this theme is also found to some extent in the writings of Joseph Ratzinger, and will be discussed in Volume Two of this work, Bergoglio's notion of God logically excludes even the possibility of a 'resurrection' understood according to the orthodox Judeo-Christian doctrine of the 'Resurrection of the Dead'; which is properly the resurrection of the physical **body** – that selfsame *body*; i.e., **"illa ista caro"**, in the words of St. Augustine, which is animated by the rational soul during its earthly sojourn. The pertinacity of Bergoglio's

---

[108] Although in 2009, when Pope Benedict XVI publicly praised Teilhard's notion of the cosmos as a "living host" he did not intend the attribution to be understood in a radical incarnational sense, which can be seen to be opposed to Ratzinger's theology, as is evident in John Allen's comment: "In a long-ago commentary on the final session of the Second Vatican Council (1962-65), a young Father Joseph Ratzinger, who would later become Pope Benedict, complained that *Gaudium et Spes*, the "Pastoral Constitution on the Church in the Modern World," played down the reality of sin because of an overly "French," and specifically "Teilhardian," influence." [John L. Allen Jr., Nov. 24 2017, in *Crux*.]

incarnationalist Naturalism, his heresy, which denies the *supernatural* mystery of the Incarnation, as well as all properly supernatural mysteries of the Christian faith, is *manifest* in his own impious words, whereas it will be shown in Volume Two that Ratzinger cannot be considered as a manifest heretic, i. e., one who is plainly and undeniably *pertinacious* in his profession of materially heretical propositions, because it cannot be proven that he has directly, immediately, contradictorily and pertinaciously denied or obstinately doubted any doctrine that must be believed with divine and Catholic faith.

Jorge Bergoglio, a veritable reincarnation of Giordano Bruno, has denied the transcendent Most High God who reveals infallible dogmas and commandments (Whom he reduces to the status of a "vague idea in the clouds"; a "God spray" which "does not exist"); and has replaced Him with an immanent "god" who is not infinitely and eternally perfect – a "god" who in some vague incarnational manner, immanent in "Mother Earth", is yet somehow conceived of as "persons", and whose revelation is not an *absolute truth* transmitted to men supernaturally by a transcendent God of infinite, absolute, and eternal perfection, but is revealed by the immanent divine principle that animates all things, and reveals itself naturally in one's own conscious experience: His religion is the Enlightenment "religion" of revelation experienced in one's heart – of an immanent "deity" which reveals itself in natural human experience (i.e. the revelation of an immanent "deity" as in the doctrine of Friedrich Schleiermacher) – the "Mother Earth" he professed on 1 June 2016, as the one who "gave us life and protects us". Thus, one understands easily what is the basis for the absolute primacy of one's own conscience in Bergoglio's doctrine rather than the authority of the Law of God, manifested by divine revelation in the Commandments of God, infallibly taught by the Church, and reflected through human reason in the natural law; because in Bergoglio's religion there is no God above us in heaven who has given the earth to the children of men (Psalm 115: 16) – but only a *deus sive natura* – a "divine" vital principle within Nature. Bergoglio's religion is patently that which is based on perfidious "liberal theology", (which originated with the 'father of liberal theology' Friedrich Schleiermacher), which itself was spawned in the lodges of Freemasonry and then sprang forth into the light of day in the faithless Enlightenment; and his moral doctrine likewise is the vague Enlightenment belief in the "Moral Sense", professed by the infidel Lord Shaftesbury, based on the notion of God as a "world soul" (*anima mundi*) that Shaftesbury professed. Shaftesbury's prayer, quoted in full by

Cornelio Fabro in his work *Introduzione all'ateismo moderno*, is addressed to God as the "universal soul."[109] Fr. Fabro explains in that work how this kind of belief system logically reduces itself and dissolves into philosophic atheism.

There cannot be salvation by means of the works of obeying one's conscience alone without supernatural faith in the supreme and eternal God who created all things visible and invisible; since justification, which brings about the transition from the state of sin to the state of sanctifying grace, cannot be accomplished by mere human works without the sanctification of justifying grace which is received by faith and not works: "For we account a man to be justified by faith, without the works of the law." (Rom. 3:28) Hence, one cannot have any participation in redemption without faith: "But without faith it is impossible to please God. For he that cometh to God, must believe that he is, and is a rewarder to them that seek him." (Heb. 11:6) According to Bergoglio there can be redemption without faith. According to Divine Revelation and Catholic dogma, there can be no redemption without faith. Bergoglio does not believe the Divine Revelation – he does not believe in the God who speaks in Revelation. Thus, Jorge Bergoglio is an infidel – he is not a Catholic, not a Christian, not a member of the Church, nor its visible head on earth.

The argument that Pope Benedict can equally be accused of heresy is utterly fallacious. In the works of Ratzinger there is a profession of belief

---

[109] Shaftesbury's doctrine of God conceived of as an *anima mundi*: «Eterno Genitore (Padre) degli uomini e di ogni cosa, Spirito, Vita e Forza (Potenza) dell'Universo, da Te (da cui) procedono l'ordine, l'antonia e la bellezza, in Te esiste ogni cosa e da He tutte le cose sono rette e governate, sì da seguire (tenere) un unico ordine e, nella varietà delle loro azioni, formare un'unità completa e perfetta. Tu sei l'artefice di tutto, in Te sono e da Te procedono tutte le cose, l'armonia e il moto dei cieli e delle sfere infinite, il vigore e la feracità (fertilità, rigoglio) di questa terra, l'universilità delle creature viventi e l'intelligenza delle anime. Piochè Tu sei (essendo Tu stesso) l'anima universale, la mente e la sagezza eterna e infinita del tutto. (Dato che) Per tua voluntà fui creato capace di conocerti (mi hai dato una natura capace di conocerti) e di contemplarti (raccogliermi in Te), fa' che sia mio pensiero e mia cura il seguirti e il vivere secondo la tua legge, ubbidiente al tuo commandamento, e perseguire nella mia natura e nella mia vita il tuo fine e il tuo scopo, giacchè questo soltanto e il fine il chi conseguimento è il bene delle creature.» PREGHIERA A DIO DI SHAFTESBURY (In *Shaftesbury Papers* G. D. 24, Vol. XXVI, 7.) in, Cornelio Fabro, *Introduzione all'ateismo moderno*, Opere Complete 21, 2013, p. 356.

in dogma, but there is also a warped understanding of dogma rooted in an Augustinian theology of faith, but circumscribed in a framework of a Rahnerian theology steeped in modern philosophy. In Bergoglio, there is the patent *dolus* of unbelief; a radical relativism which manifests itself in a conscious rejection of the "absolute truth" of dogma and the "moral absolutes". I will present a systematic exposition on the question of the Bergoglian "pontificate" vs. the true and valid pontificate of Pope Benedict XVI, in Vol. II of this work. But to those, like the editor of *Catholic Truth Scotland*, who object saying, "Why on earth you think he's [Benedict] any better than Francis"? I reply firstly that the question fallaciously and gratuitously supposes that the *indicia* of heresy in both are identical or substantially equivalent. Similarly, and with hypocritical sophistry, John Salza stridently demanded that I answer how it can be that Bergoglio is a heretic but Benedict is not; but Salza, a lawyer, made no presentation of the respective *indicia*, and offered no argument that the *indicia* in both cases are of equal value.

The "god" of Jorge "Francis" Bergoglio is the "world soul" (*anima mundi*) of Shaftesbury, Teilhard de Chardin, and the 'Ancient Mysteries' of the Pagans and Freemasons – i.e. the **pandeistic** "*deus sive natura*" of **Spinoza**. The God that Pope Benedict XVI professes is the God of Christians – the God of the apostles, prophets and philosophers; as he eloquently explained in the first part of his first major work, *Einführung in das Christentum*. Although there are problematic doctrinal formulations in that work, none of them come close to Bergoglio's stark assertions of heresy which constitute clear *indicia* of formal heresy. Bergoglio's religion worships the "god" of Spinoza in the reformed "church" of Indifferentism – the "church" of religious liberty, i.e., of equality of all religions, of doctrinal and moral relativism that is emerging out of the ruins of the "Conciliar Church" – the Bergoglian counterfeit "church" which denies the *absolute truth* of divine revelation professed by the Catholic Church[110], the "*false church of darkness*" which

---

[110] http://www.catholicherald.co.uk/news/2015/11/30/pope-francis-says-he-is-not-losing-any-sleep-over-vatican-leaks-trial/_«"Fundamentalism is a sickness that is in all religions," said the Pontiff. "We Catholics have some — and not some, many — who believe they possess the absolute truth and go ahead dirtying the other with calumny, with disinformation, and doing evil. They do evil. I say this because it is my Church." ... "You cannot cancel a whole religion because there is a group or many groups of fundamentalists at certain moments of history," the Pope said.» [*Pope Francis criticises 'fundamentalist' Catholics* – by Catholic News Service]

apes the Catholic Church and usurps its name – and which is now seen to be visibly consummating its separation from the Catholicism of the past two millennia as it emerges and morphs into the **One World Church**. Pope Benedict XVI professes and worships the true God of Catholic dogma, as does the remnant Church over which he remains the true pope and supreme Pontiff, in spite of the mass confusion among the faithful and clergy concerning the identity of the true pope. Both men, the true pope and the false pope will die, but the false "church" and the true Church will survive their deaths. It does not suffice for salvation that a Catholic resist false doctrine and personally adhere to the true dogma of faith; but one must remain within the fold of the true Church of Jesus Christ as a member of the One, Holy, Catholic, and Apostolic Church, outside of which there is neither salvation nor forgiveness of sins. The Catholic must visibly separate himself from the organization of those who visibly separate themselves from the true Catholic Church by their public defection from the faith into heresy, *but who remain as illegitimate squatters and usurpers within the visible material structural framework formerly occupied exclusively by the Catholic Church*, and which is still identified as properly belonging to it alone. St. Athanasius wrote during the Arian occupation of the buildings and places belonging to the Church: «Others have taken the churches by violence, they have the places, but you have the apostolic faith. (*Ecclesias quidem alii per violentiam tenuerunt, illi enim loca, vos vero habetis apostolicam fidem*) They are in the places, but are outside the true faith; while you are indeed outside of the places, but the faith is within you. (*Illi in locis existentes, a vera fide sunt foris: vos vero a locis quidem foris estis, fides vero intus*) [...] By so much work they are seen to hold the Church, by so much the more are they cast out. (*Quanto igitur labore videntur Ecclesiam tenere, tanto magis ejecti sunt.*)"»

Christ's religion is His Cross: the redemptive self-immolation of the Eternal High Priest offered on Calvary and renewed on the Catholic altar of Rome's *Pontifex Maximus* and of all the bishops and priests under his jurisdiction – upon which the Flesh and Blood of the slain Victim is mystically offered as the "clean oblation" – the price of redemption, offered throughout the world, "from the rising of the sun to its setting". (Malachi 1:11) That redemptive sacrifice consummated by the shedding of His Blood, mystically re-presented on the altar is the efficient cause of the justification of the hitherto unredeemed and reprobate souls of all those who participate in the fruits of His redemption, disposed to receive His saving grace of Justification by faith and repentance. Thus, by the sacrifice of the altar, the Victim is made to be the Bread of Life and the

Chalice of Salvation for those redeemed by His Blood and justified by faith in Him – the foretaste and pledge of eternal life, and thus the "consummation of the spiritual life and the end of all sacraments", as St. Thomas says in his *Commentary on the Gospel of St. John*. Thus, the Holy Sacrifice of the Mass is the heart of the true religion of Jesus Christ; and hence, its destruction would be accomplished by cutting that heart out of Christ's Mystical Body. This was the Gnostic Luther's[111] agenda, summed up in his words: *Tolle missam, tolle ecclesiam*. The cutting out of that heart of the Catholic religion is the very essence of Protestantism – it is what distinguishes Protestantism from Catholicism, as Karl Adam poignantly explained in *The Spirit of Catholicism*. The abolition of the Sacrifice was at the centre of Luther's godless agenda; and is one and the same as the agenda of Antichrist, as is revealed in the Book of Daniel. The ecumenical interfaith communion with the Protestants envisaged and planned by Bergoglio and his fellow apostate sectaries; and which is the goal of his reform, will bring about the consummation of that godless Antichrist agenda in the "mystery of iniquity". Thus, the man who placed Luther's statue in St. Peter's Square for veneration as an object of devotion makes no secret about the true nature of his reforms for the Church – reforms which he says will be "irreversible". Jorge "Francis" Bergoglio is the fulfilment of *Lamentations* 4:12: "*The kings of the earth, and all the inhabitants of the world, would not have believed that the adversary and the enemy should have entered into the gates of Jerusalem.*" In *Le jour de la colère*,

---

[111] «We cannot ignore what has been discovered in the thousands of notes written by Luther himself on the margins of books written by reputed theologians such as Augustine and Peter Lombard. The notes were written within the time periods of 1506 to 1516, and 1535 to 1545. But, they were much overlooked until the 20th century when the German scholar Theobald Beer enduringly read through the notes, studying the patriarch of Protestantism for thirty five years. Beer's research on Luther was eventually published in his 1980, 584 page publication, Der fröhliche Wechsel und Streit, in which he exposed and discoursed on the heretical gnostic beliefs and teachings of Luther. In fact, Melanchthon, a very close colleague of Luther and one of the head figures of the Protestant Reformation, criticized the German reformer as having "Manichean delirium".» [*Martin Luther and the Gnostics* https://oblongmedia-net.cdn.ampproject.org/v/s/oblongmedia.net2017/01/30/martin-luther-and-the-gnostics/amp/?amp_js_v=a2&amp_gsa=1&usqp=mq331AQCCAE%3D#referrer=https%3A%2F%2Fwww.google.com&amp_tf=From%20%251%2 4s&ampshare=https%3A%2F%2Foblongmedia.net%2F2017%2F01%2F30% 2Fmartin-luther-and-the-gnostics%2F].

Zachary mentions that Rome was being prepared for Christ's religion even before its conversion. Rome as *caput mundi*, was already the foundational idea of Augustus Cæsar's rule: the unification and centralization of the nations and peoples under Rome's *imperium* – as Adolf Harnack explained in one of his sermons – and Scripture foretold prophetically that Rome would indeed become the *caput mundi* by means of the conversion of Rome to the religion of Christ. (Matthew 21:43) By abolishing the valid celebration of the Mass, and replacing it with an invalid counterfeit rite, Bergoglio's agenda will abolish the religion of Christ and bring about the apostasy of Rome and the fulfilment of verse 4 of the same chapter cited above: "*The tongue of the sucking child hath stuck to the roof of his mouth for thirst: the little ones have asked for bread, and there was none to break it unto them.*"

Ecumenical unity is the greatest obstacle to the unity willed by Christ and declared in the Fourth Gospel: "*ut omnes unum sint.*" (John 17:21) Ecumenical 'unity' consists in an amalgamation of creeds and faiths that remain in contradiction with each other and in radical opposition to the Catholic Faith, and therefore, it is in its very nature opposed to God and to the Church's three bonds of communion — the bonds of *"One Lord, one faith, one baptism."* (Eph. 4:5); that is, the bond of unity in governance under the Vicar of Christ; the bond of *faith* – of one complete and unified creed, professing the articles of divine and Catholic faith; and the bond of *sacraments*, i.e. unity in one system of divinely instituted sacramental worship — which constitute the true unity willed, decreed and promised by Christ. Ecumenical unity will accomplish the syncretic unity of the one-world Antichrist religion against which St. Pius X warned in *Notre charge apostolique* (1904), where he spoke of "the great movement of apostasy being organized in every country for the establishment of a One-World Church which shall have neither dogmas nor hierarchy, neither discipline for the mind nor curb for the passions, and which under the pretext of freedom and human dignity, would bring back to the world the reign of legalized cunning and force, and the oppression of the weak, and all those who toil and suffer." (para. 44) When that is achieved then there will only be one great obstacle left on earth that will oppose that godless ecumenical unity of the entity which the same St. Pius X describes as "a Democracy which will be neither Catholic, nor Protestant nor Jewish" (para. 43) — that great obstacle will be the true and unreformed Catholic Church which will continue to 'hold fast to the Catholic Faith, integral and undefiled' (Athanasian Creed). Then there will be unleashed the most ferocious, intense and universal persecution of the Church that there has ever been and ever will be: the attempt to exterminate the Catholic Faith and Tradition from the face of the earth — and this bloody campaign to exterminate Catholics, depicted in the vision of the Third Secret of Fatima, will be carried out in the name of Vatican II and Ecumenism! Thus, we finally grasp what Pius XII was referring to when he said shortly after the end of World War II: "Mankind must prepare itself for sufferings such as it has never before experienced."[112] In *Le jour de la colère*, published in 1856, it is foretold when this dreadful calamity will strike the world. I mentioned above the prophecy of Sr. Jeanne de la Nativité who foretold, "Before the Antichrist arrives, the world will be afflicted with bloody wars." About one of these wars in particular, I have already commented in my earlier work, *The Mystery of Iniquity*:

> In the prophecy of Zachary — the Armenian Jew who converted to the Catholic Faith — published in 1856 was the edited text of the prophecy of the revelations that he received from God. Father A Fatacioli compiled the prophecies and published them in a book called *The Day of Anger: The Hand of God Upon an Empire*. That empire is described in its geographical dimensions as occupying the space of what became the Soviet Union and China. That is the empire that will use great guile and deception as we had in the period of detente, and the glasnost and perestroika of Gorbachev before the scheduled demolition of the Soviet Union. And then there would be the war that the prophecy refers to as "the struggle of the strong against the strong". This empire of the north — consisting of Russia and China — will go to war against North America. And this Nineteenth Century text says they will fire their missiles on North America and North America will fall and be conquered and brought into bondage. The next phrase [which I paraphrased from memory] is the most frightful thing of all. It is then that Zachary says in this text published in 1856, "and then the whole world fell under the dominion of the first-born of hell."

On page 169 of *Le jour de la colère*, that war of the great Eurasian empire comprising Russia & China against North America, which will usher in the reign of Antichrist, is described in these exact words:

> As for the people of the new world, which a great ambition and secular projects had made, at the same time too guilty, blind and crazy, I saw that after a horrible struggle between power and power, the arrogant and the arrogant, tyranny and tyranny it too [i.e. the people of the new world] fell

---

[112] Quoted by Desmond Birch in *Trial, Tribulation and Triumph*.

under the dragon and received, as the price of its mad cooperation, devouring chains. With it, too soon aged by civilization and iniquity, all the other peoples of these places fell under the dominion of the firstborn of hell, with all the islands of these two boundless seas that wrap the globe from the East to the West.[113]

That this great time of tribulation foretold in Scripture and in so many prophecies of the saints, and at Fatima is rapidly approaching and is "even at the doors" (Matt. 24:33) was strongly alluded to and virtually confirmed to by no less than Pope Benedict XVI himself in his *Address on the Occasion of Christmas Greetings to the Roman Curia*, on 20 December 2010:

> *Excita, Domine, potentiam tuam, et veni.* Repeatedly during the season of Advent the Church's liturgy prays in these or similar words. They are invocations that were probably formulated as the Roman Empire was in decline. **The disintegration of the key principles of law and of the fundamental moral attitudes underpinning them burst open the dams which until that time had protected peaceful coexistence among peoples. The sun was setting over an entire world.** Frequent natural disasters further increased this sense of insecurity. **There was no power in sight that could put a stop to this decline. All the more insistent, then, was the invocation of the power of God: the plea that he might come and protect his people from all these threats.**
>
> *Excita, Domine, potentiam tuam, et veni.* **Today too, we have many reasons to associate ourselves with this Advent prayer of the Church.** For all its new hopes and possibilities, **our world is at the same time troubled by the sense that moral consensus is collapsing, consensus without which juridical and political structures cannot function. Consequently the forces mobilized for the defence of such structures seem doomed to failure.** [114]

---

[113] «Quant au peuple du monde nouveau, qu'une ambition vaste et des projets séculaires avaient rendu, en même temps que trop coupable, aveugle et insensé, je vis qu'après une lutte horrible entre la puissance et la puissance, la superbe et la superbe, la tyrannie et la tyrannie, il tombait lui aussi sous le dragon, et recevait, pour prix de sa folle coopération, des chaînes dévorantes. Avec lui tombaient sous la domination du premier-né des enfers tous les autres peuples de ces lieux, trop tôt vieillis par la civilisation et les iniquités, avec toutes les îles de ces deux mers sans limites qui enveloppent le globe de l'Orient à l'Occident.»

[114] http://w2.vatican.va/content/benedict-xvi/en/speeches/2010/december/documents/hf_ben-xvi_spe_20101220_curia-auguri.html.

Bergoglio's reforms are transforming Rome from being the centre of Christianity to the headquarters of the mystery of iniquity under the reign of Antichrist:

> *"Where the See of the most blessed Peter and the Chair of the truth, was constituted as the light of the nations, there they have set up the throne of their abominable impiety, so that the shepherd being struck, the sheep may be dispersed."*

Bergoglio must go. He must not be tolerated in any manner. His reforms must be nullified. He is the enemy within the gate (Lamentations 4:12) – an intruder who usurps the papal throne – an impostor whose imposture must be recognized for what it is: *the usurpation of an antipope.* There exists in the Church the jurisdiction and means to remedy this unprecedented danger to the universal Church: It is that which is explained by Don Pietro Ballerini and Pope Gregory XVI – based on the teaching of St. Robert Bellarmine; which is itself founded on the ruling of Session 37 of the Council of Constance. The pastors of the Church need to act quickly – while the true pope, Benedict XVI still lives; and before Bergoglio's heretical reforms can become institutionalized and "irreversible" in a counterfeit Anti-church as he intends them to be. Pope Gregory XVI (Bartolomeo Cappellari), following Ballerini, explains that Jesus Christ infallibly conferred upon pastors of the Church the authority from God to to remove such usurpers; and that this right was exercised by the Council of Constance to depose the illegitimately elected usurper, Benedict XIII:

> Thus the Council had the whole foundation for judging, that his supporters would have known the illegitimacy and nullity of his assumption to the Apostolic See: nor should it cooperate in the continuation of the schism, leaving it in the peaceful possession of his alleged pontificate. It had therefore in this hypothesis all the right, I will even say, the obligation to provide for the safety of the whole Church, by deposing Benedict, without being able to infer from it, that it had an equal right to depose a clearly legitimate Pope. In fact, it pronounced and executed its final sentence, not on the basis of its having authority over the Pope, but on the well-founded assumption that this one was not [the pope]: in which case it is clearly certain that Jesus Christ, wanting the government founded by himself, for the safety of the faithful to be *immutable, visible and perpetual*, must have provided the Church with all means, which are necessary in order not to be governed by an illegitimate leader. Therefore he must infallibly have conferred on it the right to the power, in the uncertainty and in the reasonable and founded doubt of the legitimacy of a Pope, to proceed to the election of another.

And this, above all, if that one, whose legitimacy is reasonably suspect, were to allow it to be molested in a thousand ways, so that God should have to be accused of not having sufficiently provided for its indefectibility, if in such circumstances it did not have the appropriate faculties.[115]

The reasons why the Council considered the legitimacy of "Benedict XIII" (Pedro de Luna) to be *reasonably suspect* are precisely the same reasons why there is today *the uncertainty and the reasonable and founded doubt of the legitimacy* of the man who calls himself "Francis" (Jorge Bergoglio), namely, the doubt that Bergoglio was validly elected; and the manifestly heretical assertions which he professes. While the question of the canonical validity of Cardinal de Luna's election was not resolved by the Council, the legitimacy of his claim on the papacy was definitively disproven by his own manifest pertinacity in heresy and schism; for which reason, the Council declared him to have forfeited all ecclesiastical title, honour, dignity; and to have rendered himself unworthy; cast out and cut off by God; and deprived *ipso jure* of all right to any claim on the papacy, and cut off as a withered member from the Church.[116]

---

[115] D. Mauro Cappellari ora Gregorio XVI, *Il trionfo della santa sede e della chiesa contro gli assatti dei novatori*, Venezia, 1832, p. 46 – «Avea dunque il Concilio tutto il fondamento per giudicare, che I suoi fautori medesimi conosciuta avessero l'illegittimità e nullità della di lui assunzione alla Sede apostolica: nè doveva per altra parte cooperare alla continuazione dello scisma, lasciandolo nel pacific possesso del suo preteso pontificato. Aveva perciò in questa ipotesi tutto il diritto, dirò anzi, l'obbligo di provedere alla sicurezza di tutta la Chiesa col depor Benedetto, senza che possa da ciò inferirsi, che avesse un egual diritto a deporre un Papa evidentemente legittimo. Pronunziò esso infatti ed eseguì la sua finale sentenza, non sull'appoggio della sua autorità sopra il Papa, ma sulla fondata supposizione che tale non fosse: nel qual caso è evidentemente certa la potestà della Chiesa è evidentemente certo, che Gesù Cristo, volendo *immutabile, visibile e perpetuo* il governo da se fondato per la sicurezza dei fedeli, deve aver provveduta la Chiesa di tutti quei mezzi, che son necessarii per non lasciarsi governare da un capo illegittimo. Quindi deve infallibilmente averle conferito il diritto di potere nell'incertezza e nel dubbio ragionevole e fondato della legittimità di un Papa, procedere all'elezione di un altro. E ciò soprattutto se quello, la cui legittimità è ragionevolmente sospetta, non lasciasse di molestarla in mille guise, cosicché accusar dovrebbesi Iddio medesimo di non aver sufficientemente provveduto alla sua indefettibilità, se in tali circostanze fornita non l'avesse delle opportune facoltà.»

[116] «[...] sancta generalis synodus universalem ecclesiam repraesentans in dicta inquisitionis causa pro tribunali sedens pronunciat decernit et declarat per

St. Alphonsus explains it is certain that for an ecumenical council to be legitimate, it must be convoked by the pope; *but in such cases when it is doubtful who is the true pope, the council can be convoked by the cardinals, and by the bishops*; and then all the elected would be bound by the decision of the Council, *because in such a case the Apostolic See would be considered vacant.* [117] The Holy Doctor then continues in the next sentence, "The same would be in the case, if the pope were to fall notoriously and pertinaciously in some heresy." Pope Gregory XVI explains why this is so:

«In the times of the antipopes, as well as of the dead Pope, the form of the government ordained by Christ does not remain obscure, even in a case where there is founded doubt, so that it is not clear who should be venerated for Pope, yes in the case of sede vacante it happens in the Church what happens in different monarchies, in which in time of interregnum the government resides in some senate; as practiced also in the ancient Roman empire, in which the Roman senate commanded in time of interregnum; so in the mean while in those cases the government of the Church is aristocratic. But who does not know that this cannot be its natural state? Who can recognize him from the same dilligence that the Church gave to elect her head, suffering ill from remaining headless for a long time?»[118]

---

hanc definitivam sententiam in his scriptis **eumdem Petrum de Luna Benedictum XIII** ut praemittitur nuncupatum fuisse et esse periurum universalis ecclesiae scandalizatorem fautorem et nutritorem inveterati schismatis inveteratae scissurae et divisionis ecclesiae sanctae dei pacis et unionis eiusdem ecclesiae impeditorem et turbatorem **schismaticum et haereticum a fide devium et articuli fidei unam sanctam catholicam ecclesiam violatorem pertinacem** cum scandalo ecclesiae dei **incorrigibilem notorium et manifestum atque omni titulo gradu honore et dignitate se reddidisse indignum a deo eiectum et praecisum et omni iure eidem in papatu et Romano pontifici ac Romanae ecclesiae quomodolibet competente ipso iure privatum et ab ecclesia catholica tamquam membrum aridum praecisum.**» [Council of Constance, session XXXVII]

[117] «La seconda cosa certa si è, che quando in tempo di Scisma si dubita, chi fosse il vero Papa, in tal caso il Concilio può essere convocato da' Cardinali, e da' Vescovi; ed allora ciascuno degli eletti è tenuto di stare alla definizione del Concilio, perchè allora si tiene come vacante la Sede Apostolica.» — *Verità della Fede,* Part. III. Cap. IX. p. 457.

[118] «Nei tempi degli antipapi, come anche di Papa morto, non resta oscurata la forma del governo ordinato da Cristo, imperciocché sì nel caso in cui siavi dubbio fondato, per cui non si sappia bene chi debbasi venerare per Papa, sì nel caso di sede vacante succede nella Chiesa ciò che succede in diverse monarchie, nelle quali in tempo di interregno il governo risiede in qualche senato; come

Gregory XVI explains why the deposition of such a one *whose legitimacy is reasonably suspect* – one who allows the Church *to be molested in a thousand ways*, would not violate the primacy:

> Even so that it could be for a moment, that the Church has the authority to depose the Pontiffs: what then? ...In fact, by ceasing in this hypothesis the deposed Pope to be a true Pope, the deposition is not a prescription against the rights of the Primacy, and therefore against the current representation of the Church in the Pope recognized as such, but only against the person, who was before adorned with papal dignity... Now, the point of the question is not, if the Church can remove from one the pontifical dignity and authority, but if in the primacy it essentially includes her representation; which can never be denied when it has not been shown before that the Church has sometimes suspended in the true and subsistent Pope the exercise of his primacy, and therefore also that of representing it; and that he has nevertheless enjoyed an active, productive and effective primacy, with the essential right to make his authority felt. So long as the adversaries do not give us more convincing arguments, we can always conclude that the current representation of the Church is inseparable from the pontifical primacy. [...] Now it is clear that if there were not in the Church and in the Pope the same spirit, feelings and doctrines, there could not be in him the true representation of her. Therefore the Pontiff cannot represent the Church, who together does not necessarily represent her unity.[119]

---

praticavasi pure nell'antico impero romano, nel quale il senato romano comandava in tempo d'interregno; quindi in quei casi il governo della Chiesa è intrattanto aristocratico. Ma chi non sa, che questo non può essere lo suo stato naturale? Chi può riconoscerlo dalle stesse premure che dessi la Chiesa per eleggersi il suo capo, mal soffrendo di starsene acefala per lungo tempo?» [*Il trionfo della santa sede e della chiesa contro gli assatti dei novatori*, p. 29]

[119] "«Tuttavolta sia pure così per un momento, ed abbia pure la Chiesa l'autorità di deporre i Pontefici: che perciò? ... In fatti, cessando in questa ipotesi il Papa deposto di essere vero Papa, non è la deposizione una prescrizione contro i diritti del Primato, e quindi contro l'attuale rappresentanza della Chiesa nel Papa per tale riconosciuto, ma soltanto contro la persona, che era prima ornata di papal dignità... Ora, il punto della questione non è, se possa togliere la Chiesa ad uno la dignità ed autorità pontificia, ma se nel primato essenzialmente comprendasi la di lei rappresentanza; il che non si potrà mai negare quando prima non si dimostri che la Chiesa abbia talvolta sospeso nel vero e sussistente Papa l'esercizio dei suoi primaziali diritti, e perciò pure quello di rappresentarla; e che ciò nonostante abbia egli goduto di una primazia attiva, operosa ed efficace, col diritto essenziale di far sentire la sua autorità. Finchè

For the Church to have authority in such a case of doubt about the legitimacy of a claimant, there must be not merely a well founded *positive and probable doubt*, but the doubt must be such as makes it impossible to recognize the claimant as a certainly a valid pope. If a pope is a validly elected pope, his election cannot be nullified by the Church. Ballerini explains,

> «Idem vero primatus inest cuivis Pontifici, qui verus & legitimus sit, etiamsi ob ancipites circumstantias non constet, quis inter contendentes sit legitimus et verus. Hæc enim ignorantia potest quidem excusare eos, qui verum re ipsa Pontificem sibi invincibiliter ignotum debitis oficiis non prosequuntur; at sicut simplex ignorantia nihil juris adimit, aut adimere potest ei, qui re ipsa verus & legitimus Pontifex sit, licet aliis ignotus, ita nihil juris tribuit, aut tribuere potest in ipsum concilio quamvis œumenico: semper nimirum jus primatus manet re ipsa vero legitimoque Pontifici, qui semper hoc primatus jure re ipsa toti Ecclesiæ, & cuivis concilio superior, a jurisdictione istorum subtrahitur.»[120]

Thus, as noted above, if a false pope such as Bergoglio enjoys widespread and notorious acceptance, the true pope (Benedict XVI) does not lose his primacy because of that erroneous acceptance, nor is he bound to submit to the decrees of any council that might convene to settle the question of his legitimacy. Bordoni explains that the pope is morally bound not to cede to duress and vexations by renouncing, because it is precisely such a widespresd and notorious acceptance of a false pope and schism that will result from an illicit renunciation of a true pope who flees for fear of the wolves:

> *Tum quia verus Papa pro viribus usq. ad mortem tenetur tueri unitatem Ecclesiæ in suo capite legitimo nullum permittendo schisma in Ecclesia Dei; per renuntiationem autem*

---

adunque gli avversari non ci adducano argomenti più convincenti, potremo sempre concludere, che l'attuale rappresentanza della Chiesa è inseparabile dal pontificio primato. [...] Or egli è chiaro che, qualora non vi fosse e nella Chiesa e nel Papa medesimità di spirito, di sentimenti e di dottrine, non vi potrebbe neppur essere in questo la vera rappresentanza di quella. Dunque il Pontefice non può rappresentare la Chiesa, che insieme non ne rappresenti necessariamente l'unità.» [*Il trionfo della santa sede e della chiesa contro gli assatti dei novatori*, p. 269-270]

[120] *De Potestate Ecclesiastica Summorum Pontificum Et Conciliorum Generalium*, Auctore Petro Ballerinio Presbytero Veronensi, Augustæ Vindelicorum (Augsburg), MDCCLXX, p. 132.

permitteret schisma, ergo nullatenus renuntiare potest. Tum quia hoc renuntiare esset cedere iura Papatus intruso, quod fieri non potest, cum sit contra omnia iura, quod non Papa notorie habendus sit pro vero Papa.[121]

In the above quoted interview, Mons. Bux mentioned the difficulties involved in the removal of a heretic pope, "I do not hide, however, that what is indicated, although it is clear and smooth in theory, in practice it meets many difficulties; disadvantages also of a canonistic nature." Mons. Bux then went on to propose a more practical solution to the present crisis in the papacy:

> As you can see, there are many practical, theological and juridical difficulties to the question of the judgment of the heretical pope. Perhaps – and I say this from a practical point of view – it would be easier to examine and study more accurately the question concerning the juridical validity of Pope Benedict XVI's renunciation, i.e. whether it is full or partial ("halfway"), as someone has said) or doubtful, since the idea of a sort of collegiate papacy seems to me decidedly against the Gospel dictate. In fact, Jesus did not say "tibi dabo claves..." addressing Peter and Andrew, but he only told Peter! That's why I say that perhaps a thorough study of renunciation could be more useful and profitable, as well as helping to overcome problems that today seem insurmountable to us. It was written: "There will also come a time of the most difficult trials for the Church. Cardinals will oppose cardinals and bishops to bishops. Satan will put himself in their midst. Also in Rome there will be great changes "(Saverio Gaeta, *Fatima, The Whole Truth*, 2017, p 129). And this great change, with Pope Francis, we can see in a palpable way, given the clear intention to mark a line of discontinuity or break with the previous pontificates. This discontinuity – a revolution – generates heresies, schisms and controversies of various kinds. However, all of them can be traced back to sin. And this was already noted by Origen: "Where there is sin, there we find multiplicity, there schisms, there heresies, there the controversies. Where virtue reigns, there is unity, there communion, thanks to which all believers were one heart and one soul." (In Ezechielem homilia, 9.1, in Sources Chrétiennes 352, p.)[122]

---

[121] Bordoni, *Op. cit.*, p. 150.

[122] «Come vede, ci sono non poche difficoltà pratiche, teologiche e giuridiche alla questione del giudizio del l papa eretico. Forse – e lo dico proprio da un punto di vista pratico – sarebbe più agevole esaminare e studiare più accuratamente la questione relativa alla validità giuridica della rinuncia di papa Benedetto XVI, se cioè essa sia piena o parziale ("a metà", come qualcuno ha detto) o dubbia, giacché l'idea di una sorta di papato collegiale mi sembra

Unfortunately, without an extraordinary intervention of divine providence, Bergoglio cannot be simply neutralized like so many antipopes of past centuries, because his faction, with the backing of the sect of Freemasonry, is (humanly speaking) too powerful for a clean and tidy removal. It will be a dire struggle with dire consequences, but there exists no other viable alternative. The declaration must be issued, preferably by Pope Benedict himself together with those non-heretical cardinals who still have the Catholic faith; while there is still time. Otherwise, it will have to be issued by the cardinals alone – by those cardinals who are not of the heretical faction. The immediate consequences were described in 1969 by the future Pope Benedict XVI in a radio address on Hessischer Rundfunk in Germany: "It [the Church] will become small and will have to start pretty much all over again. It will no longer have use of the structures it built in its years of prosperity. The reduction in the number of faithful will lead to it losing an important part of its social privileges."[123] However, the tribulation will be brief, and will be followed by a glorious age of triumph for the Church, the Kingdom of God on earth. To the saintly Jesuit astronomer, Fr. Stefano Scorza S.J., was given the grace to see in a prophetic vision this glorious triumph of the Church as the "New Jerusalem" that will take place after the tribulation. We have the solemn assurance of this pronounced by

---

decisamente contro il dettato evangelico. Gesù non disse, infatti, *"tibi dabo claves…"* rivolgendosi a Pietro e ad Andrea, ma lo disse solo a Pietro! Ecco perché dico che, forse, uno studio approfondito sulla rinuncia potrebbe essere più utile e proficuo, nonché aiutare a superare problemi che oggi ci sembrano insormontabili. È stato scritto: "Giungerà anche un tempo delle prove più difficili per la Chiesa. Cardinali si opporranno a cardinali e vescovi a vescovi. Satana si metterà in mezzo a loro. Anche a Roma ci saranno grandi cambiamenti" (Saverio Gaeta, *Fatima, tutta la verità*, 2017, p. 129). E questo grande cambiamento, con papa Francesco, lo possiamo vedere in maniera palpabile, stante la chiara intenzione di segnare una linea di discontinuità o rottura con i precedenti pontificati. Questa discontinuità – una rivoluzione – genera eresie, scismi e controversie di varia natura. Tutte, però, possono ricondursi al peccato. E questo lo constatava già Origene: "Dove c'è il peccato, lì troviamo la molteplicità, lì gli scismi, lì le eresie, lì le controversie. Dove, invece, regna la virtù, lì c'è unità, lì comunione, grazie alle quali tutti i credenti erano un cuor solo e un'anima sola" (*In Ezechielem homilia*, 9,1, in *Sources Chrétiennes* 352, p. 296).»

[123] That radio address, *What Will the Church Look Like in 2000*, was reproduced in full in a book entitled *Faith and the Future*, published in 2009 by Ignatius Press.

Jesus Christ, the divine Saviour Himself: "In the world you shall have distress: but have confidence, I have overcome the world." (John 16:33)

PROLEGOMENON TO VOLUME ONE

The importance of the question of papal heresy is of far greater importance than one might first think; especially because since *Pastor Æternus*, it has been most commonly held by theologians that a pope cannot fall into formal heresy. If a man who is generally believed to hold the papal office were to manifest himself to be an obstinate heretic; the question would arise as to whether he could simply be declared to have already fallen from office *ipso jure* by the Catholic hierarchy, who would then elect a new pope; or would he need to be juridically convicted in a penal process and deposed. If he were to lose office automatically (*ipso jure*) upon manifesting pertinacity in heresy; then Catholics would have the right to refuse him recognition as pope, as well as refusing to be subject to his governance. The cardinals would only need to declare his forfeiture of office to have taken place by his defection from the Catholic faith, and then elect a new pope. Among theologians who admit at least the hypothetical possibility that a pope could fall into formal heresy, that has actually been the common opinion for more than a century. In the latter case, however, if the heretic pope would need to be juridically deposed in order to bring about his fall from office; then the heretic's removal from office would depend first of all on the question of whether or not he could be deposed at all; and if yes, it would have to be determined by what juridical procedure he could be validly deprived of office.

St. Robert Bellarmine explains in the passages of *De Romano Pontifice* which I cite in this volume, that the Church would declare deposed a manifestly heretical pope who has already fallen from the Apostolic See by himself. This principle, as mentioned above, applies for any officeholder who publicly defects into heresy, apostasy or schism. However, this is doctrine is especially pertinent in the case of a manifest heretic pope because the First See is not adjudicable, and therefore, as Gregory XVI explains, a pope cannot be deposed from office in the manner that a bishop can be deposed by the pope[124]; but a heretic could

---

[124] Cf. – D. Mauro Cappellari ora Gregorio XVI, *Il trionfo della santa sede e della chiesa contro gli assalti dei novatori*, Venezia, 1832, *Discorso Preliminare*, § 2, pp. 52-53.

only be deposed from the papacy who, as a consequence of being a public schismatic and heretic would have already "fallen from office by himself" if ever he had been elevated to that dignity.[125] Saint Alphonsus in *Truths of the Faith*[126] clearly states the same: "if God were to permit that ***a pope would be notoriously heretical and contumacious, he would cease to be pope, and the pontificate would be vacant... the See would be considered vacant*** [...] in the case, that the pope fell notoriously and pertinaciously into some heresy... ***the pope would not be deprived by the Council... he would be stripped of power immediately by Christ, becoming in fact an incapable subject***, and ***fallen from his office***". Fr. Francesco Bordoni says almost the same, but argues differently. Bordoni's argument involves itself in a contradiction, (that will be dealt with below), maintaining at the same time that the pertinaciously heretical pope, although an incapable subject already judged by God, retains his office and dignity until formally deposed by the authority of a council. The reason why he reached this conclusion is that while on the one hand he defectively argues against an *ipso iure divino* deposition by God[127], and correctly argues that an infidel or heretic would be an incapable subject; he, on the other hand demonstrates with irrefutable logic the fatal defects in the ministerial deposition theories of Suárez and Cajetan; and therefore, he arrives at what is, since the First Vatican Council's solemn dogmatic definition of the universal primacy of jurisdiction and judicial supremacy of the pope, the heretically inadmissible conclusion that only an authoritative deposition made with a superior's power of jurisdiction can have the effect of a valid deposition of a heretic pope. As I demonstrate in this volume, all theories which hold that a judgment of the Church, even to be made by an ecumenical council, is required to effect the loss of office of a heretic pope, whether that judgment be considered the act of *power of jurisdiction* of a superior over a subject, or merely the exercise of a

---

[125] *Ibid.*, p. 47.

[126] Alfonso M. De Liguori, *Verità della Fede*, Part. 3, Cap. 8, No. 10, p. 455; Part. 3, Cap. 9, No. 2, p. 457.

[127] As will be explained in its proper place, Bordoni argues that a manifest heretic would *still be a member*, but a dead and *severed member* of the Church. **Sed contra,** a member that is severed is *cut off*, and no longer an actual member of the Church; but a *former member* who has *separated himself* from the Church *by himself*, by the very act of public heresy which visibly separates a man from the Church *suapte natura*, as Pius XII teaches in *Mystici Corporis*, and effects the loss of office *ipso facto*, as is set forth in the *Code of Canon Law*.

ministerial power acting as a *dispositive cause*, are heretical insofar as they oppose the absolute judicial supremacy of the pope, who is the supreme judge *in all cases*[128] **including his own**,[129] and therefore, *without exception*, the pope *for so long as he is constituted in the papal office and dignity* cannot be judged by anyone, not even for heresy. Since the pope, while in office, is the supreme judge with universal primacy of jurisdiction, he alone is the final and infallible judge in matters of faith and morals, **against whose judgment no one may appeal, not even to an ecumenical council.**[130] Cardinal Manning observes, «Mauro Cappellari, afterwards Gregory XVI, affirms that the supreme judge of controversies is the Pontiff, "distinct and separate from all other Bishops; and that his decree in things of faith ought by them to be held without doubt."[131]» Pope Gregory bases this doctrine expressed in this proposition on the teaching of St. Thomas:[132]

---

[128] *Pastor Æternus*: «iudicem supremum… in omnibus causis ad examen ecclesiasticum spectantibus.»

[129] Innocentius III, *Sermo IV De Diversis*; Hadrianus II, *Allocutio tertia, ad Concilium Romanum*.

[130] *Pastor Æternus*: «Quare a recto veritatis tramite aberrant, qui affirmant, licere ab iudiciis Romanorum Pontificum ad oecumenicum Concilium tamquam ad auctoritatem Romano Pontifice superiorem appellare.»; *CIC 1917*: «Can. 227. §2. A sententia Romani Pontificis non datur ad Concilium Oecumenicum appellatio.»; *CIC 1983*: «Can. 333 § 3. Contra sententiam vel decretum Romani Pontificis non datur appellatio neque recursus.»

[131] «Il Trionfo della Santa Sede, Cap. v. Sect. 10, p. 124. Venezia, 1832.»

[132] *Ibid.* — «S. Tommaso per tanto offre quivi un prospetto il più minuto dei privilegi, che nel romano Pontefice si gloriano di venerare gli amanti della verità. Parlando egli del simbolo della fede, cerca chi sia il supremo giudice delle controversie, a cui appartenga la solenne *edizione* di esso simbolo, cioè della norma di nostra credenza, e conchiude: 1.° che è il Papa: 2.° distinto, e separato dagli altri Vescovi tutti, dovendo anzi da questi tenersi, *inconcussa fide*, quanto egli determina qual dogma di fede: 3.o lo prova dall'orazione e precetto di Cristo: 4.° dall'unità di fede che dee professarsi in tutta la Chiesa, la quale unità verrebbe a mancare, se il Papa non fosse il supremo giudice delle controversie, ed il solo promulgatore delle dogmatiche definizioni: 5., nè può dirsi che faccialo per usurpazione e privata autorità, nè che ciò convenga ai soli generali Concilii indipendentemente da lui: poichè tutto ciò che da essi si fa non ha forza di obbligare assolutamente, senza il concorso del Papa, da lui dipendendo e la convocazione e l'autorevole conferma degli stessi Concilii: *cuius auctoritate synodus congregatar, et eius sententia confirmatur.*»

«St. Thomas offers here a most minute prospectus of the privileges, which In the Roman Pontiff the lovers of truth in glory to venerate. Speaking of the symbol of faith, he seeks who is the supreme judge of disputes, to whom belongs the solemn edition of the symbol, that is, the norm of our belief, and concludes: 1. ° That it is the Pope: 2. ° distinct, and separate from all the other bishops, having to Indeed be held by these, *inconcussa fide*, what he determines as the dogma of faith: 3. ° He proves it from Christ's Prayer and Precept: 4. ° from the unity of faith which is to be professed throughout the Church, which unity would be lacking, if the Pope were not the supreme judge of the disputes, and the only promulgator of the dogmatic definitions: 5., nor can it be said that he does it by usurpation and private authority, nor that this should be done only by the general councils independently of him: since all that is done by them has no force to oblige absolutely, without the involvement of the Pope, from whom depends the convocation and the authoritative confirmation of the councils themselves: *cuius auctoritate synodus congregatur, et eius sententia confirmatur*».

In virtue of his office as Vicar of Christ and pastor of the universal Church, the pope is always able to freely exercise supreme, full, immediate, and universal power in the Church (*CIC 1983*, Can. 331); and therefore he alone possesses the authority to preside over a council, and to designate and constitute the business to be transacted by the council; and to transfer, suspend or dissolve the council, and to confirm its decrees. (*CIC 1917*, Can. 222. §2) The objection that says in deposing a heretical pope a council's judgment would not exercise power of jurisdiction over the pope as a superior is specious, and fatally flawed insofar as every judgment hinges directly on the power of a true jurisdiction, without which the act cannot consist, since the basis and foundation of *judgment* is **jurisdiction**, so that a judgment lacking jurisdiction would be incurable and irreparable[133]; and, furthermore, no judgment whatsoever pronounced by a council would have any juridical effect unless it would be confirmed by the pope and promulgated by his

---

[133] P. Francesco Bordoni, *Op. cit.* cap. VI, p. 154: «Deinde per illam quandam ordinarionem factam a Concilio vel intelligitur vera, & propria poteſtas, & iurisdictio Concilii in Papam, [...] vel intelligitur aliquid aliud, quod tamen conſonum non eſt, quia omnis actus iudicialis pendet à vera iurisdictione, ſine qua nullus actus conſiſtere poteſt, quia baſis, & fundamentum iudicij reputatur iurisdictio Bald. *C. ſi a compet. iud. in Rubr._Paris de confidet. q. 79. num. 22* ita quod defectus iurisdictionis dicicur infanabilis, & irreparabilis, ex Staphil. Sarnen, & Vantio ex eodem Pariſio *num. 24*.»

order.[134] In fact, an ecumenical council as such cannot validly convene and actually exist before it has been convoked by the pope;[135] and if the Apostolic See would become vacant during a council, the council would be suspended until a new pope would either order it to continue, or to dissolve it. (*CIC 1917*, Can. 227; *CIC 1983*, Can. 340) Moreover, as Bordoni amply demonstrates, the theories, whether of Suarezian or Cajetanian stripe, which posit a fall from office premised on a judgment of the Church, collapse upon themselves due to their own internal logical inconsistencies, as is shown later in this work.

In a deposition there are enumerated three acts, 1) the declaration of heresy, 2) the desisting of the papacy in the person, and 3) penal expulsion from the Church; all of which are *judicial acts*, and therefore **require the power of jurisdiction in whoever would provide the act**.[136] From this it necessarily follows, that if a manifestly pertinacious heretic pope would not fall from office entirely by himself, he would remain in office until judged and declared a heretic and deposed from the papacy by a council possessing a superior jurisdiction over him; or else he would remain in office even without any possibility of being legitimately deposed. It is *de fide* that there does not exist, nor can there exist, even by way of exception, a jurisdiction on earth superior to the pope's universal primacy of jurisdiction; and, as is amply demonstrated in the first volume of this work, it is also *de fide* that all manifestly pertinacious heretics visibly separate themselves from the Church by the nature of heresy, and not by any juridical act of ecclesiastical authority; and, as a direct consequence of being visibly severed from the body of the Church, they lose *ipso facto* by tacit renunciation whatever ecclesiastical office they may have held, without any juridical declaration by the ecclesiastical authority. Hence, it is contrary to faith to say that a manifestly pertinacious heretic could even remain in office as pope; and likewise, if the manifest heretic would still be considered to retain the

---

[134] *CIC 1917*: «Can. 227. Concilii decreta vim definitivam obligandi non habent, nisi a Romano Pontifice fuerint confirmata et eius iussu promulgata.»

[135] *CIC 1917*: «Can. 222. §1. Dari nequit Oecumenicum Concilium quod a Romano Pontifice non fuerit convocatum.»; *CIC 1983*: "Can. 338 — § 1. Unius Romani Pontificis est Concilium Oecumenicum convocare, eidem per se vel per se vel per alios praesidere, item Concilium transferre, suspendere vel dissolvere, eiusque decreta approbare."

[136] Bordoni, *Op. cit.*, p. 154 — «Numerantur autem tres actus, declarario hæresis, defitio Papatus, & eiectio extra Ecclefiam, qui omnes funt iudiciales, ac proinde requirentes iurisdictionem in eo, qui illa tria præftare debet.»

papal office and dignity before being judged by the Church, it would be contrary to faith to say that he could be deposed from the papal office by the judgment of the Church. Thus, there remain only two doctrinally orthodox opinions on the question of the deposition of a heretical pope, either, 1) that a pope cannot fall into formal heresy; or, 2) that a heretical pope would automatically fall from office once the pertinacity of the heresy becomes manifest.

In his answer to the question, "Whether a council can depose a pope," (*An Concilium possit deponere Papam.*), Fr. Bordoni responds, saying that *an obstinate heretic is already judged by God, because He who does not believe is already judged, and is to be declared to "be deposed" and deprived of the papacy; and that this is necessary that the judgment of God be published by the ministry of men, and this is most aptly done by a council, which* [according to the common opinion at that time] *is the supreme tribunal* **when the papal see is vacant**.[137] Logically, this response would not allow for the Church's judgment to be made on the pope before he would have fallen from office by himself, because before the fall from office, he would remain pope and retain the full power of jurisdiction as the supreme judge even over himself (antequam autem Papa declaretur hæreticus Papa eſt, ergò in hoc dum adhuc eſt Papa, ſupra se habet judicem) [138]; nor would there exist any rational basis for asserting that a judgment made without any jurisdiction or authority would cause either directly or indirectly the loss of papal office upon the issuing of a declaration by those same ones who lack the authority to judge.[139] Thus, the judgment of deposition for heresy could only be made if the pope would first, by the very act of his manifest heresy, vacate the see by his *ipso facto* fall from office. There exists the actual jurisdiction in the Church to judge the see vacant when a vacancy occurs, otherwise it would be impossible for the succession of popes to continue. However, only after the election of a new pope would a council's declaration of deposition gain juridical force upon ratification

---

[137] Bordoni, *Ibid.* p. 149: «Pertinax [hæreticus] vero a Deo etiam iudicatus ex illo Ioan. 3. *Num.* 18. *Qui vero non credit, iam iudicatus est*, a Concilio **declaratur depositus**, & privatus Papatu, nam necessarium est, quod Dei iudicium publicetur ministerio alicuius hominis, sed nullus aptius, & congruentius assignatur, quam Concilium, quod est supremum tribunal, quando vacat Papale.»

[138] *Ibid.*, p. 154.

[139] *Ibid.*, p. 154: «facta autem ea declaratione non video qua ratione ipſo iure ceſſet in eo Papatus, neque enim in Sacris Scripturis registratum fuit, homine perdere de ſe Papatum, vel a Deo priuari poſita declaratione hæreſis»

of the conciliar act by the new pope, (as in fact happened in the case of the deposition of Pedro de Luna by the Council of Constance), because a council possesses no jurisdiction during the vacancy of the Apostolic See. Bordoni makes it explicitly clear in his answer to the question, "Has any infidel or heretic at some time been elected pope? (*An aliquis infidelis, seu hæreticus aliquando in Papam electus fuerit?*) His answer, echoing the teaching of Innocent III in *Sermo II De Diversis*, is that God would not permit his Church to be ruled and governed by one who is ***incapable of this dignity, a putrid and severed member who cannot be the legitimate spouse and head of the Church.***[140] As I demonstrate in this volume with copious quotations from *De Romano Pontifice*, St. Robert Bellarmine, explains in precisely what qualified sense a manifestly heretical pope can be said to be *judged* and *deposed*, i.e., declared to 'be deposed' (*esse depositus*) by himself, rather than be deposed from the papacy by the authority of the Church (*deponi posse*). As Pope Gregory XVI explains (in the passage quoted below), such a judgment would not be made against the "Pope recognized as such, ***but only against the person, who was before adorned with papal dignity***".[141]

The reason why it has been the most commonly held opinion of theologians that a true pope cannot fall into formal heresy, (and as logical consequence could not be judged a heretic even after falling from office), is that the text of that above mentioned dogmatic constitution (*Pastor Æternus*), in defining the dogma of papal infallibility, premised that extraordinary charism on the promise of the divine Saviour Jesus Christ made to Peter and his successors, that their faith would not fail. It is self-evident that if the pope's faith cannot fail, then he cannot become a formal heretic, because one only becomes a formal heretic when one's faith fails. However, before the dogmatic definition was pronounced in 1870, it was not so clear in the minds of all theologians what exactly was meant by the unfailing faith of Peter and his successors as the prerequisite disposition for exercising the charism of infallibility. In the Middle Ages there was not even a clear understanding of the doctrine of papal infallibility in the minds of most theologians; but infallibility was commonly understood to be exercised in the solemn professions and

---

[140] *Ibid.*, cap. V. p. 137 – «... Deus no permitteret Ecclesiam suam regi, & gubernari ab eo, qui ***incapax est huius dignitatis***, & membrum putridum ab Ecclesia præcisum, si hæreticus, aut persona, quam numquam fuit in Ecclesia, ideo neuter potest esse legitimus sponsus, & caput Ecclesiæ.»

[141] Gregorio XVI, *Op. cit.*, p. 270.

definitions of the whole Church represented in a general council. So it comes as no surprise, that the infallible "faith of Peter" was understood to be the faith of the whole Church represented by the successor of Peter; and therefore, the unfailing faith of Peter was thought to be that of the Roman Pontiff together with the bishops in an ecumenical council, manifested in the solemn pronouncements of a council. While the notion can be shown to be logically incoherent (as I demonstrate in the main body of this volume), and was already thoroughly refuted by St. Robert Bellarmine in *Caput iii Liber iv* of *De Romano Pontifice*, it was on the basis of such a conception as this, that the theory eventually became prevalent, according to which, in matters of faith, the authority of a council would be greater than that of a pope teaching as an individual; and consequently, the next step in the development of the theory was that that a council, even without the pope, would have the juridical authority to judge the case of a heretic pope. The Fifth Lateran Council destroyed the foundation of this theory when it solemnly defined the absolute authority of the pope over a council, yet Counter-Reformation theologians attempted to circumvent that ruling by appealing to the spurious *Canon si papa* as the basis for considering the case of papal heresy as an exception to the principle of the *injudicability* of the pope. The pope, it was believed, could be judged, by way of exception, in the case of heresy; because, (it was claimed) that a council would not be exercising power over the pope, but only over the conjunction between the man and the office of the pontificate. The main flaw in this reasoning consists in the fact that such a theory still held that a juridical judgment which would exercise power over the conjunction between the man and the office would first require a prior judgment of heresy to be pronounced *juridically* upon the pope himself, while still in office, by his inferiors in order for him to fall from office for heresy. It also failed to provide a sufficient doctrinal basis that would establish only heresy as the sole exception to the principle of the injudicability of the pope; since, if one exception is admitted, other exceptions cannot be logically excluded. Thus, the opinion can be seen to clearly oppose the solemn definition of the Fifth Lateran Council, that a pope possesses absolute authority over a council (which logically excludes any exception); and directly opposes the dogmatic definition of the First Vatican Council, which, in declaring that the pope is the *supreme judge* **in all cases**, dogmatically established the absolute injudicability of the Roman Pontiff, for which reason there can be no exception. Nevertheless, the theory which can now be seen to have already been proximate to heresy after the pronouncement of the Fifth Lateran Council, was tolerated, and even persisted and survived until the late nineteenth century. The final nail in the coffin of this errant theory was hammered into it by the definition of the primacy, which solemnly pronounced that the pope is the supreme authority "*in all cases that refer to ecclesiastical examination*"; so that the proposition which held that a reigning pope *while still in office* could be judged by his inferiors, could be seen to be heretical, in that it directly opposes the doctrine set forth in the definition, whose wording logically excludes all possibility of allowing any exception to the rule, "The First See is judged by no one."

The theory, which holds that the pope, while still in office, can be judged and deposed for heresy; whether the deposition be considered as a proper act of juridical deposition, or as an act of removal of one who is considered *jure divino* removable upon having been judged guilty of the crime of heresy by competent ecclesiastical authority, and as a consequence of that judgment to have fallen from office *ipso facto*; has, since the time shortly after the First Vatican Council, been rejected with virtual unanimity by theologians, since it could be clearly seen, in the light of the absolute supremacy and injudicability of the pope set forth in solemn definition of the primacy, to be contrary to the faith of the Church.[142] Likewise, the belief that a true and valid pope could even fall into formal heresy was generally abandoned after *Pastor Æternus* taught that St. Peter *and his successors* were given the grace of unfailing faith as a requisite disposition for exercising the charism of papal infallibility. St. Robert Bellarmine had also forcefully argued this point in *Caput iii Liber iv* of *De Romano Pontifice*; but it was only after the support it received from *Pastor Æternus*, that Bellarmine's position on the question became the *opinio communissima*. Since then it has been the nearly unanimous opinion of theologians that a pope cannot fall into formal heresy. While in the Middle Ages it was the far more common opinion among theologians and canonists that a pope could fall into formal heresy, and that he could be judged for heresy by a council; conversely by the time of the Tridentine and post-Tridentine period, the great Counter-Reformation doctors, such as Cajetan, Bellarmine, Suárez, and John of St. Thomas,

---

[142] Cardinal Journet, who favoured the opinion of John of St. Thomas on the deposition of a heretic pope, was the last and lone prominent representative of the miniscule faction that dissented from what has become the morally unanimous position of theologians and canonists on this point since the late nineteenth century.

were of the opinion that a pope cannot become a formal heretic, and therefore considered the question of papal heresy as a mere hypothesis.

As I mentioned earlier, the inconsistencies in the expositions of such eminent ecclesiastical writers as St. Robert Bellarmine, Fr. Francesco Bordoni, and others on this point, ultimately cannot really be always construed to be logical inconsistencies in their own thinking, but rather serve to underscore the problematic nature intrinsic to the logical opposition existing within the notion itself of a heretic pope. The writers themselves, for the most part, proposed correctly reasoned arguments which sometimes led to contradictory conclusions, such as Bellarmine's argument that a secret heretic would necessarily remain in office as a valid pope until convicted of heresy (but he can't be convicted because he cannot be judged); and at the same time, that it is impossible for any formal heretic to be or remain in office as a valid pope. Both Bellarmine and Bordoni assert the inherent incompatibility of heresy with the papacy, so that a formally heretical pope would be an incapable subject, but from this principle both argue differently on how a public heretic would be judged and deposed. Bellarmine argued that a manifest heretic would fall from the papacy by himself *ipso facto* and then be judged and punished; while Bordoni argued that an obstinate heretic had to be judged and deposed by a general council in order to fall from the papacy. Bellarmine held that an occult heretic would remain as pope until convicted of heresy, and Bordoni held the same opinion for both the secret and the public heretic; which in both cases would logically imply that the pope is not always injudicable, and that heresy does not actually render the heretic an incapable subject. Both maintain the *injudicability* of the pope, yet Bellarmine held that the secret heretic still had to be *convicted of heresy* before he would lose office; while Bordoni followed the older Decretist opinion which held that even the notorious heretic would have to be judged and deposed by a council.[143] On the other hand, Bellarmine also says faith *simpliciter* is the necessary disposition for the conservation of the form of the papacy in the pontiff; and that with the removal of

---

[143] Bordoni, *Op. cit. cap. vi.* p. 150: «An Concilium aliquando Congregari possit sine licentia aut contra voluntatem Summi Pontificis? ... *Resp*. Concilium Generale, nolente Papa, Congregari potest a Cardinalibus in dictis duobus casibus, nimirum, in depositione Papæ pertinaciter hæretici, & in Schismate quando verus Papa ignoratur. Et in his duobus casibus Concilium habet auctoritatem de iure divino præcise deponendi Papam hæreticum pertinacem, & tollendi Schisma depositione singulorum Pontificum incertorum.»

the disposition of faith, the pope would immediately cease to be pope. Bellarmine does not really contradict himself, but reasons from what he knows to be a false and impossible premise (i.e. that a pope can be a formal heretic and still be pope), and does so only for the sake of arguing an impossible and purely absract hypothesis; and concludes *correctly* that an occult heretic could not cease by himself to be pope, but would need to first be judged and convicted before he would cease to be pope. There is no real contradiction in Bellarmine's reasoning, because on the one hand he proves the impossibility that there could even be a heretic pope *on the basis of the intrinsic impossibility per se* that a heretic could remain a valid pope; whereas he proves the impossibility of an occult heretic ceasing by himself to be pope, not from any premise based on an intrinsic impossibility, but from the *impossibility of the effect*, namely, that the whole Church would defect by being governed by one who is not the true Roman Pontiff. Bordoni concisely sums up the gist of the Bellarminian argument[144]; and then attempts to refute the argument.[145] Bordoni's refutation fails because it does not refute the intrinsic impossibility for heresy and the papacy to exist together in the same subject; but hypothetically supposes the simultaneous co-existence of them in the same subject on the basis of the *impossibility of the effect* that would ensue if the occult heretic would cease to be pope. Thus, his refutation does not disprove the intrinsic necessity of faith as a dispository habit for the conservation of the form of the pontificate in the person of the poniff, but only underscores the impossibility that the form of the pontificate could even exist in a heretic at all. Indeed, Bellarmine's own refutation (*De Romano Pontif. lib. ii cap. xxx*) of Torquemada's opinion that an occult heretic would be automatically

---

[144] *Ibid.* cap, vi. p. 152: «Probant, primo, quia ficut fe, habet vnio animæ ad corpus, quod per illam dicitur habere vitam; ita fides ad eum, qui eligitur in Papam, non enim quis affumitur ad Papatum, nifi fit fidelis, & Chriftianus, ita quod fides quafi iungit Papatum homini electo; fed fublata vnione animæ per mortem, homo non dicitur amplius habere vitam, ergò fublata fide à Papa per hærefim non amplius eft Papa.»

[145] *Ibid.* – «praeterquám quod, fi quis hæreticus occultus eligeretur in Papam, effet verè Papa, quia is defectus non deftruit dignitatem Papalem, fed cum ea ftare poteft, & hoc patet, dum omnes doctores à quonam deponendus fit Papa hæreticus, quærunt fupponentes, vtrumque fimul in eodem homine reperiri poffe. Igitur hærefis non deftruit Papam, ficut mors hominem, nam mors opponitur vitæ priuatiuè, hærefis verò nequaquam papatui.»

deposed by God hypothetically supposes the impossible, i.e., that the papal dignity and heresy could simultaneously co-exist in the same man.

Bordoni was even more explicit than Bellarmine about the false premise: *Quomodo autem deponatur Papa hæreticus?* and he replies with the words of Bonacina[146]: *respondebit Bonacina... vanam esse hanc questionem, cum falsum supponat, Papam, qui nullatenus errare potest, incidere in errorem hæresis.*[147] From the false premise of the mere hypothesis, Bordoni does eventually involve himself in the same seemingly irresolvable logical inconsistency in the case of even a notorious heretic as Bellarmine does for a secret heretic, when he arrives at the same conclusion for any heretic pope at all, saying that the heretic pope, even after being denounced, retains his dignity and power which, he only loses by deposition.[148] Bordoni is here speaking of a pope who is judged upon manifesting pertinacity, which is is evident from the above quoted passage in Chapter VI, where he prescribes that the pertinacious heretic be declared deposed and deprived of the papacy by a council, **because a council is the highest tribunal when the see is vacant**.[149] The dilemma becomes particularly obvious when one contemplates Bordoni's hairsplitting distinction between the qualified sense according to which, as an infidel compared to the faithful, the heretic pope would be considered *minor quolibet catholico*, but at the same time, retaining his power and dignity, he would *simpliciter* remain *maior quolibet catholico*.[150] The dilemma could be theoretically resolved only in the case of one who is at least a *most vehemently* or *violently suspected heretic*, who could be presumed with moral certitude to have already fallen from office, and therefore, already to be *minor quolibet catholico*, and as such could be judged on the basis of evidence to be guilty of heresy and to have already fallen from office; and to have *vacated the see* in the same manner as a manifest heretic –

---

[146] Martino Bonacina (1585 – 1631) Italian bishop and jurist.

[147] *Ibid.,* cap. v. p. 131.

[148] *Ibid.* cap, vi. p. 153: «Papa hæreticus... adhuc retinet suam dignitatem, & potestatem, licet sit etiam denuntiatus, quae duo perdit tantum per depositionem.»

[149] «... Concilium, quod est supremum tribunal, quando vacat Papale.»

[150] *Ibid.*: «Papa antem potest dici minor quolibet catholico quatenus hæreticus in eo, quod ad invicem comparati fideles, & infideles, potior, & maior est classis Christianorum, minor verò, & inferior classis infidelium, in qua adscriptus est Papa hæreticus, si verò comparado fiat quo ad potestatem, & dignitatem, quibus non caret Papa hæreticus, sine dubio Papa simpliciter est maior quolibet catholico.»

exactly as papal claimant Pedro de Luna (Antipope Benedict XIII) was judged to have already fallen from any office and dignity he may have held by himself when he was judged and declared deposed by the Council of Constance. This was in fact the solution arrived at by some of the Decretists who prescribed an *accusatio* to be brought against a secret heretic pope who would then be judged and deposed on the basis of evidence.[151]

Yet for Bordoni, the question of deposing a heretic pope is only a pure hypothesis, a *metaphysical question* with can have no practical application in the actual life of the Church: «*Sed hæc quæstio magis Metaphysica est, quam moralis, & hactenus gratia Dei favente in nullo Pontifice dominate fuit pertinacia hæresis,* **nec dominabitur, quia id Deus non permitteret**...» Only a true and certain pope is above a council, but doubtful popes and pertinacious heretics (because they are incapable subjects) are subject to a council: *solus verus & indubitatus Papa est supra Concilium, et non alii de quibus dubitatur, ergo subijciuntur Concilio.* [and here he cites the sources of the opinion]»[152] The contradiction of Bordoni's position is that on the one hand he asserts the injudicability of a certain pope: *Papa est maior omnibus ergo omnes iudicat & a nemine iudicatur* (cap. v. num. 58), and that only dubious popes and obstinate heretics can be judged because they are subject to a council (*alii de quibus dubitatur... subijciuntur Concilio*); but he does not argue that the notorious heretic would be in any manner dubious, but that even a notorious heretic, before he is judged, would certainly retain his office and dignity until judged[153], and therefore, logically, could be considered neither a dubious pope nor an incapable subject. However, according to his opinion, the council would not have jurisdiction to judge a certain pope (Papa verus

---

[151] cf. James M. Moynihan, STL, JCD; *Papal Immunity and Liability in the Writings of the Medieval Canonists*, Gregorian University Press, Roma 1961, Chapter Three, *The Decretist Doctrine on Papal Immunity and Papal Liability From the Decretum of Gratian to the Glossa Ordinaria of Johannes Teutonicus [1140 – 1220]*

[152] *Ibid.* cap. vi. p. 149.

[153] *Ibid.* p. 152 – 153: «Papa hæreticus adhuc eſt membrum Chriſti licet informe, quía non amiſit caracterem, cum ſit animæ inpreſſus indelebiliter, eſt verò præciſum, & putridum quo ad formam fidei, & caritatis, quibus caret, cum igitur adhuc retineat rationem membri, conſequenter adhuc caput eſt Eccleſiæ, ratione cuius adhuc retinet dignitatem Papatus, ſuprema poteſtatem in Eccleſia, donec Concilium congregetur virtute ex alto, [...] nam hæreticus adhuc retinet ſuam dignitatem, & poteſtatem, licet fit etiam denuntiatus, qæe duo perdit tantum per depoſitionem.»

& legitimus habitus per Cardinales, & receptus a nullo deponi potest[154]) but only a dubious one or an incapable subject, and therefore it would follow from his own premise that a council would not have the jurisdiction to judge a man who is certainly pope so that he could fall from the pontificate. Bordoni looks in vain for a remedy by appealing, on the basis of Gratian's spurious *Canon si papa*[155] to a special ordinance of divine law which would, by way of exception, grant to a council the jurisdiction to judge a heretic pope *(cap. vi. p. 151)*; and with specious, convoluted reasoning, he cites Cajetan against an *ipso facto* fall from office (Caietanus *de auctorit. Papæ* cap. 22)[156], whose opinion (as is explained in this volume) was already totally refuted by Bellarmine. As is pointed out in Part IV, there is no basis in the deposit of revelation to posit an exception in divine law that would grant a council the jurisdiction to judge a pope, while still in office, for heresy; and the argument against a *ipso iure divino* fall from the papacy[157] ignores Bellarmine's observation that the Fathers did not speak of an *ipso facto* fall on the basis of any human law, but from the nature of heresy. St. Alphonsus, whose opinion was followed by Pope Gregory XVI, argued not on the basis of any exception, but that a council would have jurisdiction because the see would be considered vacant.[158] Bellarmine provides the reason why the see would be considered vacant if the heresy were manifest, or if it could be proven that the pope is a heretic — first, because the manifest heretic would be outside the Church as a severed member; and second, because the heretic would lack the necessary disposition to retain the form of the pontificate, and would, for that reason also, become an incapable subject. Lacking that necessary disposition, he would, as an incapable subject, necessarily cease by himself to be pope, *sine alia vi externa*. This leaves no room for juridical judgment of the Church to have any role in the loss of office for heresy; because if any judgment were needed for

---

[154] *Ibid.* p. 149.

[155] *Decretum Gratiani (Concordia discordantium canonum)*, pars I, dist. 40, canon 6, *Si Papa*.

[156] Bordoni, *Op. cit.*, cap. vi. p. 153.

[157] *Ibid.*

[158] «Lo stesso (i.e. "si tiene vacante la Sede Apostolica") sarebbe nel caso, che il Papa cadesse notoriamente e pertinacemente in qualche eresia. Benchè allora [...] non sarebbe il Papa privato dal Pontificato dal Concilio... ma ne sarebbe spogliato immediatamente da Cristo, divenendo allora Soggetto affato inabile, e caduto dal suo Officio.» [Alfonso M. De Liguori, *Verità della Fede,* Part. III. Cap. IX. p. 457.]

the fall from office to take place, then even public heresy would not make the heretic an incapable subject, because even as a heretic he would still retain the form of the pontificate before judgment or if he would remain unjudged; which would mean that faith would not be a necessary disposition to conserve the form of the pontificate in the person of the pope. If faith is not a necessary disposition for a man to be pope, then even as a public heretic he could not fall from office by himself, even if he were to be judged guilty of heresy by the Church — nor could he be deposed by the Church: first, because the pope is injudicable; and second, because without faith being a necessary disposition, a heretic would not be an incapable subject, whence heresy would not be incompatible with the papal office. Therefore, either a heretic pope, as an incapable subject, necessarily falls from office automatically and entirely by himself, without any judgment or deposition by the Church; or, as a capable subject, he can neither fall from office, nor can he be deposed for heresy. However, (as is demonstrated in this volume), it is *de fide* that public heresy visibly separates a man from the body of the Church *suapte natura*, so that a public heretic would cease to be a member of the Church and thereby become an incapable subject not only for any ecclesiastical office but even for membership in the Church; and who would accordingly fall from office *ex natura hæresis* entirely by himself, *sine alia vi externa* – and therefore, he would necessarily fall from office before any judgment would be pronounced by the Church. Hence, it follows strictly from these premises that if a pope is manifestly a heretic or if his heresy is proven in such a manner that it will become public, he would necessarily fall from office *ipso facto*, before any judgment would be pronounced by the Church; since by the nature of heresy, being no longer a capable subject for membership in the Church, he would cease straightaway to be a capable subject for headship over the Church.

Today, more than a century after the opinion that a heretical pope could be judged while still holding office and deposed by the Church had been discarded and totally abandoned by theologians, since that opinion was clearly seen to oppose the dogmatic pronouncements of the *magisterium*; that opinion has resurfaced in some quarters, due to the doctrinal heterodoxy of the "Conciliar Popes" – i.e. the popes, beginning with John XXIII up to the present, who have all, without exception, distinguished themselves in the most dubious manner but in different degrees – having deviated from the rule of faith in their opinions and pronouncements. It is due, in no small measure, to the deceptive sophistry of the Conciliar Church propagandists, John Salza and Robert

Siscoe, that this heretical opinion, which holds that a pope while still in office can be judged by his inferiors in the Church, has experienced a recrudescence; and ironically, it is in the sector of the Church where the most careful attention to doctrinal rectitude is usually found, i.e. among the traditionalists, that this errant theory, which can be seen to be heretical in the light of *Pastor Æternus*, has been resurrected.

In his book, *Contra Cekadam,* the learned and highly respected rector of the Hearts of Jesus and Mary Seminary, Fr. François Chazal, has adopted the opinion of John of St. Thomas on the question of deposition of a manifest heretic pope from office. It was the opinion of John of St. Thomas that one who is manifestly a formal heretic would not fall from the papal office *ipso facto*; but would remain in office as pope until convicted of heresy by a council, and then would only fall from office upon being declared *vitandus* by the council. This is the fourth of the five opinions outlined by St. Robert Bellarmine in Book II of his *De Romano Pontifice*. Bellarmine utterly demolished this opinion in his refutation of it in chapter 30, and his own opinion (the fifth opinion) that a manifest heretic pope would straightaway fall from office *ipso facto*, was eventually incorporated into the 1917 Code of Canon Law (Canon 188. 4°); and remains in force in the 1983 Code. According to Canon 188. 4°, one who publicly defects from the faith automatically falls from whatsoever office *ipso jure*. In this volume I have demonstrated that this position is indeed, as Bellarmine called it, "the true opinion" beyond all shadow of doubt, and beyond any legitimate dispute. Unfortunately, since Fr. Chazal is refuting a *sedevacantist* in his work, he relies too heavily on the thoroughly dishonest scholarship of Salza & Siscoe in their fraudulent diatribe against Sedevacantism, *True or False Pope?* This unfortunate reliance, which is undoubtedly due to its being the most exhaustive exposition published on Sedevacantism to date, is plainly discernible in Bishop Richard Williamson's comments on Fr. Chazal's brief work.

Since it is a work against Sedevacantism, Msgr. Williamson points out that the sedevacantists' "favourite theologian is St Robert Bellarmine who held that any Pope becoming a heretic automatically ceases to be Pope." Indeed, according to Bellarmine, if it be possible for a valid pope to become a manifest heretic, he would automatically cease to be pope *ipso facto* by the act of formal heresy; because, according to the unanimous teaching of the Fathers and the doctrine of St. Thomas Aquinas, the *sin of heresy* is *per se* an act of separation by which heretics separate themselves from the body of the Church, and therefore lose office automatically, i.e.

ipso facto. But on this point, Bishop Williamson (like Fr. Chazal) is clearly led astray by the fraudulent argumentation of Salza & Siscoe when he says, "But Fr. Chazal opens the books and finds that this opinion is by no means the common opinion of Church theologians". As I document in this work, it is now the virtually unanimous opinion today among theologians who admit at least the hypothetical possibility that a pope can fall into formal heresy – and has been for more than a century, that a pope who would fall into manifestly formal heresy would immediately cease to be pope. Fr. Chazal's citation of the *Dictionaire de Théologie Catholique* is to no avail: The authors merely state their belief that "The opinion of Bellarmine is in no way [a aucun titre] guaranteed by the Church, nor adopted by the whole body of theologians." (Tome VII, col. 1714 – 1717) Since Bellarmine's "Fifth Opinion" is only a hypothesis, it would obviously not be guaranteed by the Church. The most common opinion today, and for more than a century, is that the pope cannot become a formal heretic. However, it will be shown that if the passage cited by Fr. Chazal is intended by its authors to attribute any legitimacy to the theories which postulate a power of a council to judge and depose a sitting pope for heresy, then the authors of that work would manifest themselves to be dissident theologians with respect to the authority of the ecclesiastical magisterium. The dissident opinion expressed in a single work, does not diminish in the least the moral unanimity of theologians, and especially of *canonists*, who rightly understand that Bellarmine's opinion on this point is guaranteed by the Church's supreme and ordinary magisterium, expressed in Canon 188. 4°, which is an expression of the *magisterial doctrine* of the Church. The canons of the 1917 Code are not merely a collection of *statutes*; but they set forth with precision the *canonical doctrine* of the Church on its most important points. This is a feature that is notably absent from the 1983 Code, which is based on the canonical doctrinal tradition enshrined in the 1917 Code, and which did not need to be repeated in the revised Code of 1983. Canonical doctrine pertains to Canon Law as a theological discipline in its own right; and thus, is a legitimate branch of *theology*, as Canon Law professor, Fr. Rafael Moya O.P. explained in his Canon Law lectures at the Angelicum. The canonical *doctrine* that *all* ecclesiastical offices without exception are lost by public defection from the faith *automatically*, and *without any declaration*, is plainly stated in Canon 188. 4°. The theological foundation of this doctrine is that manifest heretics separate themselves from the Church by themselves, and as a direct consequence of that separation, lose office, as I explain in this work.

The bishop then elaborates:

> For indeed, as many other famous theologians argue, the Pope is not just an individual who can lose the faith personally, but he is also head of a worldwide society which cannot function without a head. Nor does the personal loss of faith necessarily impede his headship of the Church. Therefore they argue, for the sake of the Church as a whole, God preserves the Pope's headship until the highest competent Church authorities can make a public declaration of his heresy (to prevent public chaos in the Church), and then and only then does God depose him.

The argument is an old argument, thoroughly refuted by St. Robert Bellarmine, and generally discarded after *Pastor Æternus* dogmatically pronounced the absolute *injudicability* of the Roman Pontiff in its solemn definition of the primacy. It is an abandoned opinion. Bishop Williamson continues:

> Sedevacantists also love Canon 188.4 which states that public defection from the faith on the part of a cleric means automatic loss of his office. But many other Canons and the other sections of Canon 188 clearly show that this "public defection" must include the cleric's intent to resign by such acts as, for instance, attempting marriage or joining a sect, and also there must be a warning and official monitions before the cleric loses his office.

This is a spurious argument coming straight out of the Salza & Siscoe screed, which I thoroughly refute in this work. The argument is founded on the false premise that *loss of ecclesiastical office* due to heresy takes place because heresy is a *crime* against the unity of the Church; and because it is a *crime*, it falls under the jurisdiction of the Church; and therefore loss of office cannot occur before the heretic has been juridically judged by the Church. For this reason, they argue, the heretic does not lose office without a public judgment pronounced by Church authority. Loss of ecclesiastical office, according to their argument, is a *penalty* inflicted by the authority of the Church for the crime of heresy. It does not pertain to the nature of a crime as such that the act itself, by its nature, separates one from the Church or causes the loss of office; but for the commission of a crime, one is severed from the body of the Church and is deprived of ecclesiastical office by means of a *canonical penalty*. Hence, Salza & Siscoe consider loss of office to be essentially a matter pertaining to *ecclesiastical penal law* — i.e., it is a *penalty*, in their own words: **"a severe vindictive penalty"** for the *delict* or *crime* of heresy. I provide the verbatim texts of the most authoritative commentaries on Canon Law which explain that *loss of office* for heresy is not a penalty for a crime; but on the contrary, the *fact* of public defection into heresy brings about the automatic loss of office without any regard to any prescriptions of penal law; and therefore, without warnings; without any declaration by ecclesiastical authority, and without any intent on the part of the heretic to resign his office. The reason why this is so is that heresy in its very nature is a sin opposed to faith, and therefore against the bond of the unity of the Church in the one Catholic faith; which therefore, if the sin is public, as a necessary consequence and by its very nature, visibly severs one from the body of the Church and directly brings about the loss of ecclesiastical office. St. Robert Bellarmine explains and demonstrates that it is unanimously taught by the Fathers that heretics lose all jurisdiction entirely by themselves, *ipso facto*, and not by the force of any human law, but *ex natura hæresis*. Thus, the fall from office takes place independently of the jurisdiction of the Church; and, as Suárez proves, *papal* loss of office cannot take place by the force of any human law.[159] Therefore, the administrative laws of the Church merely recognize the nature of the *ipso facto* loss of office as being *ex natura hæresis*, and accordingly statutes that such a loss of office takes place *ipso jure*.

Indeed, it is for this reason that it is explained by the expert commentators on Canon Law that the law *presumes* tacit resignation and *statutes* the loss of office solely on the basis of the public *fact* of the officeholder's defection from the faith into heresy by obstinately denying or doubting an article of faith – without joining any other sect, without explicitly rejecting the ecclesiastical magisterium as the rule of faith, without any explicit admission of heresy, and without canonical warnings. The **fact** of *public* defection into formal heresy suffices by itself for the loss of office to occur, and therefore, there is no need whatever for ecclesiastical authority to "*establish the crime*" (as Salza & Siscoe claim) for loss of office to take place; or for that fact to be established in conformity with all the specifications of penal law as a **crime** notorious by *fact*. Even in penal law, the need to establish the crime pertains to cases

---

[159] R.P. Francisci Suarez, *Opera Omnia*, Paris 1863 (Vivés), *Tomus Doudecimus, Tractatus Primus, De Fide Theologica. Disputatio X. De Summo Pontifice, Sect. VI.* p. 316: «…nec vere cadere potest Pontifex ipso facto a sua dignitate propter jus humanum, tum quia illud esset latum vel ab inferiori, scilicet concilio, vel ab æquali, nempe preedecessore Papa; at neuter horum habet vim coactivam, ut punire valeat Pontificem æqualem, vel superiorem.»

of *suspected heretics* (can. 2315), and not plainly manifest heretics (can. 2314. §1., can. 2197. 1°-2°). The actual forfeiture of ecclesiastical office for heresy ultimately has nothing to do whatever with the laws of the Church, but takes place *jure divino* as a direct consequence of the fact of public heresy itself as an act of visible separation from the Church. Ecclesiastical law merely recognizes the fact of loss of office as having taken place *ex natura hæresis*, and accordingly declares it to take place *ipso jure*.

The subterfuge of Salza & Siscoe in their book was to deliberately ignore the expert comments on the actual canon in question, which regulates *loss of office* for heresy, and instead, they interpret Canon 188. 4° in the administrative section of the Code according to the comments on canon 2314 in the *penal section* of the Code, which prescribes penalties for *crimes against the faith and the unity of the Church*. Canon 2314, which prescribes warnings before the infliction of certain *vindictive penalties*, explicitly upholds the provision of canon 188. 4° for the automatic *ipso jure* loss of office without warnings, which is decreed as a *tacit resignation from office*. Such is the devious trickery of John Salza and Robert Siscoe, who falsely state in their book that *loss of office* is a *"severe vindictive penalty"* for the *"crime of heresy"*. Loss of office, simply stated, is not a penal censure for a crime. In the 1917 Code of Canon Law, and in the revised Code of 1983, loss of office for heresy is strictly a measure pertaining to *administrative law*, and not to *penal law*; and it is founded on the unanimous teaching of the Fathers, the doctrine of St. Robert Bellarmine, Don Pietro Ballerini, Bartolomeo Cappellari (Pope Gregory XVI), and St. Thomas Aquinas – none of whom teach that such loss of office is a penalty for a crime, but who all teach that the loss of office for heresy takes place as a direct and natural consequence of heresy, because heresy is a sin which *per se* severs one from the body of the Church. Heresy, whether public or secret, whether internal or external, in its very nature is a *sin*, because it directly opposes the theological virtue of faith. Heresy, because it is a sin against faith, is a schismatic act against the unity of the Church. That the public heretic is severed from the body of the Church *"by the very nature of heresy"*, and **not** *"by legitimate authority"*, i.e. *as the penalty for a crime*, is taught explicitly by Pius XII in *Mystici Corporis*, in unison with the universal and ordinary magisterium of the Church. Hence, the loss of ecclesiastical office for heresy takes place not as a penal sanction for a delict against any ecclesiastical law, but, in Bellarmine's words, *"ex natura haeresis"*, as the direct consequence of the heretic's having visibly severed himself from the body of the Church. This is what Bellarmine teaches *De Romano Pontifice, lib ii caput xxx*; and he states explicitly, "the Holy Fathers teach in unison, that not only are heretics outside the Church, but they even lack all Ecclesiastical jurisdiction and dignity ipso facto." I provide an in-depth exposition on defection from the faith and the Church, and on the consequent loss of office for heresy in this volume.

The problem with Fr. Chazal and Bishop Williamson is that they have relied too much on the skewed and sometimes even fraudulently altered data provided by Salza & Siscoe; which presents only opinions of theologians from the Middle Ages up to just *before* Vatican I; and deliberately twists or entirely leaves out all mention of the post-Vatican I teaching. Vatican I dogmatically *defined* that the pope is the *supreme judge in all cases that refer to ecclesiastical examination*. Since then (1870) the unanimous teaching of theologians is that the pope is *injudicable*; and the Church teaches this in her canonical doctrine and in the canons themselves; and thus, it is taught unanimously in the approved commentaries on the Codes of Canon Law, in accordance with the constant teaching of the popes, that the pope, while in office, is absolutely immune from the judgment of anyone, and therefore simply cannot be judged. Canon 188. 4° also states explicitly that those who publicly defect from the faith lose **whatever offices** (*quaelibet officia*), **automatically** (*ipso facto* and *ipso jure*), and therefore, **"without any declaration"** (*sine ulla declaratione*) from the Church. The most authoritative commentaries on Canon Law explain that the loss of office (including the papal office) depends *exclusively* on the *fact* of public defection into formal heresy; and hence, independently of the opinions and judgments of anyone. The vacancy occurs *ipso jure*; and the competent authority merely declares it juridically *after the fact*. Thus, the question of how one, (including the pope if that were possible), who falls into manifestly formal heresy would lose ecclesiastical office, is no longer a matter of opinion. Since the publication of the 1917 Code of Canon Law the question is closed. Fr. Chazal's opinion was still admissible *before Vatican I* and the *codification of canon law*; but now, his opinion is plainly contrary to the magisterium of the Church, as I have proven in Part I of the first volume of this work.

In spite its major flaws, Msgr. Williamson points out the one partially redeeming merit to Fr. Chazal's critique of Sedevacantism in his comment:

Fr Cekada argues as though sedevacantism is not merely one opinion in a difficult and highly disputed question. He presents it as a dogmatic certainty, to refuse which means that one is not Catholic. Fr Chazal has a measure of sympathy for sedevacantists (he prefers them to liberals), and he shows charity towards Fr Cekada, but the great merit of "Contra Cekadam" is that he proves to any reasonable reader that, at the very least, no Catholic is obliged to accept the sedevacantist position. Fr Cekada writes as though he is a master of theology and of Canon Law, but Fr Chazal has looked up the theologians and the Canons in question and he proves that they are far from proving that the See of Rome has been vacant at any time since Vatican II.

This consideration, although important, can hardly justify Bishop Williamson's comment on Fr. Chazal's study: "Fr Cekada's arguments and opinions have acted like the grain of sand inside an oyster, which by the irritation which it produces makes the oyster produce a pearl." Unfortunately, the "pearl" is severely flawed, and in places fatally flawed. The main flaw is that Fr. Chazal attempts to refute Fr. Cekada's opinion by attacking his foundational premise, which is that public heretics automatically lose office. The premise in question, is correct. However, rather than accepting the correct premise, and exposing the logical incoherence of Fr. Cekada's application of that principle to arrive at his conclusion – a *non sequitur* conclusion, Fr. Chazal argues against the correct premise by attacking *it* with his own misapplication of provisions of penal law to a non-penal canon in a different section of the Code; and hence, fails to refute Fr.Cekada's opinion on the nature of loss of office. The correct refutation of the Sedevacantist argument is made by pointing out their misapplication of a prescription of *penal law* to the administrative provisions of Canon 188. 4°. Sedevacantists presume on the basis of Canon 2200 §2, that the *Conciliar Popes* are manifest heretics who have defected from the Catholic faith, and therefore lose office if ever they were validly elected. The canon reads, *"When an external violation of the law has been committed, malice is presumed in the external forum until the contrary is proven."*[160] *The expert commentary of Fr. Eric MacKenzie explains, "The very commission of any act which signifies heresy, e.g., the statement of some doctrine contrary or contradictory to a revealed and defined dogma, gives sufficient ground for juridical presumption of heretical depravity... Excusing circumstances have to be proved in the external forum, and the burden of proof is on the person whose*

---

[160] "Posita externa legis violatione, dolus in foro externo præsumitur, donec contrarium probetur."

action has given rise to the imputation of heresy. In the absence of such proof, all such excuses are presumed not to exist."[161] What is set forth in the canon is a provision of penal law. The accused is presumed guilty of the crime on the basis of the fact of his having committed a criminal act, and therefore he bears the onus to prove his innocence – "In the absence of such proof, all such excuses are presumed not to exist." A penal sentence of guilt is arrived at on the basis of a *presumption of guilt.* For the administrative provisions of Canon 188. 4°, *a presumption of guilt that is not morally certain does not suffice,* because the canon statutes the loss of office not on the basis of a presumption of guilt, but either on the evidence of the manifest and patent fact of one openly leaving the Church, or, if the heretic still maintains the pretence of being a Catholic, *the evidence of the manifestly patent public fact of the pertinacity*; i.e., the *dolus* or *culpa* of formal heresy. For the guilt of formal heresy to be manifest, the condition stated in Canon 2197 *3°* must be fulfilled, that the act be committed under such circumstances that by no subterfuge can the guilt be hidden, nor can there be any excuse for it extracted from the law: *"et in talibus adiunctis commissum, ut nulla tergiversatione celari nulloque iuris suffragio excusari possit".* The act must also be public, as public is defined in Canon 2197 1°, that it either be already divulged, or that it have been committed under such circumstance that it can be prudently judged that it soon will be divulged. (*Publicum, si iam divulgatum est aut talibus contigit seu versatur in adiunctis ut prudenter iudicari possit et debeat facile divulgatum iri*) It is only if these conditions have been fulfilled, that it can be seen to be *morally certain* that defection from the faith has occurred, and that the guilty individual has therefore lost office.

Regarding the interpretation of Canon 188. 4° on *Tacit Resignation of Office* due to public defection from the Catholic faith, Fr. Chazal cites the opinion of Vermeersch as his authority for adding restrictive qualifications to what is stated in an unqualified manner in the text of the canon. The cited passage reads, «One defects from the faith who denies its foundation pertinaciously, or who by some **precise fact** (facto factove) **destroys all bond with the Catholic religion,** for instance, by adhering to a heretical or a schismatic sect.» (*Epitome Iuris Canonici*, I, p. 190) Vermeersch wrongly defined defection from the faith as a *pertinacious denial of the foundation of the faith*, or the *destruction of all bond with the Catholic religion*. Now, as is fully explained if the first part of this

---

[161] Rev. Eric F. Mackenzie, A.M., S.T.L., J.C.L., *The Delict of Heresy*, Washington, D.C.: The Catholic University of America, 1932, p. 35.

volume, the formal cause of the virtue of faith is the authority of the revealing God (Pius XI, *Mortalium Animos*); and therefore, St. Thomas teaches that "the formal object of faith is the First Truth, as manifested in Holy Writ and the teaching of the Church, which proceeds from the First Truth. Consequently **whoever does not adhere, as to an infallible and Divine rule, to the teaching of the Church, which proceeds from the First Truth manifested in Holy Writ, has not the habit of faith**, but holds that which is of faith otherwise than by faith." (*II – II, Q. 5, a. 3*) For this reason he says in the same article, "**Neither living nor lifeless faith remains in a heretic who disbelieves one article of faith.**" Thus, defection from the Catholic faith already takes place in a simple act of formal heresy by obstinately denying even one article of faith, because heresy directly and *per se* opposes faith (*II^a-IIae q. 39 a. 1*); and for this reason, Pius XII teaches in *Mystici* Corporis that heresy *by its very nature* separates one from the body of the Church; and thus, heretics *"have miserably separated themselves"* from membership in the Church. Since public heretics place themselves outside the Church entirely by their own actions, they necessarily forfeit any office they held inside the Church by their own actions. Bellarmine proves that such a forfeiture for heresy is taught unanimously by the Fathers. Accordingly, therefore, Canon 188. 4° statutes an automatic loss of office *without any declaration*.

It is therefore patent that the opinion, that only *pertinacious denial of the foundation of the faith* constitutes a defection from the faith, and not pertinacious **heresy** *per se*, is indefensible, and is a grave error against the doctrine of the universal magisterium. One can only wonder how he would have argued the point to arrive at this gratuitously stated conclusion. The automatic loss of office prescribed in Canon 188. 4° is founded on the doctrine that heretics defect from the Church when they publicly defect from the faith into heresy; and therefore, they lose office as a direct and immediate consequence of their own actions. Not only was this proven by Bellarmine to be the unanimous consensus of the Fathers, but it was theologically proven by St. Thomas; and in *Mystici Corporis*, Pius XII taught the universal Church that defection from the faith and the Church is already fully accomplished *suapte natura* by the sin of manifest *heresy*. Perhaps Fr. Vermeersch could be excused for having taught his errant doctrine before the promulgation of *Mystici Corporis* in 1943, but today, there exists no possible excuse to adhere to such a grave doctrinal error.

In the continuation of the passage, Vermeersch says, "The delict is public, when it is notorious to the greater part of the community or can soon be known". From this it seems likely that Vermeersch, who explicitly refers to the act of defection as a *delict*, made the mistake of interpreting a canon in the administrative section of the Code according to the prescriptions of canons in the penal section, i.e. Canon 2314. It is easy enough to understand why Vermeersch would fall into this error in his day, so soon after the promulgation of the 1917 Code; since in the pre-1917 legislation, a form of *penal deprivation of office* had been prescribed for such a defection. The canonical innovation of Canon 188. 4° was to bring the law of the Church in line with the Patristic doctrine on automatic loss of office for defection from the faith into heresy or schism, which Bellarmine explained takes place not by any human law, but *ex natura haeresis*. The penal process prescribed in Canon 2314 begins by decreeing the *latæ sententiæ* excommunication for apostates, heretics, and schismatics. The first clause of the canon (2314. §1) properly refers to *formal heretics*, who are distinguished from *suspected heretics* (canon 2315); but the fact that some of the sections of the canon prescribe warnings is due to the fact that vindictive penalties require prior warnings; and also proves that the heretics dealt with in this canon would not only be manifestly formal heretics as such, but would also include those who having not heeded the warnings would therefore be considered *violenter* or *vehementissime* suspected of heresy; since, "*Violent* suspicion amounts to morally certain proof."[162] The penal process ends with *vindictive penalties* for the crimes if the warnings go pertinaciously unheeded, such as the added censure of *infamy* and deposition; and for joining other sects, *ipso facto* infamy, and finally *degradation* if the warnings go unheeded. If they heed the warnings and repent, the clerics can be allowed to retain the offices which they would otherwise have lost by undeclared tacit resignation; but if they do not repent, then they must be deposed according to the penal prescription. Thus, the penal process begins by prescribing warnings for suspected heretics, and inflicts the *latæ sententiæ* excommunication on those who are actually guilty of the offense (Canon 2314); and *ends* by punishing the defector with the infliction of *vindictive penalties* if warnings go unheeded. The administrative measures of Canon 188. 4° *begin* with an *already public and completed defection*; and for this reason,

---

[162] The Rev. P, Chas. Augustine, O.S.B., D.D.; *A COMMENTAY ON THE NEW CODE OF CANON LAW*, Volume VIII, St. Louis and London, 1922, p. 284.

there are no prescribed warnings, but the canon simply statutes an *ipso facto* loss of office on the basis of the already accomplished fact of the public defection.

Fr. Chazal erroneously argues that,

> «Canonists integrate **2314** and other canons to **188.4** like **Fr. Ayrinhac:** "If they have formally affiliated with a non-Catholic sect, or publicly adhere to it, they incur ipso facto the note of infamy. Clerics lose all ecclesiastical office they might hold (Canon 188.4), **and after a fruitless warning they should be deposed.**" (Penal Legislation, p. 193, 1920)»

Actually, the canonists do exactly the opposite: they do not *integrate* these canons which regulate two distinct procedures by uniting the penal procedures prescribed in penal canons and the administrative process prescribed in canon 188. 4° into one process. This is impossible because they are two different processes which follow their own prescribed procedures. Rather, what the canonists do is they *harmonize* and distinguish between the distinctly different procedures prescribed in penal law with those prescribed in the administrative section. Canon 2314. §1 — 2° prescribes that heretics who do not heed warnings are to be deprived of benefice, dignity, pension, office and any other *munus*; and are to be declared *infamous* – and after repeated warnings are to be deposed. Fr. Aryinhac explains that according to the prescription of canon 2314. §1 — 3°, that by affiliating themselves with a non-Catholic sect, clerics not only lose office *ipso facto* by tacit resignation (can. 188. 4°), but after fruitless warnings, they are to be meted out the vindictive penalty of *degradation*. If the superiors judge that an actual public defection into formal heresy has been perpetrated and completed, then all warnings and admonitions prescribed for *suspected heretics* would not be necessary to precede an administrative declaration of the cleric's loss of office, which would juridically suffice to effect his removal.

There is no reason that would necessitate an exhaustive point by point correction of all the errors in Fr. Chazal's short work; since their correction is already contained in principle in the main arguments I elaborate in this volume. Hence, I will limit myself here to only one more example. In the section on *Universal Peaceful Acceptance,* Fr. Chazal cites the Constitution, *Vacantis Apostolicae Sedis* of Pius XII, and two canons of the 1917 *Code of Canon Law* on *acceptance of the papal election* in a sense that is contrary to the letter of their obvious meaning. Fr. Chazal erroneously construes the acceptance referred to in these texts as *the pope's acceptance by the cardinals and by the universal Church*; whereas the text of the Constitution speaks explicitly of the **"*consensus electi*"** – **the consent of the pope-elect to become pope.** The Constitution prescribes that in the presence of the cardinal electors, the Cardinal Deacon must ask the **pope-elect**, "*Acceptasne electionem de te canonice factam in Summum Pontificem?*" (Do you accept your election canonically made as supreme Pontiff?) The Constitution then continues, "*Hoc consensu praestito intra terminum, quatenus opus sit, prudenti arbitrio Cardinalium per maiorem votorum numerum determinandum, illico electus est verus Papa, atque actu plenam absolutamque iurisdictionem supra totum orbem acquirit et exercere potest [73].*" What this simply states, is that once his consent is given (within the time limit determined if need be by a majority vote of the cardinals) from that instant he is constituted as the true pope with full and absolute jurisdiction over the whole world. It is precisely in this sense that the passage is expertly translated by the Canon Law Faculty of Salamanca in their commentary on page 880: "Si el elegido presta su consentimiento, desde aquel mismo instante queda constituído verdadero Papa con plena y absoluta jurisdicción sobre todo el orbe". Thus, the document does not say, as Fr. Chazal claims, «that as soon as the consent of the cardinals is given **"the elect is immediately a true pope,** and acquire by the very fact and exercise a full and absolute jurisdiction on the whole world (canon 219)". Once elected, he must be accepted...» Rather, the Constitution says exactly the opposite, and speaks explicitly of the **consent of the pope-elect, upon which he receives full power and jurisdiction; and not the other way around, as if there were any further need for the consent the cardinals who already expressed their consent by electing him.** [163] Likewise, the canons he mentions

---

[163] 100. Post electionem canonice factam, ab ultimo Cardinali Diacono accitis in aulam Conclavis S. Collegii Secretario, Praefecto Apostolicarum Caeremoniarum atque duobus Caeremoniarum Magistris, consensus electi per Cardinalem Decanum nomine totius S. Collegii his verbis: *Acceptasne electionem de te canonice factam in Summum Pontificem?* requiratur [72].

101. Hoc consensu praestito intra terminum, quatenus opus sit, prudenti arbitrio Cardinalium per maiorem votorum numerum determinandum, illico electus est verus Papa, atque actu plenam absolutamque iurisdictionem supra totum orbem acquirit et exercere potest [73]. Hinc, si quis litteras super negotiis quibuscumque confectas, quae a Romano Pontifice ante cöronationem suam emanaverint, audeat impugnare excommunicationis sententia, ipso facto incurrendae, eum innodamus [74].

(109 and 219) do not refer a need for general acceptance of the pope's election by the faithful for him to validly assume the papal office; nor do they refer to an acceptance by the *electing cardinals* to ratify the election after the pope's own acceptance of it; but canon 109[164] explicitly rules out the need for any external acceptance by the faithful or anyone else to ratify the election (**non ex populi** *vel potestatis saecularis consensu aut vocatione adleguntur*). What these canons statute is that once the cardinals elect the candidate, he validly becomes pope when *he* accepts his election to the papacy. Canon 219[165] states that he immediately receives his full jurisdiction by divine law upon his election and *his* acceptance of his own election; since he also has the right to refuse his election to the supreme pontificate. It is explicitly stated in canon 109 that clerics in general validly assume office *jure divino*, 1) in virtue of the sacrament of Orders; and, 2) either by their *canonical mission;* or for the pope, who, unlike other clerics, (who receive their canonical mission from their *superiors*), the pope validly assumes his office upon his being elected, and upon *his acceptance* of his election to the office. This is plainly explained in the 1952 commentary of the Pontifical Canon Law Faculty of Salamanca in its comment of the section *"On Election"*, and specifically on Canon 160, *"Romani Pontificis electio..."*, in which it distinguishes between elections which need to be confirmed by a superior, *or an election which is completed by the elected one's acceptance* (completándose la provisión por la aceptación del elegido).[166]

The pope-elect is not a valid pope until *he* accepts the *munus*; which the canons say is validly received *jure divino* without the consent of anyone else. How Fr. Chazal gets the idea that these canons prescribe a necessity *ad validitatam* of a post-election acceptance by the faithful or by the

---

102. De acceptatione novi Pontificis et de nomine ab Eo assumpto, Cardinali Decano interrogante: Quo nomine vis vocari? instrumentum conficitur, Praefecto Apostolicarum Caeremoniarum Notarii munere fungente, testibus adhibitis Secretario S. Collegii et duobus Caeremoniarum Magistris.

[164] «Can 109. Qui in ecclesiasticam hierarehiam cooptantur, non ex populi vel potestatis saecularis consensu aut vocatione adleguntur; sed in gradibus potestatis ordinis constituuntur sacra ordinatione; in supremo pontificatu, ipsomet iure divino, adimpleta conditione legitimae electionis eiusdemque acceptationis; in reliquis gradibus iurisdictionis, canonica missione.»

[165] Can 219. Romanus Pontifex, legitime electus, statim ab acceptata electione, obtinet, iure divino, plenam supremæ iurisdictionis potestatem.

[166] Miguelez – Alonso – Cabreros; *Código de Derecho Canónico – Bilingüe y Comentado*; Madrid, 1952, p. 67.

cardinals can only be the result of an inattentive reading of canon 109 which explicitly rules out the need for any such post-election general acceptance. Likewise, canon 219 quite obviously refers only to the pope-elect's own acceptance of his election in order to validly become pope by divine law, since only his own consent and no one else's is required *ad validitatem* after the election has taken place. The mere fact alone that the cardinals have elected a man to be pope manifests *their* acceptance of his election to the papacy. Once *he accepts his own election*, the canon says he **immediately receives full papal jurisdiction *jure divino*** (*statim ab acceptata electione obtinet, iure divino, plenam supremæ iurisdictionis potestatem*); and therefore, because he immediately receives his power directly from God, he validly assumes the papacy without any need for additional acceptance by the cardinals or any other of his subjects. Universal and peaceful acceptance provides a validating *sanatio in radice* for a canonically invalid election; but a certainly valid election of a pope has absolutely no need to be ratified by the acceptance of anyone; and to say that it does need such ratification in an error in faith.

It needs also to be mentioned that once a pope has accepted the Petrine *munus* after a canonically valid election, there exists no power on earth that can nullify his election, regardless of whether or not his election has been universally and peacefully accepted. Neither the cardinals nor anyone else have any power whatsoever to nullify the election of the man they elected, once he has accepted his election to the Supreme Pontificate. Since it is the cardinals who elect the pope, it is they who must merely confirm the fact of having elected the pope by publicly acknowledging that fact; but they have no veto power to nullify the election once the elected man has accepted the papacy. Such an attempted nullification would subject the the Roman Pontiff to a jurisdiction exercised by his inferiors; and for this reason, the proposition that a valid papal election can be nullified by an act of deposition by an imperfect council is heretical. Salza & Siscoe heretically assert on page 392 of their screed, "But in a case in which there is no peaceful and universal acceptance of an elected Pope, if the Church were to later nullify the election (e.g., by an act of deposition by an imperfect council, if the man were still living), this act would not infringe upon the Church's infallibility concerning dogmatic facts." The attempt to nullify the election of a canonically elected pope would violate the universal primacy of jurisdiction of the Roman Pontiff, solemnly defined in *Pastor Æternus*, and therefore is heretical. If a pope ceases to be pope, he ceases by himself, either by death, or by renunciation. Considered as a hypothesis, if a pope were to fall pertinaciously into manifest heresy, he would lose office by Tacit Renunciation, and thus, cease to be pope *by himself*. *No Council has ever nullified a valid papal election or attempted to depose a validly elected pope*. That does not lie within the jurisdiction of a council; which in fact possesses no jurisdiction by itself without its decisions being confirmed by the pope. Once a man accepts his election, he receives the Supreme Pontificate and its *plenitudo potetatis* immediately from God, which is supoeior to every other power on earth. The Council of Constance did not nullify the election of Pope Gregory XII, but as Ballerini observed, "One sees by what means the divine providence employed the synod of Constance to end the most tenacious schism, so that that synod did not need to exercise any power of jurisdiction by its authority to depose any true, albeit unknown, actual Pontiff."[167]

As was explained above, before the First Vatican Council, the prevalent opinion, expressed by St. Alphonsus, Ballerini, and Pope Gregory XVI, held that it would only be when the Apostolic See is judged to be vacant that a general council could be legitimately convened and act with authority to resolve a situation of multiple uncertain popes, or to depose a heretical intruder, such as one would be if he were to manifest pertinacity in heresy; and, who by that fact would manifest himself to be an invalid claimant to the papal dignity. Such a council, commonly referred to as an *imperfect council*, since it would lack a pope as its head, would in fact only exist *in potentia*, and thus would have no actual jurisdiction of its own over the universal Church. Its decrees would gain juridical force only upon subsequent confirmation by a future pope. Hence, the bishops gathered in an imperfect council during the vacancy of the Apostolic See would have no power of jurisdiction to issue a *juridical* declaration of papal heresy or of deposition; but would only be able to *recognize the fact* of the Pontiff's *defection from the faith* and the *sede vacante* it would cause.

---

[167] «Vides interim, quibus modis divina providentia usa est ad abolendum per Constantiensem synudum pertinacissimam schisma, ut ne opus esset eamdem synodum quiquam juris exercere ad deponendum sua auctoritate quempiam verum, licet ignotum, actualem Pontificem.» (*De Potestate Ecclesiastica Summorum Pontificum Et Conciliorum Generalium*, Auctore Petro Ballerinio Presbytero Veronensi, Augustæ Vindelicorum (Augsburg), MDCCLXX, p. 138)

To the question, "Whether a council can convene without the authorization of the supreme Pontiff," Bordoni[168] cites Cajetan's citation (Caiet. *Tract. 2 de auctor. Papæ, cap. 15.*) of Gerson[169], who refers to a number of cases. The first is when the see is vacant, which, according to Gerson, takes place in three ways, 1) by natural death, 2) by civil death, or, 3) by canonical deposition. Gerson specifies that civil death takes place (according to the opinion of the time), if the pope were to become insane, or be taken captive. Canonist James H. Provost wrote," Medieval canonists argued that if the pope became mentally disabled, he could no longer function as a human being and should be treated as if he were dead; a new pope would then be elected. More recent scholars have argued that the Holy Spirit would never let such a situation happen, although that seems a weak argument in light of the precedent of Urban VI (pope from 1378 to 1389), whose serious emotional or mental disturbances led the cardinals to exercise the option of electing another pope. This launched the church on the disastrous Western Schism (1378-1417)."[170] According to the modern opinion, expressed in the *Catholic Encyclopedia*, (1914, vol. 7, p.261), such a situation amounting to a civil death would include heresy, and would accordingly not merely create a situation of *sede impedita*, but of *sede vacante*: "No canonical provisions exist regulating the authority of the College of Cardinals sede Romanâ impeditâ, i.e. in case the pope became insane, **or personally a heretic**." However, on the specific question of heresy, the same *Encyclopedia* speaks not merely of a situation of *sede impedita* that would result if the pope were to become a public heretic, but the heretic would in fact *vacate the see*: "The pope himself, if notoriously guilty of heresy, would cease to be pope because he would cease to be a member of the Church." This opinion, because it is based on a generally valid doctrine of *Tacit Resignation of Office*, which Bellarmine proves (*De Romano Pontifice lib. ii cap. xxx*) to be taught unanimously by the Fathers, and which applies to all offices without exception, was enshrined as the operative canonical

---

[168] Bordoni, *Op. cit.* Cap. VI. De Sacris Conciliis, p. 150

[169] **Jean Charlier de Gerson** (13 December 1363 – 12 July 1429) was a French scholar, educator, reformer, and poet, Chancellor of the University of Paris, a guiding light of the conciliar movement and one of the most prominent theologians at the Council of Constance. He was one of the first thinkers to develop what would later come to be called natural rights theory, and was also one of the first individuals to defend Joan of Arc and proclaim her supernatural vocation as authentic. [*Wikipedia*]

[170] *America – The Jesuit Journal*, 24 January, 2013.

doctrine in can. 188. 4° of the 1917 Code of Canon Law, and remains in the provisions of Can. 196 the 1983 Code. Since there has never been any explicit provision in ecclesiastical law that would establish the canonical procedure to be followed in the eventuality of pope's public defection into heresy – an event which in fact has never occurred throughout Church history, the same *Encyclopedia* simply concludes that, "in such cases it would be necessary to consult the dictates of right reason and the teachings of history." As will be explained below, it is by consulting the dictates of right reason that the precepts of natural law become known; and it will also be explained why there exists no specific *judicial precept* of divine law, but only a general precept of *natural law* to dictate the procedure to be followed if it were to occur that a pope would fall pertinaciously into manifest heresy.

During the time of *sede vacante* or *sede impedita* of the Roman Church, there are no canonical provisions for the government of the Church except for those regarding the ordinary business of the Church.[171] *Universi Dominici Gregis* provides that during the *sede vacante*, "the government of the Church is entrusted to the College of Cardinals solely for the dispatch of ordinary business and of matters which cannot be postponed"; and the provisions limiting the powers of governance of the Cardinals during the period of *sede vacante* specify that the see becomes vacant "*after the death or valid resignation of the Pope.*" During that period, (as mentioned earlier), since the 1917 Code, a council is suspended by law, and can carry out no business whatever during the *sede vacante. Causae maiores*[172], such as judging bishops for crimes including heresy[173], or judging doctrine in matters of faith or morals for the whole Church, pertain solely to the supreme jurisdiction of the Roman Pontiff, and therefore, any judgment of heresy pronounced against a pope would lie entirely outside the jurisdiction of any synod that would attempt it.

The situation was not so clear before Vatican I. Gerson specified other cases when (according to him) a council could be convoked without the consent of the pope; such as when the pope upon request,

---

[171] "Canon 335 — Sede romana vacante aut prorsus impedita, nihil innovetur in Ecclesiae universae regimine: serventur autem leges speciales pro iisdem adiunctis latae."

[172] «Can. 220. Gravioris momenti negotia quae uni Romano Pontifici reservantur sive

natura sua, sive positiva lege, causae maiores appellantur.»

[173] *Conc. Tridentinum, Sessio XIV, Cap. VII. Canon V.*

refuses to permit a council to convene to the detriment of the Church; or if the pope, after it having been ordered by the pope to reconvene after a certain period of time, then refuses to permit a council to reconvene. In such cases, according to Gerson, the council would receive immediately from God its faculty to perform whatever is necessary in order that the council accomplish the purpose for which it was convened. Bordoni then cites *cap. 16. num. 50* of the same work of Cajetan, where it is asserted that only in two cases a council could convene without the authorization of the pope; 1) when the pope is to be deposed for heresy, and 2), when there is a plurality of popes whose elections are of uncertain validity. As I pointed out above, this was also Bordoni's own position on the question. The heretical absurdity of the opinion that anyone or any power on earth can judge the pope, even for heresy, is made manifest by the consideration that the pope, in virtue of his primacy and infallibility, possesses the supreme jurisdiction and the infallible power to judge all questions of faith and morals – even his own propositions. Hence, the proposition that a council can judge a pope's doctrine and declare it heretical; and from that premise, that the council could then judge the pope personally guilty of the crime of heresy directly opposes the dogma of pope's universal primacy of jurisdiction defined in *Pastor Æternus*.

It is to no avail whatever that it is argued by Cajetan that a council would not be judging the pope as pope, but as a private person, since, in refuting the opinion, Suárez explains that it is precisely the dignity of the person invested with the primacy of jurisdiction which strictly excludes that he can be personally judged by anyone.[174] It is in vain that John of St. Thomas attempts to refute Suárez on this point, with the assertion

---

[174] R.P. Francisci Suarez, *Op. cit. Tomus Doudecimus, Tractatus Primus, De Fide Theologica. Disputatio X. De Summo Pontifice, Sect. VI. Tertium dubium*, p. 318: «At hinc oritur tertia dubitatio, quo jure possit ab illa congregatione Papa judicari, cum esset illa superior? Qua in re Cajetanus se mire vexat, ne cogatur admittere Ecclesiam vel Concilium stare supra Papam, in casu etiam heresis; tandem vero concludit supra Papam quidem stare, ut privatam personam, non ut papam; sed non satisfacit distinctio; nam eodem modo posset affirmari Ecclesiam judicare Papam valere, atque punire, non ut Papam, sed ut privatam personam; item quia Papam superiorem esse in quantum Papam, nihil est aliud quam eam personam ratione dignitatis esse exemptam ab omni jurisdictione hominis alterius, et habere jurisdictionem in alios, ut patet de quacumque alia dignitate; et explicatur, nam dignitas pontificia non facit superiorem abstracte et metaphysice, sed revera et in individuo superiorem nulli subjectum»

that the judgment would not be an exercise of authority over the pope, but only an exercise of a ministerial power; since, as is explained below, it pertains to the nature of a judgment that it is an act of jurisdiction of a superior, and hence, lies outside the scope of a ministerial act. Similarly, for so long as the pope remains in office, a council cannot separate the Church from the pope, or the pope from the Church by exercising a ministerial power to declare a *vitandus* order, since while in office the pope retains his *munus gubernandi* in virtue of his supreme and universal *primacy of jurisdiction*, under which the whole Church is bound by divine law to be subject. It is for this reason that Bellarmine explains in his refutation of Cajetan's opinion that, "a Pope who remains the Pope cannot be shunned. How will we shun our Head? How will we recede from a member to whom we are joined?"[175] Furthermore, as is explained later in this volume, the power to declare a *vitandus* order presupposes the authority to excommunicate, since only those who have been excommunicated can be declared *vitandi*. Consequently, Bellarmine argues that since by divine precept heretics must be avoided, and since no power on earth can judge or excommunicate a pope, it follows strictly that a manifestly heretical pope is already outside the Church before any excommunication or judgment; because, "heretics are outside the Church, even before excommunication, and deprived of all jurisdiction, for they are condemned by their own judgment, as the Apostle teaches to Titus."[176]

The fallacious premise upon which such arguments as Cajetan's are founded, assumes that since the pope as pope is infallible, but as a private person can err, he can therefore be judged as a private person. However, since the pope, regardless of whether or not he can err in ignorance (which practically everyone admits), or err pertinaciously as a formal heretic (which hardly any theologian admits any more after Vatican I), he nevertheless as pope can reserve judgment of his own propositions to his own supreme and universal jurisdiction, and judge his own doctrine infallibly with the jurisdiction of the supreme judge. Since it lies within his supreme jurisdiction for so long as he is pope, to infallibly judge *all questions of faith and morals* as pope; he can pronounce as pope the infallible and final judgment even over his own propositions, which would hitherto have been his own private opinions. It is precisely for this reason, that Suárez held the opinion that a pope can err out of

---

[175] *De Romano Pontifice, lib. ii, cap. xxx.*
[176] Suarez. *Op. cit.* p. 318.

ignorance, but not out of contumacy.[177] It is quite remarkable also that Cajetan, John of St. Thomas, Bordoni, Laymann, Billuart, and all others of like mind failed to become cognizant of the fallacious nature of the premise upon which their doctrine on papal deposition collapses, since the pope's supreme magisterial authority was taught since the period of the Apostolic Fathers, and the pope's judicial supremacy and immunity from judgment was already repeatedly taught by the popes since St. Gelasius in the fifth century; and Bellarmine (in *De Romano Pontifice lib. iv. cap. ii*) attests to the fact that even in his day the belief that the pope's definitions are infallible was practically universally held by all Catholics. It was precisely because of Cajetan's dilemma concerning jurisdiction over the pope, for which reason Suárez says he "amazingly troubles himself" (*se mire vexat*), that Suárez looked for another solution – but, as will be explained below, he did so in vain.

Bordoni makes a detailed presentation of Cajetan's theory on deposition of a pope, and provides a penetrating critical analysis of it which completely demolishes Cajetan's opinion. I will summarize here only the main points. First, Cajetan argued (*cap. 20. Tract. 1. De Auctor. Papæ*) that while the Church does not possess an authoritative power over the pope, it does possess a ministerial power to depose a heretic pope. In order to prove this he points out the three aspects of the papacy: 1) the Papacy itself, 2) the person who is the pope, and 3) the conjunction between the two from which the pope results.[178] Next, he argues that the papal dignity is immediately from God, but the conjunction between the papacy and the person of the pope is not from

---

[177] *Ibid.*, p. 319: «... mihi tamen breviter et magis pium et probabilius videtur, posse quidem Papam, ut privatam personam, errare ex ignorantia, non tamen ex contumacia. Quamvis enim efficere Deus possit ut hæreticus Papa non noceat Ecclesiæ, suavior tamen modus divinæ providentiæ est, ut, quia Deus promisit Papam definientem nunqnam erraturum, consequenter provideat ne unquam ille hæreticus sit. Adde, quod hactenus in Ecclesia nunquam accidit, censendum ex Dei ordinatione et providentia accidere non posse. Vide Pighium, 1. 4 Ecclesiasticæ Hierarchiæ, c. 8; Simancas, in Institutionibus catholicis, titulo duodecimo, numero decimo quarto.»

[178] Bordoni, *Op. cit. cap. vi.* p. 154: «Tertius eſt Caietani *cap. 20. Tract. 1. De Auctor. Papæ* dicentis Eccleſiam habere poteſtatem miniſterialem deponendi Papam hæreticum, non autem auctoritatiuam ſupra illum, quia Eccleſia, & Concilíum ſupra Papam in nullo caſu habet auctoritatem. Ad hoc probandum tria præmitit. Primò, in Papa tria ſpectantur, Papatus, perſona quæ vocatur Papa, & coniunctio vtriuſq. ex qua reſultat Papa.»

Christ, but from men, the electors and the elected; since it is from the consent of the electors and the elected that there results in the elected one the effect of the conjunction with the papacy, from which the elected person is said to be pope, by the aforesaid ministry of mutual consent of the electors and the elected – thus human volition alone produces this effect of conjunction between the papacy and the person, and thus constitutes the person as pope, from which it follows, that while *the pope* depends solely from God *in esse & fieri*; nevertheless, *that person* e.g. Pope Peter, depends also from man *in fieri*, the man is made pope by men, and thus, the papacy is joined to Peter by men. Cajetan then applies the *regula iuris*, according to which, *Res per quas causas nascitur per easdem dissolvitur* – Peter becomes pope by the consent of the electors and himself, and therefore by the consent of the same the conjunction between the papacy and Peter is dissolved.[179] Secondly, Cajetan then makes the distinction between having power over the conjunction constituting or destroying the union between Peter and the papacy, and having power over the pope, since the lesser power, which, granted, is the simple power of the will of the elected and the electors over the conjunction, yet it is not over the pope, since that power is less than the papacy.[180] Thirdly, he confirms the thesis by the philosophical example of the generation of man, who consists in the conjunction of body and soul, brought into being (according to the theory of the time) by the sun

---

[179] *Ibid.* – «Secundò, dignitas Papatus eft immediatè à Deo, perfona dicitur. effe à fuo patre, coniunctio autem Papatus in perfona Papæ non eft à Chrifto, fed ab hominibus, electoribus & electo, nam ex confenfu eligentium, & electi, refultat in electo ifte effectus coniunctionis Papatus, ex quo perfona electa dicitur Papa per predictum minifterium vtriufq. confenfus electorum, & electi, fola igitur voluntas humana producit hunc effectum coniunctionis Papatus cum perfona, & fic perfonam conftituit Papam, ex quibus fequitur, quod licet Papa à folo Deo dependeat in effe, & fieri, illa tamen perfona e. g. Petrus Papa dependet etiam ab homine in fieri, fit enim Petrus Papa ab homine, & fic Papatus iungitur Petro per hominem. Tertiò demum, affert regulam iuris; Res per quas caufas nafcitur per eafdem diffolvitur; Petrus autem fit Papa ex confenfibus electorum, & proprio, ergò per eofdem diffolui poteft hæc coniunctio Papatus à Petro»

[180] *Ibid.* p. 155: «Secundo, dicit effe certum aliud effe Poffe fupra coniunctionem Petri, & Papatus conftituendam, feu deftruendam, aliud poffe fupra Papam, nam poteftas minor, quæ eft illa fimplex voluntas electi, & electorum licet poffit fupra coniunctionem, non tamen fupra Papam, cum illa poteftas fit minor Papatu.»

and man, from which a man results. The sun and man do not have power over the rational soul, which is created immediately by God, but only over the conjunction from the part of the body. Likewise in this matter, he reasons, Peter and the papacy are as the matter and form, and only Christ has power over both, but man has power only over the conjunction to the extent that he has it on Peter's part and none over the papacy; and since the pope is removed either by renunciation or deposition by the corruption of the conjunction, but not of Peter or the papacy, and thus for this is not required power higher than the pope, but only over the conjunction.[181] Finally, he says the pope is removed in three ways: deposition, renunciation, and expulsion by Christ, and in these three modes the papacy does not cease, nor does Peter, but only the conjunction between them; but with respect to Christ, the conjunction is corrupted by a superior authority, not only in respect to the conjunction, but also to the papacy.[182]

Bordoni refutes each of these points in his exposition, explaining that that ministerial power does not suffice to depose a pope; first, he points out that the ministerial power in question consists in the common consent of the electors and the elected, whereas deposition does not pertain to the cardinals, who are appointed by the pope and under the pope's authority, but the pope is not stripped of the papacy by the College of Cardinals, but even according to Cajetan's opinion, by a general council, which is different from the College of Cardinals. Second, in a deposition, the consent of the one being deposed is not required,

---

[181] *Ibid.* – «*Tertiò*, confirmat exemplo Philoſophico in generatione hominís, nam Sol & homo generant hominem, qui conſiſtit in coniunctione corporis & animæ, aut ex illa coniunctione reſultat homo, conſtat autem ſolem, & hominem non poſſe ſupra animam rationalem, quæ immediate a Deo creatur, ſed tantum ſupra coniuctionem ex parte corporis tantum. Sic in re noſtra, nam Petrus, & Papatus ſe habent vt materia, & forma, & Chriſtus Dominus ſolus ſuper vtrumque poteſt, homo verò ſolum ſuper coniunctionem quatenus ſe tenet ex parte Petrí, & nihil ſupra Papatum; & quoniam Papa amouetur renuntiatione, aut depoſtione per corruptionem illius coniunctionis, non autem Petri, aut Papatus, ideo non requiritur ad hoc poteſtas ſuperior Papæ, ſed ſupra coniunctionem tantum.»

[182] *Ibid.* – «*Quartò* demum, dícit Papam remoueri tribus: depoſitione, renuntiatíone, & eiectione per Chríſtum, & his tribus moddis non deſinit Papatus, nec Petrus, ſed ſola vtriuſq; coniunctio, reſpectu autem Chriſti, ea coniunctio corrumpitur auctorítate ſuperiorᵢ non ſolum reſpectu coniunctionis, ſed etiam reſpectu Papatus.»

because it is according to the nature of penalties that they are inflicted on the unwilling, who are of a contrary will (S. Thomas 1.2 *q. 87. art. 2. ad* 6); but according to Cajetan, this ministerial power is confected from the consent of both the electors and the elected, and therefore it follows as a logical consequence that to depose a pope his consent would be required, which is false, because such a deposition would really be a renunciation, since it involves the consent of the elected; yet even Cajetan says a heretic pope can be deposed against his will. Then also, Cajetan denies that an authoritative power is exercised in the deposition of a pope, insofar as it would be exercised over a pope regarding the papacy, but over the conjunction; and therefore it matters little whether that power by which a pope is deposed is called ministerial or authoritative; since nothing of it is exercised over the papacy but over the conjunction. Then also, there is no escape from the difficulty for this ministerial power, because the pope has no superior over him, and accordingly what is problematic for it is that every judicial act is exercised by a judge who is superior over an inferior person who is a subject, and not by the inferior over his superior, because **an inferior has no power over his superior**, as Cajetan himself admits; but the deposition of a pope is a judicial act of jurisdiction, since, according to all, it cannot be done except by a judge; therefore, such a deposition would be done by a superior over the pope as an inferior and subject, it matters little whether the power is called authoritative or ministerial, since a deposition is a judicial act by its very nature exercised by a superior over an inferior.[183] Furthermore, the threefold aspect of the papacy, the

---

[183] *Ibid.* — «Contra autem eſt primò. Tum quia illa poteſtas miniſterialis non ſufficit ad deponendum Papam, illa enim conſiſtit in communi conſenſu electorum, & electi; ſed Papa non deſtituitur per Collegium Cardinalium à quo fuit inſtitutus, ſed per concilium generale, quod aliud eſt à Collegio. Tum quia in depoſitione nullatenus requiritur conſenſus deponendi, quia pæna fertur in inuitum, ac nolentem, de de ratione ſua eſt contraria voluntati, D. Thom. I. 2* *art.* 2. Ad 6 hæc autem miniſterialis poteſtas ad Papam deponendum conficitur ſecundum Caiet. ex vtriuſque conſenſu ac proinde electi, conſequeter ad deponendum Papam concurrere debet eius conſenſus, quod falſum tamen eſt ex allegatis, præterquam quod non dicitur depoſitio, ſed renuntiatío, quando accedit confenſus electi. Tum quia, in tantum à Caiet. negatur poteſt as auctoritatiua ad deponendum Papam in quantum ea eſſet ſupra Papam in ratione Papatus, ſed ſecundum Caiet. non deponitur Papa, quo ad Papatum, ſed quo ad illam coniunctíonem, ergò parum refert quod poteſtas, per quam Papa deponitur, vocetur miniſterialís, aut auctoritaríua, cum nulla ex his dicatur

person, and the conjunction are true considered as a metaphysical speculation, but morally considered it is not applicable to the conjunction because it is absurd to say that the judge exercises authority over the conjunction to destroy it, since when the council by the penalty of deposition punishes the deposed pope, it punishes *him*, and therefore it cannot be said that the council exercises power over the conjunction, but over the person who up to that time has been conjoined to the papacy, and who would be deprived of that dignity if he were to be without the papacy, since privation supposes a habit. Thus, the council deposes the one hitherto conjoined to the papacy by depriving him of the papacy and not the conjunction. Furthermore, since, according to Cajetan, the conjunction of the form with the matter comes after the form, the conjunction is something posterior and the *esse* of the papacy is prior, and not that of the conjunction, therefore: if the conjunction is brought into being by the ministry of men, and the papacy by the authority of God, it follows that in the destruction, the *non esse* of the papacy is prior, and the disjunction of the conjunction comes after, since the disjunction of that union is brought about by the separation from the papacy; and from this is the consequence that the judge first removes the dignity from the person than that the conjunction first be destroyed.[184] Furthermore, it is contrived to posit that conjunction to be brought about by the ministry of men through election in relation to the papal dignity and power, since the electors only designate the person, upon whom God thereafter confers the dignity and authority, so that the election is not the means, by which Christ bestows the papacy upon the elected, but only the condition *sine qua non* God confers the papacy upon someone; and therefore, the conjunction is not made by the ministry of the electors, but immediately by God, lest it be said that the electors confer the papacy together with God, and thus make a man pope

---

tendere supra Papatum, sed in coniunctionem. Tum quia per hanc ministerialem potestatem non effugitur difficultas, quod Papa non habeat supra se superiorem, siquidem omnis actus iudicialis semper exercetur per superiorem iudicem in inferiorem personam, & subditam, & non per inferiorem in superiorem, quia inferior nullam habet potestatem in superiorem, *cap. Cum inferior* 16. *de maior.* ipse Caiet. hoc *cap.*20. initio; sed depositio Papæ: est actus iudicialis, & jurisdictionis, quia nonnisi per iudicem fieri potest, secundum omnes, ergò huiusmodi depositio fit per superiorem in Papam tamquam inferiorem, ac subditum, parum ergò refert, quod ea potestas vocetur auctoritatiua, siue ministerialis, si depositio est actus iudicialis ex sua natura exercitus à superiore in inferiorem.»

[184] *Ibid.* p. 155 – 156.

according to the nature of the pope. Furthermore, according to Cajetan, the conjunction comes after the form of the dignity, and therefore is its formal effect, and not, (as Cajetan would have it), of the electors. Furthermore, because if by the ministry of men, the papacy is joined to the elected man, the pope would no longer receive the dignity of the papacy immediately from God, but also from men – against the common doctrine of all canonists and theologians. And also it would follow from there that the electors conjoin the papacy to the one they elect, which is to confer upon him the dignity, like a whitewasher conjoining whiteness to a wall, and confer whiteness upon the wall; thus, likewise by Cajetan's conjunction the electors can be said to confer the papacy on the pope, which is false, because the electors designate the person, and God, by himself immediately confers the dignity and jurisdiction.[185] Furthermore, it is fallacious to say that since the conjunction between the man and the papacy was brought into being by means of the ministerial power of men, that men therefore have the power over that conjunction to destroy it by the same ministerial power; because it is by a ministerial power that a man and a woman are joined by means of the matrimonial bond, but they who exercised the ministerial power to bring that conjunction into being do not have any power to dissolve it. Furthermore, being only about halfway through Bordoni's arguments against Cajetan's conjunction theory, I leave it to the reader to read the rest of his arguments in the cited work, which is readily available as a free download. Bellarmine expressed his critique of Cajetan's conjunction theory by means of the simple Thomistic application of the principle of potentiality and act, which is also the foundation on which Bordoni's arguments rest. The ministerial power is exercised over the matter, the principle of potentiality, before the composite of matter and form (potentiality + act) come into being by virtue of the perfection of the form, which confers upon the composite its actual *esse*. In his refutation of Cajetan's conjunction theory, Bellarmine argues in *De Romano Pont. lib. ii cap. xxx*: **"For while a thing is made, the action is exercised over the matter of the thing that is going to be, not over a composite which does not yet exist, but while a thing is destroyed, the action is exercised over a composite; as is certain from natural things."** This principle, expressed by Bellarmine, is the basis of Bordoni's arguments, which explain that the ministerial power is exercised over the matter, by designating the person to become pope, but the conjunction

---

[185] *Ibid.*

between the man and the papacy is created directly by God, who conjoins the matter and form, and thereby confers the papacy on the man, creating the actual quality of the papacy inhering in the person of the pope *as a habit*. The conjunction is not a something that exists as a substance, as if it were a glue that men used to glue the man and the papacy together, and can therefore be dissolved by men – as if they were the ones who had first glued the man and the papacy together. The papacy is a *quality*, and more specifically a *habit* created by God in the man when he accepts the papacy, after which the Church possesses no jurisdiction over it, since it inheres in the pope as an accidental *quality* joined by God to the man's substance, which makes him the pope. Hence, it follow that men cannot remove the papacy from a man without acting directly on the man any more than men could remove the whiteness from a Russian or the blackness from an African without acting directly on the men to deprive them of their colour. Therefore, ministerial function has the power to act only on the matter before it is conjoined with the form; but the conjunction existing in the composite of matter and form, having been created directly by God, lies beyond the scope of the ministerial power, which can act only on the matter alone before it is conjoined with the form, but not on the conjoined composite, because that would be an exercise of power directly over the pope. Thus, Bellarmine concludes: **"what Cajetan says… that a heretical Pope who is truly Pope can be deposed by the Church, and from its authority seems no less false than the first. For, if the Church deposes a Pope against his will, certainly it is over the Pope."** Thus, the destruction of the conjunction can only be accomplished by the separation of the matter from the form by death or renunciation. Resignation is a voluntary act, which is either *directly* willed when the pope explicitly renounces his *munus*; or *indirectly* willed as an effect which follows necessarily as the natural consequence of defection from the faith or communion with the Church.

As will be shown later in this work, that although Bordoni and Bellarmine were of opposite opinions on the question of the deposition of a heretical pope, Bordoni arguing that the heretic would, by way of exception, be *deponendus* by the exceptional jurisdiction Church over the pope, and Bellarmine arguing that the manifest heretic would be *depositus per se*; both understood exactly why Cajetan was in error to believe that a deposition would not require an exercise of superior jurisdiction over the pope. It is because the whole Church is subject *jure divino* to the pope's universal jurisdiction, that the whole Church is bound or loosed exclusively by that power inherent in the primacy, exercised freely by the pope either by himself, or together with the bishops in an ecumenical council. Accordingly, it is by the pope's supreme and universal primacy of jurisdiction that he alone exercises the fullness of power to bind and loose the whole Church; and therefore it is heresy to assert that a council can bind or loose the whole Church apart from the pope; or that a council can exercise a power over the conjunction to separate and thereby *loose* the whole Church from the pope's universal jurisdiction by binding the whole Church to it own ruling against the *jure divino* precept which binds the whole Church to the pope under his universal jurisdiction.

Suárez reasoned that while others professed that in the case of heresy the Church would be superior to the pope, he rejected this opinion because Christ constituted the pope absolutely as the supreme judge; which the canons generally and indiscriminantly affirm; and thus, the Church has no power to exercise jurisdiction over the pope – nor does it confer power on him by electing him, but only designates the one on whom Christ confers the power. Therefore, he reasoned, when the Church would depose a pope, it would not do so as a superior, but by the consent of Christ, *juridically declaring him to be a heretic*, and thus unworthy of the papal dignity – for which reason, he would immediately be deposed by Christ; and being deposed, he would become inferior, and could be punished.[186] Accordingly Suárez argued that, before the declaration the Church could do nothing by way of a superior exercising jurisdiction over the heretic pope; and the Church, by its right in natural law to defend itself could coerce him if he would be injuriously scheming harmful machinations against her, or if he would attempt to prevent the convening of a general council; but once the sentence would have been

---

[186] R.P. Francisci Suarez, *Op. cit.*, p. 318: «Alii ergo fatentur Ecclesiam in casu hæresis esse Pontifice superiorem, sed difficile hoc dictu est. Nam Christus Dominus Papam constituit absolute supremum judicem; canones etiam indifferenter et generaliter id affirmant; ac tandem Ecclesia nullum actum jurisdictionis exercere valet in Papam, neque confert illi potestatem eligendo, sed personam designat cui Christus per se confert potestatem; quando ergo Ecclesia Papam hæreticum deponeret, non ipsa tanquam superior id prætaret, sed ex consensione Christi Domini juridice declararet eum heereticum esse, atque adeo prorsus indignum Pontificis dignitate; tuncque ipso facto immediate a Christo deponeretur, depositusque maneret inferior, ac posset puniri.»

pronounced, the pope would be immediately deposed *jure divino*.[187] Suárez did not see the huge flaw in his own argument, which is that before the declaration would be pronounced, the Church would not have the jurisdiction to issue the declaration – but only *after* a *juridical* declaration of heresy against the pope, which according to its nature would necessarily need to have been made with the *jurisdiction of a superior over the pope*, would his *ipso facto* fall from the pontificate then be precipitated; and the Church then would be able to exercise jurisdiction over the deposed heretic and punish him with vindictive penalties; but in order to *juridically* issue the declaration, the Church would need beforehand to already possess a superior jurisdiction than the pope's to judge the pope's doctrine to be heretical; as well as the jurisdiction to pronounce the judgment of heresy on the pope that would result in his fall from office. In the passages quoted above, Bordoni proved that the *juridical* judgment of heresy called for in the Suarezian theory would neither be in the nature of a judgment, nor would it be *juridical*, since it would not be made with an exercise of jurisdiction over the pope. Suárez's own argument against Cajetan's claim that the pope could be judged as a private person is equally applicable against his own theory, which likewise calls for a juridical judgment of heresy to be rendered against the person of the pope. The qualification that the judgment would not be an exercise of authority acting as superior *over the pope* is to no avail because it is not a qualification but a contradiction; since a *juridical judgment* is, according to its very nature, an exercise of jurisdiction by a superior over a subject.

Thus, Bordoni proved that all the theories that posit a deposition by a ministerial power are argued on the basis of logical fallacies, with the result that there are really only two opinions left to be considered: The heretic pope is either *deponendus* by authority or *depositus* entirely by himself. All of the arguments in favour of the opinion that a sitting pope can be deposed (*deponendus*) by the Church from office for the crime of heresy have been proven to be false and heretical, insofar as they depend on a juridical act of judgment made with jurisdiction over the pope. In

---

[187] *Ibid.* – «Addendum vero, quamvis Ecclesia ante suam declarationem nihil possit in hæreticum Papam, per modum superioris et habentis jurisdictionem in illum, naturali tamen jure suæ defensionis posse illum coercere, si forte nocumentum aliquod machinetur in Ecclesiam, aut congregationem Concilii generalis impedire conetur. Unde vero constet jure divino statim deponi Pontificem lata Ecclesiæ sententia»

such a proceeding, Bordoni explained, the deposition would be threefold; a composite act consisting of three moments **1)** a juridical declaration of heresy, **2)** a juridical deposition from office, **3)** a decree of separation from the Church (*excommunication*). Since according to none of the deposition theories, would the fall from office take place simply *ex natura hæresis*, and therefore entirely by itself, i.e. *ipso facto*; in a deposition properly so-called, the declaration of heresy and the act of deposition would require *jurisdiction over the pope*. Since, in a juridical deposition the act of deposition and the expulsion from the Church would not follow *ex natura* from the declaration of heresy, which, therefore, *in its nature is a juridiclly separate act* from the others, each single act would require jurisdiction over the person, and thus, *the decree of deposition from office would also require* **jurisdiction over the pope.** Only *the expulsion from the Church*, as Bordoni notes, poses no difficulty, because it would be declared or inflicted on the former pope already deposed from office and *minor quolibet catholico*.

Cajetan, Suárez, John of St. Thomas, Bordoni, as well as all other authors who reject the Bellarminian thesis that a manifest heretic pope would fall from office *ipso facto*, entirely *by himself*, reject it primarily because there exists no explicit provision in divine or ecclesiastical law that would be specifically applicable to the case of a heretic pope. However, there exists no reason why such a specific provision should be found in either the deposit of revelation or in canon law, since it is not in those places where it is to be found. Such a divine precept can only be found in Natural Law, and that is where St. Robert Bellarmine found it. When one considers the nature of the natural law precepts as in contradistinction to those of divine positive law, the reason becomes clear. The precepts of Natural Law encompass all of the *possibilia*, of nature; i.e., all that is possible *according to nature*, and thus includes all *hypothetical possibilities*; whereas the general precepts of Natural Law expressed specifically as *judicial precepts* of divine law, do not extend to mere hypothetical possibilities, because *judicial precepts* are limited only to those ordinances "which are determinations of the justice to be maintained among men" (*I.II.q.99 a.1*); and therefore are intended only to govern human actions in actual situations that will be permitted to arise according to the disposition of the divine wisdom providently directing all human actions towards their proper end according to the requirements of justice. St. Thomas explains, "it belongs to the Divine law to direct men to one another and to God. Now each of these belongs in the abstract to the dictates of the *natural law*, to which dictates the moral precepts are to be referred: yet *each of them has to be determined by Divine or human law*, because *naturally known principles are universal, both in speculative and in practical matters.*"[188] The specific determinations of the general precepts of Natural Law which direct the actions of men to one another and to God are expressed as specific statutes of ceremonial and judicial precepts: "Accordingly just as the determination of the universal principle about Divine worship is effected by the ceremonial precepts, so the determination of the general precepts of that justice which is to be observed among men is effected by the judicial precepts."[189]

There is no actual justice to be observed among men by means of specific determinations of precepts applicable only in an abstract hypothetical realm, which would govern the merely theoretical actions that would be postulated in a merely hypothetical situation of a case which divine providence is not disposed to permit. Cajetan, as Don Curzio, notes, was of the opinion that a pope cannot become a formal heretic. I quoted the passage above in which Bordoni cites passages of several authors including Suárez, whose passage I quoted above, and also Bellarmine – who all held it to be impossible or at least highly improbable that a pope can become a formal heretic. Of particular relevance to this question of divine law are Bellarmine's words in *De Romano Pont. lib. iv. cap vii* about whether a pope can become a heretic or not: "Therein it is gathered correctly that the Pope by his own nature can fall into heresy, *but not when we posit the singular assistance of God which Christ asked for him by his prayer [lest his faith would fail].*" Since *by his own nature* the pope can fall into heresy, *but not when we posit the singular assistance of God*, it becomes manifestly evident why, in the case of papal heresy, one must look only for a precept decreed by *natural law*, which extends to all *possibilia*, even to those merely hypothetical; but not for a specific *judicial precept* of divine positive law, because judicial precepts do not exist for merely hypothetical situations which, *although theoretically possible, exist only in the realm of speculation, but, will never actually be permitted by God*, and hence, for

---

[188] *I – II Q. 99 art. 4*: «Respondeo dicendum quod, sicut dictum est, ad legem divinam pertinet ut ordinet homines ad invicem et ad Deum. Utrumque autem horum in communi quidem pertinet ad dictamen legis naturae, ad quod referuntur moralia praecepta, sed oportet quod determinetur utrumque per legem divinam vel humanam, quia principia naturaliter nota sunt communia tam in speculativis quam in activis.»

[189] *Ibid.* «Sicut igitur determinatio communis praecepti de cultu divino fit per praecepta caeremonialia, sic et determinatio communis praecepti de iustitia observanda inter homines, determinatur per praecepta iudicialia.»

such a purely hypothetical case as would be a case of papal heresy, *the determination of general precepts of that justice which is to be observed among men*, would serve no purpose. It is thus in vain for one to search the sources of revelation for a divine prescription for what Ballerini affirms, is a "a mere hypothesis" – a "hypothesis... not established by any fact, since no private error ascribed to any Pontiff against any evident or defined dogma has been found, or is believed will be."[190]

The solemn teaching of *Pastor Æternus*, establishing the unfailing faith of Peter as the premise upon which the dogma of papal infallibility is founded, is the strongest proof from authority in support of the nearly certain theological opinion that a true pope cannot fall into formal heresy; and this proof from authority is confirmed by the *fact* that no specific divine precept prescribing a remedy for the case of papal heresy exists, which therefore establishes what is perhaps the strongest theological proof from reason that a pope cannot fall into formal heresy. It would contradict the divine wisdom if God were to permit that the Church should be ruled and governed by a heretical destroyer and enemy of the Church, without prescribing any clear remedy for what Bordoni calls the *necessitas maxima* of such a catastrophe. However, the conclusion that by divine law a council would be given jurisdiction to depose a heretical pope, if such a thing as a heretic pope were possible, does not follow from the premise that God would not desert his Church in a state of necessity, (as Bordoni and others before him argued on the cited Gospel passage), because there is no basis in any positive law human or divine to admit such a jurisdiction; whereas Bellarmine's application of the principles of natural law to the divinely revealed truth that *heretics are outside the Church by their own judgment*, and hence as a natural consequence they lose all office and dignity, anticipated by three centuries the canonical provision for Tacit Resignation of Office in canon 188.4° of the 1917 Code, which, in the case of a pope, does not entail a pope's act of jurisdiction against himself, nor is it a merely ecclesiastical law which, as such, would involve one pope exercising power over his successor, but is aply described by Ballerini as a *sort of abdication*, which is not a voluntary abdication, but an abandonment of an ecclesiastical office which follows necessarily *ex natura hæresis* from the act of public heresy, by which one defects from the faith and the Church, and loses office as the natural consequence of that defection.

---

[190] Pietro Ballerini, *Op. cit. Cap. IX § II.* pp. 129.

As mentioned above, the provision of canon 188.4° is not intended as a *merely ecclesiastical law* by which the pope legislates for his subjects an *ipso facto* deposition for public defection from the faith, because it is worded in such a manner so that it applies indiscriminantly to *all offices*; and therefore it necessarily applies even to the highest office. In the passage cited earlier, Suárez explained why a pope cannot fall from office *ipso facto* by the force of any merely human law, because it would either be issued by an inferior, such as would be the case if it were issued by a council, or by an equal, if it were issued by a predecessor pope. Neither of these would have the jurisdiction to exercise power over a superior or over an equal.[191] *Par in parem potestatem non habet.* Hence, insofar as the provision would be applicable to a pope (as it clearly is), it would be a provision of divine law known through reason, and incorporated into ecclesiastical legislation. An *ipso facto* effect can occur in two ways: 1) **by authority**, by means of a *latæ sententiæ* penal censure, or 2) **per se**, by the nature of the act **suapte natura**. Pius XII explains in *Mystici Corporis* that heresy separates one from the Church *suapte natura*, so that heretics separate themselves from the Church by themselves, i.e., **per se**, and not **by authority**, and are no longer numbered as members of the Church, **having miserably separated themselves**. Thus, public heretics, accordingly as both *public* and *heretic* are defined in canon law, cease automatically by themselves to be members of the Church, not by any judgment of Church authority, but entirely by themselves.

That one cannot be head who is not a member is self-evident, because to be head one must first be a member; so, membership is prior to headship; and therefore, according to nature if the head ceases to be a member he ceases to be head. Therefore it strictly follows that the head who ceases to be a member **suapte natura** by heresy, by that very act ceases **per se** to be head **ipso facto**, not by any human law but **ex natura hæresis**. Thus it is known infallibly by reason as a direct logical consequence of the revealed truth that heretics cease by themselves to be members of the Church, that a pope who would defect publicly into heresy would cease by himself to be pope. Since the fall from office is effected entirely by the nature of the act **per se**, no act of human authority is required as a dispository condition for the fall from office to take place.

---

[191] R.P. Francisci Suarez, *Op. cit., Tomus Doudecimus, Tractatus Primus, De Fide Theologica. Disputatio X. De Summo Pontifice, Sect. VI.* p. 316.

Salza & Siscoe argue on the basis of the premise that because heresy is a *crime*, the separation from the Church and the consequent fall from office do not take place without a judgment of Church authority. The argument is a *non sequitur* because regardless of whether the act is a crime or not, the *act* of heresy *suapte natura* separates one from the Church *by itself*. The separation takes place according to divine law by the nature of the act of heresy, and not by human authority by the force of ecclesiastical law, nor by the force of any explicit judicial penal precept of divine positive law. Adam & Eve were expelled from the garden by authority because they incurred the penalty of expulsion for the crime of eating the forbidden fruit. If they had walked away from the garden to take up permanent residence elsewhere without eating the forbidden fruit; they would have been banished from the garden by the nature of their own very act of desertion, without the need for any sentence to be pronounced on them by superior authority. If a pope were to expel himself from the Church by a public act of formal heresy, no declaration of Church authority would be needed to effect his expulsion from the Church and his fall from the pontificate, since these are accomplished *ex natura hæresis*. Since the pope has no superior but God, there exists no authority on earth who would have the jurisdiction to pronounce a judgment of heresy on the pope. Heresy is a crime against divine law in its very nature, but it separates one from the Church and effects the loss of office by itself *suapte natura*, because heresy is in the nature of an act of desertion, and not because it violates a judicial penal precept of divine or ecclesiastical law. It is therefore manifestly *contra rationem* to assert that a judgment of authority is needed to accomplish a separation that is accomplished by the act itself *suapte natura*.

Bellarmine explains in *De Romano Pont. lib. ii cap. xxx*, that one who ceases to be a member of the Church cannot be its head: "A non-Christian cannot in any way be Pope, as Cajetan affirms in the same book, and the reason is because he cannot be the head of that which he is not a member, and he is not a member of the Church who is not a Christian. But a manifest heretic is not a Christian, as St. Cyprian and many other Fathers clearly teach. Therefore, a manifest heretic cannot be Pope." Bordoni sums up concisely the Bellarminian argument, explaining that since a heretic is no longer a member of the Christ's body, neither can he be the head of the Church, and this argument stands because an infidel is a severed member, separated from the Church, and thus it is self-evident that because member and head are thus subordinated in such a manner that being a member is prior to being the head, because in order to be the head, the head must be a member. Therefore, since the heretic pope would no longer be a member, neither could he be the head of the Church.[192] Bordoni admits that the argument is logically consistent, but, following Cajetan, he denies that a heretic would cease altogether to be a member of the Church, and for this reason, he concludes that the heretic would still be pope until deposed by the authority of a council. Bordoni's great contribution to the question of the deposition of a heretic pope was that he exposed with an irrefutable logic the fatal flaws in the ministerial deposition theories of Cajetan and Suárez, which are the basis of all the ministerial deposition theories.

Since there is no divine precept whatsoever found in revelation specifically prescribed for a case of papal heresy, the argument against an *ipso facto* fall from office based on the fact that there is nothing explicitly set forth in divine law establishing an *ipso jure divino* fall from office for pertinacious heresy is of no value at all; because that same fact would apply equally against the argument which would attempt to demonstrate that a heretical pope could be deposed by the Church (*deponi posse ab Ecclesia*). Suárez argued against an *ipso facto* fall because it is not expressly stated in divine law, neither for heretics in general or for bishops, or especially for a pope.[193] Bordoni[194]argues against the proposition which holds that *Papam hæreticum ipso iure divino carere Papatu* solely on the basis that 1) *nullo iure id exprimitur*, and 2) *nemo tenetur in seipsum immediate exercere vim coactivam*, and 3) *nullus iurisdictionem supra se*

---

[192] Bordoni, *Op. cit.* p. 152: «*Probant secundo, quia carens fide non amplius membum Clirifti, neque proindè caput effe poteft Eccleſiæ, illud conſtat, quia infidelis eſt membrum præciſum, putridum, à Chriſto, & ab Eccleſia feparatum, cap.Sj quis 69. 1. q.1* Vide Ricciull. *lib. 5. cap. 12.* hoc de ſe patet, quia membrum, & caput eſſentialiter ita ſubordinantur, quod prius eſt membrum, quam effe caput, quia oportet caput effe membrum, ergò Papa hæretícus cum non amplius ſit membrum, neque caput erit Eccleſiæ.»

[193] «Et infra agentes de pœnis hæreticorum alios referemus, ac generaliter ostendemus jure divino non privari quempiam dignitate et jurisdictione ecclesiastica propter culpam hæresis; nuc breviter ratio a priori redditur, quia cum ea sit gravissima pœna, ut ipso facto incurratur, oportet jure divino expressam esse; nullum autem jus tale invenitur, quod vel generaliter id statuat de hæreticis, aut specialiter de episcopis, aut specialissime de Papa; nec item certa traditio de eo habetur» — R. P. Francisci Suarez, *Op. cit. Disputatio X. De Summo Pontifice, Sect. VI.* p. 316

[194] Bordoni, *Op. cit.* p. 151.

*dare potest.*¹⁹⁵ His arguments suffer the same defect as that of the early Decretists who looked exclusively to positive law for the remedy of a problem that can only be solved by seeking the remedy in natural law as Bellarmine did. However, he finds no specific remedy prescribed in divine law, but, like nearly all the other authors who held the *deponendus* opinion, he merely appeals to the words of Christ in the Gospel promising the divine assistance to the Church until the end of time: *Et ecce ego vobiscum sum omnibus diebus usque ad consummationem seculi*; and to the spurious *cap. Si Papa 6. dift. 40.*; in an attempt to prove that a council by divine law can depose a pertinaciously heretical pope (*quod concilium iure divino procedat ad depositionem papæ hæretici pertinacis*). Bordoni reasons that since God does not fail to provide for his Church in necessity, in virtue of his words, "I am with you all days even until the end of the world," by his authority which was conferred not only on Peter the head, but even to the Church gathered against the head when it is necessary, and which is of maximum necessity in those two cases of a heretic pope or an uncertain pope, the Church would be in a most dire state if it would not have a remedy, by which it could come into knowledge of its true spouse and head; or if it had no means to acquire a true and legitimate superior, having deposed the adulterers and intruders.¹⁹⁶ The cited scripture verse provides no specific remedy, and the spurious canon, although bereft of any canonical force, can be interpreted as Bellarmine did, in a concordant manner so as to not conflict with the other canons which unequivocally uphold the absolute injudicability and immunity of the Roman Pontiff. Bellarmine's doctrine on this point is nothing other than a theological formulation of the remedy already applied by the Council of Constance in its above mentioned ruling, which declared that Pedro de Luna had already forfeited all ecclesiastical office and dignity *ipso jure* by his manifest acts of schism and heresy. It is particularly

---

¹⁹⁵ *Ibid.* p. 153.

¹⁹⁶ *Ibid.* p. 151: «Tum quia, Deus in necefarijs non deeft Ecclefiæ fuæ, cum dixerit per Matth. extremis verbis. Ecce ego vobifcum sum omnibus diebus ufque ad confumationem fæculi nimirum per meam auctoritatem, quam non folum communicaui Petro capiti, fed etiam Ecclefiæ congregatæ contra caput quando id foret neceffarium, quæ neceffitas maximè accidit in his duobus cafibus de Pontifice hæretico, & incerto, cum enim caput dolet, eius membra languent & tabefcunt, ac valde infelix effet Ecclefia, fi nullum haberet remedium, per quod poffet venire in cognitionem veri fponfi, & capitis fui, aut fi nullum haberet medium, quo fibi acquirere poffet verum, & legitimum fuperiorem, depofitis adulteris, & intrufis.»

noteworthy that the Council did not cite any provision of positive law whether ecclesiastical or divine in the formulation of the ruling; but following the example of those Decretists who simply stated that the loss of office for public heresy would take place *ipso jure* without citing any specific provisions, it simply applied the provision of Natural Law as required by Natural Equity. [197] Natural Law, being derived from the Eternal Law, required that the *ipso jure* loss of office be declared in that ruling in accordance with Natural Equity, because it pertains to the *nature* of heresy and schism that the public heretic or schismatic ceases *ipso facto* to be a member of the Church, and as such, becomes an incapable subject to hold office in the Church. The solemn definition of the universal primacy of the Roman Pontiff finally laid to rest the errant opinion that a true and valid reigning pope could be deposed from office for heresy or any other reason, since that opinion, in the light of that definition, could be clearly seen to be heretical.

It is simply incredible that these utterly discredited and defunct theories, which in the light of *Pastor Æternus* can be seen to be **heretical**, have been revived more than a century after their demise, mainly due to the unceasing propagation of them by the two academically incompetent self-styled "theologians", John F. Salza and Robert J. Siscoe. Salza & Siscoe stridently accuse me of calumny for allegedly "misrepresenting" their doctrine, and of accusing them of heresies they do no profess. This is nothing but a desperate ploy. I have provided in this volume ample citations of passages in which Salza and Siscoe assert that there have been popes who were formal heretics, and that pertinaciously heretical popes can be judged and deposed by the Church. Here are two of those passages: Roberet J. Siscoe, in his *Remnant* article (Nov. 18, 2014): **"The Church must render a judgment before the pope loses his office."** On page 331 of their diatribe, Salza & Siscoe assert their heresy: "After the Church establishes that the Pope is guilty of the crime of heresy, *she renders a **judgment*** of the same (and, as we will see, *this is to be done during an **"imperfect" ecumenical council**)*." Siscoe explains in his *Catholic Family News* article, "While the Church does not possess the authority to judge a Pope, it does possess the competency and the right to judge whether or not a proposition professed by a Pope is materially heretical.

---

[197] "Natural Equity. That which is founded in natural justice, in honesty and right, and which arises ex aequo et bono. It corresponds precisely with the definition of justice or natural law, which is a constant and pepetual will to give every man what is his." (cf. https://www.lectlaw.com > def2)

This is an objective judgment, and therefore makes no difference if the proposition was professed by a pope or a non-pope". This is heresy, because it lies within the pope's universal jurisdiction as supreme teacher and judge to decide *all doctrinal questions*, so a council does not possess the competency to judge a pope's proposition. It is only by the pope's authority that a council can even exist, and none of its decisions have any juridical value if not confirmed by the pope. The wording of *Pastor Æternus* leaves absolutely no conceivable possibility to allow for an interpretation that would admit of exceptions to the pope's absolute and universal jurisdiction in all cases; and that is how all expert canonists and theologians understand the matter since 1870.

In vain Salza & Siscoe quote John of St. Thomas:

> "When Cajetan says that the Church acts with authority (*auctoritative*) on the *conjunction* or *separation* of the pontificate with the person, and ministerially on the papacy itself, we must understand it in the sense that the Church has the authority to declare the crime of the Pope, just as she has [the authority] of designating the same man to be Pope; and that what she does with authority [to the matter] by such declarations, acts, at the same time, *ministerially* on the form to either join or to separate; for of itself the Church is unable to do anything to the form, absolutely and in itself, (*absolute et in se*), since the papal power is not subject to the authority of the Church."[198]

Leaving aside the logical inconsistencies of the ministerially acting dispositively on the conjunction theory already exposed in 1648 by Francesco Bordoni, the primary and most fatal flaw in his theory is the claim that, "the Church has the authority to declare the crime of the Pope, just as she has of designating the same man to be Pope". This is heresy: Bordoni amply demonstrated that the jurisdiction of a judge as a superior is required to judge the crime of a pope. Judgment of a man's crime as a juridical act of the Church does not fall within the scope of a merely ministerial function. The ministerial power of designating the man to be pope is exercised over the matter alone – over the man who is not yet pope, disposing him to become pope; whereas juridically judging the crime of the pope is to pronounce judgment over *the pope* personally, and not merely on the matter. Thus, as Bordoni proved, to act authoritatively on the conjunction or separation cannot be performed without first exercising jurisdiction over the pope. A disposition cannot

---

[198] *Auctoritate Summi Pontificis*, Disp. II, Art. III, *De Depositione Papae*, p. 140.

be introduced into the matter without first exercising jurisdictional power of *judgment* over the pope, who is the composite of matter and form. Therefore, it is to no avail that John of St. Thomas asserts, "the Pope is deposed against his will, in a *ministerial* and *dispositive* manner by the Church, *authoritatively* by Christ the Lord, so that through Him, and not by Church, he is properly said *punished*."[199] The ministerial deposition theory collapses because the ministerial act cannot take place unless it would be preceeded by an exercise of jurisdictional judgment and magisterial authority of a superior by the council over its superior, who, as Innocent III teaches, in virtue of his primacy of jurisdiction singularly possesses the *plenitudo potestatis*, of which the bishops of the Church, singly and collectively, only possess a partial share:

> «Petrus ligare potest cæteros, sed ligari non potest a cæteris. *Tu*, inquit, *vocaberis Cephas* (Joan. 1), quod exponitur caput; quia sicut in capite consistit omnium sensuum plenitudo, in cæteris autem membris pars est aliqua plenitudinis: ita cæteri vocati sunt in partem sollicitudinis, solus autem Petrus assumptus est in plenitudinem potestatis.»[200]

Hence, the proposition stated by Salza & Siscoe on page 356 of their screed is plainly heretical:

> "The ministerial function of the Church, then, is to establish the crime, issue the declaratory sentence, and then command the faithful, by a *juridical* (and therefore binding) act, that the man must be avoided. It is this juridical act, rather than the crime itself, that induces the *disposition* into the matter that renders him incapable of sustaining the form (the pontificate)."[201]

Siscoe mendaciously says in the same above mentioned article that Pope Vigilius was, "Excommunicated by the Second Council of Constantinople, 553". This statement might pass for serious history in Alice's Wonderland, but in the real world, such statements constitute fraud. No ecumenical council ever excommunicated Pope Vigilius. A group of Eastern bishops assembled at the behest of Emperor Justinian and declared themselves to be a "council". Vigilius refused to attend, and even issued a document forbidding the council to convene without him.

---

[199] *Cursus Theologici* II-II, *De Auctoritate Summi Pontificis*, Disp. II, Art. III, *De Depositione Papae*, p. 140

[200] Innocentius III, *Sermo II, De Diversis*.

[201] Salza & Siscoe, *op. cit.*, Chapter 11, *The Deposition of a Heretical Pope*, p. 356.

At the seventh session, the bishops had Vigilius stricken from the diptychs for his refusal to appear at the council and approve its proceedings. The decisions of the council were issued in the eighth session. Vigilius approved of the decisions independently, but his papal approval of the decisions made in the eighth session had the result of making the synod an ecumenicl council. Only those decisions made in the eighth session are accepted by the Church as official pronouncements of an ecumenical council.

At the opposite extreme to the error that a pope can be judged by his subjects, is the opinion that even a manifestly formal heretic intruding onto the papal throne cannot be removed by any power on earth. This was the opinion of the nineteenth century Jesuit trained canonist, Marie Dominique Bouix, and it is also the opinion adopted by Christopher A. Ferrara. According to St. Robert Bellarmine's classification of the opinions on the deposition of a heretic pope, Mr. Ferrara's opinion is the Third Opinion:

«*The third opinion thinks that the Roman Pontiff does not automatically forfeit his power and cannot be deprived of it by deposition even for manifest heresy. This assertion is very rightly said by Bellarmine to be "extremely improbable".*» [*Jus Canonicum* by Franz Xavier Wernz S.J. and Pedro Vidal S.J. (1938) Chapter VII; and, *Jus Canonicum*, Roma, Gregoriana, 1943, vol. II, p. 517]

«*The third opinion states that even though a pope should publicly preach a heretical doctrine, he would neither be automatically deposed nor could his deposition be brought about.*» [James M. Moynihan, STL, JCD; *Papal Immunity and Liability in the Writings of the Medieval Canonists*, Gregorian University Press, Roma 1961, p. xi]

There has been no theologian of repute subscribing to the third opinion since Marie Dominique Bouix, a French canonist who died in December 1870. As I mentioned above, Bouix was the last to hold this opinion, and is only one out of 137 authors listed by Arnaldo Xavier da Silveira as having held this opinion. Yet, it is precisely this untenable opinion which is at present becoming popular among lay Catholic writers who seem unaware of the theologically problematic difficulties that beset this opinion. In his article, *A Defector Pope?*, Chris Ferrara [202] writes, «While the possibility of an heretical Pope falling from office is certainly entertained by theologians, there is no mechanism by which the universal Church could be assured that such an event has occurred during the reign of a Pope accused of heresy.» The statement is absurd

---

[202] *Fatima Perspectives* #1277.

on its face, since, if there is no means by which the Church can arrive at certitude in judging that a pope is a formal heretic, then neither is there any means by which any other baptized person can be judged with certitude to be a heretic without a solemn *ex cathedra* judgment. Mr. Ferrara argues, «Not even the idea of an "imperfect council" of cardinals to declare that an heretical Pope has deposed himself would provide the necessary surety because it would probably be contested by that Pope's loyalists should he refuse to resign, leading to something like the Great Western Schism with rival claimants to the papal throne.» This statement erroneously assumes that without a unanimous or nearly unanimous consensus, a judgment made by the College of Cardinals would not provide "the necessary surety" – as if the probability that the judgment would be contested somehow renders such a judgment uncertain.

The Church possesses the means to judge in matters of faith, and even when the Church has judged solemnly and infallibly, the judgment often has not prevented great schisms – such as the Protestant schism which has divided Christians for nearly half a millennium. It is indisputable that without an infallible papal judgment, it can be judged with moral certitude and sometimes with absolute certitude that a person is a formal heretic, by judging according to the standards and procedures established by the Church's canonical tradition. If the *indicia* of formal heresy are manifest, then it is judged beyond all shadow of doubt that the accused is guilty of the crime of heresy. If the *indicia* of *violent suspicion* of heresy are manifested in a suspect who remains obstinate even after correction, then it is morally certain that the individual is a formal heretic. Even if the judgment would be contested by that putative Pope's loyalists should he refuse to resign, that fact would not in the least degree diminish the certitude of the judgment. Mr. Ferrara then states his conclusion: «Thus, whether a given Pope has lost his office on account of heresy remains essentially an academic question while that Pope is reigning. Only a future Pope or council presided over by a Pope could declare that a predecessor Pope had fallen from office due to heresy — a declaration that has never occurred in Church history.» The statement is a hypothetical proposition founded on a false premise. The question of whether a given pope has lost his office on account of heresy is hypothetical, since it has never been proven that a pope can actually fall into formal heresy. The opinion, that a pope cannot be a heretic, (the *first opinion* outlined by Bellarmine) is the one that is most commonly taught as the most probable by the majority of theologians and Doctors: St. Robert Bellarmine, St. Alphonsus de Liguori, Francisco Suárez,

Melchior Cano, Domingo Soto, John of St. Thomas, Juan de Torquemada, Louis Billot, Joachim Salaverri, A. Maria Vellico, Charles Journet, Cardinal Tommaso de Vio "Cajetan", Francesco Bordoni, Pedro de Simanca, Domingo Bañez, and Martino Bonacina – and Bonacina cites others who were of the same opinion. For roughly a century this nearly unanimous opinion has been the most common, even among those who admit only the hypothetical possibility of a pope falling from office due to public defection into heresy. Matthæus Conte a Coronata, who believed it to be actually possible for a pope to fall from office automatically due to heresy (the *fifth opinion* outlined by Bellarmine), is the rare exception among recent authors that comes into mind. Of the *Five Opinions* outlined by Bellarmine on the question of the deposition of a heretic pope, these two, the *first*, and the *fifth* considered merely as a hypothesis, are the only two opinions still held by prominent canonists and theologians.

The question of whether or not a particular claimant is a heretic, who therefore is an incapable subject of the papacy, would not be a hypothetical question, but a simple question of *fact* — a fact that can be determined with certitude. Hence, the false premise: *Only a future Pope or council presided over by a Pope could declare that a previous claimant to the papacy had fallen from any office he may have held due to heresy.* It would also be false to assert that *such a declaration that has never occurred in Church history*, because precisely such a declaration was made by the Council of Constance in the thirty-seventh session. Thus, Chris Ferrara's prescription for the present crisis in the papacy is essentially the Bouix prescription, according to which, if the putative pope falls into heresy, he presumably retains the pontificate, but the faithful must not remain passive, but should manifest the error to the pope so that he may be corrected, without, however, being able to declare him *depositus* or to be deposed *deponendus*. This opinion has been unanimously rejected for good reason by theologians for the last one and a half centuries. Firstly, the question as to whether a public heretic automatically loses any ecclesiastical office whatsoever is now a closed question, having been decided by the papal ordinary magisterium that such loss of office for public heresy does indeed take place (Canon 188. 4°), and such loss of whatsoever offices has been infallibly prescribed as a disciplinary norm of the universal Church. Thus, it follows by strict logical implication from this rule of universal discipline that since the papacy is an *office*, a public heretic loses the papal office automatically by the very fact of his manifest heresy, without any deposition or declaration by the Church. Secondly, since all public heretics lose office *ipso facto* before any judgment or deposition, if the members of the universal Church were to remain subject to a false pope, that fact alone would constitute a defection of the Church from her divine constitution, which accordingly is defined in *Pastor Æternus* to be constituted as **"one flock under one supreme shepherd"**. Hence, it would be impossible for a future pope to declare that his predecessor had in fact fallen from office while the whole Church remained subject to him during the wait for a definitive ruling by a future pope, because the Church, having thereby defected, would then no longer exist, and accordingly a future pope could never exist either. Thirdly, the opinion supposes as a premise that God would not provide any remedy for the Church during such an extreme and maximum state of necessity that would exist if a pope were to fall into manifest heresy. Suárez explains, *"natural reason teaches thus; for it is not credible that Christ left the Church destitute of any remedy for so great a peril"*.[203] «Melchior Canus says: "Inasmuch as God promised firmness of faith to the Church, He cannot be wanting to it, so as not to bestow upon the Church prayers and other helps whereby that firmness is preserved. Nor can it be doubted that what happens in natural things, the same occurs in supernatural; namely, that he who gives the end gives the means to the end."[204]»[205]

Bordoni argues similarly, explaining that since God does not fail to provide for his Church in necessity, therefore, in virtue of his words, "I am with you all days even until the end of the world," the Lord would not fail to provide the Church with all that is necessary; and thus, by His authority which was conferred not only on Peter the head but on all the apostles, when it is necessary, and which is of maximum necessity in such cases as a heretic pope or an uncertain pope, the Church would be in a most dire state if it would not have a remedy, by which it could come into knowledge of its true spouse and head; or if it had no means to acquire a true and legitimate superior, having deposed the adulterers and

---

[203] «rationem naturalem ita docere, quia non est credendum Christum destituisse Ecclesiam omni remedio in tanto periculo; quod vero adduxi maxime accommodatum apparet causæ de qua disputamus» — Suarez, *Op. cit.* p. 318.

[204] «Cum Ecclesiæ fidei firmitatem fuerit pollicitus, deesse non potest quominus tribuat Ecclesiæ preces, cæteraque præsidia, quibus hæc firmitas conservatur. Nec vero dubitari potest, quod in rebus naturalibus contingit, idem in supernaturalibus usu venire; ut qui dat finem, det consequentia ad finem. — Melchior Canus, *De Locis Theol.*, lib. v. cap. 5, pp. 120, 131, Venice, 1776.»

[205] Cardinal Manning, *The Vatican Council and its Definitions*, p. 115.

intruders. Therefore, in virtue of Christ's promise, God cannot fail to provide a remedy.[206] Although for Bordoni, the remedy would consist in the judgment and deposition pronounced by a general council exercising jurisdiction over the pope, he made note of the fact that this opinion was not admitted by all, but that the doctors, although they all agreed that a heretical or schismatic pope could be deposed, they differed according to which means would be employed, and by what power he could be deposed, since all Catholics are in agreement that a pope is above a council and not the council above the pope.[207] Bordoni outlines four opinions on how a schismatic or heretical pope would be deposed, 1) *ipso iure* by divine law, 2) The pope pronouncing sentence upon himself, 3) Cajetan's opinion, and 4) "The pope can be deposed in cases of heresy and schism by the legitimate authority of a general council received immediately from God precisely in order to carry out the deposition, by which authority and power the council is said to be over the pope."[208] His classification of the four opinions do not correspond exactly to the Bellarmine's classification, yet there is a complete correlation between the two, which merits to be explicated, but that is outside of the scope of this work. After examining the first three opinions, arguing precisely but not always correctly, Bordoni then states his own opinion on the question, which is the fourth. After the

---

[206] Bordoni, *Op. cit.*, p. 151: «Tum quia, Deus in necesarijs non deeft Eccleſiæ ſuæ, cum dixerit per Matth. extremis verbis. Ecce ego vobiſcum sum omnibus diebus uſque ad conſumationem ſæculi... quæ neceſſitas maximè accidit in his duobus caſibus de Pontifice hæretico, & incerto, cum enim caput dolet, eius membra languent & tabeſcunt, ac valde infelix effet Eccleſia, ſi nullum haberet remedium, per quod poſſet venire in cognitionem veri ſponſi, & capitis ſui, aut ſi nullum haberet medium, quo ſibi acquirere poſſet verum, & legitimum ſuperiorem, depoſitis adulteris, & intruſis.»

[207] *Ibid.,* p. 152: «Notandum autem eſt, quod id non ab omnibus admittitur, ſed doctores, quamuis in eo conueniant, quod Papa hæreticus, & in ſchiſmate deponi poſſit, diſcrepant tamen in modo, & poteſtate deponendi illum, quia apud omnes catholicos conſtat, Papam eſſe ſupra concilium non Concilium ſupra Papam, & ideo varii ſunt modi dicendi.»

[208] 1) ipso iure divino esse depositum 2) Papam per seipsum ferret sententiam contra se 3) Tertius est Caietani 4) Quartus igitur modus asserit, Papam depone posse in casibus hæresis, & Schismatis per Concilium Generale auctoritate legitima immediate recepta a Deo præcise ad hunc effectum depositionis, per quam auctoritatem, & potestatem Concilium dicitur esse supra Papam. [cf. *Ibid.,* pp. 153-157]

condemnation of Conciliarism by the Fifth Lateran Council this fourth opinion was completely abandoned, and for that reason, Bellarmine did not even consider refuting it, but focusd on Cajetan's argument as representing the fourth of five opinions according to his classification. What is particularly noteworthy is that while rightly rejecting the Third Opinion outlined by Bellarmine, and wrongly rejecting Bellarmine's Fifth Opinion; and since Bellarmine had already refuted Cajetan's opinion (Bellarmine's Fourth), and he himself refuted it even more comprehensively – Bordoni had no option left but to adopt the Conciliarist argument, modifying it to a mitigated form of Conciliarism in what would eventually prove to be a futile effort to circumvent the definitions of the Fifth Lateran Council. Nevertheless, what is crucial to this discussion is that the opinion has been virtually unanimous among theologians and canonists that divine law has provided the Church with a remedy by which a heretical claimant to the papal throne can be removed from that throne he usurps. Cajetan, Suárez, John of St.Thomas, Laymann, Billuart, Bordoni and Bañez were among the principal representatives of the opinion which held that a heretic pope would lose office only after being judged by he Church. Bellarmine, Ballerini, Gregory XVI, Louis Billot, and Wernz were of the opposite persuasion, teaching that a manifest heretic pope would lose office automatically by himself by the very fact alone of his public heresy – but they all agreed that the Church possesses the authority and jurisdiction to remove a heretical usurper.

As outlined earlier, St. Alphonsus, Ballerini, and Pope Gregory XVI, held that it would only be when the Apostolic See is judged to be vacant that a general council could be legitimately convened and act with authority to resolve a situation of multiple uncertain popes, or to depose a heretical intruder; yet Ballerini and Gregory XVI subscribed to an even simpler remedy. Ballerini, quoted below in In Section II of Chapter IX of his above cited work devoted that entire section to the question of the remedy to be applied in the case of a pope's heresy against the faith, in which he recommends "a quicker and easier remedy" than a general council.[209] Gregory XVI explicitly endorsed Ballerini's opinion. Sydney Smith SJ (quoted below) testified in 1895 that by the late nineteenth century, Ballerini's opinion on a remedy for papal heresy had become the common opinion, namely, that a manifestly heretical pope would cease automatically to be pope, and that the Cardinals would only need

---

[209] Ballerini, *Op. cit., Cap. IX § II. De remedio in casu hæresis circa fidem*, pp. 128-9.

to issue a declaratory sentence on the one who had fallen from office. Since the First Vatican Council's definition of the Primacy of the Roman Pontiff, the Church's universal disciplinary norms expressed in the Code of Canon Law have explicitly taught that a council can only exist under the absolute power of the pope, and cannot exist at all during the period of *sede vacante*. Consequently, the very existence *in actu* of an "imperfect council" is an absolute impossibility.

On the other hand, St. Robert Bellarmine's teaching, taken from the Council of Constance, according to which all officeholder's who fall into manifest heresy or schism automatically lose office for public heresy, has been incorporated into the universal legislation of the Church; and although there exists no specified mechanism in canon law for dealing with the removal of a heretic pope, there already exists a unanimous opinion of canonists which prescribes a remedy for such an eventuality. It is precisely that unanimous *sententia* which Mr. Ferrara rejects. It is to no avail that Ferrara appeals to the "eminently simple explanation" of Fr. John Hunwicke, according to which:

> «a Pope like Francis, whose "leadership has become a danger to the faith" as even a "moderate" like Philip Lawler observes, can really *be* the Pope. The answer lies in what Cardinal Newman described as "the suspense of the functions of the Magisterium" during the Arian crisis, when it seemed almost the entire Church had embraced the Arian heresy. [...] Fr. Hunwicke argues, that the Petrine Ministry had "entered into its current 'temporary suspense'" and that "we are officially in a period in which the functions of the Papal Magisterium are in a *vacatio* which will be ended at the moment when the same Petrine Magisterial organ formally returns from dogmatic silence to the audible exercise of the functions rightly attributed to it in Catholic Tradition..." But Fr. Hunwicke does *not* say that Francis has lost his office. He says, rather, that Francis and the bishops who are failing to defend the truths of revelation in the current ecclesial crisis have abandoned the duties and limitations of their office and are essentially doing something other than what they are divinely authorized to do: "I do not, of course, in any way suggest that [Francis] and the silent or heterodox bishops have *lost* the right or capacity to use the Magisterium of his and their offices. On the contrary. Precisely as Newman did, I am simply observing that, as a matter of fact, he is not and they are not at this moment using it."»

The fatal defect in the argument consists in the failure to distinguish between *manifestly formal heretics* on the one hand and *merely suspected heretics* on the other, which is accordingly determined by properly evaluating and applying the *indicia* of heresy to each case. Canonical tradition as well as the 1917 Code of Canon Law distinguish precisely between these two categories, which are briefly outlined in Part I of this work, following the precise exposition on them by Francesco Bordoni in the ninth and tenth chapters of his above cited work. Those bishops who were infected with the Arian contagion, like those infected with the errors of Protestantism and Modernism, cannot be judged to have lost office merely for having manifested *indicia* of heresy which would render them *suspect of heresy*. Any officeholder whosoever who plainly manifests the *indicia* of *formal heresy* in a manner that would qualify the heresy canonically as *public*, loses any office he holds *ipso jure* without any judgment pronounced by the Church. This is so plainly spelled out in the post 1917 legislation, and explicitly elaborated in the most authoritative commentaries, that it is difficult to comprehend how anyone can still follow the antiquated theories of canonists who argued the point in a contrary sense, and who deduced their judgments from premises drawn from abrogated previous legislation no longer in force for more than a century.

Thus, Chris Ferrara follows the universally abandoned opinion of a lone nineteenth century canonist, Marie Dominique Bouix – an opinion which plainly manifests a lack of juridical sense. Hence, it is instructive to consider the judgment of history which the *Catholic Encyclopedia* pronounced on Fr. Bouix:

> As to his reputation as a canonist, while all must acknowledge his wonderful productivity and his high purpose, and while he has been justly called the restorer of the science of canon law in France, it must nevertheless be said that he falls short of being a great canonist; he is too often compiler rather than a genuine author, and he too frequently betrays a lack of that juridical sense which comes more from practice than from theory, and which begets the ability to pronounce justly on the lawfulness and unlawfulness of existing practices. However, the value of his works cannot be questioned, and is proved by the general favour which they still enjoy.

Also at the opposite extreme to the error that a pope can be judged by his subjects, is the opinion that any man who is uncritically accepted by the general public as pope, is therefore to be considered a valid pope who is incapable of falling into formal heresy. This is an accurate description of the opinion of Emmett O'Regan, who believes that Jorge "Francis" Bergoglio is the valid occupant of the Chair of Peter, and being the pope of Rome, is incapable of being a heretic. In his article, *The Heretical Pope Fallacy*, he manifests his bias in the opening sentence, saying, "One of the most prevalent themes currently being circulated in some extreme quarters of Catholicism revolves around the manner in which a heretical pope could be removed from the papacy." So, for Mr. O'Regan, anyone who would even think of removing a Modernist heretical intruder from the throne of Peter is to be considered an extremist. O'Regan attributes the interest in the question to "the belief that either Pope Francis has already committed heresy at various points throughout the Apostolic Exhortation *Amoris Laetitia*, or that he has been openly promoting an heretical interpretation of this document". He then offers the observation that, "One area which has been greatly neglected in this debate is whether or not a pope actually can fall into formal heresy or teach false doctrines by way of the authentic papal Magisterium."

I demonstrate in this volume that the proposition, that "a pope actually can fall into formal heresy", is *proximate to heresy*, but it is not *de fide*; and the first Vatican Council, as the *Gasser Relatio* states quite unequivocally, did not intend to define on this point. On the other hand, the proposition that a pope can "teach false doctrines by way of the authentic papal Magisterium", has always been generally accepted by theologians, even by Don Pietro Ballerini; and even after the definition on papal infallibility by the First Vatican Council, not only theologians, but even documents of the supreme magisterium admit that pronouncements of the authentic papal magisterium are not infallible, such as *Lumen Gentium 25*, which distinguishes between *ex cathedra* pronouncements which are infallible, and "the authentic magisterium of the Roman Pontiff, even when he is not speaking ex cathedra" – which is not infallible. With this consideration in mind, we can already dismiss as erroneous Mr. O'Regan's somewhat imprecisely formulated statement that, "As we shall see, according to the Fathers of the First Vatican Council, the idea of an heretical pope was definitively ruled out through the formal dogmatization of St. Robert Bellarmine's ideas on the indefectibility of the Church." The First Vatican Council did no such thing: It did not formally dogmatize Bellarmine's "ideas on the indefectibility of the Church" – but only dogmatized his *fourth opinion*: «Quarta sententia est quodammodo in medio. Pontificem, sive haereticus esse possit, sive non, non posse ullo modo definire aliquid haereticum a tota Ecclesia credendum: haec est communissima opinio fere omnium Catholicorum». According to this opinion, the pope, *regardless of whether or not he can be a heretic*, cannot in any manner define something heretical for the whole Church to believe – and this opinion, says the Holy Doctor, is the most common opinion among all Catholics. This proposition concerns only the solemn *ex cathedra* definitions of the papal extraordinary magisterium, but does not extend to the pronouncements of the authentic papal magisterium, which is non-infallible. The pope's pronouncements made when exercising his authentic magisterium in the sense that this term is used in canon 752, can contain errors, and therefore do not require an absolute assent. This point is discussed in Part III of this volume, in my exposition on Bellarmine's refutation of the second opinion on the deposition of a heretical pope.

O'Regan's observation, "According to the Official Relatio of Vatican I, which was issued in an address to the Council Fathers by Bishop Vincent Ferrer Gasser on 11th July, 1870... the debate concerning the possibility of an heretical pope was about to be definitively settled through the proposed dogmatization of St. Robert Bellarmine's incisive exposition of the doctrine of the indefectibility of the Church," is entirely erroneous. It was precisely this point which the council deliberately avoided. I have given ample treatment to this point in this volume. O'Regan goes on to say that "St. Bellarmine then goes on to list a total of four propositions outlining why the fourth opinion outlined above should be considered certain and positively asserted." The first proposition says, "The pope can never err when he teaches to the whole Church (by way of the authentic Magisterium) in matters pertaining to faith." Note that it is Emmett O'Regan, and not Robert Bellarmine, who characterizes this proposition as referring to the pope's authentic magisterium. Bellarmine is not referring to the pope's authentic magisterium in the cited passage. His language is almost maddeningly imprecise when considered according the standards of usage four centuries after his death – after two more ecumenical councils taught with precision on infallible and ordinary magisterium. Nevertheless, his meaning can be gleaned from his usage. In this proposition under consideration, he is speaking expressly on papal infallibility: "*Statuitur prima propositio de infallibili judicio summi Pontificis*"; and then states the first proposition: "*Summus Pontifex cum totam Ecclesiam docet, in his quæ ad Fidem pertinent nullo casu errare potest. Hæc est contra primam et secundam opinionem pro quarta; et probatur...*" He says this proposition, (which says nothing explicit about definitions), favours the fourth proposition, which speaks expressly of *definitions*. In treating on the second opinion,[210] which is that of Adrian VI, he specifically interprets it to refer to definitions (Pontificem ut Pontificem, posse esse haereticum, & docere haeresim, si absque generali Concilio definiat) – but the actual text of Adrian VI, while clearly intending the sense of definitive magisterial pronouncements, does not explicitly refer to definitions: *"Ad secundum principale de facto Gregorii, dico primo quod si per Ecclesiam Romanam intelligatur caput ejus, puta Pontifex, Certum est quod possit errare, etiam in his, quae tangent fidem, haeresim per suam determinationem aut Decretalem asserendo"* – yet Bellarmine clearly understands this to be Adrian's meaning; and likewise, in his above cited *prima propositio*, he does not employ the term "definition", but his intention to properly denote definitions in the expression, *"Summus Pontifex cum totam Ecclesiam docet"*, is plain enough according to the usage of his day, so that the proposition can be clearly understood to refer to *ex cathedra* definitions, and not the less solemn pronouncements of the authentic magisterium. However, in the last analysis, since *Pastor Æternus* dogmatized Bellarmine's *quarta sententia* (which speaks explicitly of definitions) using its own formula, and not that of Bellarmine; and since it did not dogmatize Bellarmine's *prima propositio* which makes no explicit mention of definitions; it is utterly futile that Mr. O'Regan attempts to extend the infallibility of the definitions of the extraordinary papal magisterium to the pronouncements of the authentic papal magisterium; and to even attempt to extend the dogma of infallibility to exclude that the pope can personally be a formal heretic. Like Mr. O'Regan, I also am in agreement with St. Robert Bellarmine that the Roman Pontiff cannot be a formal heretic. In his day, Bellarmine could only go so far as to say that his opinion on that point was "probable", and that it can easily be proven. I have argued in Part III, proving that Bellarmine's opinion on the question, since Vatican I, is more than just *probable*, but in fact is *proxima fidei*. However, from this conclusion of speculative theology, one cannot legitimately leap to the conclusion that O'Regan has fallaciously drawn from this premise; namely, that "concern over whether or not Pope

---

[210] «Secunda sententia est, Pontificem ut Pontificem, posse esse hæreticum, & docere hæresim, si absque generali Concilio definiat, & de facto aliquando accidisse. Hanc opinionem sequitur, & tuetur Nilus in suo libro adversus primatum papæ: [...] & Hadrianus VI. Papa in quæst. de confirm.; qui omnes non in Pontifice, sed in Ecclesia sive in Concilio generali tantum, constituunt infallibillitatem iudicii de rebus Fidei.»

Francis is forcing Catholics to submit their will and intellect to an heretical teaching, or has himself lapsed into heresy by extending this teaching to the level of authentic Magisterium, is somewhat misplaced, and potentially extremely harmful to the Faith"; because regardless of whether or not "some of the key issues concerning the nature of the papacy that we can see presently rising to the fore were already definitively settled during the First Vatican Council", the *fact* still remains that Jorge "Francis" Bergoglio has introduced heresy into the teaching of his (supposed) authentic magisterium, et *contra hoc factum non potest esse argumentum*. He has clearly and most certainly demonstrated himself to be a manifest formal heretic, and therefore he cannot be a true and valid pope, because **a manifest heretic cannot be pope; and therefore, the fact that Francis is a manifest heretic proves that he is not a valid pope.** Furthermore, even if Bergoglio were a valid pope, the pronouncements made by a pope exercising his *authentic magisterium* are not infallible; and, as I demonstrate in this volume, quoting the commonly held teaching set forth in approved works of Moral Theology: the obligation to give an *obsequium religiosum* to pronouncements of the pope's authentic magisterium is not absolutely binding.

Bergoglio's recent statement in the joint document he signed in Dubai simply underscores the fact that he is not a Catholic. "*The pluralism and the diversity of religions,*" he says, "*are willed by God in His wisdom*". This is a direct and immediate assertion of explicit heresy, yet some Catholic writers are desperately attempting to interpret it according to a non-heretical meaning. In a comment which appeared on Life-Site, an understandably anonymous Dominican theologian commented on such attempts to put an orthodox spin on Bergoglio's heresy. The Dominican stated bluntly that it, "in its obvious sense is false, and in fact heretical." He then elaborated, "God permits non-Catholic religions to exist; but permitting something is not a way of willing it, it is a way of not willing to prevent it. Thus God permits many innocent people to be killed, but He does not will it." The interpretational attempt to exculpate Bergoglio from the charge of heresy he called, "a strained and unnatural interpretation." There is a failure on the part of those who attempt to exculpate the Petrine pretender in this manner, to view Bergoglo's heretical propositions in their proper context, which is within the framework of his faithless belief system. If there is any article of faith that he does in fact believe, such as, "He suffered under Pontius Pilate," he believes wih something other that the virtue of faith. I have elaborated somewhat theologically on his belief system in the *Introduction*. My overall sentiments on this matter are better expressed by philosopher Flavio Cuniberto[211] than I could express them myself. To the question, «You write that the *Evangelii Gaudium* and the *Laudato sì* seem "a revolutionary program in the most Jacobin sense of the word: a post-Christian diptych." Do we have a triptych with *Amoris Laetitia*?» he replies:

> «Of course, with *Amoris Laetitia* We have a Jacobin triptych that subverts the old order to open a new era. We could introduce a new calendar: We are in the fourth year of the Bergoglio Era. [...] he behaves as if he were (a Catholic), but he is not; for reasons that can not be summarized in a short interview. The hammer blows that have led to some key points of Catholic doctrine are such that there is no point in talking about updating: it is a real demolition».

Commenting further on the destructive Jacobin character of the Bergoglian revolution, he elaborated: «The revolutionary element is not so much the Marxist ideology but the subversion of the traditional constraints (the natural family for example), the disappearance of the concept of sin and a background materialism, corrected in the pantheistic sense.» His conclusion on *Amoris Lætitia* echoes my own conclusion expressed in the *Introduction* on the Bergoglian belief system:

> «The page of the encyclical has something of the incredible... The experience of the divine is totally ignored in papal documents (it is not enough to cite the canonical sources here and there: This is protocolled routine). I see, to be honest, a creeping atheism, which arrives at the top of the hierarchy. The Pope's speech in Krakow was, in this sense, exemplary. **I would not hesitate to call it the speech of an atheist Pope.**» (emphasis added)

While Emmett O'Regan's presumably honest opinions on papal heresy are merely the result of logically defective reasoning; the same cannot be said of John Salza and Robert Siscoe; whose idolatrous worship of falsehood has rendered them blind to the truth. Indeed, the words with which St. Paul, filled with the Holy Ghost, pronounced the sentence of blindness on Elymas the magician would most aptly apply to either of them: «O full of all guile, and of all deceit, child of the devil, enemy of all justice, thou ceasest not to pervert the right ways of the Lord. And now behold, the hand of the Lord is upon thee, and thou shalt

---

[211] http://m.ilgiornale.it/news/2016/09/27/dio-non-e-cattolico-ma-forse-neppure-papa-francesco-lo-e/1311339/.

be blind» (Acts 13: 10 – 11) Salza & Siscoe are blindly entrenched in heresy, and in their blindness, seek to turn others against the faith: By deceitful sophistry, fraudulent doctoring of texts to distort, falsify, or invert their meaning; and even outright fabrication of bogus quotations, they heretically defend the thesis that a manifest heretic pope would, even as a manifest heretic remain a member of the Church, and remain in office until judged guilty by the Church (and they fraudulently argue that such a heretic pope would not actually be a manifest heretic until so judged by a public judgment of the Church, or unless he were to formally renounce the magisterial authority of the Church or explicitly admit his adherence to heresy); and they heretically maintain that the Church possesses the authority to juridically pass judgment on such a reigning Pontiff for the delict of heresy. They attempt to prove "infallibly"[212] that the manifestly heretical, Jorge Mario "Francis" Bergoglio, who publicly rejects some of the most basic and universally known dogmas of the Catholic faith, was nevertheless validly elected to the supreme pontificate; and that Bergoglio is and remains the true pope of the Catholic Church, and will remain in office as the true pope of the Catholic Church, no matter how explicitly he contradicts, expressly denies, and openly rejects the foundational principles and beliefs of Catholicism, unless he will have been judged guilty of heresy by the authority of the Church. Even if he will have openly rejected the Church as such, or have explicitly acknowledged his heresy, then perhaps, according to Salza & Siscoe, he could arguably fall from office *ipso facto*; since, according to Salza & Siscoe, it is only by heresy that is canonically *notorious by fact* (according to their own very bizarre understanding of the term), in virtue of an explicit renunciation of the Church as the rule of faith, an explicit admission of heresy, or a formal defection from the Church, that a pope would automatically be separated from the body of the Church by his heresy without first being judged guilty for the crime of heresy by the competent ecclesiastical authority. However, even then, it is still not entirely clear if, according to Salza & Siscoe, that would suffice to effect an *ipso jure* loss of office, because they equivocate on this point by maintaining that the juridical bond remains until a sentence or a *declaration of deprivation* is pronounced, so that even a public heretic would remain in office as pope until a public judgment is pronounced

---

[212] In his intellectual buffoonery, Robert J. Siscoe actually made the claim that he would "prove infallibly" that Jorge Bergoglio is the true pope of the Catholic Church.

by the Church, no matter how public or notorious by fact his heresy might be. It is by means of this kind of contradictory equivocation that Salza & Siscoe "qualify" their statements – seemingly holding at times to two mutually opposed opinions; so that whenever someone points out the error of their opinion, they scream that they have qualified their statements, and have been misrepresented and calumniated in the refutation of their position. This is exactly the *modus operandi* they employed in their *Formal Reply* to me. When they accused Dr. Peter Chojnowski of misrepresenting their position, Dr. Chojnowski asked them to plainly state their position, but this they refused to do. Dr. Chojnowski, (who holds a Ph.D. in Philosophy), being thoroughly exasperated by their evasive tactics wrote to me saying, "I have failed utterly in my attempt to have Salza and Siscoe clarify exactly what they mean with regard to their innumerable distinctions or how these distinctions apply to the real world. [...] I feel like I have stepped into the quicksand of Sophistry. [...] I however believe that I have correctly summarized their argument on my blog." On his blogsite, Dr. Chojnowski wrote

> «Sorry dear readers I have been absolutely unable to get Salza and Siscoe to clarify their position and indicate how it is exactly applicable to the current situation in the Church. When I asked Atty. Salza to answer a few basic questions with a simple yes or no answer --- using their own terminology --- all that I received back were further questions DIRECTED TOWARDS ME!»

Indeed, on innumerable occasions when Salza & Siscoe have been pressed to give a straight answer, they invariably resort to the evasive reply, "Read our book." However, when one reads their book, it becomes clear to the discerning reader that in their book, Salza & Siscoe have constructed a maze of irresolvable contradictions, and do not theologically elaborate an unequivocal and logically coherent position of their own on the questions of defection from the faith and loss of office for heresy; except that according to them, even a manifest heretic pope does not lose office without the public judgment of the Church. Their position is further obfuscated by their formulation of an unclear and self-contradictory notion of what constitutes a public judgment of the Church. Ultimately, what they say on exclusion from the Church and loss of office for heresy in their big 700-page volume is so self-contradictory that it evaporates into mere vapours of nothingness; and can only be likened to a large hall filled with smoke and mirrors in which there is nothing of substance to be found. Indeed, what conclusion can be drawn from their book, in which they say on the one hand (p. 260), that "The loss of office for a cleric is a vindictive penalty, and there is a process in Church law which must precede vindictive penalties", and in their *Formal Reply* they quote Benedict XIV, "a sentence declaratory of the offence is always necessary in the external forum"; and on the other hand they say, "a reigning Pope will not lose his office before the Church has established the crime, and most probably not before the Church issues a declaratory sentence. However, we do concede that if a Pope were to openly and publicly *leave the Church* of his own will, as opposed to simply professing heresy, a case could be made that God would sever the bond that united the man to the pontificate at the moment his public defection was acknowledged by the Church, even without a declaratory sentence of the crime (for example, if the Pope publicly declared he was no longer Catholic and then joined and became a pastor of the Lutheran sect)." (pp. 280-281) So, Salza & Siscoe «do concede... that if a Pope were to openly and publicly *leave the Church* of his own will, as opposed to simply professing heresy, **a case could be made** that God would sever the bond that united the man to the pontificate at the moment his public defection was acknowledged by the Church, **even without a declaratory sentence of the crime**» – but, as I have pointed out, the canonical doctrine of the Church teaches categorically that the loss of **"whatsoever offices"** takes place, not only by formal defection from the Church, but by **public defection from the faith,** i.e. by *simply professing manifestly formal heresy,* **"without any declaration".** St. Robert Bellarmine formulated in theological terms the doctrine on which this canonical provision is based, explaining why it is impossible for a non-Catholic to be pope: "A non-Christian cannot in any way be Pope, as Cajetan affirms in the same book, and the reason is because he cannot be the head of that which he is not a member, and he is not a member of the Church who is not a Christian. But a manifest heretic is not a Christian, as St. Cyprian and many other Fathers clearly teach. Therefore, a manifest heretic cannot be Pope." (*De Romano Pontifice lib. ii cap. xxx*)

In one of his replies to an earlier preliminary draft of this book, Salza wrote to me, "Keep the comedy hour going, Kramer, please... [Salza (incredibly) thinks my writings on this topic are comically silly!]... you repeatedly falsify our position in the face of countless corrections. For example, you continue to accuse us of holding that only the crime of heresy severs one from the Body, but in our book we QUALIFY that statement over and over again..." I have more than adequately documented in this volume that Salza & Siscoe state repeatedly, and in a categorical and unqualified manner, that *"only the crime of heresy"* separates one from the body of the Church; and that external heresy is a crime in its very nature, and that the *crime* of heresy must be public and notorious for that separation to take place without a judgment by Church authority – and then they contradict themselves elsewhere (for example, stating that even material heretics who are not subjectively guilty, [and therefore have not committed a crime because the act is not morally imputable], but who inculpably separate themselves from the Church, sever the juridical bond by themselves); and then they flip-flop again, insisting that a penal sentence of excommunication must be pronounced in order to sever the juridical bond; and that a *declaration of deprivation* or at least some form of public judgment of the Church would be necessary for the severing to take place, and for loss of office to occur, which they falsely assert to be a *vindictive penalty*. In his article, *John Salza Responds to Another Sedevacantist*, Salza states categorically that, «Canon Law requires the heresy to be public and notorious, and the determination must be made by the Church.» After stating that the determination must be made by the Church, Salza then contradicts himself, saying, «heresy includes everything from the internal sin alone, to the public crime of notorious heresy – and only the latter automatically severs a person from external union with the Church "without a declaration."» After stating flatly that *only the crime of heresy* "automatically severs a person from external union with the Church", Salza then inveighs against me: «you continue to accuse us of holding that only the crime of heresy severs one from the Body [of the Church]» Salza then seemingly reverses himself and writes to me, «In our book and articles, we also explicitly say that public (notorious) heresy severs one from the Body WITHOUT regard to "law or precept."» Public heresy considered without regard to law or precept is heresy considered formally as a *sin*, and not as a *crime*. Salza fails to see the contradiction in his own position saying on the one hand, that not the *sin of heresy*, but only the *crime of heresy* notorious by fact automatically severs one from the body of the Church; and then he says that public and notorious heresy automatically «severs one from the Body without regard to "law or precept."» Indeed, if heresy severs one from the body of the Church *without regard to law or precept*, then it does so *by its very nature as a sin*, and not because it is a crime; since there is no crime in ecclesiastical law without the violation of a *law or precept* to which is added a *penal sanction*. Salza & Siscoe then resort to the patently absurd claim that *heresy is intrinsically a crime in its very nature*; and on this basis they claim, «We never said it was based on "penal law" and always said it was the nature of the act.» ... «AND THAT MEANS SUCH HERESY DOESN'T NEED TO BE LISTED AS A CRIME IN CANON LAW TO SEVER ONE FROM THE BODY OF THE CHURCH (although it is listed as a crime). And yet that is what you falsely accuse us of holding.» Salza & Siscoe fail to grasp, that if it is not "listed as a crime", and is therefore not enumerated in ecclesiastical law as *"an external violation of a law or precept to which is added a penal sanction"*; then it is simply not a crime, but only a *sin*. Yet it is Salza's contention that «Again, Pope Pius XII is referring to the "offense" or CRIME (not SIN) of heresy, which severs one from the Body of the Church, after the formal and material elements have been proven by the Church. After the crime has been established, the heretic is automatically severed from the BODY (not SOUL) of the Church without further declaration (although most theologians maintain that the Church must also issue a declaration of deprivation)».[213] The clueless Salza also fails to grasp the inherent contradiction in a notion of crime *notorious by fact* which professes that a public crime, obvious to the mind and sight, is not to be considered notorious until the determination of notoriety is made by the official judgment of the Church – a self-contradictory notion, since then, the notorious crime would then not be *notorious by fact*, but would *de jure* notorious! It is by their fanatical and fundamentalistic *legalism* that Salza & Siscoe have fallen into a strange form of nominalism which denies that public formal heresy in an individual can be known unless that individual be convicted of the *penal delict* of heresy by a competent tribunal, or at least be publicly judged by the Church in some other manner which they seem to be unable or unwilling to clearly specifiy. I have demonstrated with copious documentation in this volume, that for one to be visibly and juridically separated from the body of the Church due to formal heresy, the Church teaches that the fact of public defection into heresy alone causes that separation *jure divino*, and therefore ecclesiastical law accordingly recognizes the separation to take place *ipso jure;* **and for this reason a juridical act of judgment is not necessary for the juridical bond to be severed.** A declaratory sentence merely confers a juridical recognition on the *ipso jure* consequence brought about

---

[213] *John Salza Responds to Another Sedevacantist.*

by the fact of separation that takes place independently of the jurisdiction of the Church by the act of defection itself. Similarly, I have amply demonstrated in this volume that it is the unequivocal position of ecclesiastical law and Church doctrine, that manifest heresy can be seen and recognized without a judgment or declaratory sentence; and without any reference whatever to penal legislation. Therefore, since it is not a matter of penal law, the *administrative statutes* in the non-penal section of the Code of Canon Law require only that there be the recognizable *public fact of defection* from the faith into heresy, *apart from all considerations of penal law*, for the actual *ipso facto* loss of ecclesiastical office to occur *ipso jure*, **without any declaration by ecclesiastical authority**. With full knowledge and obstinate deliberation, Salza and Siscoe sweep aside the expositions of the most authoritative commentaries of the expert canonists on the question of *loss of office*, by passing over them in silence; and then they fraudulently explain *loss of* office by quoting the same commentaries' expositions on the canons of the *penal section of the Code* on *penal deprivation of office*, in order to deceive their readers into thinking that *loss of office* is a "severe vindictive penalty" – i.e., a *vindictive penalty*, which is **a punishment for a penal offense that cannot take place without a declaration of deprivation made by competent authority. The supreme magisterium of the universal Church teaches exactly the opposite: public defection from the faith into heresy effects the automatic loss of office** *"without any declaration"*.

Another error Salza & Siscoe make is their belief that "only notorious heretics are excluded from the body of the Church"; and hence, a pope's heresy would need to be *public and notorious*; and therefore, it would need to actually be widely known throughout the Church, for a pope to cease to be a member of the Church. In their article, RESPONSE TO FR. KRAMER'S ERROR ON 'NOTORIOUS BY FACT", they quote a passage of Fr. Dominique Boulet of the SSPX out of context: "For the criminality of a Pope's heresy to be legally recognized, such that his heresy would be canonically Notorious, not only would a knowledge of his heresy [the material aspect] have to have spread widely through the Church, as we have seen above, but it would also have to have been widely recognized as a morally imputable crime [the formal aspect]." For a pope's heresy to be legally recognized as a *public and notorious*, i.e. *notorious by fact,* it would indeed need to have been spread widely through the Church – but it would not need to be widely diffused for his heresy to be considered *public* according to ecclesiastical law. Such an opinion is based on an antiquated notion of *public delict* that was held by some canonists before the codification of Canon Law in the 1917 Code made it obsolete. The highly authoritative 1952 canon law commentary of the Faculty of Canon Law of the Pontifical University of Salamanca (which I quote on numerous occasions in this volume), explains on page 785, that in the legislation previous to the 1917 Code, there was not yet the clear and uniform concept of *public crime*.[214] From what is set forth in the text of the canon and in the expert commentary, it is clear that according to the specifications of the canon in question that for the crime to be considered public, knowledge of the heresy would not have to have actually be publicly known, but there would only need to be the proximate danger of it becoming known; and the proximate likelihood that it would be divulged, would not have to be the danger of a divulgation that would be diffused widely throughout the greater portion of the whole Church in order for it to be considered "public". As I demonstrate irrefutably in this volume, quoting the verbatim text of the canons, and the most authoritative commentaries on the canons; that for a crime to be *public*, it suffices that the knowledge of the crime be public or *likely to soon become public* (canon 2197. 1°, "*Delictum est publicum, si iam divulgatum est aut talibus contigit aut versatur in adiunctis ut prudenter iudicari possit et debeat facile divulgatum iri*"; and a crime is *notorious by fact* (canon 2197. 3°) if the knowledge of the fact of the crime and its imputability be, 1) public (*si publice notum sit*), and, 2) that the crime be committed under such circumstances that it cannot be concealed by any subterfuge, nor excused by any excuse admitted in laws (*in talibus adiunctis commissum, ut nulla tergiversatione celari nulloque iuris suffragio excusari possit*). Similarly, for the imputability to be *notorious*, I prove in this volume that Salza & Siscoe go far beyond the letter of the law, and what

---

[214] "En el derecho anterior al Código no era claro ni uniforme el concepto de *delito público*. Hoy la publicidad puede resultar de dos capítulos: o porque ya está divulgado el delito, o porque hay peligro próximo de divulgación. 1.° *Está ya divulgado* el delito, cuando una parte notable de la comunidad tiene conociemiento del *hecho* y de su carácter *delictivo*. Con la palabra «comunidad» pretendemos designar aquí no precisamente una sociedad perfecta, una diócesis, una religion o una ciudad; sino un núcleo de fieles que pueden más directamente experimentar daño del delito o de su divulgacion, v. gr., una parroquia o una casa religiosa. En qué proporción hayan de estar los que conocen el delito para que pueda decirse que «una parte notable de la comunidad» tiene conocimiento de él, no puede definirse taxativamente…" [Miguelez – Alonso – Cabreros; *Código de Derecho Canónico – Bilingüe y Comentado*; Madrid, 1952, p. 785.]

is explained in the authoritative commentaries, specifying gratuitously and arbitrarily their own highly restrictive conditions, which according to them, must be verified for the fact of the crime of heresy and its imputability to be qualified as *notorious by fact*.[215] For an ecclesiastical officeholder to be severed from the body of the Church and to lose office, it suffices that the *fact* of defection from the faith be *public*, and thus it suffices that the publicity of the act conforms to the same conditions specified for a public delict in canon 2197. 1°.[216]

Salza & Siscoe err further when they heretically assert, against the universal and ordinary magisterium of the Church, that "How a heretical bishop or Pope loses his office, and how heresy separates a Catholic from the Church, are two separates questions, and each question has different distinctions that apply". Simply stated, according to Salza & Siscoe the *crime* of notorious heresy (i.e. "notorious" gratuitously defined according to severe and arbitrarily formulated qualifying restrictions) severs one from the body of the Church *ipso facto*; but *loss of* office (according to them) is a *vindictive penalty* which must be canonically imposed by the Church. In their *Gloria TV* interview, they bluntly assert,"heresy does not directly cause a Pope to fall from the pontificate." On their website and in their book they declare, «The sin of heresy alone, which has not been judged and declared by the Church, does not result in the loss of ecclesiastical office for a cleric. The loss of

---

[215] Salza writes, "pertinacity is established only if the Pope were to renounce the Church as the RULE of faith by PUBLIC PROFESSION"; and again, he and Siscoe state, " ... if a Catholic leaves the Church and becomes a professed atheist, or publicly joins a Protestant or Sedevacantist sect, he thereby ceases to be a member of the Body of the Church by his own act, since public apostasy, heresy and schism do sever juridical bonds which are necessary for a Catholic to retain visible union with the Church." This is how Salza & Siscoe, against the clear teaching of the magisterium, restrictively define *public heresy*, *public and notorious heresy*, and *heresy notorious by fact* – i.e. as heresy qualified by these conditions.

[216] In their *Formal Reply*, Salza & Siscoe declare: "If the culprit's heresy is not deemed to be notorious by fact, however, he must be formally judged and declared a heretic by the Church (rendering him notorious by law) before he is legally separated from the Body of the Church." **The proposition is plainly opposed to the magisterium and the letter of canon law: It suffices that the defection into heresy be *public* for the juridical bond to be visibly severed, and for the loss of office to take place *ipso jure*.** (Canon 194 § 2; Canon 188. 4°)

office for a cleric is a vindictive penalty, and there is a process in Church law which must precede vindictive penalties... This also means that the loss of office for a cleric must be imposed (ferendae sententiae) by Church authority which makes the loss of office a "vindictive penalty."»[217] Refuting all of those who held that loss of office takes place as a penalty for having violated ecclesiastical laws, St Robert Bellarmine in Book II Chapter XXX of *De Romano Pontifice* cites Aquinas, saying, **"St. Thomas teaches that schismatics *straightaway* loose all jurisdiction"**; and cites the unanimous teaching of the Fathers: **"Nor does the response which some make avail, that these Fathers speak according to ancient laws**, but now since the decree of the Council of Constance they do not lose jurisdiction, unless excommunicated by name, or if they strike clerics. I say this avails to nothing. For those Fathers, when they say that heretics lose jurisdiction, do not allege any human laws which maybe did not exist then on this matter; rather, they argued *from the nature of heresy*...** Yet heretics are outside the Church, even before excommunication, and deprived of all jurisdiction, for they are condemned by their own judgment, as the Apostle teaches to Titus; that is, they are cut from the body of the Church without excommunication, as Jerome expresses it." Thus it is patent that the opinion of Salza & Siscoe on loss of office for heresy is itself heretical, as it directly opposes the unanimous teaching of the Fathers, and the *canonical doctrine* on loss of office expressed and set forth by the *supreme magisterium* exercised by Benedict XV and John Paul II respectively in their promulgation of the 1917 and 1983 *Code of Canon Law* – which besides containing mere legislation, is also an important organ of the ordinary magisterium regarding the canonical doctrine of the Church.

As I mentioned in the Introduction to this work, I have included an entire chapter that exposes the sophistry and outright fraud in the writings of John Salza and Robert Siscoe. I have judged it necessary to devote an entire volume to expose and refute their errors, because these long discredited errors have been exhumed by Salza & Siscoe, and propagated by them with a consummate sophistry that masterfully employs the artifices of specious equivocation, deceptively conferring on them the appearance of truth. Indeed, these heretical opinions of theirs, which I already heard in the 1970s being spouted by neophytes in the study of theology and canon law, but which were summarily dismissed

---

[217] Cf. *True or False Pope – Refuting Sedevacantism and other Modern Errors*, p. 260.

by the professors of theology and canon law, have been revived and are now gaining popularity even among those who ought to know better. I have corresponded with Salza & Siscoe. I sent them copies of my earlier articles on the question of papal heresy, loss of office, and defection from the faith. Those articles, which presented in embryonic form the systematic arguments I present in this volume, have not moved Salza or Siscoe to reconsider their position, nor convinced them to retract their errors. They have responded with malice and hostility. They remain entrenched in heresy as enthusiastic partisans of the *operation of error*, and hardened in their blind adherence to false doctrine to the extent that their fanatical devotion to falsehood has distinguished them quintessentially as *The People of the Lie*.[218] Yet, though they are blind, they claim to see – so their sin remains (John 9:41) – and because their sin remains; they, with a fanatical zeal apply themselves to the accursed and futile work of their infernal masters, of *"the principalities and powers"*, of *"the rulers of the darkness of this world"* (Ephesians 6:12) – which is: **TO DECEIVE THE ELECT.** (Matthew 24:24) Therefore, in addition to this volume, two more volumes – a total of three volumes will be necessary to uphold and defend the Catholic faithful against the *"the dangers threatening the faith and the life of the Christian"*.

Vol. 1 – Provides the doctrinal basis for the Church to resolve the two-pope crisis by declaring Bergoglio to be a heretic who is therefore incapable of being validly elected, of validly assuming the papal *munus* or holding the papal office; and hence, to not validly hold the Petrine office. The opinion that the Church must presume Bergoglio to validly hold the Petrine office, and first judge him in a general council before removing him is a practical and doctrinal impossibility. It is doctrinally impossible because a pope possesses absolute authority over a council; and therefore, an ecumenical council, a Roman synod, or the College of Cardinals have no jurisdiction whatsoever to judge a validly reigning pope. It is also practically impossible, because a hierarchy thoroughly infected with the heresy of Modernism can hardly be expected to gather in council to condemn a Modernist "pope". Thus, the idea that a council could resolve the issue of a heretic pope is utterly untenable and unworkable – and would have the only foreseeable result of leaving the heretic on the papal throne, and thereby leaving the Church in what St.

---

[218] *The People of the Lie – The Hope for Healing Human Evil*, by M. Scott Peck, M.D. A 1983 study on people who do evil by attacking others instead of facing their own failures and defects.

Robert Bellarmine describes as a *most miserable condition* in his comment: "that it would be the most miserable condition of the Church, if she should be compelled to recognize a wolf, manifestly prowling, for a shepherd." (*De Romano Pontifice liber ii cap. xxx*) The Salza/Siscoe doctrine on the deposition of a heretical pope would actually leave the Church remaining in this miserable condition, because their "solution" opposes the dogma of the Catholic faith. The Church's real solution, which would simply be an application of the canonical doctrine of **Tacit Resignation of Office** is much more easily carried out, and it is based on the doctrine that a manifest heretic is simply not the pope. This doctrine is fully elaborated in this volume.

Vol. 2 – Provides the canonical basis for judging the election of Bergoglio to the papacy to have been invalid, and his pontificate null and void *ab initio*. Firstly, because Benedict XVI did not validly resign the papal office, and therefore remains in office as the only valid successor of St. Peter. All arguments in favour of a valid election of Bergoglio suffer from fatal logical defects. The Salza/Siscoe argument, that Pope Benedict validly resigned, assumes a valid resignation as a premise.[219] Their argument that a *peaceful and universal acceptance* of Bergoglio as pope infallibly proves that he validly occupies the throne of Peter, suffers multiple fatal flaws. It will be explained in Volume Two how Salza & Siscoe, in a crude and logically incoherent manner, misapply the doctrine

---

[219] In their article, *Is Francis or Benedict the True Pope?*, Salza & Siscoe begin with the question, "If his intention was not to renounce the papal office, but to expand the Petrine ministry and only renounce a portion of the exercise thereof (agendo et loquendo), would this defective intention render his resignation null?" However, they premise their answer to the question on whether Benedict XVI intended in his act of renunciation to resign the papacy or to only renounce the exercise of the active ministry by asserting, "Benedict would be the first Pontiff in over seven centuries to resign from the papacy." The conclusion is assumed in the premise – *petitio principii*. Salza & Siscoe surmise that, "**Benedict's general intention to resign** would suffice (in which case God would remove him from the papal office), even if the intention was partially deficient"; but this supposition assumes as a premise that Benedict's general intention was to resign the office; whereas Benedict, on the contrary, explicitly stated that he intended only to "renounce the active exercise of the ministry", and this intention is sufficiently expressed in his official *Declaratio*, so that Prof. Violi was able to subject the text of the *Declaratio* to an expert analysis, and conclude that Benedict's intention was not to renounce the office, but only the active exercise of its ministry.

of *universal and peaceful* acceptance to the *invalid election* of Jorge "Francis" Bergoglio. The valid application of the principle of *universal and peaceful* acceptance as proof of a valid pontificate is premised on the necessary conditions that there be a *vacant see* and *valid matter* to fill the vacancy. If the papal chair is, 1) truly vacant; and, 2) a man who is *valid matter*, i.e. a man capable of validly holding the office is elected pope; then, if, 3) he enjoys the *exclusive* universal and peaceful acceptance of the whole Church, it can be judged with certitude that he is indeed the valid holder of the papal office. The *universal and peaceful acceptance* must consist in a *general acceptance of a **Catholic** pope by the **Catholic** faithful and hierarchy*. The general acceptance of a manifest heretic or apostate during a time of general apostasy by a vast majority of clergy and laity who are '*Catholic in name only*', but *who follow the heretic into heresy or apostasy, and defect from the Catholic Church together with him*, does not constitute the universal and peaceful acceptance by **Catholics**, which theologians explain would prove a man to certainly be the valid pope of the **Catholic** Church. Volume Two will demonstrate that Bergoglio's election does not meet the necessary criteria for the valid application of the principle of *universal and peaceful* acceptance as a proof of validity of his demonstrably invalid pontificate. Thus, the solution for resolving the crisis: 1) Pope Benedict must appoint the electors who will elevate his successor to the papal throne; or, if he dies before that can be done, the much less satisfactory but sufficient solution would be that the orthodox, non-heretic cardinals would elect Pope Benedict's successor. **Francis must be juridically declared to have been invalidly elected and incapable of holding ecclesiastical office**. Volume Two will prove that this is the only legitimate solution to the present crisis occasioned by the "two-pope" situation in the Church.

Vol. 3 – Will explain and prove that the Bergoglian *Reformation* is already giving birth to the Masonic inspired *Gnostic counter-church* which already exists in gigantic fetal form as the *Conciliar Church,* as an intruder within the material space belonging properly to the true *Catholic Church,* and which is the apocalyptic *counterfeit church,* Catholic in name only; and which, by the *operation of error* (2 Thess. 2:10) would *deceive if possible even the elect.* (Matthew 24:24) The *Gnostic Antichurch* – the consummation of the "*mystery of iniquity*" (2 Thess. 2:7), which 1) had its roots already in the first heresy of the Apostolic Period, and the heresies of the succeeding centuries; 2) was institutionalized by the Protestant Reformation; and, 3) will culminate and gain universality by means of the "*great tribulation*" (Matthew 24:21; Apoc. 7:14) which is comprised of, 1) the *great apostasy*

(1 Tim. 4: 1-3[220]; 2 Thess. 2:3[221]); 2) violent global persecution of the true Church (Matthew 24; Apoc. 13:1-8); and, 3) the reign of Antichrist (Apocalypse 13).

---

[220] 1 Tim. 4:1-3: "Now the Spirit manifestly saith, that in the last times some shall depart from the faith, giving heed to spirits of error, and doctrines of devils, 2 Speaking lies in hypocrisy, and having their conscience seared, 3 Forbidding to marry, to abstain from meats, which God hath created to be received with thanksgiving by the faithful, and by them that have known the truth."

[221] 2 Thess. 2:3: "Let no man deceive you by any means, for unless there come a **revolt** first, and the man of sin be revealed, the son of perdition".

DEFECTION FROM THE FAITH & THE CHURCH:

FAITH, HERESY, AND LOSS OF OFFICE –

AN EXPOSÉ OF THE HERESY OF JOHN SALZA & ROBERT SISCOE

PART ONE

Fr. Paul Kramer B.Ph., S.T.B., M.Div., S.T.L. (Cand.)

SECTION ONE

FAITH, HERESY & LOSS OF OFFICE

The sin of manifest Heresy *per se*, like apostasy and schism, has the intrinsic effect of separating the heretic from the Church by itself, without any ecclesiastical censure or judgment; and is distinguished from other sins which do not by their very nature, separate the sinner from the body of the Church; and who, therefore, for grave offenses can only be separated from the Church by a sentence of excommunication incurred or inflicted by legitimate ecclesiastical authority. This is the infallible teaching of the universal magisterium of the Church which must be believed *de fide divina et Catholica* under pain of heresy, as is proven and demonstrated below.

St. Pius V teaches in the Roman Catechism: «Heretics and schismatics are excluded from the Church, because they have defected (*desciverunt*) from her and belong to her only as deserters belong to the army from which they have deserted»; whereas those who have not left the Church by defecting, but are excluded from the Church by excommunication, are «cut off by her sentence from the number of her children and belong not to her communion until they repent.»[222]

---

[222] Catechismus Romanus, Cap. 10,9: "Ex quo fit ut tria tantummodo hominum genera ab ea excludantur: primo infideles, deinde hæretici et schismatici, postremo excommunicati. Ethnici quidem, quod in Ecclesia numquam fuerunt, neque eam umquam cognoverunt, nec ullius sacramenti

In order to understand how it is that heretics leave the Church by themselves – i.e., that heresy *per se*, by the very nature of the transgression, separates the heretic from the body of the Church as a consequence intrinsic to the nature of the sin, (as Pius XII teaches, «*suapte natura hominem ab Ecclesiae Corpore separet*»); and that by the fully deliberate and obstinate act of heresy, the heretics have left the Church and separated themselves from union with the body of the Church: «*a Corporis compage semetipsos misere separarunt*», (as distinguished from those who for reason of a most grave fault have been cut off by the legitimate ecclesiastical authority – «*ob gravissima admissa a legitima auctoritate seiuncti sunt*» [either *a jure*, i.e. *latæ sententiæ*, or *ab homine*, i.e. *sententia ferenda*]); it is necessary first to understand how one enters the Church as a faithful member; since it is by faith that one becomes a Christian and a member of the Church, and therefore it is by defecting from the faith into heresy or apostasy that one departs from the Church and ceases by the very nature of the sin to be a member.

It is first and foremost by faith that one is a Christian, without which, (as St. Thomas teaches), no one can be said to be a Christian: «Primum quod est necessarium Christiano, est fides, sine qua nullus dicitur fidelis

---

participes in populi christiani societate facti sunt. Hæretici vero atque schismatici, quia ab Ecclesia desciverunt, neque enim illi magis ad Ecclesiam spectant quam transfugæ ad exercitum pertineant a quo defecerunt; non negandum tamen quin in Ecclesiæ potestate sint, ut qui ab ea in iudicium vocentur, puniantur et anathemate damnentur. Postremo etiam excommunicati, quod Ecclesiæ iudicio ab ea exclusi ad illius communionem non pertineant donec resipiscant."

Pope Clement XIII declared the Roman Catechism to be far removed from all danger of error, and that it sets forth the common doctrine of the Church: «Nam et illuc eam doctrinam contulerunt, quæ communis est in Ecclesia, et procul abest ab omni periculo erroris; et hanc palam populo tradendam disertissimis verbis proposuerunt» – thus, in matters of faith and morals it presents the teaching of the universal magisterium, promulgated with the authority equivalent to the authority of a dogmatic encyclical.

Doctor John Hagan, [Vice Rector & Rector of the Irish College in Rome, 1904 – 1930) writes thus: "The Roman Catechism is a work of exceptional authority. At the very least it has the same authority as a dogmatic Encyclical, – it is an authoritative exposition of Catholic doctrine given forth, and guaranteed to be orthodox by the Catholic Church and her supreme head on earth. (cf. AUTHORITY AND EXCELLENCE OF THE ROMAN CATECHISM, http://sourcebooks.fordham.edu/mod/romancat.html)

Christianus.»[223] By faith, even before baptism (Acts 10:47), one can be united to the soul of the Church, and become a member not *"in re"* but *"in voto"* (as St. Robert Bellarmine teaches[224]). This is, as St. Thomas explains, in virtue of the effects of faith: 1) It is by faith that the soul is first united to God: «Primum est quod per fidem anima coniungitur Deo: nam per fidem anima Christiana facit quasi quoddam matrimonium cum Deo»;[2] and for that reason it is that one who is baptised must first profess the faith: «Et inde est quod quando homo baptizatur, primo confitetur fidem, cum dicitur ei, credis in Deum?».[2] And thus it is that Baptism is first a sacrament of faith: «Quia Baptismus est primum *sacramentum fidei.*» – and for this reason Baptism is said to be "the door", the *vitæ spiritualis ianua* and the door to the other sacraments[225]; for it is by this sacrament of faith that one enters the Church, and without faith the sacrament is of no benefit: «Baptismus enim sine fide non prodest.» [1] From there it becomes clear that in order to be a member of the Church, it is necessary, (as St. Pius X teaches), to be baptised, and to believe and profess the doctrine of Jesus Christ («Per esser membro della Chiesa è necessario esser battezzato, credere e professare la dottrina di Gesù Cristo»)[226]; since the Church is «the congregation of all baptized persons united in the same true faith, the same sacraments, and the same sacrifice, under the authority of the Sovereign Pontiff and the bishops in communion with him» – and therefore, «To remain a real member of the Church after Baptism a person must profess the one true faith and must not withdraw from the unity of the body of the Church in schism or heresy or be excommunicated by legitimate authority because of serious sins.»[227]

---

[223] Sancti Thomæ de Aquino; *Expositio in Symbolum Apostolorum,* PROOEMIUM

[224] *De Ecclesia Militante*, Cap. III, IV – «there are those who belong to the soul and not the body, as catechumens or the excommunicated, if indeed they have charity, which can happen.» – and, «Catechumens however if not in re at least in voto are in the Church and are therefore able to be saved.»

[225] «Holy Baptism is the basis of the whole Christian life, the gateway to life in the Spirit (vitæ spiritualis ianua), [Council Of Florence: DS 1314: vitæ spiritualis ianua], and the door which gives access to the other sacraments.» – *Catechism of the Catholic Church*, 1213.

[226] San Pio X, *Catechismo Maggiore*

[227] *Baltimore Catechism No. 3*, 1949, Official Revised Edition, p. 78; annotated by Rev. Francis J. Connell C.ss.R., S.T.D.

Thus, the heretic, schismatic, and apostate withdraw from unity and leave the Church, and thereby cease to be members, as St. Pius X teaches (in Question 200), Whoever would not believe in the solemn definitions of faith or would doubt them, would sin against faith; and remaining obstinate in unbelief, would no longer be a Catholic, but a heretic. («Chi non credesse alle definizioni solenni del Papa, o anche solo ne dubitasse, peccherebbe contro la fede, e se rimanesse ostinato in questa incredulità, non sarebbe più cattolico, ma eretico.») Heretics are not only those who stubbornly doubt or deny any solemn definitions; but the same Pontiff teaches that they are heretics who refuse to believe any truth revealed by God which the Catholic Church teaches as *"de fide"*: «Gli eretici sono i battezzati che ricusano con pertinacia di credere qualche verità rivelata da Dio e insegnata come di fede dalla Chiesa cattolica» (Q. 228).

The doctrine that not only the solemn definitions, but all that has been taught by the universal and ordinary magisterium of the Church as divinely revealed must be believed with divine and Catholic faith was set forth with precision in the Dogmatic Constitution «*Dei Filius*» by the First Vatican Council: «Further, by divine and Catholic faith, all those things must be believed which are contained in the written word of God and in tradition, and those which are proposed by the Church, either in a solemn pronouncement or in her ordinary and universal teaching power, to be believed as divinely revealed.»[228] Thus it follows that heresy consists not only in the denial or refusal to believe solemnly defined dogmas, but any revealed truth taught by the universal magisterium that must be believed with divine and Catholic faith: «Can. 751 — Dicitur haeresis, pertinax, post receptum baptismum, alicuius veritatis divina et catholica credendae denegatio, aut de eadem pertinax dubitatio; apostasia, fidei christianae ex toto repudiatio». (*Codex Iuris Canonici*)

It is to be noted that in both extraordinary and ordinary Magisterium, the doctrine must either be proclaimed with a "definitive act" (extraordinary) or it is agreed that it is "to be held as defininive." The teaching of both the extraordinary and the universal and ordinary Magisterium are defined doctrines[i]. Any doctrine that is not defined does not pertain formally to the infallible Magisterium of the Church. The definitions of the *extraordinary magisterium*, as well as of the *universal and ordinary magisterium* are of equal authority: commenting on Canon 1323

---

[228] "Porro fide divina et catholica ea omnia credenda sunt, quæ in verbo Dei scripto vel tradito continentur, et ab Ecclesia sive solemni iudicio sive ordinario et universali magisterio tamquam divinitus revelata credenda proponuntur."

of the 1917 Code of Canon Law, the Faculty of Canon Law of the Pontifical Ecclesiastical University of Salamanca explains «**1323** El magisterio *ordinario y universal* de la Iglesia es el ejercido por todos los obispos del mundo en sus diócesis bajo la dependencia del Romano Pontifice. Las enseñanzas del magisterio *ordinario* tienen igual valor que las del solemne.»[229]

Francisco Marin-Sola O.P. explains:

> «The Church's doctrinal authority or magisterium has for its proper and specific purpose the conservation and exposition of the revealed deposit. To determine or to fix infallibly the true meaning of the divine deposit is called a definition of faith by the Church...»
>
> «These two ways of exercising the magisterium on the content and the meaning of the revealed deposit are of equal dogmatic value, and both are true definitions of faith. Between them there exists only an accidental difference, to wit, that the magisterium exercised by the Ecumenical Council or by the Pope speaking ex cathedra is done with a greater solemnity and show of formulae and is easily discernible by all; on the other hand, the ordinary magisterium is exercised through the universal teaching of the Church without any special display or set formulae, and at times it is not so easy to determine its scope and signification.»[230]

Since, as Marin-Sola observes, the definitions of he *extraordinary magisterium* are «done with a greater solemnity and show of formulae and is easily discernible by all»; while those of the *ordinary magisterium* are «without any special display or set formulae, and at times it is not so easy to determine its scope and signification»; I have included in the first endnote a brief exposition on the criteria that are used for determining whether or not a doctrine pertains to the *universal and ordinary magisterium.*

A precise and official formulation on Magisterium and that which must be believed *de fide* is to be found in Canons 749 and 750 of the 1983 Code of Canon Law: Can 749 § 1. «The Supreme Pontiff, in virtue of his office, possesses infallible teaching authority when, as supreme pastor

---

[229] Miguelez – Alonso – Cabreros; *CÓDIGO DE DERECHO CAONICO Y LEGISLACIÓN COMPLEMENTARIA, TEXTO LATINO Y VERSION CASTELLANA CON JURISPRUDENCIA Y COMENTARIOS POR LOS CATEDRÁTICOS DE TEXTO DEL CÓDIGO EN LA PONTIFICIA UNIVERSIDAD ECLESIÁSTICA DE SALAMANCA*, Madrid, 1952, p. 498.

[230] Francisco Marin-Sola, O.P., *The Homogeneous Evolution of Catholic Dogma*, Manila, 1988, p. 288.

and teacher of all the faithful... he proclaims with a definitive act that a doctrine of faith or morals is to be held as such.»

§2. «The college of bishops also possesses infallible teaching authority when the bishops exercise their teaching office gathered together in an ecumenical council when, as teachers and judges of faith and morals, they declare that for the universal Church a doctrine of faith or morals must be definitively held; they also exercise it scattered throughout the world but united in a bond of communion among themselves and with the Successor of Peter when together with that same Roman Pontiff in their capacity as authentic teachers of faith and morals they agree on an opinion to be held as definitive.»

«Can. 750 §1. A person must believe with divine and Catholic faith all those things contained in the word of God, written or handed on, that is, in the one deposit of faith entrusted to the Church, and at the same time proposed as divinely revealed either by the solemn magisterium of the Church or by its ordinary and universal magisterium which is manifested by the common adherence of the Christian faithful under the leadership of the sacred magisterium; therefore all are bound to avoid any doctrines whatsoever contrary to them.»

«§2. Each and every thing which is proposed definitively by the magisterium of the Church concerning the doctrine of faith and morals, that is, each and every thing which is required to safeguard reverently and to expound faithfully the same deposit of faith, is also to be firmly embraced and retained; therefore, one who rejects those propositions which are to be held definitively is opposed to the doctrine of the Catholic Church.»[231]

---

[231] Can. 749 — § 1. Infallibiitate in magisterio, vi muneris sui gaudet Summus Pontifex quando ut supremus omnium christifidelium Pastor et Doctor, cuius est fratres suos in fide confirmare, doctrinam de fide vel de moribus tenendam definitivo actus proclamat.

§ 2. Infallibiitate in magisterio pollet quoque Collegium Episcoporum quando magisterium exercent Episcopi in Concilio Oecumenico coadunati, qui, ut fidei et morum doctores et iudices, pro universa Ecclesia doctrinam de fide vel de moribus definitive tenendam declarant aut quando per orbem dispersi, communionis nexum inter se et cum Petri successore servantes, una cum eodem Romano Pontifice authentice res fidei vel morum docentes, in unam sententiam tamquam definitive tenendam conveniunt.

Can. 750 — § 1. Fide divina et catholica ea omnia credenda sunt quæ verbo Dei scripto vel tradito, uno scilicet fidei deposito Ecclesiæ commisso, continentur, et insimul ut divinitus revelata proponuntur sive ab Ecclesiæ magisterio sollemni, sive ab eius magisterio ordinario et universali, quod quidem

«The truths of faith taught by the Magisterium must be understood according to the mind of the Church with the same unchanging meaning: «For the doctrine of the faith which God has revealed... has been entrusted as a divine deposit to the spouse of Christ, to be faithfully guarded and infallibly interpreted. Hence, also, that understanding of its sacred dogmas must be perpetually retained, which Holy Mother Church has once declared; and there must never be a recession from that meaning under the specious name of a deeper understanding.»

«Therefore... let the understanding, the knowledge, and wisdom of individuals as of all, of one man as of the whole Church, grow and progress strongly with the passage of the ages and the centuries; but let it be solely in its own genus, namely in the same dogma, with the same sense and the same understanding (St. Vincent of Lérins).» (Dei Filius)[232]

The importance of this clause just quoted, *"Crescat igitur et multum vehementerque proficiat, tam singulorum, quam omnium, tam unius hominis, quam totius Ecclesiæ, ætatum ac sæculorum gradibus, intelligentia, scientia, sapientia; sed in suo dumtaxat genere, in eodem scilicet dogmate, eodem sensu, eademque sententia* (Vinc. Lir. Common, n. 28),*"* is such that it must be rightly understood according to the mind of the Church, so that it will not be minimalized in such a manner as to negate the Church's dogma on the ordinary and universal magisterium in the manner that Robert Siscoe has done in his article, *The Infallibility of the Ordinary and Extraordinary Magisterium*, which appeared in the October 2018 issue of the *Catholic Family News*. In that

---

communi adhæsione christifidelium sub ductu sacri magisterii manifestatur; tenentur igitur omnes quascumque devitare doctrinas iisdem contrarias.

§ 2. Firmiter etiam amplectenda ac retinenda sunt omnia et singula quæ circa doctrinam de fide vel moribus ab Ecclesiæ magisterio definitive proponuntur, scilicet quæ ad idem fidei depositum sancte custodiendum et fideliter exponendum requiruntur; ideoque doctrinæ Ecclesiæ catholicæ adversatur qui easdem propositiones definitive tenendas recusat.

[232] «Neque enim fidei doctrina, quam Deus revelavit, velut philosophicum inventum proposita est humanis ingeniis perficienda, sed tamquam divinum depositum Christi Sponsæ tradita, fideliter custodienda et infallibiliter declaranda. Hinc sacrorum quoque dogmatum is sensus perpetuo est retinendus, quem semel declaravit Sancta Mater Ecclesia, nec umquam ab eo sensu, altior intelligentiæ specie et nomine, recedendum. Crescat igitur et multum vehementerque proficiat, tam singulorum, quam omnium, tam unius hominis, quam totius Ecclesiæ, ætatum ac sæculorum gradibus, intelligentia, scientia, sapientia; sed in suo dumtaxat genere, in eodem scilicet dogmate, eodem sensu, eademque sententia (Vinc. Lir. Common, n. 28).»

article, Siscoe states, "Due to the difficulty of a non-defined doctrine obtaining a definitive character, practically speaking the OUM [ordinary and universal magisterium] can only effectively serve as an organ of infallibility for basic doctrines of the faith." The proposition that the "ordinary and universal magisterium can only effectively serve as an organ of infallibility for basic doctrines of the faith" is *heretical* in so far as it denies that in practice the ordinary and universal magisterium can, with equal authority, like the extraordinary magisterium, infallibly explicate the the divinely revealed truths and propose them to be believed with an assent of faith. There is a growth *secundum quid* in the material object of faith[233] contained in the deposit of revelation, the truths of which are set forth and explicated not only by the extraordinary magisterium, *but also and with equal authority by the universal and ordinary magisterium*; but this is denied *by denying that in practice it can be determined when the ordinary magisterium definitively explicates and proposes in a recognizably infallible manner that which is implicitly contained in the already definitively proposed basic revealed truths of faith*. Pronouncements of the ordinary magisterium that cannot be recognized to be definitive and infallible are in fact not infallible, because any definition that cannot be known to be infallible is, for that very reason, judged to be *not infallible*, i.e. **subject to error**: *"Infallihiliter definita nulla intelligitur doctrina, nisi id manifesto constiterit."* (Can. 749 § 3) Hence, in practice, only the extraordinary magisterium would be able to infallibly explicate and define any of the revealed truths of faith beyond the most basic truths explicitly taught since antiquity; *but then this function, which in fact is proper to both the extraordinary and the ordinary universal magisterium*[234], *would not lie within the practical scope of the ordinary and universal magisterium*; in which case it could not be said, as the Church has perpetually taught, that, *"the universal ordinary magisterium... can truly be considered as the usual expression of the Church's infallibility"* (Pope John Paul II on 15 Oct. 1988) In fact, if Siscoe's proposition were true, the

---

[233] G. Van Noort, *Tractatus de Fontibus Revelationis nec non de Fide Divina*, Caput I De Objecto Fidei Divinae, Art. IV, De Incremento Objiecti Materialis Fidei Catholicae, Prop. 2., Bussum in Hollandia, 1920, N. 217, p. 153.

[234] "This magisterium is not above the divine word but serves it with a specific carisma veritatis certum, which includes the charism of infallibility, present not only in the solemn definitions of the Roman Pontiff and of Ecumenical Councils, but also in the universal ordinary magisterium, which can truly be considered as the usual expression of the Church's infallibility." [Address of The Holy Father John Paul II to the Bishops from The United States Of America On Their «*Ad Limina*» Visit Thursday, 15 October 1988]

universal and ordinary magisterium as a vehicle of proposing infallible definitions could not be considered as the usual expression of the Church's infallibility, but would be far more rare and extraordinary than the extraordinary magisterium; and in practice its object would not be co-extensive with that of the extraordinary magisterium, but the restricted scope of its infallible definitions would be limited in practice to the restating of the basic truths of faith definitively taught by the ordinary magisterium since antiquity, beyond which its object could not practically extend.

Siscoe fraudulently twists the meaning of Msgr. Van Noort's words in order to make it appear that Van Noort agrees with Siscoe's heretical deviation. He quotes Van Noort, [*The Sources of Revelation*, (Westminster, Maryland: Newman Press, 1961), p. 222], "Now since a definitive proposal of this sort [i.e. of the ordinary and universal magisterium] must blossom forth from countless activities which individually are neither definitive nor infallible, the existence of such a [definitive] proposal (*with the exception of some fundamental truth*) is frequently enough not too obvious." Now the statement that the existence of a definitive proposal of that sort, "is frequently not too obvious", only means that in many cases some diligent effort is required so that the criteria for determining whether or not a proposal is definitive can be rigorously applied.

Siscoe then errantly applies a passage of the *Catholic Encyclopedia* [*Catholic Encyclopedia* (1913), vol. VII, p. 795], which he quotes: "And while for subsequent ages down to our own day it continues to be *theoretically true* that the Church *may*, by the exercise of this ordinary teaching authority arrive at a final and infallible decision regarding doctrinal questions, *it is true at the same time that in practice it may be impossible to prove conclusively that such unanimity as may exist has a strictly definitive value in any particular case.*" This passage does not state or imply that "practically speaking the OUM [ordinary and universal magisterium] can only effectively serve as an organ of infallibility for basic doctrines of the faith," as Siscoe claims, but clearly, it only means that in any given particular case it may not be possible to prove that there is the requisite unanimity for a doctrine to be considered as definitively taught. Siscoe's conclusion is a howling *non sequitur*. Van Noort explicitly upholds and flatly states the Church's doctrine that such definitive proposals are made *in two ways*: "Propositio per ecclesiam, qualem supra descripsimus, teste conc. Vatic., *duplici modo* haberi potest, np. aut *solemni judicio*, aut *ordinario et universali magisterio.*"²³⁵ He does not suggest or imply that the ordinary and universal magisterium "can only effectively serve as an organ of infallibility for basic doctrines of the faith," as Siscoe heretically states. Van Noort also mentions the more easily recognizable indications of such definitive proposals of the ordinary and universal magisterium: "Praecipua ejus *signa* sunt, si res ubique terrarum in catechismis popularibus docetur, et magis adhuc si universali et constanti consensus theologorum tamquam ad fidem pertinens retinetur."²³⁶ A more complete exposition of the criteria for determining which doctrines are definitively taught by the ordinary and universal magisterium by Adolphe Tanquerey, under the title, *The Ordinary and Universal Magisterium*, taken from his *Manual of Dogmatic Theology*, can be found in the endnote at the end of this volume.

Robert Siscoe's doctrinal deviations on the ordinary magisterium are not limited only to his errant opinions on the Church's ordinary and universal magisterium, but extend also to his heterodox opinions on the papal magisterium. In the same above cited article, Siscoe begins by saying, "The *organs* through which the Church teaches infallibly are (a) the pope, (b) a general council, and (c) the ordinary and universal magisterium (OUM), which consists of the bishops dispersed throughout the world, teaching in union with the pope. Each of these organs *can* teach infallibly, and indeed will do so, provided the necessary conditions are met, but infallibility will not prevent them from erring if the conditions are not satisfied." Unfortunately, Siscoe then deviates from Catholic doctrine by asserting that the pope teaches infallibly *only* when defining doctrine *ex cathedra*: "The Pope is not infallible as a private person, or as a public person in relation to a part of the Church, but only as a public person *in relation to the entire Church*. Hence, to be preserved from error he must be teaching the *entire* Church, *as Pope*, and he must do so with the *express intention of defining a doctrine*. These two conditions are required, and together constitute, and ex cathedra teaching." And even more explicitly: "Only when a pope 1) exercises his supreme apostolic authority, as teacher of all Christians, with the 2) clear intent of defining a doctrine, is he preserved from error. Papal infallibility will not prevent a pope from erring when these conditions are not met."

---

²³⁵ G. Van Noort, *Op. cit., Caput I De Objecto Fidei Divinae, Art. III De Objecto Materiali Fidei Divino-Catholicae*, Bussum in Hollandia, 1920, N. 206, p. 145.
²³⁶ *Ibid.*, N. 207, p. 146.

Siscoe's very grave error against Catholic Doctrine on this point limits papal infallibility exclusively to solemn *ex cathedra* definitions, and thereby eliminates the papal infallibility that flows from the pope's ordinary magisterium. However, *Pastor Æternus* did not define that only the pope's *ex cathedra* definitions are infallible, as if to limit the scope of infallibility, so as to exclude that the pope does not exercise infallibility in any other way. It is manifestly clear from the wording of the definition[237] that it concerns only one point of infallibility, limiting not the scope of infallibility, but limiting the scope of the definition to the infallibility of papal *ex cathedra* definitions by defining that the papal *ex cathedra* definitions are indeed infallible; but not defining that no other papal act is infallible. In fact, the dogmatic formula defines and specifies that the pope's *ex cathedra* definitions are an exercise of that broader infallibility with which Christ equiped the Church in defining doctrine: *ea infallibilitate pollere, qua divinus Redemptor Ecclesiam suam in definienda doctrina de fide vel moribus instructam esse voluit*. In fact, Msgr. Gerardus Van Noort, in *De Ecclesia Christi*,[238] *Caput III De Proprietatibus Ecclesiæ, art. I, De Ecclesiæ Infallibilitate*, § 2. *Infallibilitas Objectum*, provides a precise exposition on the *object of infallibility* in which he enumerates the other ways the Church exercises the charism of infallibility. The pope is not only infallible when defining revealed truths, but it is theologically certain his infallibility also extends to, 1) judgments on *theological conclusions*,[239] 2) to judgments on dogmatic facts,[240] 3) to the ordinances of *general discipline of the Church*,[241] and, 4) to the approbation of religious orders.[242] It was Van Noort's opinion, and the common opinion of theologians in his day, that infallibility also extends to the canonization of saints.[243]

---

[237] "definimus: Romanum Pontificem, cum ex Cathedra loquitur… ea infallibilitate pollere, qua divinus Redemptor Ecclesiam suam in definienda doctrina de fide vel moribus instructam esse voluit."

[238] G. Van Noort; *De Ecclesia Christi*, Hilversum in Hollandia, 1932.

[239] "*Infallibilitas ecclesiæ se extendit ad conclusiones theologicas* — Theologice certum est." (N. 88 p. 99)

[240] "Infallibilitas *ecclesiæ se* extendit *ad facta dogmatica* — Theologice certum est." (N. 89 p. 100)

[241] "*Infallibilitas ecclesiæ se extendit ad disciplinam generalem ecclesiæ.* — Theologice certum est." (N. 90 p. 103)

[242] "*Infallibilitas ecclesiæ se extendit ad approbationem Ordinum religiosorum.* — Theologice certum est." (N. 93 p. 105)

[243] *Infallibilitas ecclesiæ se extendit ad canonizationem Sanctorum.* (N. 93 p. 106)

In an article entitled, *"Clear ideas on the pope's infallible magisterium"*, published by the Priestly Fraternity of St. Pius X (originally printed in the January 2002 issue of the *SiSiNoNo*), there is described the "the error by excess of those who extend papal infallibility to all acts of the pope, without distinction; and **the error by defect of those who restrict infallibility to definitions that have been uttered *ex cathedra*.**" It is precisely this latter error, the *error by defect*, which is the error Siscoe asserts in the above quoted passages of his article, *The Infallibility of the Ordinary and Extraordinary Magisterium*. The article elaborates:

«These two opposing errors are not new. They were denounced even before Vatican II. In 1954, Fr. Labourdette, O.P., wrote: "Many persons have retained very naive ideas about what they learned concerning the personal infallibility of the sovereign pontiff in the solemn and abnormal exercise of his power of teaching. For some, every word of the supreme pontiff will in some way partake of the value of an infallible teaching, requiring the absolute assent of theological faith; for others, acts which are not presented with the manifest conditions of a definition *ex cathedra* will seem to have no greater authority than that of any private teacher." (*Revue Thomiste* LIV, 1954, p. 196)»

The article then sets forth the very crucial critical distinction:

«The "Authentic Magisterium" cannot be so simply identified with the Ordinary Magisterium. In fact, the Ordinary Magisterium can be infallible and non-infallible, and it is only in this second case that it is called the "Authentic Magisterium." *The Dictionnaire de Theologie Catholique* [hereafter referred to as *DTC*—Ed.] under the heading of "papal infallibility" (vol. VII, col. 1699ff) makes the following distinctions:

1. there is the *"infallible or* ex cathedra *papal definition in the sense defined by Vatican I"* (col.1699);
2. there is the *"infallible papal teaching which flows from the pope's Ordinary Magisterium"* (col.1705);
3. there is *"non-infallible papal teaching"* (col.1709).

Similarly, Salaverri, in his *Sacrae Theologiae Summa* (vol. I, 5th ed., Madrid, B.A.C.) distinguishes the following:

1. Extraordinary Infallible Papal Magisterium (no. 592 ff);
2. Ordinary Infallible Papal Magisterium (no. 645 ff);

Papal Magisterium that is mere *authenticum*, that is, only "authentic" or "authorized" as regards the person himself, not as regards his infallibility (no. 659 ff).»

The author then comments:

«Unfortunately this three-fold distinction between the Extraordinary Magisterium, the Ordinary Infallible Magisterium, and the authentic non-infallible Magisterium, has fallen into oblivion. This has resulted in two opposite errors in the crisis situation of the Church at the present time: the error by excess of those who extend papal infallibility to all acts of the pope, without distinction; and the error by defect of those who restrict infallibility to definitions that have been uttered *ex cathedra*.»

The author then quotes Dom Paul Nau to account for how this situation came about:

«By a strange reversal, while the personal infallibility of the pope in a solemn judgment, so long disputed, was definitely placed beyond all controversy, it is the Ordinary Magisterium of the Roman Church, which seems to have been lost sight of. [On the temporary fading of a doctrine from Catholic consciousness, see the entry "*dogme*" in DTC (vol. IV).] It all happened—as is not unheard of elsewhere in the history of doctrine—as if the very brilliance of the Vatican I definition had cast into shadow the truth hitherto universally recognized; we might almost say, as if the definition of the infallibility of the solemn judgments made these henceforth the unique method by which the sovereign pontiff would put forward the rule of faith." [*Pope or Church?*, Angelus Press, 1998, p.13] ... Dom Nau considered from where this phenomenon had developed: "Since 1870 [the year of Vatican I—Ed.], manuals of theology have taken the formulae in which their statements of doctrine have been framed from the actual wording of the Council text. None of these treated in its own right of the ordinary teaching of the pope, which has accordingly, little by little, slipped out of sight and all pontifical teaching has seemed to be reduced solely to solemn definitions *ex cathedra*. Once attention was entirely directed to these, it became customary to consider the doctrinal interventions of the Holy See solely from the standpoint of the solemn judgment, that of a judgment which ought in itself to bring to the doctrine all the necessary guarantees of certainty." (*ibid.*, p.13) This is partly true, but we should not forget that liberal theology had already been advertising its reductive agenda. That is why Pius IX, even before Vatican I (1870) felt obliged to warn German theologians that divine faith's submission *"must not be restricted only to those points which have been defined*" (Letter to Archbishop of Munich, Dec. 21, 1863).»

Thus it must be borne in mind that only the conditions for the infallibility of the pope's solemn definitions when exercising his extraordinary magisterium were set forth in the definition of papal infallibility in *Pastor Æternus*; but in so doing, the Council did not teach that only solemn definitions are infallible, or that papal infallibility is restricted to only this solemn manner of defining, so as to deny the Church's doctrine on the *infallible ordinary magisterium* of the pope. Only when a pope exercises his extraordinary magisterium is his infallibility absolute in the sense that his definitions are infallible *per se*, and hence, *by the very act*; and therefore, as the Council defined, they are *ex sese irreformabiles*. The pope is therefore absolutely prevented from erring when solemnly defining by himself *ex cathedra*; but he is still nonetheless prevented from erring when he exercises his *infallible ordinary magisterium* under the conditions necessary for that infallible magisterium to be exercised; which is not infallible by the act itself, but must be made in conjunction with the bishops of the whole Church in exercising the universal and ordinary magisterium.

It is also to be noted that Siscoe's agenda is exposed and becomes transparent by his own words, and is seen to be identical to the "reductive agenda" of liberal theology, when one considers his assertion, "If a pope errs when not defining a doctrine, in no way does it suggest that he lacks papal authority, or is not the Pope." Van Noort, in the above quoted passages, enumerated by which acts the charism of infallibility is exercised. If a putative pope were to err in such an act, it would prove that he is not in possession of that charism, and consequently, that he is not a valid pope.

St. Vincent of Lérins in his Commonitory lays down the rules that must be observed in order to identify and safeguard the sacred doctrine so that its authentic meaning can be perpetually retained:

> «*Moreover, in the Catholic Church itself, all possible care must be taken, that we hold that faith which has been believed everywhere, always, by all. For that is truly and in the strictest sense Catholic which, as the name itself and the reason of the thing declare, comprehends all universally. This rule we shall observe if we follow universality, antiquity, consent. We shall follow universality if we confess that one faith to be true, which the whole Church throughout the world confesses; antiquity, if we in no wise depart from those interpretations which it is manifest were notoriously held by our holy ancestors and fathers;*

consent, in like manner, if in antiquity itself we adhere to the consentient definitions and determinations of all, or at the least of almost all priests and doctors.»

The universality, antiquity and consensus on points of doctrine which distinguish them as being of divine origin are pre-eminently to be found where there is the unanimous consensus of the Fathers on a point of doctrine. In matters of faith and morals the true sense of sacred scripture is to be understood as the Church, which has the authority to interpret and judge, has understood and understands it; and no one may interpret them contrary to this sense; and it is permitted to no one to interpret the scriptures contrary to the unanimous consent of the Fathers:

> «*Nos, ... hanc illius mentem esse declaramus, ut in rebus fidei et morum, ad aedificationem doctrinae Christianae pertinentium, is pro vero sensu sacrae Scripturae habendus sit, quem tenuit ac tenet Sancta Mater Ecclesia, cuius est iudicare de vero sensu et interpretatione Scripturarum sanctarum; atque ideo nemini licere contra hunc sensum, aut etiam contra unanimem consensum Patrum ipsam Scripturam sacram interpretari.»*
> – «*Dei Filius*»

Steve Ray, in «*Unanimous Consent of the Fathers*», (written for the *Catholic Dictionary of Apologetics and Evangelism* by Ignatius Press), says, on the authority of ecclesiastical writers, «Where the Fathers speak in harmony, with one mind overall-not necessarily each and every one agreeing on every detail but by consensus and general agreement-we have 'unanimous consent'.»

Unanimous consent in interpreting scripture cannot be intelligibly understood in the fundamentalistic sense of unanimous interpretation of many Fathers of individual scriptural texts and verses, (which is rare), but is understood by the Church to denote a moral unanimity of the Fathers agreeing or consenting on points of doctrine that are derived from various texts of scripture.

Thus, (Cardinal) Yves Congar writes, «In fact, a complete consensus is unnecessary: quite often, that which is appealed to as sufficient for dogmatic points does not go beyond what is encountered in the interpretation of many texts.»[244] On the consensus of the Fathers, Fr. Bernard Schid writes,

---

[244] Yves Congar on the «*Unanimous Consent of the Fathers*» in, Tradition and Traditions; McMillan Company, New York, 1966.

«[T]he unanimity of the Fathers (Consensus Patrum), in matters of faith and morals, begets complete certainty and commands assent, because they, as a body, bear witness to the teaching and belief of the infallible Church, representing the Church herself. So the authority of the Fathers is binding only when they all agree upon a question of faith and morals. The consensus, however, need not be absolute; a moral agreement suffices, as, for instance, when some of the greatest Fathers testify to a doctrine of the Church, and the rest, though quite aware of it, do not positively oppose it.»[245]

On this point Congar states, «As a matter of fact, a few testimonies sufficed, even that of one single man if his particular situation or the consideration accorded him by the Church were such as to give to what he said the value of coming from a quasi-personification of the whole Church at that time.» [11] On this point of what constitutes "consensus" or "moral unanimity", there is no disagreement among theologians. Benedict Lemeer O.P., who had been Dean of the Faculty of Theology at the Pontifical University of St. Thomas Aquinas in Rome for many years explained it this way in his lectures, as did Fr. De Simone, professor of Patristics in his Angelicum lectures. I mention this here, because John Salza continues with his repeated *ad hominem* ridicule against me for having quoted Yves Congar and Steve Ray – but never once expressing disagreement with their opinion in this matter.

The Catholic doctrine on heresy as an act of defection is stated in scripture, interpreted unanimously by the Fathers, explicated by the Doctors and theologians, defined by the universal and ordinary Magisterium of the Church, and taught by the Supreme Pontiffs to the whole Church in their ordinary magisterium. The basis of the doctrine, as St. Thomas explains, is that heresy is essentially schismatic in its nature; and schism is *per se* by its very nature an act of separation – of severing (*scissio*), by which one separates himself from the body of the Church. Schism, heresy and apostasy all directly and *per se* sever communion with the Church. By refusing submission to the pope the schismatic departs from communion with the Church by severing the bond of ecclesiastical governance – of unity under the vicar of Christ, the visible head of the Mystical Body of the Church. By visibly separating himself from the common worship of participation in the sacred rites; the schismatic withdraws from communion with the Church by severing

---

[245] *Manual of Patrology*, Rev. Bernard Schid, O.S. B, Herder Book Co., 1917, p. 31.

the bond of worship. Heresy (and *a fortiori* apostasy) is also in its essence an act of schism, because it severs the bond of unity in the one faith by which one is united to the body of the Church. By rejecting the teaching authority of the Church, the heretic (and *a fortiori* the apostate) severs the bond of ecclesiastical governance. Hence, as is elaborated further on in this section, St. Thomas explains that every heretic is a schismatic; but every schismatic is not a heretic.

The doctrine that, «The public sin of manifest heresy *per se*, like apostasy and schism, by its very nature has the intrinsic effect of separating the heretic from the Church by itself, without any ecclesiastical censures or judgment; and is distinguished from other sins which do not by their very nature, separate the sinner from the body of the Church; and who, therefore, for grave offenses can only be separated from the Church by a sentence of excommunication incurred or inflicted by legitimate ecclesiastical authority», is taught plainly and explicitly in *Mystici Corporis*:

> «*In Ecclesiae autem membris reapse ii soli annumerandi sunt, qui regenerationis lavacrum receperunt veramque fidem profitentur, neque a Corporis compage semet ipsos misere separarunt, vel ob gravissima admissa a legitima auctoritate seiuncti sunt.*» and, «*Siquidem non omne admissum, etsi grave scelus, eiusmodi est ut — sicut schisma, vel haeresis, vel apostasia faciunt — suapte natura hominem ab Ecclesiae Corpore separet.*»

The common and general meaning of the word *"admissum"* is defined by Lewis & Short as a "voluntary fault", and only in certain specific instances can it be understood to mean "crime", when the particular context in which it is used supports that interpretation. Salza & Siscoe gratuitously interpret the term as used in *Mystici Corporis* to mean "offense" as in "crime" – a canonical delict or transgression of ecclesiastical law which, in the case of heresy by ecclesiastical authority incurs the penalty of excommunication *latæ sententiæ*. It is quite impossible, and in fact, *contra rationem*, for the word *"admissum"* to be understood as meaning only the act of of heresy, schism, or apostasy *suapte natura* in virtue of its being a canonical *delict*, separates a man from the Church, but not that the manifest external sin *per se* by its very nature accomplishes that separation in the context that it is used in this passage of *Mystici Corporis*, because that would render the meaning of the passage unintelligible and entirely irrational.

Salza & Siscoe go to great lengths to insist that in *Mystici Corporis*, the words *"admissa"* and *"admissum"* mean, "crime(s)", and not "sin(s)"[246]; but when you examine the syntax of text very carefully, **it makes no difference how you translate the terms.** Read the Latin text very carefully – it says: «And thus not every fault (*admissum*: sin, fault, crime), even a gravely evil deed (*scelus*: an evil deed; a wicked, heinous, or impious action; a crime, sin, enormity) does such – as schism, heresy, and apostasy do – by their very nature separate a man from unity of the body the Church.» There it is: Others are separated from the Church by *excommunication* – «*by the legitimate authority of the Church*» for having committed excommunicatable *penal offenses*, i.e. **crimes**; as opposed to those who «*miserably separate themselves from union with the body*» of the Church by heresy, schism, or apostasy, which separate them *not* for their being crimes punishable *by the authority of the Church*, but because they are of the nature of *sins opposed to the unity of the Church*; which therefore, **according to their nature (suapte natura)** separate the perpetrator from the body of the Church. In Canon Law, it pertains to the nature of a crime *per se* that it is a *penal* violation – a violation of a law or precept that is of ecclesiasticasl character; and, if the transgression is public, and if there is added to the law or precept the *penal cenure* of excommunication, it results in the separation of the offender from the Church by means of the penalty of excommunication, incurred or inflicted by the authority of the Church. Pius XII teaches, (in conformity with the constant teaching of the universal magisterium), that heresy, schism and apostasy, are the sole exceptions, because, although they in fact happen to be crimes; heretics, schismatics, or apostates are not separated from the body of the Church "by legitimate authority", i.e. because they committed *crimes*; but because these **sins by their very nature are directly and per se opposed to the unity of the Church**; and accordingly, schismatics, heretics and apostates have «**miserably separated themselves from the unity of the Body**» of the Church *(a Corporis compage semet ipsos misere separarunt)*. The reason why this is so (as

---

[246] «Again, Pope Pius XII is referring to the "offense" or CRIME (not SIN) of heresy, which severs one from the Body of the Church, after the formal and material elements have been proven by the Church. After the crime has been established, the heretic is automatically severed from the BODY (not SOUL) of the Church without further declaration (although most theologians maintain that the Church must also issue a declaration of deprivation)» – *John Salza Responds to Another Sedevacantist.*

is explained below) is because the *specific nature* of each of these *sins*, i.e. of heresy, schism, (and *a fortiori* apostasy), is such that they *directly* and *per se* separate one from the unity of the Church. (II^a-IIae q. 39 a. 1 ad 3) On the other hand, criminal acts considered under their formal aspect as *crimes*, i.e., according to the nature of *crimes*, do not directly and *per se* separate one from the Church; but according to the nature of crimes as such, it is only by means of *juridical authority* that the separation would take place, being that they are crimes carrying the penalty of *excommunication*.

Salza & Siscoe interpret this papal magisterial text of *Mystici Corporis* by conflating it with the doctrinally obsolete and no longer admissible private opinion of John of St. Thomas[247], in order to support their *heretical belief* that the *sin* of manifest formal heresy by itself does not *suapte natura* separate a man from the Church unless there is pronounced a judgment of the Church for the *crime* of heresy[248], but *"without an additional censure"* – (according to them), there must be some judgment, condemnation or penal censure, but not the additional censure. i.e. a declared excommunication or a *vitandus* declaration. Their words directed against me on their *True or False Pope?* website make their meaning explicitly and unmistakably clear: "If Fr. Kramer would have read our book, he would have learned that the Pope was not teaching that the sin of heresy automatically causes the loss of ecclesiastical office, but rather that the nature of the crime of heresy requires no additional censure to sever one from the Body. But this does not nullify the necessity of the Church – who alone has the authority to judge whether a person is guilty of the crime of heresy – rendering a judgment, and most certainly in the case of a person who continues to present himself as a Catholic (as opposed to one who openly left the Church)." (As will be shown below, after I exposed the heterodoxy of this opinion, Salza

---

[247] The opinion of John of St. Thomas can be seen to be heterodox in the light of the teaching of *Mystici Corporis*, and because St. Robert Bellarmine demonstrates that it is contrary to the unanimous consensus of the Fathers.

[248] In Part II of their *Formal Reply*, Salza & Siscoe state: "If the culprit's heresy is not deemed to be notorious by fact, however, he must be formally judged and declared a heretic by the Church (rendering him notorious by law) before he is legally separated from the Body of the Church." **As will be amply demonstrated, it suffices that the defection into heresy be a *public fact* (not *notorious by fact* according to the prescriptions of penal law) for the juridical bond to be visibly severed, and for the loss of office to take place *ipso jure*, without any declaration.**

& Siscoe then assert that I falsely accuse them of holding it, although it was so explicitly asserted by them on their website, and then, they will contradict this position and claim that notorious heresy *suapte natura* severs one from membership in the Church; and then they will assert again the opinion that one remains a juridical member of the Church until the "legal bond" is severed by means of a declared sentence.) According to them, it must be a *crime*, i.e. a *delict* – *a penal offense* judged by the Church for heresy to separate a man from the Church *"suapte natura".*[249] However, if there is **any judgment or censure at all**, then the heretics are separated by the *"legitimate authority of the Church"*, and therefore not by heresy *suapte natura*, which is to say, the act of heresy *simpliciter*, by which they "miserably separated themselves from the unity of the body" of the Church. One is either separated from the body of the Church by *excommunication*, i.e. "by legitimate authority", or by one's own sinful act of desertion, which according to its very nature separates one from the body of the Church *per se*, as St. Pius V and St. Pius X teach in their catechisms. There exists no third way out of the Church, by which one is separated from the body of the Church for manifest heresy only upon some unspecified form of "public judgment" before being excommunicated or declared *vitandus*. Thus, their interpretation of the passage of *Mystici Corporis* would render it entirely irrational. Now, the *act* of formal heresy, because it is directly opposed to faith, is a **mortal sin *ex toto genere suo*;** and therefore, heresy, properly considered *in its nature*, is the **SIN** of heresy, and not the ecclesiastical *crime of heresy*, since heresy in its nature is not an *ecclesiastical crime* – so when Pius XII wrote saying that heresy *suapte natura* separates one from the body of the Church, he wrote specifically of the external *sin* of manifest heresy, and not heresy considered under the formal aspect of its being an ecclesiastical *crime* or *delict*, for which one would be excluded from Church membership *"by legitimate authority"*, as Pius explained.

---

[249] Salza & Siscoe later modified their position, stating in their *Formal Reply* that heresy is in its very nature a *crime*, even if it not listed as a penal offense or given any mention in ecclesiastical law. This opinion, which is dealt with later in this section, is a ridiculous opinion that is contrary to all the expert commentaries on canon law, and it is manifestly contrtary to the canonical doctrine of the Church. If an act is not listed as a penal offense or given any mention in ecclesiastical law, then it is simply not a crime according to ecclesiastical law.

The Salza/Siscoe conclusion on this point, is a *non sequitur* based on a passage of Benedict XIV, (which I deal with more fully later in this section), which they cite and take entirely out of its proper context: "a sentence declaratory of the offence is always necessary in the external forum". In this passage, Benedict writes exclusively on a point of *penal law*, to wit, on the canonical penalty of excommunication, explaining that it cannot simply be presumed that one has incurred the canonical penalty for a penal offense without at least a declaratory sentence of the crime. This ruling has absolutely no bearing whatever on the question of the severing of the juridical bond of faith and communion with the Church, which takes place *ipso jure* in virtue of the nature of an act of manifest heresy which in its very essence *according to the nature of the sin* is an act of separation from the body of the Church. Since it is according to the very nature (*suapte natura*) of the manifest act itself of defection from the faith into heresy that the juridical bond uniting one to the Church is severed, it is necessarily severed *ipso facto*; and hence, the resulting effect of *loss of office*, as will be explained more fully below, is understood by the Church to be necessarily the *ipso facto* natural consequence of that separation from the body of the Church. Hence, the loss of office, since it takes place *ipso facto* as a natural consequence of the separation from the body of the Church by such an act of defection into heresy, it is recognized in canon law as taking place *ipso jure*; and therefore, it is not a question *penal deprivation of office*, which is dealt with in the penal section of the Code, but *loss of office* is dealt with in the non-penal administrative laws in a different section of the Code under the title, *Loss of Office*. Here, as always, Salza & Siscoe misconstrue *loss of office* as a penalty, "a severe vindictive penalty"[250], as Salza says In the above cited article – Salza & Siscoe repeatedly state in their book, that a heretic pope's loss of office would be a "punishment" for the "crime of heresy"; or again, as they explain on page 265 of their book "If a Pope has shown himself incorrigible by remaining obstinate in the face of a public warning, the crime of heresy would be sufficiently established. This would pave the way for the divine punishment (loss of office), which would then be followed by the human punishment (excommunication)." A vindictive penalty (expiatory penalty in the 1983 Code) can only be inflicted by the authority of a *superior* who possesses *jurisdiction*. Thus, they say that for the separation from the body of the Church and loss of office to take place, "most theologians maintain that the Church must also issue a declaration of

---

[250] And it is stated also in *True or False Pope?*, p. 260.

deprivation"; and accordingly, they cite Pope Benedict XIV's ruling of penal law on excommunication: "a sentence declaratory of the offence is always necessary in the external forum".

As can be seen from the above quoted text of St. Pius V's Catechism, heretics withdraw (descisco, desciscere, descivi, descitum – withdraw, leave, revolt from, desert defect), they leave the Church on their own, as opposed to the *excommunicati*, who are expelled by act of authority. By the act of heresy, i.e., by the sin of defecting from the Catholic faith by an external act of manifest formal heresy, the heretic, by that act of heresy *suapte natura*[251], i.e., by the effect that is intrinsic to the nature of the act of manifest formal heresy, leaves the Church and ceases to be a member of it. It is not by the force of law in virtue of a *latæ sententiæ* excommunication, or in any manner by means of, or after any ecclesiastical judgment, that the heretic ceases to be a member of the Church by having been expelled from the Church by the authority of ecclesiastical law (*ob gravissima admissa a legitima auctoritate seiuncti sunt*), nor is it necessary for a heretic to formally declare his separation from the Church, join another religious sect or denomination, or explicitly admit that he is in heresy, but the desertion itself that is intrinsic to the nature of the public act of formal heresy, *suapte natura*, separates the heretic from the body of the Church, so that any judgment or censure does not in any manner separate the heretic, or play any role in the heretic's *ipso jure* separation from the Church, nor does it merely dispose the heretic to be actually separated from the Church, but only gives juridical recognition and adds force of law to the *fact* of separation accomplished *suapte natura* by heresy. The severing of the juridical bond is accomplished by the heretic *per se* by his own actions. Consequently, any censure merely gives juridical recognition to the *fact* of separation, and thus imposes the obligation of absolution from the censure as a condition for reconciliation with the Church.

---

[251] The term *"suapte natura"* simply means "by or of its own nature". The meaning in law is identical: "Lat. In its own nature. Suapte natura sterilis, barren in its own nature and quality; intrinsically barren." – Black's Law Dictionary (online) The act of desertion from the Church is intrinsic to the nature of the manifest sin of heresy, apostasy or schism, committed as an external act; whereas the act of separating oneself from the Church is not intrinsic to the nature other crimes, but the separation takes place by the authority of the Church.

If the Salza/Siscoe interpretation of *Mystici Corporis* were correct,[252] i.e., that only the *crime* of heresy *suapte natura*, but not the manifest *sin* of heresy, (apart from any consideration of heresy considered under its formal aspect as a *crime*), *suapte natura* severs the heretic from the body of the Church, then the distinction between those who depart from the Church by their own act of desertion into heresy or schism, and those who are expelled from the Church by legitimate authority would not exist, since all sinners separated from the Church for being guilty of a delict, including heretics and schismatics, would then be separated from the Church by legitimate authority – by a judgment of guilt, or a sentence of excommunication incurred or inflicted by legitimate ecclesiastical authority; and not by the very nature of the act of desertion. It is also quite absurd to say that the crime of heresy only, but not the sin, (which is identical in essence to the sin, and defined in both Canon Law and Moral Theology in identical terms), *suapte natura* severs the perpetrator from the Church; and that it accomplishes this separation in some manner different than by which other crimes separate the offender from the Church, since under the formal aspect of *crime*, i.e. *according to the nature of a crime*, no criminal act, formally considered under that aspect, severs the perpetrator from the Church *suapte natura*, but only *by legitimate authority*. It is only the penal censure added to heresy in ecclesiastical law, and not the nature of the act that makes the external sin of heresy a crime; and therefore, considered under its formal aspect as as a crime, heresy is a crime according to the definition of crime in Canon Law, and as such is indistinguishable in nature from any other crime; and all crimes, according to the nature of a crime, separate the offender from the Church *by legitimate authority*, and not *suapte natura*. Only Schism, heresy and apostasy are the sole exceptions, which accomplish that

---

[252] The Salza/Siscoe interpreration of Mystici Corporis is not shared by any academically qualified theologian in the world. Mons. Van Noort wrote:

"b. Public heretics (and a fortiori, apostates) are not members of the Church. They are not members because they separate themselves from the unity of Catholic faith and from the external profession of that faith. Obviously, therefore, they lack one of three factors—baptism, profession of the same faith, union with the hierarchy—pointed out by Pius XII as requisite for membership in the Church. The same pontiff has explicitly pointed out that, unlike other sins, heresy, schism, and apostasy automatically sever a man from the Church. 'For not every sin, however grave and enormous it be, is such as to sever a man automatically from the Body of the Church, as does schism or heresy or apostasy'." (Dogmatic Theology, Volume II, Christ's Church, p. 241-242.)

separation *suapte natura*, because these sins themselves in their very nature are intrinsically acts of separation from the Church.

It is also patent that in *Mystici Corporis*, where it teaches on the question of the separation from the Church brought about by heresy schism and apostasy *suapte natura*, these acts are considered in themselves according to their intrinsic nature, i.e. as *sins*, and not according to their formal aspect of being canonical *crimes*, which is extrinsic to their nature as acts, since it is stated therein that it is a matter, not of human law, but of divine law (***iubente Domino***) that those who refuse to hear the Church are cut off:

> «*Sicut igitur in vero christifidelium coetu unum tantummodo habetur Corpus, unus Spiritus, unus Dominus et unum Baptisma, sic haberi non potest nisi una fides; 18 atque adeo qui Ecclesiam audire renuerit, iubente Domino habendus est ut ethnicus et publicanus. 19 Quamobrem qui fide vel regimine invicem dividuntur, in uno eiusmodi Corpore atque uno eius divino Spiritu vivere nequeunt.*»

And thus he says in the following paragraph, that hence, literally, *siquidem*, i.e., "accordingly" not all sins as do schism, heresy, or apostasy separate by their very nature a man from the body of the Church: «*20 Siquidem non omne admissum, etsi grave scelus, eiusmodi est ut — sicut schisma, vel haeresis, vel apostasia faciunt — suapte natura hominem ab Ecclesiae Corpore separet.*»

Finally, if the Salza/Siscoe opinion that only the *crime* of heresy by its very nature (but not the public *sin* by its very nature), severs the heretic from the Church, then the perpetual teaching of the Church, namely, that the sin of heresy *per se* according to its intrinsic nature as an act of separation severs the heretic from the body of the Church, and not heresy merely considered as an ecclesiastical crime (which is extrinsic to the nature of heresy), would be an error. St. Robert Bellarmine, commenting on the fourth opinion in *De Romano Pontifice liber ii cap. xxx*, quotes St. Jerome (d. 420 AD), one of the four major Latin Fathers, who teaches with the unanimous consensus of the Fathers, «Jerome comments on the same place, saying that *other sinners, through a judgment of excommunication are excluded from the Church; heretics, however, leave by themselves and are cut from the body of Christ*». Bellarmine states explicitly that the heretic is cut off from the body of the Church before any sentence of excommunication comes into effect: «Yet heretics are outside the Church, even before excommunication, and deprived of all jurisdiction, for they are condemned by their own judgment, as the Apostle teaches to Titus; that is, they are cut from the body of the Church without excommunication, as Jerome expresses it.»

St. Robert Bellarmine teaches most explicitly (*De Romano Pontifice, lib. ii. cap. xxx*) that it is **heresy by its very nature, (*ex natura haeresis*), which severs the heretic from the Church, and causes the immediate loss of ecclesiastical office:** «Thenceforth, **the Holy Fathers teach in unison, that not only are heretics outside the Church, but they even lack all Ecclesiastical jurisdiction and dignity *ipso facto*.**» In *De Ecclesia Militante* Bellarmine says it is demonstrated by the testimony of the Fathers who teach with a common consensus that those who are outside the Church have no authority or jurisdiction in the Church;[253] and quoting St. Augustine, Bellarmine declares that *all heretics* and *all schismatics* have departed from the Church.[254] Salza & Siscoe desperately attempt to interpret the Fathers as teaching that the heretic's severing himself from the Church and the subsequent loss of office does not take place without the authority of the Church, but result from an ecclesiastical censure or judgment of the crime. Bellarmine, in his refutation of the Fourth Opinion utterly destroys that argument:

> «Nor does the response which some make avail, that these Fathers speak according to ancient laws, but now since the decree of the Council of Constance they do not lose jurisdiction, unless excommunicated by name, or if they strike clerics. I say this avails to nothing. ***For those Fathers, when they say that heretics lose jurisdiction, do not allege any human laws which maybe did not exist then on this matter; rather, they argued from the nature of heresy.*** Moreover, the Council of Constance does not speak except on the excommunicates, that is, on these who lose jurisdiction through a judgment of the Church. Yet ***heretics are outside the Church, even before excommunication, and deprived of all jurisdiction, for they are condemned by their own judgment***, as the Apostle teaches to Titus; that is, ***they are cut from the body of the Church without excommunication, as Jerome expresses it.***»

---

[253] «Secundo demonstratur hoc idem ex testimoniis eorum Partum, qui communi consensu docent, eos qui sunt extra Ecclesiam, nullam habere auctoritatem aut jurisdictionem in Ecclesiam.» [*De Controversiis Christianae Fidei Adversus Hujus Temporis Haereticos, Tomus Secundus, Liber Tertius, De Ecclesia Militante Toto Orbe Difusa, Cap. X,* Neapoli, 1837, p. 90.]

[254] «s. Augustinus… Sic enim ait… *Omnes hæretici, omnes schismatici ex nobis exierunt idest, ex Ecclesia exierunt*» [*Ibid.* p. 89.]

(Neque valet, quod quidam respondent, istos Patres loqui *secundum antiqua jura,* nunc autem ex decreto Concilii Constantiensis non amittere jurisdictionem, nisi nominatim excommunicatos, & percussores clericorum; hoc, inquam, nihil valet. Nam Patres illi cum dicunt haereticos amittere jurisdictionem, **non allegant ulla jura humana**, quae etiam forte tunc nulla extabant de hac re: **sed argumentantur ex natura haeresis**. Concilium autem Constantiense, non loquitur *nisi de excommunicatis*, id est, de his, qui per sententiam Ecclesiae amiserunt jurisdictionem. Haeretici autem etiam ante excummunicationem sunt extra Ecclesiam, & privati omni jurisdictione: sunt enim proprio judicio condemnati, ut docet Apostolus ad Titum3. V. II. Hoc est: praecisi a corpore Ecclesiae, sine excommunicatione, ut Hieronymus exponit.) Thus, St. Robert Bellarmine proves that it is the teaching of scripture, interpreted unanimously by the Fathers, that heretics are outside the Church and lose all jurisdiction entirely by themselves – straightaway (*mox perdere omnem jurisdictionem*). On this point, he is also following the *Doctor Communis*: *"Potestas autem iurisdictionalis est quae ex simplici iniunctione hominis confertur. Et talis potestas non immobiliter adhaeret. Unde in schismaticis et haereticis non manet. Unde non possunt nec absolvere nec excommunicare nec indulgentias facere, aut aliquid huiusmodi, quod si fecerint, nihil est actum."* (*Summa Theol.* 2 – 2 Q. 39 a. 3) In his argument Bellarmine cites this article of St. Thomas explicitly: «Denique etiam D. *Thomas* 2. 2. Q. 39. art. 3. docet schismaticos mox perdere omnem jurisdictionem, et irrita esse, si quae ex jurisdictione agere conentur.»

In this article, St. Thomas explains that the spiritual power is twofold (*duplex est spiritualis potestas*): *sacramental* and *jurisdictional* (*una quidem sacramentalis; alia iurisdictionalis*). The sacramental power remains even in those who fall into schism or heresy; and he explains why this is so;[255] but he also explains why schismatics and heretics lose the right to exercise the sacramental power.[256] Then, in the above cited passage, the

---

[255] «Sacramentalis quidem potestas est quæ per aliquam consecrationem confertur. Omnes autem consecrationes Ecclesiæ sunt immobiles, manente re quæ consecratur, sicut patet etiam in rebus inanimatis, nam altare semel consecratum non consecratur iterum nisi fuerit dissipatum. Et ideo talis potestas secundum suam essentiam remanet in homine qui per consecrationem eam est adeptus quandiu vivit, sive in schisma sive in hæresim labatur, quod patet ex hoc quod rediens ad Ecclesiam non iterum consecratur.»

[256] «Sed quia potestas inferior non debet exire in actum nisi secundum quod movetur a potestate superiori, ut etiam in rebus naturalibus patet; inde est quod tales usum potestatis amittunt, ita scilicet quod non liceat eis sua potestate uti.

Angelic Doctor explains why one who falls into schism or heresy (*in schisma sive in haeresim labatur*) simply loses the power of jurisdiction. In this teching, St. Thomas provides the theological foundation for the teaching of Pope St. Celestine on a heretic's loss of jurisdiction: "For he who had defected from the faith with such preachings, cannot depose or remove anyone whatsoever."[257]

The foundation of this doctrine of automatic loss of all jurisdiction by heretics and schismatics is that *it pertains to the very nature of the sins of heresy and schism* that they *per se* separate one from the unity of the Church. Schism is opposed to unity, whence it is said that the **sin** of schism is **directly** and ***per se*** opposed to unity. Now that which is intended *per se* constitutes the *species* of the act; and thus *schism is properly a special sin in that it intends directly to separate one from the unity of the Church*.[258] Both sins, schism and heresy, are *per se* opposed to the unity of the Church, since heresy is *per se* opposed to the unity of the one faith; and schism is *per se* opposed to the unity of ecclesiastical charity; and for which reason, every heretic is a schismatic, but not vice versa.[259] Thus, a schismatic act,

---

Si tamen usi fuerint, eorum potestas effectum habet in sacramentalibus, quia in his homo non operatur nisi sicut instrumentum Dei; unde effectus sacramentales non excluduntur propter culpam quamcumque conferentis sacramentum.»

[257] Fr. Gerald McDevitt, in *The Renunciation of an Ecclesiastical Office*: "And in a letter to the clergy of Constantinople, Pope St. Celestine I says: The authority of Our Apostolic See has determined that the bishop, cleric, or simple Christian who had been deposed or excommunicated by Nestorius or his followers, after the latter began to preach heresy shall not be considered deposed or excommunicated. For he who had defected from the faith with such preachings, cannot depose or remove anyone whatsoever." Fr. McDevitt's exposition on this point is provided later in this work.

[258] «Scissio autem unitati opponitur. Unde peccatum schismatis dicitur quod directe et per se opponitur unitati, sicut enim in rebus naturalibus id quod est per accidens non constituit speciem, ita etiam nec in rebus moralibus. In quibus id quod est intentum est per se, quod autem sequitur præter intentionem est quasi per accidens. Et ideo peccatum schismatis proprie est speciale peccatum ex eo quod intendit se ab unitate separare quam caritas facit.» [*II^a-II^æ q. 39 a. 1 co.*]

[259] «hæresis et schisma distinguuntur secundum ea quibus utrumque per se et directe opponitur. Nam hæresis per se opponitur fidei, schisma autem per se opponitur unitati ecclesiasticæ caritatis. Et ideo sicut fides et caritas sunt diversæ virtutes, quamvis quicumque careat fide careat caritate; ita etiam schisma et

whether it be an act of pure schism, or schism connected with heresy, in its very nature separates the schismatic from the body of the Church because it separates one *per se* from the unity of the Church. The Church is *One* in virtue of her unity: 1) unity of faith, 2) unity of cult, 3) unity under one visible head. Thus Canon Law states that "Those baptised are fully in communion with the Catholic Church on this earth who are joined with Christ in its visible structure by the bonds of profession of faith, of the sacraments and of ecclessiastical governance." (can. 205). When one commits an act that *per se* visibly severs any one of those bonds of communion, one is separated by that act from the unity of the body of the Church. Thus, schismatics, heretics and apostates *miserably separate themselves* from the unity of the Church; whereas those who are separated for other crimes, are expelled *by legitimate authority*, as *Mystici Corporis* teaches. Referring specifically to the expulsion from the Church of heretics, schismatics, and apostates, the Canon Law Society Commentary explains, "The Church, does not expel persons from its midst. Essentially the apostate, heretic, or schismatic withdraws those bonds (of full communion) by a personal act. The Church recognises this in declaring the bonds severed..."[260]

It is also shown by reason – by the very meaning of the words schism, heresy, apostasy *suapte natura* in *Mystici Corporis*, and and *ex natura haeresis* in *De Romano Pontifice*, that what is being spoken of is heresy in itself, *in its very own nature*, and not heresy considered as a violation of ecclesiastical law; because a thing considered in its nature, is considered formally as a *principium motus in eo quod est*. St. Thomas takes this definition straight from the Physics of Aristotle (Aristotle, Physics, III, I, 201 a 10 s.); and says, «*Naturalia enim sunt quorum principium motus in ipsis est.*» (*Sancti Thomae de Aquino, De motu cordis ad magistrum Philippum de Castro Caeli*) Thus to speak of heresy *suapte natura*, or of heresy *ex natura haeresis*, refers to it as a principle of motion that is intrinsic to itself, and by which it separates the heretic from the Church, and not by any extrinsic principle such as the force of ecclesiastical law or of a declaration of a judge.

Thus, as explained above, it is by faith that one is first united to God; and by the external profession of faith, and the sacrament of faith, that

---

hæresis sunt diversa vitia, quamvis quicumque est hæreticus sit etiam schismaticus, sed non convertitur.» [II[a]-IIæ q. 39 a. 1 ad 3]

[260] James A. Coriden, Thomas J. Green, Donald E. Heintschel; *THE CODE OF CANON LAW, A Text and Commentary*, Commissioned by THE CANON LAW SOCIETY OF AMERICA, et al., p. 128.

one enters the Church, because it pertains properly to the nature of faith that it unites one to God and to his Church; and it is by the contrary disposition of the sin of infidelity – of heresy or apostasy, by which one, with an external act, rejects faith, and leaves the Church. Such is the motion proper to each nature, as St. Thomas explains, that the natural motion of fire is upward, and of earth downward (*motus autem naturalis ad unam partem est, ut ignis sursum, et terrae deorsum*); so likewise, the motion of faith brings one into the Church, and heresy *suapte natura* takes one out.

Bellarmine explains that even bad Catholics are united to the Church and are members, they are united by the soul through faith, and by the body through the confession of faith and the visible participation of the sacraments. (*Nam Catholici enim mali sunt uniti, & sunt membra; animo, per fidem; corpore per confessionem fidei, & visibilium Sacramentorum participationem*); and secret heretics are united and are members only by external union, but a manifest heretic is not a member of the Church in any manner, by neither soul nor body, neither by internal nor external union. (*haereticus manifestus, nullo modo est membrum Ecclesiae, id est, neque animo, neque corpore, sive neque unione interna, neque externa*)

Applying this doctrine to the hypothetical case of a manifestly heretical pope, Bellarmine explains (nn. 9, 10, and 11 of his exposition on Opinion No. 4), in what manner faith is *simpliciter* a necessary disposition for one to be pope; and faith being removed, by its contrary disposition, which is heresy, the pope would straightaway cease to be pope, with the necessary disposition for the form of the papacy not being able to be preserved. (*ista dispositione sublata per contrariam quae est haeresis, mox papa desinit esse; neque enim potest forma conservari sine necessariis dispositionibus.*) It is therefore on this theological foundation that Bellarmine judges the fifth opinion to be the "true opinion", and according to it that Bellarmine's explication of it must be interpreted. **Bellarmine explains, and states explicitly and categorically that without the necessary disposition of faith, the loss of papal office would take place *immediately* and *entirely without the involvement of any other external agent*.** «*Deinde*, quae habent ultimam dispositionem ad interitum, Paulo post desinunt esse, sine alia vi externa, ut patet; igitur et Papa haereticus sine alia depositione *per se* desinit esse Papa.» Thus, when Bellarmine comments in his exposition of the third opinion, according to which a heretical pope cannot be "deposed" (*"esse depositum aut deponi posse"*), it is clearly his meaning when he says that this opinion is "exceedingly improbable" (*opinio valde* *improbabilis*) that he does not judge against the opinion that there cannot be the deposition of a pope while still in office (*deponendus*), as is manifestly evident from his exposition on the fourth and fifth opinions; but he judges highly improbable that opinion which denies that a heretic would cease to be pope entirely by himself (*depositus*), i.e. *"per se"* and without the intervention of any external agent (*sine alia vi externa*); or, as Pope Gregory XVI expressed it of the claimant Pedro De Luna (Benedict XIII), if ever he was pope, would have already "fallen" ("decaduto") by himself (*"per se"*) from the papal throne for having attacked the dogma *"unam sanctam"*.[261]

The correct understanding of the doctrine of St Robert Bellarmine, which exposes the absurdity of the Salza & Siscoe interpretation of Bellarmine's doctrine on the question of a heretic pope, is explained by the Jesuit canonists Franz Xavier Wernz S.J. and Pedro Vidal S.J. in, *Jus Canonicum* (1938) Chapter VII:

> **453. By heresy which is notorious and openly made known. The Roman Pontiff should he fall into it is by that very fact even before any declaratory sentence of the Church deprived of his power of**

---

[261] "Ora quali molestie non riceveva ella la Chiesa da Benedetto, che pertinacemente col fatto impugnava l'articolo unam, sanctam? Fulminava questi i più terribili anatemi contro il Concilio, e contro gli aderenti agli altri Pontefici, e praticava tutti I più precipitosi attentati onde conservarsi sul trono illegitimmante occupato; pretendendo che la Chiesa di Gesù Cristo perita in tutte le altre parti del mondo, si trovasse ristretta nella sola Paniscola, come rispose ai legati del Concolio: Ibi non est Ecclesia, sed in Paniscola est vera, inquam, Ecclesia… hic est arca Noe (1). Ond'è che poteasi, come osserva il Ballerini, considerarlo quale pubblico scismatico e eretico, ed in conseguenza per se decaduto dal pontificato, se anche ad esso fosse stato validamente inalzato." (*Il trionfo della santa sede e della chiesa contro gli assatti dei novatori*, p. 46-47) Translation: "Now what harassments did she, the Church, not receive from Benedict, who obstinately by his deeds attacked the article unam, sancatm? He fulminated these most terrible anathemas against the Council, and against adherents to other Pontiffs, and made the more precipitous attacks in order to keep himself on the illegitimately occupied throne; claiming that the Church of Jesus Christ to have perished in all other parts of the world, and that it was restricted only in Paniscola, as he said to the legates of the Council: 'That is not a Church, but in Paniscola, I say, is the true Church… This is Noah's Ark'. So then he could be considered, as noted by Ballerini, to have been a public schismatic and heretic, and consequently to have fallen from the papacy by himself, even if he had been validly elevated to it."

jurisdiction. (*Per haeresim notoriam et palam divulgatam R. Pontifex si in illam incidat, ipso facto etiam ante omnem sententiam declaratoriam Ecclesiae sua potestate iurisdictionis privatus existit*) Concerning this matter there are five Opinions of which the first denies the hypothesis upon which the entire question is based, namely that a Pope even as a private doctor can fall into heresy. This opinion although pious and probable cannot be said to be certain and common. For this reason the hypothesis is to be accepted and the question resolved.»[262] [NB – The term *notorious* in the expression, *by heresy which is notorious and openly made known*, is clearly denoting the common meaning of the word, (equivalent to public, manifest, evident or known[263]) in the context that the authors are using it,

---

[262] It is Bellarmine's position in his day which is explained with the words, "This opinion although pious and probable cannot be said to be certain and common." Since the First Vatican Council the First Opinion has become the *opinio communissima*, as Don Curzio Nitoglia (quoted in Part III Section II) points out; and is arguably (as will be explained in Part III Section III) not merely probable, but *theologically certain or nearly certain*. Fr Jean-Michel Gleize points out (in his article *The Question of Papal Heresy*) in reply to the question, "Can a pope fall into heresy?": "In fact, the negative answer to this question is the **common opinion** of theologians of the modern era."

[263] **Notorious** – «Ordinarily it is equivalent to public, manifest, evident, known; all these terms have something in common, they signify that a thing, far from being secret, may be easily known by many. Notoriety, in addition to this common idea, involves the idea of indisputable proof, so that what is notorious is held as proved and serves as a basis for the conclusions and acts of those in authority, especially judges. To be as precise as is possible, "public" means what any one may easily prove or ascertain, what is done openly; what many persons know and hold as certain, is "manifest"; what a greater or less number of persons have learnt, no matter how, is "known"; what is to be held as certain and may no longer be called in question is "notorious"... Whatever is easily shown and is known by a sufficient number of persons to be free from reasonable doubt is notorious in fact. This kind of notoriety may refer either to a transitory fact, e.g., Caius was assassinated; or permanent facts, e.g., Titius is parish priest of this parish; or recurring facts, e.g. Sempronius engages in usurious transactions. Whatever has been judicially ascertained, viz., judicial admissions, an affair fully proved, and the judgment rendered in a lawsuit, is notorious in law; the judge accepts the fact as certain without investigation; nor will he allow, except in certain well-specified cases, the matter to be called in question. "Notorious" is then used as more or less synonymous with "official". Such also are facts recorded in official documents, as civil or ecclesiastical registries of births, deaths, or marriages, notarial records. Lastly, whatever arises from a rule of law based on a "violent" presumption, for instance, paternity and

and not according to the strict canonical definition of the term as it is defined in penal law, as some authors arbitrarily interpret it; seizing upon the word *notorious*, and uncritically assuming it to denote a canonical *delict* that a *judge* has pronounced by a *judicial sentence* – (something that is impossible in the case of a manifestly heretical pope); or denoting a notoriety in the strict sense of a notorious *delict*, that would need to conform to the strict criteria of a *delict notorious by fact* in penal law – and in fact, (as will be shown later), according to Salza & Siscoe, the delict would have to conform to stricter criteria than those set forth in the 1917 Code of Canon Law for a crime to be considered *notorious by fact*. Thus it is manifestly evident that Wernz and Vidal do not apply the term *notorious* in its strictly canonical sense of a *delict* that is canonically *notorious by fact*; but in its ordinary sense that, apart from the strict considerations of penal law, they construe the term *notorious* to denote the *fact of defection* that is public and manifest; since in this instance the authors, in the cited passage, are not expounding what is properly a point of canon law, but of *speculative theology* intimately connected with canon law; namely, the loss of office *ex natura haeresis*, as is manifestly evident from the context of Bellarmine's explicitly stated exposition on the fifth opinion. What is *canonically notorious* is a question of law[264], and is therefore determined by legislation, jurisprudence, and principles of law. Although in Moral Theology, as far as the moral imputability of the act is concerned, the definition of *notorious heresy* in the sense of not merely material heresy of a Catholic who errs in ignorance, but of *formal heresy*, would be more or less but not entirely materially equivalent[265], to the definition of notorious heresy in the case of a delict of heresy as it is understood in its penal/canonical connotation of *notoriety of fact*; the moral-theological definition is nevertheless formally distinguished from the penal/canonical definition by the fact that it is not a question of law determined by legalities, but is determined by the moral object of the act, and according to the nature of that which morally constitutes the sin of

---

filiation in case of a legitimate marriage, is presumptively notorious.» (*Catholic Encyclopedia*)

[264] Rev. Stanislaus Woywod. O.F.M.; *A Commentary and Summary of the New Code of Canon Law; New York, London, 1918, The Fifth Book, Offenses and Penalties*, p. 162: "**The nature of an offence is to be judged from the subject matter of the law.** The greater or lesser culpability depends not only on the gravity of the law which is violated, but also on the degree of sinfulness of the action and the harm caused. (Canon 2196.) 1481."

[265] *Ibid.*, p. 162: "1. **Public**, if it actually has been divulged or circumstances are such that it easily can and must become public; […] 3. **Notorious** by notoriety of fact, if the offence is publicly known and has been committed under such circumstances that it cannot be kept secret by any artifice, nor can be excused by any subterfuge of law".

heresy as a notorious act. It is in this moral-theological sense, that an act of formal heresy can plainly be considered to be notorious when the act of obstinate denial or doubt of a revealed truth of faith is *public*, and concerns: 1) a revealed truth that pertains to natural law[266]; 2) a universally known dogma that no Catholic is ignorant of[267]; 3) heresy under such circumstances under which the heretic acknowledges that his belief is contrary to dogma; 4) obstinate doubt or denial that persists after correction.]

«A second opinion holds that the Roman Pontiff forfeits his power automatically even on account of occult heresy. This opinion is rightly said by Bellarmine to be based upon a false supposition, namely that even occult heretics are completely separated from the body of the Church... The third opinion thinks that the Roman Pontiff does not automatically forfeit his power and cannot be deprived of it by deposition even for manifest heresy. This assertion is very rightly said by Bellarmine to be 'extremely improbable'.»

«The fourth opinion, with Suarez, Cajetan and others, contends that a Pope is not automatically deposed even for manifest heresy, but that he can and must be deposed by at least a declaratory sentence of the crime. 'Which opinion in my judgment is indefensible', as Bellarmine teaches.»

«Finally, there is the fifth opinion – that of Bellarmine himself – which was expressed initially and is rightly defended by Tanner and others as the best proven and the most common. For he who is no longer a member of the body of the Church, i.e. the Church as a visible society, cannot be the head of the Universal Church. **But a Pope who fell into public heresy would cease by that very fact to be a member of the Church. Therefore he would also cease by that very fact to be the head of the Church.**»

«Indeed, a publicly heretical Pope, who, by the commandment of Christ and the Apostle must even be avoided because of the danger to the Church, must be deprived of his power as almost all admit. But he cannot be deprived by a merely declaratory sentence... Wherefore, *it must be firmly stated that a heretical Roman Pontiff would by that very fact forfeit his power*. Although a declaratory sentence of the crime which is not to be

---

[266] It is impossible that one would be to any degree inculpable for reason of ignoance for denying any of the most basic revealed truths of faith, such as the necessity of faith for salvation, because that pertains to the Natural Law which is written in the heart (Rom. 2:15): *"Certum est hominem teneri ex lege naturali ad Deum per Fidem, Spem et Charitatem se convertere, et ideo elicere earum virtutum actus" (S. Alphonsus de Liguri, Opera Moralia, Lib. II, Tract. I, De Præcepto Fidei. cap. II)* – and therefore, besides the patent matter of heresy, there would necessarily be present the pertinacity, which is the inexcusable form of the sin of heresy, since, "whoever shall have sinned without the law shall perish without the law". (Rom. 2:12).

[267] *De Lugo, disp. XX, sect. IV, n. 157-158.*

rejected in so far as it is merely declaratory would be such that *the heretical pope would not be judged, but would rather be shown to have been judged.*»

Thus, the great Jesuit canonists of the Gregorian University explain that Opinion No. 5 of St. Robert Bellarmine is based on the doctrine of Pope Innocent III, who said in *Sermo IV De Diversis*, "Since the Roman Pontiff has no other superior than God... who could cast him out or trample him under foot? ... But he ought not vainly flatter himself because of his power... because the less he is judged by men, the more he is judged by God. I say the less, because he can be judged by men, or rather he **can be shown to be already judged**, if he should wither away into heresy; because «*he who does not believe has already been judged (John III)*»"[268] Again, in another passage, in Sermo II: «*In tantum enim fides mihi necessaria est ut cum de caeteris peccatis solum Deum judicem habeam, propter solum peccatum quod in fide committitur possem ab Ecclesia judicari.* **Nam qui non credit, iam iudicatus est.** *(Joh.3 18).*»

Thus it is not an exception to the principle, *Apostolica Sedes a nemine iudicatur*, as many had taught before the solemn definition of the universal papal primacy of jurisdiction by the First Vatican Council made such an interpretation inadmissible, but rather, as Paul Hinschius explained in his monumental work on Canon Law[269], **a series of Catholic writers**, and already **Innocent III and St. Robert Bellarmine, see no exception** to that rule, **because a pope who falls into heresy would already leave the Church and forfeit the Pontificate**, so that a council could no longer depose him (in the proper sense of a juridical deposition of a reigning Pontiff), but could only declare that the loss of office had taken place:

«Eine Reihe katholischer Schriftsteller wollen aber darin keine Ausnahme von der gedachten Regel finden, weil der in Ketzerei verfallene Papst sich dadurch selbst von der Kirche ausscheide, damit weiter den

---

[268] «Unde, cum Romanus pontifex non habeat alium dominum nisi Deum... quis potest eum foras mittere aut pedibus conculcari?... Verum non frustra sibi blandiatur de potestate, neque de sublimitate vel honore temere glorietur; quia quanto minus judicatur ab homine, tanto magis judicatur a Deo. Minus dico; quia potest ab hominibus judicari, *vel potius judicatus ostendi*» – Sermo IV De Diversis

[269] *System des katholischen Kirchenrechts mit besonderer Rücksicht auf Deutschland, Erster Band*, Berlin, 1869, p. 307.

Pontifikat verwirke und also das Konzil keine Deposition mehr verhängen könne, sondern nur die Thatsache des erfolgten Verlustes der Päpstlichen Würde zu konstatiren habe. [3] (Dieser Gedanke tritt schon bei Innocenz III. auf (im Sermo IV. In consecrat. pontiff. opp. Colon. 1575. 1. 197): «Potest (pontifex) ab hominibus iudicari vel potius iudicatus ostendi, si videlicet evanescat in haeresim, quoniam qui non credit, iam iudicatus est») Vgl. ferner Bellarmin, christ. Fidei controv. gen. III. De Romano pontifice II. 30. (ed. Ingolstadt. 1605. 1083): «Est ergo opinio quinta vera, papam haereticum manifestum per se desinere esse [papam et caput, sicut per se desinit esse] christianus et membrum corporis Ecclesiae; quare ab ecclesia posse eum iudicari et puniri. Haec est sententia omnium veterum patrum qui docent haereticos manifestos mox amittere omnem jurisdictionem»; Fagnan. comm. Ad c. 4. X. de elect. I. 6. n. 70 ff; Fragosi, regimen reipubl. Christianae lib. II. c. I. §. 2. n. 21 (Lugduni. 1648. 2, 11); Kober, Deposition. S. 585.» (see translation in Part II)

With an arrogant stupidity that nearly defies belief, Salza and Siscoe say that it is I who have not understood the teaching of St. Robert Bellarmine correctly, in spite of the fact that all the great scholars, canonists, jurists and theologians of recent centuries have unanimously understood Bellarmine's doctrine in the manner that I have explained it; yet it is on the basis of their own grotesquely inverted interpretation of Bellarmine and of *Mystici Corporis* that they obstinately justify their heretical doctrine, that heresy by itself does not separate the heretic from the Church and directly cause the loss of office without an ecclesiastical censure or judgment – whereas it is plainly set forth and proven by Bellarmine that it is the unanimous teaching of the Fathers interpreting scripture that heresy in its very nature severs one from the Church, and directly brings about the loss of ecclesiastical office before and even without any judgment of the Church; and being the unanimous teaching of the Fathers, it must be believed *de fide*.

Salza and Siscoe still adamantly maintain, that, «As we explain in great detail in our book, Bellarmine and Suarez teach that the Pope will lose his office, ipso facto, once he is judged by the Church to be a heretic, without the additional juridical act of vitandus declaration.» Wernz and Vidal have explained that the opinion of Suárez is not that of Bellarmine, who says Opinon No. 5 is the "true opinion", but that Suárez subscribed to Opinion No. 4. Thus, Salza and Siscoe quote Suárez to justify their errant doctrine, claiming that those who follow Bellarmine in saying that the loss of office takes place before any judgment, «have erred [...] by interpreting the ipso facto loss of office to be similar to an "ipso facto" latae sententiæ excommunication, which occurs automatically (or ipso facto), when one commits an offense that carries the penalty, without requiring an antecedent judgment by the Church. But this is not at all what Bellarmine and Suarez meant by the ipso facto loss of office. What they meant is that the ipso facto loss of office occurs after the Church judges the Pope to be a heretic and before any additional juridical sentence or excommunication (which differs from Cajetan's opinion). In other words, after the Church establishes "the fact" that the Pope is a manifest heretic, he, according to this opinion, is deemed to lose his office ipso facto ("by the fact"). This is clear from the following quotation from Suarez who wrote: "Therefore, others [e.g., Azorius] affirm the Church is superior to the Pope in the case of heresy, but this is difficult to say. For Christ the Lord constituted the Pope as supreme judge absolutely; even the canons indifferently and generally affirm this; and at length the Church does not validly exercise any act of jurisdiction against the Pope; nor is the power conferred to him by election, rather [the Church] merely designates a person upon whom Christ confers the power by himself; Therefore on deposing a heretical Pope, the Church would not act as superior to him, but juridically and by the consent of Christ she would declare him a heretic and therefore unworthy of Pontifical honors; he would THEN ipso facto and immediately be deposed by Christ..."»

Incredibly, Salza and Siscoe have interpreted Bellarmine by quoting Suárez (and John of St. Thomas)! In order to arrive at Bellarmine's meaning, it is necessary to make a critical examination of Bellarmine's own words; but Salza and Siscoe attempt to determine Bellarmine's meaning by quoting Suárez and John of St. Thomas — and these are the men who say, Fr. Kramer is an amateur! I will provide a critical commentary on St. Robert Bellarmine's teaching on this question in a later segment of this work. Since it may be necessary to devote entire sections of chapters to the five opinions, I will only comment on them briefly here; since Salza and Siscoe have expounded on this topic so ignorantly, that a full refutation of their errors needs to be done.

In their insolent ignorance, these mere dilettantes (Salza and Siscoe), who have no formal education in Sacred Theology or in Canon Law, and who cannot read theological works in Latin (the language of Sacred Theology)[270], have even gone so far as to say that the above mentioned

---

[270] In their book and on their website, Salza & Siscoe refer to the *munus Petrinum* as the "munus petrinus" – thereby manifesting their ignorance of

eminent canonists of the Pontifical Gregorian University have wrongly interpreted Suárez and Bellarmine, saying that they equate the opinion of Suárez with Cajetan; whereas in reality they did no such thing. What they did say is that Suárez and Cajetan were both of Opinion No. 4. Each had his own variation of the Fourth Opinion, but both of them opined that a manifest heretic pope would not lose office until judged by the Church – according to Cajetan by deposition, and according to Suárez, the logically incoherent opinion that the heretic pope would lose office *ipso facto* for heresy, but only after having been judged juridically by the Church, which amounts to a form of deposition. Wernz and Vidal correctly explain Bellarmine's Opinion No. 5, which holds that «***a Pope who fell into public heresy would cease by that very fact to be a member of the Church*** [...] he cannot be deprived by a merely declaratory sentence... Wherefore, ***it must be firmly stated that a heretical Roman Pontiff would by that very fact [of falling into heresy] forfeit his power.***» This is exactly what Bellarmine says, to wit, that a manifest heretic pope ceases to be pope, a Christian, and a member of the Church **by himself** (*per se*), having left the Church and the pontificate *by his own judgment*, and not after the judgment of others: "the true opinion is the fifth, according to which the Pope who is manifestly a heretic ceases by himself to be Pope and head, in the same way as he ceases to be a Christian and a member of the body of the Church"[271]; and, "heretics are outside the Church, even before excommunication, and deprived of all jurisdiction, for they are condemned by their own judgment"[272]. Salza & Siscoe simplistically equate the fourth opinion exclusively with the opinion of Cajetan, oblivious of the fact that many variations of the fourth opinion had already been formulated by medieval canonists centuries before Cajetan. That opinion had achieved its classical formulation from Cajetan in the 16th Century, so in refuting Opinion No. 4, Bellarmine zeroed in on Cajetan's formulation of it.

Opinion No. 2 differs essentially from Opinion No. 5 in that in the case of a secret heretic, unlike the manifest heretic who can be judged to have separated himself from the Church and fallen from office, the secret heretic does not pronounce judgment against himself, and therefore *cannot be judged by men* to have separated himself from the

---

elementary level Latin grammar that even a first-year student of High Scool Latin would know.

[271] *De Romano Pontifice lib. ii cap. xxx*, on the fifth opinion.
[272] *Ibid.*, on the fourth opinion.

Church, and to have fallen from office by means of tacit resignation of office. He would remain united to the Church by external union only; so, as a practical hypothesis, he would not cease being pope for the sin of occult heresy, because *he cannot be judged by men* to have fallen from office by tacit resignation, *nor does he resign voluntarily* – and, *since the occult heretic was made pope by means of the cooperation of men, neither he nor his jurisdiction can be removed except through men*. Since he receives his jurisdiction directly from God, *there exists no jurisdiction in the Church to deprive him of his office or jurisdiction*. Therefore, only God can remove his jurisdiction; but since *neither can he be deposed from office by men, nor can his jurisdiction be removed from him by men*; it is only if he were to visibly condemn himself as a heretic that he would be seen and judged by men to have forfeited his office and to have had his jurisdiction removed by God. Bellarmine states explicitly, «*Nam iurisdictio datur quidem Pontifici a Deo, sed hominum opera concurrente, ut patet; quia ab hominibus habet iste homo, qui ante non erat Papa, ut incipiat esse Papa; igitur non aufertur a Deo nisi per hominem,* **at hæreticus occultus non potest ab homine iudicari; nec ipse sponte eam potestatem vult relinquere**.»

The reason why God cannot secretly depose a heretic pope is that *it is impossible for the visible head of the Church on earth who was visibly made pope through men, to be invisibly removed without the involvement of men*; and therefore, if he is to be removed, he must be removed by men in a visible manner; since jurisdiction is given to the pope by God through men, and therefore it cannot be taken away from him except through the instrumentality of men, but a secret heretic cannot be judged by men. In saying this, Bellarmine is not saying that a reigning pontiff can actually be judged by men, (in *cap. xxvi* he absolutely excludes that a pope can ever be judged by anyone); but he is only explaining why a pope cannot be invisibly deposed by God. In *De Ecclesia Militante Cap. X*, Bellarmine explains at some length why it is that a secret heretic cannot be invisibly deposed from the pontificate. In his explanation of Opinion No. 5 and his refutation of Opinion No. 4, Bellarmine explained how a heretic pope would be visibly fall from from the Pontificate and have his jurisdiction taken away: the manifest heretic pope would cease to be pope "by himself" *(per se)*, i.e., **by his own judgment of condemnation against himself and not by the judgment of others**; and then, having already fallen from the pontificate and lost all jurisdiction as a direct result of his own judgment against himself, he could then be judged and punished by the Church. He explains at some length and argues most forcefully in his exposition on the fourth opinion in *De Romano Pontifice* *liber ii cap. xxx* why a pope while still in office **cannot be judged and deposed by the bishops or the cardinals**; and states categorically in *liber iv cap. vii* that **"the pope cannot be judged"**. Indeed, Bellarmine devotes an entire chapter (*lib. ii cap. xxvi*) to prove the thesis that, "The supreme Pontiff is judged by no one" – and he categoricaly states that, "the Roman Pontiff cannot be judged by anyone on earth."[273] In that chapter, he declares his judgment in the most absolute terms and in such language that excludes the possibility of any exception. Bellarmine's refutation of Opinion No. 2 must be understood according to the unequivocal doctrine he sets forh in his expositions on of Opinions No. 4 and No. 5, namely, that the manifest heretic pope would cease "by himself" to be pope, a Christian, and a member of the Church; and **"for which reason"** (*quare*) having ceased to be pope, "he may be judged and punished by the Church." The *judgment of men* he speaks of as necessary in order to bring about the manifest heretic's removal of jurisdiction and deposition from the papal office can only be *his own judgment against himself.* For however long his heresy would remain hidden or known only to a few, the occult heretic pronounces no judgment against himself, and remains in office as the visible head of the Church.

---

[273] «Argumentum decimum sumitur ex eo quod Romanus Pontifex a nemine in terris judicari potest. Non enim potest evidentius ostendi principatus ejus, quam si ostendatur ita omnibus prelatus, ut nemini sit subjectus. ... Loquimur ergo de Pontifice ratione solius pontificatus; ac dicimus eum, etiam si ditionem temporalem nullam haberet, non posse ullo modo judicari in terris ab ullo Principe christiano, sive saeculari, sive ecclesiastico; neque ab omnibus simul in Concilio congregatis. ... Observandum est tertio, rationem praecipuam, cur Papa judicari non possit, esse, quia Princeps est Ecclesiae totius, et proinde superiorem in terris non habet, nam quia summus Princeps est Ecclesiae, non potest judicari ab ullo Ecclesiastico Antistite, et rursum, quia respublica Ecclesiastica spiritualis est, ac proinde major, ac sublimior quavis republica temporali, propterea summus Princeps Ecclesiae dirigere et judicare summum Principem reipublicae temporalis; non autem ab eo dirigi, aut judicari debet, nisi rectus ordo, et ipsa rerum natura pervertatur. Haec, inquam, est ratio primaria; et, ut Scholae loquuntur, a priori: tamen, quia haec ratio assumit id, quod in tota haec disputatione probare nitimur; videlicet Romanum Pontificem Principem esse totius Ecclesiae: idcirco hac, et similibus rationibus praetermissis, ex testimoniis Conciliorum, Pontificum, Imperatorum, ac Doctorum Ecclesiae demonstrabimus, Romanum Praesulem judicari non posse: ut inde confirmemus primariam nostrum thesim; quae est, Romanum Pontificem caput et principem esse Ecclesiae universae.»

The only juridical judgment that can be made by others against him is the judgment made *post factum* after the heretic's pertinacity has been proven, and thereby his separation from the Church by his own judgment against himself would be made manifest. Thus, a judgment of men made by others, which would effect the secret heretic's unwilling loss of office and removal of his jurisdiction, **is a judgment that cannot be made by men.** In Chapter XXVI, Bellarmine categorically ruled out any possibility for a validly reigning pope to be judged. Therefore, Bellarmine explains that a pope, would not lose jurisdiction, nor dignity, nor the name of the head of the Church, either until he would manifestly separate himself from the Church by his public heresy, or; by having his secret heresy exposed and proven, his heresy would be made manifest, and he would thereby be separated against his will.[274] Hence, the only public judgment that can be made by men with juridical force would be the pronouncement of a ***declaratory sentence* that the man who was pope has lost office**, and not a **penal sentence**, i.e. a **judicial verdict of guilt on the pope while still in office,** which judges him as a superior and deposes him directly; or indirectly deposes him as a dispositive cause; (whether by separating the Church from him, or by disposing his *ipso facto* loss of office), **because such a judgment requires the jurisdiction of a superior**, and therefore is impossible to be made by non-superiors who lack jurisdiction. Since the solemn definition of the papal primacy, it is no longer admissible to hold the opinion that a pope while in office can be judged; and the opinion can be seen to be heretical, acoring to which a pope while still in office can be judged by anyone on earth for any reason, because *papal immunity* pertains to the very essence of the *judicial supremacy* of the primacy as solemnly defined by the First Vatican Council, and it has been repeatedly taught by the popes that the pope cannot be judged by anyone. Bellarmine definitely did not hold any form or variation of any opinion which would allow that a pope could be judged while still in office. When he declared that the pope's jurisdiction cannot be removed except through men, *he was explaining why the secret heretic's jurisdiction cannot be invisibly removed by God*, but in saying that, *he was not saying that it can actually be removed by the judgment of his inferiors.* He explains in the texts I have cited,

---

[274] «Certum est autem… si episcopus, aut etiam summus pontifex esset, non amittere jurisdictionem; nec dignitatem, aut nomen capitis in Ecclesia, donec aut ipse se ab Eccclesia publice separet, aut convictus hæreseos invitus separetur.» [*De Ecclesia Militante* Cap. X, p. 90.]

exactly why a manifest heretic pope cannot be deposed, nor have his jurisdiction removed by the judgment of the bishops, or of the cardinals, or by the judgment of anyone other than himself. Nevertheless, Salza and Siscoe stubbornly claim that it was Bellarmine's opinion expressed in Chapter 30 that the pope can be judged for heresy while still in office; and this is their justification to obstinately hold to their heretical opinion that a heretic pope would not lose office unless he is first judged by the public judgment of the Church. This opinion is heretical, because it directly opposes the doctrine of the injudicability of the pope (which Bellarmine argued and proved in Chapter 26); and which is set forth in the definition of the dogma of the universal primacy of jurisdiction of the Roman Pontiff in *Pastor Æternus*.

As I pointed out above, the observation of Hinschius that many Catholic authors had already avoided the conflict between the problematic doctrine that a pope, by way of exception, can be judged by the Church and deposed for heresy, and the principle opposed to it, namely, **Apostolica Sedes a nemine iudicatur**, by advancing the opinion that the manifest heretic pope falls from office by himself before any judgment is made against him by the Church, so that a Council would not be able to depose him, but would only declare the fact that the pope had fallen from the pontificate; and he quotes Innocent III and Belarmine as holding this opinion. It remains here only to be said, that Pope Gregory XVI (quoted above) was also of this same opinion as Bellarmine, and he based his opinion on the doctrine of Ballerini, who explained it with great erudition in his work, *De Potestate ecclesiastica Summorum Pontificum et Conciliorum generalium*. Gregory XVI, in the passage cited in the *Introduction*, wrote, "the deposition is not a prescription against the rights of the Primacy, and therefore against the current representation of the Church in the Pope recognized as such, but only against the person, who was before adorned with papal dignity." Pope Gregory had said of papal claimant Benedict XIII, "So then he could be considered, as noted by Ballerini, to have been a public schismatic and heretic, and consequently to have fallen from papacy by himself, even if he had been validly elevated to it." Ballerini wrote of this same case saying, "For this double reason of schism and heresy Benedict XIII (if one believes him to have been a true Pontiff), by his own will ipso facto abdicated the primacy and the pontificate, [and] rightly and legitimately was able to be deposed by the Council as a schismatic and heretic, which was not the case with John XXIII, which in the sentence passed against him was not stated. One sees by what means the divine providence employed the synod of Constance to end the most tenacious schism, so that that synod did not need to exercise any power of jurisdiction by its authority to depose any true, albeit unknown, actual Pontiff."[275] Ballerini says here that if Benedict XIII had been a valid pope; by his heresy and schism he would have *ipso facto* **of his own volition (*sua voluntate*) "abdicated the primacy and the pontificate"** *(primatu et pontificatu exauctoratus)*; and for that reason the Council could rightly and correctly depose him. However, this abdication having taken place before any judgment or canonical warnings, (the warnings were not canonical admonitions, but were made only in charity) by the Council, the Council in its judgment declared that he had shown himself to be a schismatic and heretic, therefore, Ballerini explains, the Council did not declare that it had "deposed" him, but simply that he was deposed (*depositum declaruit potius quam deposuit*). Hence, the Council did not depose him but declared him deposed **"as a precautionary measure"** (*"ad omnem cautelam"*), and that he had been automatically cast out by God, and deprived of all office and ecclesiastical dignity *ipso jure* due to obstinate heresy and schism. Thus the council's judgment (Session 37) did not depose or in any way cause him to lose office, but merely declared it *post factum*:

> "For, how greatly he has sinned against God's church and the entire christian people, fostering, and continuing the schism and division of God's church How ardent and frequent have been the devout and humble prayers, exhortations and requests of kings, princes and prelates with which he has been warned in charity, in accordance with the teaching of the gospel, to bring peace to the church, to heal its wounds and to reconstitute its divided parts into one structure and one body, as he had sworn to do, and as for a long time it was within his power to do! He was unwilling, however, to listen to their charitable admonitions. How many were the persons afterwards sent to attest to him! Because he did not listen at all even to these, it has been necessary, in accordance with the aforesaid evangelical teaching of Christ, to say to the church, since he has not listened even to her, that he should be

---

[275] «Hac itaque duplici schismate & hæresis causa Benedictus XIII, (si verum Pontificem fuisse existimes) ipso facto sua voluntate primatu & pontificatu exauctoratus, rite ac legitime deponi potuit a Concilio tamquam schismaticus & hæreticus; quod non congrueret Joanni XXIII, in sententia contra hunc edita declaratum non legitur. 18 Vides interim, quibus modis divina providentia usa est ad abolendum per Constantiensem synudum pertinacissimam schisma, ut ne opus esset eamdem synodum quiquam juris exercere ad deponendum sua auctoritate quempiam verum, licet ignotum, actualem Pontificem.» (p. 138)

treated as a heathen and a publican. All these things have been clearly proved by the articles coming from the inquiry into faith and the schism held before this present synod, regarding the above and other matters brought against him, as well as by their truth and notoriety. The proceedings have been correct and canonical, all the acts have been correctly and carefully examined and there has been mature deliberation. Therefore this same holy general synod, representing the universal church and sitting as a tribunal in the aforesaid inquiry, pronounces, decrees and declares by this definitive sentence written here, that the same Peter de Luna, called Benedict XIII as has been said, has been and is a perjurer, a cause of scandal to the universal church, a promoter and breeder of the ancient schism, that long established fission and division in God's holy church, an obstructer of the peace and unity of the said church, a schismatic disturber and a heretic, a deviator from the faith, a persistent violator of the article of the faith One holy catholic church, incorrigible, notorious and manifest in his scandal to God's church, and that he has rendered himself unworthy of every title, rank, honour and dignity, rejected and cut off by God, deprived by the law itself of every right in any way belonging to him in the papacy or pertaining to the Roman pontiff and the Roman church, and cut off from the catholic church like a withered member. This same holy synod, moreover, as a precautionary measure, since according to himself he actually holds the papacy, deprives, deposes and casts out the said Peter from the papacy and from being the supreme pontiff of the Roman church and from every title, rank, honour, dignity, benefice and office whatsoever. It forbids him to act henceforth as the pope or as the supreme and Roman pontiff. It absolves and declares to be absolved all Christ's faithful from obedience to him, and from every duty of obedience to him and from oaths and obligations in any way made to him. It forbids each and every one of Christ's faithful to obey, respond to or attend to, as if he were pope, the said Peter de Luna, who is a notorious, declared and deposed schismatic and incorrigible heretic, or to sustain or harbour him in any way contrary to the aforesaid, or to offer him help, advice or good will."[276]

---

[276] «Qui quantum in ecclesiam dei et universum populum christianum peccaverit schisma et divisionem ecclesiæ dei fovens nutriens atque continuans: quantis quam que frequentibus devotis et humilibus regum principum et prælatorum precibus exhortationibus et requisitionibus charitative iuxta doctrinam evangelicam admonitus fuerit ut pacem daret ecclesiæ et illius sanaret vulnera et eius partes divisas in unam compaginem et corpus unum reficeret quemadmodum ipse iuraverat erat que et diu fuit in sua potestate: quos tamen charitative corripientes nullatenus voluit exaudire quot sint postmodum testes adhibiti quibus etiam minime exauditis necesse fuit secundum prædictam christi evangelicam doctrinam dicere ecclesiae quam quia etiam non audivit habendus sit tamquam ethnicus et publicanus: capitula in causa inquisitionis fidei et

Thus, the doctrine that a heretic pope would lose office by himself, before any sentence, judgment, or declaration, was already affirmed and applied by the Council of Constance, in the decree that cleared the way for the election of Pope Martin V. As Hinschius observed in the above cited passage, this opinion is supported by the doctrine of Pope Innocent III, expressed in the words: «*Potest (pontifex) ab hominibus iudicari vel potius iudicatus ostendi, si videlicet evanescat in hæresim, quoniam qui non credit, iam iudicatus est*» – that the pontiff can be judged or rather that he can be

---

schismatis coram praesenti sancta synodo generali super praemissis et aliis contra eum edita ac illorum veritas et notorietas declaravit manifeste.»

«Super quibus rite et canonice processo ac omnibus rite actis ac diligenter inspectis habita que super ipsis deliberatione matura eadem sancta generalis synodus universalem ecclesiam repraesentans in dicta inquisitionis causa pro tribunali sedens pronunciat decernit et declarat per hanc definitivam sententiam in his scriptis eumdem Petrum de Luna Benedictum XIII ut praemittitur nuncupatum fuisse et esse periurum universalis ecclesiae scandalizatorem fautorem et nutritorem inveterati schismatis inveteratae scissurae et divisionis ecclesiae sanctae dei pacis et unionis eiusdem ecclesiae impeditorem et turbatorem schismaticum et haereticum a fide devium et articuli fidei unam sanctam catholicam ecclesiam violatorem pertinacem cum scandalo ecclesiae dei incorrigibilem notorium et manifestum atque omni titulo gradu honore et dignitate se reddidisse indignum a deo eiectum et praecisum et omni iure eidem in papatu et Romano pontifici ac Romanae ecclesiae quomodolibet competente ipso iure privatum et ab ecclesia catholica tamquam membrum aridum praecisum.»

«Ipsum que Petrum quatenus de facto papatum secundum se tenet eadem sancta synodus papatu et summo ecclesiae Romanae pontificio omni que titulo gradu honore dignitate beneficiis et officiis quibuscumque ad omnem cautelam privat et deponit et abiicit.»

«Eidem que inhibet ne deinceps pro papa aut Romano et summo pontifice se gerat omnes que christicolas ab eius oboedientia et omni debito oboedientiae ipsius atque iuramentis et obligationibus eidem quomodolibet praestitis absolvit et absolutos fore declarat ac omnibus et singulis christi fidelibus inhibet sub poena fautoriae schismatis et haeresis atque privationis omnium beneficiorum dignitatum et honorum ecclesiasticorum et mundanorum et aliis poenis iuris etiam si episcopalis et patriarchalis cardinalatus regalis sit dignitas ac imperialis quibus si contra hanc inhibitionem fecerint sint auctoritate huius decreti et sententiae ipso facto privati et alias iuris incurrant poenas ne eidem Petro de Luna schismatico et haeretico incorrigibili notorio declarato et deposito tamquam papae oboediant pareant vel intendant aut eum quovis modo contra praemissa sustineant vel receptent sibi que praestent auxilium consilium vel favorem.»

shown to be judged"; and thus Wernz and Vidal cited above, "Wherefore, it must be firmly stated that a heretical Roman Pontiff would by that very fact forfeit his power. Although a declaratory sentence of the crime which is not to be rejected in so far as it is merely declaratory would be such that the heretical pope would not be judged, but would rather be shown to have been judged."

Ballerini, however, is equally explicit as Bellarmine in stating that the fall of a manifest heretic pope takes place *per se*, without involving any judgment of the Church. With the Latin text of the book in front of me and the chapter on this topic before my eyes, I cite the key passage:

> «For any person, even a private person, the words of Saint Paul to Titus hold: *"A man that is a heretic, after the first and second admonition avoid: knowing that he that is such an one, is subverted, and sinneth, being condemned by his own judgment."* (Tit. 3, 10-11). He forsooth, who having been once or twice corrected, does not repent, but remains obstinate in a belief contrary to a manifest or defined dogma; by this his public pertinacity which for no reason can be excused, since pertinacity properly pertains to heresy, **he declares himself to be a heretic, i.e. to have withdrawn from the Catholic faith and the Church by his own will, so that no declaration or sentence from anyone would be necessary**. Conspicuous in this matter is the explanation of St. Jerome on the commended words of Paul. *Therefore, by himself [the heretic] is said to be condemned, because the fornicator, adulterer, murderer, and those guilty of other misdeeds are driven out from the Church by the Priests: but heretics deliver the sentence upon themselves, departing from the Church by their own will: this departure is seen to be the condemnation by their own conscience.* Therefore a Pontiff, who after such a solemn and public admonition from the Cardinals, Roman Clergy, or even a synod would maintain himself hardened in heresy, and have openly departed from the Church, according to the precept of Paul he would have to be avoided; and lest the ruin be brought to the rest, his heresy and contumacy, and thus his sentence which he brought upon himself, would have to be publicly pronounced, made known to the whole Church, that he by his own will departed, making known to be severed from the body of the Church, and **in some manner to have abdicated the Pontificate**, which no one holds or can hold, who is not in the Church.»[277]

---

[277] «*Quemcumque vel privatum respiciunt illa Pauli ad Titum: Haereticum Hominem post unam et alteram correptionem devita, sciens quia subversus est, qui ejusmodi est, et delinquit, cum sit proprio judicio condemnatus.* Qui nimirum semel & bis correctus non resipiscit, sed pertinax est in sententia dogmati manifesto aut definito contraria; hac sua publica pertinacia, cum ab haeresi proprie dicta, quae pertinaciam requirit, excusari nulla ratione potest; tum vero semetipsum palam

It is ironic and quite simply incredible that Salza and Siscoe quote this text in support of their opinion that a manifest heretic pope does not lose office unless he is first given official ecclesiastical warning by the Church, and then, if he remains obstinate in heresy, he would then lose office only upon being judged by the Church. Firstly, Ballerini is clearly presenting this argument against those who maintain that it is necessary in order that the Church render a judgment, such a manifest heretic pope must be judged by an ecumenical council. In Section II of Chapter IX, he asks why not resort to a simpler solution than convoking a general synod when there is the most grave and present danger of a heretic pope: «But why is it to be believed, that the remedy is to be expected from the not so easily done convocation of a general synod, when a most present and gravest of all dangers for the faith, which, impending from a Pontiff espousing heresy even in his private judgment, would not be able to be endured through lengthy delays?»[278] And he says in the case of a pope falling into heresy there is a faster and easier remedy: «Remedium in casu hæresis, in quam Pontifex incideret, promtius & facilius suppetit.» He quotes St. Paul to Titus, saying a heretic after a first and second warning is to be avoided, and that such a one is condemned by his own judgment, and this can be done by any private person, and so it could even be done by cardinals, the Roman clergy, or even a (local) synod of bishops – and

---

declarat haereticum, hoc est a fide catholica, & ab Ecclesia voluntate propria recessisse, ita ut ad eum praecidendum a corpore Eccleaiae nulla cujusquam declaratio aut sententia necessaria sit. Perspicua hac in re est S. Hieronimi ratio in laudata Pauli verba, *Propterea a semetipso dicitur esse damnatus, quia fornicator, adulter, homicida, et cetera vitia per sacerdotes ex Ecclesia propelluntur: haeretici autem in semetipsis sententiam ferunt, suo arbitrio de Ecclesia recedentes: quae recessio propriae conscientiae videtur esse damnatio.* Pontifex ergo, qui post solemnem & publicam Cardinalium, Romani Cleri, vel etiam synodi monitionem se se obfirmatum praeferret in haeresi, & de Ecclesia palam recessisset, iuxta praeceptum Pauli esset vitandus; & ne aliis perniciem afferret, in publicum proferenda esset ejus haeresis, & contumacia, ut omnes similiter ab eo caverent, sicque sententia, quam in se ipsum tulit, toti Ecclesiae proposita, cum sua voluntate recessisse, & ab Ecclesiae corpore declararet avulsum, atque abdicasse quodammodo Pontificatum, quo nemo fruitur, nec frui potest, qui non sit in Ecclesia.» (p. 127-128)

[278] «Cur vero in praesentissimo omniumque gravissimo periculo fidei, quod ex Pontifice haeresim privato licet judicio propugnante impendens, diuturniores moras non pateretur, remedium ex generalis synodi non ita facili convocatione expectandum credatur?» (p. 128)

if he does not retract, but remains obstinate in his opinion either contrary to a manifest or a defined dogma, such pertinacity not being able to be excused, he declares himself openly to be a heretic, to have withdrawn from the Catholic faith by his own will, cutting himself off from the body of the Church, without any declaration or sentence being made. In support of this opinion, he quotes St. Jerome, exactly as did Bellarmine.

When I explained in an e-mail to John Salza, "The point at issue is about the loss of office without any declaration or sentence by the Church – the public heretic ceases to be pope and member of the Church BY HIMSELF (as Bellarmine says), 'so that no declaration or sentence from anyone would be necessary' (as Ballerini says)"; Salza answered with the incredibly ignorant reply: "Your response proves that you don't even understand our position. WE DO NOT HOLD THAT A DECLARATORY SENTENCE IS REQUIRED FOR LOSS OF OFFICE! And yet you continually accuse us of this falsehood! Thus, it is you who uses straw men arguments and red-herrings, and you do so either out of profound ignorance or malice, God knows. You confuse the *public judgment* of pertinacity with a *declaratory sentence* of the crime, which shows you don't know the material. As I said in the last email, whether a declaratory sentence is required after the Church establishes the fact of public pertinacity is irrelevant." This is not an expression of mere, blind ignorance: In their book, Salza & Siscoe explicitly declare that loss of office for a cleric is a vindictive penalty that "must be imposed (ferendae sententiae) by Church authority".[279] Salza's explicitly stated position is that the loss of office does not take place without the *public judgment* of the Church; but there can be no juridically valid *public judgment of the Church against a person* unless there is a *judicial act exercising jurisdiction;* and for the judgment to be *public,* there must be a *penal sentence*, or at least a merely *declaratory sentence*. Materially "determining the crime" is not a judgment of the Church. For there to be a public judgment of the Church, the material determination of the crime must be followed by a formal *judicial act* made *with jurisdiction*. Hence, Ballerini's words, "so that no declaration or sentence from anyone would be necessary" plainly state his position that **no public judgment of the Church is necessary** for the loss of office to take place; yet Salza & Siscoe adamantly and stubbornly insist that a public judgment of the Church is necessary for a heretic pope to fall from office *ipso facto*; and they claim that this is also

---

[279] *True or False Pope – Refuting Sedevacantism and other Modern Errors*, p. 260.

the opinion of Ballerini! Salza says, "[W]hether a declaratory sentence is required after the Church establishes the fact of public pertinacity is irrelevant", **but it would only be by a declaratory sentence that the Church could make a public judgment that would juridically estsblish the fact of public pertinacity; since without the promulgation of a declaratory sentence, there would be no public judgment of the Church having any juridical effect!** A more mendacious expression of consummate sophistry can scarcely be imagined than the explanation given by John Salza. Incredibly, Salza later contradicted his own position in the Salza/Siscoe *Formal Reply*, citing a decree of Benedict XIV which declared, "a sentence declaratory of the offence is always necessary in the external forum".

John Salza apparently does not know what is a declaratory sentence: A **public judgment** of the Church against a person is either a *juridical act* which is merely declaratory – a "*declaratory sentence*" made by an individual or a body in possession of *competent jurisdiction to judge*, which, with juridical effect, merely declares a judgment of fact, such as that one has incurred a penalty or that one has already lost office due to manifest defection from the faith and the Church; **or it is a juridical act pronouncing a penal sentence on a subject** by one who has jurisdiction over a person to pronounce a *judicial sentence* of guilt on that person for a crime and inflict a penal sanction. **Without either of these juridical acts, a declaratory sentence, or a penal sentence,** *the Church makes no public judgment of pertinacity*. Salza, the Doctor of Law, in the footnote on page 275 of his and Siscoe's *magnum opus* most ignorantly declares: "**A merely declaratory sentence of the crime is not a juridical act.**" A *declaratory sentence*, however, since it is a clear cut example of administration of the law, to wit, a public judgment of the Church, it is a *juridical act*,[280] the execution of which pertains to the

---

[280] *Merriam-Webster*, **juridical**: "of or relating to the administration of justice or the office of a judge". According to the *Oxford Dictionaries*, 'juridical' means: "relating to judicial proceedings and the administration of the law." The *Dictionary of Canon Law*, compiled by the Faculty of Canon Law of the University of Seville explains: "ACTOS ADMINISTRATIVOS. Son los actos jurídicos puestos por la autoridad que posee la potestad administrativa. CC. 16 &3, 479 &1. (Cf. Potestad administrativa)." [*VOCABULARIO DE SIGNIFICACIONES DE DERECHO CANÓNICO* (Universidad de Sevilla) p. 5]

administrative power.[281] In order for it to be a valid juridical act, it must be promulgated by one who has the authority to pronounce it,[282] and to have force of law it must be declared in such a manner so that it is validly promulgated.[283] If any of these elements are lacking, there is simply no valid act of official judgment of the Church. Therefore, I reply to Salza with his own words: "You are not making even the most basic, elementary distinctions. You are not capable of discussing the finer points of this theology because you don't even know the basics." Ballerini's position is manifestly and indisputably this: that upon the manifestation of pertinacity of a heretic pope, the pope manifests that he has "*abdicated the primacy and the pontificate*", or, (as Bellarmine says, "ceased to be pope ***by himself***"), before any judgement by the Church; and the public judgment of the Church is merely a declaration after the fact, that the loss of office has taken place. Ballerini also makes it explicitly clear in the above quoted passage, that pertinacity in formal heresy, the obstinate rejection of a dogma, is all that is required for the heretic to depart from the body of the Church, when he explained that the pope who "would maintain himself hardened in heresy", i.e.that he "remains obstinate in his opinion either contrary to a manifest or a defined dogma" would thereby "have openly departed from the Church [...] i.e. to have withdrawn from the Catholic faith and the Church by his own will, so that no declaration or sentence from anyone would be necessary."

---

[281] "POTESTAD ADMINISTRATIVA. Funciòn de gobernar, inspirar, guiar e incluso santificar. En este sentido, poseen la potestad administrativa no sòlo los que ya tienen la potestad ejecutiva sino incluso el legislador. Es que, en la Iglesia, el legislador no sòlo legisla sino que a veces desempeña funciones que estrictamente pertenecen a la potestad ejecutiva. P. e: el obispo econòmo. La diferencia fundamental entre la potestad ejecutiva y la administrativa está en que esta última se refiere a la administraciòn de toda la Iglesia mientras que la potestad ejecutiva es parte de la potestad administrativa porque sirve para urgir el uso y la aplicaciòn de las leyes. En consecuencia, poseen la potestad administrativa los moderadores supremos (superiores y superioras generales) de los institutos de vida consagrada e incluso, de las sociedades de vida apostòlica." [*Ibid.,* pp. 119, 120]

[282] **Can. 124** — § 1. Ad validitatem actus iuridici requiritur ut a persona habili sit positus, atque in eodem adsint quae actum ipsum essentialiter constituunt, necnon sollemnia et requisita iure ad validitatem actus imposita.

[283] **Can. 7** — Lex instituitur cum promulgatur. [Can 8 §1. Leges instituuntur, cum promulgantur. (1917 Code)]

Ballerini's explanation of this point coincides exactly with the Church's magisterial teaching. The Church's definition of heresy is set forth in the Code of Canon Law: "Can. 751 — *Dicitur hæresis, pertinax, post receptum baptismum, alicuius veritatis divina et catholica credendæ denegatio, aut de eadem pertinax dubitatio; apostasia, fidei christianæ ex toto repudiatio*". The 1917 code of Canon Law defines what a heretic is in precisely the same terms: Can. 1325 §2 — *"Post receptum baptismum si quis, nomen retinens christianum, pertinaciter aliquam ex veritatibus fide divina et catholica credendis denegat aut de ea dubitat, hæreticus...est."* The canon makes it clear that even those who still claim to be Catholic, but who pertinaciously deny or doubt any truth which must be believed with divine and Caholic faith are *heretics*. When the Church declares that heretics are outside the Church, she understands the term 'heretics' according to this definition as it has traditionally been understood, and which remains applicable even under the 1983 Code: Canon 6 § 2 — *"Canones huius Codicis, quatenus ius vetus referunt, æstimandi sunt ratione etiam canonicæ traditionis habita."* **All** who are guilty of this offense are heretics, and are therefore, if the sin is public, they are **all** severed from the body of the Church and cease to be members according to the very natue of heresy; and for this reason, in addition to the *ipso jure* loss of office and severance from the body of the Church for public heresy, **all, and every single heretic, (as well as apostates and schismatics) incur the penalty of excommunication:** Can. 2314. §1 — *"Omnes a christiana fide apostatæ et omnes et singuli hæretici aut schismatici: 1° Incurrunt ipso facto excommunicationem"*.

Salza manifests his abysmal ignorance again in his failure to understand what it means to reject the magisterium as the rule of faith. Salza, in his delusional mendacity states,

> «Cardinal Billot and the rest of the Church's real theologians teach exactly the opposite of you – that pertinacity is established only if the Pope were to renounce the Church as the RULE of faith by PUBLIC PROFESSION (*sic*). You explicitly reject this unanimous opinion of the theologians (*sic*). You say heresy is established "by a public external act," but Cardinal Billot says heresy is **NOT** established "**by those who indeed manifest their heresy by external signs**.»

Here one may reasonably ask if heresy is not established by the heretic's public words and actions, then how is it established – by mental telepathy? Of far greater authority than the personal opinion of Cardinal Billot, a dogmatic theologian, on such a question of law as the severing of the juridical bond of membership in the Church, is the consensus of the *catedráticos* of the Faculty of Canon Law of the Pontifical and Ecclesiastical University of Salamanca. Since this matter is a question of law, the canonical doctrine of the **expert canonists**[284] – i.e. the *communi constantique doctorum sententia*[285] must be followed, and not the private opinions of theologians. The *doctores de derecho* of Salamanca explain that what the Church understands by the word 'heretics' is defined in canon 1325; and that the crime of heresy is determined through its external manifestation by actions or words: «**2314** *Figuras del delito:* 1) La apostasía; 2) la herejía, y 3) el cisma, cuyas definiciones se hallan contenidas en el canon 1325, § 1; mas para que haya *delito* es preciso que la apostasía, la herejía, o el cisma se manifesten exteriormente por medio de hechos o de palabras.»[286]

What the Salamanca canonists explain on this point in their commentary is in total agreement with the canonical doctrine and tradition of the Church. Cardinal Billot was simply wrong on this point. Fr. Francesco Bordoni, a *qualificator* of the Universal Inquisition in the seventeenth century and an eminent jurist and canonist who wrote two highly authoritative works on the investigation and prosecution of heretics and suspected heretics; is indisputably a much higher authority on these points of law than Cardinal Louis Billot, who distinguished himself as a dogmatic theologian. First, in Bordoni's earlier work published in 1648, he defines heresy according to a formulation which he points out is in essence in agreement with those definitions that have been handed down by the doctors, to which he provides a reference to the verbal formulation: «Est error intellectus voluntarie assertus ab homine Baptizato ex parte contrarius fidei Catholicæ. Hæc definitio in re non discrepat ab aliis per doctores traditis quas ad verbum refert Farin.

---

[284] Miguelez – Alonso – Cabreros; *Op. cit.*, Madrid, 1952, p. 11 – «*El parecer común y constante de los doctores* o verdaderamente peritos en la ciencia del derecho.»

[285] 1983 Code: Can. 19 – Si certa de re desit expressum legis sive universalis sive particularis praescriptum aut consuetudo, causa, nisi sit poenalis, dirimenda est attentis legibus latis in similibus, generalibus iuris principiis cum aequitate canonica servatis, iurisprudentia et praxi Curiae Romanae, communi constantique doctorum sententia. 1917 Code: Can. 20 – Si certa de re desit expressum praescriptum legis sive generalis sive particularis, norma sumenda est, nisi agatur de poenis applicandis, a legibus latis in similibus; a generalibus iuris principiis cum aequitate canonica servatis; a stylo et praxi Curiae Romanae; a communi constantique sententia doctorum.

[286] Miguelez – Alonso – Cabreros, *Op. cit.*, Madrid, 1952, p. 836.

Q. 178. Initio.»²⁸⁷ Again, in his posthumously published work (1693), he defines heresy in essentially the same terms: «Est error intellectus ex parte contrarius fidei, voluntarie, & pertinaciter assertus ab Homine usum rationis habente, valide baptizato aqua fluminis.»²⁸⁸ In the definition I quoted in the *Introduction*, St. Alphonsus, in the following century, defined heresy with a formulation nearly identical to that of Fr. Bordoni: «Hæresis est error intellectus, et pertinax contra Fidem, in eo qui Fidem suscepit.» In the mentioned passage of St. Alphonsus, references are provided to passages in the works of two Spanish theologians, Gabriel Vásquez SJ (1549 or 1551-1604) and Tomás Sánchez SJ (1550 – 1610). Both of them are also frequently cited by Fr. Bordoni. Fr. Bordoni then explains individually the terms which together make up the definition of heresy, and first, that it is *an error of the intellect* according to which one thinks something to be true which is actually false; and thus consists in the disbelief of those things which are taught by divine faith.²⁸⁹ Heresy is in part but not in the whole against faith, since he who disbelieves all of the articles, and thus the entire substance of faith from which it is composed, is not merely said to be a heretic, but is properly an apostate, such as one who from being a Christian would become a Jew, a Pagan, a Turk or a Gentile.²⁹⁰ It is an asserted error (*error assertus*) for one does not end up as a heretic for the mere narrating of heresy, and thus heresy consists in assertively judging or saying something knowingly against faith, but not doing something against it, such as tearing up images, worshipping idols, etc.; but indeed, such deeds

---

²⁸⁷ P. Francesco Bordoni, *Sacrum Tribunal Iuducum In Causis Sanctæ Fidei Contra Hæreticos Et Hæresi Suspectos, Caput Nonum De Hæresi et Hæreticis*, Romæ, MDCXLVIII p. 188.

²⁸⁸ P. Francesco Bordoni, *MANUALE CONSULTORUM In Causis S. Officii contra Hæreticum pravitatem refertum quamplurimis dubiis novis, & veteribus resolutis*, Parmæ, MDCXCIII, p. 32.

²⁸⁹ «Dixi 1. Quod hæresis est *error Intellectus*, errat enim Intellectus, dum putat esse verum, quod revera falsum est, quia errare est unum pro alio putare, *ex d. Aug. relato cap. In quibus 6. 22 q. 2.* Error ergo huius generis consistit in discredere ea, quæ docet divina Fides.» (*MANUALE CONSULTORUM* p. 32)

²⁹⁰ «Dixi sexto, qoud hæresis ex parte, & non in totum est contraria fidei, quia qui discrederet omnes articulos, ac proinde omnem fidei rationem, quæ ex illis componitur, non diceretur simplex hæreticus, sed proprie Apostata, ut si quis ex Christiano fieret Iudeus, vel Paganus, Turca, vel Gentilis...» [Bordoni, *SACRUM TRIBUNAL IUDUCUM IN CAUSIS SANCTÆ FIDEI CONTRA HÆRETICOS ET HÆRESI SUSPECTOS*, p. 190]

are significative of heresy, and render those who perpetrate them violently suspect of heresy, as is taught by all.291 Secondly, it is voluntarily asserted (*voluntarie assertus*), and since it is a sin it must be voluntary, which pertains to the substance of sin, since, according to Augustine and Chrysostom, there is no sin unless it is voluntary – and voluntary, according to Aristotle, is that which is in the agent knowing the individual things that are in an action, so that for one to be said to have committed the sin of heresy, it is necessary that he know and be aware that he errs in faith, and disbelieves in something of those things which the Church commands must be believed, otherwise the error would not be voluntary if the one making it would not know that his words and error are contrary to determinate points of faith. Whence to say that heresy is a voluntary error is to say the same that it is pertinacious, for one is said to be a pertinacious heretic who knows and is aware that what he says or doubts is something against faith, but nevertheless wills to hold the error against faith. Therefore one is a willful and pertinacious heretic who holds or doubts something he knows to be against the Catholic faith, or who knows his opinion to be contrary to the Catholic Church.292

---

291 «Dixi tertio, quod hæresis est error assertus, nam quis non evadit hæreticus per solem narrationem hæresis... Ex quo infertur, hæresim consistere in iudicando, seu dicendo assertive aliquid scienter contra fidem, non autem faciendo aliquid contra eandem, ut lacerando imagines, adoranda Idola &c. Verum quidem est quod similia facta sunt signitiva hæresis reddentia perpetrantes illa suspectos vehementissime de hæresi, ut docent omnes...» [*Ibid.* p. 189]

292 «Dixi secundo, quod hæresis est error voluntarius, quia cum iste error sit peccatum, necessrium est, quod sit voluntarium, siquidem voluntarium est de substantia peccati, quia nullum peccatum nisi voluntarium secundum Aug. & D. Chrysostomum... Voluntarium secundum Aristot. Est id, quod est in agente cognoscente singula, in quibus est actio, ut quis dicatur commisse peccatum hæresis, necesse est, quod sciat, & advertat se errare in fide, & discredere aliquid eorum, quæ Ecclesia præciput esse credenda, aliter actus huius erroris non esset voluntarius, si errans ignoraret suum dictum, & errorem esse contrarium determinatis de fide. Unde dicere, quod hæresis est error voluntaruius idem est ac dicere, est error pertinax, nam ille dicitur hæreticus pertinax qui licet sciat, & advertat, seu dubitet se dicere aliquid contra fidem, nihilominus vult tenere errorem contra fidem. Ille igitur est hæreticus voluntarius, & pertinax qui tenet aliquid quod scit, vel dubitat esse contra Catholicam fidem, seu qui scit suam opinionem esse contrariam Ecclesiæ Catholicæ. Sed de hac pertinacia infrs, *quæst. 5*» [*Ibid.* p. 189]

Pertinacity consists in this, that one firmly consents in something or doubts, what he knows to be against faith, and determined by the Church. Thus, pertinacity is the voluntary consent of something, consciously or dubitatively against what one actually knows to be against faith.[293] Thus it is deduced that heresy does not involve perseverance and permanence in the false assertion, since with the error being known the judgment can be made in an instant, such as one who knowingly wills something without a duration of time, therefore the will and the intellect can produce their acts in an instant, be they true and good, or false and evil – therefore also heresy.[294]

With great precision, Fr. Bordoni explains exactly what is the pertinacity of heresy:

> «*Pertinaciter*, ille autem dicitur Pertinax in suo Dogmate, qui scit, & actu advertit, dum illud asserit, esse contrarium definitis de Fide ab Ecclesia Romana. Pertinacia ergo est assensus Intellectus, & Voluntatis consensus in aliquid, quod cognoscitur actu, & advertenter esse contra Fidem Romanam. Hæresis ergo non contingit sine Pertinacia cum hæc illi sit essentialis, ut docent omnes... *Ioannes Alberghinus in suo manuali Qualificatorum cap. 1. Num. 7. & 8.* ubi rem clare explicat in eo, quod Pertincia habet esse ab Intellectu cognoscente se contrariare definitis de Fide, & a voluntate, quæ ab Intellectu male edocta, vult nihilominus persistere in suo errore, & resistere determinatis ab Ecclesia, cuius auctoritati non vult se subijcere *Ricciul. Lib. 5. Cap. 2.* dicit, pertinaciam versari circa malum, & opponi Perseverantiæ, quæ habet pro obiecto bonum. Ad hoc autem ut quis fiat formaliter hæreticus non est necesse, quod diu perseveret in errore; sed sufficit, quod per momentum scienter discredit alicui propositioni de Fide; eo enim ipso consumavit in corde suo suam Hæresim, assensus enim, & consensus in momento recipient esse, *Filliuc. part. 2. tract. 32. cap. 6. num. 135. Molfesius tract. 11. cap. 2. num. 41. Carena part. 2. num. 12. Bellonus Papien. lib. 1. de his qua fiunt incontin. cap. 193. num. 4.*»[295]

---

[293] «Pertinacia autem in eo consistit, quod quis consentiat firmiter in aliquid, quod scit vel dubitat esse contra fidem, & determinationem Ecclesiæ, pertinacia igitur est voluntarius consensus in aliquid, quod cognoscitur actu, & advertenter, vel dubitative esse contra fidem» [*Ibid.* p. 193]

[294] «Deducitur ex his primo, pertinaciam non importare perseverantiam, & permantiam in asserto falso, cum hæresis posita cognitione erroris fieri possit in instanti, sicut quis potest scienter velle aliquid sine temporis diuturnitate, voluntas igitur, & intellectus in instanti suos actus tam veros, & bonos, quam falsos, & malos producere possunt, ergo & hæresim.» [*Ibid.* pp. 193-194]

[295] *MANUALE CONSULTORUM* p. 33.

According to the canonical doctrine and universal practice of the Roman Church, heresy is established by the *indicia* of heresy, which are the words and deeds that constitute the evidence of heresy.296 Fr. Francesco Bordoni explains in the tenth chapter of his work on prosecuting heretics, that according to the *indicia* of heresy, one is either a *formal* heretic, or a *suspected heretic*.297 A *formal heretic*, Fr. Bordoni explains, is one who firmly asserts his disbelief in a certain and defined article of faith, which has been proposed to be believed by all, and which he knows to be such.298 Thus, what a *formal heretic* is, is unanimously defined by all without exception: *"Formalis Hæreticus est ille, qui discredit aliquid, quod expresse, & explicite scit esse contra Fidem ab Ecclesia declaratum. In hac enim Scientia consistit Pertinacia constituens Hæreticum formalem. Et in hoc omnes convenient nullo contradicente."*299 Such a one is manifestly a formal heretic, and no previous warnings or admonitions are necessary to judge such a one to be guilty of formal heresy.300 They simply fall under the penalty: Can. 2314. §1 — *"Omnes a christiana fide apostatæ et* **omnes et singuli hæretici** *aut schismatici: 1° Incurrunt ipso facto excommunicationem"*. Any office they may have held are lost *ipso jure*; yet, since there is a fine line between *violenter suspectus*, which falls under canon 2314, and *vehementer suspectus*, which falls under canon 2315, there is a penal process prescribed in canon 2314 that gives allowance to those who repent to

---

296 «Indicium est signum probativum inducens iudicem in cognitionem delicti... [idest] ex verbis, vel factis» [Padre Francesco Bordoni, *SACRUM TRIBUNAL IUDUCUM IN CAUSIS SANCTÆ FIDEI CONTRA HÆRETICOS ET HÆRESI SUSPECTOS*, p. 223]

297 «Hæretici quatum facit ad explicationen huius capitis, sunt in duplici differentia, alii vocantur Formales, alii tantum Suspecti.» [*Ibid.* p. 221]

298 «Formalis autem hæreticus dicitur ille, qui negavit firmiter, & ex corde aliquem articulum de fide certum, & expresse definitum, quem scit esse talem, ab ecclesia propositum ab omnibus credendum, exprimendum se illum non credere» [*Ibid.* p. 221]

299 Bordoni, *MANUALE CONSULTORUM In Causis S. Officii contra Hæreticum pravitatem*, pp. 34-35.

300 «Quaeritur 6. An ad Pertinaciam requiratur praevia monitio... & nihilominus in sua Opinione persistens incipiat tunc esse pertinax, & formalis Haereticus? R. Nullam require monitionem, sed esse Haereticum formaliter hoc ipso, quod aserit aliquo pro vero, quod scit esse contra Fidem, in hoc enim formaliter consistit Pertinacia, quae non datur sine Scientia illius obiecti, contra quod est ipsa Pertinacia, quae includit Scientiam, ergo frustra praemonetur, qui scit se scire illud, cui adversatur; monitio enim fit ignorantibus, non scientibus.» [*MANUALE CONSULTORUM*, p. 35]

retain the offices which were lost *ipso facto*. Admonitions are for *suspected heretics*. In the 1907 edition of the *Catholic Encyclopedia*, under "Canonical Admonitions," these are defined as, "A preliminary means used by the Church towards a suspected person, as a preventive of harm or a remedy of evil" (Burtsell). Mention is made of an *Instruction* by Pope Leo XIII which states that, "Among the preservative measures are chiefly to be reckoned the spiritual retreat, admonitions, and injunctions." This Instruction also says, "the canonical admonitions may be made in a paternal and private manner (even by letter or by an intermediary person), or in legal form, but always in such a way that proof of their having been made shall remain on record." It then states further that these admonitions are founded on *suspicion*: "after an investigation to be made by one having due authority, with the result of establishing a reasonable basis for the suspicion." The first admonition is a paternal admonition: "the prelate either personally or through a confidential delegate informs the suspected person of what has been said about him, without mentioning the source of information, and without threat, but urges amendment." If the paternal admonition goes unheeded, then a legal warning is issued which is, "to a great extent akin to the summons to judgment."

One who is a suspect of heresy is one who has been proven to have said or done something from which one is reasonably inclined to believe him to be a heretic; and since this belief is not certain knowledge, but is only suspicion and presumption that he is a heretic, it pertains to the office of the judge to verify what was intended by those words or deeds.[301] F. Charles Augustine comments on canon 2315 (Suspicion of Heresy):

> Suspicion in the psychological sense, is doubt, coupled with a positive leaning to one side; In law it may be expressed by presumption or circumstantial evidence. It is therefore a judgment formed about some one without sufficient evidence on the ground of certain *indicia*.

---

[301] «Suspectus de hæresi dicitur ille, qui probatur dixisse, vel fecisse aliquid, ex quo iudex rationabiliter movetur ad credemndum illum hæreticum esse, & quia hæc credulitas non est certa scientia, sed solum suspicio, & presumptio, quod ille sit hæreticus, ideo ut iudex se certificet de hac re, sic exigente eius officio, indicit torturam reo præsumpto hæretico, ut venire possit in cognitionem qualis fuerit eius intentio, consequenter reus hæresis presumptus tortura purgat suspicionem.» [P. Francesco Bordoni, *Op. cit., Caput Decimum De Suspectis de Hæresi*, p. 221]

Three kinds of suspicion are generally distinguished: light, vehement, and violent. *Light* suspicion admits of no conclusion, because it is based on absolutely insufficient *indicia*. *Vehement* suspicion rests on effective signs and conclusions. *Violent* suspicion amounts to morally certain proof.

The Decretals, from which the notion "suspicion of heresy" is taken, have in view vehement suspicion, and no doubt this is here to be understood. Light suspicion often amounts to no more than rash judgment, whilst violent suspicion is to be considered as a positive proof, and therefore falls under can. 2314. That the limits between vehement and violent suspicion cannot be clearly set off, is owing to the nature of circumstantial evidence.[302]

For there to be suspicion of heresy, there must be the sufficient *indicia* from which one may reasonably presume from the words or deeds, since not everything that is said or done is such that it would lead one to the prudent judgment of suspicion of heresy; but only that which necessarily indicates heresy, which is rare, or more often words or actions that are clearly connected to heresy.[303] Suspicion is a conjectural judgment of something that is apparently true but still uncertain, which proceeds from the nature of the matter or its circumstances or the person.[304] Suspicion, therefore, is the opinion of wrongdoing which proceeds from *indicia*; which is properly a *light suspicion* if it is based on *indicia* from which the suspicion can be judged to be at least *probable*, otherwise it would only amount to a rash judgment.[305] Hence, light suspicion is defined as

---

[302] The Rev. P, Chas. Augustine, O.S.B., D.D., *A COMMENTAY ON THE NEW CODE OF CANON LAW.*, Vol. VIII, St. Louis and London, 1922, pp. 284-285.

[303] «Dixi secundo, *ex quo rationabiliter iudex movetur*, non enim omne id, quod dicitur, aut fit, potest esse sufficiens indicium, & signum ad præsumendum aliquem ex suo dictu, vel facto esse hæreticum, sed ea tantum dicta, vel facta iudicem habent prudenter ducere in suspicionem hæresis, quæ aliqua ratione referri, seu ordinari possunt ad ipsam hæresim, siue ex necessaria, seu contingenti raro, vel sæpius connexione dicti vel facti cum hæresi, ut apparebit in exemplis infra referendis.» [P. Francesco Bordoni, *Op. cit., Caput Decimum De Suspectis de Hæresi*, p. 221.]

[304] «Præsumptio est verisimilis coniectura rei dubiæ, quae ex natura rei, vel circumstantiis negotiorum, aut personarum procedit...» [*Ibid.*, p. 223]

[305] «Suspicio est opinio mali ex levibus indiciis proveniens, quæ si sunt probabilia faciunt suspicionem probabilem, per quam pervenitur ad præsumptionem, aliter dicitur iudicium temerarium.» [*Ibid.*, p. 223]

that which arises from a moderate but reasonable conjecture.[306] *Vehement suspicion* arises from words or actions which frequently and most often indicate that the one who says or does them is a heretic. Thus, *vehement suspicion* is commonly defined: "*Doctores communiter eam definiunt, quod sit illa, quæ sepe, frequenter, & ut plurimum oritur ex Indiciis eam inferentibus.*"[307] *Crass* or *affected ignorance* of that which is commonly know to all results in vehement suspicion. Religious observance of false ceremonies leads to at least vehement suspicion of heresy, but more properly pertains to *violent suspicion*.[308] *Violent suspicion* arises from words or deeds from which it is gathered that the one saying or doing them is presumed to be a heretic, since they are *necessarily connected to heresy*. Examples of violent suspicion of heresy are, 1) those who go back to their previous sect; 2) supporters, patrons, and defenders of heretics; 3) those who publicly assert heretical propositions; 4) worshippers of idols, or those who render to them similar acts of *latria*, are violently suspect of heresy.[309] Furthermore, two *indicia* of vehement suspicion amount to *violent suspicion of heresy*.[310]

Thus it is proven that according to Catholic Doctrine, for one to be considered a formal heretic, it is not necessary that he, "renounce the

---

[306] «Levis suspicio est illa, quæ oritur ex modiciis coniecturis.» [*Ibid.*, p. 225]

[307] Bordoni, *Manuale Consultorum*, p. 138.

[308] «Suspicio vehemens est illa, quæ oritur ex verbis, vel factis, ex quibus frequenter, & ut plurimum deducitur, eum qui talia, dicit, vel facit, esse hæreticum. Est communis omnium… ex quo differ a levi, quod vehementem actus frequenter inducunt, levem raro, … exempla… *primo*, Ignorantia crassa, seu affectata inducit vehementem suspicionem in eum, qui ignorat ea. Quæ communiter omnes sciunt … Secundo, observatio falsarum cæremoniarum inducit vehementem suspicionem, quamquam hoc exemplum potius spectat ad violentem…» [*Ibid.*, p. 225]

[309] «Suspicio violenta est illa, quæ oritur ex verbis, seu factis, ex quibus fere semper colligitur, quod illa dicens, seu faciens est hæreticus præsumptus, & ex eo, quod habent necessariam connexionem cum hæresi. … Exempla sint *Primo*, qui transit ad sectum antiquam est violenter suspectus de hæresi… *Secundo*, fautores, & defensores hæreticorum… *Tertio*, publice asserentes propositiones hæreticas… *Quarto*, adorantem idola, & similes actus latriæ illis præstando, esse violenter suspectus de fide» [*Ibid.*, p. 225]

[310] «Quæritur *9*. An ex duabus levibus oriatur Vehemens? Ex duabus vero vehementibus Violenta? R. Affirmative, quia plus operari debent simul quam singulæ seorsim acceptæ ergo inducunt vehementem… Sicut ergo duæ leves producunt Vehementem, ita duæ vehementes unam Violentam.» [*Manuale Consultorum*, p. 140]

Church as the RULE of faith by PUBLIC PROFESSION", or explicitly admit that one is knowingly in heresy; but it suffices that one either 1) assertively state his disbelief in one single article of faith, because, one who offends against even one article is guilty of all, because disbelieving in one destroys the formal cause of faith from which that article depends;[311] or, that the nature or circumstances of ones words or deeds constitute *moral certitude* of formal heresy. Hence, Cardinal Robert Bellarmine, who was a high official of the Roman Inquisition, and is a Doctor of the Church, teaches that, *"men are not bound*, or able to read hearts; but when they see that someone is a heretic by his external works, they judge him to be a heretic pure and simple [*simpliciter*], and condemn him as a heretic."[312]

Salza utterly fails to make the critical distinction between a *formal act of defection from the* **Church** (canons 1086, § 1, 1117 and 1124), by which one formally declares oneself to have separated from the Church; and *public defection from the Catholic* **faith** (can. 171, § 1, 4°; 194, § 1, 2°; 316, § 1; 694, § 1, 1°; 1071, § 1, 4° and § 2) – which comprises the "virtual" forms of "notoriously" or "publicly" abandoning the faith that are deduced from behavior.[313] Public defection from the faith by means of formal heresy or apostasy by their very nature (*suapte natura*) sever one from membership in the body of the Church and effects the *ipso jure* loss of ecclesiastical office; but the canonical consequences of such a defection are not as far reaching as a *formal act of defection from the Church*, as the cited document explains.[314]

---

[311] «Sufficit autem unicum negare articulum, ut quis dicatur formaliter hæreticus, quia in uno offendens factus est omnium reus, in quantum destruit rationem formalem fidei, a qua dependet articulus negatus.» [*Ibid.* p. 222]

[312] «Non enim homines tenentur, aut corda possunt scrutari; sed quem externis operibus hæreticum esse vident, simpliciter hæreticum iudicant, ac ut hæreticum damnant.» (*De Romano Pontifice, lib. iv, cap. ix*)

[313] Cf. Pontifical Council for Legislative Texts, *ACTUS FORMALIS DEFECTIONIS AB ECCLESIA CATHOLICA, Prot. N. 10279/2006*, 13 March 2006.

[314] There are passages in the cited document which could be twisted in order to distort its meaning, so that it would appear to say something other than that meaning which is intended by the authors of the document; one of which particularly relates directly to the question of defection from the Catholic faith: «On the other hand, heresy (whether formal or material), schism and apostasy do not in themselves constitute a formal act of defection if they are not externally concretized and manifested to the ecclesiastical authority in the

Salza continues his errant rant: «Again, he [Billot] also requires a renunciation of the Magisterium as the RULE of faith by PUBLIC PROFESSION. You stand alone (*sic*) in disagreeing with Billot. You reject Billot's teaching by saying "it is not necessary that such a one explicitly reject the Church as the rule of faith," even though Cardinal Billot says "heresy by its nature **REQUIRES departure from the**

required manner.» Public defection from the Catholic faith by means of formal heresy or apostasy is by definition, and therefore in its very nature a *formal* act of defection from the faith, as well as a *canonical delict*; and consequently, such an act *suapte natura* separates one from the body of the Church, and incurs the penalty of excommunication *latae sententiae*; as is set forth in Canon 1364 — § 1: "*Apostata a fide, haereticus vel schismaticus in excommunicationem latae sententiae incurrit, firmo praescripto can. 194, § 1, n. 2; clericus praeterea potest poenis, de quibus in can. 1336, § 1, nn. 1, 2 et 3, puniri.*". Hence, *formal heresy* does indeed constitute a *formal act of defection from the faith*, with the real consequence of severing one from the body of the Church, and the canonical consequence of incurring excommunication; but does not constitute canonically a *formal act of defection from the Church*, in the strict sence according to which this act of formal defection is conceived, which is «new to canonical legislation and is distinct from the other – rather "virtual" (that is, deduced from behaviors) – forms of "notoriously" or "publicly" abandoning the faith (cfr. can. 171, § 1, 4°; 194, § 1, 2°; 316, § 1; 694, § 1, 1°; 1071, § 1, 4° and § 2).» Hence, the statement, «Consequently, only the convergence of the two elements – the theological content of the interior act and its manifestation in the manner defined above – constitutes the actus formalis defectionis ab Ecclesia catholica, with the corresponding canonical penalties (cfr. can. 1364, § 1)», is not intended to mean that the *de facto* defection of public formal heresy does not incur the penalty of *latae sententiae* excommunication; but merely intends to make clear that the mere «juridical-administrative act of abandoning the Church», (i.e. «the removal of one's name from a Church membership registry maintained by the government in order to produce certain civil consequences»), does not incur the penalty of excommunication, because, «The juridical-administrative act of abandoning the Church does not per se constitute a formal act of defection as understood in the Code, given that there could still be the will to remain in the communion of the faith.» Canon 1364 *must* be understood according to its literal meaning: "Can. 17 — *Leges ecclesiasticae intellegendae sunt secundum propriam verborum significationem in textu et contextu consideratam*"; and in accordance with canonical tradition since it repeats what has been set forth for centuries in previous legislation: Canon 6 § 2 — "*Canones huius Codicis, quatenus ius vetus referunt, aestimandi sunt ratione etiam canonicae traditionis habita.*" The document clearly does not attempt to alter the proper meaning of Canon 1364 as it is understood according to canonical tradition.

RULE of the ecclesiastical magisterium."» As mentioned above, heresy is in its nature a *partial* departure that is contrary *ex parte* but not *in totum* against the rule of faith, as the above cited passage of Bordoni explains: «hæresis ex parte, & non in totum est contraria fidei». Salza does not understand what is meant by the words, "departure from the rule of the ecclesiastical magisterium". Salza fundamentalistically construes Billot's words to mean that separation from the body of the Church requires a *total* departure from the rule of faith, i.e., a *renunciation of the magisterium as the rule of faith*; whereas Billot, in unanimous agreement with all theologians, speaks of heresy in the passage cited by Salza only as a *departure* from the rule of faith. Tanquerey explains, "All theologians teach that publicly known heretics, that is, those who belong to a heterodox sect through public profession, **or those who refuse the infallible teaching authority of the Church**, are excluded from the body of the Church, even if their heresy is only material heresy."[315] However, anyone who knowingly rejects even **a single article of faith** is included among those who refuse the infallible teaching authority of the Church. St. Thomas Aquinas explains in II – II, Q. 5, a. 3:

> "**Neither living nor lifeless faith remains in a heretic who disbelieves *one article of faith*.** The reason of this is that the species of every habit depends on the formal aspect of the object, without which the species of the habit cannot remain. Now the formal object of faith is the First Truth, as manifested in Holy Writ and the teaching of the Church, which proceeds from the First Truth. Consequently ***whoever does not adhere, as to an infallible and Divine rule, to the teaching of the Church, which proceeds from the First Truth manifested in Holy Writ, has not the habit of faith***, but holds that which is of faith otherwise than by faith."

---

[315] Adolphe D. Tanquerey, A Manual of Dogmatic Theology, (Desclée: 1959), vol. 1 n. 271 p. 160 N.B. – It is to be borne in mind that Tanquerey uses here the term 'material heresy' according to the improper novel sense of the term as it was commonly used by early twentieth-century theologians to denote only the heresy of non-Catholics visibly outside the Church. He does not refer to what are properly material heretics; i.e., those who ignorantly profess heretical opinions, but have not left the Church, and remain in the Church subject to the magisterial authority of the Church. Material heresy, if not qualified by schism which places one outside the Church, does not separate one from the Church, nor does it effect the loss of office *ex natura haeresis*, because it does not formally oppose the faith of the Church.

Elaborating on this teaching of St. Thomas, Msgr. Paul Glenn wrote:

«To reject any article of the faith is to reject the faith itself. This is like pulling one stone out of an arch; it is like putting one hole in the hull of a ship. The whole arch tumbles down; the whole ship sinks. A man who has the faith, accepts God's word. Now, God's word has set up the Church as man's infallible teacher and guide. If a man, therefore, rejects one article of the faith, and says that he believes in all the other articles, he believes these by his own choice and opinion, not by faith. Rejecting one article of the faith, he rejects the whole authority of the Church, and he rejects the authority of God which has set up and authorized the Church to teach truth. Hence, it is entirely incorrect to say that a man may have lifeless or formless faith in some articles of the Creed while he rejects others; such a man has not the faith at all, living or lifeless.»[316]

On page 281 and 282 of their screed, Salza & Siscoe declare: «*By referring to heretics as those who "separate themselves from the Church," who "turn away from the Church," and who "depart by themselves from her," Bellarmine is referring not to those who merely profess a heretical proposition, but to those who openly leave the Church (no longer accepting the Church as the rule of faith).*» This proposition is manifestly a fallacious artifice of sophistry. As I mentioned earlier, St. Robert Bellarmine was a high official of the Inquisition. He knew perfectly well that one who professes a heretical proposition without pertinacity is not guilty of formal heresy; but if there are present the *indicia* of formal heresy then formal heresy is certain; or if the *indicia* are of *violent suspicion*, then the one who asserts the heretical proposition is judged with moral certitude to be a formal heretic, and thereby to have severed himself from the body of the Church. In reading the works of St. Robert Bellarmine, one is particularly impressed by his adherence to the doctrine of St. Thomas, which constitutes the foundation of his own theology on this point. It is patent from the teaching of St. Thomas that heretics are not merely those who openly declare themselves to leave the Church as manifest schismatics; but St. Thomas explains in *II-II 11.1*, "heresy is a species of unbelief, belonging to those who profess the Christian faith, but corrupt its dogmas." Thus, it pertains properly to heretics that they profess to be Catholic and maintain the pretense of remaining within the Church, but they corrupt its dogmas by their unbelief in one or more articles of faith. As has been

---

[316] Paul J. Glenn, *COLLECTION*, Aeterna Press.

shown above, *it pertains to the very nature of formal heresy as a conscious denial of even a single article of faith, that* **it is a rejection of the ecclesiastical magisterium as the rule of faith**, and hence, heresy, *suapte natura,* visibly separates *all public heretics* from the body of the Church, and not just those who expressly reject the Church or her magisterial authority. Bellarmine, as quoted above, states categorically on the authority of St. Augustine, that **all heretics have departed from the Church.** ("s. Augustinus... *Omnes hæretici... ex nobis exierunt idest, ex Ecclesia exierunt*") Thus it is explicitly clear in the teaching of St. Robert Bellarmine based on the unanimous teaching of the Fathers, that not only those heretics who expressly renounce the Church or explicitly reject the authority of the ecclesiastical magisterium, separate themselves from the Church and automatically lose all ecclesiastical jurisdiction and dignity, but *all manifest heretics*, by the public act of formal heresy, depart from the Church and automatically forfeit any ecclesiastical office and jurisdiction they may have held.

From Bellarmine's own words quoted above, we gather that same clear meaning as I have explained it, when he says that heretics are outside the Church, and lose jurisdiction and all ecclesiastical dignity **"ex natura hæresis"**. ***Heresy in its nature is the obstinate denial or doubt of even a single dogma, and therefore, manifest heresy, by its very nature separates the heretic from the body of the Church.*** If some additional qualifying circumstance, such as explicitly renouncing the Church as the rule of faith, or formally declaring oneself separated from the Church, or joining some other denomination or sect, were to be necessary for a heretic to be separated from the body of the Church (as Salza & Siscoe maintain); then heresy would not *suapte natura* separate one from the Church (as Pius XII teaches), but only heresy qualified by the additional circumstance of explicit schism that would alter the species of the act of heresy. If that were the case, the doctrine taught in *Mystici Corporis*, that heresy *by its own nature* severs the heretic from membership in the Church, would be erroneous. However, the words, "heresy *suapte natura*", and *"ex natura hæresis"* mean precisely this: that heresy itself, according to its very nature as a rejection of an article of faith, and therefore *by itself*, **without any other qualifying circumstance that would alter the species of the sin (such as formally rejecting the Church)**, separates the heretic from membership in the Church. This is also explicitly clear in the teaching of Ballerini, quoted above. Let us consider again the cited text, paying close attention to the bolded and italicized phrases:

«He… who having been once or twice corrected, does not repent, but **remains obstinate in a belief contrary to a manifest or defined dogma**; by this his public pertinacity which for no reason can be excused, since pertinacity properly pertains to heresy, **he declares himself to be a heretic, i.e. to have withdrawn from the Catholic faith and the Church by his own will**, so that no declaration or sentence from anyone would be necessary. […] Therefore a Pontiff, who after such a solemn and public admonition from the Cardinals, Roman Clergy, or even a synod would maintain himself hardened in heresy, **and have openly departed from the Church**, according to the precept of Paul he would have to be avoided; and lest the ruin be brought to the rest, his heresy and contumacy, and thus his sentence which he brought upon himself, would have to be publicly pronounced, made known to the whole Church, **that he by his own will departed, making known to be severed from the body of the Church, and in some manner to have abdicated the Pontificate**, which no one holds or can hold, who is not in the Church.»

Ballerini explains quite explicitly, in unison with the universal and ordinary magisterium of the Church, that **all** manifest heretics, by the very fact of their heresy, i.e. by remaining **"obstinate in a belief contrary to a manifest or defined dogma"**, without any additional qualification of explicit schism, such as the plainly stated rejection of the magisterium etc., are deserters who **have have "openly departed from the Church"**. Bellarmine and Ballerini also prove from the authority of scripture and the Fathers, that heretics, **by their manifest heresy alone, leave the Church and lose office on their own, without any judgment from the Church**. The Church only confirms the fact of defection from the Church and loss of office *post factum*, and juridically declares the loss of office as already having happened. Salza and Siscoe base their opinion on loss of office on their heretical belief that heresy by itself does not separate the heretic from the Church by itself *suapte natura*, and as a direct consequence thereof cause the loss of office; but separation from the Church and the loss of office, according to them, only take place upon the authoritative judgment of the Church, or separation from the Church after the formally schismatic and public acts of expressly rejecting the teaching authority of the Church, or by inscribing oneself as a member of some other religious sect. If that were true, then heresy would not separate the heretic from the Church *suapte natura*, because the nature of heresy simply consists in the pertinacious rejection of an article of faith: «*Hæresis est* **error intellectus, et pertinax** *contra Fidem, in eo qui Fidem suscepit*».[317] If Salza & Siscoe were correct in saying that manifest heresy by itself, without any further qualification, judgment or censure of the Church does not separate the heretic from the body of the Church, then Pius XII would be in error for teaching that heresy separates one from the Church *suapte natura*, and the Church would already have defected in the Fifth Century, because that is what St. Jerome and the Fathers unanimously taught (as Bellarmine demonstrated in the earlier cited text). Bellarmine is unequivocal and explicit in affirming that the pertinacity of the heretic alone expels him from the body of the Church:

> «Præterea ad Tit. 3. *Hæreticum hominem post unam et alteram correptionem devita, sciens, quia subversus est qui ejusmodi est, et delinquit cum sit proprio judicio condemnatus.* Ubi apostolus episcopi præcipit, ut hæreticum vitet, quod certe non juberet, si esset intra Ecclesiam. Debet enim pastor non vitare, sed curare eos, qui ad suum gregem pertinent. Et addit rationem, quia **talis pertinax hæreticus** est, proprio judicio condemnatus, idest (ut Hieronymus exponit) non est ejectus ab Ecclesia per excommunicationem, ut multi alii peccatores, sed ipse seipsum ab Ecclesia ejecit.»[318]

Now **pertinacity is simply this**, as St. Alphonsus explains: *for one to consciously remain in an error against the faith after it has been sufficiently explained to him that it is contrary to the faith of the universal Church*: «pertinaciter errare... est eum [errorem] retinere, postquam contrarium est sufficienter propositum: sive quando scit contrarium teneri a reliqua universali Christi in terris Ecclesia, cui suum iudicium præferat»[319] **Thus it is demonstrated to be a revealed truth of divine and Catholic faith, that the manifestly pertinacious denial of a single article of faith by itself separates one from the body of the Church, visibly severs the heretic from membership in the Catholic Church, and by itself brings about the loss of ecclesiastical office.**

Salza also strays from the teaching of the universal magisterium on the nature of the *pertinacity* of heresy: Salza wrote to me, saying,

---

[317] St. Alphonsus M. De Liguori, *Lib. II. Tract. I. De præcepto Fidei. Dubium III.*

[318] *De Ecclesia Militante*, Cap. IV. p. 76.

[319] St. Alphonsus M. De Liguori, *Lib. II. Tract. I. De præcepto Fidei. Dubium III.*

«"Public formal heresy" requires "public pertinacity." **This is your key error**, because pertinacity will be considered public *only* if the person **publicly renounced the Church as the infallible RULE of faith** – either by publicly defecting from the Catholic religion, or publicly admitting that he knowingly and willfully rejects a dogma of Faith.»

In their book and in their articles, Salza & Siscoe state quite plainly that for them, "publicly defecting from the Catholic religion" means that one *"publicly defects from the Faith by joining a non-Catholic sect"*, or by *expressly renouncing the Church as the rule of faith*, or by *explicitly admitting that one's belief is heretical*. I have just quoted St. Alphonsus, the greatest single authority in Moral Theology who explained that pertinacity is established when it can be seen that one consciously remains in an error against the faith after having been sufficiently explained to the heretic that his belief is contrary to the faith of the Church. De Lugo, who St. Alphonsus considered to be the of the highest authority after St. Thomas, in disp. XX, sect. IV, n. 157-158, elaborates similarly: "For if it could be established, […] given that the doctrine is well known, given the kind of person involved and given the other circumstances, that the accused could not have been unaware that his thesis was opposed to the Church, he would be considered as a heretic from this fact".

Another huge error they make in their book (p. 281) is that, «*"public heresy"* and *"public defection from the faith"* are two different things»; and they erroneously base this assertion on their deceptively conflated interpretation of a provision of administrative law according to a completely different provision of penal law that is non-applicable to the administrative canon: «As we will see below in our discussion on canon 188, §4, the old 1917 Code of Canon Law taught that in the extreme case in which a prelate publicly defects from the Faith by joining a non-Catholic sect, he is deposed *without the need of a declaratory sentence*.» (p. 281) The 1917 Code taught no such thing. The Salza/Siscoe "discussion on canon 188, §4", which is one portion of the canon that sets forth the provisions for loss of office in the *administrative section* of the Code, is in fact entirely focused on Canon 2314 in Title XI of the *penal section* of the Code that prescribes *vindictive penalties* for *"Crimes Against Faith and the Unity of the Church"*. Canon 188. 4° simply statutes an *ipso jure* **tacit resignation of office**, "without any declaration", for public defection from the faith. It does not say that a cleric is *deposed* without the need of a declaratory sentence for joining a non-Catholic sect. Deposition is a penal deprivation of office – a *vindictive penalty* which cannot take place without being *inflicted* according to the prescriptions of penal law. It is not a tacit resignation of office, which takes place automatically. What the 1917 Code prescribed in that "extreme case" is not provided for in Canon 188. 4°, but is a penal prescription of Canon 2314 in the *penal section* of the Code: «Can. 2314. §1 — 3° *Si sectæ acatholicæ nomen dederint vel publice adhæserint, ipso facto infames sunt et, firmo præscripto can. 188, n. 4, clerici, monitione incassum præmissa, degradentur.*» The canon states that those who join non-Catholic sects or adhere to them are *ipso facto* infamous; and the phrase, "*firmo præscripto can. 188, n. 4*", means that the *ipso jure* provision for tacit resignation in Canon 188. 4° remains in force; and after unheeded warnings clerics are to be degraded to the lay state. The canon states that the need for warnings before inflicting the penalty of degradation does not prevent the automatic provision of Canon 188. 4° from being incurred. What that means is that the penalty of degradation must be preceded by warnings, but since the administrative provision of Canon 188. 4° remains in force, the need for warnings in the penal process of degradation does not prevent the automatic loss of office provided for in Canon 188. 4° from taking place even before the warnings are given. On page 139 of *The Renunciation of an Ecclesiastical Office*, Fr. Gerald McDevitt writes: "The defection of faith must be public. It is to be noted immediately that **adherence to or inscription in a non-catholic sect is not required to constitute the publicity that the canon demands.**" The Very Rev. H. A. Ayrinhac comments on Canon 2197 in his General Legislation in the New Code of Canon Law (pp. 349-350), that public defection from the faith means: "Public defection from the faith, by formal heresy or apostasy, with or without affiliation with another religious society. The offense must be public, that is, generally known or liable to become so before long. (Can. 2197)" Nor is it required that one formally declare oneself to have left the Church.[320] This point is underscored by the very wording of Can. 2314. §1 — 3° in the penal section of the 1917 Code, which explicitly upholds the non-penal prescription of can. 188 4°, in mentioning that clerics who

---

[320] "A formal act [i.e. a declaration that one has left the Church] is not required for the defection in canon 194; the only requirement is that it be public (known or likely to become known).[114] Neither is it required that the officeholder join another religion, although this could be an objective indication of defection. [[114] Socha, in *Münster Com, 194/2-3;* Urrutia, n. 925, confuses this with "notorious".]" – (John P. Beal, *New Commentary on the Code of Canon Law* pp. 226-7)

join a non-Catholic sect are *ipso facto* infamous; and are to be degraded to the lay state if warnings go unheeded.[321] Fr. Charles Augustine explains how defection from the faith takes place: "Defection from the Catholic faith, if public, deprives one of all ecclesiastical ofices he may hold; [C. 9, X, V, 7.] not, however, mere schism, if unconnected with heresy." [322] Heresy alone, and not joining a non-Catholic sect or formally renouncing the Church, is all that is required for the defection from the faith to take place; and therefore public heretics, are defectors from the faith according to can. 188 4° –

> «*heretics* who, having been bapized, retain the name of Christians, but obstinately deny or doubt some of the truths that must be believed by divine or Catholic faith… a heretic is one who wilfully rejects or doubts only the one or or other truth revealed and proposed by the Catholic Church… Obstinacy may be assumed when a revealed truth has been proposed with sufficient clearness and force to convince a reasonable man.»[323]

This is all that is required for loss of office to take place: **the external act of defection into heresy** that is public or liable to become public, before any judgment, and without any *judgment* pronounced by the Church.

Fr. Gerald McDevitt elaborates on defection from the faith faith in canon 188. 4° on pp. 136-140 of *The Renunciation of an Ecclesiastical Office*:

> Since it is not only incongruous that one who has publicly defected from the faith should remain in an ecclesiastical office, but since such a condition might also be the source of serious spiritual harm when the care of souls is concerned, the Code prescribes that a cleric tacitly renounces his office by public defection from the faith. Prior to the Code the law imposed a privation of office and benefice on a cleric for such a crime. This penalty was certainly imposed upon those clerics who were publicly guilty of heresy and of apostasy, but because of two apparently contradictory laws it was disputed whether the penalty applied also to those who were publicly guilty of schism. The present law attaches a tacit renunciation instead of a privation of office to a public defection from the faith. Since canon 188, n.

---

[321] Can. 2314. §1 — 3° *Si sectae acatholicae nomen dederint vel publice adhaeserint, ipso facto infames sunt et, firmo praescripto can. 188, n. 4, clerici, monitione incassum praemissa, degradentur.*

[322] The Rev. P, Chas. Augustine, O.S.B., D.D.; *A COMMENTARY ON THE NEW CODE OF CANON LAW.*, Vol. II, St. Louis and London, 1919, p. 159.

[323] *Ibid.* Vol. VI, St. Louis and London, 1921, p. 335.

4, uses a general terminology, it necessary to determine the meaning of defection of faith and also to determine the extent of publicity that is required if the act of defection is to become the basis for a tacit renunciation of office.

Since three specific crimes, namely, heresy, apostasy and schism, will enter this discussion, it is necessary to give the definitions of them as found in the Code. These definitions are contained in canon 1325, §2, which reads as follows:

Post receptum baptismum si quis, nomen retinens christianum, pertinaciter aliquam ex veritatibus fide divina et catholica credendis denegat aut de ea dubitat, haereticus; si a fide Christiana totaliter recedit, apostata; si denique subess renuit Summo Pontifici aut cum membris Ecclesiae ei subiectis communicare recusat, schismaticus est.

These definitions are quite clear. Apostasy is a total defection from the faith, while heresy is only a partial defection, but as MacKenzie remarks (The Delict of Heresy in Its Commission, Penalization, Absolution, The Catholic University of America Canon Law Studies, n. 77 (Washington, D.C.: The Catholic University of America, 1932), p. 19), they are essentially the same, since the rejection of any one truth involves the same blasphemous attitude towards God that is involved in a denial of all the truths.

The authors are not in agreement as to whether schism is to be included in the meaning of the term "defection of faith," as used in canon 188, n. 4. Augustine, Blat, Toso and Coronata do not regard schism as constituting a defection from the faith as understood in canon 188, n. 4. since schism as such does not essentially militate against the possible retention of the faith even in its entirety. Maroto, Vermeersch-Creusen, Cocchi and Sipos, on the other hand, consider schism pure and simple as sufficient to constitute a defection from the faith and hence to call for the application of the sanction enacted in canon 188, n. 4. Heneghan includes those who are guilty purely of schism in his interpretation of the clause, "qui notorie aut catholicam fidem abjecerunt," in canon 1065, § 1. The expression which Heneghan interprets in this manner is substantially the same as the expression employed in canon 188, n. 4, which reads as follows: "A fide catholica publice defecerit."

According to the strict interpretation of the words contained in canon 188, n. 4, and of the definition of schism, it must be admitted that the canon does not indisputably comprehend the condition of pure schism, since in its essence schism does not denote defection from the faith, but rather connotes a violation of obedience and charity. However, one could doubt that the law intends to exclude the consideration of schism from this canon, for in canon 2314, §1, n. 3, which provides penalties for the public adherence to a non-catholic sect, cognizance is taken of canon 188, n. 4, with the words "firmo praescripto can. 188, n. 4." Since the wording of canon 2314, § 1, n. 3, applies to a schismatical sect as well as to a heretical one, and since the application of canon 188, n. 4, is confirmed in this canon, on could reasonably be led to conclude that the wording of canon 188, n. 4, means to comprise also the condition of pure schism.

In practice it will be extremely rare that a case of pure schism will arise, for almost invariably and all but inevitably some heresy will be joined to it. This is especially true since the time of the solemn definition of the primacy and the infallibility of the Roman Pontiff. If, however, there should arise a case of pure schism on the part of a cleric, the writer believes that the cleric would not lose his office by a tacit renunciation since the sanction of canon 188, n. 4, is of but doubtful efficacy in view of its questionable comprehension of the condition of pure schism, and especially since the effective application of that sanction involves the forfeiture of a vested right.

The defection of faith must be public. It is to be noted immediately that adherence to or inscription in a non-catholic sect is not required to constitute the publicity that the canon demands. The defection must be public according to the definition of publicity which is found in canon 2197, n. 1:

Delictum est publicum, si iam divulgatum est aut talibus contigit aut versatur in adiunctis ut prudenter iudicari possit et debeat facile divulgatum iri.

The authors are in agreement that this is the type of publicity postulated for making the defection a public one. Thus the defection from the faith may be public by reason of the fact that it is already known to a notable part of the community. The law does not prescribe any special number as being necessary to constitute a notable part of the community. Determination of this point is left to man's prudent judgment. Besides being public by reason of actual divulgation, the defection from the faith may be public also because of the fact that the circumstances force one to conclude that it will be easily divulged in the future. Thus if even only a few loquacious persons witnessed the defection from the faith, or if the sole and only witness was a taciturn person who later threatened to divulge the crime because of an enmity that has arisen between him and the delinquent, the delict would be public in the sense of canon 2197, n. 1.

A cleric, then, if he is to occasion the tacit renunciation of his office, must have defected from the faith by apostasy or heresy in a public manner according to the explanation just given. Since the writer holds the opinion that tacit renunciation is not of the nature of a penalty, he holds also that the prescriptions of canon 2229 concerning excusing causes with reference to latae sententiae penalties do not apply to the case of a tacit renunciation of office on the part of a cleric who has perpetrated the act which is mentioned in canon 188, n. 4. Thus the writer believes that even if it were thinkable that a cleric was excused from incurring excommunication involved in a defection from the faith in view of the prescriptions of canon 2229, § 3, n. 1, he still would lose his office by a tacit renunciation. In this regard a tacit renunciation is like an irregularity, which, while in many respects it looks like a penalty, is nevertheless not a penalty in a truly canonical sense.

Any confusion that there may have been on this point is entirely cleared up in the 1983 Code, which speaks not only of defection from the faith as effecting loss of office, but of defection from communion with the Church (*a communione Ecclesiæ*), which takes place by an act of heresy, schism or apostasy. Penal sanctions, such as privation of office and deposition, mentioned in the above cited canon (Can. 2314. §1 — 2°)[324], have never been considered applicable in a case of tacit renunciation of office, beause they are applicable only as penal sanctions for canonical delicts, and so are dealt with separately in the section of penal law, i.e. *"secundum præscripta canonum de iure poenali"*. (Canon 196 — § 2 1983 CIC) Tacit resignation is not a penalty, but, as Fr. Augustine explains, "Besides express or explicit resignation, both the old and the new law admit also a TACIT RESIGNATION, which is brought about and signified by a fact, especially one upon which the law itself has decreed the loss of an ecclesiastical office."[325] He then continues on Canon 188: "This canon presumes resignation, to which it applies the effect which *certain facts* are supposed to produce under the law. This effect is vacancy of the office held, whether adduced by privation, as a punishment, [Really it would be privation, but the Code presumes resignation *ipso facto*.] or simply due to the incompatibility of certain offices with the newly chosen state in life or other offices. Hence: […] (4) *Defection* from the Catholic faith, if public, deprives one of all ecclesiastical offices he may hold".[326] This dispenses witht the nonsensical objection made by Fr. Brian Harrison, who, quoted by Salza & Siscoe, says,

> «This particular cause of losing an ecclesiastical office is found in that section of the Code dealing with the resignation of such an office (cc. 184-191), and is part of a canon which lists eight sorts of actions which the law treats as 'tacit resignations.' In other words, they are the sorts of actions

---

[324] *"Nisi moniti resipuerint, priventur beneficio, dignitate, pensione, officio aliove munere, si quod in Ecclesia habeant, infames declarentur, et clerici, iterata monitione, deponantur."*
[325] *Ibid.* p. 159.
[326] *Ibid.*, pp. 160, 161.

which can safely be taken as evidence that the cleric in question does not even to want to continue in the office he held up till that time, even though he may never have bothered to put his resignation or abdication in writing.»

Whether or not the cleric intends to remain in office or not is of no consequence whatever, since like all canons, they must be understood according to the proper signification of their terms (Can. 18); and the canon in question makes no consideration whatever of whether or not the defecting cleric intends to remain in office, but the sole considerarion specified is *public defection from the Catholic faith*, and *presumes resignation* on the basis of this sole *fact*.

As I mentioned on page one of this work, "St. Pius V teaches in the Roman Catechism: 'Heretics and schismatics are excluded from the Church, because they have defected (desciverunt) from her and belong to her only as deserters belong to the army from which they have deserted.'" Defection from the faith is intrinsic to the act of heresy, which consists in the obstinate denial of some revealed truth of faith which must be believed with divine and Catholic faith; and therefore, defection from the faith cannot be understood to take place only when one joins some other sect or denomination; or when one openly declares oneself explicitly to have left the Church. Ecclesiastical laws must be understood according to the proper signification of the terms considered in their text and context[327] (Can. 17; and Canon 18 in the 1917 Code). Thus, the expression, 'defection from the faith' must be understood as the Church defines it, and not according to the arbitrary whims of fundamentalists such as Salza and Siscoe, who gratuitously define the terms themselves in such a manner to make them appear to confirm the errant legalism of their heretical doctrines. According to the expert commentaries of the Schools and scholars of Canon Law, public formal heresy suffices for the loss of office to take place. Salza & Siscoe write on page 286, «*A simple review of the explanation of this canon, as found in the canonical manuals, explains precisely what the Church means by "public defection from the faith."*» However, instead of providing such a "simple review of the explanation of this canon" (i.e. 188. 4°), Salza & Siscoe deceptively engage in verbal sleight of hand by quoting a lengthy comment of Fr.

---

[327] **Can. 17 — *Leges ecclesiasticae intellegendae sunt secundum propriam verborum significationem in textu et contextu consideratam*,** quae si dubia et obscura manserit, ad locos parallelos, si qui sint, ad legis finem ac circumstantias et ad mentem legislatoris est recurrendum.

Charles Augustine on the vindictive penalties prescribed in Canon 2314 for crimes against the faith and the unity of the Church, while claiming that they are discussing Canon 188. 4°. Thus, it is precisely such a 'simple review' of the expert commentaries on Canon 188. 4° that they have studiously omitted, in order to propagate the lie that 'defection from the Catholic faith' means joining some other religion or sect, or expressly rejecting the Church. They also engage in the fraudulent trickery of interpreting the non-penal Can 188. 4° on tacit resignation of office (which presupposes only a *fact* but not the *commission of a crime*), according to the commentaries on Can. 2314 in the *penal section* of the Code, in which are enumerated the canons which prescribe various medicinal and vindictive penalties for crimes against the faith and unity of the Church.[328]

---

[328] «Tacit resignation for public defection from the faith occurs when a prelate joins a non-Cathlic sect, not when he simply makes a heretical statement (judged so by private judgment). Canon 2314, §3 confirms this when it provides:
"Canon 2314: (3) if they have joined a non-Catholic sect (Si sectae acatholicae nomen dederint) or publicly adhered to it (vel publice adhaeserint), they are ipso facto infamous, and clerics, in addition to being considered to have tacitly renounced any office they may hold, according to canon 188.4, are, if previous warning proves fruitless, to be degraded" (emphasis added). Furthermore, as noted above in Canon 2314 and in the quotation from Fr. Augustine, even in this extreme case in which a cleric publicly defects from the faith by joining a non-Catholic sect, the prelate must be duly warned before being degraded or "deposed." Thus, even when a cleric openly leaves the Church (by joining another religion), thereby abandoning his office (which is de facto vacant due to his "tacit resignation"), he must first be warned by ecclesiastical authority before he is formally deposed (or degraded) by the Church.

This is also confirmed by Fr. Ayrinhac's commentary on the 1917 Code, wherein he notes that a cleric who "formally affiliates with a non-Catholic sect, or publicly adheres to it" is only deposed after being warned. Wrote Fr. Ayrinhac:

"If they have been formally affiliated with a non-Catholic sect, or publicly adhere to it, they incur ipso facto the note of infamy; clerics lose all ecclesiastical offices they might hold (Canon 188.4), and after a fruitless warning they should be deposed."139 [Footnote139] Ayrinhac, Penal Legislation in the New Code of Canon Law, p. 193. Note: "A deposition is an ecclesiastical vindictive penalty by which a cleric is forever deprived of his office or benefice and of the right of exercising the functions of his orders." Catholic Encyclopedia (1913), vol. IV, p. 737.» (*True or False Pope?* pp. 284-286)

It must also be borne in mind that what is set forth in Canon Law on the nature of defection from the faith or from communion with the Church, and on the consequent loss of office resulting from such a defection, is not a matter of "merely ecclesiastical law" (as mere provisions of purely human positive law in the Code are referred to in Canon 11), but pertain to divine law revealed by God, and that these precepts of divine law are merely enshrined in the provisions of Canon Law that treat of loss of ecclesiastical office due to defection from the faith. That heresy, apostasy, and schism (as demonstrated above) according to their very nature constitute defection from the faith or from communion with the Church, and accordingly sever a man from the body of the Church by themselves, apart from any human law, and therefore without any judgment or censure by ecclesiastical authority, must be believed with *divine and Catholic faith*. It is plainly set forth and proven by Bellarmine that it is the unanimous teaching of the Fathers interpreting scripture, that *heresy in its very nature not only severs one from the Church, but also directly brings about the loss of ecclesiastical office before and even without any judgment of the Church*; and being the unanimous teaching of the Fathers, it must be believed *de fide*. This has also been demonstrated above in this work. Thus, the commentaries of the canonists which explain that defection from the faith takes place by acts of heresy, even without a formal act of defection from the Church, or joining some other sect; and that the consequent loss of office takes place *ipso facto* (as an act of tacit renunciation of office), and that since it is first and foremost a matter of Church teaching and not a mere question of law, it does not require any sentence or declaration by ecclesiastical authority to take place; do not express mere opinions on these points, but truths of faith which require an assent of faith. John Salza and Robert Siscoe have explicitly denied these truths of faith in their articles, in their interviews, and in their book, *True Or False Pope?*.

True or False Pope website: 1) "After explaining the bonds that unite man to the true Church, the authors explain the distinction between heresy and lesser errors, and how **the sin of heresy alone does not sever one from the Church**." 2) «Our work speaks for itself, and the process that is currently underway in Rome, with the Cardinals formally confronting Pope Francis about his errors (all the while they recognize him as Pope), is following precisely the process that we describe in our book – **a heretical Pope is still the Pope, until the Church's authorities judge him to be a formal heretic**.»

Thus it can be plainly seen that John Salza and Robert Siscoe are in heresy. Their entire doctrine on heresy and loss of office is based on their heretical proposition, (which I copied straight from their website): «*heresy alone does not sever one from the Church.*» Their objection, that they qualify their statement by professing that heresy which is public and notorious (not according to the letter of the canons of the Church, but according to their own understanding of "public and notorious", i.e. according to the above enumerated circumstances, which according to them, qualifies heresy as public and notorious), severs one from the body of the Church without there being made a judgment by ecclesiastical authority, does not render their opinion any less heretical; because they insist that **only** heresy that is public **and notorious** (according to their own specifications which go far beyond public and notorious heresy, and in fact, amount to what is tantamount to a formal defection from the Church), severs the heretic automatically from the body of the Church without a judgment by ecclesiastical authority – and that **public heresy**, which is *only* public, but is not *notorious by fact* according to their understanding of the term, does not automatically separate the heretic from the body of the Church *suapte natura*; but for that separation to take place, Salza & Siscoe profess that a public judgment of the Church is necessary. Now that proposition is plainly heretical. It has been perpetually and generally held in the Catholic Church, that not only those convicted of the *crime* of heresy, or those who are guilty of heresy canonically qualified as a *crime notorious by fact*, but **all** who obstinately and willfully persist in *manifest heresy* (i.e. public heresy as canonically defined that is in fact manifestly formal) are cut off from the body of the Church before any judgmengt is made. This belief was already plainly reflected in the *Codex Justinianus* (1: 5: 12), which declared to be heretics, "everyone who is not devoted to the Catholic Church *and to our Orthodox holy Faith*". As St. Jerome explained, in unanimous consensus with the other ancient Fathers, that heretics leave the Church on their own, and are not expelled by judgment of the Church. Now heretics are by definition ALL who obstinately deviate from even one article of faith; and therefore, not only those who join heretical sects or publicly renounce the Church, or publicly admit that that they are in heresy defect from the Church by themselves, but ALL who publicly deviate from even one article of faith in a manner that is patently obstinate, separate themselves from the body of the Church. The unanimous opinion of the Fathers, as Bellarmine demonstrates in his refutation of Opinion No. 4, and which is affirmed by Ballerini, Cappellari (Gregory XVI), the Council of Constance, and both the 1917 and 1983 Code of Canon Law, is that heretics are those who obstinately reject even one article of faith, or profess even one heretical doctrine (Can. 751 in the 1983 Code; Can. 1325 §2 in the 1917 Code); and by the fact of that very act of manifestly obstinate heresy, if it be *public* (as *public* is defineded in canon 2197 n. 1; and **not** *notorious by fact* as that is defined in canon 2197 n. 3), they leave the Church by themselves and are separated from the Body of the Church by the very act of heresy *suapte natura*; and lose office and all ecclesiastical dignity **automatically** [first and foremost, *ex natura hæresis*, i.e. by the very nature of heresy apart from the law as Bellarmine explains; and therefore *ipso facto* "without any declaration" (Canon 188. 4° in the 1917 Code); as well as *ipso jure*, i.e. "by operation of the law itself" (Canon 194 § 2 in the 1983 Code], even before any judgment of the Church is made (*"sine ulla declaratione"* Canon 188. 4° in the 1917 Code). So what has been John Salza's response to me on this point? All he can say is, "You haven't addressed Cardinal Billot's teaching, who was an adherent to Bellarmine's Fifth Opinion on the loss of office for a heretical Pope... you are not equipped to have this debate with us. You are in way over your head." Having run out of arguments, Salza writes to Dr. Peter Chojnowski, "Fr Kramer is blind. Only public and notorious heresy separates one from the Body of the Church."

Since Salza and Siscoe remain blindly adamant that I have interpreted both St. Robert Bellarmine and Don Pietro Ballerini incorrectly, an alleged misinterpretation which they maliciously attribute to diminished mental capacity and ignorance, I point out here that my interpretation of Ballerini is exactly that which was expressed by Pope Gregory XVI in the above cited passage of his book: "***the deposition is not a prescription... against the current representation of the Church in the Pope recognized as such, but only against the person, who was before adorned with papal dignity.***" I also include here the learned opinion of Don Curzio Nitoglia on Ballerini's doctrine on a heretic pope's loss of office, and his commentary on the interpretation of Frs. Wernz & Vidal on Bellarmine's doctrine on Opinion No. 5. First, Don Nitoglia on the Wernz-Vidal interpretation of Bellarmine:

> «Secondo il Bellarmino (De Romano Pontifice, lib. II, cap. 30, p. 420), siccome gli eretici manifesti, notori e pubblici perdono ipso facto la giurisdizione, ammesso e non concesso che il Papa possa cadere in eresia, in caso di eventuale eresia manifesta egli perderebbe immediatamente l'autorità papale. Questa è l'interpretazione della posizione bellarminiana

data dai padri gesuiti Franz Xavier Wernz e Pedro Vidal (Jus Canonicum, Roma, Gregoriana, 1943, vol. II, p. 517> Secondo il Da Silveira (op. cit., p. 37) Francisco Suarez (De Fide, disp. X, sect. VI, n. 11, Parigi, Vivès, tomo XII, 1858, p. 319) e S. Roberto Bellarmino (De Romano Pontifice, lib. IV, cap. 7, Milano, Battezzati, vol. II, 1858) difendono la medesima tesi del Billot, ma in maniera meno rigida. Infatti il Billot (Tractatus de Ecclesia Christi, Prato, Giachetti, 1909, tomo I, pp. 617-618) la ritiene esplicitamente una "mera ipotesi, *mai traducibile in atto*. [...]. A priori si può ritenere che *Dio non lo permetterebbe mai*". Suarez e Bellarmino impiegano termini meno forti, però la sostanza della loro tesi coincide con quella del Billot, ossia secondo i due Dottori controriformistici il Papa come dottore privato può ipoteticamente e per una pura possibilità o al massimo per una probabilità e mai per una certezza teologica cadere in eresia materiale o favorire l'eresia.» [«According to Bellarmine, since the manifest, notorious and public heretics lose jurisdiction ipso facto, granted but not conceded that the pope can fall into heresy, in the case of an eventual manifest heresy, he would immediately lose all papal authority. This is the position of Bellarmine given by the Jesuit Fathers Franz Xavier Wernz and Pedro Vidal. According to Da Silveira (op. cit., p. 37) Francisco Suarez (De Fide, disp. X, sect. VI, n. 11, Parigi, Vivès, tomo XII, 1858, p. 319) and St. Robert Bellarmine (De Romano Pontifice, lib. IV, cap. 7, Milano, Battezzati, vol. II, 1858) defend the same thesis as Billot, but in a less rigid manner. In fact, Billot (Tractatus de Ecclesia Christi, Prato, Giachetti, 1909, tomo I, pp. 617-618) explicitly holds it to be a "mere hypothesis *that can never become actual* [...] A priori one can maintain that *God would never permit it*". Suarez and Bellarmine use less forceful terms, but in substance their theses coincide with that of Billot, or rather according to the two Counter-Reformation Doctors, the pope as a private doctor could fall into objective heresy or favour heresy hypothetically and as a pure possibility, or at most probably, but never as a theological certainty».]

The statement, "Suarez and Bellarmine use less forceful terms, but in substance their theses coincide with that of Billot," does not claim that all three were of Opinion No. 5, but only that "according to the two Counter-Reformation Doctors, the pope as a private doctor could fall into objective heresy or favour heresy hypothetically and as a pure possibility, or at most probably, but never as a theological certainty"; and on this point only, "*in substance their theses coincide with that of Billot*". Ballerini likewise admits formal papal heresy as a theoretical possibility; but doubts it will ever happen: "But this hypothesis is not established by any fact, since no private error ascribed to any Pontiff against any evident or defined dogma has been found, or is believed will be."³²⁹ Billot, like Bellarmine, is clearly of Opinion No. 5, which holds that a manifest heretic pope would automatically fall from office by the very act of his heresy before any judgment is pronounced; whereas Suárez held that the heretic pope would only fall from office upon being judged by the Church, which is Opinion No. 4. As I will show later in this work, **all of the expert canonists and theologians who expound on the five opinions are unanimous in stating that the difference between Opinion No. 4 and No. 5 is that No. 4 requires a judgment to be made by the Church before the pope falls from office, whereas No. 5 holds that the fall from office is automatic, and takes place independently of and before any judgment is made.** In order to support their erroneous opinion on this point, Salza & Siscoe in Chapter 11 of their book quote the ambiguously stated opinion of Fr. Sebastian Smith (Elements of Ecclesiastical Law, p. 210. 68 Ibid., Preface, p. xi.), who wrote in 1881, "Question: Is a Pope who falls into heresy deprived, ipso jure, of the Pontificate? Answer: There are two opinions: one holds that he is by virtue of divine appointment, divested ipso facto, of the Pontificate; the other, that he is, jure divino, only removable. Both opinions agree that he must at least be declared guilty of heresy by the Church – i.e., by an ecumenical council or the College of Cardinals." It is first to be pointed out that Fr. Smith states ambiguously that there are "two opinions" on the question (there have been five opinions, but only two which admit the removal of a manifest heretic pope); and he says, "Both opinions agree that he must at least be declared guilty of heresy by the Church". This statement, "Both opinions agree that he must at least be declared guilty of heresy by the Church", simply means that in the case of an *ipso jure* loss of office which takes place automatically even before the declaration and independently of it; and the case of *jure divino* "only removable" opinion, in which the loss of office is said to take place immediately upon the declaration: in both cases, a declaratory sentence would be required to enforce the removal and authorize the election of a new pope. Expressed in the manner that it is formulated, the statement can superficially be misinterpreted to mean, (in the manner that Salza & Siscoe opportunistically misinterpret it for their own purpose), that the

---

³²⁹ «Sed haec hypothesis nullo facto comprobatur; siquidem nullus vel privatus error cuipiam Pontifici adscriptus contra ullum dogma evidens aut definitum hactenus inventus est, aut futurus putatur.» [*De Potestate ecclesiastica Summorum Pontificum et Conciliorum generalium*; p. 129.]

declaration would be required in order for the loss of office to take place. As they do with so many authors (as will be shown later in this work), Salza & Siscoe twist the meaning of a passage to make it appear to say exactly the opposite from what a critical examination of the words demonstrates to be their authentic meaning. Smith is clearly referring to Opinion No. 5 when he says, "one holds that he is by virtue of divine appointment, divested ipso facto, of the Pontificate"; since he writes in answer to the question, "Is a Pope who falls into heresy deprived, ipso jure, of the Pontificate?" Now in Canon Law, the expression that one is deprived *ipso jure* means that it is automatic – it takes place *ipso facto* **before** any judgment is prounounced. This is exactly how the medieval Decretists employed the term in the earliest formulations of Opinion No. 5, and it is employed in exactly the same manner by the Council of Constance when it deposed Pedro de Luna "as a precautionary measure", and declared that he had already fallen from every ecclesiastical dignity and had been severed from the body of the Church *ipso jure* before any judgment was pronounced. The term is again employed in exactly the same manner in the 1983 Code of Canon Law of Pope John Paul II. When Smith says of "the other", i.e. "that he is, jure divino, only removable", he is clearly speaking of Opinion No. 4 in its less radical formulation (Suárez), according to which the Church would deliberatively determine that the pope is a heretic, and upon the juridical declaration of guilt, the pope would immediately fall from office. If Smith had meant by, "Both opinions agree that he must at least be declared guilty of heresy by the Church", that in both cases a declaration of guilt would be necessary for the fall from to take place; that would mean that there would not be two opinions on the question, but only one, namely, "that he is, jure divino, only removable". Yet this absurd interpretation of the passage is exactly how it is understood by Salza & Siscoe in Chapter 11 of their book: «Fr. Smith expressly states that "both opinions agree" that he must at least be declared guilty of heresy by the Church. If he is not found guilty, he remains a true and valid Pope."». Then they state their *non sequitur* conclusion: «The teaching of Fr. Smith confirms John of St. Thomas' understanding of Bellarmine and Suarez's position, since he [John of St. Thomas] stated that "Bellarmine and Suarez" both held that a heretical Pope loses his office only if he is "declared incorrigible."» In reality, what Fr. Smith's teaching confirms is that John of St. Thomas failed to correctly understand Bellarmine's exposition on the question; and that Salza & Siscoe have understood neither Bellarmine's exposition on Opinion No. 5, nor have they understood the opinion as it has been elaborated by theologians and canonists for more than eight centuries. In the first of the "two opinions" in which the heretic pope would lose office *ipso jure* (automatically) the Church would possess the jurisdiction to declare the See vacant, in the manner that the Council of Constance declared "Benedict XIII" to have already lost all ecclesiastical dignity and to have severed himself from the body of the Church, thus removing the last remaining claimant to the papal throne, and juridically establishing the *sede vacante*. In the second of the "two opinions", the Church would not be able to declare the pope guilty of heresy, because an official judgment of guilt of an individual pronounced by the Church absolutely requires jurisdiction to judge that person; but neither the cardinals, nor a synod, and not even a general council possess the jurisdiction to make such an official, *juridical* declaration – so any judgment a council would make would not be a public *juridical act* of the *Church*, but would be a non-juridic statement of *churchmen* utterly devoid of any force of law or juridical value whatsoever. This is the fatal flaw in all the variations of Opinion No. 4, which holds that a heretic pope does not lose his office until he is **judged** by the Church. John of St. Thomas, who held this opinion, admitted himself the problematic aspect of the opinion when he wrote: *"Concerning the second point, namely by whose authority the declaration and deposition is to be made, there is dissent among theologians, and it does not appear by whom such a deposition is to be made, because it is an act of* **judgment***, and* **jurisdiction***, which can be exercised by* **no one over** *the pope."*[330]

Salza & Siscoe then carry the absurdity even further:

> «Because the "two opinions" agree that a heretical Pope "must at least be declared guilty of the crime of heresy by the Church," there are actually three opinions to be noted, which, for the sake of simplicity and easy recall, could be classified as follows: 1) the "Jesuit" opinion (of Bellarmine/Suarez), 2) the "Dominican" opinion (of Cajetan/John of St. Thomas), and 3) the unanimous opinion. The Jesuit opinion is that a heretical Pope falls from office after the crime of heresy has been established by the Church. The Dominican opinion is that a heretical Pope falls from office only after the Church commands the faithful to avoid him. But the unanimous opinion is that "he must at least be declared guilty by the Church."»

---

[330] *De Auctoritate Summi Pontificis" Disputatio III, Articulus II XVII De Depositione Papae & Seq.*

The belief that there was a single "Jesuit opinion" is the result of an uncritical failure to distinguish between two of the oldest opinions on the question of the deposition or removal of a heretic pope. As Moynihan demonstrates[331], among the early Decretists there were those, who maintained that a heretic pope would remain in office until judged guilty of heresy by the Church; and others, mainly of the French school of canonists who advocated the opinion that a heretic pope would by his very heresy automatically lose office by himself, *ipso jure*. It was among the early Decretists that these opinions, enumerated by Bellarmine as No. 4 and No. 5 originated. Bellarmine argued in favour of the fifth opinion which held that a heretic pope would automatically fall from office *ipso facto* or (as the Decretists would say), *ipso jure*; while Suárez followed the fourth opinion, which held that the heretic would remain in office until judged guilty of heresy by the Church. By the late 19th Century, the fourth opinion had been universally abandoned; and since then, the fifth opinion (as will be shown below), has been the morally unanimous opinion among theologians who admit, at least hypothetically, that a pope can become a heretic. Salza & Siscoe have totally inverted the truth in this matter, hysterically claiming that those who follow what is now the virtually unanimous opinion among those theologians who admit at least as a hypothesis, that a pope can become a heretic, (No. 5), (in the manner that it is explained by all of the eminent scholars who have examined each of the five opinions), 'nonsensically reject the unanimous opinion' one cannot hold the Jesuit opinion (the Pope loses his office ipso facto), without also holding the unanimous opinion (the Pope must at least be declared guilty of the crime of heresy by the Church)." They then conclude against what has been established and is held with a unanimous consensus of scholars that the "rejection of [what is according to them] the unanimous opinion is clearly not the fruit of sound, scholarly research of the question, but rather a rash and superficial judgment based, in many cases, on snippets read on the internet". (!)

Bellarmine explained that the manifest heretic pope would cease "by himself" to be pope, a Christian, and a member of the Church; and **"for which reason"** (*quare*) having ceased to be pope, "he may be judged and punished by the Church." It is unmistakably clear from the explicit wording of the text that Bellarmine is saying that the manifest heretic

---

[331] James M. Moynihan, STL, JCD; *Papal Immunity and Liability in the Writings of the Medieval Canonists*, Gregorian University Press, Roma 1961, Chapter Three.

pope, completely by himself, i.e. by his own act of defection from the faith, *"sine alia vi externa"*, ceases to be pope, a Christian and a member of the Church; and precisely because he would cease to be pope, he, having fallen from office, could then be judged and punished by the Church. Ballerini, following Bellamine, is more explicit in saying that the heretic pope, upon manifesting his pertinacity, would have *"abdicated the primacy and the pontificate"*, ceasing automatically to be pope, without any judgment, but explains the pastoral reason why a declaratory sentence would need to be made. Pope Gregory XVI explicitly endorsed Ballerini's opinion. A declaratory sentence is absolutely necessary not only for the pastoral reason given by Ballerini, (so that the faithful may be warned about the heretic), but more importantly, because unless the heretic intruder be visibly and juridically declared to have fallen from office and to have *vacated the chair*, a manifestly and certainly valid pope could not be elected and universally accepted by the whole Church for so long as the intruder is allowed to carry on with his imposture.

As they do with the passage of Fr. Sebastian Smith, similarly Salza & Siscoe twist the words of Bellarmine and Ballerini, even falsifying the text of the latter (as is shown later in this work) to fit their own meaning. All three of these authors mentioned in the previous paragraph (Bellarmine, Ballerini and Gregory XVI), were following the ruling of the Council of Constance, which declared that Pedro de Luna had already lost all office and ecclesiastical dignity by himself, prior to his being judged by the Council. By the late 19th Century, Fr. Sydney Smith SJ (in 1895) testified that it had already become the *common opinion* that a manifestly heretical pope would cease automatically to be pope, and that in such a case the Cardinals, being duly informed, would only need to issue a declaratory sentence on the one who was no longer pope.[332] (This is also the explicitly stated opinion of Cardinal Raymond Burke[333]). Thus,

---

[332] "[I]t has been **generally held** that, **given the possibility of a personally heretical Pope, he would *ipso facto* cease to be Pope by ceasing to be a member of the Church.** The Church in that case, as represented by the Cardinals or otherwise, could **on due information of the *fact*** pass a **declaratory sentence** on one who being no longer Pope was no longer its superior, and **then take measures to remove him from the see in which he had become an intruder.**" (*Dr. Littledale's Theory of the Disappearance of the Papacy* – Sydney F. Smith S.J. Catholic Truth Society, London, 1896.)

[333] "If a Pope would formally profess heresy he would cease, by that act, to be the Pope. It's automatic. And so, that could happen. […] It would have to

it would seem highly unlikely that Fr. Sebastian Smith would have been so ignorant as to mean by saying, "Both opinions agree that he must at least be declared guilty of heresy by the Church", that both opinions held that the fall from office would only take place upon judgment by the Church, as Salza & Siscoe maintain. What his words clearly indicate, if one examines them critically, is that whether the pope would be "divested ipso facto, of the Pontificate" (Opinion No. 5), or, "that he is, jure divino, only removable" (Opinion No. 4), **a declaratory sentence would be necessary in order to enforce the loss of office and facilitate the election of a new pope in the former case;** and at least a declaratory sentence as opposed to penal judgment and deposition by a tribunal, would be necessary to effect the removal of the heretic pope from office in the latter. Thus, Smith uses the term "removable" in the same manner as it is used in By Bellarmine in his refutation of Opinion No. 2, rather than that a reigning pope could be juridically judged and deposed from office. What this shows, is that Sebastian Smith is testifying that in his day (1881), the classical position of Opinion No. 4 formulated by Cajetan during the Reformation, which held in favour of a juridical deposition of a heretical pope, had already been universally abandoned, and was replaced by a less radical version of the opinion; which held, contrary to the vast majority who favoured Opinion No. 5, that a heretic pope would fall from office upon the issuance of a merely declaratory sentence after a merely deliberative inquiry. The flaw in this theory is that a mere declaration pronounced on actually reigning pontiff by his subjects would lack all jurisdiction, and would therefore not be an official judgment of the Church, because so long as he is pope, the pontiff, who is solemnly defined to be the supreme and final judge in all cases, is the only one who has the authority to judge his own case. Without jurisdiction to pronounce judgment on the pope, a council's judgment would not be a judgment of the Church, but a mere opinion of men, who would invalidly presume to convene in a council and pronounce a judgment they are juridically incompetent to make. The belief that the Cardinals, or even an ecumenical council would be competent to judge a pope juridically is a heresy that directly offends against the judicial supremacy and injudicability of the Roman Pontiff, solemnly defined in *Pastor Æternus*; against the repeated declarations of the popes teaching that the pope cannot be judgd by anyone, as well as

---

be members of the College of Cardinals [to declare him to be in heresy]." Interview with Catholic World Report, December 8 2016.

against the solemn pronouncement of the Fifth Lateran Council that the pope has absolute authority over a council[334]. Bellarmine refuted this opinion in his exposition on Opinion No. 4 demolishing the argument, by explaining that neither the bishops nor the cardinals have any power over a pope, and to pronounce official judgment *on* a pope is to exercise *power of jurisdiction* **over** a pope. Wernz and Vidal most conclusively refute and utterly demolish the theory that a council could even pronounce a merely declaratory sentence on a reigning pope:

> Finally there is the fifth view of Bellarmine which was expressed at the outset in the assertion [above] and which is rightly defended by Tanner and others as being more approved and more common. For he who is no longer a member of the body of the Church, that is, of the Church as a visible body, cannot be the head of the universal Church. **But a pope who falls into public heresy would by that fact cease to be a member of the Church; therefore he would also, upon that fact, cease to be the head of Church.**
>
> So, a publicly heretical pope, who by the mandate of Christ and of the Apostle should be avoided because of danger to the Church, must be deprived of his power, as nearly everyone admits. **But he cannot be deprived of his power by a merely declaratory sentence.**
>
> For every judicial sentence of privation supposes a superior jurisdiction over him against whom the sentence is laid. But a general council, in the opinion of adversaries, does not have a higher jurisdiction than does a heretical pope. For he, by their supposition, before the declaratory sentence of a general council, retains his papal jurisdiction; therefore a general council cannot pass a declaratory sentence by which a Roman Pontiff is actually deprived of his power; for that would be a sentence laid by an inferior against the true Roman Pontiff. In sum, it needs to be said clearly that a [publicly] heretical Roman Pontiff loses his power upon the very fact. Meanwhile a declaratory criminal sentence, although it is merely declaratory, should not be disregarded, for it brings it about, not that a pope is "judged" to be a heretic, but rather, that he is shown to have been found heretical, that is, a general council declares the fact of the crime by which a pope has separated himself from the Church and has lost his rank.[335]

---

[334] "... the Roman Pontiff alone, possessing as it were authority over all Councils, has full right and power of proclaiming Councils, or transferring and dissolving them" (The reference is provided below with the text of the full paragraph.)

[335] Wernz-Vidal, *IUS CANONICUM II* (1928), n. 453

Following the doctrine of Innocent III[336], who taught that the pope, *as pope*, cannot be judged; Bellarmine says in Book Four, Chapter Seven of *De Romano Pontifice*, "**the Pope cannot be judged**", but only upon having fallen from office *"by himself"* (he explains in Book Two Chapter Thirty) **he could then be *judged and punished by the Church*.** It suffices to say that if even a council may not judge a pope, then *a fortiori* neither can any other group or individual which would be less than a council, judge a pope, but could only declare in such a manner that he may be "shown to be already judged" (Innocent III), to have already fallen, to already have lost any office and all ecclesiastical dignity *ipso jure* (Council of Constance) to have "abdicated the primacy and the pontificate" (Ballerini), and to have "fallen from the pontificate by himself" (Gregory XVI). Ballerini states in the most explicit of terms that, a general council has no power to judge a pope, since the pope receives his power not from his electors or from the Church, but immediately from God; by which he is the Pontiff over the whole Church, and superior over general councils, and therefore is entirely removed from the jurisdiction of all others who are inferior to him, and precisely for this reason, the machinations of Basel against Eugenius IV ended up in open schism:

> «... contra certum Pontificium jus nulla vel generalis concilii potestas est: cum ob idem jus non ab electoribus, nec ab Ecclesia, sed a Deo immediate tributum, verus Pontifex toti Ecclesiæ, & generalibus quoque synodis (ut probavimus) superior, ab aliorum omnium sibi inferiorum jurisdictione subtrahatur. Hac quidem de causa Basileensium molimina & gesta contra Eugenium IV. unicum certumque Pontificem illegitima & inania nihil potuerunt ad ipsum deponendum, & in apertum schisma deflexerunt.»[337]

Ballerini's formulation leaves absolutely no room for the sole exception for heresy theory that had been formulated by canonists since the time of the Decretists, according to which, a council would have the authority to depose a certain pope from office for the crime of heresy.

---

[336] «Qui autem judicat, dominus est» (I *Cor.* IV)." And again: "The Roman Pontiff has no superior but God. Who, therefore, should a pope 'lose his savour', could cast him out or trample him under foot". The doctrine of Innocent III is dealt with in Part II.

[337] *De Potestate Ecclesiastica. De casu Schismatis, quo duo vel plures se se gerant tamquam Pontifices;* p. 130.

On page 132 of the same work, Ballerini declares, «Ideo enim (ut antea probatum est) supra certum pontificem jus nullum est concilio etiam generali, quia verus Pontifex est, & primate fruitur, ob quem toti Ecclesiæ etiam collective sumptæ, & in concilio adunatæ jure divino superior est; nec inferiori in superiorem suum coactivum jus esse potest.»

Peters[338] attests to the fact that the opinion that a heretic pope would remain in office until even a merely declaratory sentence would effect his removal as a dispositive cause for his fall from office has been entirely abandoned in his article where he says, «I know of no author coming after Wernz who disputes this analysis [of Wernz and Vidal]. See, e.g., Ayrinhac, CONSTITUTION (1930) 33; Sipos, ENCHIRIDION (1954) 156; Regatillo, INSTITUTIONES I (1961) 299; Palazzini, DMC III (1966) 573; and Wrenn[339] (2001) above. As for the lack of detailed canonical examination of the *mechanics* for assessing possible papal heresy, Cocchi, COMMENTARIUM II/2 (1931) n. 155, ascribes it to the fact that law provides for common cases and adapts for rarer; may I say again, heretical popes are about as rare as rare can be and yet still be. In sum, and while additional important points could be offered on this matter, **in the view of modern canonists from Wernz to Wrenn**, however remote is the possibility of a pope actually falling into heresy and however difficult it might be to determine whether a pope has so fallen, **such a catastrophe, Deus vetet, would result in the loss of papal office**.» Incredibly, Salza & Siscoe adamantly and delusionally insist that the common opinion today is that a manifest heretic pope would not fall from office until he is judged by the Church; and, according to them, the opinion which was originated by the Decretists of the early 1180s, namely, the *Fifth Opinion* which holds that a manifest heretic pope would automatically fall from office *ipso facto* by the act of formal heresy itself before any judgment by the Church, is nothing but an opinion of sedevacantists who do not understand Bellarmine! As I

---

[338] https://canonlawblog.wordpress.com/2016/12/16/a-canonical-primer-on-popes-and-heresy/

[339] *Ibid.* «Wrenn, writing in the CLSA NEW COMM (2001) at 1618 states: "Canon 1404 is not a statement of personal impeccability or inerrancy of the Holy Father. Should, indeed, the pope fall into heresy, it is understood that he would lose his office. To fall from Peter's faith is to fall from his chair."»[339] An earlier edition of that same commentary says, "Communion becomes a real issue when it is threatened or even lost. This occurs especially through heresy, apostasy and schism. Classical canonists discussed the question whether a pope, in his private or personal opinions, could go into heresy, apostasy or schism."

just quoted Peters, "I know of no author coming after Wernz who disputes this analysis [of Wernz and Vidal]"; yet the two armchair theologians – the tax lawyer and the businessman, who have no formal education in Canon Law or Theology presume to differ with the unanimous opinion of canonists and theologians on papal loss of office, and their learned understanding of Opinion No. 5.

On the opinion of Ballerini, Don Curzio comments,

> «In breve ciò che don Pietro Ballerini mantiene come certissimo è che il Papa nel definire non errerà mai; infine come ipotesi investigativa "ammesso e non concesso" che il Papa cada in errore contrario alla fede, dovrebbe essere ammonito e corretto e dopo due ammonizioni, se si ostina nell'errore, si dichiara da se stesso eretico e decaduto dal Pontificato, ma tutto ciò deve essere opera non di giurisdizione bensì di carità (De Potestate ecclesiastica Summorum Pontificum et Conciliorum generalium, Verona, 1765, cap. 9, nn. 3-8; cap. 15, n. 21; cfr. T. Facchini, Il Papato principio di unità e Pietro Ballerini di Verona, Padova, Il Messaggero di S Antonio, 1950, pp. 126-128).»

[«Briefly, that which Don Pietro Ballerini maintains as most certain is that in defining the pope will never err; finally as an investigative hypothesis, "granted but not conceded" that should the pope fall into error against the faith, he ought to be warned and corrected, and after two warnings, and if he remains obstinate in error, **he declares himself to be a heretic and fallen from the pontificate**, but this must not be an act of jurisdiction but a work of charity.»]

Thus Don Curzio Nitoglia explains the doctrine of Ballerini exactly as I have: *there is not even a hint made that the heretic pope would be officially warned by "the Church", but by individuals as an act of charity*, not acting in an official capacity (which requires the authority of a superior), and not pronouncing a judicial verdict or even a declaratory sentence while the pope remains in office (which requires jurisdiction). The judgment of condemnation is pronounced by the self-judging heretic, who falls from the pontificate by his own self condemnation before any juridical *post factum* judgment is made by the Church. This is precisely what the Council of Constance explicitly declared to have taken place in the case of Pedro de Luna (Benedict XIII).

The proposition stated explicitly by Salza and Siscoe on their website, purportedly refuting my "erroneous" interpretation of Bellarmine, in which they assert that the Church may judge a pope for heresy while still in office, directly opposes the dogma of the universal papal primacy of jurisdiction defined by Vatican I, and which declares most solemnly that no one on earth may judge the pope. Don Nitoglia points out that this is the defined article of faith that the pope cannot be judged by anyone:

> «Ma il Concilio Vaticano I (IV sessione, 18 luglio 1870, Costituzione dogmatica Pastor Aeternus) ha stabilito la definizione dogmatica circa il principio della ingiudicabilità del Papa: "Insegniamo e dichiariamo che secondo il diritto divino del primato papale, il Romano Pontefice è il giudice supremo di tutti i fedeli [...]" (DS, 3063-3064). Il CIC del 1917 al canone 1556 riprendendo la definizione dogmatica del Vaticano I ha stabilito il principio: "Prima Sedes a nemine iudicatur", ripreso tale e quale dal CIC del 1983, canone 1404.»
>
> ["But the First Vatican Council (Session IV, 18 July 1870, Dogmatic Constitution Pastor Aeternus) has established the dogmatic definition on the principle of the injudicability of the pope: 'We teach and declare that according to divine right of the papal primacy, the Roman Pontiff is the supreme judge of all the faithful [...]'. (DS, 3063- 3064). The CIC of 1917 in Canon 1556 reiterating the dogmatic definition of Vatican I established the principle: 'Prima Sedes a nemine iudicatur', repeated exactly the same in the CIC of 1983, Canon 1404."]

The doctrine that the Apostolic See may never be judged by anyone was already proclaimed in the Fifth Century by Pope St. Gelasius. Hinschius observes:

> «Schon im fünften Jahrhundert, in welchem die Stellung des Römischen Bischofs sich zu einer wirchlichen Obergewalt umzubilden anfängt, wird indessen aus der demselben beigelegten höchsten Jurisdiction über die Kirche von Papst Gelasius I. der Satz hergeleitet, dass die Römische Kirche dem Gerichte Niemandes unterstehe. [4]»
>
> «[4] c. 16 (Gelasius I. a. 493) C. IX. qu. 3: *"Ipsi sunt canones qui appellationes totius ecclesiæ ad huius sedis examen voluere deferri. Ab ipsa vero nusquam prorsus appellari debere sanxerunt ac per hoc illam de tota ecclesia iudicare, ipsam ad nullius commeare iudicium nec de eius unquam præceperunt iudicio iudicari"*; c. 17 (idem a. 498) ead.: *"Cuncta per mundum novit ecclesia, quod sacrosancta Romana ecclesia fas de omnibus habet iudicandi neque cuiquam de eius liceat iudicare iudicio."*»[340]

In the phrase, «*ipsam ad nullius commeare iudicium*», the **injudicability of the Roman Pontiff** is declared, a principle which is restated by Pope St. Gregory VII around the year 1075 in *Dictatus 19* of his *Dictatus*

---

[340] Hinschius, *Op. cit.* p. 297.

Papæ[341]: «***Quod a nemine ipse* (the pope) iudicari debeat**», and again Paul IV in 1559 declared that the Roman Pontiff, «*omnesque iudicat, a nemine in hoc sæculo iudicandus.*» This *injudicability* pertains essentially to the very nature of the *judicial supremacy* of the **primacy**, as Moynihan explains, "This doctrine of papal immunity is incontrovertible [...] the authority of the pope is supreme, and by virtue of his own primacy of jurisdiction, no one else is competent to be his judge."[342] Hence, it is a proposition against the very nature of the primacy to assert that the pope can ever be judged by anyone, even for the crime of heresy; unless "judging the pope" be understood in a qualified sense, according to which, the manifestly heretical pope would, by the very act of his heresy, cease by himself straightaway to be pope and a member of the Church; and *for that reason*, (as Bellarmine states) he could then be judged and punished by the Church, i.e. shown to be already judged. Thus it is according to the same qualification and meaning, as both Hinschius observes (in the earlier cited passage), and Moynihan explains (citing the same passage as Hinschius), that Innocent III teaches, if the pope were to fall into heresy, he could be "judged by men"; but only in the qualified sense that he "can be shown to be already judged". Moynihan explains: "Innocent in this passage is making a veiled reference to the principle elaborated by his teacher, Huguccio of Pisa, who wrote, «*Cum papa cadit in heresim, non iam maior sed minor quolibet catholico intelligitur*»"[343]. According to this principle as elaborated by Huguccio, a heretic pope would automatically cease to be pope, and would therefore no longer be greater than any Catholic, but less than any Catholic. This principle had already been elaborated less systematically earlier by the authors of the *Summa Et est sciendum*[344] and the Gloss *Ecce uicit leo*[345]. According to this principle elaborated by these early

---

[341] Sources are provided in the reference given by Moynihan on page 7 of his work.

[342] Moynihan, *Op. cit.* p.8

[343] *Ibid.* p. 81.

[344] *Ibid.* p. 64, footnote 69 – «Sed quare est in haeresi speciale? Quia caetera peccata unitatem ecclesiae non rumpunt. Cum caeteris enim uicis potest esse homo membrum ecclesiae licet putridum. Haeresis uero uel scisma ipsam uiololant (sic) unitatem et fundamentum fidei maculant et corrumpunt, unde cum sit haereticus est quolibet catholico minor».

[345] *Ibid.* p. 90 footnote 117: «Tercia est exceptio quando papa est in heresim lapsus est (sic) tunc potest a minori excommunicari et iudicari ut di. X. *Si papa* (D. XL, c. 6) quondam non uero hec exceptio, quia ex quo est hereticus est

Decretists, a pope who becomes a heretic, ceases automatically to be pope (*ipso jure*) and a member of the Church; and being no longer a member of the Church, (excommunicated *ipso iure* as the author of the Gloss *Ecce uicit leo* states[346]) he is no longer *greater than any Catholic*, but is *less than any Catholic*. Hence, he can, as Innocent III teaches, be "shown to be already judged", and "cast out and trampled underfoot by men" – "deposed", as I explain in Part II of this work. So, explains Moynihan,

> "In this connection [i.e. on the automatic fall from office for heresy] it is interesting to note the difference of opinion on this question between Huguccio and Innocent III (1198 – 1216). The latter had been a pupil of Huguccio's at Bologna. [...] he could not agree with Huguccio that a pope could be deposed for notorious crimes, but rather only for heresy. There is a veiled attempt at avoiding a papal trial in the following words: «Romanus Pontifex... potest ab hominibus judicari, vel potius judicatus ostendi». [...] (Sermo IV)."[347]

Thus, it is the constant teaching of the Church going back to the explicit formulations of Pope St. Gelasius, that for so long as the pope is still the validly reigning pope, he is the **supreme judge in all cases – including his own**, as Pope Innocent III teaches (see Part II); and cannot be judged by anyone. He can only be judged by his inferiors if he were to consent to being judged; or if a future occupant of the Apostolic See were to consent to the judgment of his predecessor, as Pope Hadrian II taught in his *Allocutio tertia, ad Concilium Romanum*.[348] Fr. Salvatore Vacca elaborates:

---

minor quolibet catholico». Footnote 114: «Si nouam et eam iam predicare cepit similiter cadit a iurisdictione sua ipso iure [...] Credo quia sine eo debeat ecclesia deliberative non iudicialiter disceptare et eo inuento quod heresis sit, papa correctus, nisi resipiscat papa desinit esse ipso iure».

[346] *Ibid.* Footnote 119: «Item si papa incidid heresim dampnatam estne excommunicatus? Uidetur quod si incidit in talem heresim quod ipso iure excommunicatus est».

[347] *Ibid.*, p. 81, footnote 103.

[348] *Ibid.* p. 34: «Siquidem Romanum pontificem de omnium ecclesiarum praesulibus judicasse legimus; de e overo quemquam judicasse non legimus: licet enim Honorio ab orientalibus post mortem anathema sit dictum, sciendum tamen est quia fuerat super haeresi accusatus, propter quam solam licitum est minoribus majorum suorum motibus resistendi, vel pravos sensus libere respuendi: quamvis et ibi **nec patriarcharum nec antistitum cuipiam de eo quemlibet fas fuerit proferendi sententiam, nisi ejusdem primae sedis**

The Roman council condemned that one of Constantinople of 867, including Photius and the Greek Fathers who had participated in it, because it had launched a condemnation against Pope Nicholas I. Unfortunately, the acts of the Constantinople of 867 were destroyed. During the Roman Council, Pope Adrian II defined the decision of the Council of Constantinople as arrogant and intolerable, since he could not condemn the bishop of Rome.

Nobody, in fact, had ever dared to do it and never had heard of such a thing. The pontiff states: *We read that only the Roman Pontiff judged the bishops of all the Churches; but we do not read that he was judged by someone: even if Pope Honorius, after his death, was condemned by the Easterners, this was due to the fact that he had been accused of heresy, the only reason that allows the subjects to oppose their superiors and to reject their perverse sentiments: but even in this case no patriarch or any bishop is allowed to utter a sentence against the pontiff of the first see, if first he does not have the prior consent and authority.*

According to Hadrian II, the papal legates, when they left in 680 for the sixth ecumenical council, had instructions from Pope Agatho (678 – 681) on the various conciliar decisions. This means that there was something fundamental that needed to be clarified and pointed out. Hadrian II, more for a technical-juridical than an ecclesiological concern, maintains that the pope can be condemned only for heresy, and with the prior authorization of the pontiff of the same First See: hence the priority of the condemnation of Honorius by Agatho on that pronounced by the Orientals. Ultimately, it is always the pope who determines what to do with his person or the bishop of Rome. Hadrian II glimpses that Pope Honorius, now dead, was condemned only because of the unofficial consent of his successor, Agatho. And on this juridical disposition the papal legates would have been prepared before and during the VI Ecumenical Council. Therefore, only in case of heresy can the Pope be judged. But it is always himself that establishes and fixes the possibility of being judged. He could always remain the bishop of Rome, if he were not to admit himself to be judged by a council of bishops.[349]

---

pontificis consensus praecessisset auctoritas». [HADRIANUS PAPA II, *Allocutio tertia, ad Concilium Romanum, a. 869,* in Mansi, 16, 126.]

[349] Salvatore Vacca, O.F.M. Cap., *PRIMA SEDES A NEMINE IUDICATUR Genesi e sviluppo storico dell'assioma fino al Decreto di Graziano,* Editrice Pontificia Università Gregoriana, Roma, 1993, pp. 122 – 123: «Il concilio romano condannò quello costantinopolitano del'867, compreso Fozio e I Padri greci che vi avevano partecipato, perché aveva lanciato una condanna contra papa Niccolò I. Purtroppo, gli atti del costantinopolitano del'867 sono stati distrutti. Durante il concilio romano, papa Adriano II definisce arrogante ed intollerabile la decisione del concilio di Costantinopoli, poiché non poteva condannare il vescovo di Roma.

Moynihan mentions that, "The acts of this Roman council, including the papal allocutions, were read by the Roman legates at the Fourth Council of Constantinple (869 – 870) and incorporated into its acts." (Mansi, XVI, cols. 373 ff.)[350] He then comments, "In this reference to the celebrated case of the posthumous condemnation of Pope Honorius, Hadrian makes it very clear that the case in question was one of heresy, and that heresy is the only reason which would justify the judgment of superiors by their subjects. Furthermore, Hadrian notes that the proceedings were legal only insofar as Agatho, the pope reigning at the time, had given his consent to them."[351] However, such a condemnation of a pope made by his subjects with his consent would not constitute a true act of deposition, but of abdication only. Bordoni explains, that deposition is of its very nature a judicial act exercised by a superior over his inferior (depoſitio eſt actus iudicialis ex ſua natura exercitus à

Nessuno, infatti, aveva mai osato farlo e mai si era udita una cosa simile. Il pontifice afferma: *Leggiamo che solo il Romano Pontefice ha giudicato I presuli di tutte le Chiese; ma non leggiamo che questi sia stato giudicato da qualcuno: anche se papa Onorio, dopo la sua morte, è stato condannato dagli orientali, ciò fu dovuto al fatto che questi era stato accusato di eresia, unica motivazione che permetta ai sudditi di opporsi ai loro superiori e di respingere I loro sentimenti perversi: ma anche in questo caso a nessun patriarcha né a nessun vescovo è permesso di proferire una sentenza contro il pontefice della prima sede, se prima questi non ne abbia il preliminare consenso e l'autorità.*

Adriano II fa intendere, circa la condanna di papa Onorio, che I legati papali, quando sono partiti nel 680 per il VI concilio ecumenico, avevano istruzioni da parte del papa Agatone (678-681) sulle diverse deliberazioni conciliari. Ciò significa che c'era qualcosa di fondamentale che bisognava chiarire e puntualizzare. Adriano II, più per una preoccupazione technico-giuridica che ecclesiologica, sostiene che il papa può essere condannato solo per eresia, e con la previa autorizzazione del pontefice della stessa Prima Sede: da qui la priorità della condanna di Onorio da parte di Agatone su quella pronunciata dagli orientali. In definitive, è sempre il papa a stabilire il da farsi in ordine alla sua persona o al vescovo di Roma. Adriano II fa intravedere che papa Onorio, ormai morto, è stato condannato solo perché c'è stat oil consenso ufficioso del suo successore, Agatone. E su questa disposizione giuridica I legati papali sarebbero stati preparati prima e durante il VI Concilio ecumenico. Pertanto, solo in caso di eresia il papa può essere giudicato. Ma è sempre lui stesso a stabilire e a fissare la possibilità d'essere giudicato. Potrebbe rimanere sempre il vescovo di Roma, se non fosse lui ad ammetere di farsi giudicare da un concilio di vescovi.»

[350] Moynihan, *Op. cit.* p. 34.
[351] *Ibid.*

ſuperíore in inferiorem) – it is "a judicial act of jurisdiction which, according to all (authors), cannot be done except by a judge" (eſt actus iudícialís, & jurisdictíonis, quia nonniſi per iudicem fieri poteſt, ſecundum omnes), and, according to St. Thomas, by its nature it is done against one's will (de ratione ſua eſt contraria voluntati, D. Thom. I. 2. q.87. art.2. ad.6); and therefore, if the act would be done by or with the consent of the legitimately elected pope, it would not be an act of deposition but of renunciation (non dicitur depoſitio, ſed renuntiatío, quando accedit conſenſus electi).[352] Hence,

> "*no one can be deposed except by his superior*, for *deposition is a judicial act of jurisdiction to be exercised only by a superior, but no one is superior to a pope, except God, therefore he can be deposed by no one*, for he judges all, and is judged by no one *cap. Si Papa diſt.* 40. *cap. Duo ſunt diſt.* 96. Also because the members do not judge their head, from which they have the influx, whence it is understood that the members are destroyed with the head being destroyed, and not conversely *l. cum in diuerſis ff. de relig.* [...] *ſumpt. fin.* And the members must follow the head and not the head to follow the members, *cap.* I. *diſt.* 12. But a council consists of its members, whose head is the pope as is proven *q.* 5 *therefore he cannot be deposed by a council.* And in this there is no difficulty."[353]

It is precisely on this point that all the variations of the Fourth Opinion collapse: 1) The *Conciliarist* opinion which holds that in matters of doctrine a council is superior to a pope is heretical because it directly opposes the pope's universal primacy of jurisdiction; 2) The opinion of *Mitigated Conciliarism*, which holds that by way of exception a council is superior to a pope only in the case of heresy is heretical for the same reason, since there is no clear basis in the deposit of revelation, nor in any magisterial pronouncement of the supreme magisterium for such an

---

[352] P. Francesco Bordoni, *Op. cit., cap. VI De Sacris Conciliis*, p. 155.

[353] *Ibid.* p. 149 — «Tum quia nullus deponi potest niſi à ſuo ſuperiore, depoſitio enim est actus iudicialis iuriſdictionis exercendus per ſolum ſuperiorem; ſed ſupra Papam nullus est ſuperior, præter Deum, ergo à nullo deponi potest, ille enim omnes iudicat, & a nemine iudicatur, *cap. Si Papa diſt.* 40. *cap. Duo ſunt* [...] *diſt.* 96. Tum quia membra non iudicant ſuum caput, à quo habent influxum, vnde membra intelliguntur deſtructa capite deſtructo, non è contra, *l. cum in diuerſis ff. de relig.* [...] *ſumpt. fin.* & membra debent ſequi caput, non caput membra, *cap.* I. *diſt.* 12. Sed Concilium constat ex membris, quorum capur est Papa ex probatis *q.5.* ergò à Concilio deponi non potest. Et ịn hoc nulla Difficultas.»

exception which would grant to inferiors the power of jurisdiction to judge an actually reigning Supreme Pontiff; while the constant teaching of the papal magisterium affirms the contrary, i.e., asserting the absolute judicial supremacy and injudicability of an actually reigning pontiff; 3) The opinion of *Mitigated Conciliarism* which holds that a council may depose a heretic pope by exercising power not over the pope as a superior, but as a dispositive cause in disjoining the conjunction between the man and the papacy is heretical; *because the action of such a dispositive cause in such a deposition is conditioned absolutely on the prerequisite judgment of heresy which can only be pronounced on the pope by an individual or body which exercises the jurisdiction of a superior*; 4) The opinion of *Mitigated Conciliarism* which holds that a council may depose a heretic pope by *judging him guilty of heresy*, and thereby disposing him to fall from office *ipso facto* is heretical for the same reason, namely, that the *ipso facto* fall from office would only take place upon a *juridical judgment against the actually reigning pontiff*, which would dispose him to fall by himself from office. Such a fall from office would not actually be an *ipso facto* fall (by the fact of heresy itself), which of its very nature takes place *by itself*, and therefore *sine alia vi externa*, but would be the result of an act of deposition which would take place by means of the external agency of a dispositive cause, namely, *the judgment of a council acting with the jurisdiction of a superior*.

The only opinion allowing for the deposition of a heretic pope which does not involve itself in heresy, is the one which holds that in the event that a pope's formal heresy would become manifest with certitude, the heretic pope would cease by himself to be pope, a Christian, and a member of the Church; and to already have fallen from office by himself and to have become *minor quolibet catholico*. Thus, the only "exception" is not an exception at all, but only if a pope were to cease entirely by himself to be a member of the Church because of manifest heresy, Schism or apostasy, he would by that very act, publicly defect from communion with the Church, cease to be a member of the Church; and therefore, according to the prescription of Canon 194 §1. 2°[354] (Canon

---

[354] Can. 194 — § 1. Ipso iure ab ecclesiastico officio amovetur: [...]2° qui a fide catholica aut a communione Ecclesiae publice defecerit; [...] § 2. Amotio, de qua in nn. 2 et 3, urgeri tantum potest, si de eadem auctoritatis competentis declaratione constet.

Can. 194 §1. The following are removed from an ecclesiastical office by the law itself: [...] 2° a person who has publicly defected from the Catholic faith or from the communion of the Church; [...] §2. The removal mentioned in nn. 2

188. 4° in the 1917 Code[355]); he would lose office automatically *(ipso jure)*; and the loss of office would then be enforced juridically by a merely declaratory sentence (Canon 194 §2). On this point, the canon is absolutely clear and unequivocal: "Can. 194 §1. The following are removed from an ecclesiastical office by the law itself: [...] 2° a person who has publicly defected from the Catholic faith or from the communion of the Church; [...]§2. The removal mentioned in nn. 2 and 3 can be enforced only if it is established by the declaration of a competent authority." In the commentary on the Code of Canon Law composed by the Canon Law faculty of the University of Navarre, it is explained: "In the 2nd and 3rd cases, the act of the ecclesiastical authority is declarative, and it is necessary, not to provoke the vacating of the right of the office, but so that the removal can legally be demanded (also for the purposes of 1381 § 2), and consequently the conferral of the office to a new officeholder can be carried out (cfr. C. 154)."[356] Since the loss of office takes place *ipso jure*, it does not depend in any way on the subsequent declaration which merely enforces it; and for this reason, as the quoted canon of the 1917 Code explains, **the actual loss of whatsoever office by tacit renunciation takes place ipso facto without any declaration ("Ob tacitam renuntiationem ab ipso iure admissam quælibet officia vacant ipso facto et sine ulla declaratione").** The Canon Law commentary of the Pontifical Faculty

---

and 3 can be enforced only if it is established by the declaration of a competent authority.

[355] Can. 188. *"Ob tacitam renuntiationem ab ipso iure admissam quaelibet officia vacant ipso facto et sine ulla declaratione, si clericus: [...] 4° A fide catholica publice defecerit".*

[356] "Remoción ipso iure es la decretada por el propio derecho en los casos taxativamente determinados en el § 1. Todos ellos requieren, sin embargo, algún grado de intervención de la autoridad eclesiástica para que la remoción tenga plena eficacia jurídica. En el supuesto 1.° es preciso que se decrete la pérdida del estado clerical (cfr. cc. 290, 1336 § 1, 5.°) para que, como efecto reflejo, se produzca ipso iure la remoción del oficio. En los casos 2.° y 3.°, el acto de la autoridad eclesiástica es declarativo, y se hace necesario, no para provocar la vacación de derecho del oficio, sino para que pueda exigirse jurídicamente la remoción (también a los efectos del c. 1381 § 2), y consiguientemente pueda llevarse a cabo la colación del oficio a un nuevo titular (cfr. c. 154)." – *CÓDIGO DE DERECHO CANÓNICO EDICIÓN BILINGÜE Y ANOTADA UNIVERSIDAD DE NAVARRA, FACULTAD DE DERECHO CANÓNICO*, Sexta edición revisada y actualizada, p. 176.

of Canon Law of the University of Salamanca explains that the sole necessary condition for such a loss of office to take place, is that the act be freely committed, and then the loss of office follows necessarily: "El hecho por el que se presupone la renuncia debe ser puesto voluntariamente, a tenor del canon 185; pero, cumplida esta condición, la perdida del oficio se produce necesariamente."[357] That the canon is applicable to **all ecclesiastical offices is stated explicitly with the words,** *"quælibet officia vacant ipso facto"* **– and therefore necessarily includes the office of the Supeme Pontiff.** The Very Rev. H. A. Ayrinhac explained, in his *General Legislation in the New Code of Canon Law,* on *Loss of Ecclesiastical Offices,* that such loss of office (Canons 185-191) "applies to all offices, the lowest and the highest, not excepting the Supreme Pontificate." (p. 346)

There exists only one case in the entire history of the Church that a papal claimant has been validly and legitimately deposed by ecclesiastical authority, and that was the deposition of Benedict XIII (Pedro de Luna) by the Council of Constance (Sess. 37), which followed the same procedure as rhat which is prescribed in the canons in force at present. The Council did not presume to remove him by any judicial act of judgment, but rather, it followed and applied the teaching of Innocent III, and declared him to have already lost all office and ecclesiastical dignity by himself *ipso jure*; and thus, having already been reduced to the state of *minor quolibet catholico* by his own actions, the Council then deposed him "as a precautionary measure" (*ad omnem cautelam privat et deponit et abiicit*).[358]

---

[357] Miguelez – Alonso – Cabreros, *Op. cit.* p. 78.

[358] "Therefore this same holy general synod, representing the universal church and sitting as a tribunal in the aforesaid inquiry, pronounces, decrees and declares by this definitive sentence written here, that the same Peter de Luna, called Benedict XIII [...] a schismatic disturber and a heretic, a deviator from the faith, a persistent violator of the article of the faith One holy catholic church, incorrigible, notorious and manifest in his scandal to God's church, and that he has rendered himself unworthy of every title, rank, honour and dignity, rejected and cut off by God, deprived by the law itself (*ipso jure*) of every right in any way belonging to him in the papacy or pertaining to the Roman pontiff and the Roman church, and cut off from the catholic church like a withered member. This same holy synod, moreover, as a precautionary measure, since according to himself he actually holds the papacy, deprives, deposes and casts out the said Peter from the papacy and from being the supreme pontiff of the

The subsequent developments brought it about, that the Conciliaristic tendency on the part of the hierarchy to attempt to limit papal power by means of creating exceptions to immunity were overcome, so that, (as Hinschius observed already in 1869[359]), "The course of the further development, however, has, as is known, eliminated episcopalism in the Catholic Church, and the principle, apostolica sedes a nemine iudicatur is now in full force." Based on the foundation of the doctrine of Pope Innocent III and its application by the Council of Constance, St. Robert Bellarmine formulated his exposition on the doctrine of the automatic loss of office of a manifest heretic pope, which he briefly stated in *De Romano Pontifice lib. II cap. xxx* as Opinion No. 5. Pietro Ballerini elaborated the same opinion more systematically, basing it explicitly on the firm foundation of the ruling of the Council of Constance; and Pope Gregory XVI explicitly endorsed Ballerini's doctrine on the question of a heretic pope in his book, saying such a heretic would have "fallen from the pontificate by himself"[360]. After the First Vatican Council infallibly defined the dogma of papal primacy, thus giving dogmatic force to the principle of papal injudicability, the principle *"Prima sedes a nemine judicatur"* was incorporated into the Code of Canon Law; and has been interpreted according to the mind of the Church, and in conformity with the constant teaching of the ordinary magisterium, by the officially approved commentaries on Canon Law, to admit no exceptions.

After all my lengthy argumentation and copious documentation, Salza & Siscoe remain entrenched in their position. Salza's chronic and habitual dishonesty comes to the fore in his most recent piece of sophistry, an e-mail message which blindly ignores the arguments which expose his fallacious (and fraudulent) reasoning, and simply re-affirms his thoroughly refuted, errant propositions:

Roman church and from every title, rank, honour, dignity, benefice and office whatsoever."

[359] Hinschius, *Op. cit.*, p. 306: "Der Verlauf der weiteren Entwicklung hat aber, wie bekannt, den Episkopalismus in der katolischen Kirche beseitigt, und so steht heute wieder der Satz: apostolica sedes a nemine iudicatur in voller Geltung."

[360] «Ond'è che poteasi, come osserva il Ballerini, considerarlo quale pubblico scismatico e eretico, ed in conseguenza **per se decaduto dal pontificato**, se anche ad esso fosse stato validamente inalzato.» (*Il trionfo della santa sede e della chiesa contro gli assatti dei novatori*, p. 47)

«Every apologist for the Sedevacantist sect asserts that it is the "nature" of heresy, and not any declaration from Church authorities, that severs one from the Church.»

This is a glaring red-herring argument. It is not a doctrine concocted by Sedevacantists, but is taught by the Fathers, by St. Robert Bellarmine, and most explicitly by Pius XII in *Mystici Corporis*. I have amply demonstrated in this work, from the most explicit magisterial pronouncements and the texts of the popes, Fathers and Doctors of the Church, that it is in the nature of manifest heresy that it is *per se* a defection from the faith and the Church; and that therefore, by the very act of manifest formal heresy, one ceases to be a member of the Church. **This is the clear and explicit teaching of Pius XII in *Mystici Corporis*.** Salza & Siscoe falsify the teaching of that encyclical, modifying and changing it by adding their own qualifications to the teaching which do not pertain to the simple and unqualified doctrine expressed in that document.

Salza quotes his faulty translation of Pius XII, and misinterprets the passage with a gramatically flawed and logically impossible hermeneutic: «For not every offense, although it may be a grave evil, is such as by its very own nature to sever a man from the Body of the Church, as does schism or heresy or apostasy.» According to Salza & Siscoe, it is only the *crime* of heresy but not the *sin* of heresy which *suapte natura* separates one from the body of the Church. Salza & Siscoe falsely assert that it pertains to the *nature* of the *sin of heresy* that it is *internal*, as opposed to *external heresy* which they say is in its *nature* a *crime*. Accordingly, they reason, internal heresy and external heresy, being of two different natures, are acts of two different species. Hence, according to their errant doctrine, it is only the *crime*, but not the *sin* of heresy that separates one from the body of the Church *suapte natura*. The principal fallacy of this argument lies in its failure to consider that heresy, is in fact, *one species of sin*, whether internal or external, and is in its nature a *sin*, and *is* **one species** *of sin*, **because it directly and per se opposes the virtue of faith**. Heresy, whether internal or external, in its nature is a *sin*; but it is not intrinsic to internal nor external heresy that either one is in its essential nature a *crime*, as *crime* is defined in canon law (can. 2195. §1).

Salza, therefore, translates the word *"admissum"* as "offense" in order to gratuitously interpret it strictly to mean *"crime"* in the canonical sense of a *delict*, and then, against the rules of grammar, attempts to qualify the phrase later on in the sentence with that strict modification, whereby the unqualified words *"schisma, vel heresis, vel apostasia faciunt suapte natura"* stated *simpliciter*, are no longer to be understood according to their clear and proper signification of the actions *per se* as sins; but are errantly and gratuitously qualified to designate these sins only in so far as they are *ecclesiastical crimes*, i.e. *delicts* – which is to say, *in so far as they pertain to the genus of crimes*. Schism, heresy and apostasy are not canonical offenses according to their nature, they are not crimes *per se* in their very essence; but are crimes only in virtue of *penal legislation*, which is extrinsic to their nature. Thus it is not in the nature of crimes, that *by their very nature* they sever a man from the Church, as do schism, heresy or apostasy, but *only by the authority of the Church* do they sever one from the body of the Church; whereas according to the nature of schism, heresy and apostasy, i.e. **according to the intrinsic nature of the sin as a visible act of separation, it is an act of defection from communion with the Church**, that *by itself* visibly severs one from the body of the Church apart from anyone else's judgment, or any act or judgment of ecclesiastical authority; and without any need of further qualification such as, 1) explicit formal defection from the *Church*, 2) formal rejection of the Church's magisterial authority as the rule of faith; or, 3) joining another religion – because the act of formal heresy is in its very nature, a rejection of the authority of the Church, as St. Thomas explains in the above cited passage. I have already sufficiently explained this point and exposed the sophistry employed by Salza as the basis of his bogus interpretation of *Mystici Corporis*. Pius XII clearly and explicitly distinguishes between the sins which by themselves, according to their very nature (*suapte natura*) cut one off from the body of the Church, and all other sins, which do not effect the separation from the body of the Church *suapte natura*, but only in virtue of their being crimes – "by the legitimate authority of the Church", i.e. by *excommunication*, because they are *penal offenses*. If one interprets the words, "schism, heresy, and apostasy — *suapte natura*" to denote these species of sins under their formal aspect as crimes, i.e. according to the accidental quality of their being *ecclesiastical crimes*, or according to the patently false belief that by the nature of their *genus* as external acts they are crimes *in their very nature*, then the distinction made by Pius XII in that paragraph between the *specific* acts which by themselves, by their own *specific nature* separate one from the Church, and *all other species of acts* which separate one by legitimate ecclesiastical authority is thereby destroyed, making irrational nonsense of Pacelli's magisterium on this point; *since all crimes without exception pertain to the genus of external acts, and in their generic nature as external* *acts are* **absolutely identical.** If Pius XII's words are interpreted to mean that by their *generic nature* as external acts, schism, heresy and apostasy are *crimes* that separate one from the Church *suapte* natura, then **all external sins** would by their very nature separare the perpetrator from the body of the Church – yet it is precisely **only** these three species of the *sin of infidelity* that the encyclical teaches, separate one from the body of the Church *suapte natura,* and for all others, men are "severed by the legitimate authority" of the Church: «*ob gravissima admissa a legitima auctoritate seiuncti sunt.*» Thus, Salza & Siscoe do violence to the teaching of the Church on the nature of heresy; and against the clear pronouncement of the Supreme Magisterium in 1943, Salza appeals to a previously expressed opinion written before the question was definitively closed, such as that of Cardinal Billot (which errs on the specific nature of the matter of heresy, confusing it with the generic nature of *infidelity*)[361], and the clearly contrary opinion of John of St. Thomas. The opinion of John of St. Thomas, which holds that even for heresy, the judgment of the Church is required for the heretic to be severed from the body of the Church is explicitly contrary to the teaching of Pius XII, who explained in *Mystici Corporis,* that according to its very nature, heresy by itself separates one from the body of the Church, so that while those guilty of other crimes are severed from the body of the Church, *by legitimate authority,* heretics, according to the nature of heresy (*suapte natura*), *miserably separate themselves from the unity of the body.* The idea advanced by John of St. Thomas and advocated by Salza & Siscoe, namely, that the judgment of authority is required for the heretic to be separated from the body of the Church, is diametrically opposed to the teaching of *Mystici Corporis,* **which explicitly excludes that the separation takes place by authority,** and hence, the Salza/Siscoe doctrine is patently opposed to this clearly expressed papal doctrine which pertains to the universal and ordinary magisterium. The proposition of John of St. Thomas, affirmed by Salza & Siscoe, that the Church, *"judges the quality of the crime that excludes from the Church without any over added censure, as long as it is declared by the Church",* is **plainly contrary**

---

[361] Cardinal Billot wrote, "the nature of heresy consists in withdrawal from the rule of the ecclesiastical Magisterium", which is false: **The *nature* of heresy, in its *matter,* is the denial or doubt of an article of faith, *even if one professes, or sincerely believes he is faithful to the magisterium.*** This point will be discussed later in this section.

to the explicitly stated doctrine of Pius XII in Mystici Corporis and the teaching of the universal and ordinary magisterium.

In the above cited texts, I have quoted the verbatim translations (of the passage of *Mystici Corporis*), and the commentaries of two of Salza's favorite authors, Msgrs. Van Noort and Fenton, both distinguished theologians who translate and interpret the passage of *Mystici Corporis* exactly as I do; yet Salza continues to blindly and obstinately insinuate that such an interpretation is a sedevacantist "abuse" of *Mystici Corporis* (which would mean that Salza, who does not know Latin, translated the passage correctly, and Fenton, Van Noort and the official website of the Apostolic See translated it wrongly).[362] Thus, Salza is not only wrong, but is plainly blind and obstinate against the mind of the Church.

It is the *act of manifest formal heresy by itself*, i.e. the *manifestation of pertinacity*, without any additional qualifications or conditions, and without any censure or judgment of authority, *which separates the manifest heretic from the body of the Church*, and takes place **ipso facto** *according to the very nature of heresy* (*suapte natura*), and hence, juridically *ipso jure*, by the operation of the law itself, (as I have amply explained and documented), and therefore severs both the spiritual and visible bond with the Church; thus accomplishing the juridical separation *per se,* without the need for any judgment to be pronounced by the Church.

Siscoe likewise remains entrenched in heresy, "I applied the Thomistic distinction of quoad se/quoad nos to show that, just because heresy *of its nature* severs a person from the Church (spiritually), does not mean heresy, *of its nature*, causes a person to cease being a *member* of the Church (legally). And I quoted the great John of St. Thomas **who explained it exactly the way I did.**" Siscoe elaborates:

> "Did you even read John Salza's recent article that prompted this e-mail exchange? John and I both contributed to that article so it represents both of our opinions. We both affirm that the sin of heresy, of its nature, separates a person from the Church quoad se (of itself), but **the sin of heresy, of its nature, does not result in a separation from the**

---

[362] Salza & Siscoe have subsequently contradicted their position on this point, and have since claimed that it doesn't matter how you translate the word *admissum*; and that I misrepresent their doctrine. Nevertheless, they still adamantly insist that the passage in question denotes only the *crimes* of schism, heresy, and apostasy as separating one from the Church *suapte natura*, and not the external sins *per se* as *sins*.

Church quoad nos (according to us), nor does it result in the loss of office. [...] As long as a person remains a member of the Church quoad nos – even if he has committed the sin of heresy and has lost the faith – he remains a legal member of the Church, and if the person in question is a bishop or Pope, he retains his office until the crime has been legally established by the proper authorities."

Then he quotes John of St. Thomas:

«[J]ust as the Church, by designating the man, proposed him juridically to all as the elected Pope, so too, it is necessary that she depose him by declaring him a heretic and proposing him as vitandus (one to be avoided). Hence, we see from the practice of the Church that this is how it has been done; for, in the case of the deposition of a Pope, his cause was handled in a general Council before he was considered not to be Pope, as we have related above. It is not true, then, that the Pope ceases to be Pope by the very fact [ipso facto] that he is a heretic, even a public one, before any sentence of the Church and before she proposes him to the faithful as one who is to be avoided. ***Nor does Jerome exclude the judgment of the Church (especially in so grave a matter as the deposition of a Pope) when he says that a heretic departs from the body of Christ of his own accord***, rather, he is judging the quality of the crime, which of its very nature excludes one from the Church—***provided that the crime is declared by the Church***—without the need for any superadded censure; for, ***although heresy separates one from the Church by its very nature, nevertheless, this separation is not thought to have been made, as far as we are concerned [quoad nos], without that declaration.***»

Siscoe then comments,

"Before continuing, notice the point he makes about heresy, of its nature, severing a person from the Church without the need for any additional censure. *This is how heresy, schism and apostasy differ from other mortal sins, which, of their nature, deprive a person from sanctifying grace,* but do not separate them from the Church. It requires **an additional censure for other sins to sever a person from the Church**. For example, abortion severs a person from the Church, not by the nature of the sin, but due to the censure of excommunication that has been attached to it by the Church."

Siscoe is simply saying that other sins require the additional censure of excommunication for one to be cut off from membership in the Church, but for heresy, schism and apostasy, excommunication is not necessary, but only the judgment of the Church by which one is declared a heretic. He again quotes John of St. Thomas:

> "Likewise, we respond to his reasoning in this way: one who is not a Christian, both in himself (quoad se) and in relation to us (quoad nos), cannot be Pope; however, if in himself he is not a Christian (because he has lost the faith) *but in relation to us has not yet been juridically declared as an infidel or heretic (no matter how manifestly heretical he is according to private judgment), he is still a member of the Church as far as we are concerned (quoad nos)*; and consequently he is its head. *It is necessary, therefore, to have the judgment of the Church, by which he is proposed to us as someone who is not a Christian*, and who is to be avoided; and at that point he ceases to be Pope in relation to us (quoad nos); and we further conclude that he had not ceased to be Pope before [the declaration], even in himself, since all of his acts were valid in themselves."

Siscoe concludes: "If you disagree with the great John of St. Thomas – who was known, even in his own day as the second Thomas' – explain why he is wrong." It is not difficult to understand why the "second Thomas" is wrong – one need only compare his teaching on this point with the doctrine of **St. Thomas** (quoted above) to see exactly how the "second Thomas" went astray: John of St. Thomas teaches that the manifest heretic remains a member of the Church, who *"has not yet been juridically declared as an infidel or heretic"* and, *he is still a member of the Church as far as we are concerned (quoad nos)"*, since *"It is necessary, therefore, to have the judgment of the Church, by which he is proposed to us as someone who is not a Christian"*. Thus, John of St. Thomas teaches that even heretics are severed from the body of the Church and cease to be members, *but not without the authority of the Church*. This is *diametrically opposed to the doctrine of St. Thomas Aquinas* quoted and elaborated above. Pius XII teaches in unison with St. Thomas, St. Robert Bellarmine, the unanimous consensus of the Fathers, and the universal and ordinary magisterium of the Church, that *all other sins*, which result in the separation of one from the body of the Church, do not cause that separation *per se* according to their own nature, but the separation is effected "by legitimate authority"; but heresy, schism and apostasy do *not* result in the separation of one from the body of the Church by legitimate authority, but separate one *suapte natura*, and thus by divine law (*jubente Domino*) public heretics visibly and juridically, "miserably separate themselves" from the body of the Church.

Salza & Siscoe reply in their Formal Reply Part II:

«Dispositive vs. Formal Separation: This distinction explains different ways of understanding how heresy severs a person from the Body of the Church, without considering a separate unity with the Soul of the Church. According to this explanation, the sin of heresy, of its nature, severs a person from the Body of the Church dispositively, but not formally. The formal separation from the Body of the Church occurs when the juridical bond is severed by the public act (crime) of notorious heresy (notorious by fact), or when the crime has been judged and declared by the Church (notorious by law).»

According to the bizarre doctrine of Salza & Siscoe, the *sin* of heresy is an internal sin only, and *the external **act*** (not sin) of heresy is in its nature a *crime*. Salza & Siscoe speak only of *internal heresy* as the "*sin of heresy*"; but for them, since "*sin is internal*" and external heresy is intrinsically in the nature of a crime; it follows that external heresy is not an *external sin*, but "externalized internal sin", or "the sin of heresy externalized as a crime". Such a usage of the terms and the doctrine they convey is contrary to the common and perpetual usage of theologians, who distinguish between *internal sins* and *external sins,* and is against Catholic doctrine; but according to the skewed thinking of Salza & Siscoe, *any sin committed with an external act is in the nature of a crime, because it is a violation of divine law*. This error is dealt with more fully below. Cardinal Manning wrote, "Theology, like chancery law, has its technical language; and the common sense of Englishmen would keep them from using it in any other meaning."[363] It is this basic common sense that is entirely lacking in the strange theology of John Salza and Robert Siscoe.

To willfully profess heresy or to commit murder are equally *external sins*. The external profession of heresy is not an *internal sin externalized by an external act* (as Salza & Siscoe repeatedly claim), but external heresy is an **external sin in the same manner that murder is an external sin.** Both the *internal* and the *external sin* of heresy are intrinsically mortally sinful acts, which, by definition, are of the *same species*, i.e. of *identical specific nature*, to wit, **an obstinate denial or doubt of a revealed truth which must be believed with divine and Catholic faith**. In their Formal Reply, Salza & Siscoe obfuscate on this point by quoting Cajetan who pointed out the **generic difference** *between the nature of the* **genus** *of internal acts and the* **genus** *of external acts*[364], which distinguishes only the

---

[363] Cardinal Manning, *The Vatican Council and is Definitions*, p. 109.

[364] "[I]f anyone falls into heresy internally and, being alone, expresses that heresy to himself with spoken words in the merest whisper, he is

material species between an internal and external act; and on that basis they draw the absurd conclusion that the *internal sin of heresy* is of a different **specific nature,** i.e. of a **different species** than the *external sin of heresy*. As is explained below, **according to St. Thomas (*I^a-II^ae q. 18 a. 6 s c*), it is the *form*, which is the *internal component of a* sin, which constitutes the *species* of the act**; for which reason, ***internal heresy and external heresy are acts of the same species*. There is nothing morally specific in the material species of the external act that would distinguish it from the species of the internal sin.** They then, even more absurdly claim on the false premise that external heresy, being of a different species, is a *crime in its very nature*. Since heresy as a sin **specifically**, whether internal or external, directly opposes the virtue of faith, both internal and external heresy are defined by one definition, which expresses its *species* and *nature*. Thus, both the internal sin and the external sin of heresy, which are only different in their *material species*, are of the same *specific nature*. Hence, *heresy as such, whether internal or external, is directly and per se opposed to faith*, and therefore *heresy, committed internally or externally is of the same species*, and is a mortal sin *ex toto genere suo*. No sin is *in its nature* a crime, because the criminality of an act is not intrinsic to the nature of the act, but the criminality of the act exists solely in virtue of penal legislation extrinsic to its nature, which *per accidens* qualifies it as a crime, *but does not enter into the definition of the act*, and therefore the criminality of an act is extrinsic to its nature.

Earlier I wrote, «Salza & Siscoe now claim: "The external act of heresy is, by its nature, a crime." This proposition is patently false: The nature of a crime *in ecclesiastical law* is of an external and *morally imputable violation* of a law or precept. It does not pertain to the *nature* of heresy that it is "an *external* and *morally imputable* violation of a law [*an ecclesiastical law*] or precept"; and therefore, the proposition is false. The external act of heresy is a sin, and not a crime.» The context of my words make it unequivocally clear that my meaning is that the external act of heresy is

---

excommunicated, even though it is entirely hidden, because the act of speaking it aloud itself subjects him to human judgment, as such, even though the act lacks witnesses. (...) internal acts are not judged according to their nature as purely internal, but rather in so far as they are cases of external commission... Many have erred in this matter due to ignorance of this distinction... Purely internal acts are in the **genus** of things hidden by their natures, because they are unknowable to human knowledge of their own nature. External acts are of the **genus** of things... accessible to human knowledge."

in its nature a sin, but it is not a crime *in its nature*. Since I knew very well that the congenital con-artists, Salza & Siscoe, would twist my words to give them quite another meaning, I repeated the same paragraph in my next communication, but with the more explicit wording with the qualifying words in brackets: "The external act of heresy is [in its nature] a sin, and not a crime." Nevertheless, in spite of my explicit qualification, they twisted my words and falsified my meaning in order to make it appear that I had changed my previous position and was now claiming that external heresy is not an ecclesiastical crime! Here is what they wrote:

> «Here is the argument in Fr. Kramer's own words. He sent the following out via e-mail, after the publication of Part I of this series of articles, and then posted it online, as his official "refutation" of our statement that "external heresy is, by its nature, a crime." […] "Salza & Siscoe now claim: 'The external act of heresy is, by its nature, a crime.' This is patently false: The nature of a crime in ecclesiastical law is of an *external* and *morally imputable* violation of a law or precept. It does not pertain to the nature of heresy that it is 'an *external* and *morally imputable* violation of a law or precept'; and therefore, the proposition is false. The external act of heresy is a sin, and not a crime." Now, it should be obvious that there is a problem somewhere in Fr. Kramer's reasoning, since external heresy is a crime punishable by Canon Law (Canon 2314, 1917 Code; Canon 1364.1, 1983 Code), which would not be the case if it did not meet the canonical definition for the nature of a crime.»

Nowhere have I ever stated or implied, that the gravely imputable external act of heresy is not a crime according to Canon Law, but is only not a crime *in its very nature*; yet that is exactly what Salza & Siscoe deliberately attempt to deceive their readers into thinking in order to distort my arguments and obfuscate my meaning.

The fallacious Salza/Siscoe argument that external heresy is in its nature an ecclesiastical crime, is that since, according to Canon Law the external act of heresy conforms to the specifications required for an act to qualify as a crime, external heresy is therefore, in its nature a crime. The nonsensical fallacy of their thinking is exposed in the consideration that what pertains to the definition of a crime, **does not intrinsically pertain to the nature of exernal heresy** (whether considered formally in its specific nature as heresy or materially in its generic nature as an external act); and therefore, the external act of heresy is not in its nature a crime. Heresy in its nature is directly and *per se* opposed to faith, but it is not in its nature intrinsically opposed to ecclesiastical law, since the penal sanction added to it in ecclesiastical law is an accidental circumstance extrinsic to its nature. Salza & Siscoe fallaciously argue that since external heresy falls within the parameters of the definition of a crime in canon law (i.e. an external violation of a law or precept, etc.), external heresy is consequently by definition a crime, and therefore it is in its intrinsic nature a crime. The false conclusion is based on an elementary error of logic: External heresy is indeed a crime because it falls within the parameters of the canonical definition of a delict; but that only *accidently qualifies* external heresy as a crime, because the specifications of the nature of a crime which fall within the canonical definition of a crime do not fall within the canonical or theological definition of heresy. Being a crime is an accidental quality of external heresy due to the circumstance that external heresy is a delict according to ecclesiastical law; but that quality does not pertain *per se* to the essential nature of external heresy, because its being an external violation of a penal law does not pertain to the definition of external heresy as it is defined in canon law and moral theology. Furthermore, to be a crime, the external act must be *morally imputable*; and hence, the merely material and therefore inculpable external act of heresy is not a crime; and therefore, it follows necessarily that the act of external heresy is manifestly not in its nature a crime. Additionally (as is explained below), to be a crime, it does not suffice that it violate a precept of divine law, but it must also violate an *ecclesiastical* law or precept; and therefore, without a law or precept of ecclesiastical law, or at least a divine law to which is added a *penal censure*, the external act is not a *delict*, nor is it punishable in the external forum by the Church. Thus, it is patent, that the external act of heresy *per* se, is not in its nature a crime. The fallacy is seen to be patent in their own words:

> «We respond, firstly, by noting that the definition of heresy, as such, may be defined the same for the sin of heresy in Moral Theology and for the crime of heresy in Canon Law, but the definition of the nature of the act that qualifies as a sin, and the nature of the act that qualifies as a crime, are not the same, since, as we have seen, an internal act alone suffices for the sin, whereas "an external and morally imputable" act is required to meet the definition of the nature of a crime (Canon 2195.1, 1917 Code). This is why Fr. Kramer's reference to the definition of heresy from Moral Theology and Canon Law does not support his position.»

As I explained above, the definition of the nature of the act that qualifies it as a crime only *qualifies* it *accidentally* as a crime according to canon law, because that act as it is defined, conforms to the specifications of law which qualify it as a crime according to the definition of a crime. Those specifications which qualify an act as a crime do not pertain to the definition of the act itself, which alone defines its *nature*. External heresy pertains properly to the *generic nature and material species of the act* as an *external act*, which falls within the parameters of that which qualifies it as a crime; but that which qualifies it as a crime, qualifies it *accidentally* as a crime, and does not pertain to that which, according to the definition of heresy, is therein defined as constituting the essential *nature* of the act of *heresy*. Thus it is clear that just because the generic nature of an internal act differs from that of an external act, and consequently the *species* of an internal act differs *materially* from the species of an external act, it does not follow that the *specific nature* of an internal sin differs *formally* from the specific nature of an external sin of the same species; nor does it follow from these premises that the external act is intrinsically in its nature a *crime* – yet this is the canard that Salza & Siscoe have cooked up for their readers.

St. Thomas, as mentioned before, explains in *II-II 11.1*, "heresy is a species of unbelief, belonging to those who profess the Christian faith, but corrupt its dogmas." Thus, heresy is of *one species*, and therefore *internal and external heresy are of one and the same specific nature*. As St. Thomas explained in the above cited passage, that which is intended is *per se* (*id quod est intentum est per se*), and therefore constitutes the *species* of the act; and hence, the *nature of heresy*, consists in that which constitutes the *species of the sin of heresy*; namely, that heresy *per se* opposes faith: "*Nam hæresis per se opponitur fidei*" (*II^a-II^æ q. 39 a. 1 co.*). Therefore, the sin of heresy, regardless of whether committed as an internal act or an external act, is of the same nature, since the species of the sin is one and the same. The Salza/Siscoe proposition that the internal act and the external acts of heresy are of different species and nature[365] is nonsensical and is entirely foreign to Catholic teaching; since, as faith, which is one species of virtue, so therefore heresy, whether internal or external, is the one species sin which directly and *per se* opposes the virtue of faith, and is therefore of one and the same species of unbelief. Hence, *heresy*, a species of infidelity, is taught by the Church to be one species of sin, because

---

[365] "*The interior act of heresy is to disbelieve (or refuse to assent); since the external act is to deny (or to express a doubt about) the faith.*"

the nature of heresy, whether internal or external, is to opposed to the one virtue of faith.

The Salza/Siscoe sophistry comes to the fore in their attempt to refute the doctrine of St. Thomas which I have merely adopted as my position on the question: "… since Fr. Kramer attempted to defend his position using Thomistic metaphysics (i.e., "qualitative accidental circumstances", "species") we will refute his argument in like manner by noting that an internal act and an external act are two different physical acts, with two different objects, proceeding from two different principles." This consideration has absolutely no bearing whatever on the question; because the internal and external act remain formally of the same species. Then they try to support their errant opinion with a quote from St. Thomas: "The principle of the interior act is the interior apprehensive or appetitive power of the soul; whereas the principle of the external action is the power that accomplishes the movement. Now where the principles of action are different, the actions themselves are different. (St. Thomas I-II, q. 20, a. 3, ad 1)" In the quoted passage, St. Thomas explained the generic difference between every kind of internal and external act; and according to which the external act is *materially* of a different species than the internal act – which has nothing to do with the specific nature of a sin; since it is the *end*, i.e. that which is intended *per se*, which pertains properly to the *internal component of a* sin, which formally constitutes the *species* of the act: **«actus humani habent speciem a fine»**[366].

Then St. Thomas concludes the corpus of the article explaining why this is so: The formal component of an external act is what comes internally from the will; for which reason what is proper to the material species of external acts has nothing of the nature of morality except for being voluntary; and therefore, the species of human acts are formally considered according to their end.[367] This is why heresy is externally and internally only *one species* of sin, and not *two*.

---

[366] *I^a-IIae q. 18 a. 6 s c* – Salza & Siscoe quoted passages from this article, but conveniently left this one out.

[367] «Ita autem quod est ex parte voluntatis, se habet ut formale ad id quod est ex parte exterioris actus, quia voluntas utitur membris ad agendum, sicut instrumentis; neque actus exteriores habent rationem moralitatis, nisi inquantum sunt voluntarii. Et ideo actus humani species formaliter consideratur secundum finem, materialiter autem secundum obiectum exterioris actus.» [*I^a-IIae q. 18 a. 6 co.*]

Then they again quote St. Thomas and go on to say, «To illustrate this point, the interior act of faith is to believe; [St. Thomas I-II, q. 2, a. 1.] the external act is to confess the faith. [St. Thomas I-II, q. 3, a. 1.] The interior act of heresy is to disbelieve (or refuse to assent); the external act is to deny (or to express a doubt about) the faith.» What they fail to grasp is that only the generic and material nature of the acts are different, one being internal, and the other being external; but the internal act of faith expresses one's assent to divine revelation with the internal word of the mind; and the external confession of faith *formally* expresses the same identical belief in the revealed truths by externally expressing it *materially* in a manner perceptible to the senses. The internal act of faith and the external act of faith, are not acts of two different virtues, but have the same specific nature of the one *theological virtue* of faith, because virtues (which are habits) are known through their acts, and acts through their objects,[368] and both internal and external faith are acts which directly and *per se* have the same *formal object*, namely, **God**, who is the object of the theological virtues (*virtutum theologicarum obiectum est Deus*[369]), the *summa et prima veritas* (*Summa Theol. Ia.16.6*) which is the *formal object of faith*[370], to which is given assent through the *material object of faith*[371], i.e. that which is *proponitur nobis ad credendum* (*IIa IIæ Q. 2 a. 2*). Thus, the *species* of both the internal and external acts of faith, formally considered, are one and the same, and therefore, formally considered as moral acts, are of the same identical nature.

Thus the *species* of a human act morally considered, i.e. the *specific nature* of an act, whether an internal act or an external act, is *one species* determined by the *form*, and not the *matter*. In nature, it is the *form* which determines and specifies the essence of things, and the matter which receives the form and is thereby brought from potentiality to act; hence, the *nature*, which is the essence in act, considered as a *principium motus* is determined and specified by the *form*, and not the matter. The same is

---

[368] «*habitus cognoscuntur per actus, et actus per obiecta*» – [*Quaestiones Disputate de Virtutibus, q. 4 a. 1 co.*]

[369] *Quaestiones Disputate de Virtutibus; Q. 4, a. 1, ad 6.*

[370] «Sic igitur in fide, si consideremus formalem rationem obiecti, nihil est aliud quam **veritas prima**, non enim fides de qua loquimur assentit alicui nisi quia est a Deo revelatum; unde ipsi veritati divinae innititur tanquam medio.» – [*II^a-IIae q. 1 a. 1 co.*]

[371] «*Sic igitur, sicut formale obiectum fidei est veritas prima, per quam sicut per quoddam medium assentit his quae creduntur, quae sunt materiale obiectum fidei*» – [*De virtutibus, q. 4 a. 1 co.*]

true for human actions. In both internal and external human acts morally considered, the species is determined by the *end*, which pertains to the *form* of the act. That is why the nature of a sin is determined by the *form*, which is the *internal* constitutive principle of the act, and not the *material object* or the *principle* of the external act. Hence, neither the *principle* nor the *material object* of the external act determine the species of an act. Since it is only the *principle of the external act* and its *material object* which distinguishes an external sin from an internal sin, and not the form, which is identical in both, the act itself of a crime *per se* is distinguished from an internal sin solely by the external *material* element; and not the form which determines the moral *nature* and *species* of the act; and hence, the *nature* of the internal and external act are identical, being of one and the same *species*. Therefore a *crime*, considered under its formal aspect of an *external act*, differs only materially from the internal act; but morally is of the same species as the internal act; and thus, the *nature* of a sin and of a crime, according to the species of the act, are the same. However, even if they really were of different species, that would not make an external act a crime in its nature.

The nature of a thing does not differ from the *essence* of the thing *per se*, but nature differs only from essence according to its formal aspect, i.e. in so far the definition expresses the quidity of a thing, and nature is the essence considered as a *principium motus*. In substance they are one and the same. That substance is the composite of matter and form, whose essence is expressed in the definition of the thing. (*Definitio declarat essentiam*). The definition, signified by words (*verbum significat definitionem*) expresses that which constitutes the *nature* of a thing. St. Thomas, quoted above, explains that *id quod est per se* constitutes the species and not *id quod est per accidens*. That which is *per se* is the *matter* and the *form*, which constitute the essence and determine the *nature* of things, whether they be substances or human actions. That which is *per se* is expressed in the definition, which is signified by the words of the definition. The 'legal element', which makes an external act a crime, does not enter into the definition of any act considered *per se*, i.e. in its *nature*. An external act is a crime not by *id quod est per se*, i.e. the composite of matter and form; but by *id quod est per accidens*, i.e. the mere accidental circumstance that the act violates a penal law. The accidental circumstance of being an *"externa et moraliter imputabilis legis violatio cui addita sit sanctio canonica saltem indeterminata"*, does not enter into the definition of *heresy* or any other sin, and therefore does not pertain to the nature of any act. The Salza/Siscoe proposition, namely, that the external act of heresy is a crime in its very nature, is patently absurd. It is the desperate product of desperate minds of men who are desperate to persuade their readers that their heretical opinions on defection from the faith and the Church, and on loss of office, are the orthodox expressions of the mind of the Church.

Salza & Siscoe then employ verbal sleight of hand by quoting Van Noort on *internal heresy*, who explains that *internal heresy* separates one *potentially* from the body of the Church: «"Internal heresy, since it destroys that interior unity of faith from which unity of profession is born, separates from the body of the Church dispositively, but not yet formally." (Dogmatic Theology, Volume II, Christ's Church, p. 242.)» In this passage Van Noort speaks of the manner in which *internal heresy* separates one from the body of the Church *dispositively*, which is to say *potentially* without causing the separation *in actu*. This was also my meaning when I explained that *internal heresy* separates one spiritually from the *soul* of the Church. It is the act of visible manifest heresy which *actually* separates one from the body of the Church *suapte natura*. It is this latter sense according to which *public heresy* actually causes the separation *suapte natura* that is intended in the passage of Van Noort that I quoted: «Public heretics (and a fortiori, apostates) are not members of the Church. They are not members because they separate themselves from the unity of Catholic faith and from the external profession of that faith.» Van Noort, whom I quoted above, rightly understood that Pius XII was referring specifically to the *external sin* of public heresy, when he commented: «The same pontiff has explicitly pointed out that, unlike other sins, heresy, schism, and apostasy automatically sever a man from the Church. 'For not every sin [admissum], however grave and enormous it be, is such as to sever a man automatically from the Body of the Church, as does schism or heresy or apostasy'. (*Dogmatic Theology, Volume II, Christ's Church*, p. 241 – 242.)» Now to say that public heretics are not members of the Church, because Pius XII teaches that *not every sin however grave and enormous it be is such as to sever a man automatically from the Body of the Church, as does schism or heresy or apostasy*, most patently does not refer to a merely dispositive act that only disposes one *potentially* to be separated, but does not *actually* separate one from membership in the Church; but Pius XII, in the quoted passage, manifestly refers to an *external sin* which *actually separates* one from the body of the Church. This is clearly the unequivocal meaning of Pope Pacelli's teaching in that passage, because the context and verbal tense of those words refer specifically to those who have *actually separated themselves* from the Church, or have been separated from the Church by authority, in such a manner that they are no longer members: «*In Ecclesiæ autem membris reapse ii soli annumerandi sunt, qui regenerationis lavacrum receperunt veramque fidem profitentur, neque a Corporis compage semet ipsos misere* **separarunt**, *vel ob gravissima admissa a legitima auctoritate* **seiuncti sunt**.» And who, according to the text of the encyclical, are those who **are no longer members of the Church**? They are those who *have miserably separated themselves* (semet ipsos misere **separarunt**), and those who *have been cut off for most grave sins by legitimate authority*: (ob gravissima admissa **a legitima auctoritate seiuncti sunt**). The use of the perfect tense logically and grammatically excludes the possibility that Pius XII was saying that *those who* **have separated themselves** in such a manner that they are *no longer members of the Church*, had only **disposed themselves to be separated potentially,** *but were* **not yet actually separated** – yet this is exactly how Salza & Siscoe fraudulently interpret the text, and claim that their fraudulent interpretation explains its authentic meaning! Now, who are those, who *unlike all others who are cut off from the Church by legitimate authority* (i.e. those who have been excommunicated by the Church), **have separated themselves** in such a manner that they are *no longer members of the Church?* They are the **schismatics, heretics, and apostates,** because, "not every sin, however grave and enormous it be, is such as to sever a man by its very nature from the Body of the Church, as does schism or heresy or apostasy" – «Siquidem *non omne admissum, etsi grave scelus, eiusmodi est ut — sicut schisma, vel hæresis, vel apostasia faciunt — suapte natura hominem ab Ecclesiæ Corpore separet.*»

Furthermore, since Pius XII in the quoted passage distinguishes between the *nature* of schism, heresy, apostasy as opposed to *all other sins*, he is clearly referring to heresy *formally* according to its *specific nature* as a single species, and not to the nature of the *material species* of the external act which materially distinguishes the nature of the external act from that of the internal act; since it is not by the nature of the *material species* of the external act, (which is morally indistinguishable from all other acts of the genus of external acts), that heresy, schism and apostasy *per se* intend against the unity of the Church, but by the nature of what *formally* constitutes the *species* that they, *suapte natura* separate one from the body of the Church; as opposed to sins of all other species which do not accomplish that separation *suapte natura*. St. Thomas explains that there is nothing of morality in the material species of an act except that the the act is voluntary, and is therefore a human act. Hence, there is no moral content in the material species of an external act to distinguish it from the internal act of the same species, nor from the external acts of every other species in the genus of external acts to which all delicts pertain. It is therefore not according to the nature of the *material species,* but according to what is properly and *formally* the nature of the species that schism, heresy, and apostasy differ in their nature from the nature of sins of all other species. Hence, Pope Pius distinguishes *formally* the nature of these three *species* of infidelity from the nature of sins of all other species; and not according to the nature of the *material species* of the external act, since there is nothing of morality in the material species of the external act that would distinguish it in its nature from the internal act; and most importantly,there is nothing of morality in the material species of heresy, apostasy or schism that would distinguish them from any other sin in the genus of external acts. Thus, the plain sense of the quoted passage of *Mystici Corporis* is that unlike other sins, the sins of schism, heresy, and apostasy, if public, separate one from the body of the Church *suapte natura,* because acts of these species are *formally* acts of separation according to their nature, and not because they, in their *material species*, are materially of the nature of external acts, since, in their material species they are morally indistinguishable from the external acts of any other species of any other sin or criminal act. Therefore, it is not that these external sins are crimes in their material species unlike any other crimes, that they separate one from the body of the Church *suapte natura,* since considered under the formal aspect of what constitutes them as crimes, they are indistinguishable from any other crimes; but it is because of what formally distinguishes their species, by that which is *formally* specific to the nature of the *sins* of schism, heresy, and apostasy that they separate one from the body of the Church *suapte natura.* Thus, it is because of the physical difference between the material species of the internal and external acts of schism, heresy, and apostasy, that only the external acts of these species are crimes; but it is in virtue of the *formal* difference of nature of these species of acts from all other species, that they *per se,* by their intrinsic nature as acts of separation, and not because they are crimes, that they effect the separation of a man from the Church.

Salza & Siscoe throw around such terms as "Thomistic metaphysics" etc. To try to con their readers into thinking they have some degree of expertise in Thomistic doctrine; but it is nothing but a charade. They conclude their attempt to refute my position, (which is taken straight out the writings of St. Thomas), with a fraudulently altered passage of my own words:

«Fr. Kramer: "Salza's error...[is this]: 'Separation from the Soul of the Church is intrinsic to the nature of the internal act of heresy, and separation from the Body of the Church is intrinsic to the nature of the external act of [notorious] heresy, even if external heresy were not a crime in canon law.'»

Nowhere have I ever stated that the cited proposition is an error. What I actually wrote was quite different: «Salza's error [*the internal sin and the external sin are not of the same nature*]: ...» Thus, I explained that Salza's error consists precisely in the *non sequitur* which says the conclusion, *that the internal act of heresy and the external act of heresy are not acts of the same specific nature*, logically follows from the premise, "'Separation from the Soul of the Church is intrinsic to the nature of the internal act of heresy, and separation from the Body of the Church is intrinsic to the nature of the external act of [notorious] heresy, even if external heresy were not a crime in canon law." From what has been elaborated above, it can be clearly seen that the internal and external acts of heresy are of the same specific nature, and therefore Salza's argument is a *non sequitur*. Then they quote me further:

> "The false premise on which [Salza's] proposition is based is that the internal act and the external act are each of a different nature... However, the nature of both is one and the same. ... It is for this reason that Pius XII does not qualify his teaching by saying that only the external acts of heresy, schism, and apostasy by their very nature separate a man from the Body of the Church... The specific nature of the internal act, the occult external act, and the public act of heresy is identical, and is expressed in the definition of heresy [given in Moral Theology and Canon Law]: the 'pertinacious denial or doubt of a revealed truth that must be believed with divine and Catholic faith'. The qualitative accidental cirumstance [sic] of the act being internal or external is therefore extrinsic to the specific nature of the act of heresy." (...) "The specific nature of the sin of heresy and that of what is properly defined as notorious heresy are one and the same nature: they are both of the same species of heresy."

I have amply demonstrated that "The specific nature of the internal act, the occult external act, and the public act of heresy is identical, and is expressed in the definition of heresy". Furthermore, in relation to the specific nature of heresy, the circumstance of the act being internal or external is qualitative and accidental, and in no manner distinguishes the species between them. The Salza/Siscoe first objection, «but the definition of the nature of the act that qualifies as a sin, and the nature of the act that qualifies as a crime, are not the same, since, as we have seen, an internal act alone suffices for the sin, whereas "an external and morally imputable" act is required to meet the definition of the nature of a crime (Canon 2195.1, 1917 Code)» has been demonstrated to be false. The specific nature of both is the same, and they differ only in their generic nature – one pertaining to the genus of internal acts and the other to the genus of external acts. As I have already explained, the "definition of the nature of a crime" – that it is an "external violation of a law [etc.] …", does not enter into the definition of heresy, whether it be internal or external. Circumstances are the part of an act that do not pertain to the essence of an act. The circumstance of being an ecclesiastical crime; i.e. a punishable, external penal offense, does not pertain to that which defines the nature and essence of heresy whether external or inrernal – it is accidental to the nature of heresy.

Their second objection, [«*Second*, since Fr. Kramer attempted to defend his position using Thomistic metaphysics (i.e., "qualitative accidental circumstances", "species"), we will refute his argument in like manner by noting that an internal act and an external act are two different physical acts, with two different objects, proceeding from two different principles.»], has already been adequately dealt with by what has been stated above. Nothing in this objection has any bearing on the essential nature of heresy as a *species of sin*; but only concerns the difference between the *material species* of the internal and external acts, as explained above, which does not alter the species.

Their third objection: «Now, while it is true that interior and exterior acts combine to form one thing in the moral order, and that the combined acts are of the same moral species (since an act derives its species for its formal object), the natural genus of the internal act alone is distinct from the natural genus of the two acts when combined. This latter point is what refutes Fr. Kramer's error, as we will now see.» As also pointed out above, this distinction between the natural genus of the internal and external acts concerns only the *material species*, and does not alter the nature of the act as a moral act, which alone would result in an alteration of the species of the sin. The objection, "that the internal and external actions are different in the physical order", likewise concerns the difference of *material species* only, and therefore does not differentiate the essential nature of external heresy as a separate species of sin. All of these objections are what in logic are called "red herrings" – none of them are *ad rem*.

It is also of extreme importance to bear in mind that Salza & Siscoe insist that it is only the *crime* and not the *sin* of heresy that severs one from membership in the Church, because (according to them) *sin* is *internal* and therefore cannot be judged by the Church in the external forum; but *crime* is external, and therefore external heresy, and even manifestly formal public heresy, that is not canonically *notorious by fact* must be juridically judged by the Church to be severed from the body of the Church – and therefore, even the manifest heretic, according to their reasoning, remains a member of the Church and remains in office until the Church renders a public judgment in the competent forum. The dilemma that this theory creates is that the Church teaches that the sin of manifestly formal heresy by its very nature is a species of act that *per se* severs one from the body of the Church and thereby expels one from ecclesiastical office; and therefore, if it were only the *crime* of heresy *suapte natura* that would cause one to be severed from membership in the Church, and effect the loss of office *ex natura hæresis*, then the external act of manifest heresy would have to be in its very nature a *crime* according to its species, in order that the act sever the heretic from the body of the Church *suapte natura*, and cause the loss of office to take place by itself *ipso facto*. Hence, Salza & Siscoe assert the absurd proposition that external heresy is a crime in its nature, and is a distinct species of sin, different from the species internal heresy which is not a crime in its specific nature. However, it is self-evident from the very definition of heresy that it does not pertain to the species of either the internal or external act of heresy that it is a *crime – a morally imputable external violation of a law or precept* **to which is added a canonical sanction** (i.e. a *crime* as defined in can. 2195. §1), and for that reason extenal heresy is not in its nature a crime.

Faced with this impossible dilemma, Salza & Siscoe have resorted to the desperate tactic of obfuscation: «We should also note that a crime (delictum) is not limited to an offense against "merely ecclesiastical laws" (human positive law), but also includes offenses against divine law.[22] External heresy is a violation of both ecclesiastical law and divine law.» [(22) "*Delictum* is taken from the word *delinquere* (*de* and *linquere*, to forsake, to leave, to omit) and means an offence in the general sense. However, by common usage the term is restricted to a public offence or crime against the juridical order or law. Therefore it is called <u>a transgression of the law,</u> **whether divine or human**, i.e., merely ecclesiastical. ... the transgression which the ecclesiastical law considers is not merely the guilty mind (mens rea)... it is essential to the notion of a delictum that it be an external act..." ~ Fr. Augustine, A Commentary on the New Code of Canon Law, (London: Herder Book Co., 1918) p. 11.]

Judging by the cherry-picked truncated segments of text joined together by ellipses, one would easily get the impression that the eminent commentator on Canon Law quoted in the footnote teaches that absolutely anything that violates divine law and is committed with an external act is classified as a canonical crime in ecclesiastical law. That would destroy the distinction between merely external sins and crimes; with the result that *all morally imputable external sins without exception would be crimes*, since all sins violate the divine law. What Salza & Siscoe fail to mention is that for an external violation of divine law to be considered a crime in ecclesiastical law, the law must be of an *ecclesiastical character*; and in order for a precept of natural or divine law to be of ecclesiastical character, it would suffice that the Church sanction its violation with a canonical penalty (as is explained below). An external violation of *divine law* is not *per se* a crime in its nature, but to qualify as a crime in *ecclesiastical law*, it must be an "externa et moraliter imputabilis legis violatio **cui addita sit sanctio canonica saltem indeterminata**". A morally imputable violation of divine law, whether internal or external, is by definition, and therefore in its very nature a **sin**[372], but not a **crime**. It is thus, patently clear that by leaving out the important material in the cited section of Fr. Augustine's work, Salza & Siscoe deliberately intend to deceive their readers into thinking that Fr. Augustine says exactly the opposite of what he actually says. When one reads the text of Fr. Augustine's commentary on canon 2195[373] in its proper context, the fraudulent verbal sleight off hand becomes obvious:

On page 10-11:

> «A *crime*, in ecclesiastical law, is an external and morally imputable transgression of a law to which is attached a canonical sanction, at least in general. *Delictum* is taken from the word *delinquere* (*de* and *linquere*, to forsake, to leave, to omit) and means an offense in the general sense. However, by common usage the term is restricted to a public offense or crime against the

---

[372] St. Augustine (*Contra Faustum* XXII 27): «Dictum, factum vel concupitum contra legem æternam»

[373] Can. 2195. §1. Nomine delicti, iure ecclesiastico, intelligitur externa et moraliter imputabilis legis violatio cui addita sit sanctio canonica saltem indeterminata.

§2. Nisi ex adiunctis aliud appareat, quae dicuntur de delictis, applicantur etiam violationibus praecepti cui poenalis sanctio adnexa sit.

juridical order or law. Therefore it is called a *transgression of the law*, whether divine or human, *i.e.*, merely ecclesiastical. It is the law, either eternal or positive, that governs order, the relation of man to God and of man to man, and any defection from that order constitutes a frustration of the designs of Providence.»

«2. But the transgression which the ecclesiastical law considers is not merely the guilty mind (*mens rea*), but the *act*, – i.e., an outward manifestation of a vicious intention, or a breach of the law as externally apprehensible... It is essential to the notion of *delictum* that it be an *external act*, either of speech or deed, although it is not necessary to be provable.»

After the paragraph on *externality*, Fr. Augustine then elaborates on the *legal element* on page 12, 13 and 14:

«4. But what does the addition *"cui addita sit sanctio canonica saltem indeterminata"* mean? The transgression is accompanied by penal sanction, at least in general terms. This means that there is neither crime nor punishment without a penal law.4 [*"Nullum crimen, nulla poena sine lege poenali,"* was the adage of the School; Eichmann, *l. c.,* p. 27.] It is therefore, as stated above, the law which is infringed and which punishes. [...] Take, for instance, the reading of forbidden books, which is not punished generally (can. 1395) but only in particular cases (can. 2318); hunting by clergymen (can.138), etc. Yet these forbidden actions cannot be called crimes in the sense of ecclesiastical law." [...] The *sanctio canonica indeterminata* signifies a penalty to be meted out according to the good pleasure of the judge or superior (can. 2217, § I, n. I). It follows that, although no special penalty is provided for the transgression of a law, yet if that law embodies the provision that the punishment of the transgressor is left to the prudent judgment of the Ordinary, this is sufficient to mark the transgression as a crime, provided that the other necessary marks are not wanting.»[374]

Thus, one of the great authorities on Canon Law explains those marks and elements necessary for a sin to be considered a cime in ecclesiastical law; and all of those marks and elements together do not pertain to the intrinsic nature of any external sin.

The commentary of the Salamanca Canon Law Faculty explains on page 783, the definition of a crime in essentially the same sense as Fr. Augustine, but expounding on the necessary elements that constitute a delict in ecclesiastical law more concisely and with greater precision:

---

[374] Augustine, *Op. cit.*, Volume VIII, pp. 10 – 11, 12, 13, 14, B. HERDER BOOK CO., St. Louis, London, 1922.

«**2195** Tres son los elementos constitutivos del delito por derecho eclesiástico: *a)* violación externa de una ley; *b)* que la violación sea moralmente imputable, y *c)* que la ley lleve aneja una sanción canonica, por lo menos indeterminada. A estos tres elementos suelen los autores llamarles, respectivamente, elemento *objetivo*, elemento *subjetivo* y elemento *legal*. A dicha terminología nos atendremos, por ser la más común.»

Those three elements necessary for a sin to be constituted as a crime in ecclesiastical law are 1) the external violation of a law (the objective element), 2) moral imputability of the violation (the subjective element), 3) a penal sanction connected to the law (legal element). The objective element is comprised of a) an external violation, b) of a law, c) that damages the juridico-social order of the Church[375]. The canon uses the word 'law' in the broad sense of an *obligatory norm of objective law*, which includes in its scope a law properly so-called, or a simple jurisdictional precept or admonition. The law must be *ecclesiastical*, it does not suffice for a *crime* that a law merely *natural* or divine be transgressed, however grave it might be. In order for a natural or divine law to be of ecclesiastical character, it would suffice that the Church sanction it with a canonical penalty.[376]

Also pertaining essentially to the nature of a crime, is the *legal element*, as Fr. Augustine explained (in the portion of the text that Salza & Siscoe left out when quoting it), and summed up with the words, "This means that there is neither crime nor punishment without a penal law." The *catedráticos* of the Canon Law faculty of Salamanca elaborate even more fully on this point, and what is most essential is that,

> «[P]or derecho eclesiástico, lo mismo que ocurre en la legislación de los Estados, la violación no constituye *delito*, aunque pueda ser *pecado externo*, si no hay una norma legal objetiva – en sentido lato, según hemos expuesto –

---

[375] Miguelez – Alonso – Cabreros, *Op. cit.* p. 783: «ELEMENTO OBJETIVO: Exige a su vez: *a)* violación externa; *b)* de una ley; *c)* con daño social»

[376] *Ibid.*, p. 783: «2° *Violación de una ley:* La palabra «ley» se toma aquí en sentido lato, en quanto que signifìca «norma obligtoria del derecho objetivo» ya sea *ley* propiamenta dicha o simplemente *precepto* jurisdiccional o *amonestación* canónica…La ley ha de ser *eclesiástica*, no bastando para el delito que se viole una ley *meramente natural* o *divina*, por grave que ésta sea. Ahora bien, para que una ley natural o divina tenga a la vez el character de ley eclesiástica, basta que la Iglesia haya sancionado con alguna pena *canonica* la violación de dicha ley, como ocurre, v. gr., con el homocidio, la blasfemia, el perjurio, etc.»

que amenace previamente con una pena. De no ser asi, se daría lugar a inumerables arbitrariedades, lo que cedería en ultimo lugar en detrimento mayor y trastorno del orden social.»[377]

In this passage, the Salamanca canonists explain why it is that the *legal element* necessarily pertains essentially to the nature of a crime – and that is because it is necessary for a penalty to be connected to the violation of a law, for the violation to constitute a crime; because it is essential to the preservation of the social order which necessarily requires it. Hence, the mere omission of any mention of the *legal element* in the characterization of a crime in the 1983 Code (which falls short of a proper definition), cannot imply that the absence of inclusion of the *legal element* in the canons of the 1983 Code alters the essential definition of a crime; firstly because the *legal element* pertains *intrinsically* to the nature of a crime, which lies outside of the power of a legislator to eliminate; and secondly [as the Canon Law faculty of Navarre explain in the passage cited below] because one of the general principles applied in the 1983 revision of the Code of Canon Law was the elimination of all the definitions that were given in the 1917 Code, since they pertain to canonical doctrine rather than legislation; and thus remain applicable for the interpretation of the canons of the 1983 Code.

Salza & Siscoe fail to make the most elementary distinctions when they say in Part II of their Formal Reply:

> The only distinction that can be made when considering the nature of heresy is between: (1) the <u>sin</u> of heresy that is completely concealed in the heart and has never been externalized *at all*, and (2) the <u>crime</u> of heresy that *has* been externalized, *even if no one was around to hear it* (i.e., external, occult heresy). Cajetan explains that the reason the two are distinct, *according to their nature*, is because the <u>sin</u> of heresy that remains *entirely* hidden in the heart can only be judged by God, according to 1 Kings 16:7 – "man seeth the things that appear, but God beholdeth the heart," whereas the crime of heresy that has been externalized (the external act renders it a crime *by its nature*) is subject to the judgment of men – even if, due to the circumstances (e.g., no one around to hear it) it cannot be judged. In other words, the former is not divulged at all (hidden by its nature); the latter is divulged (external by its nature), even if no one heard it. The former is judgeable only by God; the latter can be judged by men. Heresy that has not been externalized at all is a sin, but not a crime; heresy that has been externalized (even if no one was around to hear it), is both a sin and a crime. Hence, the

---

[377] *Ibid.*, p. 784.

crime of heresy is more restrictive in its meaning than is the sin of heresy; and the external act is what makes it a crime, *by its nature.*

The first distinction they fail to make is between the *internal sin* and the *external sin*; and the second is the distinction between the *external sin* and the *crime*. The second I have already sufficiently explained above; so it will suffice here to point out firstly, that an act that in its nature is only a crime against divine law, but does not in any manner violate an ecclesiastical law, does not fall under the jurisdiction of the Church in the external forum as a *crime*; and therefore, is not subject to the public penal judgment of the Church. Secondly, although every crime is an external sin, every exernal sin is not a crime in the sense of an ecclesiastical *delict* that is subject to the public penal judgment of the Church. Thirdly, the Salza/Siscoe self-contradictory notion of an "*externalized internal sin*", is a failed oxymoron, based on the *non sequitur* that since the formal component of sin is internal; therefore sin is internal, even if it is committed with an external act. This grave error against Catholic moral doctrine fails to recognize that sin is in its essential nature a composite act consisting of two constituent components: *matter* and *form*. **The form alone is not the sin**, but **the composite of the form and the matter together constitute the essence of a sin**, which specifies its *nature*. All sins are *actions* – thoughts, words or deeds; actions which are either internal or external. The *matter* of the sin is *the action itself which transgresses the law of God*, as St. Alphonsus (quoted below) explains; and if that action is *external*, then the sin is an *external sin*. The classic definition of *sin* is that of St. Augustine (*Contra Faustum* XXII 27): «Dictum, factum vel concupitum contra legem æternam». The *form*, consists in the *intention of the will to knowingly commit an act of transgression against the divine law*, and is the *principle* from which the sinful action is brought into being. *Internal sin* is an *action* which terminates within the mind in such a manner that there does not proceed from the act of the will an action which is perceptible to the senses. *External sin* is a transgression of the law of God which *begins* in the will, as do all sins, and *terminates* in the external commission of words or deeds that are perceptible to the senses. The *form* of a sin is only a *constitutive component* of the sin, but not the sin itself; because the sinful action itself is the *matter* of the transgression which specifies the *nature* of the sin. Form without matter is a mere abstraction – a principle without any specific determination of any transgression of divine law; and therefore, there is no sin without both matter and form. Hence, if the action is internal, the sin is internal; but if the action is external, then the sin is an *external sin*.[378]

On the basis of their bizarre doctrine that the *sin* of heresy is internal, and is of a different specific nature than the external sin, i.e. the *crime* of heresy; and that only the *crime* of heresy, but not the act of public heresy considered formally as a *sin*, separates one from the body of the Church; Salza & Siscoe, heretically interpret the words of *Mystici Corporis* to mean that only the canonical ecclesiastical crime of notorious heresy (i.e. according to their own uncanonical definition of "notorious heresy") separates one from membership in the Church by its own nature by severing the juridical bond of membership in the Church, *without a public judgment of the Church*. From this point of departure, they eventually arrive at the conclusion that for anything less than canonically notorious heresy (according to their own definition of the term), the juridical bond that unites one to the Church is not actually severed until a judgment of the *crime* is pronounced. In their Formal Reply, they begin by quoting their own book: *True or False Pope?*, explaining that it is,

> «the public offense (the crime) of heresy, which, of its nature, severs a person from the Body of the Church with no further censure attached to the offense. (…) Jerome is referring to the nature of the crime [of heresy], which severs one from the body of the Church with no additional censure attached to it. In this sense, the crime of heresy differs in its nature from other crimes, such as physically striking the Pope or procuring an abortion, which are crimes that only sever a person from the Church by virtue of the additional censure attached to the act.»

They continue by arguing that *only* the *crime* of *notorious heresy* separates one from the body of the Church:

> «The Crime of Notorious Heresy: What separates a Catholic from external union with the Body of the Church is not the nature of the sin of heresy (again, as Kramer argues above), but rather the nature of the external act (crime[4]) [[4] The external act of heresy is, *by its nature*, a crime.]

---

[378] The matter of a sin, formally considered as a sin, is a voluntary human act, and therefore, the essential nature, i.e. the *species* of the sin is derived from its matter, and is the same species as the species of the human act. Considered not under the formal aspect of sin but considered as such as a human *act*, the form of the human act is that which is willed directly and *per se*, and is that which constitutes the species of the act, whose matter is the action materially considered in itself apart from what is formally willed.

of notorious heresy.» «This is confirmed by Cardinal Billot, who said "only notorious heretics are excluded from the body of the Church." (De Ecclesia, Thesis II). The reason notorious heresy, of its nature, separates a Catholic from the Body of the Church is because it severs the juridical bond[5] [[5] See *Mystici Corporis Christi*, No. 70.] The legal separation from the Church has nothing to do with the nature of the sin of heresy, and everything to do with the nature of the public act (crime) of notorious heresy. This is confirmed from the fact that Bellarmine, Cajetan and John of St. Thomas unanimously teach that a notoriously heretical Pope can be deposed, or declared deposed, even if, per accidens, he is not subjectively guilty of the sin.»

In the quoted paragraph, Salza & Siscoe have just provided the premises for their own refutation. Firstly, as mentioned above, *material heresy*, if not qualified by *schism*, which places one outside the Church, does not separate one from the Church, nor does it effect the loss of office *ex natura hæresis*, because merely material heresy does not formally oppose the faith of the Church, and therefore does not sever the juridical bond. Salza & Siscoe say, "Bellarmine, Cajetan and John of St. Thomas unanimously teach that a notoriously heretical Pope can be deposed, or declared deposed, even if, per accidens, he is not subjectively guilty of the sin"; but they do not provide any direct quotation or reference to back up this claim; so, from the information provided, it is not possible to determine exactly what these authors really wrote nor determine what was their meaning. In Part III of this work I quote Bellarmine in *lib. iv cap. ii* of *De Romano Pontifice*, where he says that all authors, Catholic and non-Catholic are in agreement that a pope can be materially in heresy due to ignorance. So, no matter how notoriously known the materially heretical opinion of a pope may be; he is not properly a heretic, and therefore not a *"notorious heretic"* as the Church understands that term, unless he visibly separates himself from the Church; thus qualifying his material heresy by a visible act of schism. Secondly, according to the definition of *'crime'* in canon 2195 § 1, and what is prescribed concerning *imputability* and *dolus* of crime in cann. 2199 and 2200; heresy cannot be considered a crime notorious by fact, nor is it even a crime at all if there is no *moral imputability*, which only exists when there is *subjective guilt*. If one is not *subjectively guilty of the sin*, then *there is no crime*; because, there is lacking in the act the *grave moral imputability*, which depends directly on the *dolus*, (i.e. «*deliberata voluntas violandi legem*») or *culpability* that are *intrinsic to the nature of a crime*, as defined in the canons; and without which the material act would not fulfil the conditions necessary for the act to be qualified as, and actually be constituted as a *crime*. Nevertheless, one who formally defects from the Catholic faith or communion with the Church, expressly rejecting the authority of the Church *inculpably*, separates himself from visible union with the Church and severs the juridical bond without committing the crime of heresy, schism, or apostasy; since there is no crime without grave moral imputability. Furthermore, mere *material heresy on one or several points of doctrine*, no matter how publicly or notoriously known, does not separate a Catholic from the Church, nor effect the loss of office; because an officeholder who is only *materially* in heresy has not defected from the faith by rejecting its formal cause, nor has he intended to leave the Church; nevertheless, given that the external violation of the law has occurred, the *dolus* of crime, which is defined as *the deliberate intention to violate the law* (Can. 2200. §1),[379] is presumed in the 1917 Code until the contrary is proven (2200. §2): «*Posita externa legis violatione, dolus in foro externo præsumitur, donec contrarium probetur.*» In the 1983 Code it is presumed *unless it appears otherwise.* (*nisi aliud appareat* — Can. 1321 § 1) Yet, heresy schismatically qualified as *a public act of formal defection from the Church* (as opposed to simple heresy), committed by one who happens to not be subjectively guilty of sin but who wilfully departs from the Church, although *not having committed an actual crime*, is nevertheless visibly and juridically separated from the body of the Church, *by the very nature of the defection*; and therefore loses office *ipso jure* (can. 194; 188. 4° in the 1917 Code), apart from any consideration of penal legislation, or the lack of *dolus* or *culpa* which would need to be present to make the act a grave and morally imputable *crime*. Thus, it can be seen that Salza & Siscoe contradict themselves again when they assert, «heresy includes everything from the internal sin alone, to the public crime of notorious heresy – and **only the latter** [i.e. the ***crime***] automatically severs a person from external union with the Church "without a declaration."» So, the premise, "the fact that Bellarmine, Cajetan and John of St. Thomas unanimously teach that a notoriously heretical Pope can be deposed, or declared deposed, even if, per accidens, he is not subjectively guilty of the sin," *does **not** prove* or confirm that "the legal separation from the Church has nothing to do with the nature of the sin of heresy, and everything to do with the nature of the public act (crime) of notorious heresy;" – but *what it **does** prove*, is that **the juridical bond that unites one to the Church as an actual member is sundered ipso jure as a direct result of the fact of the**

---

[379] «deliberata voluntas violandi legem»

severing of the visible external bond, which is accomplished per se by the act of public defection; regardless of whether or not that act be also a sin or a crime. The public sin of manifest formal heresy, by its very nature as a visible rejection of the formal cause of faith, and not because it is a crime in ecclesiastical law, but because it *per se* severs the visible external bond of faith that formerly united the heretic to the Church as a visible member, *suapte natura* dissolves the juridical bond, and separates the heretic from the body of the Church in such a manner that heretics (as *Mystici Corporis* teaches) *"miserably separate themselves"* from the body of the Church by that very sin; and **not** *"by legitimate authority"* for having committeed a *crime*. This is precisely what Pius XII taught in *Mystici Corporis*, and not that the "offense", (considered only under its formal aspect as a *crime* in ecclesiastical law), separates one *suapte natura* from the body of the Church; as Salza & Siscoe heretically assert against the clear and perpetual teaching of the universal and ordinary magisterium of the Church.

The latter quoted statement of Salza & Siscoe is also plainly false, because not only an act of *notorious* heresy, but even *public heresy* separates one from the Church, and as a direct consequence, results in an *ipso jure* loss of office: In its Prot. N. 10279/2006 (*Actus Formalis Defecionis ab Ecclesia Catholica*) approved by the Supreme Pontiff, Benedict XVI, the Pontifical Council for Legislative Texts. on 13 March 2006, clarified the Church's position on formal defection from the Church, explaining,

> «The concept therein presented is new to canonical legislation and is distinct from the other – rather "virtual" (that is, deduced from behaviors) – forms of "notoriously" or "publicly" abandoning the faith (cfr. can. 171, § 1, 4°; **194, § 1, 2°**; 316, § 1; 694, § 1, 1°; 1071, § 1, 4° and § 2).[380] In the latter circumstances, those who have been baptized or received into the Catholic Church continue to be bound by merely ecclesiastical laws (cfr. can. 11).»

The document distinguishes between «forms of "notoriously" or "publicly" abandoning the faith», both of which constitute a defection from the Church, and effect the *ipso jure* loss of office. This proves that it is not only canonically notorious heretics who are outside the Church, as Salza & Siscoe claim, (quoting Billot, who uses the word according to its common meaning, synonymous with "public": "only notorious heretics are excluded from the body of the Church."); but also *public heretics*. Furthermore, whoever publicly defects from the Catholic faith, apart from any consideration of penal law, crime, or the imputability of the act, loses office *ipso jure* according to the prescription of Canon 194, § 1, 2°. The *ipso jure* loss of office takes place "by the action of the law itself", and as Canon 188. 4° prescribed, "automatically" (*ipso facto*) and "without any declaration" (*sine ulla declaratione*), and from "whatsoever offices" (*quælibet officia*), because the loss of office ultimately does not result from any human law, but **from the nature of heresy**, as Bellarmine explains in the earlier cited passage: "Nam Patres illi cum dicunt hæreticos amittere jurisdictionem, non allegant ulla jura humana, quæ etiam forte tunc nulla extabant de hac re: sed argumentantur *ex natura hæresis*."

Salza & Siscoe continue:

> «It should be further noted – and this is also a critical point – that notorious heresy does not sever a person from the Church because it is listed as a crime (delict) in canon law, or because of the censure of excommunication that the Church attaches to the crime…Rather, notorious heresy separates a person from the Church due to the nature of the public act itself, which severs a juridical bond (i.e., "profession of the faith"). Notorious heresy would sever a person from the Church even if it were not listed as a crime in canon law."»

First of all, if it were not *listed as a crime in canon law*, then heresy would not be an ecclesiastical *delict*, and would therefore not be judicable and punishable in the external forum by the Church. Furthermore, as I explained above, it is in the *nature* of notorious heresy, (as the word 'notorious' is commonly understood as interchangeable with 'public'), *as being intrinsically an act of public defection* (i.e. as a *fact*), and not because it is a *crime* (i.e. a *penal offense* or *delict*), that it severs the juridical bond *ipso jure* apart from any penal laws. Since Salza & Siscoe profess that the external act of heresy is in its nature a *crime*, according to them, the *crime* of notorious heresy severs the juridical bond and thus separates heretic from the body of the Church without a declaration – but if the *crime* is not *public and notorious, then, according to Salza & Siscoe, the juridical bond is not severed automatically, but only by a penal sentence pronounced by Church authority.*

«Now, in the case of a Catholic who is guilty of the sin of heresy and has even externalized his heresy, yet who is not deemed to be a notorious heretic by fact, he would still incur the censure of excommunication ipso facto (since the censure is even incurred by external occult heretics) but, in such a case, it would require a "pronounced judgment of the Church" (rendering him notorious by law), before he would be legally severed from the Body of the Church. The ipso facto excommunication he incurred (in the internal forum) would not, per se, have the juridical effect (in the external forum) of legally separating him from the visible society of the Church since, as Pope Benedict IV said, "a sentence declaratory of the offence is always necessary in the external forum, since in this tribunal no one is presumed to be excommunicated unless convicted of a crime that entails such a penalty."»[381]

The Salza/Siscoe conclusion is a *non sequitur*, because in the cited passage, Benedict XIV does not state or imply that a declaratory sentence of a penal offense is necessary for the juridical bond with the Church to be severed; but only that *no one is to be presumed to have incurred the penalty of excommunication without a declaratory sentence of the crime*. For the public crime of heresy, the juridical bond is not severed by the penalty of excommunication, but is severed *suapte natura* by the act of public heresy. Thus it is that Salza and Siscoe have fallen into heresy for their clearly heretical opinion that holds that a manifest formal heretic who is guilty of the *public sin of heresy*, but is not guilty of the *crime* of heresy *canonically notorious by fact* (as they understand it), remains a member of the Church until he is juridically judged to be a heretic, unless 1) he has left the Church by an explicit act of formal defection, or 2) has explicitly rejected the magisterium as the rule of faith, 3) has expressly admitted that his opinion is heretical. Those guilty of heresy, as heretics are defined in Canon 1325 § 2, if the sin is public (Canon 2197. 1°), have *publicly defected from the Catholic faith*, and are therefore by the very nature of that act of defection, separated from the body of the Church, apart from the *latæ sententiæ* excommunication prescribed in the canon. Such a defection provokes the *ipso jure* removal from ecclesiastical office (Canon 194, § 1, 2°). The proposition, «The ipso facto excommunication he incurred (in the internal forum) would not, per se, have the juridical effect (in the external forum) of legally separating him from the visible society of the Church since, as Pope Benedict IV said, "a sentence declaratory of the offence is always necessary in the external forum, since in this tribunal

---

[381] *Formal Reply*, Part I.

no one is presumed to be excommunicated unless convicted of a crime that entails such a penalty,» is fallacious in so far as it presumes 1) on the basis of the previous sentence, that the "externalized" public sin of heresy, incurs an *ipso facto* excommunication "in the internal forum", because "sin is internal" – and "the Church does not judge internals". In fact, the public sin of heresy is an external sin, and because it publicly violates an ecclesiastical law, its excommunication pertains to the *external forum*. However, notwithstanding the fact of the *crime* of external heresy and *the penalty incurred by it*, 2) the public sin of heresy, *as an act of public defection from the Catholic faith*, by its very nature severs the juridical bond of union with the Church apart from any penal censure or any human law, as has been amply demonstrated above, and therefore, as Bellarmine explained in the above quoted passage, "heretics are outside the Church, *even before excommunication, and deprived of all jurisdiction, for they are condemned by their own judgment*, as the Apostle teaches to Titus; that is, **they are cut from the body of the Church without excommunication,** as Jerome expresses it." For this reason, the public sin of manifest formal heresy of itself severs the juridical bond, and thus *suapte natura* produces the effect of *separating the heretic from the visible society of the Church* **ipso jure,** notwithstanding the merely penal requirement mentioned by Benedict XIV, ("a sentence declaratory of the offence is always necessary in the external forum, since in this tribunal no one is presumed to be excommunicated unless convicted of a crime that entails such a penalty"), which is merely necessary to confirm the penalty of excommunication, *but not to effect the severing of the juridical bond* – **because heresy already directly and *per se* separates one from the Church without any excommunication,** i.e. *by its very nature;* and not *"by legitimate authority"*, i.e. *by excommunication,* as Pius XII teaches in *Mystici Corporis*. **It is this last consideration which exposes the absurdity of the Salza/Siscoe thesis which would reason against reason, arguing that since external heresy is in its nature a crime, therefore a public judgment of the Church would be necessary for the juridical bond to be severed, and for the heretic to lose office. However, even if we grant solely for the sake of argument that the external act of heresy is in its nature a crime; it remains that the very act of manifestly formal heresy *suapte natura*, as an act of severing the bonds of communion, *directly and per se* severs the heretic visibly from the body of the Church *entirely by itself*, and therefore *directly and per se* severs the juridical bond *ipso jure* and causes the loss of office; and therefore necessarily it does so** without any judgment of Church authority. An action which actually accomplishes the severing of the bonds of communion *directly* and *per se*, is manifestly not merely dispositive in nature, disposing the heretic to be severed upon judgment by the Church, since the act itself *by its own nature* accomplishes that severing entirely by itself. The further obfuscations, equivocations, contradictions that Salza & Siscoe elaborate on this point, is dealt with in Part V under the heading, "THE LATEST SALZA/SISCOE FRAUD".

Salza & Siscoe have also fallen into heresy in their belief that a pope while in office, can be judged by the Church for the crime of heresy, since this opinion opposes the doctrine of the primacy of the pope as the **supreme judge in all cases**:

Constitutio Dogmatica *«Pastor Æternus»* Concilii Vaticani I: Et quoniam divino Apostolici primatus iure Romanus Pontifex universæ Ecclesiæ præest, docemus etiam et declaramus, **eum esse iudicem supremum** fidelium (Pii PP. VI Breve, *Super soliditate* d. 28 Nov. 1786), et *in omnibus causis ad examen ecclesiasticum spectantibus* ad ipsius posse iudicium recurri (Concil. Oecum. Lugdun. II); *Sedis vero Apostolicæ, cuius auctoritate maior non est, iudicium a nemine fore retractandum, neque cuiquam de eius licere iudicare iudicio* (Ep. Nicolai 1 ad Michælem Imporatorem). *Quare a recto veritatis tramite aberrant, qui affirmant, licere ab iudiciis Romanorum Pontificum ad oecumenicum Concilium tamquam ad auctoritatem Romano Pontifice superiorem appellare.*

That, however, has already been adequately dealt with in this chapter, and will be discussed further in a later chapter of this work.

EX SUPRADICTIS PATET:

Sententia hæretica — «After the **Church establishes that the Pope is guilty of the crime of heresy, she renders a judgment** of the same (and, as we will see, **this is to be done during an *"imperfect"* ecumenical council**).» – *True or False Pope?* p. 331

Sententia hæretica — «The Church must render a judgment before the pope loses his office.» – [Robert J. Siscoe, Article in *The Remnant* (Nov. 18, 2014)]

Sententia hæretica — «But only the Church possesses the authority to render such a judgment and make any consequent declarations.» [Salza & Siscoe in *Paul Kramer a Father of Lies?*]

Sententia hæretica — «the sin of heresy alone does not sever one from the Church.»

Sententia hæretica — That not the public sin of heresy alone, but heresy after judgment is pronounced by the Church is required to sever the heretic from the Church:

«Again, Pope Pius XII is referring to the "offense" or CRIME (not SIN) *[sic]* of heresy, which severs one from the Body of the Church, after the formal and material elements have been proven by the Church *(sic)*. After the crime has been established *(sic)*, the heretic is automatically severed from the BODY (not SOUL) of the Church without further declaration (although most theologians maintain that the Church must also issue a declaration of deprivation)» [382] *[sic]*

N.B. – Besides the heretical belief that the sin of manifest heresy by itself and without any censure or judgment, publicly committed, does not separate one from the Church, there are here in John Salza's proposition additional errors, 1) that Pius XII in the cited passage of Mystici Corporis refers to the canonical delict of heresy and not the public sin per se; 2) that the heretic is separated from the Church only after the fact has been proven by the Church (Heresy *suapte natura* severs one from the Church when the sin is committed, not when it is judged post factum by the Church; 3) that the one guilty of the crime of heresy is separated from the body, but not from the soul of the Church. In fact, one who is guilty of public formal heresy is united neither internally nor externally to the Church; and is severed from both the body and the soul of the Church (As St. Robert Bellarmine explains at the end of Ch. XXX of De Romano Pontifice.).

Sententia hæretica – «**The sin of heresy alone does NOT 'sever the person from the Body of the Church'** because sin is a matter of the internal forum»[383]; and «the sin of heresy alone does not "automatically expel" one from the body of the Church»;[384] «The correct interpretation of Pope Pius XII's teaching is not that he was referring to the internal sin of heresy alone, but to the public offense (the crime) of heresy, which, of its nature, severs a person from the Body of the Church with no further censure attached to the offense.»[385] [It is de fide that the sin of heresy alone, committed as an external, public act severs the person from the body of the Church, without any Church judgment or

---

[382] In *John Salza Responds to Another Sedevacantist*
[383] *Ibid*
[384] *Ibid*
[385] *True or False Pope*, p. 159.

any canonical censure, and would have the effect of severing the heretic even if there were no canonical penalty attached to the sin.] Salza & Siscoe manifest a profound ignorance of Fundamental Moral Theology in this proposition:

> «In other words, the sin of heresy disposes a person to be separated from the visible Church *(sic)*, but the actual separation does not take place until the Church itself renders a judgment *[sic]* (unless, of course, the person himself rendered the judgment by openly leaving the Church [15]). Because the Church, itself, does not judge internals *[sic]* (de internis ecclesia non judica *[sic]*), for the sin to be judged, it must be public; and needless to say the judgment of the public sin must proceed from the proper authorities *(sic)*, not from the individual Catholic in the pew».
>
> *Sententia hæretica*: «The sin of heresy alone does not cause the loss of office» (Contrary to the doctrine of the Universal and Ordinary Magisterium)[386]
>
> *Error in fide*: Siscoe/Salza: «Yes, that is correct. [...] heresy does nòt directly cause a Pope to fall from the pontificate.» (Gloria TV interview)
>
> «The sin of heresy alone, which has not been judged and declared by the Church, does not result in the loss of ecclesiastical office for a cleric. [*sententia hæretica*] The loss of office for a cleric is a vindictive penalty [*sententia erronea*], and there is a process in Church law which must precede vindictive penalties...
>
> «This also means that the loss of office for a cleric must be imposed (ferendae sententiae) *(sic)* by Church authority [70] which makes the loss of office a "vindictive penalty." *(sic)* [Footnote 70] – In the old 1917 Code, there was an exception to this rule for the more severe vindictive penalty (canon 188, §4). *(sic)*»[387]

Salza & Siscoe manifest a profound confusion on the distinction between internal and external sin throughout their writings. Their heretical proposition that «*the sin of heresy alone does not sever one from the Church*», is founded on the heterodox belief that it pertains to the distinction between *sin* and *crime* that *sin is a matter of the internal forum*. They attempt to justify their indefensible position by appealing to the canonical distinction between an act that is materially and formally public, and an act that is materially public but formally occult. On the basis of this distinction, they errantly judge that a sin which is *materially* public, but *formally occult*, is an *internal sin*; and therefore beyond the scope

---

[386] *True or False Pope?*, p. 149.

[387] *True or False Pope – Refuting Sedevacantism and other Modern Errors*, p. 260.

of Canon Law, because "the Church does not judge internals". On this utterly spurious foundation, Salza & Siscoe errantly declare that one who flagrantly and publicly professes even the most blatant and inexcusable heresy cannot be considered to have *ipso facto* defected from the faith, or fallen from office, or ceased to be a member of he Church unless he explicitly admits that his doctrine is heretical, explicitly rejects the Church as the rule of faith, or obstinately persists in heresy after ecclesiastical warnings. Their crude obfuscation of the distinction between internal and external sin becomes manifestly apparent when one considers the manner in which it is explained and applied in the canons of the Church. Canon 1321 § 1 of the 1983 Code describes a canonical crime as an *"externa legis vel præcepti violatio"*, which is *"graviter imputabilis ex dolo vel ex culpa"*; and the 1917 Code likewise defines a canonical delict: «*Can. 2195. §1. Nomine delicti, iure ecclesiastico, intelligitur externa et moraliter imputabilis legis violatio cui addita sit sanctio canonica saltem indeterminata.*» An *"externa legis vel præcepti violatio"*, which is *"graviter imputabilis ex dolo vel ex culpa"* is an *external mortal sin* – it is not an "externalized internal sin". The 1983 Code on the nature of canonical crime essentially repeats, with minor alteration, the canons of the 1917 Code, and therefore, as set forth in the above quoted Canon 6 of the 1983 Code, it must on these points be understood according to canonical tradition, which is enshrined in the *definitions* given in the 1917 Code. The above quoted commentary of the Canon Law Faculty of Navarre also points out that one of the general principles applied in the revision of the Code of Canon Law was the elimination of all the definitions that were given in the 1917 Code, since they pertain to canonical doctrine rather than legislation; and thus remain applicable for the interpretation of the canons of the 1983 Code.[388]

Next to be considered is the meaning of *"externa et moraliter imputabilis legis violatio"*. First, as the above cited Salamanca commentary explains, the violation must be *external*: which means the act must be perceivable by the senses, so that if someone were present, they would be able to

---

[388] «1312 Como quedó dicho, uno de los principios generales que informan la revisión del Código es la supresión de todas las definiciones, ya que ello es tarea más de la doctrina que de la legislación. Por eso el c., en el § 1, se limita a enunciar la división fundamental de las penas canónicas —censuras y penas expiatorias—, remitiendo a los cc. respectivos lo que a su regulación se refiere.» UNIVERSIDAD DE NAVARRA, FACULTAD DE DERECHO CANÓNICO; *Op. cit.* p. 817.

perceive it. The merely *internal violation* of the law is never a crime because it cannot disturb the juridico-social order of the Church. However, the *external* violation must not be confused with the *public* violation of the law: there can be a crime even if the criminal act were to take place in a most hidden manner, even if no one were present, and there did not exist the possibility that anyone could come into knowledge of it.[389] Second, the violation must be *morally imputable.* Canon 1321 § 3 sets forth that if an external violation has been committed, the violation is presumed to be *"graviter imputabilis ex dolo vel ex culpa"* (§ 1) unless it appears otherwise: «*Posita externa violatione, imputabilitas præsumitur, nisi aliud appareat.*» By the term *dolus*, is meant the deliberate will to violate the law, as is defined in the 1917 Code: *"deliberata voluntas violandi legem"* (Can 2200); and the same canon, states that *dolus* is presumed until the contrary is proven: *"Posita externa legis violatione, dolus in foro externo præsumitur, donec contrarium probetur."* The Salamanca commentary explains on page 787, that there are two elements which constitute *dolus*: 1) *on the part of the understanding* the knowledge of the law is required, and the obligation it imposes; and 2) *on the part of the will*, the positive intention to commit an act that is known to be opposed to the law, or to the rights which the law protects. For this it suffices that the said intention has for its direct object the commission or omission of an act that is either prohibited or mandated by the law; so that it is not necessary that there be the formal intention of breaking the law as such.[390] The 1983 Code

---

[389] «1° *Violación externa*: El acto debe ser externo o sensible, de tal manera que pueda percibirse por los sentidos, si alguno estuviera presente cuando se realiza. La violación *meramente interna* de la ley jamás es delito, porque con ella no puede perturbarse el orden jurídicosocial de la Iglesia. No debe confundirse la violación *externa* con la violación *publica* de la ley. Puede haber delito, aunque el hecho delictivo se realice ocultíssimamente sin que nadie lo presencie y aun sin que haya posibilidad de que nadie llegue a tener conocimiento de él.» Miguelez – Alonso – Cabreros *Op. cit.* p. 783.

[390] «**2200** — Dos elementos integran el dolo en materia criminal: 1) *por parte del entendimiento,* se requiere conoscimiento de la ley y de la obligación que ésta impone y conciencia de que el acto que se va a realizar es lesivo de los bienes o derechos que por la ley están protegidos; 2) *por parte de la voluntad*, intención positiva de realizar un acto que se sabe es opuesto a la ley, o sea a los derechos que la ley protege. No es, por consiguiente, requisito indispensable del dolo que la intención del agente vaya directamente dirigida al quebrantamiento de la ley *formalmente* considerada, como tal; Basta que dicha intención tenga por objeto directo la realización u omisión de un acto que está proibido o mandado por la

states explicitly that the moral imputaility resulting from culpability *or* dolus is presumed; so if an ecclesiastical officeholder of any rank whatsoever were to publicly commit an external act of manifest heresy, in which not only the *matter* of the sin is explicitly expressed, but the pertinacity is manifestly evident, then defection from the faith into heresy and its consequent loss of office *ipso jure* would be presumed according to the law. Imputability is presumed, because, «The vicious act, therefore, presupposes a guilty mind (*mens rea*) [English lawyers for nearly 800 years have been familiar with the maxim: "*Actus non facit reum nisi mens sit rea,*" the origin of which is attributed to St. Augustine; see: Kenny-Webb, *Outlines of Criminal Law*, 1907, p. 33.] Why? A transgression of the law is an act, and the transgressor, therefore, is an agent, and when that agent is intelligent and free, and acts as such, we say that the effects caused by such an agent are to be imputed or credited to him. Because an intelligent being has dominion over its actions, it is capable of moral proprietorship in the praise or blame justly due to its deliberate acts, according as they are seen to be good or bad. [W. Hill, S.J., *Ethics*, 8th ed., p. 47.] In this feature crime shares the notion of sin, for every crime is a sin, though not conversely.»[391]

Salza & Siscoe again manifest their profound confusion on the distinction between internal and external sin in a passage on their website:

> «Not wishing to be pinned down, he [Fr. Anthony Cekada] carefully avoids defining his concocted terminology, but it is clear that by the "public sin" of heresy, he essentially means the internal sin of heresy that the person manifests to many by his external actions (but actions that are not public heresy, as such, as we will explain later). These external actions are what lead others to conclude that he is guilty of the sin of heresy, which, Cekada claims, places the perpetrator outside the Church.»

These two ignorant dilettantes have obviously never properly studied Fundamental Moral Theology. I studied Philosophy and Theology at the Angelicum in Rome under the old Dominican Thomist professors in the 70s, and I have 14 well read volumes of Moral Theology in my personal

---

ley. Tampoco se requiere, para que haya dolo, conociemiento de la pena o del carácter penal de la ley que we quebranta; pero la ignorancia de esto disminuye la imputabilitad del delito y excusa de ciertas penas.» Miguelez – Alonso – Cabreros; *Op. cit.* p. 787.

[391] The Rev. P, Chas. Augustine, O.S.B., D.D.; *Op. cit.*, Volume VIII, p. 11.

library. Salza & Siscoe fail to understand the basic distinction between an internal sin and an external sin. An internal sin is a sin of thought or an act that is not perceptible to the senses, as opposed to an external sin which is a sin of words or deeds – an act perceptible to the senses. An external sin is occult if the sin is not known by anyone, or only by very few individuals. An external sin is public if was done in public, and is sufficiently widely known or soon will be, so that it is considered to be a public sin.

It is the matter and not the form which determines whether a sin is internal or external; and it is the form or lack thereof, and not the matter which determines whether the sin is pertinacious, merely culpable but not pertinacious, or inculpable (i.e. material sin). St. Alphonsus explains the difference between *material* sin and *formal* sin, distinguishing between the **matter**, which is the *action that transgresses the moral law*; and the **form**, which consists in the intention to violate the law. The holy Doctor explains that material sin is the action which would be the matter of sin if the transgressor had knowledge of the law: «*il peccato materiale non è altro, che un'azione che sarebbe materia di peccato, se vi fosse la cognizione della legge, ma essendo la legge invincibilmente ignota (poichè nel contrasto di due probabili non è nota la legge, ma solamente il dubbio della legge), pertanto la trasgressione non è colpevole.*»[392] Thus the *form* of the sin is to the moral law more or less equivalent to what *dolus* is in ecclesiastical law; consequently, there is an intimate connection between *culpa* and *dolus* in the determination of what constitutes *moral imputability* of a crime in canon law. The error of material heresy can be inculpable; or culpable and vincible, but without pertinacity: "*Et quia illa ignorantia, vel error potest esse, aut inculpabilis, aut culpabilis & vincibilis, eaque vel levis, vel lata, crassa, supina, vel denique etiam affectata, & directe voluntaria, ideo triplicis gradus distingui possunt hæretici materiales.*"[393] The error of formal heresy is culpable and pertinacious; the error of material heresy is not pertinacious, but in both cases, it is the matter alone that determines whether the sin is internal or external.

So, when Salza says that Fr. Cekada, "avoids defining his concocted terminology, but it is clear that by the 'public sin' of heresy, he essentially means the internal sin of heresy that the person manifests to many by his external actions"; Salza is saying that a public sin is only an internal sin manifested by external actions. He adamantly refuses to admit the

---

[392] Alfonso Maria de Liguori; *Opere Morali*, volume decimosesto, Torino 1829, pp. 66-7.
[393] Patritius Sporer, *Theologia Moralis Super Decalogum*, Salzburg, 1722, p. 175.

distinction between one who sins internally commits an internal sin of thought, and that one who sins externally commits an *external sin* of word or deed. The motive of Salza & Siscoe for formulating this unorthodox doctrinal aberration is transparently obvious: By professing the error that "sin is internal", they justify their error of distinguishing *sin*, which they define as an internal act; from *crime*, which they define as any external violation of divine law. On the basis of this bogus distinction, Salza & Siscoe can then claim that even the gravest sin, *committed in public*, if it is not a *notorious crime*, pertains to the *internal forum*, and not to the *external forum*. Thus, according to this errant doctrine which opposes the constant teaching of the Church, it is only when the ecclesiastical authority *determines the crime* by means of a *public judgment* in the external forum, that the "externalized sin" of heresy has been determined to be a *crime of heresy*, and that the juridical bond has been severed; and that the one hitherto privately judged to be a manifest heretic has been juridically severed from membership in the Church by means of a public judgment; and as a consequence thereof, it can be argued that the heretic has fallen from office.

Fr. Cekada employs in this cited instance, the accepted usage of theological terms; so it is ironic, and even comical in a pathetic way, that Salza accuses Fr. Cekada of manufacturing "concocted terminology".

A public sin is crime if it falls within the parameters set forth in Canon 2195 § 1 of the 1917 Code; and is *notorious by fact* if the act and its moral imputability are publicly known according to the prescription of Canon 2197. 3°; and it is public, if, according to the prescription of Canon 2197. 1°, it is publicly known or can be prudently judged that it will soon be publicly known. The law presumes that the transgressor knowingly and wilfully transgresses the law; and therefore in the case of heresy, it is presumed that he is sufficiently informed that his error is contrary to the dogma of faith, and therefore, unless there is evidence to the contrary, the notoriety or publicity of the fact of the crime by itself suffices; for a private individuals to judge as a matter of conscience, by way of personal judgment, without any pretense to usurp ecclesiastical jurisdiction or to judge with force of law; that the heretic in question is guilty of the crime of manifest heresy; even before any official pronouncement is made by competent ecclesiastical authority. If the moral imputability of public heresy is manifest, the law presumes loss of office, which therefore suffices for a private individuals to judge as a matter of conscience that the defector has forfeited his office. Only the juridically competent authority has the jurisdiction to declare the loss of office with force of law; which in the case of one who is presumably pope, would first and foremost be the college of cardinals, since they have the jurisdiction to pronounce on a vacancy of the Roman see. Otherwise, a general council, or even a Roman synod would be competent to make the judgment (as Ballerini explains). The moral imputability of heresy must be manifest for tacit resignation to take place; so if there exists positive doubt about the moral imputability of the transgression; then the pope would have to be corrected before a judgement could be made that the papal see is truly vacant; since by the public crime of manifest heresy, the heretic does indeed pronounce judgment on himself by leaving the Church, as Bellarmine, Ballerini, and Gregory XVI explain. And since it is taught unanimously by the Fathers, (as Bellarmine demonstrates in *lib. ii cap. xxx* of *De Romano Pontifice*), and is therefore a teaching of the universal and ordinary magisterium; and it is taught in scripture, (as Ballerini demonstrates in the above cited passage), it is a revealed truth that must be believed with divine and Catholic faith, that a manifest heretic leaves the Church by himself if he shows himself obstinate in adhering to a doctrine contrary to a revealed dogma of the Catholic faith. When Salza & Siscoe quote St. Thomas against private individuals making judgment, they err, not grasping from the plainly worded text that St. Thomas is not treating on the question of private judgment of conscience, but of private individuals usurping the public judicial function. Thus they crudely misinterpreted the moral teaching of St Thomas.

If the heresy and its pertinacity are manifest or at least apparent without evidence to the contrary, then private individuals have the right to prudently judge privately and state their private opinions in a prudent manner even in public; but as private individuals they may not presume to judge in any official capacity. It is because the loss of office takes place *ex natura hæresis*, according to divine law, and therefore takes place independently of any ecclesiastical law or act of jurisdiction, that the individual has the right in conscience to form an opinion even before a judgment is pronounced by Church authority. As Christopher Ferrara explains in *Fatima Perspectives*, "It is an axiom of our religion that no person on earth can judge the Pope in the sense of a penal sentence with juridical effect."[394] Since ecclesiastical law recognizes the *ipso facto* loss of office to take place *ipso jure*, it pertains strictly to ecclesiastical jurisdiction for a judgment to be pronounced with juridical effect.

---

[394] http://archive.fatima.org/perspectives/fe/perspective1068.asp

Salza & Siscoe are totally in error on all the points I have elaborated in this chapter. Their main problem is that they have attempted to teach Catholic theology without first having learned it properly by means of a disciplined academic formation. If my memory doesn't betray me, I believe it was Herbert Thurston S.J. who said of the Modernist, George Tyrell, that he needed to have first learned doctrine before attempting to teach it. Salza and Siscoe err in the same manner. There are many more grave errors in their various presentations that will be dealt with in later in this work. Salza & Siscoe have reacted to an earlier draft of this chapter in a manner that reveals their total spiritual blindness — what St. Thomas calls *insipientia*. When I sent a copy of the first revision to them, this is the pathetic response I received from Salza in a copy of his message to his partner in iniquity: "Robert, I am laughing out loud right now, at how easy it will be to refute this desperate novus ordo priest's attempt at theology, classic petitio principii, which we have already refuted. Lets have some fun with this." To this gesture of abject clownery, what more need be said, but the most apt reply which is expressed in the words from Act One of Leoncavallo's *Pagliacci* – "Ridi, pagliaccio, e ognun applaudirá!"[395] Whenever Salza is totally stumped, he clumsily constructs a bogus case of *petitio principii* which he builds on the foundation of his own distorted caricature of his adversary's argument. Like a mindless talking bird, Salza replies with those two words in order to deflect attention away from the fact that his argument has been demolished. Anyone with a sane mind can grasp easily enough that there is no "question begging" in the arguments I have presented. Salza certainly knows that too, but his desperate hope is to get his readers to believe his lie. As they say in baseball, he has thrown that pitch too many times. Like Salza, Siscoe also manifests a total disregard for truth, even divine truth. They both subscribe to the same creed: "No Salvation Outside of My Opinion". It was Siscoe who wrote, "for the sin [of heresy] to be judged, it must be public; and needless to say the judgment of the public sin must proceed from the proper authorities, not from the individual Catholic in the pew". He does not believe in his own doctrine. This was his reply to me on 14 October 2016, not long after I sent him an earlier draft of this chapter: "Due to your heretical ecclesiology, you are now a sworn enemy of the Church, and that is how you will be treated." In his hypocrisy, he has repeatedly accused me of openly leaving the Church for professing propositions that he as a private

---

[395] "Laugh, clown, and everyone will clap!"

layman believes are heretical, but which the Church has never condemned, and which many approved authors have professed; yet, he is the one who insists that one cannot judge another to be a heretic simply for having uttered propositions privately judged to be heretical.[396] Siscoe's explicit words in that same message: "**WE** recognize you as being outside of the Church due to your public sin of heresy, even though the Church has not yet declared you to be a heretic" — the key word being, **«WE»**. Thus, the calumnious condemnatory judgment against me stated in Siscoe's message was expressly the opinion of both Siscoe and Salza. Thus spoke the self-appointed lay vigilante inquisitors who, for all other cases, say the Church must judge, and not the individual Catholic. An ample sampling of the arrogantly pronounced anathemas pronounced by the self-appointed lay inquisitors against me appears at the end of the *Appendix to Part V*.

---

[396] Salza & Siscoe were compelled to be less vitriolic in expressing their public condemnations posted on their website, due to the glaring self-contradiction that the more explicit expression of their judgments against me would create; since it remains their stated opinion that only the Church can judge in cases of heresy, except (of course) for heresy that Salza & Siscoe judge to be "public and notorious" – and that means any publicly expressed opinion that conflicts with their own bizarre dogmatic beliefs. Nevertheless, their less explicit but still clearly expressed judgments of heresy against me remain posted on their website.

SECTION TWO

HERETICS

In addressing the question of the possibility of a heretical pope, and if such a thing is possible, whether or not a heretic pope could be deposed or judged by the Church, one must first distinguish the various senses in which the term "heretic" has been employed by ecclesiastical writers and understood by the Church. Giuseppe de Luca[397] explains that the term «heresy» (αἵρεσις) which denotes a choice, selection, election, or a preference for one position rather than another, was a term used in classical Greek; and in Alexandrian Greek it began to be typically applied to philosophical, political, and religious doctrines. In Josephus Flavius, it already acquired the meaning of "sect", although without any connotation of condemnation or disapproval. In the New Testament, the word αἵρεσις occurs nine times, and the word αἱρετικός, once, and the connotation in which it is used is always one of condemnation and reproach. In 1 Cor. 11:19, there already appears to be a clear distinction between heresy and schism, and throughout the New Testament, its signification is one of heinously grievous culpability. In Acts 24:14, St. Paul rejects the Jewish attribution of the term to the nascent Christianity of the Church.

St. Irenæus gave the term a more widespread usage due to his work, *Adversus Hæreses*, in which he referred to the Catholic doctrine as "orthodox", and the Gnostic beliefs (Valentinians, Marcosians, etc.) as "heresy". The term gained more precision during the period of the Apostolic Fathers, and was properly defined by Tertullian in Chapter VI of *De Præscriptione*, in which he explains the Greek origin of the term, and contrasts the self-condemnation of the heretic by his willful choice of doctrines in opposition to the teaching of the Apostles, which was not the result of their choice or preference, but was received from Christ and faithfully transmitted to the nations; and therefore, if an angel from heaven should preach a different Gospel, he would be anathematized. (*hæreses dictæ græca uoce ex interpretatione electionis qua quis maxime siue ad instituendas siue ad suscipiendas eas utitur. [3] Ideo et sibi damnatum dixit hæreticum quia et in quo damnatur sibi elegit. Nobis uero nihil ex nostro arbitrio inducere licet sed nec eligere quod aliquis de arbitrio suo induxerit. [4] Apostolos*

---

[397] *Enciclopedia Italiana* 1932.

Domini habemus auctores qui nec ipsi quicquam ex suo arbitrio quod inducerent, elegerunt, sed acceptam a Christo disciplinam fideliter nationibus adsignauerunt. [5] Itaque etiamsi angelus de cœlis aliter euangelizaret, anathema diceretur a nobis.)

I have explained in the previous section the Catholic teaching on heresy, and present here what is the most common definition of heresy, given by Albert Michel in the *Dictionnarire de théologie catholique*[398], where it is said of heresy that, "It is a doctrine that immediately, directly, and contradictorily opposes the truths revealed by God and authentically set forth as such by the Church." In his above cited article, de Luca sums up the distinctions commonly made by theologians in their works, between the "internal" and "external" heretic, the former keeps the heresy within himself, the latter manifests it to others; the external heretic is "occult" (secret) who manifests the heresy to only a few (or even to no one, but commits external acts of heresy), and "public" if the heresy is manifested to a sufficient number of persons. There is also the distinction between "formal heretic" and "material heretic"; material when one denies or doubts an article of faith without being aware of denying or doubting an article of faith, or does it without obstinacy or full consent of the will; formal when it is done with full knowledge and deliberation. De Luca, in 1932, rightly mentions that the distinction between formal and material heretics is of the maximum importance, and gave the common understanding of them. Quoting a 21st Century author, Wikipedia also defines these terms according to what is the common understanding of these terms today:

> «In traditional Catholic theology, the term material heresy refers to an opinion that is objectively contradictory to the teachings of the Church, and as such heretical, but which is uttered by a person without the subjective knowledge of its being so. A person who holds a material heresy may therefore not be a "heretic" in the strict sense. Material heresy is distinguished from "formal heresy", i.e. a heretical opinion proposed deliberately by a person who is aware of its being against the doctrine of the Church.»[399]

I have given particular emphasis to express what is even today the commonly understood distinctions between the terms "formal heretic" and "material heretic"; as well as "internal" and "external" heresy,

---

[398] *Dictionnarire de théologie catholique*, VI, ii.

[399] Oderberg, David S. (2011). "Heresies". In Kurian, George T. *The Encyclopedia of Christian Civilization*. 1. Malden: Wiley-Blackwell. p. 1119.

because the common understanding of the terms is firmly rooted in Catholic traditional usage. John Salza and Robert Siscoe have deviated from the signification of these terms as they have traditionally been understood for centuries in Catholic theology, (calling the traditional scholastic usage of the term 'material heretic' "perverted"), and have made use of the relatively recent and novel definition of "material heretic"; as well as inventing their own deviant and totally erroneous distinction between external and internal heresy, in order to more persuasively argue their own heretical doctrines. Most notably, as I pointed out in the previous section of this work, Salza & Siscoe have used their deviant understanding of the "sin of heresy", to make it appear that the external sin of heresy pertains to the internal forum as an "externalized internal sin", which (according to their convoluted heretical reasoning) by itself, *suapte natura*, does not separate the heretic from the body of the Church, but only does so after judgment has been pronounced on the "crime of heresy" by Church authority. It is the matter and not the form of the sin which determines whether heresy is an internal or external; and it is the form or lack thereof, and not the matter which determines whether the sin is pertinacious, merely culpable but not pertinacious, or inculpable (i.e. material sin). Salza & Siscoe have totally distorted the Catholic doctrine on heresy by speaking of "the internal sin of heresy that the person manifests to many by his external actions (but actions that are not public heresy, as such [...]). These external actions are what lead others to conclude that he is guilty of the sin of heresy." The error of formal heresy is culpable and pertinacious; the error of material heresy is not pertinacious, but in both cases, it is the matter alone that determines whether the sin is internal or external. **It is not the form that determines whether a sin is internal or external.** Such a totally muddled notion of internal and external sin of heresy as expounded by John Salza and Robert Siscoe is worthy of the Dictionary of Voodoo Theology, but Salza and Siscoe attempt to convince their readers that their heretically errant theological deviations are faithful to the magisterium of the Church.

So, having given what is the common understanding of heresy and the distinctions related to it, I will proceed to demonstrate that these terms as they are commonly understood, faithfully represent the doctrine of St. Thomas Aquinas, St. Alphonsus de Liguori, and the theologians who have followed their teaching for centuries. Only then will it be precisely understood what is meant by the terms, "manifest heretic" and "heretical" or "heretic pope".

Salza, ignorantly challenging me on the definition of the term, "material heretic" wrote to me on 12 July 2014: «An ignorant Catholic is not a heretic (formal or material) because he possesses divine faith and is invincibly ignorant of his heresy through no fault of his own. A material heretic is also invincibly ignorant of his heresy, but does not possess divine faith *(sic)*, thus rendering him a material heretic.» Trying to express their doctrine with at least some semblance of theological coherence, Salza and Siscoe resort to the weakest of arguments, the argument from authority – not the magisterial authority of the Church, which is the strongest argument in theology, but the private authority of an "expert witness", writing on their website:

> What we see is that Fr. Kramer understands the term "material heretic" to refer to Catholics – "faithful sons of the Church" – who err materially in good faith. He says that such persons are only material heretic (sic) since they do not "prefer their own judgment to the teaching of the Church." But is this the correct use of the term "material heretic," or has Fr. Kramer "entirely perverted" the "legitimate use of the expression"? We will allow Cardinal Billot to answer this question for us.

In the following citation, we will see that, according to one of the greatest Thomists of the 20th Century, a material heretic is not a Catholic who errs in good faith, but rather a non-Catholic – that is, one who has chosen something other than the Church's Magisterium as his rule of faith (e.g., the "bible alone", a local Protestant minister, etc.).

Here is Cardinal Billot's definition of a material heretic and a formal heretic:

> Cardinal Louis Billot S.J., De Ecclesia Christi: "Heretics are divided into formal and material. Formal heretics are those to whom the authority of the Church is sufficiently known; while material heretics are those who, being in invincible ignorance of the Church herself, in good faith choose some other guiding rule. So the heresy of material heretics is not imputable as sin and indeed it is not necessarily incompatible with that supernatural faith which is the beginning and root of all justification. For they may explicitly believe the principal articles, and believe the others, though not explicitly, yet implicitly, through their disposition of mind and good will to adhere to whatever is sufficiently proposed to them as having been revealed by God. In fact they can still belong to the body of the Church by desire and fulfill the other conditions necessary for salvation. Nonetheless, as to their [i.e., the material heretics] actual incorporation in the visible Church of Christ, which is our present subject, our thesis makes no distinction between formal

and material heretics [in other words, neither material or formal heretics are members of the visible Church], understanding everything in accordance with the notion of material heresy just given, which indeed is the only true and genuine one. For, if you understand by the expression material heretic one who, while professing subjection to the Church's Magisterium in matters of faith [i.e. a professing Catholic], nevertheless still denies something defined by the Church because he did not know it was defined, or, by the same token, holds an opinion opposed to Catholic doctrine because he falsely thinks that the Church teaches it, it would be quite absurd to place material heretics outside the body of the true Church; but on this understanding the legitimate use of the expression would be entirely perverted. For a material sin is said to exist only when what belongs to the nature of the sin takes place materially, but without advertence or deliberate will. But the nature of heresy consists in withdrawal from the rule of the ecclesiastical Magisterium and this does not take place in the case, since this is a simple error of fact concerning what the rule dictates. And therefore there is no scope for heresy, even materially" (Cardinal Louis Billot S.J., De Ecclesia Christi).

Firstly, Cardinal Billot errs when he imprecisely defines and restricts the term "material heretics" to "those who, being in invincible ignorance of the Church herself, in good faith choose some other guiding rule." St. Pius V teaches in the earlier quoted passage of the Roman Catechism that those who are ignorant of the Church herself and have never taken part in the sacramental life of the Church are the *infidels*, and are distinguished from *heretics*, who have *left the Church*.[400] By extension, those who belong to *sects* that were founded by heretics who rejected and left the Church are also reckoned among heretics, because they also reject the Church. Accordingly, St. Pius X explains, in his *Catechismo Maggiore* (quoted below), that heretics are the baptized who pertinaciously refuse to believe any truth revealed by God and taught by the Church as *de fide*, such as "the Arians, the Nestorians, and the various sects of Protestants". In the previous section I quoted the passages of St. Jerome and St. Augustine who likewise taught that heretics are those who have

---

[400] «Ex quo fit ut tria tantummodo hominum genera ab ea excludantur: primo infideles, deinde haeretici et schismatici, postremo excommunicati. *Ethnici quidem, quod in Ecclesia numquam fuerunt,* **neque eam umquam cognoverunt**, *nec ullius sacramenti participes in populi christiani societate facti sunt.* **Haeretici** *vero atque* **schismatici**, quia **ab Ecclesia desciverunt**, neque enim illi magis ad Ecclesiam spectant quam transfugae ad exercitum pertineant a quo **defecerunt**.»

left the Church. Those who have inculpably left the Church or the baptized who consciously reject her teaching even inculpably are still to be classified as heretics, because they are all heretics who consciously reject the Church's magisterium as the rule of faith, even if they are invincibly ignorant of the fact that in so doing, they are rejecting divinely revealed truths. Hence, even if they err innocently, there is still in them what Billot says is the nature of heresy, namely, "the nature of heresy consists in withdrawal from the rule of the ecclesiastical Magisterium". Secondly, Billot, in this passage cited by Salza & Siscoe, errs on the nature of heresy by confusing what is common to apostasy and heresy, with the specific nature of heresy. It is not specifically that, "the nature of heresy consists in with the withdrawal from the rule of the ecclesiastical Magisterium" (which pertains properly to the form of the sin and not the species), as Billot asserts, but heresy specifically consists in the obstinate denial or doubt of some article of faith. However, since the *obstinate* denial or doubt of even a single article of faith can only be accomplished by one who is conscious that his opinion opposes the authority of the ecclesiastical magisterium, one who does so withdraws in principle from the rule of the magisterium and effectively rejects the authority of the Church as the rule of faith. Hence, the withdrawal from the rule of the magisterium pertains properly to the *pertinacity*, which is the *form* of heresy, but it is not the specific nature of the sin as a whole, which is defined according to its form and matter as a composite. The *matter* of heresy is an error against faith. **Therefore, a *material heretic* is properly defined as *one who professes an error against faith without the form of the sin*,** which consists in the withdrawal from the rule of the magisterium by a wilful and conscious preference of one's own opinion to an article of faith proposed by the magisterium of the Church. In *formal* heresy, there is the *withdrawal from the authority of the ecclesiastical magisterium*, even in one who claims to be Catholic but rejects even one article of faith. In material heresy, there is the denial of an article of faith committed without the withdrawal from the magisterial authority of the Church. Hence, those who being invincibly ignorant that the Catholic Church is the true Church, and who would even inculpably but knowingly reject or *withdraw from the teaching authority of the Catholic Church* and "choose some other guiding rule", fall outside of what are properly the defining parameters of the term "material heretics", (who are not properly heretics because they do *not* withdraw from the rule of the magisterium), and therefore are properly designated simply as "heretics". In his above cited Manual, Fr. Bordoni explains that those who were baptized as infants but were never instructed in the rudiments of the faith; and were brought up in pagan territories; or those of heretics, where there are no Catholics; and where Catholicism is neither practiced nor preached, are material heretics, and are excused from the crime of heresy;[401] *and also included in the genus of material heretics are those Catholics who are ignorant of some things pertaining to faith*, such as one who invincibly believes the Father to be greater than the Son, because it is so among humans; or that the Trinity is a female (human), because Trinity is a feminine sounding word.[402] Hence, as Abbé F.X. de Feller[403] states, material heretics are faithful sons of the Church: "Gli eretici materiali sono figliuoli della chiesa."[404]

Following the doctrine of St. Thomas, St. Alphonsus states the definition of heresy: «*Hæresis est* **error intellectus, et pertinax contra Fidem, in eo qui Fidem suscepit**» Thus, the nature of heresy is **1) the pertinacious error of the intellect against faith, 2) in one *who has***

---

[401] «Haereticus materialis dicitur ille, qui licet baptizatus ab infantia, quia tamen a nullo fuit unquam instructus in rudimentis Fidei; ut quia nutritus fuit in terries Paganorum, vel Haereticorum, cum quibus non sunt mixti catholici, apud quos nec Catholica Fides colitur, nec praedicatur Evangelium, nec docentur rudimenta Fidei, excusatur a crimine Haeresis, si non credit, quia in eo fides infusa nihil operator ad hoc, nisi per instructionem...»

[402] «Sub hoc genere Hæretici materialis comprehendi potest ignorans quaedam ad Fidem pertinentia non solum indirecte, sed etiam directe, ut si quis invincibiliter credat Patrem esse maiorem Filio, quia in humanis res ita se habet; ut si quis rudis credat Trinitatem esse fœminam, quia profertur sono fœmineo...», p. 34.

[403] **François-Xavier de Feller S.J.** – (1735 – 1802) He was born at Brussels. In 1752 he entered a school of the Jesuits at Reims, where he manifested a great aptitude for mathematics and physical science. In 1764 he was appointed to the professorship of theology at Tyrnau in Hungary, but in 1771 he returned to Belgium and continued to discharge his professorial duties at Liege till the suppression of the Jesuit Order in 1773. Among his works are *Catéchisme philosophique*; *Cours de morale chrétienne et de littérature religieuse* (Paris, 1826); and his principal work *Dictionnaire historique et littéraire* (published in 1781 at Liege in volumes, and afterwards several times reprinted and continued down to 1848). – c. f. *Wikipedia*.

[404] *Catechismo filosofico (Catéchisme philosophique), o raccolta d'osservazioni atte a difendere la religione cristiana contro de' suoi nemici. Opera del sig. abate F. X. De Feller tradotta dal francese secondo la terza edizione di Liegi corretta, e notabilmente accresciuta, num. 414*; Tomo III, Milano, 1828, p. 203.

received the faith. St. Alphonsus distinguishes between the **matter** and the **form** of heresy:

> «Hæresis est error intellectus, et pertinax contra Fidem, in eo qui Fidem suscepit. ... Unde patet, ad Hæresim, ut et Apostasiam, duo requiri, 1. **Judicium erroneum, quod est ejus quasi materiale.** 2. **Pertinaciam; quæ est quasi formale**. Porro pertinaciter errare non est hic acriter, et mordicus suum errorem tueri; sed est eum retinere, postquam contrarium est sufficienter propositum: sive quando scit contrarium teneri a reliqua universali Christi in terris Ecclesia, cui suum iudicium præferat»[405].

Thus, the **matter** of the sin is the **erroneous judgment**; and the form is the **pertinacity,** *by which one withdraws from the rule of the ecclesiastical magisterium even in rejecting a single article of faith*. The *pertinacity* of heresy is the *form*, which consists in the retaining of the matter of heresy (i.e. the error against faith) even after one has been sufficiently informed that the error transgresses against the faith of the Church. Since material sin, as St. Alphonsus explains, is the action which would be the matter of sin if the transgressor had knowledge of the law; one who understands that his error is opposed to the *lex credendi* of the Church consciously rejects the material object of faith which consists in articles of faith taught by the authority of the Church; and is accordingly judged to be a formal heretic for the very fact that he is sufficiently aware that his error offends against the faith of the Catholic Church, and thus withdraws from the rule of the ecclesiastical magisterium. Material heresy, therefore, properly considered in its nature, is *per se* an act of the species of heresy which lacks the *formal element* of the *sin, by which one withdraws from the rule of the magisterium* — an act committed without sufficient knowledge that the error offends against an article of faith taught by the Church. Thus, *withdrawal from the rule of the magisterium* pertains essentially to *formal* heresy; but not to *material* heresy, in which the withdrawal from the rule of the magisterium is absent. However, being wilfully outside or separated from the Church even inculpably, does not pertain to the notion of material heresy, (since material heresy is defined as the professing of *error against the faith by one who has received the faith* of the Catholic Church, but is unaware that his error opposes the teaching and magisterial authority of the Church); but those who even inculpably but consciously choose some other rule of faith are **schismatics**, who wilfully separate themselves from the Church by

---

[405] St. Alphonsus M. De Liguori, *Lib. II. Tract. I. De præcepto Fidei. Dubium III.*

consciously withdrawing from the rule of the ecclesiastical magisterium. Accordingly therefore, the term *material heretic* strictly considered, is not logically applicable to members of Protestant or other sects (or to non-denominational and non-affiliated individuals) who innocently but wilfully remain schismatically outside or separate themselves from the Catholic Church. The notion, therefore, of *material heretic* logically and properly denotes one of her own who is ignorant of her teaching; but is commonly extended *secundum quid* to one who has faith, but is invincibly ignorant of the Church or her teaching, and is *per accidens* visibly outside the Church. However, none of those among the baptized who have reached the age of judgment and belong to a heretical sect because they deny some article of faith which they know the Catholic Church teaches, and for which reason they choose some other creed or rule of faith, are, according to to the proper signification of the term, "material heretics", but are simply referred to as "heretics"; because they have the form of heresy in virtue of their knowingly rejecting articles of the Catholic faith and the magisterial authority of the Church. Accordingly, in Canon Law and Catholic doctrine, they are rightly understood to be outside of the Catholic faith, and presumed to be guilty of heresy unless there is evidence that suggests otherwise; although some of them in invincible ignorance might have divine faith, and thus belong to the soul of the Church.

The opinion that there are to be generally found among members of non-Catholic sects, invincibly ignorant adult material heretics, who retain the virtue of faith; and who consciously reject the teaching authority of the Church, while remaining in a permanent state of invincible ignorance of the Church's teaching, seems scarcely believable, smacks of heresy; and is refuted by St. Alphonsus de Liguori, who explains that, "unbelievers who arrive at the use of reason, and are not converted to the Faith, cannot be excused, because though they do not receive sufficient proximate grace, still they are not deprived of remote grace, as a means of becoming converted."[406] Thus, Bishop George Hay expounds on those who say invincible ignorance will save a man,

---

[406] "11. Si risponde pertanto ai Semipelagiani che gl'infedeli i quali giunti all'uso di ragione non si convertono alla fede non sono degni di scusa; perché, quantunque non ricevano la grazia sufficiente prossima, almeno non sono destituiti della grazia rimota e mediata per convertirsi alla fede. E qual è questa grazia rimota? È quella che insegna il dottore Angelico1, il quale scrive: Si quis nutritus in silvis, vel inter bruta animalia ductum rationis naturalis sequeretur in

«will bring him to salvation;" saying, "[T]hey suppose that a man may be a member of the true Church in the sight of God, though not born with her in communion, as all baptised children are, though born in heresy, at least till they come to the age of judging for themselves. Their mistake here lies in not reflecting that all adults who are in a false religion, can be members of the Church in the sight of God, in no other sense than those were of whom our Saviour says, "Other sheep I have who are not of this fold." But as he expressly declares, that it was necessary to bring even those to the communion of the Church; this evidently shows that they and all such are not members of the Church in such a way as that they can be saved in their present state without being joined in her communion.»[407]

Of those who deny some article of faith, but who profess themselves to be Catholics and members of the Catholic Church, St. Thomas makes the distinction between such persons, some of whom, who might be called heretics either because they err solely from ignorance, who are therefore not excommunicated; and others who, because erring through obstinacy and trying to subvert others, then fall under the excommunication *latæ sententiæ*:

«Sed numquid ex hoc sunt excommunicati omnes hæretici? Videtur quod non, quia dicitur Tit. III, 10: *hæreticum hominem post primam et secundam correctionem devita*, et cetera. Respondeo. Dicendum est, quod hæreticus potest dici aliquis, vel quia simpliciter errat ex ignorantia, et ex hoc non est excommunicatus; vel quia errat ex pertinacia et alios nititur pervertere, et tunc incurrit in canonem latæ sententiæ.»[408]

---

appetitu boni et fuga mali, certissime est credendum quod ei Deus vel per internam inspirationem revelaret ea, quae sunt ad credendum necessaria; vel aliquem fidei praedicatorem ad eum dirigeret, sicut misit Petrum ad Cornelium. Sicché secondo s. Tommaso agl'infedeli che son giunti all'uso di ragione almeno vien data da Dio la grazia rimotamente sufficiente per salvarsi; la quale grazia consiste in una certa istruzione della mente ed in una mozion della volontà ad osservar la legge naturale; alla quale mozione se coopera l'infedele, osservando i precetti della natura, con astenersi dai peccati gravi, riceverà appresso certamente per i meriti di Gesù Cristo la grazia prossimamente sufficiente ad abbracciar la fede ed a salvarsi." (Sant'Alfonso Maria de Liguori, *Storia delle Eresie*; I edizione – Maggio 2003, p. 313.)

[407] Bishop George Hay; *The Sincere Christian Instructed in the Faith of Christ*; Dublin, 1822, p. 341-2.

[408] *Commentarium Sancti Thomæ Aq. super ep. S. Pauli ad Galatas*, cap. I, lect. ii.

Since St. Thomas speaks in this passage of canonical warnings and the ecclesiastical censure of excommunication, he is clearly not speaking of persons who are members of some non-Catholic sect, or of persons who have never known the Church, but distinguishes here between Catholics who become formal heretics, and incur the excommunication; and those Catholics whom he calls "heretics", but who err against the faith in ignorance as merely material heretics: "It is to be said that one can be called a heretic because he simply errs out of ignorance, and therefore is not excommunicated." Such an ignorant Catholic, who errs out of ignorance, and who therefore does not incur the excommunication, is called a "heretic", but not properly in the sense of a 'formal heretic', who "errs out of pertinacity and tries to pervert others", and therefore is not properly a heretic, but is called a 'material heretic' in traditional Catholic usage. From this passage of the Angelic Doctor alone, one sees how far Cardinal Billot drifted away from the doctrine of St. Thomas and St. Alphonsus on heresy.

Salza & Siscoe are quite unaware of the fact that it is precisely because the material heretic retains the formal cause of faith and professes in principle the material object of faith, that he still has the *Catholic* faith, and is not one who is ignorant of the Church. The material heretic believes in revelation on divine authority, and; because he does not knowingly reject the material object of faith proposed by the Church, he does not reject the formal cause of faith – "*supernaturalis enim virtus fidei causam formalem habet, Dei revelantis auctoritatem*" (Pius XI – *Mortalium Animos*).

The material heretic believes in the authority of the Church, accepts the authority of the revealing God, professes the Creed, and thus does not reject the formal object of faith, but, errs ignorantly on some *matter* of faith, being unaware that his opinion *materially* opposes some truth of revelation. Such a one still adheres to the formal object of faith; but it is the formal heretic who rejects the doctrine of the Church as an infallible and divine rule: "*Formale autem obiectum fidei est veritas prima secundum quod manifestatur in Scripturis sacris et doctrinæ Ecclesiæ. Unde quicumque non inhæret, sicut infallibili et divinæ regulæ, doctrinæ Ecclesiæ, quæ procedit ex veritate prima in Scripturis sacris manifestata, ille non habet habitum fidei, sed ea quæ sunt fidei alio modo tenet quam per fidem.*"[409] The one who is properly a material heretic adheres formally to the doctrine of the Church as an infallible and divine rule, assenting on divine authority to the divinely revealed truths, but errs

---

[409] St. Thomas, *Summa Theol.*, IIa IIae, q.5, a. 3.

objectively in ignorance regarding the matter of some article(s) of faith: "[W]hoever does not adhere to the doctrine of the Church, as an infallible and divine rule does not have the habit of faith, but holds to matters of faith in some other manner than by faith."

The material heretic retains the formal cause of the virtue of faith, because the form of heresy which is contrary to that virtue is absent in material heretics, who do not err out of pertinacity, but out of simplicity or ignorance, as Reiffenstuel explains, "*Hæretici materiales (qui autem iuxta S. Augustinum...nequaquam sunt inter hæreticos deputandi) dicuntur illi, qui non ex malo animo aut pertinacia, sed ex simplicitate, aut defectu debitæ informationis, errant circa Fidem.*"[410]

Those who because of simplicity and ignorance err materially do not deliberately prefer their own judgment to the teaching of the Church, in which consists the sin of infidelity and the form of heresy, as St. Alphonsus explains: "*Porro pertinaciter errare (quæ est formale)...est eum [errorem] retinere, postquam contrarium est sufficienter propositum: sive quando scit contrarium teneri a reliqua universali Christi in terris Ecclesia, cui suum iudicium præferat*". Therefore it is only the formal heretic who is properly called a heretic because he has defected from the faith by refusing to believe what he knows to be taught as the faith of the universal Church, and thus no longer has the virtue of faith — but the material heretic still has divine and Catholic faith but errs out of ignorance of what the Church teaches. Material heresy is properly a "material sin". As explained in the previous chapter, the term, "material sin" is defined by St. Alphonsus de Liguori as an action that would be matter of sin but without the knowledge of the law, and therefore inculpable: (*il peccato materiale non è altro, che un'azione che sarebbe materia di peccato, se vi fosse la cognizione della legge*). Hence, "material heresy" is the inculpable, or at least not gravely culpable act of heresy, because of ignorance of the material object of faith, and thus "material heretics" accordingly are defined and distinguished from "formal heretics" by theologians: "*Qui cum sua culpa veritatem de fide negant, formales hæretici vocantur, qui id sine sua culpa faciunt, materiales hæretici dicuntur.*"[411] (Those who culpably deny a truth of faith are called formal

---

[410] *Theologia Moralis*, P. F. Anaclet Reiffenstuel, Munich, 1715, p. 202.

[411] THEOLOGIAE FUNDAMENTALIS *Tractatus prior. Demonstratio christiano-catholica contra adversarios generatim omnes* TRACTATUS DUO. – SAC. F. H. REINERDING, H. ET. PH. DR. ET TH. PROF. IN SEMINARIO FULDENSI, Monasterii Guestphalorum. SUMPTIBUS LIBRARIAE ASCHENDORFFIANAE.

heretics, those who do so without fault are said to be material heretics.) As is plainly self evident, this definition of the term 'material heretic' properly specifies with precise determination the essence of what it is for one to be a 'material heretic'. Those who fall under this heading are properly members of the Church, in the manner of those 'heretics' described in the above passage of St. Thomas, who, regarding the material object of faith, err out of ignorance and are not excommunicated. Those who have been innocently led astray and brought into the congregations of heretics, are not members of the Church, and are not properly material heretics because they are schismatics who know that their opinions oppose the *lex credendi* of the Church — they inculpably reject what they know to be proposed for belief by the magisterium; yet, as St. Augustine (quoted below) teaches, are not to be reckoned as heretics (*nequaquam sunt inter hæreticos deputandi*), because they still have the formal cause of faith, and are material heretics *secundum quid*, in that they knowingly reject the material object of faith, but do so not knowing that their error opposes the *prima veritas*. Thus explains Abbé F.X. de Feller that the term *material heretics* includes "*all invincibly ignorant Christians, those drawn into error by false teachers, and who believe with good faith that they profess the truth, are really, because of their good disposition, children of the true Church.*"[412]

The error of material heresy is not always entirely inculpable, but can be culpable and vincible, but without pertinacity, as one of the classical

---

[412] «Aggiungeremo che ne' paesi eretici tutt'I fanciulli battezzati, il cui intelletto non è ancora capace di giudicare della seta, in cui sono nati; che tutti I Cristiani invincibilmente indotti in error da' falsi dottori, e che credono con buona fede di professare la verità, sono realmente per la buona disposizione loro figuoli della vera chiesa (1)» «(1) In questo numero certamente non si comprendono gli eretici ben istruiti, nè quelli che senza aver grandi lumi hanno però de' motivi di dubitare, nè sono senza mezzi per istruirsi; molto meno poi I ministri che non possono sinceramente aderire a delle sette, delle quali conoscono l'insussistenza. Codesti son d' ordinario Tolleranti o Deisti. Molti internamenti conoscono la verità della religione Cattolica; ma legati da rispetti umani e da interessi temporali, non hanno il coraggio di professarla: sono nel caso di quell pastore mercenario, il quale non poteva nè server volentieri, nè abbandonar il servaggio, a cui erasi obbligato. Egli vedeva da un lato gli Dei, e l'interesse dall'altro. *Quid facerem? Neque servitio me exire licebat, Nec tam præsentes alibi cognoscere Divos.* Virg. *Eclog. 1.*» [F. X. De Feller, *Op. cit.,* pp. 339-340.]

authors of Moral Theology, Patritius Sporer[413] explains the three degrees of material heresy: "*Et quia illa ignorantia, vel error potest esse, aut inculpabilis, aut culpabilis & vincibilis, eaque vel levis, vel lata, crassa, supina, vel denique etiam affectata, & directe voluntaria, ideo triplicis gradus distingui possunt hæretici materiales.*" [414] Those described in the third category, i.e., of ignorance directly willed, can hardly be considered excused of sin, or even be considered invincibly ignorant according to some authors[415] even if not guilty of pertinacious and directly expressed explicit heresy; and therefore cannot be saved if they die in that state if they are fully aware of their negligence. Indeed, those whose ignorance results from the maximum degree of negligence, together with temerity and *dolus*, would not be excused by that ignorance from formal heresy; nor would they be excused from censures, irregularities, or other penalties.[416] However,

---

[413] **Patritius Sporer** († 29 May 1683) was a German Franciscan moral theologian. Sporer was born and died at Passau, in the Electorate of Bavaria. In 1637 he entered the Order of Friars Minor in the convent of his native town, which then belonged to the religious Province of Strasburg. He taught theology for many years, obtained the title of Lector jubilatus, and was also the theologian of the Bishop of Passau. Alphonsus Liguori often quotes him and Lehmkuhl numbers him amongst the classical authors of moral theology. (*Wikipedia*)

[414] Patritius Sporer, *Theologia Moralis Super Decalogum*, Salzburg, 1722, p. 175.

[415] «Sive ergo ignorantia sit iuris, sive facti ut non inducat peccatum præsertim in foro conscientiæ debet esse probabilis, & inculpabilis, seu invincibilis, hæc enim sola excusat a peccato presertim mortali, ut docent omnes, & deducitur ex Sacra Scriptura, Genes. *Cap.* 20. *n.* 4. *Domine num gentem ignorantem, & iustam interficies.*» and, «Hæc ignorantia non solum excusat a peccato, sed etiam a censuris, & irregularitate ex delicto… Sed ignorantia invincibilis ex supra dictis excusat a culpa, & peccato, ergo etiam a pena quacumque ex prædictis & ita docent omnes…» [Bordoni, *Sacrum Tribunal Iudicum In Causis Sanctæ Fidei Contra Hæreticos Et Hæresi Suspectos*, p. 195]

[416] «Hæc ignorantia non solum excusat a peccato, sed etiam a censuris, & irregularitate ex delicto… Sed ignorantia invincibilis ex supra dictis excusat a culpa, & peccato, ergo etiam a pena quacumque ex prædictis & ita docent omnes… Crassa ignorantia est illa quæ procedit ex maxima, vel magna negligentia, & temeritate sciendi necessaria quæ potuit scire a se prævisa: Vel est illa, qua quis ignorat publica, manifesta, & ea, quæ omnes fere eiusdem professionis sciunt. Dicitur crassa ex similitudine crassorum, qui multum negligentes sunt in suis operibus; supina vocatur, quia homines ita dispositi censentur otiosi, … Hæc autem inducit peccatum mortale, quia fundatur in magna negligentia, & temeritate, ita quod neque a peccato, neque a censuris,

those in the second category, i.e. only slightly culpable of supine ignorance, if the degree of ignorance is such that they are not sufficiently conscious of being in the state of supine ignorance, so that they would be morally capable of overcoming the obstacle of ignorance, would still have to be considered invincibly ignorant; at least until they become sufficiently aware of the defective nature of their own opinions and seek to properly inform their conscience. Nevertheless, since the degree of culpability that would qualify one as a material heretic is strictly an internal matter, the Church presumes members of non-Catholic denominations in general to be formal heretics, according to their external profession of heresy and rejection of the Church's doctrine, as is patent in the earlier partially quoted passage of St. Pius X: "Gli eretici sono i battezzati che ricusano con pertinacia di credere qualche verità rivelata da Dio e insegnata come di fede dalla Chiesa cattolica, per esempio gli ariani, i nestoriani, e le varie sette dei protestanti."[417] The reason for this is that virtually all members of non-Catholic sects consciously and wilfully refuse to assent to the *lex credendi* of the Catholic Church; whereas material heretics are judged to be only material heretics, and not *formal* heretics precisely because they are ignorant of the Church's law of belief. There are exceptions which need to be judged on an individual basis, when the *bona fides* of the individual is manifested.

Salza & Siscoe uncritically and gratuitously assert that *their* definition of "material heretic", which became popular among some early 20th Century theologians, is the correct one, and that the traditional and theologically correct definition of the term is "perverted". As their authority, they quote a text of Cardinal Billot which offers no argumentation on the point, but merely asserts his own gratuitously

---

irregularitate (196) et aliis penis excusat, expresse *cap. 2. De constit. In 6 cap. Apostolicæ 9. De cler. excom.* Sanch. *lib. 9. disp. 32. num. 31* Portellus *ver. Ignorantia num. 27.* Bonac. *q. 2. De cens. In genere p. 1. num. 10* Diana *part. 3. tract. 5 resol. 13. part. 4. tract. 2. resol. 85.* Cœlestinus ex nostris in suo Comped. Theol. *moral. tract. 3. cap. 5. num. 2* Limita prædicta, nam quando ad incurrendam censuram lex præscribit scientiam, ausum, præsumptionem, aut temeritatem, non sufficit quæcumque ignorantia crassa, sed ea, quæ coniuncta est cum maxima negligentia, temeritate, & dolo, ita docui cum Sanch. Curiel. Henriq. Auilam. & Molinam. Sed oppositam sententiam Tolet. *lib. 1. cap. 48.* Alterius *disp. 11. de cens. de susp. cap. 5. S. Hoc autem,* & multi alii, nullam ignorantiam crassam excusare a censuris, sicut non excusat a peccato, longe probabiliorem putant, quia est conformis viri pluribus in locis..." [*Ibid.*, p. 195-196]

[417] *Catechismo Maggiore,* Q. 228.

stated belief that the traditional definition of the term, "material heretic", is "perverted", based on a flawed understanding of the nature of heresy. Cardinal Billot and the other early 20th Century theologians who restricted the attribution of the term 'material heretics' exclusively to those outside the Church, have never sufficiently explained why, in their opinion, only those who are *secundum quid* but not properly material heretics, i.e. *those who are not members of the Catholic Church because they reject the authority of the magisterium*, should be called 'material heretics'; and those Catholics who are properly in material but not formal heresy, should not be called 'material heretics'. The explanation he provides is plainly deficient and erroneous, since he errs on the nature of heresy when he says, "But the *nature of heresy consists in withdrawal from the rule of the ecclesiastical Magisterium* and *this does not take place in the case, since this is a simple error of fact concerning what the rule dictates*. And therefore there is no scope for heresy, even materially". What Billot says is the nature of heresy properly pertains only to *formal* heresy; and the *"simple error of fact concerning what the rule dictates"*, which Billot says does not fall within the scope of heresy, is precisely the *matter* of *material heresy*. Billot, as I explained above, does not properly specify the nature of heresy; which is not the *withdrawal from the rule of the ecclesiastical Magisterium*, but is the **erroneous judgment**, as St. Alphonsus defines, the nature of heresy as the **error intellectus pertinax contra fidem**, and the matter is the **Judicium erroneum, quod est ejus quasi materiale**. However, the traditional usage of the term as I understand and employ it, which, unlike Billot's usage of it, is based on the proper definition of heresy, is still commonly employed by theologians of the late 20th and 21st Centuries. In the pontifical universities where I studied in the 70s and 80s, it was commonplace to hear the term used as I use it. In his series of articles, Fr. Jean-Michel Gleize, Professor of Theology at the SSPX seminary in Ecône employs the term precisely according to the same traditional usage as I employ it: "At first glance it would seem that this is an improbable thesis [i.e. that a pope can become a formal heretic]. In fact, the negative answer to this question is the common opinion of theologians of the modern era. They say, in effect, that the pope could not become a formal, obstinate heretic, in other words a deliberate, culpable heretic, although he could become a **material heretic**, through non-culpable ignorance or because of a simple error and not by reason of ill will."[418] Salza & Siscoe say on their website, "Cardinal Billot

---

[418] Fr. Jean-Michel Gleize, *The Question of Papal Heresy*, Part 3.

declares Fr. Kramer's use of the term material heretic to be 'perverted'". Salza & Siscoe seem to be totally unconcerned with the hypocrisy they manifest by saying only that Fr. Kramer's use of the term is perverted, but not Fr. Gleize's identical use of the same.

Having examined the question as to whether there can even be adult "material heretics" with faith and justifying grace, but in invincible ignorance, as members of non-Catholic sects; there remains the question as to whether or not there can be adult members of non-Catholic sects, who, although not invincibly ignorant, would still qualify as material heretics who would nevertheless belong to the Church because their culpable ignorance would not be gravely culpable, and not amount to pertinacity; and thus would in some manner belong to the Church, without being formally incorporated as visible members of the Church. According to Sebestiano Fraghi, in his 1937 Angelicum doctoral dissertation, *De Membris Ecclesiæ* (p. 85 ff.), there are two opinions, and there is not a consensus among theologians whether such material heretics are or are not members of the Church: "Some deny they are members of the Church;[1] others, however, affirm they are, and Suarez is also among them, as a result of his general principle regarding the nature of a member of the Church;[2] others distinguish, affirming them to be members of the Church in the internal forum and by the judgment of God, but in the external forum and by the judgement of the Church they are presumed heretics[3]".[419] Belonging to the latter category was notably Cardinal Franzelin.

Fraghi himself considered the first to be more probable, "Nos ut probabiliorem primam sententiam tenemus." First, he considers the usage of the term "heretics" by the Fathers: "When the Fathers speak of heretics, generally they intend to speak of formal and pertinacious heretics; sometimes, however, some of them are seen to excuse those who bona fide are outside the Church." And he quotes St. Augustine:

> "Those who maintain their own opinion, however false and perverted, without obstinate ill will, especially those who have not originated their own error by bold presumption, but have received it from parents who had been led astray and had lapsed, those who seek truth with careful industry, ready to be corrected when they have found it, are not to be rated among heretics

---

[419] Fraghi's references: 1. Cf. Aem. Dobsch, De Eccl. Chr., p. 495; Card. Billot, De Eccl. Chr., thes. XI, p. 292; 2. Cf. De Fide, d. IX, s. 1, 13; 3. Cf. Card. Franzelin, De Eccl. Chr., Thes. XXIII, II, 10.

(*nequaquam sunt inter hæreticos deputandi*). Therefore, if I did not believe you to be such, I would probably not send you any letters."[420]

Fraghi then makes the observation that *all heretics who entered into the bad congregations of the heresiarchs*[421] are "outside the Church":

> "But also the Fathers often teach that even material heretics are turned outside the Church (*etiam hæreticos materiales versari extra Ecclesiam*). For they explicitly say that all heretics, even those seduced by heresiarchs who entered into their bad congregations, do not pertain to the mystical body of Christ (*non pertinere ad corpus Christi mysticum*), putting no distinction between them who voluntarily and them who bona fide participate in their errors."

It would be somewhat extreme to say that those not gravely culpable ignorant material heretics who belong to the *congregatiunculæ* of the heretics do not pertain in any way to the mystical body of Christ, and are thus totally outside the Church (and that certainly does not appear to be Fraghi's meaning), because they, as St. Augustine says, "seek truth with careful industry, ready to be corrected when they have found it"(*quærunt autem cauta sollicitudine veritatem, corrigi parati cum invenerint*); and therefore they can be said to belong to the soul of the Church in the manner described by Pope St Pius X.[422] St Robert Bellarmine explained the

---

[420] "*Qui sententiam suam, quamvis falsam atque perversam, nulla pertinaci animositate defendunt, praesertim quam non audacia praesumptionis suae pepererunt, sed a seductis atque in errorem lapsis parentibus acceperunt, quaerunt autem cauta sollicitudine veritatem, corrigi parati cum invenerint, nequaquam sunt inter haereticos deputandi. Tales ergo vos nisi esse crederem, nullas fortasse vobis litteras mitterem.*" [*Ad Glorium*, epist. 43, 1; ML 33, 160.]

[421] "Illos qui seducti ab haeresiarchis in eorum congregatiunculas ingressi sint, non pertinere ad corpus Christi mysticum"

[422] CATECHISMO DELLA DOTTRINA CATTOLICA: 132. Chi è fuori della Chiesa si salva? Chi è fuori della Chiesa per propria colpa e muore senza dolore perfetto, non si salva; ma chi ci si trovi senza propria colpa e viva bene, può salvarsi con l'amor di carità, che unisce a Dio, e, in spirito, anche alla Chiesa, cioè all'anima di lei.

CATECHISMO MAGGIORE: 163 D. Come è costituita la Chiesa di Gesù Cristo? R. La Chiesa di Gesù Cristo è costituita come una vera e perfetta società; ed in essa, come in una persona morale possiamo distinguere l'anima e il corpo.

164 D. In che consiste l'anima della Chiesa? R. L'anima della Chiesa consiste in ciò che essa ha d'interno e spirituale, cioè la fede, la speranza, la carità, i doni della grazia e dello Spirito Santo e tutti i celesti tesori che le sono derivati pei meriti di Cristo Redentore e dei Santi.

doctrine of the soul of the Church taught by St. Augustine who explained that the Church is a *living* body, and therefore is comprised of a body and a soul:

> "*Notandum autem est ex Augistino in breviculo collationis. Collat. 3.* **Ecclesiam esse corpus vivum, in quo est anima et corpus**, *et quidem* **anima sunt interna dona Spiritus sancti, fides, spes, charitas etc.** *Corpus sunt externa professio fidei, et communicatio sacramentorum. Ex quo fit, ut quidam sint de anima et de corpore Ecclesiæ, et proinde uniti Christo capiti interius et exterius; sunt enim quasi membra viva in corpore [...] Rursum aliqua sint de anima, et non de corpore, ut catechumeni, vel excommunicati, si fidem et charitatem habeant, quod fieri potest.*"[423]

This is precisely the same teaching which St. Pius X teaches magisterially in his *Catechismo Maggiore*, that in the Church there is body and soul: "*La Chiesa di Gesù Cristo è costituita come una vera e perfetta società; ed in essa, come in una persona morale possiamo distinguere l'anima e il corpo.*" He likewise defines the soul of the Church in identical terms: "*L'anima della Chiesa consiste in ciò che essa ha d'interno e spirituale, cioè la fede, la speranza, la carità, i doni della grazia e dello Spirito Santo e tutti i celesti tesori che le sono derivati pei meriti di Cristo Redentore e dei Santi.*" Following St. Augustine and St. Robert Bellarmine, St. Pius X teaches that the soul of the Church consists of faith, hope and charity, the gifts of the Holy Ghost, and all the heavenly treasures. St. Pius X then asks if one who is outside the church can be saved: "*Chi è fuori della Chiesa si salva?*" He then makes the critical distinction between those who die outside the Church unrepentant, and those who find themselves materially outside without fault and spiritually in the Church; living the life of sanctifying grace which unites them to God, and spiritually also to the Church, i.e. to the 'soul of the Church': "*Chi è fuori della Chiesa per propria colpa e muore senza dolore perfetto, non si salva; ma chi ci si trovi senza propria colpa e viva bene, può salvarsi con l'amor di carità, che unisce a Dio, e, in spirito, anche alla Chiesa, cioè all'anima di lei.*"

---

171 D. Ma chi si trovasse, senza sua colpa, fuori della Chiesa, potrebbe salvarsi? R. Chi, trovandosi senza sua colpa, ossia in buona fede, fuori della Chiesa, avesse ricevuto il Battesimo, o ne avesse il desiderio almeno implicito; cercasse inoltre sinceramente la verità e compisse la volontà di Dio come meglio può; benché separato dal corpo della Chiesa, sarebbe unito all'anima di lei e quindi in via di salute.

[423] *De Ecclesia Militante, Caput II. p. 75.*

Thus it is that those who are only material heretics but not united to the Church by visible, external union can be united to the Church by internal union; i.e. by faith and sanctifying grace, and therefoe can be said to belong to the Church, and be in the Church, although not incorporated as members by external union. They can therefore be said to be in the Church not as members *in actu*, but *in potentia*, as St. Robert Bellarmine explains, and can therefore be saved for the same reason as the catechumens[424] who die in the state of grace, who, not having been sacramentally baptized with water, are not actual members of the Church, but are members *in voto*: "*si non re, saltem voto sunt in Ecclesia, ideo salvari possunt*". This is the doctrine of the Council of Trent, which defined that the grace of justification can be received by the sacraments or the resolve (*votum*) for them[425]; and in accordance with the manifest dogma of the universal Church, in Chapter fourteen of the *Decree on*

---

[424] "De Catechumenis [...] sunt fideles, et salvari possunt, si moriantur in eo statu, et tamen extra Ecclesiam nemo salvatur, sicut nec extra arcam Noe, iuxta illud Concilii Lateranensis, cap. 1. *Una est fidelium universalis Ecclesia, extra quam nullus omnino salvatur*. At nihilominus certum est, Catechumenos non esse in Ecclesia actu et proprie, sed tantum in potentia, quomodo homo conceptus, sed nondum formatus, et natus, non dicitur homo, nisi in potentia. Nam legimus Actor. 2 *Qui ergo receperunt verbum, baptizati sunt, et appositae sunt in die illa animae circiter tria millia*. Item Concilium Florentinum in instructione Armenorum, docet, homines fieri membrii Christi, ac de corpore Ecclesiae, cum baptizantur. Idem et Patres docent [...] RESPONDEO igitur, quod dicitur, extra Ecclesiam neminem salvari, intelligi debere de iis, qui neque re ipsa, nec desiderio sunt de Ecclesia: sicut de Baptismo communiter loquuntur Theologi. Quoniam autem Catechumeni si non re, saltem voto sunt in Ecclesia, ideo salvari possunt. Neque repugnat similitudo arcae Noe, extra quam nemo salvabatur, etiamsi in voto in ea fuisset: nam similitudines non in omnibus convenient. Quodcirca 1. Pet. 3 Baptismus comparator arcae Noe, et tamen constat, sine Baptismo in re, aliquos salvari." [*De Ecclesia Militante*, Cap. III. p. 75.]

"At, inquies, Aug. tract. 4. In Ioan dicit, Catechumenos esse in Ecclesia; Verum est, sed ibidem separet eos a fidelibus. Voluit ergo dicere, esse in Ecclesia non actu, sed potentia, quod idem ipse explicuit initio libri secondi de Symbolo, ubi comparat Catechumenos hominibus conceptis, non natis." [*De Ecclesia Militante*, Cap. III. p. 76.]

[425] Session VII Canon 4: "Si quis dixerit sacramenta novae legis non esse ad salutem necessaria sed superflua et sine eis aut eorum voto per solam fidem homines a Deo gratiam iustificationis adipisci licet omnia singulis necessaria non sint: a[nathema] s[it]."

Justification, it is defined[426] that whoever dies in the justified state enters eternal life.[427] The objection, therefore, made by Fr. Leonard Feeney SJ,

---

[426] The entire doctrine on justification in the Decree is given dogmatic force in virtue of canon 33: "33. *Si quis dixerit per hanc doctrinam catholicam de iustificatione a sancta Synodo hoc praesenti decreto expressam* aliqua ex parte gloriae Dei vel meritis Iesu Christi Domini nostri derogari et *non potius veritatem fidei nostrae Dei denique ac Christi Iesu gloriam illustrari: a[nathema] s[it]*."

[427] The Council of Trent's Decree on Justification (Ch. 4) sets forth the infallible truth that one can be justified, and sasved and by the sacrament of water or by the resolve (votum) to receive Baptism (as is explained in the Roman Catechism of St. Pius V):

"Quibus verbis iustificationis impii descriptio insinuatur ut sit translatio ab eo statu in quo homo nascitur filius primi Adae in statum gratiae et adoptionis filiorum Dei per secundum Adam Iesum Christum salvatorem nostrum; quae quidem translatio post Evangelium promulgatum sine lavacro regenerationis aut eius voto fieri non potest sicut scriptum est: nisi quis renatus fuerit ex aqua et Spiritu Sancto non potest introire in regnum Dei."

In English: "By which words, a description of the Justification of the impious is indicated, as being a translation, from that state wherein man is born a child of the first Adam, to the state of grace, and of the adoption of the sons of God, through the second Adam, Jesus Christ, our Saviour. And this translation, since the promulgation of the Gospel, cannot be effected, without the laver of regeneration, or the desire thereof, as it is written; unless a man be born again of water and the Holy Ghost, he cannot enter into the Kingdom of God."

And again (Sess. VII can. iv): "Si quis dixerit sacramenta novae legis non esse ad salutem necessaria sed superflua et sine eis aut eorum voto per solam fidem homines a Deo gratiam iustificationis adipisci licet omnia singulis necessaria non sint: a[nathema] s[it]."

In English: "CANON IV.-If any one saith, that the sacraments of the New Law are not necessary unto salvation, but superfluous; and that, without them, or without the desire thereof, men obtain of God, through faith alone, the grace of justification; though all (the sacraments) are not ineed necessary for every individual; let him be anathema."

The grace of Justification makes one an heir to the hope of eternal life in this life (Decree on Justification Ch. 7): "Hanc dispositionem seu praeparationem iustificatio ipsa consequitur quae non est sola peccatorum remissio sed et sanctificatio et renovatio interioris hominis per voluntariam susceptionem gratiae et donorum unde homo ex iniusto fit iustus et ex inimico amicus ut sit haeres secundum spem vitae aeternae."

that those who have been justified by "votum" (i.e. the resolve to receive the sacrament) but die without the actual water of baptism remain outside the Church, and therefore cannot be saved[428], is heretical; because it is a dogma that all who die in the justified state have had their

---

In English: "This disposition, or preparation, is followed by Justification itself, which is not remission of sins merely, but also the sanctification and renewal of the inward man, through the voluntary reception of the grace, and of the gifts, whereby man of unjust becomes just, and of an enemy a friend, that so he may be an heir according to hope of life everlasting."

And those who appear before the divine Judge in possession of that grace will "have eternal life": "Itaque veram et christianam iustitiam accipientes eam ceu primam stolam pro illa quam Adam sua inobedientia sibi et nobis perdidit per Christum Iesum illis donatam candidam et immaculatam iubentur statim renati conservare ut eam perferant ante tribunal Domini nostri Iesu Christi et habeant vitam aeternam." (Ch. 7)

In English: "Wherefore, when receiving true and Christian justice, they are bidden, immediately on being born again, to preserve it pure and spotless, as the first robe given them through Jesus Christ in lieu of that which Adam, by his disobedience, lost for himself and for us, that so they may bear it before the judgment-seat of our Lord Jesus Christ, and may have life everlasting."

Chapter 16 teaches explicitly that the justified have fulfilled the law of God, and in order to enter heaven, only one thing is required: that they die in the state of grace: Cum enim ille ipse Christus Iesus tamquam caput in membra et tamquam vitis in palmites in ipsos iustificatos iugiter virtutem influat quae virtus bona eorum opera semper antecedit comitatur et subsequitur et sine qua nullo pacto Deo grata et meritoria esse possent nihil ipsis iustificatis amplius deesse credendum est quominus plene illis quidem operibus quae in Deo sunt facta divinae legi pro huius vitae statu satisfecisse et vitam aeternam suo etiam tempore (si tamen in gratia decesserint) consequendam vere promeruisse censeantur. (Decree on Justification Ch. 16)

In English: "For, whereas Jesus Christ Himself continually infuses his virtue into the said justified,-as the head into the members, and the vine into the branches,-and this virtue always precedes and accompanies and follows their good works, which without it could not in any wise be pleasing and meritorious before God,-we must believe that nothing further is wanting to the justified, to prevent their being accounted to have, by those very works which have been done in God, fully satisfied the divine law according to the state of this life, and to have truly merited eternal life, to be obtained also in its (due) time, if so be, however, that they depart in grace: ..."

[428] "It is now: Baptism of Water, or damntion! If you do not desire tht Water, you cannot be justified. And if you do not get it, you cannot be saved." Fr. Leonard Feeney in *Bread of Life*, p. 25.

sins remitted and were justified by sanctifying grace. The heretical conclusion is based on the heretical premise that those justified only by the resolve to receive baptism remain outside the Church. However, the infallible dogma of faith professes that there is **outside the Church neither salvation nor remission of sins**: «Unam sanctam ecclesiam catholicam et ipsam apostolicam urgente fide credere cogimur et tenere, nosque hanc firmiter credimus et simpliciter confitemur, **extra quam nec salus est, nec remissio peccatorum**».[429]

From the above considerations, it can be properly understood in what manner material heretics, who are not visible members of the Church (*in re*), can be properly said to be members of the Church in a qualified sense (*in voto*). Cardinal Franzelin, as noted above, affirmed them to be members of the Church in the internal forum and by the judgment of God, but in the external forum and by the judgement of the Church they are presumed and held to be heretics.[430] Fraghi notes the objection of Ludovicus De San, who said, "This cannot be said [...] for in the judgement of God, which is infallible, material heretics and schismatics cannot in actuality be but what they truly are; if they in the judgement of God be members of the Church, it follows they are true members of the Church, which appears to be most false".[431] It is scarcely conceivable that a theologian of such preeminence as Johannes Baptiste Franzelin SJ would have fallen into such a crude contradiction as De San attributes to him. Franzelin was a vastly learned *Jesuit theologian*, who would have obviously intended the expression "members of the Church in the internal forum and by the judgment of God" to denote membership in the qualified sense of *internal union* with the soul of the Church, elaborated by that other vastly learned *Jesuit theologian*, St. Robert Bellarmine SJ; thus denoting that qualified sense of membership *in voto*, and denying them membership in the proper sense of the term *in re* by saying, "in the external forum they are presumed and held by the Church to be heretics". Nor can it be deemed improper on the part of the

---

[429] Bonifacius VIII «*Unam Sanctam*», 18 novembris 1302.

[430] "[H]aeretici materiales in foro externo ab Eccle besia praesumuntur et habentur ut haeretici, sed in foro interno et coram Deo manent membra Ecclesiae." [*De Eccl. et Romano Pontif.*, n. 359]

[431] "Hoc dici non potest [...] cum enim in iudicio Dei, quod est infallibile, haeretici et schismatici materiales non possint actu esse nisi id quod vere sunt, si ipsi in iudicio Dei essent membra Ecclesiae, sequeretur eos esse vera Ecclesiae membra, quod falsissimum patet esse".

Church's judgment to presume those to be heretics who might invisibly belong to the Church by internal union only; but who inculpably profess heresy externally, and, being ignorant of the fact of the divinely constituted authority of the Roman Church, do not submit to the judgment of the ecclesiastical magisterium of that Church with the assent required by the law of Christ. God, "Who will have all men to be saved, and to come to the knowledge of the truth", (1 Tim. 2:4), provides sufficient grace to all men to come into the revealed truths of the Catholic faith in order that they may be saved.[432] So, while God gives the grace to all, each one is free to cooperate or resist that grace, and hence, St. Augustine says: "He who made thee without thee, does not justify thee without thee. Therefore He made the unknowing one, He justifies the willing one. "[433] For so long as the grace, even the remote grace, is given but resisted, the soul distances itself from God and his Church, and thus the grace is gradually withdrawn: "he that contemneth small things, shall fall by little and little" (Ecclesiasticus 19:1) – the soul falls away little by little, until it becomes hardened in heresy.

Thus, with a clear understanding of heresy as understood according to the mind of the Church, we can safely proceed to the exposition on papal heresy and the five opinions on the question of the deposition of a heretic pope.

---

[432] "Grace is given which is truly yet merely sufficient: "truly" because it really confers the power; "merely" because, through the fault of the will, it fails in its effect, with respect to which it is said to be inefficacious, but sufficient. This doctrine of the Church is formulated against the Predestinationists and later, much more explicitly, against the Jansenists. (Cf. *De praedestinianismo*, Denz., nos. 316 ff., 320 ff.)" [Reginald Garigou-Lagrange OP, *Commentary on the Summa Theologica*, Chapter Five; 2 The Doctrine of the Church on Sufficient Grace]

[433] *Sermo XV de Verb. Apost.*, chap. II, no. 13; *PL*, XXXVIII, 923: «Qui ergo fecit te sine te, non te justificat sine te. Ergo fecit nescientem, justificat volentem.»

PART TWO

THE FIRST PAPAL TEACHING ON A HERETIC POPE'S LOSS OF OFFICE

The virtue of faith, as I explained in the first part of this article, is essential to the office of the Supreme Pontificate; thus, as St. Robert Bellarmine explains; faith is *simpliciter* a necessary disposition for one to be pope; and faith being removed, by its contrary disposition, which is heresy, the pope would straightaway cease to be pope, since the necessary dispositions for the form of the papacy could no longer be preserved: *"ista dispositione sublata per contrariam quæ est hæresis, mox papa desinit esse; neque enim potest forma conservari sine necessariis dispositionibus"*. Bellarmine's doctrine **that faith is a necessary disposition for the papal office is based on the teaching of Pope Innocent III; that faith pertains so essentially to the Petrine office that Christ conferred upon Peter and his successors in that office, the grace of unfailing faith**: "... Unless I am grounded in faith, how can I make others firm in faith? It is certain that faith belongs **especially to my office. The Lord publicly proclaimed it**: 'I', he said, 'have prayed for you Peter that your faith may not fail, and you, once being converted, must confirm your brothers'... For this reason **the Faith of the Apostolic See has never failed even during turbulent times**, but has remained whole and unharmed, so that the privilege of Peter continues to be unshaken.[434]

Thus, Pope Innocent teaches that the prayer of Christ for the grace that the faith of Peter not fail, does not limit itself to a personal charism of Simon Peter that is not passed on to his successors, but that charism pertains essentially to the exercise of the Petrine office, and therefore is a *gratia gratis data* given to every holder of that office. That the prayer of Christ for the charism of unfailing faith refers to the holder of the Petrine

---

[434] "Nisi enim ego solidaltus essem in fide, quomodo possem alios in fide firmare? Quod ad officium meum noscitur specialiter pertinere, Domino protestante: «Ego, inquit, pro te rogavi, Petre, ut non deficiat fides tua, et tu aliquando conversus, confirma fratres tuos (*Luc*.xxii).» Rogavit, et impetravit: quoniam exauditus est in omnibus pro sua reverentia. Et ideo fides apostolicae sedis in nulla nunquam turbatione defecit, sed integra semper et illibata permansit: ut Petri privilegium persisteret inconcussum." (*Sermo II, De Diversis*)

Primacy, and most specifically to his duty of office to confirm his brethren in the Catholic faith, is clearly established in the words of the same Innocent III again in his letter:

> "Deus homo, Christus Jesus (1 *Tim.* II), apostolicæ sedis primatum in Beato Petro apostolorum principe stabilivit, qui et ante passionem inquit ad ipsum: *Tu es Petrus, et super hanc petram ædificabo Ecclesiam meam, et quodcumque ligaveris super terram erit ligatum et in cœlis, et quodcumque solveris super terram, erit solutum et in cœlis* (*Matth.* XVI). Et circa passionem suam dixit eidem: *Simon, expetivit vos ut cribraret sicut triticum; sed ego pro te rogavi ut non deficiat fides tua, et tu aliquando conversus confirma fratres tuos* (*Luc.* XXII) Et post passionem suam, vocabulo tertio repetito præcepit *Simon Joannis, diliges me plus his? Pasce oves meas* (*Joan.* XXI); non distinguens inter has oves et illas; ut ab ovile Christi se sciat esse penitus alienum, qui beatum Petrum recusat habere pastorem, et qui claves ejus contemnit, ipse sibi regni cœlestis januam intercludit, nec Satanæ potest cribrum effugere, qui per eum renuit in fide catholica confirmari."[435]

Hence, Innocent concludes in *Sermo III*, that he would not easily believe that God would permit the Roman Pontiff to err in faith (*Ego tamen facile non crederim, ut Deus permitteret Romanum pontificem contra fidem errare*), for whom He spiritually prayed in Peter, *I have prayed for thee Peter, etc.* (Luke 22), Therefore, *he who has the bride, is the bridegroom*, and this bride did not wed vacuously, but granted him [the pope] the priceless dowry of spiritual plenitude. Others are called to a partial share in the solicitude, but only Peter was taken up into the fullness of power (*solus autem Petrus assumptus est in plenitudinem potestatis*). Thus, Innocent III teaches that Faith is necessary for the exercise the *munus* of the Petrine office, and therefore it seems unlikely that God would permit the Roman Pontiff to defect from the faith.

In the first *Hauptstück* of the second volume of his *Fundamentaltheologie*, Prof. Dr. Albert Lang[436] observes, that the grace of

---

[435] Ep. Nobili viro W., Meganippano Serviæ, 1203 Likewise Pope St. Agatho in his response to Sergius: "Let your clemency therefore consider that the Lord and Saviour of all, to whom faith belongs, **who promised that the faith of Peter should not fail**, admonished him to strengthen his brethren; and it is known to all men that the apostolic pontiffs, the predecessors of my littleness, have always done this with confidence…"

[436] Albert Lang (1890-1973) was Professor of Fundamental Theology in Bonn from 1939 to 1959 and thus predecessor to Joseph Ratzinger on that chair. He is the author of the well-known, two-volume *Fundamentaltheologie*.

unfailing faith could not be merely a personal privilege for the Apostle, but was given to equip him for the fulfillment of his official duty to confirm the faith of his brethren: "This could not be a personal privilege for the apostle, but equipment for his ministry, which obliges him to strengthen his brothers in faith. He can fulfill this task only if he is able to influence the brothers in a guiding, admonishing and preventive manner in order to preserve and direct their faith. The Confirmator fratrum must have the power of teaching and jurisdiction over the brothers."[437] Christ's prayer was an efficacious prayer that to Peter, to whom was given the task of leading the Church through all dangers, was also given the assurance that his faith would not fail: "To Peter he has given the task to guide the Church safely through all the dangers. In the farewell hour he gives him the task of strengthening the brothers in the faith in the times of danger, but to him he also gives the assurance that his assistance in the fulfillment of this task will not be lacking. Through his prayer, which can only be understood as an effective prayer, Jesus has accomplished that ***the faith of Peter will not waver.***"[438] Thus, faith pertains essentially to the Petrine office.

With the removal of that necessary disposition of faith, which belongs essentially to the exercise of the charism of the papal office, Bellarmine, applying the principle set forth by Innocent III, concludes as a purely abstract hypothesis, that if it be possible for that essential disposition which is faith, to be lost, then the pope would straightaway cease to be pope (*mox Papa desinit esse*). If he were to publicly defect from the faith by professing heresy, then, as a theoretically possible hypothesis with real pracical applicability; the pope, having already pronounced

---

[437] Albert Lang, *Fundamentaltheologie*, Band II *Der Auftrag der Kirche*, München, 1962, p. 80: «Das soll nicht ein persönliches Privileg für den Apostel sein, sondern eine Ausrüstung für sein Amt, die ihn verpflichtet, nun seinerseits die Brüder im Glauben zu stärken. Diesem Auftrag kann er nur nachkommen, wenn er leitend, mahnend und vorbeugend auf die Brüder einwirken kann, um ihren Glauben zu bewahren und zu lenken. Dem Confirmator fratrum muß Lehr-und Jurisdiktionsgewalt über die Brüder zustehen.»

[438] *Ibid.* — «Dem Petrus hat er die Aufgabe zugedacht, die Kirche sicher durch alle Fährnisse zu leiten. In der Abschiedsstunde gibt er ihm den Auftrag, in den Zeiten der Gefahr die Brüder im Glauben zu stärken, gibt ihm aber auch die Versicherung, daß ihm sein Beistand bei der Erfüllung dieser Aufgabe nicht fehlen werde. Durch sein Gebet, das hier nur als ein wirksames Gebet verstanden werden kann, hat Jesus erreicht, daß der Glaube des Petrus nicht wanken wird.»

judgment upon himself and thus having been judged by God and having fallen from the supreme pontificate *"by himself"*, he could then be judged and punished by the Church. This proposition of the Holy Doctor is an explicit restatement and concise application of the teaching of Pope Innocent III, who teaches that the pope has no superior but God (*post Deum alium superiorem non habet [Sermo III]*) to judge him; thus, "Vir autem iste [Romanus Pontifex] alligatus uxori, [Ecclesiæ Romanæ] [...] non deponitur; nam «*suo domino aut stat, aut cadit*» (*Rom.* XIV). – «Qui autem judicat, dominus est» (I *Cor.* IV)." And again:

> "The Roman Pontiff has no superior but God. Who, therefore, should a pope 'lose his savour', could cast him out or trample him under foot — since of the pope it is said 'gather thy case (causa)[439] into thy fold' [fold of the toga over the breast]? Truly, he should not flatter himself about his power, nor should he rashly glory in his honour and high estate, because the less he is judged by man, the more he is judged by God. I say less, because he can be judged by men, **or rather, can be shown to be already judged**, if for example he should wither away into heresy; **because he who does not believe is already judged.** In such a case it should be said of him: *If salt should lose its savour, it is good for nothing but to be cast out and trampled underfoot by men.*"[440]

By "cast out", Innocent means "deposed", and by "trampled underfoot by men, "despised by the people": (*mittatur foras,* id est ab officio deponatur*: et concucetur ab hominibus*, id est a populo contemnatur). He clearly teaches that the pope *as pope* cannot be judged by men, since the servant is judged by his own superior, and the Roman Pontiff has no

---

[439] "causa" – case, lawsuit, contention – Thus, "Collige causam tuam in sinum tuum" = "Gather thy case into thine own bosom."

[440] "Servus enim, secundum Apostolum, «suo domino stat aut cadit (Rom. xiv).» Propter quod idem Apostolus ait; «Tu quis es, qui judicas alienum servum?» (Ibid.) Unde cum Romanus pontifex non habeat alium dominum nisi Deum, quantumlibet evanescat, quis potest eum foras mittere, aut pedibus conculcare? Cum illi dicatur: «Collige causam tuam in sinum tuum?» Verum non frustra sibi blandiatur de potestate, neque de sublimitate vel honore temere glorietur; quia quanto minus judicatur ab homine, tanto magis judicatur a Deo. Minus dico; quia potest ab hominibus judicari, vel potius judicatus ostendi, si videlicet evanescat in haeresim; quoniam «qui non credit, jam judicatus est» (*Joan.* iii). In hoc siquidem casu debet intelligi de illo, *quod si sal evanuerit, ad nihilum valet ultra, nisi ut mittatur foras, et conculcetur ab homninibus*." (*Sermo IV De Diversis*)

superior but God: "Servus enim, secundum Apostolum, «*suo domino stat aut cadit (Rom.* xiv).» Propter quod idem Apostolus ait; «*Tu quis es, qui judicas alienum servum?*» (*Ibid.*) Unde cum Romanus pontifex non habeat alium dominum nisi Deum, quantumlibet evanescat, quis potest eum foras mittere, aut pedibus conculcare?" So, the pope asks, "Since the Roman Pontiff has no superior but God, if he were to lapse, who can cast him out and trample him underfoot?"

The answer he gives explains, quoting St. John, that as a heretic, he is already judged (quoniam «*qui non credit, jam judicatus est*» (*Joan.* iii).), and therefore, for reason of fornication, not carnal but the error of infidelity, the Roman Church can divorce the Roman Pontiff; since the matrimony can only exist between legitimate persons (*solus consensus inter legitimas personas efficit matrimonium*). By the sin of infidelity, the necessary disposition for the spiritual matrimonial union between the Roman Pontiff and the Church ceases to exist; and thus the heretic, no longer a legitimate spouse, would cease to be pope, and could then be judged by men. This is what St. Robert Bellarmine teaches in *De Romano Pontifice lib. ii cap. xxx*: "*Est ergo quinta opinio vera, papam hæreticum manifestum per se desinere esse papam et caput, sicut per se desinit esse christianus et membrum corporis Ecclesiæ; quare ab Ecclesia posse eum judicari et puniri. Hæc est sententia omnium veterum Patrum, qui docent, hæreticos manifestos mox amittere omnem jurisdictionem.*"

"Therefore, the true opinion is the fifth, according to which the Pope who is manifestly a heretic ceases by himself to be Pope and head, in the same way as he ceases to be a Christian and a member of the body of the Church; and for this reason he can be judged and punished by the Church. This is the opinion of all the ancient Fathers, who teach that manifest heretics immediately lose all jurisdiction."

In this manner, the pope, who has no judge but God, can be judged by men upon having ceased to be pope:

> «*Fundamentum hujus sententiæ est quoniam hæreticus manifestus nullo modo est membrum Ecclesiæ, idest, neque animo neque corpore, sive neque unione interna, neque externa.*»

"The foundation of this argument is that the manifest heretic is not in any way a member of the Church, that is, neither spiritually nor corporally, which signifies that he is not such by internal union nor by external union."

In order to attack this doctrine, which they ignorantly dismiss as a "sedevacantist argument", John Salza and Robert Siscoe have blindly declared that my exposition on Bellarmine's doctrine proves that I have never even read Bellarmine (!); and in their attempt to refute the argument, as I already explained, they have fallen into two heresies: 1) They have denied a revealed truth of the universal magisterium pertaining to the divine constitution of the Church regarding heresy, apostasy and schism; and 2) They have denied the injudicability of the Roman Pontiff, which pertains essentially to the dogma of papal primacy.

The heretical doctrine of Salza and Siscoe, that a pope while still in office can be judged by the Church is ultimately founded on and hinges on their heretical interpretation of the doctrine on the nature of heresy, apostasy and schism taught by Pius XII in *Mystici Corporis*. Salza & Siscoe speak of my, "erroneous opinion", which according to them is based on, "a misreading/misapplication of Pope Pius XII's Mystici Corporis Christi [...] in which the Pope says 'For not every offense (admissum), although it may be a grave evil, is such as by its very own nature to sever a man from the Body of the Church, as does schism or heresy or apostasy.'" [6] According to them, the teaching in this passage is that "Pope Pius XII is referring to the **'*offense*' or *CRIME (not SIN) of heresy, which severs one from the Body of the Church, after the formal and material elements have been proven by the Church.*"** It is their explicitly stated position that,

> "the nature of the ***crime of heresy*** requires no additional censure to sever one from the Body. But this does not nullify the necessity of the Church – who alone has the authority to judge whether a person is guilty of the crime of heresy – rendering a judgment, and most certainly in the case of a person who continues to present himself as a Catholic (as opposed to one who openly left the Church)."

What Salza and Siscoe are saying here quite explicitly is that heresy as such does not *suapte natura* sever the heretic from the body of the Church by itself without the judgment of the Church, but only the *canonical crime of heresy* according to **ecclesiastical law**, severs the heretic from the body of the Church, after the Church has judged, **without any additional censure.** Notwithstanding that in the first part of this work, I have demonstrated the absurdity of this heretical interpretation of the doctrine on the nature of heresy; and that this teaching of Pius XII pertains not to ecclesiastical law but to divine law *(Deo iubente)*, Salza and Siscoe remain entrenched in their heretical belief. However, even without the explanation I have given, it should already have been obvious enough to Salza and Siscoe just from reading the opening words of the encyclical; that, in the passage in question, Pius XII would not be expounding a distinction on a point of ecclesiastical law concerning the delict of heresy in a dogmatic encyclical on the divine constitution of the Church. Those opening words are:

> "*LITTERAE ENCYCLICAE AD VENERABILES FRATRES PATRIARCHAS, PRIMATES, ARCHIEPISCOPOS, EPISCOPOS ALIOSQUE LOCORUM ORDINARIOS PACEM ET COMMUNIONEM CUM APOSTOLICA SEDE HABENTES: DE MYSTICO IESU CHRISTI CORPORE DEQUE NOSTRA IN EO CUM CHRISTO CONIUNCTIONE.*"

Thus it is clear that this is a **doctrinal encyclical** addressed to all the bishops of the universal Church, on the Mystical Body of Jesus Christ and our union with Him in IT. In that encyclical Pius XII explains, what has already been a manifest dogma of the universal magisterium, that there are two ways that a person can be separated from the body of the Church; 1) **excommunication** by the authority of the Church, and; 2) **heresy, apostasy or schism**, which by themselves, *suapte natura*, sever one from the body of the Church. For all other sins and offenses, one is severed from the body of the Church only upon being excommunicated by legitimate ecclesiastical authority. Heresy, schism and apostasy by the very nature of the sin, effect the separation of the culprit from the body of the Church, without any penalty, censure or judgment of the ecclesiastical authority. Msgr. Van Noort comments:

> "b. Public heretics (and a fortiori, apostates) are not members of the Church. They are not members because they separate themselves from the unity of Catholic faith and from the external profession of that faith. Obviously, therefore, they lack one of three factors—baptism, profession of the same faith, union with the hierarchy—pointed out by Pius XII as requisite for membership in the Church. The same pontiff has explicitly pointed out that, unlike other sins, heresy, schism, and apostasy automatically sever a man from the Church. 'For not every sin, however grave and enormous it be, is such as to sever a man automatically from the Body of the Church, as does schism or heresy or apostasy'."[441]

---

[441] Dogmatic Theology, Volume II, Christ's Church, pp. 241-242.

John Salza and Robert J. Siscoe, (as their own words state quite plainly), categorically, adamantly, and explicitly reject this doctrine of the universal and ordinary magisterium of the Church; and, according to their convoluted reasoning, they have professed a ***third way*** for sinners to be separated from the Church: by, 1) openly renouncing or leaving the Church (such as one who joins another sect or religion); or, 2) by being excommunicated by the authority of the Church; and also, 3) by heresy – by which they are severed from the body of the Church only when the Church will have established the crime in its judgment, and not before. On the basis of their heretical interpretation of *Mystici Corporis*, and the legalistic fundamentalism of their interpretation of the Canon *Si papa (Decretum Gratiani)*, (which has never had any statutory force nor has ever been officially recognized[442]), they have resurrected the universally abandoned opinions which held that a manifestly heretical pope would remain in office until he would have been judged by the Church, by proper Church authorities; and only upon being judged by the Church, he would fall from office. Since the solemn definition of the primacy in *Pastor Æternus*, those opinions had to be abandoned because they directly conflicted with the doctrine of the injudicability of the Roman Pontiff set forth and solemnly declared in that dogmatic constitution.

Robert Siscoe's reply, which appeared on the *True or False Pope?* website, desperately attempts to sidestep the undeniable point that the injudicability of the Roman Pontiff is a *defined dogma* by making a futile defense of the non-existent juridical force of the *Canon Si papa*:

---

[442] «It was about 1150 that the Camaldolese monk, Gratian, professor of theology at the University of Bologna, to obviate the difficulties which beset the study of practical, external theology (theologia practica externa), i.e. canon law, composed the work entitled by himself "Concordia discordantium canonum", but called by others "Nova collectio", "Decreta", "Corpus juris canonici", also "Decretum Gratiani", the latter being now the commonly accepted name. In spite of its great reputation the "Decretum" has never been recognized by the Church as an official collection.» — *Catholic Encyclopedia*

«The "Corpus Juris Canonici" was now, indeed, complete, but it contained collections of widely different juridical value. Considered as collections, the "Decree" of Gratian, the "Extravagantes Joannis XXII", and the "Extravagantes communes" have not, and never had, a legal value, but the documents which they contain may possess and, as a matter of fact, often do possess, very great authority.» — *Catholic Encyclopedia*

Siscoe: The Canon Si Papa, which Fr. Kramer tries to dismiss, is found in the Decretum Gratiani (12th century), which is the first part of a collection of six legal texts that together became known as the Corpus Juris Canonici. The canon was on the books for eight centuries and is cited regularly by the theologians who discuss the loss of office for a heretical pope. It is treated as an authoritative canon by them all, including St. Robert Bellarmine. The reason Fr. Kramer is attempting to dismiss this canon is because it explicitly states that a pope (not a former pope) can be judged in the case of heresy (not punished, but judged), which is a teaching that Fr. Kramer declares to be heretical. He thinks this teaching is contrary to the famous axiom "Prima sedes a nemine iudicatur" (the First See is judged by no one). What he doesn't realize is that heresy is the exception to the rule, and it has always been considered as such. Si Papa explicitly states that a pope can be judged in the case of heresy, and this is how the canon has been interpreted by theologians for centuries.

The great 17th century canonist, Fr Paul Laymann, S.J., (who is recognized as one of the greatest canonists of his day), also acknowledges the authority of Si Papa. "He wrote: [...] And in Si Papa d. 40, it is reported from Archbishop Boniface: 'He who is to judge all men is to be judged by none, unless he be found by chance to be deviating from the Faith'."»

The following is Cajetan's commentary on Si Papa: "Next that of Boniface, pope and martyr, as found in Si Papa [D. 40, c. 6], where he says, 'Unless the pope is deviant from the faith, no mortal presumes to convict him of his faults,' where only the crime of unbelief entails subjection to a judge by whom the pope can be judged, which is recognized to be the universal Church or the general council." [Cajetan, De Comparatione Auctoritatis Papae et Concilii, English Translation in Conciliarism & Papalism, by Burns & Izbicki (New York: Cambridge University Press, 1997), p. 103.]

They all interpret Si Papa is meaning that heresy is the exception to the rule, which permits the Church to render a judgment concerning the pope in the case of heresy.

Suarez also confirms that heresy is the exception to the rule that "the pope is judged by no one". He wrote:"If you ask what gives us certainty that, by Divine Law, a Pontiff is deposed as soon as a sentence is pronounced by the Church [contrary to the teaching of Cajetan]: I respond, in the first place, that I have already produced the testimony of [Pope] Clement, which is from the mouth of Peter; in the second place... it is the common consensus of the Church and the Pontiffs. (...) "I say fourthly: outside of the case of heresy, a true and undoubted Pontiff, even if he be extremely wicked, cannot be deprived of his dignity. (...) Therefore all the Pontiffs cited above, while affirming that the Church can pass judgment on the Supreme Pontiff in the case of heresy, deny absolutely that she can pass judgment on him outside of that case; and it is in this sense that the often say that the Pope is judged by no one."

It is first to be noted, as Don Curzio Nitoglia points out, that the *Canon si Papa*, "has been demonstrated to be spurious, *and today, no canonist accepts it any more as a proof of authority*."[443] It is also to be pointed out that Siscoe quotes only antiquated opinions of Counter-Reformation theologians, whose opinions were based on the false premise that the *Canon Si papa*, which never had been accorded any official recognition of having force of law, and was discovered to be spuriously attributed to St. Boniface, established judgment for heresy as an exception to papal injudicability. Those opinions eventually were totally and unanimously abandoned after The First Vatican Council defined the *injudicability of the pope* as pertaining to the dogma of the universal primacy of jurisdiction of the Roman Pontiff; and that injudicability which is the dogmatic basis of total *papal immunity from judgment*, was incorporated into the Code of Canon Law.

It pertains to the very nature of heresy that by professing manifest heresy, one ceases to be a Christian and a member of the Church; and, as I have explained, heresy as a species of infidelity, in its nature takes one out of the Church. One is a Christian by faith, united to God by belief, and to the Church by the external profession of faith. This is the nature of heresy, that it takes one out of the Church, and as such, does not admit of exceptions, any more than man, having the nature of a rational animal, could be a dog; or that a dog, according to its nature an irrational animal, could be a rational man.

Hence, it is contrary to Christian belief that a heretic can be pope, because a Christian is a professing believer in Christ, and a heretic is an unbelieving infidel dog (Matth. 7:6, 15:26; Mark 7:27; Philip. 3:2; Apoc. 22:15); and an infidel dog can no more be the head of the Church – the highest and chief member of the Church, than a dog could be king over a nation of humans; because by nature a dog is not a man, and a heretic is not a member of the Church.

Thus it is that a pope who falls into manifest heresy ceases by that very fall to be a member of the Church, because the natural motion of heresy removes one from the body of the Church. Hence, Bellarmine,

---

[443] «Tuttavia i due Dottori [Cajetan and John of St. Thomas] si rifanno al Decreto di Gratiano (pars I, dist. 40, canon 6 "Si Papa"), che è stato dimostrato spurio *ed oggi nessun canonista prende più come un argomento d'autorità*.»

Ballerini, and Gregory XVI teach that such a pope would pronounce judgment upon himself, cease *per se* to be pope, and of his own volition would have in some manner abdicated.

Thus, no longer a pope or member of the Church, the manifest heretic would be already deposed, and could therefore be so declared by the Church to "be deposed" (*esse depositum*) and not that he can be deposed (*deponi posse*) by the Church. This critical distinction between *esse depositum* and *deponi posse* is made by Bellarmine in his exposition on the third opinion, and by Ballerini in the earlier quoted passage on the deposition of "Benedict XIII": «*depositum declaruit potius quam deposuit*». Hence, Salza and Siscoe err in saying that according to Bellarmine, a pope who is a manifest heretic can be deposed by the Church. Such a pope, in the doctrine of Bellarmine, would be like the king who renounces his royalty, yet refuses to give up the throne. By renouncing his royalty, he becomes a commoner and ceases to be king; and therefore the State has the authority to remove him from the throne if he is unwilling to give it up. As king, he was the head of state, and none in his realm would have the authority to remove him. Likewise, a pope who becomes a manifest heretic renounces his membership in the royal priesthood of Christ; and loses all claim to any prerogative pertaining to it. Having abdicated his membership in the royal family of God's household, he thereby forfeits all claim to the throne of Christ's Vicar, and becomes a mere usurper who must be evicted.

All of the adherents of the variations of Opinion No. 4 argue against the nature of heresy as taught in *Mystici Corporis*; by saying that the manifest heretic pope remains in office until he is judged by the Church; since heresy, *suapte natura*, would sever him from membership in the Church; and as a necessary logical corollary, *ex natura hæresis*, would effect the immediate loss of office *ipso facto*, as is taught by the Fathers. They also argue against the dogma of the Primacy which defines the pope is the supreme judge who is judged by no one. The pope is the monarch who cannot be judged by his subjects, any more than a secular king of an absolute monarchy can be judged by his subjects.[444] The subjects do

---

[444] «Quis autem sum ego, aut quæ domus patris mei, ut sedeam excellentior regibus et solium gloriæ teneam? Mihi namque dicitur in Propheta: «Constitui te super gentes et regna, ut evellas et destruas et disperdas et dissipes, et ædifices st plantes» (Jer.l).»

«Cum autem soli Petro loqueretur, universaliter ait: Quodcumque ligaveris super terram, erit ligatum et in ccelis, etc.; quia Petrus ligare potest cæteros, sed

not possess the authority. There is no office or institution possessed of the authority to judge a pope, so it is absurd to maintain that any individual or body can officially warn or judge the pope. Only if the pope has forfeited his office and ceased to be pope, can he be judged by those who were his subjects, but now have authority over him. All variations of Opinion No. 4, whether of Cajetan, Suárez, John of St. Thomas, Billuart, Laymann, etc., are no longer admissible, because they offend against the doctrine of *Mystici Corporis* on the nature of heresy severing one *suapte natura* from the Church; and offend against the injudicability of the pope defined in *Pastor Æternus*.

The same can be said of Opinion No. 3, that it cannot be considered admissible to subscribe to that opinion, because it professes that a manifest heretic would remain in office, as the visible head of the Church, and thus conflicts with the doctrine of *Mystici Corporis* that heretics are cut off from membership in the Church according to the very nature of heresy; and conflicts with the Church's canonical doctrine on Tacit Resignation of Office (can. 188 4°); which Bellarmine demonstrated is the unanimous teaching of the Fathers, namely, that heretics are outside the Church and immediately lose all jurisdiction, not by any human law, but *ex natura hæresis*.

Opinion No. 2 has been universally abandoned, because it is untenable: It is founded on the erroneous belief that even a secret heretic ceases entirely to be a member of the Church. If that were the case, then there would never be any way of knowing whether the pope was a true pope, or a counterfeit heretic who has fallen from the pontificate, and the Church would thereby be deprived of the certitude of having a visible head. Bellarmine demonstrates this point in *De Ecclesia Militante, Cap. X*. It would also bring about a defection of the Church because it pertains to the divine constitution of the Church that it is under the governance of the pope, and therefore it would be a defection if the whole Church

---

ligari non porest a cæteris. «Tu, inquit, vocaberis Cephas (Joan. 1), quod exponitur caput; quia sicut in capite consistit omnium sensuum plenitudo, in cæteris autem membris pars est aliqua plenitudinis: ita cæteri vocati sunt in partem sollicitudinis, solus autem Petrus assumptus est in plenitudinem potestatis. Jam ergo videtis quis iste servus, qui super familiam constituitur, profecto vicarius Jesu Christi, successor Petri, Christus Domini, Deus Pharaonis: inter Deum et hominem medius constitutus, citra Deum, sed ultra hominem: minor Deo, sed major homine: qui de omnibus judicat, et a nemine judicatur: Apostoli voce pronuntians, «qui me judicat, Dominus est (ICor. iv).»
– Innocent III, *Sermo II, De Diversis*.

would fall under the power of a secret heretical impostor. Since Christ conferred indefectibility on the Church, it is impossible for God's providence to permit a pope to secretly fall into formal heresy and invisibly lose office. Thus, it is either impossible altogether for a pope to be a heretic, or if he is a secret heretic, he would remain in office. The second opinion, therefore, is objectionable, although it was the opinion of Cardinal Juan de Torquemada, the theologian of Pope Eugenius IV at the time of the Council of Florence; and *appears* at first glance also to have been the opinion of Pope Paul IV (but in fact it was not).

In my judgment, Opinion No. 5, as a pure hypothesis, is the true opinion, that a pope who is a manifest heretic would immediately lose office **by himself**. Any public sin or crime is established *per se* if the form of the sin is unmistakably manifest; and therefore, the opinion that the Church authorities would have to first "establish the crime" before the heretic would lose office is nonsensical, since the heretic manifestly establishes the crime by pronouncing the public judgment of heresy against himself. Salza & Siscoe have distorted the Catholic doctrine on the nature of heresy in order to make the Church's doctrine appear to conform with their heretical doctrine that holds that the public sin of heresy, committed as an external act, is a matter pertaining to the internal forum; and that the "crime" of heresy needs to be "established" by the judgment of ecclesiastical authority before the manifest heretic is cut off from the body of the Church. According to Salza and Siscoe, «for a Pope to lose his office for heresy, the Church first judges him a heretic, and then God removes him from office (and in the "Third Opinion," Bellarmine explicitly says that a heretical pope "can be judged by the Church").»[445]

Against the heresy that the pope can be judged by anyone, Fr. E. Sylvester Berry quotes St. Robert Bellarmine:

> «The Roman Pontiff is not subject to any power on earth whether civil or ecclesiastical. This follows of necessity from his position as supreme head of the Church, which is subject to no authority save that of Christ alone. "Being supreme head of the Church, he cannot be judged by any other ecclesiastical power, and as the Church is a spiritual society superior to any temporal power whatever, he cannot be judged by any temporal ruler. Therefore, the supreme head of the Church can direct and judge the rulers of temporal powers, but he can neither be directed nor judged by them without a perversion of due order founded in the very nature of things" [St.

---

[445] Salza & Siscoe in *OUR REPLIES TO FR. PAUL KRAMER, PART II.*

Robert Bellarmine, *De Romano Pontifice*, Book 2, Ch. 26]. This doctrine is taught by the Fathers and incorporated in the canons of the Church: "The first See is judged by no one" [Canon 1556]. A synod of bishops held in Rome in 503, to investigate charges against Pope Symmachus, declared that "God wished the causes of other men to be decided by men, but He reserved to His own tribunal, without question, the ruler of this See."»[446]

Likewise, Rev. Charles Augustine:

«The first or primatial see is subject to no one's judgment. This proposition must be taken in the fullest extent, not only with regard to the object of infallibility. For in matters of faith and morals it was always customary to receive the final sentence from the Apostolic See, whose judgment no one dared to dispute, as the tradition of the Fathers demonstrates. Neither was it ever allowed to reconsider questions or controversies once settled by the Holy See. But even the person of the Supreme Pontiff was ever considered as unamenable to human judgment, he being responsible and answerable to God alone, even though accused of personal misdeeds and crimes. A remarkable instance is that of Pope Symmachus (498-514). He, indeed, submitted to the convocation of a council (the *Synodus Palmaris*, 502), because he deemed it his duty to see to it that no stain was inflicted upon his character, but that synod itself is a splendid vindication of our canon. The synod adopted the Apology of Ennodius of Pavia, in which occurs the noteworthy sentence: "God wished the causes of other men to be decided by men; but He has reserved to His own tribunal, without question, the ruler of this see." No further argument for the traditional view is required. A general council could not judge the Pope, because, unless convoked or ratified by him, it could not render a valid sentence. Hence nothing is left but an appeal to God, who will take care of His Church and its head.»[447]

Similarly Fr. Stanislaus Woywod:

«The Primatial See can be judged by no one (Canon 1556). The Supreme Pontiff has the highest legislative, administrative and judicial power in the Church. The Code states that the Roman Pontiff cannot be brought to trial by anyone. The very idea of the trial of a person supposes that the court

---

[446] Rev. E. Sylvester Berry, *The Church of Christ: An Apologetic and Dogmatic Treatise*, London, 1927, pp. 544-45.

[447] Rev. Charles Augustine, *A Commentary on the New Code of Canon Law*, Vol. VII, St. Louis and London, 1921, pp. 11-12.

conducting the trial has jurisdiction over the person, but the Pope has no superior, wherefore no court has power to subject him to judicial trial.»[448]

Thus, the expert commentaries on Canon Law provide us with a certain understanding of the doctrine defined at the First Vatican Council:

> «And since the Roman Pontiff is at the head of the universal Church by the divine right of apostolic primacy, We teach and declare also that he is the supreme judge of the faithful, and that in all cases pertaining to ecclesiastical examination recourse can be had to his judgment; moreover, that the judgment of the Apostolic See, whose authority is not surpassed, is to be disclaimed by no one, nor is anyone permitted to pass judgment on its judgment. Therefore, they stray from the straight path of truth who affirm that it is permitted to appeal from the judgments of the Roman Pontiffs to an ecumenical Council, as to an authority higher than the Roman Pontiff.»[449]

THE POPE, WHILE IN OFFICE, MAY NEVER BE JUDGED BY ANYONE ON EARTH:

> The Roman Pontiff has received from Christ supreme authority over the whole Church, and it follows from this very fact that he, in the direction of the faithful to eternal salvation, possesses full jurisdiction and all its attributes. He alone, or together with a Council called by him, can make laws for the universal Church, abrogate them or derogate from them, grant privileges, appoint, depose, judge or punish Bishops. He is the supreme judge by whom all causes are to be tried; he is the supreme judge whom no one may try.
>
> ... It is not becoming that the supreme legislator [i.e. the Pope] should be subject to other laws, except to those which emanate from the Sovereign Pontificate; it is not becoming that he who constitutes the tribunal of appeal for all men, rulers as well as subjects, should be judged by his inferiors....
>
> The divine law upon which rests pontifical immunity in spiritual things, is also the foundation upon which is built the ecclesiastical law in things partly spiritual and partly temporal. That the Apostolic See is subject to no judgment is affirmed by Boniface VIII in these terms, "The superiority of the Church and ecclesiastical power over the State and civil power is verified by the prophecy of Jeremias, 'I have set thee this day over the nations, and

---

[448] Rev. Stanislaus Woywod, *A Practical Commentary on the Code of Canon Law*, revised by Rev. Callistus Smith New York, 1952, n. 1549, p. 225.

[449] First Vatican Council, Dogmatic Constitution *Pastor Æternus*, Ch. 3; Denz. 1830.

over kingdoms to root up, and to pull down, and to waste, and to destroy, and to build, and to plant' [Jer 1:10]. Therefore, if the earthly power shall go astray, it shall be judged by the spiritual; and if a lesser spiritual power shall go astray, by its superior: but if the supreme power shall go astray, he can be judged by God alone, not by man, according to the Apostle, 'The spiritual man judgeth all things, and he himself is judged of no man'" [Bull Unam Sanctam].

The Roman Pontiff is declared to be free from subjection to any forum or tribunal by the first Canon in De Fore Competente. "Prima Sedes a nemine judicatur" [Canon 1556]. By the Prima Sedes is meant the Roman Pontiff, as is apparent from the nature of the thing [cf. Canon 7]. The Sacred Congregations, Tribunals and Offices by means of which the Pope is wont to transact the affairs of the Church are not included in this immunity, and their members may be judged by the Pope himself or by his delegate. The reason why the Pope can be judged by no one is evident. No one can be judged by another unless he is subject to that person, at least with respect to the subject matter of the trial. Now, the Roman Pontiff is the Vicar of Jesus Christ, who is the King of Kings and the Lord of Lords, and to him has been entrusted the commission to feed His lambs and His sheep. In no way, therefore, can he be subjected to any man or to any forum, but is entirely immune from any human judgment. This principle, whether taken juridically or dogmatically suffers no exception.[450]

"The Roman Pontiff is declared to be free from subjection to any forum or tribunal by the first Canon in De Fore Competente. "Prima Sedes a nemine judicatur" [Canon 1556]. By the Prima Sedes is meant the Roman Pontiff, as is apparent from the nature of the thing [cf. Canon 7]."

What Fr. Burke states in this passage with the words, "By the Prima Sedes is meant the Roman Pontiff, as is apparent from the nature of the thing [cf. Canon 7]," is explained by Cardinal Manning, commenting on a passage of Ballerini: "***This primacy of chief jurisdiction***, not of mere order, in St. Peter and the Roman Pontiffs his successors, ***is personal, that is, attached to their person; and therefore a supreme personal right, which is communicated to no other, is contained in the primacy.***"

Manning then elaborates:

---

[450] Rev. Thomas Joseph Burke, *Competence in Ecclesiastical Tribunals*, Washington, D.C., Catholic University of America Press, 1922, pp. 85-87.

«Hence, when there is question of the rights and the jurisdiction proper to the primacy, and when these are ascribed to the Roman See, or Cathedra, or Church of St. Peter; by the name of the Roman See, or Cathedra, or Church, to which this primacy of jurisdiction is ascribed, the single person of the Roman Pontiff is to be understood, to whom alone the same primacy is attached.

"Hence again it follows, that whatsoever belongs to the Roman See or Cathedra or Church, by reason of the primacy, is so to be ascribed to the person of the Roman Pontiffs that they need help or association of none for the exercise of that right."*[451] From this passage three conclusions flow: I. First, that the Primacy is a personal privilege in Peter and his successors.

2. Secondly, that this personal privilege attaches to Peter and to the Roman Pontiffs alone. 3. Thirdly, that in exercising this same primacy the Roman Pontiff needs the help and society of no other. Ballerini then adds: "That what was personal in Peter by reason of the primacy, is to be declared personal in his successors the Roman Pontiffs, on whom the same primacy of Peter with the same jurisdiction has devolved, no one can deny." Therefore to Peter alone, and to the person alone of his successors, the dignity and jurisdiction of the Primacy is so attached, that it can be ascribed to no other Bishop, even though of the Chief Sees; and much less can it be ascribed to any number whatsoever of Bishops congregated together; nor in that essential jurisdiction of the primacy ought the Roman Pontiff to depend on any one whomsoever; nor can he; especially as the jurisdiction received from Christ was instituted by Christ uncircumscribed by any condition, and personal in Peter alone and his successors: like as He

---

[451] cf. Manning, *The Vatican Council and its Definitions*, p. 101: «* "Hic præcipuae jurisdictionis et non meri ordinis primatus S. Petri et Romanorum Pontificum ejus successorum personalis est, seu ipsorum personæ alligatus; ac proinde jus quoddam præcipuum ipsorum personale, id est, nulli alii commune, in eo primatu contineri debet. Hinc cum de jure, seu jurisdictione propria primatus agitur, hæcque Romanæ S. Petri sedi, cathedræ, vel Ecclesiæ tribuitur; sedis cathedræ vel Ecclesiæ Romanæ nomine, cui ea jurisdictio primatus propria asseratur, una Romani Pontificis persona intelligenda est, cui uni idem primatus est alligatus. Hinc quoque sequitur, quidquid juris ratione primatus Romanæ sedi cathedræ, vel Ecclesiæ competit, Romanorum Pontificum personæ ita esse tribuendum ut nullius adjutorio vel societate ad idem jus exercendum indigeant."» — Ballerini, *de Vi et Ratione Primatus*, cap. iii. propositio 3, p. 10.

instituted the primacy of jurisdiction to be personal, which without personal jurisdiction is unintelligible."*452»453

Cardinal Manning therefore concludes, "Ballerini has declared that whatsoever is ascribed to the Roman See, Cathedra, or Church is to be ascribed to the Person of the Roman Pontiff only." 454

The supreme judicial authority of the pope, to whom particularly grave crimes are reserved for judgment, is already clearly set forth by the Council of Trent:

> «*Magnopere vero ad christiani populi disciplinam pertinere sanctissimis patribus nostris visum est ut atrociora quædam et graviora crimina non a quibusvis sed a summis dumtaxat sacerdotibus absolverentur unde merito pontifices maximi pro suprema potestate sibi in Ecclesia universa tradita causas aliquas criminum graviores suo potuerunt peculiari iudicio reservare.*»455

The more grave criminal cases against bishops, including heresy, are reserved for judgment by the pope alone: «*Causæ criminales graviores contra episcopos etiam hæresis (quod absit) quæ depositione aut privatione dignæ sunt: ab ipso tantum summo Romano Pontifice cognoscantur et terminentur.*»456

I have already quoted the canons of Pope St. Gelasius457 which state starkly that the Roman Church judges all, and is judged by no one, and

---

452 «* "Quod autem personale in Petro fuit rations primatus, idem in successoribus ejus Romanis Pontificibus, in quos idem primatus Petri cum eadem jurisdictione transivit, personale esse dicendum, inficiari potest nemo. Soli igitur Petro et soli successorum ejus personæ ita alligata est propria primatus dignitas et jurisdictio ut nulli alii Episcopo præstantiorum licet sedium, et minus multo pluribus aliis Episcopis quantumvis in unum collectis, possit adscribi: neque in ea jurisdictione primatus essentiali Romanus Pontifex dependere ab alio quopiam debet aut potest, cum præsertim jpsam a Christo acceptam idem Christus nulla conditione circumscriptam, personalem solius Petri ac successorum esse instituerit, uti primatum jurisdictionis instituit personalem, qui sine personali jurisdictions intelligi nequit." — Ballerini, *de Vi et Ratione Primatus*, cap. iii. sect. 4, p. 13.»
453 Cardinal Manning, *The Vatican Council and its Definitions*, pp. 101 – 102.
454 *Ibid.*, p. 104.
455 Sesio XIV, Cap. VII.
456 *Ibid.* Canon V.
457 c. 16 (Gelasius I. a. 493) C. IX. qu. 3: "Ipsi sunt canones qui appellationes totius ecclesiae ad huius sedis examen voluere deferri. Ab ipsa vero nusquam prorsus appellari debere sanxerunt ac per hoc illam de tota ecclesia iudicare, ipsam ad nullius commeare iudicium nec de eius unquam præceperunt iudicio

Pope St. Gregory VII who declared that the pope cannot be judged by anyone; so, (as Pope Innocent III asked), who could cast out the pope and trample him underfoot? The answer provided by Innocent III, and by Bellarmine in Opinion No. 5, was also endorsed by the Apostolic See at the First Vatican Council under Pope Pius IX. On this point, we have the testimony of Archbishop John Purcell who was present at that Council:

«The question was also raised by a Cardinal, "What is to be done with the Pope if he becomes a heretic?" It was answered that there has never been such a case; the Council of Bishops could depose him for heresy, for from the moment he becomes a heretic he is not the head or even a member of the Church. The Church would not be, for a moment, obliged to listen to him when he begins to teach a doctrine the Church knows to be a false doctrine, and he would cease to be Pope, being deposed by God Himself.»

«If the Pope, for instance, were to say that the belief in God is false, you would not be obliged to believe him, or if he were to deny the rest of the creed, "I believe in Christ," etc. The supposition is injurious to the Holy Father in the very idea, but serves to show you the fullness with which the subject has been considered and the ample thought given to every possibility. If he denies any dogma of the Church held by every true believer, he is no more Pope than either you or I; and so in this respect the dogma of infallibility amounts to nothing as an article of temporal government or cover for heresy.»[458]

Thus, the official position of the Apostolic See at the First Vatican Council on the question of a heretic pope was Bellarmine's Opinion No. 5, exactly as I have explained it, but which John Salza and Robert Siscoe dismiss as a sedevacantists' misinterpretation of Bellarmine! The controversy between myself and Salza began when I wrote, "With or without the law, the heretic by the very nature of the sin of heresy ceases to be a Catholic and is incapable of holding office. Bellarmine explains this in *De Romano Pontifice*." With an almost unfathomable stupidity, Salza replied: "with this utterly erroneous assertion it does not seem possible that he has even read Bellarmine's De Romano Pontifice."

Catholic Encyclopedia, 1914, v.7, p. 261: "The pope himself, if notoriously guilty of heresy, would cease to be pope because he would cease to be a member of the Church."

---

iudicari"; c. 17 (idem a. 498) ead.: "Cuncta per mundum novit ecclesia, quod sacrosancta Romana ecclesia fas de omnibus habet iudicandi neque cuiquam de eius liceat iudicare iudicio." (Hinschius Op. Cit. p. 297)

[458] Archbishop John B. Purcell, quoted in Rev. James J. McGovern, *Life and Life Work of Pope Leo XIII* [Chicago, 1903, p. 241.

PART THREE

THE FIVE OPINIONS ON A HERETICAL POPE

SECTION ONE

THE FIVE OPINIONS

The eminent canonists Wernz and Vidal outline the five opinions[459]:

«Concerning this matter there are five Opinions of which the first denies the hypothesis upon which the entire question is based, namely that a Pope even as a private doctor can fall into heresy. This opinion although pious and probable cannot be said to be certain and common. For this reason the hypothesis is to be accepted and the question resolved.»

«A second opinion holds that the Roman Pontiff forfeits his power automatically even on account of occult heresy. This opinion is rightly said by Bellarmine to be based upon a false supposition, namely that even occult heretics are completely separated from the body of the Church.»

«The third opinion thinks that the Roman Pontiff does not automatically forfeit his power and cannot be deprived of it by deposition even for manifest heresy. This assertion is very rightly said by Bellarmine to be "extremely improbable".»

«The fourth opinion, with Suarez, Cajetan and others, contends that a Pope is not automatically deposed even for manifest heresy, but that he can and must be deposed by at least a declaratory sentence of the crime. "Which opinion in my judgment is indefensible" as Bellarmine teaches.»

«Finally, there is the fifth opinion – that of Bellarmine himself – whichh was expressed initially and is rightly defended by Tanner and others as the best proven and the most common. For he who is no longer a member of the body of the Church, i.e. the Church as a visible society, cannot be the head of the Universal Church. But a Pope who fell into public heresy would cease by that very fact to be a member of the Church. Therefore he would also cease by that very fact to be the head of the Church.»

They state their own position on the question: «By heresy which is notorious and openly made known. The Roman Pontiff should he fall

---

[459] *Jus Canonicum* by Franz Xavier Wernz S.J. and Pedro Vidal S.J. (1938) Chapter VII; and, *Jus Canonicum*, Roma, Gregoriana, 1943, vol. II, p. 517

into it is by that very fact even before any declaratory sentence of the Church deprived of his power of jurisdiction.» And conclude,

«Indeed, a publicly heretical Pope, who, by the commandment of Christ and the Apostle must even be avoided because of the danger to the Church, must be deprived of his power as almost all admit. But he cannot be deprived by a merely declaratory sentence... Wherefore, it must be firmly stated that a heretical Roman Pontiff would by that very fact forfeit his power. Although a declaratory sentence of the crime which is not to be rejected in so far as it is merely declaratory would be such, that the heretical Pope would not be judged, but would rather be shown to have been judged.»

Moynihan, in the preface of his above cited work explains, in

"Wernz-Vidal, five modern-day opinions are cited regarding the procedure to be followed in the event that a pope should lapse into heresy. The first opinion denies the supposition, namely that a pope in the role of a private individual is able to preach a doctrine which is heretical. The second maintains that a pontiff who secretly professes a heretical belief is automatically deprived of the papacy. The third opinion states that even though a pope should publicly preach a heretical doctrine, he would neither be automatically deposed nor could his deposition be brought about. Those in favor of the fourth opinion say that should a pope publicly profess a heretical doctrine he would not be automatically deposed, but his deposition could be brought about by a declaratory sentence. The fifth and last opinion Wernz-Vidal regard as *communior*. According to this view, a pope notoriously preaching a heretical doctrine would be automatically excommunicated and deprived of the papacy. The principal argument for this last opinion is based upon the fact that a pope who by his heresy is no longer a member of the Church, is *a fortiori* no longer the Head of the Church. Hence this opinion would admit of a declaratory sentence, but it would have to be one that was merely declaratory and nothing more."[460]

Similarly, Eduardus F. Regatillo:

"The Roman Pontiff ceases in office: ... (4) Through notorious public heresy? Five answers have been given: 1. 'The pope cannot be a heretic even as a private teacher.' A pious thought, but essentially unfounded. 2. 'The pope loses office even through secret heresy.' False, because a secret heretic can be a member of the Church. 3. 'The pope does not lose office because of public heresy.' Objectionable. 4. 'The pope loses office by a judicial sentence because

---

[460] Moynihan; *Op. cit.*; p. xi.

of public heresy.' But who would issue the sentence? The See of Peter is judged by no one (Canon 1556). 5. 'The pope loses office ipso facto because of public heresy.' This is the more common teaching, because a pope would not be a member of the Church, and hence far less could be its head."[461]

It is to be noted, that all of the Five Opinions existed historically before the lifetime of St. Robert Bellarmine; the first being the most recent, the opinion of Albert Pigghe (Albertus Pighius) who died in the same year (1542) that Bellarmine was born. Bellarmine mentions that the second opinion was held by Juan de Torquemada (1388-1468), but we find the origins of that opinion already in the works of the early Decretists, some of whom wrote expressly on the question of the deposition of a pope discovered to be an occult heretic. The origins of fourth opinion are already present in the writings of the earliest Decretists, writing between 1141-1180; and among whom are some who speak of the accusation of heresy as an exception to the rule of papal injudicability. Notably, the author of the *Summa De Iure Canonico Tractaturus* adopts the position that a council was superior in authority to a pope; and that the council's sentence must be awaited (*expectanda est*); and it is the council which decides whether or not the pope's doctrine is heretical.[462] The fifth opinion had its beginning in the *Decretum* itself, in which (as Moynihan explains), "Gratian had pointed out (C. xxiv, q. 1, dict. A. c. 1) that no condemnation was necessary in the case of a man who followed a heresy already condemned, for such a man was held to have wilfully included himself in that previous condemnation."[463] On that basis the authors of the 1180s, of the *Summa Reverentia sacrorum canonum*, the *Summa Et est sciendum*, and the Gloss, *Ecce uicit leo*, applied the principle that the heretic pope, having become *minor quolibet catholico*, would be self-condemned and would thereby lose office without any formal accusation or criminal trial. In the *Summa* of Huguccio, "All the arguments which had been assembled down through the years on the question of a heretical pope were recapitulated and expanded upon in the *Summa* of Huguccio, the greatest of the twelfth-century commentators on the *Dectetum*".[464] Moynihan explains,

> "Huguccio's presentation is so clear that it calls for little in the way of explanation. As in the *Summa Et est sciendum* and in the *summa Omnis qui iuste*,

---

[461] *Institutiones Iuris Canonici*. 5th ed. Santander: Sal Terrae, 1956. 1:396
[462] Moynihan; *Op. cit.*, p. 66.
[463] Moynihan; *Ibid.* p. 66.
[464] *Ibid.* p. 75.

Huguccio seeks to unravel all the intricate problems involved in bringing a pope to trial by eliminating the need or a trial as such. Taking his cue from the authors of these earlier works as well as from Gratian, Huguccio comprehensively determined the circumstances in which a pope could be presumed guilty of heresy, and so no longer a true pope, without any trial being held. He accepted Gratian's view that superiors could not be judged by inferiors, but in the question of a papal heretic, he reasoned that this rule was no longer valid, «cum hæreticus catholico minor sit» (C. II, q. 1. C. 20) [...] «Cum papa cadit in hæresim non iam maior sed minor quolibet catholico intelligitur».[465]

Moynihan makes the important observation that, "medieval canonists placed a great value upon arguments drawn from positive law. On the particular question of papal immunity and a heretical pope, citations from the Decretum of Gratian and the Decretals of Gregory IX and even from Justinian's Code formed the basis of most of their statements."[466] The legalism is apparent in the treatment of the question of an already condemned heresy and a new heresy; as if what mattered most in a case of papal heresy was the legal question of determining the authority to condemn a heresy, rather than the obvious theological consideration that what ultimately determines a pope's doctrine to be heretical is not whether or by what authority the pope's doctrine had been previously condemned, but whether or not it manifestly opposes a defined article of faith, even if previously the doctrine had never been professed by anyone nor condemned by the Church (as happened in the case of Arius, who was condemned at Alexandria in 321 by his diocesan bishop in a synod of nearly one hundred Egyptian and Libyan bishops before the solemn profession against his heresy at the Council of Nicaea in 325). In contrast, Innocent III's exposition of his own doctrine on this point, although derived in its essential points from the doctrine of Huguccio, is entirely based on a solid doctrinal foundation and set forth with theologically coherent argumentation; and therefore understandably it became the basis for the classical formulations of Opinion No. 5 in the doctrine of Bellarmine, Ballerini, Gregory XVI, and the others of that series of authors mentioned but not named by Hinschius – and finally Wernz & Vidal, who in the exposition of their own position (Opinion No. 5) quote almost verbatim the words of Innocent, saying that "the heretical Pope would not be judged, but would rather be shown to have been judged."

---

[465] Moynihan, *Ibid.* p. 80, 81.
[466] Moynihan, *Ibid.*, p. 143.

SECTION TWO

COMMENTARY ON THE FIVE OPINIONS

The doctrine of St. Robert Bellarmine is of the greatest importance to the Church's teaching on the papacy, since the First Vatican Council to a great extent based its doctrine on the primacy and infallibility of the Roman Pontiff on his doctrine. Pope Pius XI declared in *Providentissimus Deus*,

> «But it is an outstanding achievement of St Robert, that the rights and privileges divinely bestowed upon the Supreme Pontiff, and those also which were not yet recognised by all the children of the Church at that time, such as the infallible magisterium of the Pontiff speaking ex cathedra, he both invincibly proved and most learnedly defended against his adversaries. Moreover he appeared even up to our times as a defender of the Roman Pontiff of such authority that the Fathers of the [1870] Vatican Council employed his writings and opinions to the greatest possible extent.»[467]

Particularly concerning the primacy of the pope, Bellarmine's doctrine during his lifetime on the absolute injudicability of the pope while still in office had not yet been adopted by the First Vatican Council, which definitively settled and closed the question forever in a solemn decree of the extraordinary magisterium; but was still treated as an open question by theologians in Bellarmine's day. Similarly it can also be said about his doctrine on the loss of office in specific relation to the pronouncement on the nature of heresy by Pius XII in *Mystici Corporis*, in which is set forth more definitively the doctrine of the universal magisterium, but not *ex cathedra*, that heresy *suapte natura* severs the heretic from the body of the Church – in both cases Bellarmine demonstrated that these not yet solemnly defined teachings were already fulfilling the criteria of *de fide* doctrines of the universal and ordinary magisterium (what Ballerini called "manifest dogma" of the Church as distinguished from "defined dogma" of the extraordinary magisterium). So, while the five opinions were all accorded various degrees of

---

[467] Pope Pius XI, Decree *Providentissimus Deus* (declaring St. Robert Bellarmine a Doctor of the Church), 17 Sept, 1931.

legitimacy by theologians in the Seventeenth Century, and were at least tolerated by the magisterium, the same can no longer be said today of the third and fourth opinions, since there have been subsequent magisterial pronouncements which render them untenable and inadmissible, and therefore theologically antiquated. I have already explained the doctrinally problematic nature of the second opinion earlier in this work; so that leaves us with only the first and fifth opinions as theologically viable and legitimate. Thus, having given ample consideration to the fifth opinion earlier, I will focus here primarily on the first opinion, and Bellarmine's analysis of the fourth opinion in the next section, in which he provides his theological foundation for the fifth opinion.

First to be considered is in what manner a pope can be considered to be a heretic. The question is whether a pope can properly be a heretic; that is, a formal heretic, since all, Catholics and non-Catholics, says Bellarmine in *De Romano Pontifice lib. iv. cap. ii*, are in agreement that a pope can be materially in heresy due to ignorance: «Posse pontificem ut privatum Doctorem errare, etiam in quæstionibus juris universalibus, tam Fidei, quam morum, idque ex ignorantia, ut aliis Doctoribus interdum accidit.» The Holy Doctor then focuses on four opinions:

> «Prima (sententia) est, Pontificem etiam ut Pontificem, etiamsi cum generali Concilio definiret aliquid, posse esse hæreticum in se, & docere alios hæresim, & de facto ita aliquando accidisse. Hæc est hæreticorum omnium huius temporis, et præcipue Lutheri [...] & Calvini.»

This opinion, says Bellarmine, that the pope can himself be heretical and teach others heresy, even when defining with an ecumenical council, and that this has actually happened, is the opinion of all heretics, and particularly of Luther and Calvin.

> «Secunda sententia est, Pontificem ut Pontificem, posse esse hæreticum, & docere hæresim, si absque generali Concilio definiat, & de facto aliquando accidisse. Hanc opinionem sequitur, & tuetur Nilus in suo libro adversus primatum papæ: [...] & Hadrianus VI. Papa in quæst. de confirm.; qui omnes non in Pontifice, sed in Ecclesia sive in Concilio generali tantum, constituunt infallibillitatem iudicii de rebus Fidei.»

The second opinion is that the pope can be a heretic and teach heresy, if he defines without a general council, because infallibility in matters of faith and morals pertains not to the pontiff but to the Church in a general council; and he mentions that this was the opinion of Pope Adrian VI.

> «Tertia sententia est in alio extremo, Pontificem non posse ullo modo esse hæreticum, nec docere publice hæresim, etiamsi solus rem aliquam definiat. Ita Albertus Pighius lib. 4. Hier. Eccles. Cap. 8.»

The third opinion is of the opposite extreme, that of Albert Pighius, which holds that a pope cannot in any manner be a heretic, nor teach heresy, even when defining by himself.

> «Quarta sententia est quodammodo in medio. Pontificem, sive hæreticus esse possit, sive non, non posse ullo modo definire aliquid hæreticum a tota Ecclesia credendum: hæc est comunissima opinio fere omnium Catholicorum.»

The fourth opinion occupies the middle ground; the pope, regardless of whether or not he can be a heretic, cannot in any manner define something heretical for the whole Church to believe – and this opinion, says the Holy Doctor, is the most common opinion of nearly all Catholics.

He then pronounces his verdict on each of the four opinions:

> «Ex his quatuor opinionibus prima est hæretica; secunda non est proprie hæretica: nam adhuc videmus ab Ecclesia tolerari, qui illam sententiam sequuntur; tamen videtur omnino erronea & hæresi proxima; tertia probabilis est, non tamen certa; quarta certissima est et asserenda, ac ut ea facilius intelligi & confirmari possit, statuemus aliquot propositiones.»

The first, he says, is heretical; the second, while not properly heretical, because the Church still tolerates (i.e. in Bellarmine's day) those who follow this opinion; but it appears to be entirely erroneous and proximate to heresy; the third is probable; the fourth is most certain and is to be held. Since the definition of Vatican I on papal infallibility, the second opinion is now to be judged as heretical, and the fourth as *de fide definita*.

In Book II Chapter XXX of *De Romano Pontifice*, Bellarmine proposes the solution to the question on whether a heretic pope can be deposed. He first states the thesis: "A Pope can be judged and deposed by the Church in the case of heresy; as is clear from Dist. 40, can. Si Papa: therefore, the Pontiff is subject to human judgment, at least in some case." (Pontifex in casu hæresis potest ab Ecclesia judicari, et deponi, up patet distinct. 40. Can. *Si Papa*. Igitur, Pontifex est subjectus humano judicio, saltem in aliquot casu.); and then introduces his response, saying there are five opinions on this matter.

The Holy Doctor's response to the first opinion is brief and plainly stated in the original Latin, and in the precise English translation of Ryan Grant: «Prima est Alberti Pighii lib. 4 cap. 8 hierarchiæ Ecclesiasticæ; ubi contendit, Papam non posse esse hæreticum, proinde nec deponi in ullo casu; quæ sententia probabilis est, & defendi potest facile, ut postea suo loco ostendemus».[468] What he means by "in its proper place", is Book Four Chapter Six & Seven of the same work. There Bellarmine explains:

> «Nam Pontifex non solum non debet, nec potest hæresim prædicare, sed etiam debet veritatem semper docere, & sine dubio id faciet, cum Dominus illi jusserit confirmare fratres suos, & propterea addiderit, *Rogavi pro te, ut non deficiat fides tua*, idest, ut saltem non deficiat in throno tuo prædicatio veræ Fidei: at quomodo, quæso, confirmabit fratres in Fide, & veram Fidem semper prædicabit Pontifex hæreticus? Potest quidem Deus ex corde hæretico extorquere veræ Fidei confessionem, sicut verba posuit quondam in ore asinæ Balaam: at violentum erit, & non secundum morem providentiæ Dei suaviter disponentis omnia.»[469]

The question, «at quomodo, quæso, confirmabit fratres in Fide, & veram Fidem semper prædicabit Pontifex hæreticus?» (How, I ask, will a heretical Pope confirm the brethren in faith and always preach the true

---

[468] "The first is of Albert Pighius, who contends that the Pope cannot be a heretic, and hence would not be deposed in any case [319]: such an opinion is probable, and can easily be defended, as we will show in its proper place. Still, because it is not certain, and the common opinion is to the contrary, it will be worthwhile to see what the response should be if the Pope could be a heretic."

[469] «It is proved: 1) because it seems to require the sweet disposition of the providence of God. For the Pope not only should not, but cannot preach heresy, but rather should always preach the truth. He will certainly do that, since the Lord commanded him to confirm his brethren, and for that reason added: "I have prayed for thee, that thy faith shall not fail," that is, that at least the preaching of the true faith shall not fail in thy throne. How, I ask, will a heretical Pope confirm the brethren in faith and always preach the true faith? Certainly God can wrench the confession of the true faith out of the heart of a heretic just as he placed the words in the mouth of Balaam's ass. Still, this will be a great violence, and not in keeping with the providence of God that sweetly disposes all things.»

faith?), is of the greatest importance, because faith, (as Bellarmine explains in Book II Ch. XXX on the fourth opinion), which is the necessary disposition to retain the form of the supreme pontificate, would be utterly lacking in a heretic, who therefore would be incapable of preserving the form of the papacy in himself, and would therefore cease to be pope straightaway. A heretic would necessarily cease to be pope because even if he were only externally a member of the Church, he would lack faith as the necessary disposition to exercise the charism of Infallibility, since Christ did not confer a magical power of infallibility on Peter (and his successors), but He conferred on him the gift of unfailing faith as the necessary disposition to exercise the charism of Infallibility. Then there is the further consideration, as, Bellarmine remarks, "Certainly God can wrench the confession of the true faith out of the heart of a heretic just as he placed the words in the mouth of Balaam's ass. Still, this will be a great violence, and not in keeping with the providence of God that sweetly disposes all things"; but such a confession would not require, nor would proceed from unfailing faith as the **disposition** on which the exercise of the charism of Infallibility is based and in which it is rooted; and it would be contrary to the nature of man which is constituted of free will, and therefore **would not be a human act proceeding from the soul as the principle of the operation** of the exercise of a charism – the exercise of the supernatural charism of infallibly defining the true faith, given by Christ as the free and infallible exercise of that charism hinged upon and rooted in the virtue of unfailing faith as its necessary disposition. If God were to wrench the confession of the true faith out of a heretic in whom faith is absent, that heretic would not be exercising the charism of Infallibility any more than the ass of Balaam was exercising the prophetic charism, **because the act would not proceed from the soul as its principle making use of the organs of speech, exercising the faculty of speech, but God would be using the mouth of the heretical Pontiff in the same manner that He used the mouth of the ass, which did not possess the faculty of speech.**[470] (Numbers 22: 28-30)

---

[470] 28 «And the Lord opened the mouth of the ass, and she said: What have I done to thee? Why strikest thou me, lo, now this third time?29 Balaam answered: Because thou hast deserved it, and hast served me ill: I would I had a sword that I might kill thee. 30 The ass said: Am not I thy beast, on which thou hast been always accustomed to ride until this present day? tell me if I ever did the like thing to thee. But he said: Never.»

Faith would be utterly unnecessary for a Pontiff to profess the faith infallibly in such a manner as that; and therefore the grace of unfailing faith, which was promised by Christ to the Pontiff precisely for the purpose of enabling him to confirm the faith of his brethren, would have been given by Christ to serve no purpose, and would be utterly superfluous if the *confirmator fratrum* could exercise the charism of Infallibility with no faith at all; but since Christ gave to Peter and his successors the gift of unfailing faith precisely for the purpose of disposing them to confirm the faith of the brethren, faith is seen, therefore, to be the absolutely necessary disposition for the exercise of the charism of Infallibility, and hence, pertains essentially to the form of the Supreme Pontificate, and is therefore the necessary disposition for the form of the Pontificate to be conserved in the person of the Pontiff, and remain united to him.

As I have explained, the "necessary disposition", which Bellarmine says is faith, is necessary, because, the exercise of the charism of Infallibility depends entirely on the grace of unfailing personal faith of the pope, which *Pastor Æternus* declares Christ promised to Peter and his successors in order that they may fulfill the office of *confirmator fratrum*. The argument proving this *ex ratione* is based philosophically on St. Thomas' doctrine on the operation of the powers of the soul and the necessary dispositions that are sometimes required for these operations to accomplish their purpose. The application of St. Thomas' teaching on the relation of virtue to the operation of the powers of the soul, to the exercise of the papal charism of Infallibility is as follows.

Distinguishing between the essence of the soul and its powers, Aquinas explains that the powers of the soul are rooted in the potentiality and act of the substance of the soul, which, in its essence as form is act, but is in potentiality as the principle of the operation of the powers of the soul. [471] In *Article 2*, St. Thomas explains that the soul has

---

[471] «Respondeo dicendum quod impossibile est dicere quod essentia animae sit eius potentia; licet hoc quidam posuerint. Et hoc dupliciter ostenditur, quantum ad praesens. Primo quia, cum potentia et actus dividant ens et quodlibet genus entis, oportet quod ad idem genus referatur potentia et actus. Et ideo, si actus non est in genere substantiae, potentia quae dicitur ad illum actum, non potest esse in genere substantiae. Operatio autem animae non est in genere substantiae; sed in solo Deo, cuius operatio est eius substantia. Unde Dei potentia, quae est operationis principium, est ipsa Dei essentia. Quod non potest esse verum neque in anima, neque in aliqua creatura; ut supra etiam de Angelo dictum est. Secundo, hoc etiam impossibile apparet in anima. Nam

many and various powers because many operations are required for the soul to accomplish its end, which is beatitude, and why men, being of a lower order of nature than angels, require a greater number of operations to attain that end.[472] In article three, it is explained how the powers are of necessity distinguished by their acts and objects; and in the fourth article is explained the order between the higher and lower powers, and the dependence of the lower on the higher.[473] St. Thomas elaborates in

---

anima secundum suam essentiam est actus. Si ergo ipsa essentia animae esset immediatum operationis principium, semper habens animam actu haberet opera vitae; sicut semper habens animam actu est vivum. Non enim, inquantum est forma, est actus ordinatus ad ulteriorem actum, sed est ultimus terminus generationis. Unde quod sit in potentia adhuc ad alium actum, hoc non competit ei secundum suam essentiam, inquantum est forma; sed secundum suam potentiam. Et sic ipsa anima, secundum quod subest suae potentiae, dicitur actus primus, ordinatus ad actum secundum. Invenitur autem habens animam non semper esse in actu operum vitae. Unde etiam in definitione animae dicitur quod est actus corporis potentia vitam habentis, quae tamen potentia non abiicit animam. Relinquitur ergo quod essentia animae non est eius potentia. Nihil enim est in potentia secundum actum, inquantum est actus.» (*Summa Theol.* 1.77.1)

[472] «Respondeo dicendum quod necesse est ponere plures animae potentias. Ad cuius evidentiam, considerandum est quod, sicut philosophus dicit in II de caelo, quae sunt in rebus infima, non possunt consequi perfectam bonitatem, sed aliquam imperfectam consequuntur paucis motibus; superiora vero his adipiscuntur perfectam bonitatem motibus multis; his autem superiora sunt quae adipiscuntur perfectam bonitatem motibus paucis; summa vero perfectio invenitur in his quae absque motu perfectam possident bonitatem. Sicut infime est ad sanitatem **dispositus** qui non potest perfectam consequi sanitatem, sed aliquam modicam consequitur paucis remediis melius autem **dispositus est** qui potest perfectam consequi sanitatem, sed remediis multis; **et adhuc melius**, qui remediis paucis; optime autem, qui absque remedio perfectam sanitatem habet.»

[473] «Respondeo dicendum quod, **cum anima sit una, potentiae vero plures; ordine autem quodam ab uno in multitudinem procedatur; necesse est inter potentias animae ordinem esse.** Triplex autem ordo inter eas attenditur. **Quorum duo considerantur secundum dependentiam unius potentiae ab altera**, tertius autem accipitur secundum ordinem obiectorum. Dependentia autem unius potentiae ab altera dupliciter accipi potest, **uno modo, secundum naturae ordinem, prout perfecta sunt naturaliter imperfectis priora**; alio modo, secundum ordinem generationis et temporis, prout ex imperfecto ad perfectum venitur. Secundum igitur primum potentiarum ordinem, potentiae intellectivae sunt

Article 5 on the operation of the powers of the soul, distinguishing between those powers which exist in the soul as their subject, and those which have for their subject the conjoined body and soul, and therefore not proper to just the soul or the body:

> "from what we have said above (I:75:3; I:76:1 ad 1), that some operations of the soul are performed without a corporeal organ, as understanding and will. Hence the powers of these operations are in the soul as their subject. But some operations of the soul are performed by means of corporeal organs; as sight by the eye, and hearing by the ear. And so it is with all the other operations of the nutritive and sensitive parts. Therefore the powers which are the principles of these operations have their subject in the composite, and not in the soul alone."[474]

And finally, "All the powers are said to belong to the soul, not as their subject, but as their principle; because it is by the soul that the composite has the power to perform such operations."[475] It is evident, therefore,

---

priores potentiis sensitivis, unde dirigunt eas et imperant eis. Et similiter potentiae sensitivae hoc ordine sunt priores potentiis animae nutritivae. Secundum vero ordinem secundum, e converso se habet. Nam potentiae animae nutritivae sunt priores, in via generationis, potentiis animae sensitivae, unde ad earum actiones praeparant corpus. Et similiter est de potentiis sensitivis respectu intellectivarum. Secundum autem ordinem tertium, ordinantur quaedam vires sensitivae ad invicem, scilicet visus, auditus et olfactus. Nam visibile est prius naturaliter, quia est commune superioribus et inferioribus corporibus. Sonus autem audibilis fit in aere, qui est naturaliter prior commixtione elementorum, quam consequitur odor.»

[474] Iª q. 77 a. 5: «Respondeo dicendum quod illud est subiectum operativæ potentiæ, quod est potens operari, omne enim accidens denominat proprium subiectum. Idem autem est quod potest operari, et quod operatur. Unde oportet quod eius sit potentia sicut subiecti, cuius est operatio; ut etiam philosophus dicit, in principio de somno et vigilia. Manifestum est autem ex supra dictis quod **quædam operationes sunt animæ, quæ exercentur sine organo corporali, ut intelligere et velle. Unde potentiæ quæ sunt harum operationum principia, sunt in anima sicut in subiecto.** Quædam vero **operationes sunt animæ, quæ exercentur per organa corporalia**; sicut visio per oculum, et auditus per aurem. Et simile est de omnibus aliis operationibus nutritivæ et sensitivæ partis. Et ideo potentiæ quæ sunt talium operationum principia, sunt in coniuncto sicut in subiecto, et non in anima sola.»

[475] Iª q. 77 a. 5 ad 1: «Ad primum ergo dicendum quod **omnes potentiæ dicuntur esse animæ, non sicut subiecti, sed sicut *principii*,** quia per animam coniunctum habet quod tales operationes operari possit.»

that all operations proceed from the powers of the soul as principles of those operations, whether they be operations only of the soul, or of the composite of body and soul. Thus, for the pope to exercise the charism of Infallibility, the principle of the operation must be an internal power, of the soul, and not an external power such as the power which produced speech from the mouth of Balaam's ass. However, it does not lie within the power of the human soul to accomplish an operation that exceeds its natural power, and therefore, such an operation requires a supernatural virtue as a necessary disposition. Thus St. Thomas explains,

> "Since the habit perfects the power in reference to act, then does the power need a habit perfecting it unto doing well, which habit is a virtue, when the power's own proper nature does not suffice for the purpose. [...] Now the proper nature of a power is seen in its relation to its object. Since, therefore, as we have said above (I-II:19:3), the object of the will is the good of reason proportionate to the will, in respect of this the will does not need a virtue perfecting it. But if man's will is confronted with a good that exceeds its capacity, whether as regards the whole human species, such as Divine good, which transcends the limits of human nature, or as regards the individual, such as the good of one's neighbour, then does the will need virtue."[476]

To teach the faith infallibly is a "Divine good, which transcends the limits of human nature", for which, therefore, "then does the will need virtue."

Thus, according to the nature of the operation of the powers of the soul, the operation of the soul's power in the exercise of a supernatural charism presupposes and builds upon the natural power; and necessarily the operation of the charism of Infallibility requires a subject in which is

---

[476] Respondeo dicendum quod, cum **per habitum perficiatur potentia** ad agendum, **ibi indiget potentia habitu perficiente ad bene agendum, qui quidem habitus est virtus, ubi ad hoc non sufficit propria ratio potentiae.** Omnis autem potentiae propria ratio attenditur in ordine ad obiectum. Unde cum, sicut dictum est, obiectum voluntati sit bonum rationis voluntati proportionatum, quantum ad hoc non indiget voluntas virtute perficiente. **Sed si quod bonum immineat homini volendum, quod excedat proportionem volentis; sive quantum ad totam speciem humanam, sicut bonum divinum, quod transcendit limites humanae naturae, sive quantum ad individuum, sicut bonum proximi; ibi voluntas indiget virtute.** Et ideo huiusmodi virtutes quae ordinant affectum hominis in Deum vel in proximum, sunt in voluntate sicut in subiecto; ut caritas, iustitia et huiusmodi. (Ia IIæ 56 a.6)

present the habit of faith as the necessary disposition for the operation, in order that the soul attain to that divine truth, which transcends the limits of human nature, so that faith functioning as the supernatural disposition in the soul, enables the natural power of the soul to operate the supernatural power of the charism of the fullness of the power of faith; exercised by the soul as a human act of the composite of body and soul ***through the natural powers of the soul*** aided by grace. Thus it is that *for the exercise of the charism of Infallibility to be properly a human act of the Pontiff*, faith is the necessary disposition for the form of the supreme pontificate, to which pertains the charism of Infallibility, in which there is not just a participation in the power of the virtue of faith, but the plenitude of power (as Pope Innocent III says[477]): the plenitude of power – in which plenitude there is unfailing faith as the basis upon which depends the operation of the charism to infallibly teach and bind in matters of faith. Thus from reason, from considering the nature of the powers of the soul, one understands why both Pope Innocent III[478] and St. Robert Bellarmine[479] were correct in their belief that the Roman Pontiff cannot personally confirm the faith of others if that virtue is lacking in the Pontiff himself, because ***faith is necessary as a disposition of the soul and must be in the soul as its subject for the soul to be the principle of the operation of the charism of***

---

[477] «Ego tamen facile non crediderim, ut Deus permitteret Romanum pontificem contra fidem errare: pro quo spiritualiter oravit in Petro: <Ego, inquit, pro te rogavi, Petre, etc. (Luc.xxii),> Ergo *qui habet sponsam, sponsus est.* Haec autem sponsa non nupsit vacua, sed dotem mihi tribuit absque pretio pretiosam, **spirilualium videlicet plenitudinem** et latitudinem temporalium, magnitndinem et multiudinem utrorumque. Nam caeteri vocati sunt in partem sollicitudinis, solus autem Petrus assumptus est in **plenitudinem potesatis.**» (*Sermo III De Deversis*); «*Tu*, inquit, *vocaberis Cephas* (*Joan.* 1), quod exponitur caput; quia sicut in capite consistit **omnium sensuum plenitudo, in cæteris autem membris pars est aliqua plenitudinis: ita cæteri vocati sunt in partem sollicitudinis, solus autem Petrus assumptus est in plenitudinem potestatis.**» (*Sermo II De Diversis*)

[478] «Nisi enim ego solidaltus essem in fide, quomodo possem alios in fide firmare?» (*Sermo II, De Diversis*); «Ego tamen facile non crediderim, ut Deus permitteret Romanum pontificem contra fidem errare» (*Sermo III De Deversis*)

[479] «Nam Pontifex non solum non debet, nec potest haeresim praedicare, sed etiam debet veritatem semper docere, & sine dubio id faciet, [...] at quomodo, quaeso, confirmabit fratres in Fide, & veram Fidem semper praedicabit Pontifex haereticus?»

Infallibility. It is also plainly evident from the above considerations, that the merely external profession of faith of a faithless heretic, is in its very essence, entirely lacking the nature of a dispositive habit in the manner that the virtue of faith would dispose the soul of the pontiff to teach infallibly; since a false and lying profession of faith does not pertain even in the most remote and general way to faith, but to infidelity, and hence is a blasphemy against the Holy Ghost that hardens the soul in the error of infidelity and disposes it for eternal perdition. Now it is patent that a lying act of hypocritical profession, such as would be a fictitious and feigned profession of faith, cannot dispose the pope to teach the faith infallibly even if he would wish to do so, because that can only be accomplished by the power of a theological virtue; and thus *simpliciter*, it is not a disposition to preserve the form of the pontificate in a man. It follows therefore, that the merely feigned external profession of faith of one in whom the virtue of faith is entirely absent does not suffice to preserve the form of the Supreme Pontificate in him; because **if God were to wrench an infallible definition of faith from a faithless pontiff, that profession would not be a human act of the pope**, but would be an act of God **doing violence to human nature** – it would be God speaking through the mouth of the pontiff in exactly the same manner that God spoke through the mouth of the ass of Balaam. This is what Bellarmine was pointing out when he said, "Still, this will be a great violence…". Hence, it is not the merely material verbal pronouncing of the articles of faith alone that disposes a man to be and remain united to the form of the Pontificate, but only that external profession, if it be elicited by the power of the theological virtue of faith, *disposes the natural powers of the soul to exercise the charism of Infallibility*, and thereby dispose the soul of the pontiff to conserve the form of the pontificate within him.

The "spiritual plenitude" which, according to the teaching of Innocent III is given to the Roman Pontiff is the plenitude of power which includes the charism of the fullness of faith to teach the faith infallibly. In order to teach and define the faith infallibly the pope must have the *intention* to exercise the power of the keys to bind the whole Church with a definition of a matter that pertains to the *deposit of revelation*, which is believed on *divine authority*. Thus, the *moral object* of the act of defining requires the *intentional defining of doctrine pertaining to the revealed truths of the deposit of faith believed on divine authority*. A heretic is without faith because he rejects the authority of divine revelation, and therefore does not believe any of the revealed truths on divine authority, *but professes his beliefs by something other than faith.* Thus, for so long as he remains hardened in heresy and believes contrary errors, he lacks the dispositive habit of faith, and cannot be disposed to profess the revealed truths of faith, which can only be infallibly professed on the basis of faith founded on the divine authority he rejects – that faith in divine authority by which, if he had faith, he would believe and profess all the revealed truths, and by which he would therefore be disposed to infallibly define the revealed doctrine he believes by faith. And thus, with this explanation is answered Bellarmine's question, "How, I ask, will a heretical Pope confirm the brethren in faith and always preach the true faith?" Indeed, how can the heretic profess the opposite of what he obstinately believes? God cannot force the pope to profess the revealed truth he rejects, but He can give him the grace to prevent him from heretically rejecting the authority of the Revealing God, and thereby dispose him to teach the revealed truth infallibly.

This entire argument is premised on the promise of Christ to Peter of the gift of unfailing faith so that he may confirm the faith of his brethren, and thus that unfailing faith is the necessary disposition for Peter's operation of the charism of Infallibility. Christ did not simply bestow infallibility on Peter to speak in such a mnner that God would speak through Peter in the same manner that God spoke through the ass of Balaam; but He gave him the unfailing virtue of faith as the basis and necessary disposition for **Peter himself**, to exercise the charism of Infallibility by means of the natural powers of the soul aided by grace, thus constituting **him** as the *confirmator fratrum*; and thus it is, that the charism cannot be exercised in one in whom the virtue of faith is absent, and as a consequence, the form of the Supreme Pontificate cannot be retained in the person of a heretic Pope.

The opposing opinion was expressed already by Cardinal Enrico da Susa (a.k.a. Ostiene or Ostiense), and was explained by Cardinal Alfons Stickler, as Roberto de Mattei relates:

> «Professor Jamin recalls in particular Ostiene's commenting of these words relating to the Pope, "Nec deficiat fides eius". According to the Cardinal Bishop of Ostia: "The faith of Peter is not exclusively his "faith" meant as a personal act, but as the faith of the entire Church of which he is the spokesman and the Prince of the Apostles. Christ prays therefore, for the faith of the entire Church in persona tantum Petri, since it is the faith of the Church, professed by Peter, which never fails et propterea ecclesia non presumitur posse errare" (op. cit. p. 223).»

This notion of the unfailing faith of Peter not being meant as a personal act, but is the faith of entire Church, is the basis of Opinions Nos. 4 and 5. De Mattei continues,

> «Ostiene's thought matches that of all the great medieval canonists. The greatest scholar of these authors, Cardinal Alfonso Maria Stickler, points out that "the prerogative of infallibility of office does not impede the Pope, as an individual, from sin and thus become personally heretical (...). In the case of an obstinate and public profession of certain heresy, since it is condemned by the Church, the Pope becomes "minor quolibet catholico" (a common phrase of canonists) and ceases to be pope (...). This fact of a heretic Pope does not touch then Pontifical infallibility since it does not signify impeccability or inerrancy in the person of the Pontiff, [or] inerrancy in establishing forcefully from his office a truth of the faith or an immutable principle of Christian life (...). The canonists knew very well how to distinguish between the person of the Pope and his office. If then they declared the Pope dethroned, when certainly and obstinately heretical, they admit implicitly that from this personal fact not only is the infallibility of the office not compromised, but that it is somewhat defended and affirmed: any 'papal' decision whatever against a truth already decided is automatically rendered impossible" (A. M. Stickler, Sulle origini dell'infallibilità papale, "Rivista Storica della Chiesa in Italia", 28 (1974), pp. 586-587)."»[480]

This erroneous belief (that papal infallibility depended not on the pontiff's personal unfailing faith, but on the unfailing faith of the Church) was founded on the commonly held but false medieval belief that only a pope in council representing the faith of the whole Church is infallible, and that therefore a council is superior to a pope in doctrinal authority, as Moynihan explains. He also demonstrates that it was *this medieval belief in conciliar superiority in doctrine over a pope teaching alone, which became the basis of the even more radical opinion that a council could judge and depose a pope for heresy; and thus formed the basis for Opinion No. 4.*

The fatal defect in the notion of the unfailing faith of Peter being not the personal faith of Peter, but the faith of the entire Church represented *in persona tantum Petri*, is its foundation on an incomplete, and therefore defective notion of infallibility. It was not yet the common opinion during the time of the Decretists and Decretalists that the pope could define infallibly by himself *ex cathedra*. It was believed by many that a pope together with a council was superior to the pope alone in doctrinal

---

[480] http://rorate-caeli.blogspot.ie/2016/12/de-mattei-irrevocable-duties-of.html?m=1.

matters; and there were some who outright denied that the pope by himself could define infallibly. Yet the popes exercised their primacy in deciding doctrinal questions by themselves alone, and outside of any council, as Pope Alexander III did in 1170. Rowan Williams relates, "theologies that understated or diminished the substantive reality of Jesus' humanity were condemned: in 1170, Pope Alexander III ruled against the teaching that Christ's humanity was *nihil* nothing in itself, and reaffirmed that it must be *aliquid*. And although Peter Lombard himself did not go so far as this, the *habitus* theory [which minimized and tended to negate the substance of Christ's human nature[481]] was seen as inadequate to the logic of the basic basic Christian proposition that God became *homo*, a human being like others."[482] It was unanimously agreed that the pope together with the bishops in an ecumenical council were infallible in professing the faith; and in this manner, the pope was recognized as the spokesman for all the bishops, and thus the faith of the entire Church was considered to be represented *in persona tantum Petri*. However, *papal infallibility is not a collective charism, but pertains to the one individual who teaches from the chair of Peter;* and hence, when one considers the nature of the Infallibility of the Church as pertaining not only to the universal magisterium of the Church of the bishops in communion with the pope, but in a special way pertaining *personally* to the holder of the

---

[481] Rowan Williams, *Christ the Heart of Creation*, Cambridge, 2018, p. 23: "A second opinion focuses on the meaning of the word 'subsist' and 'subsistence': the Word continues to subsist as God, unchanged, but comes simultaneously to subsist as a human individual, being essentially unchanged by its union with a created soul and body. Lombard prefers a third approach, less likely to compromise or confuse our discourse about divine unchangeability: we could say that the Word in the Incarnation is in a state of 'having' a human being (*habens hominem*), rather like an individual putting on a coat or otherwise acquiring a characteristic which does not affect who or what they are. This *habitus* theory allows us to hold on to the unchanging nature of God and specifically of God the Word, but it also involves making a clear distinction between two things – the relation of the Word to its divine nature and the relation of the Word to the human nature it assumes. The former is intrinsic and necessary, such that the Word is inconceivable unless understood as wholly identical with the essence of God; the latter is more like an 'accidental' relation, something that comes to be true in a limited sense for a limited period without affecting the subject. The problem with it is that it makes the humanity dangerously like an assemblage of qualities with no identity as a finite reality."

[482] *Ibid.*

Petrine office as an individual, who even exercises that charism exclusively by himself when defining *ex cathedra*, the logical inapplicability of this notion of Infallibility as the faith of the whole Church represented *in persona tantum Petri* becomes manifest, since the collective faith of the entire Church, not being a *dispositio animæ*, is incapable of exerting any infallible power direct or indirect on the soul of the pope, by which power he would infallibly define *ex cathedra*. Since the charism of Infallibility can be exercised by the pope alone, without a council, the pope therefore exercises it not as a mere spokesman and chief representative of the Church which collectively teaches infallibly; thus merely representing the faith of the whole Church *in persona tantum Petri*; but he defines in matters of faith by himself alone as an individual – as the singularly infallible successor of the Prince of Apostles, to whose definitions all members of the Church must give an assent of faith. With the charism of Infallibility understood in this manner, i.e. as it is defined in *Pastor Æternus*, the impossibility becomes patent for the faith of the entire Church to play any role in the pope's exercise of the charism of papal Infallibility in such a manner that the faith of the Church would merely be represented in the person of Peter through the collective charism of Infallibility, because the faith of the whole Church is not a *dispositio animæ* disposing the pope to define infallibly; and therefore, faith must exist as a *habit* in the soul of the successor of Peter as its subject, thus uniting his soul to the *Prima Veritas* as a supernatural principle; and thereby *disposing the soul of the Pontiff, (the natural principle of operation), for the operation of the power of the charism of unfailing faith*, the charism of the *spiritual fullness of power* given only to Peter[483], which is the charism of Infallibility; by which he *by himself* defines infallibly: «*modus actionis sequitur dispositionem agentis, unumquodque enim quale est, talia operatur. Et ideo, cum virtus sit principium aliqualis operationis, oportet quod in operante præexistat secundum virtutem aliqua conformis dispositio.*» (1a 2æ q. 55. A. 1 ad 1) The virtue of faith is a *quality of soul*[484] and, as all human virtues, a habit (I – II 55 a.2); by which the rational power, which is a *power of the soul*, is determinate to

---

[483] Innocent III: «… sed [Deus] dotem mihi tribuit absque pretio pretiosam, **spirilualium videlicet plenitudinem** et latitudinem temporalium, magnitndinem et multiudinem utrorumque. Nam caeteri vocati sunt in partem sollicitudinis, **solus autem Petrus assumptus est in plenitudinem potesatis.**» (Sermo III *De Deversis*)

[484] «virtus est bona qualitas mentis, qua recte vivitur, qua nullus male utitur, quam Deus in nobis sine nobis operatur.» I – II Q. 55 a.4.

its operation by means of that habit which is faith, in the manner that the rational powers are determined to their operations by habits (I-II:49:4). Focusing on the key words, «*cum virtus sit principium aliqualis operationis, oportet quod in operante præexistat secundum virtutem aliqua conformis dispositio*» – it is seen that the *virtus*, understood in its general sense as a *power*; and in the case of the charism of Infallibility, a power which pertains essentially to a habit as a modification of that habit, then it cannot operate without that habit as its *conformis dispositio*. The charism of Infallibility is a special *power*, to wit, the fullness of the power of faith, i.e. the *fullness of the spiritual power*, which, as the fullness of the power of faith, cannot operate without the essence of the power of the habit of faith existing in the soul of the subject as its *necessary disposition*. Thus faith, to which is added the power to exercise that charism which consists in the fullness of power (*plenitude potestatis*) of faith, must be understood as the basic principle of operation of the extraordinary power of the charism of Infallibility. Hence, that charism cannot be operative unless there pre-exist in the soul of the operating subject the disposition which is the habit of faith by which the power of the soul is disposed to the optimal operation of the virtue of faith, and is thus brought into conformity with and determined to that particular operation of the fullness of the spiritual power, which is to define the faith infallibly. Hence, the charism of Infallibility given singularly to Peter and his successors, which consists not in the collective exercise, but in the singular exercise of the fullness of the power of the virtue of faith, cannot operate in the soul where that virtue, as a dispositive habit ordered to the operation of that charism, is totally absent; and thus, the virtue of faith is the necessary disposition which must be present as a *"dispositio animæ"* in the soul as its subject *(in anima sicut in subiecto)*[485] for that charism to be operative; and therefore, the virtue of faith existing in the soul of the pope as its subject is the necessary disposition for the preservation of the form of the supreme pontificate in the person of the pope. It follows therefore as a strict corollary that were it possible for the pope's faith to fail, then, as Bellarmine says, «*ista dispositione sublata per contrariam quæ est hæresis, mox papa desinit esse; neque enim potest forma conservari sine necessariis dispositionibus.*» (*De Romano Pontifice lib. ii cap. xxx*)

Bellarmine explains why this would be so:

---

[485] It is more fully explained elsewhere in this volume why it must be that **potentiae quae sunt harum operationum principia, sunt in anima sicut in subiecto**, as St. Thomas teaches.

"either faith is a necessary disposition as one (*simpliciter*) for this purpose, that someone should be Pope, or it is merely that he be a good Pope. If the first, therefore, after that disposition has been abolished through its opposite, which is heresy, and soon after the Pope ceases to be Pope: for the form cannot be preserved without its necessary dispositions. If the second, then a Pope cannot be deposed on account of heresy. On the other hand, in general, he ought to be deposed even on account of ignorance and wickedness, and other dispositions which are necessary to be a good Pope, and besides, Cajetan affirms that the Pope cannot be deposed from a defect of dispositions that are not necessary as one (*non necessarium simpliciter*), but merely necessary for one to be a good Pope (*ad bene esse*)."

Bellarmine then responds to Cajetan's objection:

"Cajetan responds that faith is a necessary disposition simply, but in part not in total, and hence with faith being absent the Pope still remains Pope, on account of another part of the disposition which is called the character, and that still remains. But on the other hand, either the total disposition which is the character and faith, is necessary as one unit, or it is not, and a partial disposition suffices. If the first, then without faith, the necessary disposition does not remain any longer as one, because the whole was necessary as one unit and now it is no longer total. If the second, then faith is not required except to be good (*fides non requiritur nisi ad bene esse*), and hence on account of his defect, a Pope cannot be deposed. Thereupon, those things which have the final disposition to ruin (*quæ habent ultimam dispositionem ad interitum*), soon after cease to exist, without another external force (*sine alia vi externa*), as is clear (*ut patet*); therefore, even a heretical Pope, without any deposition ceases to be Pope through himself. (Papa hæreticum sine alia depositione *per se* desinit esse Papa.")

Bellarmine argues here of faith *simpliciter* as a necessary disposition in order that the form of the pontificate be conserved in the pope. Now faith *simpliciter* is faith properly understood according to its essence as the theological virtue by which one assents to the divinely reveled truths of faith; and not faith *secundum quid*, as an occult heretic's merely lying external profession of the *content* of the revealed truths of faith without assent to their substance; which, without the internal habit of faith is not properly faith (*simpliciter*), but would be faith *secundum quid*, i.e., a faithless profession of the faith made not by faith, but by some other merely human power for purely natural human motives. For the pope to remain united to the Church as visible member by means of the public confession of faith, the merely external profession suffices; but to conserve the form of the pontificate in him, both the *character*, (which is internal), and faith *simpliciter* (which is the *virtue* of faith by which is made by the internal assent and the external profession) are necessary. The logic of Bellarmine's argument is airtight and unassailable; but since the internal virtue is not visible, it only proves beyond legitimate dispute that if a pope were to become a public heretic, he would cease automatically to be pope. However, the merely external profession of faith as a necessary disposition to remain in the Church as a visible member does not suffice to conserve the form of the pontificate in the person of the pope; but faith *simpliciter*, the **virtue** of faith as a *principium operationis* is necessary to be in the soul of person of the pope as its subject *in order to receive and preserve within himself the form of the supreme pontificate*. As I mentioned earlier, St. Thomas explains that, «*Primum est quod per fidem anima coniungitur Deo*»; and therefore, «*Baptismus enim sine fide non prodest*»; and thus, as Bellarmine notes, «ex *B. Thoma,* qui 3. part. q. 8. dicit, eos qui fide carent, non esse unitos Christo actu, sed *in potentia* tantum», and therefore, «*secundum B. Thomam, solus character non unit actu hominem cum Christo*» – and thus not being united to Christ by faith *simpliciter*, and therefore *in actu*, a heretic pope would lack the necessary internal disposition to fulfil the function of *confirmator fratrum*, which is to exercise the the charism of the fullness of the power of faith, which is the charism of Infallibility. A faithless heretic, incapable of exercising the charism of of the fullness of the power of faith, would therefore lack *the necessary disposition to conserve in himself the form of the papacy*. In Bellarmine's own words, lacking the necessary disposition to conserve the form of the papacy, «Papa hæreticus sine alia depositione *per se* desinit esse Papa»; because, «ista dispositione sublata per contrariam quæ est hæresis, mox papa desinit esse; neque enim potest forma conservari sine necessariis dispositionibus.»

Simply stated, the charism of Infallibility depends on the virtue of faith as its necessary disposition, because it consists of the fullness of power of the unfailing virtue of faith; and therefore, it would clearly be *impossible* for one to be a valid Roman Pontiff without the virtue of faith; nor would it be possible for a Pontiff, who possesses the gift of unfailing faith as the requisite disposition to exercise the fullness of the power of faith, to fail in his faith and to defect from the faith by falling into heresy. The reason why this is so, is that a merely external act of profession cannot dispose the soul internally to operate in a certain manner; since for that, an internal disposition is necessary. Hence, the merely external profession of the objective content of faith is incapable of internally disposing the soul of the pontiff to externally profess the faith infallibly, because all operations of the composite of body and soul begin in the soul; and therefore, that disposition which disposes and orders the soul of the pope to that operation which is to teach the faith infallibly; and therefore is, as Bellarmine says, *the necessary disposition to conserve the form of the pontificate in the person of the pope*, must necessarily be the *virtue* of faith acting internally in the soul as a *dispositio animæ*: "*Facit autem virtus operationem ordinatam. Et ideo ipsa virtus est quædam dispoitio ordinata in anima.*" (I – II Q. 53 a. 2) The virtue of faith is an internal *dispositive habit* which enables one to profess the faith externally; and is therefore the necessary disposition for the pope to profess the faith infallibly. *A merely external profession of a faithless pope is not a dispositive habit in the soul, because it is not a virtue*; and therefore does not enable one to profess the faith infallibly; because in whichever manner the motion of the human mind would reach God, that motion pertains to virtue: «*motus humanæ mentis qualitercumque Deum attingeret, ad virtutem pertinent.*»[486] Therefore, Bellarmine says, in a heretic pope, the *necessary disposition* to profess the faith infallibly, and thus *to conserve the form of the pontificate in the person of the pope* would be utterly lacking and absent; for which reason, «*ista dispositione sublata per contrariam quæ est hæresis, mox papa desinit esse; neque enim potest forma conservari sine necessariis dispositionibus.*»

The virtue of faith as the absolutely necessary disposition for a man to validly receive and preserve the form of the Supreme Pontificate can also clearly be seen to be the basis of the teaching of Paul IV in **Cum ex apostolatus officio**, which, although not dogmatically defined[487], was the basis of disciplinary canonical provisions set forth in that decree which clearly remained in force until 1983 (and some of which can be argued to remain in force even after the 1983 code), **but its doctrinal basis, founded on divine law, remains perpetually valid**. The doctrine expressed in that decree teaches that if one who has been elected pope is discovered to have been a heretic before his election, that election would be invalid. This teaching was already found in the writings of some of the early Decretists. The problematic aspect of its teaching would only be its applicability, insofar as it appears to be unenforceable, and remaining unenforced, it would result, in some cases, in a defection of the Church if it were not ever to be found out that that the man

---

[486] *Quaestiones Disputatae de Virtutibus* Q. 4 a 1 ad 6.

[487] cf. — Christopher Conlon; The Non-Infallibility of Cum Ex Apostolatus Officio.

elected was an occult heretic. However, divine providence would easily provide a remedy, because God is omnipotent: Either God will convert the elected internal heretic to the faith so that he can be disposed to receive the form of the papacy, or, if he has faith, God will provide the sufficient efficacious grace to prevent him from falling into heresy. However, the earlier mentioned arguments of Suárez and Bordoni provide sufficient foundation to judge that God would never permit a heretic to be pope; and therefore, if a heretic were to be canonically elected, God would necessarily provide the Church with the proof that the elect is a heretical intruder to be deposed in similar manner as Pedro de Luna was deposed. As a pure hypothesis, the same doctrine would *seem* to constitute a valid basis for Opinion No. 2 (but in fact it is not), according to which even a pope who is a secret heretic would cease to be pope, but not because he would thereby cease altogether to be a member of the Church (which is the foundation of Opinion No. 2), but more correctly because the heretic can neither receive nor conserve the form of the papacy. However, since a secret heretic could neither be pope, nor could it be known and judged that he is not a valid pope, and therefore he could not be removed by men, (as Bellarmine points out), the papacy would cease to be a visible institution, because it could not ever be known whether or not the pope is a true and visible head of the Church, or if he is secretly a counterfeit heretic impostor. There would also be the further problem of a defection of the Church from its divine constitution, in so far as the Church is constituted of the faithful of the world under the governance of the pope; and that constitution would be destroyed if the whole Church were to fall under the governance of an invalid papal impostor. Thus, the necessity of personal faith as the premise and doctrinal basis of the teaching in **Cum ex apostolatus officio** on heresy as a criterion for valid disqualification of a papal candidate from an otherwise valid election, would only superficially appear to provide a theological basis for opinion no. 2; whereas in reality, **it underscores and confirms the validity of Opinion No. One**, and manifests the irresolvable problematic aspect of Opinion No. 2, which plainly demonstrates it to be utterly inapplicable in reality, and thus, logically incoherent even as a practical hypothesis, since the pope is by definition the visible head of the Church, and that visibility would not exist in the papacy if a heretic who is not the pope would visibly govern the Church. Hence, it is clear that Opinion No. One, and not Opinion No. 2 (which only superficially appears to be), was the basis for Paul IV's doctrine in that decree, which defines that even one who would otherwise be duly elected pope would not be a valid pope if it were to be later found out that the man in question was a heretic. The question of a true and valid pope falling into heresy is not even considered as a possibility in *Cum ex apostolatus officio*, which simply declares that the pope is judged by no one and presumes that he is not a heretic – and thus the doctrinal basis of its teaching is clearly Opinion No. One. Since God is infinite in wisdom and power; and He guarantees through the prayer of his onlybegotten Son that the pope's faith will not fail; it would be vain and presumptuous to suspect that a valid pope who errs only materially in matters of faith would ever fail in his faith and fall into formal heresy. The question of whether a manifest heretic would ever have been a valid pope at all, or a valid pope who fell from office, is still be disputed; but what is beyond legitimate dispute is that a man who is manifestly a formal heretic, is simply not a true pope.

In *Cum ex apostolatus officio*, Paul IV solemnly declares the injudicability of the Roman Pontiff, "who is the representative upon earth of God and our God and Lord Jesus Christ, who holds the fullness of power over peoples and kingdoms, **who may judge all and be judged by none** in this world, may nonetheless be contradicted if he be found to have deviated from the Faith."[488] He may be refuted and contradicted for material heresy but can be judged by no one if he is a true and valid pope; but one who was already a (formal) heretic before election may be removed if it is discovered that he had been a heretic before his election, because that election would be invalid:

> *"if ever at any time it shall appear that [...] the Roman Pontiff, prior to his promotion or his elevation as Cardinal or Roman Pontiff, has deviated from the Catholic Faith or fallen into some heresy: (i) the promotion or elevation, even if it shall have been uncontested and by the unanimous assent of all the Cardinals, shall be null, void and worthless; (ii) it shall not be possible for it to acquire validity (nor for it to be said that it has thus acquired validity) through the acceptance of the office, of consecration, of subsequent authority, nor through possession of administration, nor through the putative enthronement of a Roman Pontiff, or veneration, or obedience accorded to such by all, nor through the lapse of any period of time in the foregoing situation; (iii) it shall not be held as partially legitimate in any way; (iv) to any so promoted to be [...] Roman Pontiff, no authority shall have been granted, nor shall it be considered to have been so granted either in the*

---

[488] "... Romanus Pontifex, qui Dei, et Domini Nostri Iesu Christ vices gerit in terris, et super gentes, et regna plenitudinem obtinet potestatis, **omnesque iudicat, a nemine in hoc saeculo iudicandus**, possit, si deprehendatur a fide devius, redargui..."

spiritual or the temporal domain; (v) each and all of their words, deeds, actions and enactments, howsoever made, and anything whatsoever to which these may give rise, shall be without force and shall grant no stability whatsoever nor any right to anyone; (vi) those thus promoted or elevated shall be deprived automatically, and without need for any further declaration, of all dignity, position, honour, title, authority, office and power."[489]

Thus the doctrine on which the legislation of the decree is based is set forth in the decree itself: a heretic cannot validly become pope; but a true and valid pope cannot be judged by anyone. One who is discovered to already have been a heretic before election is declared incapable of validly assuming the papacy even if granted universal acceptance and obedience, yet a true pope cannot be judged by anyone. This leaves only two practical, hypothetical possibilities: 1) that a pope cannot become a heretic (Opinion No. One); or, 2) that a pope who falls into manifest heresy (or whose occult heresy becomes manifest), because he cannot ever be judged by anyone as pope; can only be judged as one who has already fallen from office automatically, *ipso jure*, as a result of the *suapte natura* consequence of his manifest heresy, by which he separated himself from the body of the Church and ceased to be pope, and "for which reason he may be judged and punished by the Church" (Bellarmine); and for which reason Innocent III teaches, "I say the less (he is judged by men), because he can be judged by men, or rather can be shown to be

---

[489] "*6. Adiicientes quod si ullo umquam tempore apparuerit aliquem Episcopum, etiam pro Archiepiscopo, seu Patriarcha, vel Primate se gerentem, aut praedictae Romanae Ecclesiae Cardinalem, etiam ut praefertur, Legatum, seu etiam Romanum Pontificem ante eius promotionem, vel in Cardinalem, seu Romanum Pontificem assumptionem a fide Catholica deviasse, aut in aliquam haeresim incidisse, (i) promotio, seu assumptio de eo etiam in concordia, et de unanimi omnium Cardinalium assensu facta, nulla, irrita, (ii) et inanis existat, nec per susceptionem muneris, consecrationis, aut subsecutam regiminis, et administrationis possessionem, seu quasi, vel ipsius Romani Pontificis inthronizationem, aut adorationem, seu ei praestitam ab omnibus obedientiam, et cuiusvis temporis in praemissis cursum, convaluisse dici, aut convalescere possit, (iii) nec pro legitima in aliqua sui parte habeatur, (iv) nullamque talibus in Episcopos, seu Archiepiscopos, vel Patriarchas aut Primates promotis, seu in Cardinales, vel Romanum Pontificem assumptis, in spiritualibus, vel temporalibus administrandi facultatem tribuisse, (v) aut tribuere censeatur, sed omnia, et singula per eos quomodolibet dicta, facta, gesta, et administrata, ac inde secuta quaecumque viribus careant, et nullam prorsus firmitatem, nec ius alicui tribuant,(vi) sintque ipsi sic promoti, et assumpti, eo ipso absque aliqua desuper facienda declaratione, omni dignitate, loco, honore, titulo, auctoritate, officio, et potestate privati, liceatque omnibus, et singulis sic promotis, et assumptis, si a fide antea non deviassent, nec haeretici fuissent, neque schisma incurrissent, aut excitassent, vel commisissent.*"

already judged."⁴⁹⁰ The premise upon which both of these propositions are based is that a heretic cannot be pope, and the pope cannot be a heretic, because a heretic is incapable of assuming the form of the Supreme Pontificate or of conserving it.

2) «Secundo probatur ab eventu; nam hactenus nullus fuit hæreticus, vel certe de nullo probari potest, quod hæreticus fuerit; ergo signum est, non posse esse.»⁴⁹¹ St. Alphonsus, following Bellarmine, comments saying, «That some Pontififfs have fallen into heresy, some have tried to prove it, but have never proven it, nor will they ever prove it; and we will clearly prove the opposite in the end of Chapter X. Moreover, if God allowed, that a Pope was notoriously heretical and contumacious, he would cease to be Pope, and he would vacate the Pontificate. But if it were a hidden heretic, and did not propose any false dogma to the Church, then no harm would come to the Church: but we must rightly presume, as Cardinal Bellarmine says, that God will never allow any of the Roman Pontiffs, even as private men, become a heretic, notorious, or hidden.»⁴⁹² The reason, explains St. Alphonsus, why the public heretic would cease to be pope, is that because of his heresy, he would "by becoming an incapable subject [have] fallen from his office"⁴⁹³; and in this he follows Bellarmine who explained that faith is a necessary disposition *simpliciter* for a man to conserve in himself the form of the Pontificate, and that a heretic is incapable of conserving it; for which reason if he be deprived of the virtue of faith, he would become an incapable subject, and straightaway would cease to be pope, *sine alia vi*

---

⁴⁹⁰ «Minus dico; *quia potest ab hominibus judicari,* **vel potius judicatus ostendi.**»

⁴⁹¹ "2) It is proved *ab eventu*. For to this point no [Pontiff] has been a heretic, or certainly it cannot be proven that any of them were heretics; therefore it is a sign that such a thing cannot be [410]."

⁴⁹² «Che poi alcuni Pontifici sieno caduti in eresia, taluni han cercato di provarlo, ma non mai l'han provato, nè mai lo proveranno; e noi chiaramente proveremo il contrario nella fine del *Capo X*. Del resto, se Dio permettesse, che un Papa fosse notoriamente eretico e contumace, egli cesserebbe d'essere Papa, e vacherebbe il Pontificato. Ma se fosse eretico occulto, e non proponesse alla Chiesa alcun falso Dogma, allora niun danno alla Chiesa recherebbe: ma dobbiam giustamente presumere, come dice il Cardinal Bellarmino, che Iddio non mai permetterà che alcuno de' Pontefici Romani, anche come uomo private, diventi eretico nè notorio, nè occulto.» [*Verità della Fede,* p. 455]

⁴⁹³ «divenendo allora Soggetto affato inabile, e caduto dal suo Officio.» [*Verità della Fede,* Part. III. Cap. IX. p. 457.

externa. Since faith is the necessary disposition *simpliciter* for the pope to retain the form of the Pontificate, "God will never allow any of the Roman Pontiffs, even as private men, [to] become a heretic, notorious, or hidden," because even if the pope were to secretly defect from the faith as a private person, he would become an incapable subject to retain the form of the Pontificate; and would cease to be pope straightaway, and the Church would defect by adhering to a false head. For this reason, *a true pope cannot become a heretic*; and therefore *formal heresy, whether manifest, or occult, if proven, demonstrates beyond all shadow of doubt that a man is not a valid pope.*

Dr. Edward Peters, in *A Canon Lawyer's Blog* notes, «Beste, (Introductio (1961) 242), "In history no example of this can be found." And the great Felix Cappello, Summa Iuris I (1949) n. 309, thought that the possibility of a pope falling into public heresy should be "entirely dismissed given the special love of God for the Church of Christ [lest] the Church fall into the greatest danger."»[494] Not only does St. Robert Bellarmine affirm that no pope has ever fallen into heresy, but Innocent III cleady stated the same: «Et ideo fides apostolicæ sedis in nulla nunquam turbatione defecit, sed integra semper et illibata permansit: ut Petri privilegium persisteret inconcussum.»[495]; and, Pope St. Agatho in his response to Sergius: "Let your clemency therefore consider that the Lord and Saviour of all, to whom faith belongs, **who promised that the faith of Peter should not fail**, admonished him to strengthen his brethren; and it is known to all men that **the apostolic pontiffs, the predecessors of my littleness, have always done this with confidence…**"[496]

Citing the work of Da Silveira, Don Curzio Nitoglia explains that the first opinion, that a pope cannot be a heretic, is the one that is most commonly taught as the most probable by the majority of theologians and Doctors: Bellarmine, Francisco Suárez, Melchior Cano, Domingo Soto, John of St. Thomas, Juan de Torquemada, Louis Billot, Joachim Salaverri, A. Maria Vellico, Charles Journet (and Cajetan who is not cited by Da Silveira, but is demonstrated by Msgr. Vittorio Mondello in *La dottrina del Gaetano sul Romano Pontefice*, Messina, Istituto Arti Grafiche di

---

[494] **A canonical primer on popes and heresy** (https://canonlawblog.wordpress.com/2016/12/16/a-canonical-primer-on-popes-and-heresy/).

[495] *Sermo II, De Diversis*

[496] Rev. Joseph L. Iannuzzi, STD, Ph.D.; *Can a Pope Become a Heretic?*, Chapter IV, p. 19.

Sicilia, 1965, cap. V, pp. 163-194 e cap. VI, pp. 195-224). According to this opinion, the pope as pope cannot fall into formal heresy, whereas he can favour heresy or fall into material heresy as a private doctor or also as pope, but only in the non-defining magisterium, which in neither infallible nor [absolutely] binding.[497] Bordoni, who held the opinion to be "very probable", cites Suárez, Pedro de Simanca, Domingo Bañez, and Bellarmine to be of this opinion; and mentions that Bonacina, cites others who were of the same opinion, explaining that they (as well as he) based their opinion on the belief that the words, *Ut non deficiat fides tua* were spoken *simpliciter*, and therefore without distinction between the public or the private person.[498] Bordoni also argued extensively on the notable disputed cases proving that none of those popes was a formal heretic.

Commenting on Ballerini, Don Curzio explains,

> "If one studies well the thought of don Pietro Ballerini, one sees that according to him, the pope is obligated to place himself under supernatural faith, and the natural moral law as well as the divine law; there is no human authority over him, but his power is limited to that which God has given to

---

[497] «da *prima opinione* o meglio l'antecedente, che è quella insegnata comunemente come la più probabile dalla maggior parte dei teologi e dei Dottori: S. Roberto Bellarmino, Francisco Suarez, Melchior Cano, Domingo Soto, Giovanni da San Tommaso, Juan de Torquemada, Louis Billot, Joachim Salaverri, A. Maria Vellico, Charles Journet (ed anche il Gaetano non citato dal Da Silveira, ma lo dimostra mons. Vittorio Mondello, ne *La dottrina del Gaetano sul Romano Pontefice*, Messina, Istituto Arti Grafiche di Sicilia, 1965, cap. V, pp. 163-194 e cap. VI, pp. 195-224) è che il Papa come Papa non può cadere in eresia formale, mentre può favorire l'eresia o cadere in eresia materiale come dottore privato oppure come Papa, ma solo nel magistero non definitorio, non obbligante e quindi non infallibile (cfr. A. X. Da Silveira, p. 33, nota 1; cfr. B. Gherardini, *Concilio Ecumenico Vaticano II. Un discorso da fare*, Frigento, Casa Mariana Editrice, 2009; *Tradidi quod et accepi. La Tradizione, vita e giovinezza della Chiesa*, Frigento, Casa Mariana Editrice, 2010; *Concilio Vaticano II. Il discorso mancato*, Torino, Lindau, 2011; *Quaecumque dixero vobis. Parola di Dio e Tradizione a confronto con la storia e la teologia*, Torino, Lindau, 2011; *La Cattolica. Lineamenti d'ecclesiologia agostiniana*, Torino, Lindau, 2011).»

[498] Bordoni, *Sacrum Tribunal Iuducum*, cap. v. p. 131 – «Quartum quod multum probabile sit errare non posse ut privatum, docent Suar. *Disp.* 10 *sect sect.* 6 *dub.*4; Siman. Bannes, Bellarm. cum aliis quos pro se citat Bonacina in Bullam *disp.* 13 *q.2p.*1 *num.* 12 quia putant illa verba. *Ut non deficiat fides tua.* Dicta sunt simpliciter, ac proinde sine ulla distinction personæ publicæ aut privatæ…»

him who is his vicar on earth, which is only when he defines and infallibly binds; but when expressing opinions on manners not yet defined, he can err; and in an *eventual* and *possible* case of external heresy, Ballerini is not opposed to the *possibility* that the pope could fall, not dealing with definitions, but he maintains that *it has never happened in all the history of the Church and will never happen.*"⁴⁹⁹

For a long time opinions have been divided among eminent theologians and canonists between opinion no 1 that a pope simply cannot fall into heresy, and the opinion that a pope could fall into heresy. Peters, observes,

> «Wrenn, writing in the CLSA NEW COMM (2001) at 1618 states: "Canon 1404 is not a statement of personal impeccability or inerrancy of the Holy Father. Should, indeed, the pope fall into heresy, it is understood that he would lose his office. To fall from Peter's faith is to fall from his chair."»⁵⁰⁰

An earlier edition of that same commentary says, "Communion becomes a real issue when it is threatened or even lost. This occurs especially through heresy, apostasy and schism. Classical canonists discussed the question whether a pope, in his private or personal opinions, could go into heresy, apostasy or schism." The footnote refers to S. Sipos, Enchiridion Iuris Canonici, 7th ed. (Rome: Herder, 1960), who "cites Bellarmine and Wernz in support of this position; this view, however, is termed 'antiquated' by F. Cappello, Summa Iuris Canonici

---

⁴⁹⁹ «Se si studia bene il pensiero di don Pietro Ballerini si vede che secondo lui il Papa è obbligato a sottomettersi alla fede soprannaturale e alla morale naturale e divina; non ha nessuna autorità umano/ecclesiastica sopra di lui, ma il suo potere è limitato da quello di Dio di cui è il Vicario in terra; soltanto quando definisce e obbliga a credere è infallibile; come dottore privato opinando su questioni non ancora definite può errare; infine in caso di *eventuale e possibile* eresia esterna il Ballerini non si oppone alla *possibilità* che il Papa vi cada, non trattandosi di definizioni, ma ritiene che ciò *non si è mai verificato nella corso della storia della Chiesa e non si verificherà mai*.» Ballerini: «Sed haec hypothesis nullo facto comprobatur; siquidem nullus vel privatus error cuipiam Pontifici adscriptus contra ullum dogma evidens aut definitum hactenus inventus est, aut futurus putatur.» [*De Potestate ecclesiastica Summorum Pontificum et Conciliorum generalium*; p. 129.]

⁵⁰⁰ https://canonlawblog.wordpress.com/2016/12/16/a-canonical-primer-on-popes-and-heresy/.

(Rome: Pontificia Universitas Gregoriana, 1961), 297." The Commentary continues,

> "If he were to do so in a notoriously and widely publicised manner, he would break communion and, according to an accepted opinion, lose his office ipso facto (c. 194 par. 1, n. 2). Since no one can judge the pope (c. 1404) no one could depose a pope for such crimes, and the authors are divided as to how his loss of office would be declared in such a way that a vacancy could then be filled by a new election."[501]

Bellarmine states in his comment on Opinion No. 1, that he accepted this opinion (no.5) as a hypothesis, but considered Opinion No. 1 one as the more probable: "Still, because it is not certain, and the common opinion is to the contrary, it will be worthwhile to see what the response should be if the Pope could be a heretic."

I have already quoted above, Cardinal Stickler ("the prerogative of infallibility of office does not impede the Pope, as an individual, from sin and thus become personally heretical"), and most recently, Cardinal Raymond Burke, "If a Pope would formally profess heresy he would cease, by that act, to be the Pope. It's automatic. And so, that could happen."[502]

Dominic Prummer openly doubts that it can be possible for a pope to become a heretic: "The power of the Roman Pontiff is lost... (c) By his perpetual insanity or by formal heresy. And this at least probably. ... The authors indeed commonly teach that a pope loses his power through certain and notorious heresy, *but whether this case is really possible is rightly doubted.*"[503]

Matthæus Conte a Coronata clearly believed it is possible, but based his judgment of this opinion on statements of Innocent III which do not actually admit that a pope could in fact become a heretic, but admit of the possibility as a hypothesis (as I have shown in Part II):

> "2. Loss of office of the Roman Pontiff. This can occur in various ways:...c) Notorious heresy. Certain authors deny the supposition that the Roman Pontiff can become a heretic. It cannot be proven however that the

---

[501] James A. Coriden, Thomas J. Green, Donald E. Heintschel; *THE CODE OF CANON LAW, A Text and Commentary*, Commissioned by THE CANON LAW SOCIETY OF AMERICA, et al., p. 272.

[502] Interview with Catholic World Report, December 8 2016

[503] *Manuale Iuris Canonci*. Freiburg im Briesgau: Herder 1927. p. 95

Roman Pontiff, as a private teacher, cannot become a heretic – if, for example, he would contumaciously deny a previously defined dogma. Such impeccability was never promised by God. Indeed, Pope Innocent III expressly admits such a case is possible. If indeed such a situation would happen, he would, by divine law, fall from office without any sentence, indeed, without even a declaratory one. He who openly professes heresy places himself outside the Church, and it is not likely that Christ would preserve the Primacy of His Church in one so unworthy. Wherefore, if the Roman Pontiff were to profess heresy, before any condemnatory sentence (which would be impossible anyway) he would lose his authority."[504]

The contrary opinion is expressed by St. Robert Bellarmine, who first states the argument:

"Many canons teach that the Pope cannot be judged unless he may be discovered to have deviated from the faith, therefore he can deviate from the faith. Otherwise these canons would be to no effect. It is clear from the preceding canon, *Si Papa*, dist. 40, from the 5th Council under Symachus, from the Eighth general council, act 7, from the third epistle of Anacletus, the second epistle of Eusebius, and from Innocent III [411]."[505]

He then tersely refutes it: "Therein it is gathered correctly that the Pope by his own nature can fall into heresy, *but not when we posit the singular assistance of God which Christ asked for him by his prayer*. Furthermore, Christ prayed lest his faith would fail, not lest he would fall into vice."[506] Thus, Bellarmine answers the impeccability objection according to which Christ did not promise such impeccability that the pope cannot become a heretic. By that singular assistance, the pope remains *in his nature* capable of heresy, but the infallibly efficacious grace promised by Christ prevents such a fall. The efficacious grace would not negate the freedom

---

[504] *Institutiones Iuris Canonici*. Rome: Marietti 1950. I:312, p. 316

[505] «Multi canones docent, Pontificem non posse judicari, nisi inveniatur a fide devius; ergo potest deviare a Fide: alioqui frustra essent illi canones. Antecedens patet ex can. Si Papa dist. 40. Ex Concilio V sub Symmacho, ex Concilioi VIII. Generali act. 7. Ex Anacleto epist. 3. Eusebio epist. 2. Ex Innocentio III. In serm. 2. De consecrate. Pontif.»

[506] «Respondeo ad primum argumentum: inde recte colligi, posse Papam ex natura sua incidere in haeresim, non tamen posita singulari Dei assistentia, quam Christus oration sua illi impetravit: oravit autem Christus, ne dificeret Fides ejus, non autem ne incideret in alia vitia.» (*De Romano Pontifice, Lib. IV, Cap. VII*)

of the pope's will, because that would be contrary to the nature of efficacious grace, which infallibly helps the will, and therefore does not take away its liberty, as St. Augustine says: «neque enim voluntatis arbitrium ideo tollitur, quia iuvatur, sed ideo iuvatur, quia non tollitur».[507]

Not only does St. Robert Bellarmine argue that there has never been any pope proven to have been a heretic, but it was the position of the Apostolic See during the First Vatican Council under Pope Pius IX, as Archbishop Purcell testified (in the earlier cited passage on the query of a cardinal on a heretic pope), "It was answered that there has never been such a case". St. Robert also argues that it cannot be gathered from those canons that a pope can in fact become a heretic, but (says Bellarmine in the same chapter VII), "I say those canons do not mean the Pope can err as a private person but only that *the Pope cannot be judged*; it is still not altogether certain whether the Pontiff could be a heretic or not. Thus, they add the condition 'if he might become a heretic' for greater caution."[508] These words of the Holy Doctor, «*sed tantum non posse Pontificem judicari*», provide a key for understanding the distinctions he makes in refuting opinion no. 3 and 4, and the basis of opinion no. 5.

"THE POPE CANNOT BE JUDGED"

De Romano Pontifice, Lib. IV, Cap. VII

Needless to say, St. Robert Bellarmine's declaration that "the Pope cannot be judged", directly refutes the interpretation of John Salza and Robert Siscoe, who say that according to Bellarmine, a heretical pope would not lose office unless he would be judged to be a heretic by the Church. In their hysterical article, *RESPONDING TO FR. KRAMER'S ERRONEOUS INTERPRETATION OF BELLARMINE*, Salza & Siscoe quote my statement: «Bellarmine does not refute the argument that a pope who is a manifest heretic loses office [by himself] – he is speaking specifically of removal of the pope when he says the judgment

---

[507] S. Augustinus, *Ep. 157, c. 2, n. 10*.

[508] «Canones autem citati loquuntur expresse de haeresi; igitur non loquuntur de errore judiciali, sed personali Pontificis. Secundo dico; canones illos non velle dicere, Pontificem etiam ut privatam personam posse errare, sed tantum non posse Pontificem judicari: quia tamen non est omnino certum, an possit necne esse haereticus Pontifex; ideo ad majorem cautelam, addunt conditionem, nisi fiat haereticus.»

of men is required to remove him. The fact of loss of office occurs *ipso facto*, but the heretic "pope" must be **removed** by the judgment of the Church. (Non *aufertur* a Deo nisi per hominem)» Salza & Siscoe then comment, "Fr. Kramer says that the heretical Pope is only 'judged by men,' after he has fallen from office. In other words, according to Fr. Kramer, Bellarmine teaches that Christ secretly deposes the Pope (removes him from office) and then the man who is 'judged' is no longer the Pope. The 'judgment of men,' he claims, simply concerns the Church's physical removal of the former Pope from office."[509] I have already explained in the first part of this work, the manner in which the loss of office would take place in the case of a heretical pope, as set forth by Bellarmine, Ballerini, and Pope Gregory XVI; and **nowhere have I ever even remotely suggested that "Christ secretly deposes the Pope"**, but that according to their doctrine, the heretic pope would by the very act of heresy **fall from office "*by himself*"**, having **pronounced a public judgment upon himself;** and the fall from office would take place **without any judgment by the Church**, as Ballerini explicitly states.[510] As I explained earlier, the act of public defection into manifestly formal heresy constitutes an act of *tacit resignation from* office, which Ballerini explains is an act of *abdication*: «*sicque sententia, quam in se ipsum tulit, toti Ecclesiæ proposita, cum sua voluntate recessisse, & ab Ecclesiæ corpore declararet avulsum, atque* **abdicasse** *quodammodo Pontificatum.*» The loss of office would take place *jure divino*, and entirely independently of any human law; and therefore, the only question of law would not be concerned with how the loss of office would come about, (since that question is already definitively settled), but with the means and procedures by which the Church would declare the heretic's fall from office to have taken place, so that the vacancy could be filled.

Salza and Siscoe also write most stupidly in their *magnum opus* of, "Pope Honorius, who has been declared a heretic by the Church (albeit after his death)!"[511] The Church has never judged Pope Honorius to have actually been guilty of the crime of heresy. Salza in particular most ignorantly pontificates that there have been historical examples of popes

---

[509] *RESPONDING TO FR. KRAMER'S ERRONEOUS INTERPRETATION OF BELLARMINE.*

[510] «semetipsum palam declarat haereticum, hoc est a fide catholica, & ab Ecclesia voluntate propria recessisse, ita ut ad eum praecidendum a corpore Eccleaiae **nulla cujusquam declaratio aut sententia necessaria sit.**»

[511] True or False Pope, p. 220

who were formal heretics, claiming that there have been "several historical examples".[512]

Bellarmine deals with the question of judging a pope, and of Pope Honorius in particular in his commentary on the third opinion:

> "The third opinion is on another extreme, that the Pope is not and cannot be deposed either by secret or manifest heresy. Turrecremata in the aforementioned citation relates and refutes this opinion, and rightly so, for it is exceedingly improbable. Firstly, because that a heretical Pope can be judged is expressly held in the Canon, Si Papa, dist. 40, and with Innocent. And what is more, in the Fourth Council of Constantinople, Act 7, the acts of the Roman Council under Hadrian are recited, and in those it was contained that Pope Honorius appeared to be legally anathematized, because he had been convicted of heresy, the only reason where it is lawful for inferiors to judge superiors. Here the fact must be remarked upon that, although it is probable that Honorius was not a heretic, and that Pope Hadrian II was deceived by corrupted copies of the Sixth Council, which falsely reckoned Honorius was a heretic, we still cannot deny that Hadrian, with the Roman Council, and the whole Eighth Synod sensed that in the case of heresy, a Roman Pontiff can be judged. Add, that it would be the most miserable condition of the Church, if she should be compelled to recognize a wolf, manifestly prowling, for a shepherd."

A fundamentalistic interpretation of Bellarmine's refutation of Opinion No. 3, (such as that of Salza and Siscoe), simplistically applies the *Canon Si papa* like a blunt instrument, with a total disregard for the subtly nuanced understanding of the canon as it was understood by Medieval canonists and interpreted by Bellarmine. Siscoe most ignorantly states, in his Remnant article, replying to those who would

> object by saying, since a pope cannot be judged by a council, Bellarmine could not have meant that a council would depose a heretical Pope. They will then insist that this is why Bellarmine taught that a heretical pope loses his office automatically. But this is clearly not the case, since Bellarmine himself defended the opinion that a heretical Pope can be judged by a council. He wrote: "Firstly, that a heretical Pope can be judged is expressly held in Can. Si Papa dist. 40, and by Innocent III (Serm. II de Consec. Pontif.) Furthermore, in the 8th Council, (act. 7) the acts of the Roman

---

[512] «Nevertheless, even conceding the possibility that a Pope could fall into formal heresy (which I do, based on the teaching of Pope Innocent III **and several historical examples**).» [John Salza Replies to Another Sedevacantist] (emphasis qadded)

Council under Pope Hadrian are recited, in which one finds that Pope Honorius appears to be justly anathematized, because he had been convicted of heresy, which is the only case in which inferiors are permitted to judge superiors." (79)

Indeed, if Bellarmine were invoking that canon as a justification for a pope's inferiors to judge a reigning Pontiff for heresy, then he would have involved himself in an irreconcilable contradiction, having stated in Book IV that "the pope cannot be judged"; as well as having explained in his refutation of Opinion No. 4 in *liber ii caput xxx* that neither the cardinals nor the bishops have the power to judge the pope. In *lib. ii cap. xxvi* of the same work, Bellarmine categorically states in the passage I quoted earlier, that the pope cannot be judged by any power or anyone on earth (*Romanus Pontifex a nemine in terris judicari potest.*), and most explicitly, not by a **Council**: «non posse ullo modo judicari in terris ab ullo Principe christiano, sive saeculari, sive ecclesiastico; **neque ab omnibus simul in Concilio congregatis.**» He explains the principal reason why a true pope cannot ever be judged:

> «*Observandum est tertio, rationem praecipuam, cur Papa judicari non possit, esse, quia Princeps est Ecclesiae totius, et proinde superiorem in terris non habet, nam quia summus Princeps est Ecclesiae, non potest judicari ab ullo Ecclesiastico Antistite, et rursum, quia respublica Ecclesiastica spiritualis est, ac proinde major, ac sublimior quavis republica temporali, propterea summus Princeps Ecclesiae dirigere et judicare summum Principem reipublicae temporalis; non autem ab eo dirigi, aut judicari debet, nisi rectus ordo, et ipsa rerum natura pervertatur.*»

In fact, the citation of "the acts of the Roman Council under Pope Hadrian", by Bellarmine in his refutation of the Third Opinion in Chapter XXX, which Salza & Siscoe cite as proof that "Bellarmine himself defended the opinion that a heretical Pope can be judged by a council", is precisely the same that Bellarmine cites in Chapter XXVI as proof that a pope cannot be judged by a council, nor by anyone else on earth: «Concilium Romanum sub Adriano Papa II. cujus verba referuntur in VIII. Synodo, act. 7. sic ait: *Romanum Pontificem de omnium Ecclesiarum Praesulibus judicasse legimus: de eo vero quemquam judicasse, non legimus.* Quod sane de legitimo judicio intelligendum est.»

Salza and Siscoe completely overlook the critical distinction between *deponendus* and *depositus* that Bellarmine and Ballerini make, and according to which a pope cannot be judged and deposed (*deponi posse*), but can be judged to be already deposed (*esse depositum*), as I have already pointed out earlier. Don Curzio also explains this distinction:

> «the third opinion has been taken into consideration by only one French theologian of the Nineteenth Century (D. Bouix, *Tractatus de Papa*, Parigi/Lione, Lecoffre, 1869) out of 137 authors, according to which if the pope, as a hypothesis, falls into heresy he retains the pontificate, but the faithful must not remain passive, but should manifest the error to the pope so that he may be corrected, without, however, being able to declare him "depositus" or to be deposed "deponendus" (cfr. A. X. Da Silveira, *Qual è l'autorità dottrinale dei documenti pontifici e conciliari?*, "Cristianità", n. 9, 1975; Id., *È lecita la resistenza a decisioni dell'Autorità ecclesiastica?*, "Cristianità", n. 10, 1975; Id., *Può esservi l'errore nei documenti del Magistero ecclesiastico?*, "Cristianità", n. 13, 1975) This third opinion is not shared by any "approved" theologians".»[513]

Accordingly Bellarmine presents the third opinion thus, "Papam neque per hæresim occultam, neque per manifestam, **esse depositum** aut **deponi posse**". Thus Bellarmine rejects this opinion not on the basis of a pope being able to be judged and deposed by the Church (*deponi posse*), but to be judged as having fallen from office and to simply "be deposed" (*esse depositum*) by his own actions, and thus not deposed by the Church, but *per se* to have fallen from office. Don Curzio concludes, «In reality, Bellarmine treats of the pure hypothesis of a heretic pope, "admitted but not conceded", but holding speculatively, as an investigative hypothesis – that the pope would be deposed *ipso facto* (*"depositus"*) and not to be deposed (*"deponendus"*) after a declaration of the bishops or the Sacred College of Cardinals.»[514]

---

[513] «La *terza opinione* è stata presa in esame da un solo teologo francese del XIX secolo (D. Bouix, *Tractatus de Papa*, Parigi/Lione, Lecoffre, 1869) su oltre 137 autori; essa ritiene che il Papa se per ipotesi cade in eresia mantiene egualmente il Pontificato, ma i fedeli non devono restare passivi, manifestando al Papa il suo errore affinché si corregga (cfr. A. X. Da Silveira, *Qual è l'autorità dottrinale dei documenti pontifici e conciliari?*, "Cristianità", n. 9, 1975; Id., *È lecita la resistenza a decisioni dell'Autorità ecclesiastica?*, "Cristianità", n. 10, 1975; Id., *Può esservi l'errore nei documenti del Magistero ecclesiastico?*, "Cristianità", n. 13, 1975) senza tuttavia poterlo dichiarare deposto (*"depositus"*) o deponendo (*"deponendus"*); questa terza opinione non è condivisa da tutti i teologi *"probati"*.»

[514] «In realtà il Bellarmino tratta della pura ipotesi dell'eresia del Papa, "ammessa e non concessa" la quale, ritiene – solo speculativamente, indagativamente e ipoteticamente – che il Papa sarebbe deposto *ipso facto*

One of the great medieval canonists was Pope Innocent III, whose sermons strongly support Opinion No. One, but who at least hypothetically admitted Opinion No. 5 as well. It is absolutely clear from Innocent's teaching that, so long as the pope holds office, he cannot be judged by anyone, and no judgment of the Church pronounced on the pope would be of any effect:

> «Petrus ligare potest cæteros, sed ligari non potest a cæteris. *Tu*, inquit, *vocaberis Cephas* (Joan. 1), quod exponitur caput; quia sicut in capite consistit omnium sensuum plenitudo, in cæteris autem membris pars est aliqua plenitudinis: ita cæteri vocati sunt in partem sollicitudinis, solus autem Petrus assumptus est in plenitudinem potestatis. Jam ergo videtis quis iste servus, qui super familiam constituitur, profecto vicarius Jesu Christi, successor Petri, Christus Domini, **Deus Pharaonis**: inter Deum et hominem medius constitutus, citra Deum, sed ultra hominem: **minor Deo, sed major homine: qui de omnibus judicat, et a nemine judicatur**: Apostoli voce pronuntians, *qui me judicat, Dominus est* (I Cor. iv).»[515]

The Pope is the **divine pharaoh**, he is **less than God but more than man, who pronounces with the voice of the Apostle,** *He who judges me is the Lord.* (1 Cor. 4) Being *"minor Deo sed major homine"*, he is judged by **no one** – *"a nemine judicatur"*.

However, if a pope were to become a heretic, he would, according to some Medieval canonists, (as Cardinal Stickler explains), "cease to be pope", and thus would no longer be *major homine,* but as a heretic who is no longer a member of the Church would become *minor quolibet catholico*: from being **more than man**, he would become **less than any Catholic**, since (as Bellarmine would later explain) he would no longer be pope, a Christian, or a member of the Church. Having fallen from office – from the highest position to the lowest, i.e., *minor quolibet catholico*, **he can be shown to be already judged**, (as Innocent III says) and having been already judged by God and having ceased to be pope, **he can then be judged and punished by the Church (as Bellarmine says).** Don Curzio Nitoglia[516] writes,

---

(*"depositus"*) e non da deporsi (*"deponendus"*) dopo dichiarazione dell'Episcopato o del S. Collegio cardinalizio»

[515] Innocent III, *Sermo II, De Diversis.*

[516] http://www.unavox.it/ArtDiversi/DIV1628_Nitoglia_Questione_Papa_eretico.htm

«Monsignor Vittorio Mondello (*La dottrina del Gaetano sul Romano Pontefice*, cit., pp. 163-194) explains that the hypothesis of the possibility of a heretic pope derives from the Decree of Gratian (dist. XL, cap. 6, col. 146) written between 1140 and 1150, in which is found a fragment erroneously believed to be of St. Boniface, († 5 June 754), a Benedictine monk of Exeter in England sent by Pope Gregory II to evangelize Germany, consecrated Archbishop of Mainz, and martyred in Freising, who is considered to be the apostle of Germany, and whose body rests in Fulda.»[517]

«This fragment,» continues Don Curzio, «has the title, '*Si Papa*', and expresses the doctrine according to which [the pope] '*a nemine est iudicandus, nisi deprehendatur a Fide devius*, cannot be judged by any human authority, except if he has fallen into heresy'.»[518] «Basing themselves on this spurious decree erroneously attributed to St. Boniface and accepted at face value by Gratian,» continues Don Curzio,

«the Medieval and Counter-Reformation theologians maintained as possible the hypothesis but not the certitude of the possibility of a heretic pope. At this point they are divided in how to resolve the question of a pope who eventually falls into heresy as a private person (cfr. A. M. Vellico, *De Ecclesia Christi*, Roma, 1940, p. 395, n. 557, in footnote 560 there is an ample bibliography). Cardinal Charles Journet (*L'Église du Verbe Incarné*, Bruges, Desclée, II ed., 1995, vol. I, p. 626) maintains that the opinion according to which the pope cannot fall into heresy "is gaining ascendency above all due to the progress of historical studies. Bellarmine (*De Romano Pontifice*, lib. II, cap. 30) was one of the supporters of this thesis. The opinion that admits of the possibility of papal heresy has its remote origin from the already cited Decree of Gratian, which brings up again a spurious text attributed to St. Boniface" (cited in V. Mondello, *op. cit.*, p. 164).»[519]

---

[517] Monsignor Vittorio Mondello (*La dottrina del Gaetano sul Romano Pontefice*, cit., pp. 163-194) spiega che l'ipotesi della possibilità del Papa eretico deriva dal Decreto di Graziano (dist. XL, cap. 6, col. 146) composto tra il 1140 e il 1150, in cui si trova riportato un frammento creduto erroneamente di S. Bonifacio († 5 giugno 754), un monaco benedettino dell'Exeter in Inghilterra inviato da papa Gregorio II ad evangelizzare la Germania, consacrato arcivescovo di Magonza e martirizzato dai Frisoni, che è considerato l'apostolo della Germania e il cui corpo riposa a Fulda.

[518] «Questo frammento si intitola "*Si Papa*" ed esprime la dottrina secondo cui "*a nemine est iudicandus, nisi deprehendatur a Fide devius* / non può essere giudicato da nessuna autorità umana, tranne che sia caduto in eresia".»

[519] «A partire da questo decreto spurio attribuito erroneamente a San Bonifacio e ripreso come tale da Graziano i teologi medievali e

«Now the eventual condemnation of a pope in the sole case of heresy by an imperfect Council (of bishops only),» continues Don Curzio,

> «is the thesis of mitigated Conciliarism, condemned as heretical and the child of radical Conciliarism, which holds that the Council is always superior to the pope, and which has been condemned per se as heretical. Msgr. Antonio Piolante writes, 'Conciliarism is an ecclesiological error, according to which an ecumenical Council is superior to the pope. The remote origin of Conciliarism is found in the juridical principle of the *Decree of Gratian* (dist. XL, cap. 6) according to which the pope can be judged by the Church (the bishops or the cardinals) in case of heresy. [...] this error was condemned by the Council of Trent and received its coup de grâce from the First Vatican Council' (*Dizionario di teologia dommatica*, Roma, Studium, IV ed., 1957, pp. 82-84, voce *Conciliarismo*).»[520]

I have already quoted verbatim the relevant texts of Trent and Vatican I earlier in this work.

---

controriformistici hanno ritenuto possibile la ipotesi e non la certezza del Papa eretico. Da qui si sono divisi nel discettare come risolvere la questione di un Papa eventualmente caduto in eresia come persona privata (cfr. A. M. Vellico, *De Ecclesia Christi*, Roma, 1940, p. 395, n. 557, nella nota 560 vi è un'amplia bibliografia). Il cardinal Charles Journet (*L' Église du Verbe Incarné*, Bruges, Desclée, II ed., 1995, vol. I, p. 626) ritiene che la sentenza secondo cui il Papa non può cadere in eresia "va oggi divulgandosi grazie soprattutto al progresso degli studi storici. Il Bellarmino (*De Romano Pontifice*, lib. II, cap. 30) è stato uno dei sostenitori di questa tesi. La sentenza che ammette la possibilità dell'eresia del Papa trae la sua lontana origine dal già citato Decreto di Graziano, che riporta un testo spurio attribuito a San Bonifacio" (citato in V. Mondello, *op. cit.*, p. 164).»

[520] «Ora la eventuale condanna del Papa solo in caso di eresia da parte del Concilio imperfetto (i soli Vescovi) è la tesi del conciliarismo mitigato, condannato come ereticale e figlio del conciliarismo radicale, che ritiene il Concilio superiore al Papa sempre e per sé ed è stato anch'esso condannato come ereticale. Mons. Antonio Piolanti scrive: "il Conciliarismo è un errore ecclesiologico, secondo cui il Concilio ecumenico è superiore al Papa. L'origine remota del Conciliarismo si trova nel principio giuridico del *Decreto di Graziano* (dist. XL, cap. 6) secondo il quale il Papa può essere giudicato dalla Chiesa (l'Episcopato o i Cardinali) in caso di eresia. [...]. Il Papa può errare e persino cadere in eresia, dovrà in tal caso essere corretto ed anche deposto. [...] quest'errore fu condannato dal Concilio di Trento e ricevette il colpo di grazia dal Concilio Vaticano I" (*Dizionario di teologia dommatica*, Roma, Studium, IV ed., 1957, pp. 82-84, voce *Conciliarismo*).»

In spite of their protestations that they refrain from holding a position in these matters which (according to them) have not been decided by the ecclesiastical magisterium, Salza and Siscoe have emphatically stated and elaborated their heretical position on the question of a heretical pope. In their Gloria TV interview, Salza and Siscoe emphatically declare in response to the question, "So, are you saying that heresy itself would not cause a Pope to fall from office?": (Salza and Siscoe) – "Yes, that is correct. In the book, we use the metaphysics of Thomas to explain why it is that heresy does not directly cause a Pope to fall from the pontificate." (*error in fide*) Robert J. Siscoe states with unequivocal clarity his heretical mitigated Conciliarist opinion in his *Remnant* article (Nov. 18, 2014): **"The Church must render a judgment before the pope loses his office."** — Robert J. Siscoe (*sententia hæretica*)

Clueless Robert Siscoe still cannot grasp the simple notion of an **automatic** loss of office that does not take place by either private judgment of the laity, or official judgment by the Church, but is an act of abdication intrinsic to the public act of formal heresy itself, which, consequently, takes place independently of the judgment of others, but is pronounced as a judgment of self-condemnation by the heretic upon himself, so that he loses office "straightaway", as Bellarmine teaches: "by himself" (*per se*), and ***ipso facto***, which means **"by the very act itself"**, and therefore **"immediately", "automatically" or "straightaway"**, as Bellarmine explains. Ballerini explicitly states that by his pertinacity, the pope would manifest that he had "*in some manner abdicated*". Cardinal Raymond Burke, unlike John Salza and Robert Siscoe, does not suffer from the hang-up about automatic loss of office for heresy (which Salza & Siscoe repeatedly declare to be "sedevacantist theology" and a "misinterpretation" and "distortion" of the teaching of St Robert Bellarmine), but understands the clear and unequivocal teaching of St. Bellarmine in his presentation of opinion no. 5, so Cardinal Burke simply states, "If a Pope would formally profess heresy he would cease, by that act, to be the Pope. It's automatic. And so, that could happen." In such a case, the judgment declared by the Church would add juridical enforcement to the loss of office that would have already taken place *ipso jure*.

Salza & Siscoe have become so desperately obsessed with their heretical Conciliarist belief that a pope who falls into heresy must first be judged by the Church, that they have resorted to a plainly irrational argument against the plainly expressed position of Bellarmine, which I have interpreted and understood in the manner of Cardinal Burke and *all the expert commentators of recent centuries*. Here is Salza & Siscoe's moronically heretical argument against what is universally understood as Opinion No. 5:

> «Suffice it to say that not a single theologian has ever taught the laity, or individual priest, are permitted render such a judgment or make such public declarations on their own authority. Before a person can conclude that a Pope has lost his office for heresy, it requires an antecedent (prior) judgment that he has, in fact, fallen into heresy. The antecedent judgment must be rendered by the Church before the consequent judgment can be declared. And if the antecedent judgment is forbidden, as Kramer now argues *[sic]* ("a Pope cannot be judged, even for heresy") how could the consequent judgment (that he lost his office for heresy) ever be determined? If the Church was not permitted to render a judgment of heresy concerning a pope, it would be equally forbidden to declare that a Pope had lost his office for heresy. This explains why the famous axiom "the first see is judged by no one" has been understood to include the exception "unless he is accused of heresy." But only the Church possesses the authority to render such a judgment and make any consequent declarations.»[521]

First, to the statement, "that not a single theologian has ever taught the laity, or individual priest, are permitted render such a judgment or make such public declarations on their own authority." St. Robert Bellarmine says:

> "For although Liberius was not a heretic, nevertheless he was considered one, on account of the peace he made with the Arians, [...] *for men are not bound*, or able to read hearts; but when they see that someone is a heretic by his external works, they judge him to be a heretic pure and simple [simpliciter], and condemn him as a heretic."[522]

No authority is required to express an opinion on a manifest fact, such as formal heresy that is plainly manifest. That is a basic right of natural law. The loss of office that directly results from manifest heresy takes place *jure divino*, independently of any human jurisdiction; and

---

[521] Salza & Siscoe in *Paul Kramer a Father of Lies?*

[522] «Tametsi enim Liberius hæreticus non erat, tamen habebatur, propter pacem cum Arianis factam, hæreticus, [...] Non enim homines tenentur, aut corda possunt scrutari; sed quem externis operibus hæreticum esse vident, simpliciter hæreticum iudicant, ac ut hæreticum damnant.» (Lib. IV, Cap. IX)

therefore, one does not usurp or infringe upon the jurisdiction of the Church by expressing an opinion on the matter of papal loss of office for heresy. Now here is the Salza/Siscoe lunacy:

> *"Before a person can conclude that a Pope has lost his office for heresy, it requires an antecedent (prior) judgment that he has, in fact, fallen into heresy. The antecedent judgment must be rendered by the Church before the consequent judgment can be declared. And if the antecedent judgment is forbidden, as Kramer now argues **[sic]** ('a Pope cannot be judged, even for heresy') how could the consequent judgment (that he lost his office for heresy) ever be determined?"* **[As Kramer now argues? What nonsensical silliness!]**

Salza & Siscoe speak of those (i.e. "sedevacantists") who "have misunderstood (and abused) the quote from St. Robert Bellarmine, who said 'the manifest heretic is ipso facto deposed,' as if Bellarmine actually meant that a cleric or Pope automatically loses his office when a person privately judges him to be a heretic." In fact, it is Salza and Siscoe who crudely misinterpret Bellarmine, who does not say that a heretic pope loses office *ipso facto* "when a person privately judges him" to be a heretic, but says he loses office "straightaway", "by himself", when he publicly pronounces judgment upon himself. It is, as Ballerini says, in some manner an *abdication* — an act of tacit resignation according to Canon Law. It is at this point when, as Bellarmine says, "men are not bound, or able to read hearts; but when they see that someone is a heretic by his external works, they judge him to be a heretic pure and simple [simpliciter], and condemn him as a heretic." As both Bellarmine and Ballerini have plainly stated in the quotations I have cited earlier in this work, the loss of office would take place automatically and independently of anyone else's judgment when the heretic would pronounce judgment upon himself; and the judgment of the Church and that of private individuals would take place after the *ipso facto* loss of office had already taken place. All of the decrees and canons (such as Canon 10 of the Fourth Council of Constantinople) cited by Salza and Siscoe, which forbid subjects to depose their prelates, are clearly not applicable, and were not intended to be applied to such a case as would take place when a holder of ecclesiastical office publicly defects from the Catholic faith by manifest heresy. This is most evident from the clear wording of that Canon 10 of Constantinople, which says, "As divine scripture clearly proclaims, 'Do not find fault before you investigate, and understand first and then find fault'. And does our law judge a person without first giving him a hearing and learning what he does?'" This text clearly refers to suspected crimes and not manifest or notorious crimes, and thus is not applicable to a person who pronounces a public judgment of heresy upon himself, and is not to be found among the canons dealing with heresy, but is in a different section dealing with other crimes. The Church did not excommunicate those who refused to be in communion with Nestorius, but vindicated them by declaring their excommunications to have been null and void. What it means can be clearly understood from the words of Christopher A. Ferrara, who wrote, "It is an axiom of our religion that no person on earth can judge the Pope in the sense of a penal sentence with juridical effect."[523]

It is one thing for a subject to presume to judge his superior, but it is quite another, and there has always been the belief in the Church that subjects have the right to judge in conscience, and in the case of heresy, to withdraw straightaway their alliegance from their superiors, even from a pope, if the superiors manifest themselves to be heretics. Moynihan mentions that there was such "a tradition already prevalent as far back as the seventh century."[524] Moynihan elaborates that at the time when rumors were circulating against the orthodoxy of Pope Boniface IV (608-615), St. Columban wrote to him, assuring him that he believed none of it, but the saint was careful to add:

> "Si enim hæc certa magis quam fabulosa sunt, versa vice filii vestri *in caput* conversi sunt, vos vero in *caudam* (Deut. 28, 44); quod etiam dici dolor est: ideo et vestri erunt judices qui semper orthodoxam fidem servaverunt, quicumque illi fuerint, etiamsi juniores vestri videantur. Ipsi autem orthodoxi et veri catholici, qui neque hæreticos neque suspectos aliquos aliquando receperunt neque defenderunt, sed in zelo veræ fidei permanserunt."[525]

With the words, "*neque hæreticos neque suspectos aliquos*"; the saint makes it clear that the subjects have the right in conscience to judge and reject (literally to not receive[526]) not only superiors who are notoriously *manifest*

---

[523] *Fatima Perspectives – Perspective No. 1068*.
[524] Moynihan, *Op. cit.*, p. 33.
[525] *MPL*, LXXX, col. 278
[526] St. Columban's use of the term "*receperunt*" in the phrase, *neque suspectos aliquos aliquando receperunt neque defenderunt*, is a clear allusion to the apostolic teaching that heretics and infidels are to be absolutely shunned and avoided, "If any man come to you, and bring not this doctrine, receive him not into the house, nor say to him, God speed you." (II John 10).

heretics, but also those who positively manifest themselves to be reasonably considered *suspected heretics*. In the latter case, if the suspicion is sufficiently grave, the pontiff would no longer enjoy the status of a certainly valid pope, but would have become a *papa dubius*, and thus there would be positive doubt as to whether the papal *cathedra* was occupied or vacant. In the case of a *papa dubius*, no one is bound to be subject to him, to be in communion with him, or to accept him as a valid pope. In unison with all the eminent commentators on Canon Law, Wernz & Vidal explain, "Finally one cannot consider as schismatics those who refuse to obey the Roman Pontiff because they would hold his person suspect or, because of widespread rumors, doubtfully elected (as happened after the election of Urban VI)..."[527] Under such circumstances, therefore, it would be licit for one to consider the Apostolic See to be vacant.

Siscoe also makes an errant application of Bellarmine's words on the deposition of bishops to the question of the deposition of a pope in his *Remnant* article when he says,

> «St. Bellarmine himself explained that a heretical bishop must be deposed by the proper authorities. After explaining how a false prophet (meaning heretical pastor) can be spotted, he wrote: "... if the pastor is a bishop, they [the faithful] cannot depose him and put another in his place. For Our Lord and the Apostles only lay down that false prophets are not to be listened to by the people, and not that they depose them. And it is certain that the practice of the Church has always been that heretical bishops be deposed by bishop's councils, or by the Sovereign Pontiff."»

For Bellarmine, the process of deposing a bishop is quite different from the process for removing a manifestly hereticl pope. As noted above, Pope Gregory XVI, who followed the opinion of Ballerini, who himself subscribed to Bellarmine's opinion, explained that a pope cannot be deposed from office in the manner that a bishop can be deposed by the pope.[528] It is also patent from the explicitly expressed doctrine of Bellarmine in this text, that he is not treating of matters of opinion, but of acts of jurisdiction, to wit, the jurisdiction to depose which the faithful do not possess. One has the natural right in conscience to judge as a

---

[527] Wernz-Vidal, *Ius Canonicum*, Rome, Gregorian Univ. 1937, Vol. II, p. 398.

[528] Cf. – D. Mauro Cappellari ora Gregorio XVI, *Il trionfo della santa sede e della chiesa contro gli assalti dei novatori*, Venezia, 1832, *Discorso Preliminare*, § 2, pp. 52 – 53.

matter of opinion that a manifest heretic who openly rejects dogma has lost office; but private individuals do not have the right to juridically enforce their private opinions, but the loss of office can only be enforced by proper authority upon declaration by ecclesiastical authority. (Canon 194 § 2)[529]

The position of the Apostolic See at the First Vatican Council was quite different from that of Salza and Siscoe, and did not concern private judgment of a heretical pope, but the plainly evident fact of manifest heresy, as Archbishop Purcell related: "If he denies any dogma of the Church held by every true believer, he is no more Pope than either you or I". No 'antecedent judgment' is required or even possible, because by the very fact of public heresy, the heretic would have already fallen from office, and thus there can be no antecedent judgment. An individual person or the Church can only understand and judge that a manifest heretic, who openly denies the faith, is in fact a heretic after the fact of the manifest formal heresy and the immediately consequent fall from office. The Church must declare the fact officially so that the vacancy can be filled, and to protect the souls of the faithful from the heretical wolf, but there is no reason why men would be morally forbidden from forming their own opinions in the matter before the Church makes its official pronouncement: "*men are not bound* or able to read hearts; but when they see that someone is a heretic by his external works, they judge him to be a heretic pure and simple [simpliciter], and condemn him as a heretic."

Salza and Siscoe say, *The antecedent judgment must be rendered by the Church before the consequent judgment can be declared.* Really? But there is no antecedent judgment that can be made before the fall from office – it is *impossible*, because the pope remains in office so long as he is not a public heretic, and *cannot be judged*. According to Bellarmine, and all who hold to Opinion No. 5, *the first judgment is pronounced by the heretic upon himself, who automatically falls from office without any judgment by the Church*. This is patently manifest in Bellarmine's own words:

> "Therefore, the true opinion is the fifth, according to which the Pope who is manifestly a heretic *ceases by himself* to be Pope and head, in the same way as he ceases to be a Christian and a member of the body of the Church; *and for this reason* he can be judged and punished by the Church. This is the

---

[529] Canon 194 § 2. Amotio, de qua in nn. 2 et 3, urgeri tantum potest, si de eadem auctoritatis competentis declaratione constet.

opinion of all the ancient Fathers, who teach that manifest heretics *immediately lose all jurisdiction.*"

It is at this point, after the fall from office, that, as Bellarmine says, "when they [men] see that someone is a heretic by his external works, they judge him to be a heretic pure and simple, and condemn him as a heretic." The Church would only judge a pope after the fact of his public defection from the faith and the Church, and who would thereby have fallen *ipso facto* from office entirely by himself and become "*minor quolibet catholico*". Hence, only after the fall from office would have taken place, would the Church then judge juridically that the fall from office had already taken place, and then proceed to punish the fallen heretic. Individuals are also morally permitted in a case of manifest heresy to judge according to their own private opinion, according to a properly informed conscience, but the private judgment of individuals does not have any juridical effect of removal or deposition.

As Gregory XVI (quoted earlier) explained, such a one would have "fallen" from office "by himself" (*per se decaduto dal pontificato*). Similarly, St. Alphonsus: "After all, if God were to permit that a pope would be notoriously heretical and contumacious, he would cease to be pope, and the pontificate would be vacant." [530] And again in the same work,

> "The same (i.e. 'the See would be considered vacant') would be in the case, if the pope were to fall notoriously and pertinaciously in some heresy. Since then, ... the pope would not be deprived by the Council... but would be immediately stripped by Christ, having in fact become an incapable subject, and fallen from his office."[531]

Thus, the very justification for the Church to convene in a synod to judge the heretical pope would be the fact that the See would already be considered to have been vacated by the heretic pope, who would have

---

[530] «Del resto, se Dio permettesse che un papa fosse notoriamente eretico e contumace, egli cesserebbe d'essere papa, e vacherebbe il pontificato.» *Verità della Fede*, part 3, ch. 8, no. 10. In: *Opere dommatiche di S. Alfonso de Liguori* (Torino, G. Marietti, 1848), p. 720. (Opere di S. Alfonso Maria de Liguori, v. 8)

[531] «Lo stesso (i.e. "si tiene vacante la Sede Apostolica") sarebbe nel caso, che il Papa cadesse notoriamente e pertinacemente in qualche eresia. Benchè allora [...] non sarebbe il Papa privato dal Pontificato dal Concilio... ma ne sarebbe spogliato immediatamente da Cristo, divenendo allora Soggetto affatto inabile, e caduto dal suo Officio.» [*Verità della Fede,* Part. III. Cap. IX. p. 457.]

become an incapable subject to retain the papacy, and would have already fallen from office. The proposition that one is morally bound not to acknowledge such a fact, and to believe the falsehood that a heretic is still the pope until the Church will have declared otherwise, is absurd on its face, and is a perverted belief. No one can ever be bound to believe a falsehood until the Church declares it is false; and that would also leave the wolf free to prowl and destroy souls for however so long it would take for the negligent pastors of the Church to finally get their act together and render a judgment – *quod esset miserrima conditio Ecclesiæ, si lupum manifeste grassantem, pro pastore agnoscere cogeretur. (Bellarminus)*

What takes place *ipso facto* can be *ex natura*; it can be *ipso jure*, or it can be both. As I have already explained earlier, an *ipso facto* loss of office according to the very nature of an *ipso faco* effect, takes place **immediately** by the very act itself, and **by that fact alone without the intervention of any other external agent,** *otherwise it is not ipso facto.* In either case, whether *ex natura* or *ipso jure,* if an *ipso facto* fall from office does not take place immediately **by the fact itself,** but only after a judgment pronounced by the Church, **then *it is not ipso facto,*** because the term *"ipso facto"*, according to the proper signification of those very words *"ipso facto"*, means, **"by the fact itself"**; and consequently, if the fact of public heresy has already taken place in reality, but the heretic does not yet fall from office **by that fact itself without the active intervention of any other agent, then the fall from office itself is not *ipso facto.*** The very notion of an *ipso facto* fall from office due to heresy, that does not take place entirely by the very fact of heresy alone, i.e., *per se,* but only after the intervention of another agent, such as a *public judgment of the Church,* is a self-contradictory notion. *This is how the teaching of St. Robert Bellarmine is explained unanimously by ecclesiastical scholars who comment on the Five Opinions* – that the *ipso facto* fall from office is **automatic,** and is not in any way dependent on an intervening judgment by the Church. In Bellarmine's own words, the *ipso facto* fall from office takes place *"sine alia vi externa".* These words absolutely exclude the possibility of any involvement of any dispositive ministerial judgment of the Church in the *ipso facto* fall from office.

"According to Bellarmine," explains Don Curzio Nitoglia, "(De Romano Pontifice lib. II. Cap. 30, p. 420), since notorious and public manifest heretics lose jurisdiction ipso facto, granted but not conceded that the pope can fall into heresy, in the eventual case of manifest heresy, he would immediately lose the papal authority. This is the interpretation of the Bellarminian position given by the Jesuit Fathers Franz Xavier

Wernz and Pedro Vidal. (Jus Canonicum), Rome, Gregorian, 1943, vol. II, p. 517)"[532] Then Don Curzio points out that the same interpretation is given by other eminent authorities as well: "(cfr. also L. Billot, Tractatus de Ecclesia Christi, Prato, Giachetti, 1909, tomo II, p. 617; J. Salaverri, De Ecclesia Christi, Madrid, BAC, 1958, p. 879, n. 1047)." [533]

Against this unanimous interpretation of commentators on Bellarmine made by eminent theologians and canonists who have expounded on the Five Opinions in recent centuries, Salza and Siscoe most stupidly declare:

---

[532] «Secondo il Bellarmino (De Romano Pontifice, lib. II, cap. 30, p. 420), siccome gli eretici manifesti, notori e pubblici perdono ipso facto la giurisdizione, ammesso e non concesso che il Papa possa cadere in eresia, in caso di eventuale eresia manifesta egli perderebbe immediatamente l'autorità papale. Questa è l'interpretazione della posizione bellarminiana data dai padri gesuiti Franz Xavier Wernz e Pedro Vidal (Jus Canonicum, Roma, Gregoriana, 1943, vol. II, p. 517).»

[533] Don Curzio explains that the opinion of Ballerini follows that of Bellarmine, as I have already explained earlier, that the heretic pope would declare himself a heretic and fall from office by himself: «In breve ciò che don Pietro Ballerini mantiene come certissimo è che il Papa nel definire non errerà mai; infine come ipotesi investigativa "ammesso e non concesso" che il Papa cada in errore contrario alla fede, dovrebbe essere ammonito e corretto e dopo due ammonizioni, se si ostina nell'errore, *si dichiara da se stesso eretico e decaduto dal Pontificato*, ma tutto ciò deve essere opera non di giurisdizione bensì di carità (*De Potestate ecclesiastica Summorum Pontificum et Conciliorum generalium*, Verona, 1765, cap. 9, nn. 3-8; cap. 15, n. 21; cfr. T. Facchini, *Il Papato principio di unità e Pietro Ballerini di Verona*, Padova, Il Messaggero di S Antonio, 1950, pp. 126-128). Anche dallo studio testé citato di padre Tarcisio Facchini si capisce bene che l'ipotesi di don Pietro Ballerini segue l'opinione del Bellarmino» The warnings given are of the nature of fraternal correction, and are not canonical warnings (which are impossible, because they are properly the act of a superior), as Salza & Siscoe mendaciously claim. As I have demonstrated above from Ballerini's exposition on Pedro de Luna (Benedict XIII), since the warnings are not canonical, if the heretic pope manifests his pertinacity *sponte sua* without warnings, he would fall from office even without being warned. Both Bellarmine and Ballerini speak of the necessity of the warnings not in terms of a canonical procedure, but only for the practical necessity of establishing pertinacity; and at which point the heretic would fall entirely by himself *ipso facto* without being judged by the Church, and before any merely declaratory sentence confirming the fact could be made.

«Bellarmine and Suarez (two Jesuits) disagree with the opinion of Cajetan and John of St. Thomas (the Dominicans). As we explain in great detail in our book, Bellarmine and Suarez teach that the Pope will lose his office, ipso facto, *once he is judged by the Church to be a heretic*, without the additional juridical act of vitandus declaration.» (emphasis added)

And then they explain what (according to them) is the "erroneous interpretation of Bellarmine" which they characterize as the "sedevacantist interpretation of Bellarmine", which, (they say), Fr. Kramer has swallowed "hook, line and sinker":

«Where the Sedevacantists have erred is by interpreting the ipso facto loss of office to be similar to an "ipso facto" latae sententiæ excommunication, which occurs automatically (or ipso facto), when one commits an offense that carries the penalty, without requiring an antecedent judgment by the Church. But this is not at all what Bellarmine and Suarez meant by the ipso facto loss of office. What they meant is that the ipso facto loss of office occurs after the Church judges the Pope to be a heretic and before any additional juridical sentence or excommunication (which differs from Cajetan's opinion). In other words, after the Church establishes "the fact" that the Pope is a manifest heretic, he, according to this opinion, is deemed to lose his office ipso facto ("by the fact"). This is clear from the following quotation from Suarez who wrote: ....»

It is unanimously explained by expert canonists and theologians that according to Opinion No. 4, a judgment must be made by the Church for the heretic pope to fall from office; and according to Opinion No 5, the heretic pope falls automatically by himself from the pontificate by the very act itself of manifest formal heresy, without any judgment being pronounced by the Church. Both of these opinions were already expressed by canonists in the early 1180s, as Moynihan documents in his earlier cited work. That essential difference which distinguishes between the fourth and fifth opinions was clearly understood by theologians and canonists in Bellarmine's day. It simply beggars belief that anyone would seriously claim that the eminent scholars who have written unanimously on this question are wrong – that they have misinterpreted Bellarmine, and they have not understood Opinion No. 5 correctly. This is exactly what Salza & Siscoe do when they say that Suárez and Bellarmine are both of Opinion No. 5, which according to them, requires the judgment of the Church for the loss of office to take place. It is quite simply inconceivable that Bellarmine would have been ignorant of the long established opinion which held that the pope who falls into heresy falls automatically by himself from the pontificate by the very act itself of manifest formal heresy, without any judgment being pronounced by the Church; and that he would have not included it as one of the five opinions. Either Salza & Siscoe do not understand Opinion No. 5, or Bellarmine did not understand it correctly; and that would mean that all of the expert commentators on the Five Opinions have not correctly understood it either!

Incredibly, Salza and Siscoe would attempt to interpret the meaning of Bellarmine, not by strictly analyzing Bellarmine's own words, but by quoting Suárez, who, according to all the expert canonists and theologians subscribed to Opinion No. 4. Salza & Siscoe say that all those eminent authors are wrong, and that Suárez actually followed Opinion No. 5! Don Curzio comments,

> "The fourth opinion, studied above all by Cardinal Tommaso de Vio 'Cajetan', by John of St. Thomas, (*De aucttoritate Summi Pontificis*, Quebec, Laval University, 1947) and also by Francisco Suárez (who examines the first and the fourth, but maintains the first more probable than the fourth); according to the fourth opinion there must be a declaration of heresy of the pope by the bishops or the College of Cardinals."[534]

That is exactly what Suárez maintained, to wit, that «**the Pope would cease to be Pope just when a sentence was passed against him for his crime**, by the legitimate jurisdiction of the Church.» [535] All commentators, whether theologians or canonists, distinguish between Opinion No. 4 and no. 5 on the basis that in Opinion No. 4, a judgment of the Church is necessary for a manifest heretic pope to fall from office, and in Opinion No. 5 the fall is automatic, without any judgment by the Church. This is the opinion of Cardinal Burke, whom I have quoted

---

[534] «La *quarta opinione* è stata studiata soprattutto dal cardinal Tommaso de Vio detto il Gaetano, da Giovanni di San Tommaso (*De auctoritate Summi Pontificis*, Québec, Università di Laval, 1947) e anche da Francisco Suarez (che esamina la prima e la quarta, ma ritiene più probabile la prima della quarta); secondo la quarta opinione occorre che vi sia una dichiarazione dell'eresia del Papa da parte dell'Episcopato o del Collegio cardinalizio»

[535] «Dico tertio: si Papa sit hæreticus et incorrigibilis, cum primum per legitimam Ecclesiæ jurisdictionem sententia declaratoria criminis in eum profertur, desinit esse Papa.» [Suarez, *De Fide Theologica. Disputatio X. De Summo Pontifice, Sect. VI.* p. 317.]

earlier saying the fall would be "automatic". According to Salza & Siscoe, they are all wrong, and their interpretation of Opinion No. 5 is "sedevacantist theology"— and they ignorantly insist that both Suárez and Bellarmine were of Opinion No. 5, which they interpret to mean that the heretic pope would fall from office after a judgment by the Church. Furthermore, according to the private pontifications of the Salza/Siscoe Vigilante Inquisition, no matter how explicitly, directly, immediately, and contradictorily the Argentinian claimant brazenly asserts his perverted propositions against Catholic dogma, no one may privately express the belief that that same one, Bergoglio, has fallen from office before the Church finishes the juridical process of declaring him a public heretic – and for that reason, by their non-existent authority, Salza & Siscoe solemnly declare a moral judgment, namely: that until the formal deposition process is completed, "Francis still remains Pope, and no Catholic can claim otherwise without sinning against the Faith."[536]

It is by their fraudulent and grotesquely distorted misinterpretation of Bellarmine and Ballerini, that Salza and Siscoe attempt to make it appear that Bellarmine, Cajetan, Suárez, John of St. Thomas, Billuart, Laymann, and all the other doctors of theology and canon law were in unanimous agreement that a judgment of the Church would first be necessary before a manifest heretic pope would fall from office, and they perversely maintain that this universally abandoned opinion is the common opinion today, which must be followed under pain of mortal sin against faith! That opinion, that a manifestly and formally heretical pope would remain in office and retain jurisdiction *until judged by the Church* is a *heresy,* because it directly opposes the pope's absolute *judicial supremacy* infallibly defined in the solemn dogmatic pronouncement on the Primacy of the Roman Pontiff at the First Vatican Council; and it professes *directly* against the dogma of *papal immunity and injudicability* taught repeatedly (in the declarations cited earlier in this work) by the popes in their *ordinary magisterium,* such as the explicit declaration of Pope St. Gregory VII, **that a pope cannot be judged by anyone** – «**Quod a nemine ipse (the pope) iudicari debeat**». This is the same doctrine which St. Robert Bellarmine demonstrated to be the teaching of the Fathers, Doctors, Popes, and Councils in *lib. ii cap. xxvi* of *De Romano Pontifice.* The opinion is also an *error in fide,* by its it opposition to the teaching of the universal magisterium that a heretic is severed from the

---

[536] Salza & Siscoe in *Pope Francis Refuses to Answer the Dubia – What Happens Next.*

body of the Church *suapte natura* by the public act of formal heresy; and it is contrary to the unanimous teaching of the Fathers that heretics lose office *ex natura hæresis*, as Bellarmine plainly demonstrates in the passages I have cited earlier in this work. To directly deny that teaching is heresy, and to deny its applicability to the papacy in the hypothetical case of a manifestly heretical pope is an *error in faith*. Salza and Siscoe make a desperate attempt to salvage their heretical doctrine on these points by appealing to the teaching of Billuart, who misapplies the provisions of *Ad evitanda scandala* (Martin V) to the case of a heretic pope. This topic will be dealt with in the next section.

SECTION THREE

ST. ROBERT BELLARMINE'S TREATMENT OF THE FIVE OPINIONS

PRELIMINARY REMARKS

St. Robert's exposition on the Five Opinions follows an orderly sequence in its line of argumentation: First he states the thesis; and then he presents the five opinions on the question. He briefly explains why the first opinion is probable, but (in his day) not certain. He rejects the second, because the visible head of the Church is visibly chosen for that office by men; and therefore, a secret heretic cannot be invisibly deposed by God, because he remains a visible member of the Church; and hence, must be visibly removed by men only upon having had his heresy proven, (and thus made manifest), and then judged. Once the fact of his obstinate defection from the faith has been proven, his heresy is made manifest, and he ceases to be pope and a visible member of the Church by his own judgment of self-condemnation in accordance with Opinion No. 5. He can then be judged to have fallen from office. Bellarmine rejects the third opinion which holds that a manifest heretic pope can neither "be deposed", (in the intransitive sense of *esse depositum*); nor is it that he "can be deposed" (in the transitive sense of *deponi posse*, i.e. can be deposed by the Church). Bellarmine explains that the provision exists in the *Decretum Gratiani* to judge a pope for heresy; but, in his refutation of the fourth opinion, he explains that for so long as he is pope he cannot be judged or deposed by the Church (*deponendus*); but a manifest heretic visibly ceases by himself to be a Christian and a member of the Church; and therefore (according to "the fifth and true opinion") ceases entirely by himself, to be pope *ipso facto* (*depositus*); for which reason he can be judged and punished by the Church.

ON OPINION NO. ONE:

THE POPE CANNOT BE A FORMAL HERETIC

I have presented St. Robert Bellarmine's exposition on the First Opinion, that a pope cannot be a heretic, in the previous section, and also presented my own argument proving this opinion to be the correct one. Bellarmine says of this opinion, "such an opinion is probable, and can easily be defended", but, he adds, "it is not certain". As has been pointed out already, the more common belief of the Middle Ages that a pope could fall into heresy had its origin in the spurious Canon *Si papa*, which heavily influenced the medieval canonists, and even influnced most of the theologians and canonists in Bellarmine's day to consider the question at least as a highly improbable hypothesis. That this canon was the basis for that opinion is clear from the manner that Bellarmine presents the topic for discussion: "The tenth thesis. A Pope can be judged and deposed by the Church in the case of heresy; as is clear from Dist. 40, can. Si Papa: therefore, the Pontiff is subject to human judgment, at least in some case." One must bear in mind that in this passage, Bellarmine is only presenting the *thesis* to be discussed in the chapter, and ***not stating his own opinion on the question***. This is obvious enough from the context, since he then says, "I respond: there are five opinions on this matter." The reason I mention this here is because Salza & Siscoe very deceptively quote this passage by leaving out the words, "The tenth thesis", which present the passage as merely introducing the thesis to be discussed; and by omitting those words, they subtly create the appearance that in stating the thesis, Bellarmine was not merely presenting the topic to be discussed, but was actually stating own opinion in the matter. On their website, Salza & Siscoe misleadingly write:

> «Before providing and commenting on the "Five Opinions" in his De Romano Pontifice, Bellarmine begins with this proposition: "A Pope can be judged and deposed by the Church in the case of heresy; as is clear from Dist. 40, can. Si Papa: therefore, the Pontiff is subject to human judgment, at least in some case."»[537]

---

[537] *RESPONDING TO FR. KRAMER'S ERRONEOUS INTERPRETATION OF BELLARMINE*: «As we saw above, in this latest blurb Fr. Kramer says that the heretical Pope is only "judged by men," *after* he has *fallen* from office. In other words, according to Fr. Kramer, Bellarmine

In fact, Bellarmine did not begin by *stating a proposition*, as if he were stating his own conclusion at the onset of the discussion of the question, but he begins the discussion by presenting the *topic*, i.e., the *argumentum* to be discussed: "The tenth thesis (*argumentum*). A Pope can be judged and deposed by the Church in the case of heresy; as is clear from Dist. 40, can. Si Papa: therefore, the Pontiff is subject to human judgment, at least in some case."

Bellarmine's own opinion was that a pope cannot fall into heresy and cannot be judged; and that hypothetically, if a pope could fall into manifest heresy, he would cease to be pope by that very fall, and only then could he be judged by the Church. I quoted the passage earlier, where he said, "I say those canons do not mean the Pope can err as a private person but only that *the Pope cannot be judged*; it is still not altogether certain whether the Pontiff could be a heretic or not. Thus, they add the condition 'if he might become a heretic' for greater caution"; and then the passage in which he most emphatically declares, "the Pope by his own nature can fall into heresy, but not when we posit the singular assistance of God which Christ asked for him by his prayer. Furthermore, Christ prayed lest his faith would fail". It is clear that for St. Robert Bellarmine, the pope cannot be judged for heresy because, 1) while in office he cannot be judged by anyone, and, 2) he cannot be judged for heresy because he cannot become a heretic. Nevertheless, he says, "it is still not altogether certain whether the Pontiff could be a heretic or not." Although St. Robert knew the teaching of Innocent III,

---

teaches that Christ secretly deposes the Pope (removes him from office) and then the man who is "judged" *is no longer the Pope*. The "judgment of men," he claims, simply concerns the Church's physical removal of the *former* Pope from office.

Is this what St. Bellarmine taught? No, he taught the contrary! And these bipolar positions of Bellarmine and Kramer give us reason to believe that Fr. Kramer has not even read Bellarmine's treatment of the issue. Unfortunately, however, that wouldn't stop Fr. Kramer from opining on Bellarmine's theology, just as it hasn't stopped him from denouncing our book, **which he has not read**. Before providing and commenting on the "Five Opinions" in his *De Romano Pontifice*, Bellarmine begins with this proposition: "**A Pope can be judged and deposed by the Church in the case of heresy**; as is clear from Dist. 40, can. Si Papa: therefore, **the Pontiff is subject to human judgment**, at least in some case." Notice, the issue Bellarmine is addressing is the deposition of a **Pope**, and whether the **Pope** (not a *former* Pope) "is subject to human judgment" in some cases, specifically, in the case of heresy.»

that the grace of unfailing faith pertains essentially to the holder of the Petrine office, he did not yet have the solemn definition of the dogma of Infallibility pronounced by the First Vatican Council, which established the promise of unfailing faith of the Pontiff as the premise and basis of the definition, and therefore the necessary disposition for Papal Infallibility:

> «*Quorum quidem apostolicam doctrinam omnes venerabiles Patres amplexi et sancti Doctores orthodoxi venerati atque secuti sunt; plenissime scientes,* **hanc sancti Petri Sedem ab omni semper errore illibatam permanere, secundum Domini Salvatoris nostri divinam pollicitationem discipulorum suorum principi factam: Ego rogavi pro te, ut non deficiat fides tua**, *et tu aliquando conversus confirma fratres tuos.*»[538]

So, while the Vatican Council did not define papal inerrancy, or that a pope cannot fall into heresy; nevertheless, the Council did magisterially establish that the infallibility of the See of Peter is premised on the promised grace of unfailing personal faith of the Pontiff, which logically would prevent him from falling into pertinacious heresy. Fr. Gleize's observations in his article on Papal Heresy, 1) "that the facts of history are undeniable. There have been in the Church one or two popes who favored heresy, and there are today, since Vatican II, popes who have caused serious problems for the conscience of Catholics, who are rightly perplexed"; and, 2) "it is clear that since Vatican II, Popes Paul VI, John Paul II. and Benedict XVI have taught—and Pope Francis still teaches—theological opinions that would be difficult to reconcile with the substance of Catholic dogma", have absolutely no bearing on the question of whether or not a pope can fall into formal heresy, because these observations merely make note of the material fact of heresy, and therefore do not even constitute a probable argument in favour of the opinion that a pope could become a formal heretic. Fr. Gleize concludes, "the first opinion that regards as improbable the fall of a pope into heresy is itself improbable. In other words, the arguments from theological authority along the lines of a negative answer to the question posed are insufficient to win adherence. It must still be shown, therefore, how right reason, enlightened by faith, could justify an affirmative answer." I believe I have sufficiently, and even more than adequately demonstrated how right reason enlightened by faith does indeed jusify an afffimative answer. However, without there having been in his day a

---

[538] *Pastor Æternus*

dogmatic definition of papal infallibility and a clear magisterial pronouncement establishing the unfailing faith of the Pontiff absolutely as a necessary premise for the exercise of the charism of papal Infallibility, Bellarmine did not consider his own opinion to be altogether certain, and therefore says, "it will be worthwhile to see what the response should be if the Pope could be a heretic."

ON OPINION NO. TWO:

THE POPE WHO IS VISIBLY ELEVATED TO THE PONTIFICATE BY MEN CANNOT BE INVISIBLY DEPOSED BY GOD

Proceeding to the Second Opinion, Bellarmine states that opinion: "Thus, the second opinion is that the Pope, in the very instant in which he falls into heresy, even if it is only interior, is outside the Church and deposed by God, for which reason he can be judged by the Church." The glaring defect in this opinion is that according to it, the one who falls into interior heresy can be judged by the Church; since the Church authorities could not possibly know that he is a secret heretic, and that he has been deposed by God, and therefore there would be no way they could judge and remove him, as Bellarmine notes, "But a secret heretic cannot be judged by men". Thus it would be quite impossible for him to be "declared [by the Church] deposed by divine law, and deposed de facto, if he still refused to yield". If such a heretic pope were to be deposed by God, he would be deposed invisibly, and that would be to no avail, because no one would know he had fallen from the pontificate, and he would therefore remain illegitimately in power as a usurper, in such a manner that he could not be removed. Hence, Bellarmine says, "For jurisdiction is certainly given to the Pontiff by God, but with the agreement of men, as is obvious; because this man, who beforehand was not Pope, has from men that he would begin to be Pope, therefore, it is not removed by God unless it is through men." It is clear therefore, that for a pope to be removed by some act other than death (or permanent insanity which is equivalent to death), he must be removed by men, and such a process of removal is first accomplished by the *renunciation* of the papacy either expressly or tacitly, which effects the *loss of office*. In the case of tacit renunciation, it is only by such visible actions as acts of manifest heresy, which constitute a visible and obvious defection from the faith and the Church, that bring about the automatic loss of office, so that the pope can be judged to have left office *by himself*, as Bellarmine puts it; or, as Ballerini says, to have "*ipso facto* by his own will *abdicated* the primacy and the pontificate".[539] Thus it is that a pope can be *judged by men* to have tacitly abdicated by defecting into public heresy, and as a public heretic, (and not as a secret heretic as Torquemada[540] maintained), be "*judged by the Church*, that is, *he is declared deposed by divine law*, and deposed *de facto*, if he still refused to yield." Thus the heretic who loses office by himself can be judged to have *lost office* and be effectively *removed by men*. Such automatic loss of office, according to Bellarmine, would only take place in the case of a manifestly heretical pope (Opinion No. 5); and not in the case of a pope who falls into occult heresy (Opinion No. 2). However, in either case, the "necessary disposition" to preserve the form of the pontificate, which is *faith simpliciter* (as Bellarmine explains in his refutation of Opinion No. 4), would be lost; but practically considered, while in the case of a manifest heretic, Bellarmine says by the removal of that necessary disposition and the severing of the visible bond with the Church, the heretic would straightaway cease to be pope; but in the case of a secret heretic pope, he would not cease to be pope until his heresy is proven, and, thus being manifested, he would thereby cease to be a visible member of the Church.

At first glance, it might appear that the Holy Doctor had contradicted himself, but it was not Bellarmine who asserted a contradictory position on the question, but rather Bellarmine himself was only too aware of the intrinsically problematic nature of Opinion No. 2, and the irresolvable paradox its premise, and therefore its refutation, creates. St. Robert Bellarmine demonstrated conclusively, that in accordance with divine revelation, external acts of manifest heresy bring about a visible

---

[539] "ipso facto sua voluntate primatu & pontificatu exauctoratus"

[540] According to Bellarmine, it would not appear that Torquemada intended to exclude from Church membership those who lacked the internal virtue of faith, but was only trying to say that faith is requird for one be internally united to the body of Christ: «Restant postremo infidels occulti, idest ii, qui nec fidem internam, nec ullam christianam virtutem habent, et tamen exterius propter temporale aliquod commodum fidem catholicam profitentur, et communionem sacramentorum veris fidelibus permiscentur; quos quidem nullo modo ad veram Ecclesiam pertinere non solum Confessionistae et Calvinistae docent, sed etiam aliqui ex catholicis, quorum unus est Joan. de Turrecremata, lib. 4. De Ecclesia; par. 2. c. 20. **Quamquam hic auctor nihil fortasse aliud dicere voluit, nisi requiri fidem, ut quis unitus dici possit interna unione corpori Christi**, quod quidem verissimum est.» [*De Ecclesia Militante*, Cap. X. p. 89.]

separation from the Church and a consequent automatic loss of office; and therefore if a pope were to fall into manifest heresy, according to "the fifth and true opinion", he would immediately cease to be pope and could then be judged by the Church; but in the case of occult heresy, "it is not proven to me", because such an impostor as a counterfeit heretic pope could not be judged and removed from the throne, and, he adds, "that the foundation of this opinion is that secret heretics are outside the Church, which is false, and we will amply demonstrate this in our tract de Ecclesia."[541] Quite rightly, Bellarmine expressed his belief and

---

[541] «Nostra autem sententia est, Ecclesiam unam tantum esse, non duas, et illam unam et veram esse coetum hominum ejusdem christianae fidei professione, et eorundem sacramentorum communion colligatum, sub regimine legitimorum pastorum, ac precipue unius Christi in terris vicarii romani pontificis. Ex qua definition facile colligi potest, qui homines ad Ecclesiam pertineant. Tres enim sunt partes hujus definitionis. Professio verae fidei, sacramentorum communion, et subjection ad legitimum pastorem romanum pontificem. Ratione primae partis excluduntur omnes infidels tam qui numquam fuerunt in Ecclesia [...] tam qui fuerunt et recesserunt, ut haeretici et apostatae. Ratione secundae, excluduntur catechumeni et excommunicati, quoniam illi non sunt admissi ad sacramentorum communionem, isti sunt dimissi. Ratione tertiae, excluduntur schismatici, qui habent fidem et sacramenta, sed non subduntur legitimo pastori, et ideo foris profitentur fidem, et sacramenta percipient. Includuntur autem omnes alii, etiamsi reprobi, scelesti et impii.

Atque hoc interest inter sententiam nostrum et alias omnes, quod omnes aliae requirunt internas virtutes ad constituendum aliquem in Ecclesia, et propterea Ecclesiam vera invisibilem faciunt, nos autem, et credimus in Ecclesia inveniri omnes virtutes, fidem, spem, charitatem, et caeteras; tamen ut aliquis aliquot modo dici possit pars verae Ecclesiae, de qua Scripturae loquuntur, non putamus require ullam internam virtutem, sed tantum externum professionem fidei, et sacramentorum communionem, quae sensu ipso percipitur. Ecclesia enim est coetus hominum ita visibilis et palpabilis, ut est populi romani, vel regnum Galliae, aut respublica Venetorum.

Notandum autem est ex Augustino in breviculo collationis. Collat. 3. Ecclesiam esse corpus vivum, in quo est anima et corpus, et quidem anima sunt interna dona Spiritus sancti, fides, spes, charitas etc. Corpus sunt externa professio fidei, et communicatio sacramentorum. Ex quo fit, ut quidam sint de anima et de corpore Ecclesiae, et proinde uniti Christo capiti interius et exterius; sunt enim quasi membra viva in corpore [...] Rursum aliqua sint de anima, et non de corpore, ut catechumeni, vel excommunicati, si fidem et charitatem habeant, quod fieri potest. Denique, aliqui sint de corpore, et non de anima, ut qui nullam habent internam virtutem, et tamen spe, aut timore aliquot temporali

presented proofs (which he judged not to be altogether certain), that such a thing as a heretic pope is impossible; and this is especially borne out by the fact that a secret heretic pope could not confirm the faith of his brethren (as Bellarmine himself believed), being cut off (internally) from the unity of the Church[542], and therefore incapable of exercising the charism of Infallibility and carrying out his *munus* of *confirmator fratrum*, he would, (lacking the necessary disposition to preserve the form of the papacy), necessarily cease to be pope; while at the same time, remaining a visible but atrophied member of the Church by a merely external and material union, he would necessarily remain pope as the visible head, (because he could not be visibly removed by men), but incapable of exercising his *munus*. However, since the dogma of Infallibility had not yet been defined, Bellarmine was clearly not disposed to declare the first opinion as certain on the sole basis of the *ex ratione* argument that for the pope to exercise his *munus* the faith of the pontiff must necessarily be permanent and unfailing, otherwise there would take place the of loss of papal office due to the removal of the necessary disposition (faith) to preserve the form of the pontificate in the person of the pope; since that disposition is necessary to preserve the form of the Pontificate in the person of the Pontiff precisely because it is the necessary disposition to exercise the charism of Papal Infallibility – and thus the proof of Opinion No. One would not have been certain until

---

profitentur fidem, et in sacramentis communicant sub regimine pastorum, et tales sunt sicut capilli, aut ungues, aut mali humores in corpore humano.

Definitio igitur nostra solum comprehendit hunc ultimum modum existendi in Ecclesia, quia hic requiritur ut minimum; ut quis possit dici esse pars visibilis Ecclesiae» [*De Ecclesia Militante,* Cap. II. p. 75]

[542] This opinion is confirmed in Ineffabilis Deus: «*Quapropter si qui secus ac a Nobis definitum est, quod Deus avertat, præsumpserint corde sentire, ii noverint, ac porro sciant, se proprio judicio condemnatos, naufragium circa fidem passos esse, et ab unitate Ecclesiæ defecisse, ac præterea facto ipso suo semet pœnis a jure statutis subjicere si quod corde sentiunt, verbo aut scripto, vel alio quovis externo modo significare ausi fuerint.*»

"Wherefore if any persons should have the presumption, which God forbid, of thinking in their hearts contrary to what has been in this respect defined by us, let them be made aware, and let them further know, that they are by their own decision condemned; that they have suffered shipwreck of the faith, and have fallen away from the unity of the Church, and that moreover, by their own act itself, they subject themselves to the penalties imposed by the law, if they should either by word written or oral, or by any other external sign, attempt to give outward expression to the erroneous views they form in their hearts."

the certain existence of the charism itself had been infallibly defined. For this reason, he judged the first opinion, which rules out the premise of the second opinion, to be not entirely certain, but only probable; and therefore, he had to consider the hypothesis of an occult heretic pope, which is the premise of the second opinion. The contradiction implicit in its premise which leads to the irresolvable dilemma that the refutation Opinion No. 2 creates (that a secret heretic for one reason necessarily remains pope, and for another equally compelling reason necessarily ceases to be pope), demonstrates the impossibility that there can even exist a secret heretic pope; and as a logical corollary, that there can exist a heretic pope *simpliciter*. However, before *Pastor Æternus*, it could not be argued with certitude that the secret heretic's loss of faith by itself would necessarily result in the loss of the necessary disposition for the conservation of the form of the pontificate in him, whereby he would cease to be pope; and therefore in his day, Bellarmine was compelled to conclude that the secret heretic would necessarily remain in office as pope, since in his judgment, the reason why he would also necessarily fall from office could not yet be proven with certitude; because the premise upon which the proof is founded, the charism of Infallibility, could not yet be proven *from authority*, but could only be demonstrated *ex ratione*; and in fact, many theologians even centuries before *Pastor Æternus* had convincingly argued in favour of papal infallibility *ex ratione*. This leads to a further consideration: If a pope could become a manifest heretic, that would establish that a pope can become a heretic *simpliciter*, which would mean that he could also be a secret heretic, which is impossible; and therefore, it is certain that a pope cannot become a heretic.

Elsewhere, (in my e-mail reply[543] to the rabid but weak-brained Salza cheerleader, Paul Folbrecht), I wrote:

> «Unlike Opinion No 5, *Opinion No. 2*, which holds that even an occult heretic would automatically cease to be pope is *not even valid as a [practical] hypothesis*, because the refutation of its foundational principle (*that an occult heretic would not be a member of the Church*), results in an outcome consisting of logically opposed effects. Bellarmine refutes the opinion by pointing out that, contrary to Torquemada's argument, *an occult heretic cannot be judged and removed by the Church*. The reason why the heretic would need to be judged and removed, is NOT (as Salza & Siscoe believe) because *the loss of office*

---

[543] I have slightly edited this reply merely for the sake of clarity, without altering the essential content in the least.

cannot take place without judgment (Bellarmine, as quoted above, explains that the pope cannot be judged, but precisely because the manifest heretic pope falls from office by himself, he may then be judged); but rather **because the fall from office of a secret heretic could not be judged to have taken place,** *he would thus cease to be pope without the possibility of being removed, and for this reason, the papacy would cease as a visible institution of the Church* (which is contrary to the divine constitution of the Church), *and the whole Church would defect by being subject to a false Pontiff,* (which is also contrary to the divine constitution of the Church). Thus, a secret heretic cannot be judged to have fallen from the papacy and then be removed by men, and therefore, the secret heretic cannot invisibly cease to be pope without causing a defection from the divine constitution of the Church; since it would appear that the fallen secret heretic pope would still remain in office after his fall from office, and for that reason the Church, against its divine constitution, would no longer be governed by the Roman Pontiff, [but by an impostor]. *Hence, the only possible solution to the problematic Opinion No. 2, is not that the secret heretic would either cease to be pope or remain validly in the Pontificate, but that the pope cannot become a heretic in the first place: OPINION NO. 1 – Bellarmine's opinion, and the most common opinion today.*»

Siscoe's latest reply to this argumentation consists in a mendacious obfuscation; by making it appear that I have contradicted myself:

Siscoe says: «[Y]ou accuse us of being dishonest and misrepresenting your position when *everything we have "accused" you of is backed up by what you are on record as holding?* Here is one example. You wrote:

Fr. Kramer: "the Salza/Siscoe long and convoluted argument is of no avail in its attempt, by means of fraudulent sophistry, to make me falsely appear to contradict myself; **and to deceive their readers into falsely believing that I hold the Opinion No. 2 which Bellarmine (and I too) have refuted.**"

What is Opinion No. 2? It is this: in the hypotheses of a pope falling into heresy and losing "the virtue of faith," he would automatically lose his office. That is Opinion No. 2. Here's your position in your own words:

Fr. Kramer: "Finally, and for the record, I do indeed hold that hypothetically, losing **the virtue of faith**, the pope would lose office."

And again:

Fr. Kramer: "**the virtue of faith** existing in the soul of the pope as its subject is the necessary disposition for the preservation of the form of the supreme pontificate in the person of the pope. (…) **Faith, not merely the material and external profession of the objective content of faith,** but **the virtue of faith** as a principium operationis **is necessary to be in the** soul of person of the pope as its subject in order to receive and **preserve within himself the form of the supreme pontificate** (…) it would clearly be impossible for one to be a valid Roman Pontiff without **the virtue of faith.**" (…) A heretic would necessarily cease to be pope because **even if he were only externally a member of the Church, he would lack [the virtue of] faith.**"

No matter how you try to spin in, you cannot escape the fact that what you wrote above is identical to Opinion No. 2.

And as evidence that I did not use "fraudulent sophistry" to twist your position, I provided the quotations in which you **directly contradict** yourself and gave you *multiple opportunities* to clarify your position. Instead of even trying to do so, you responded by calling us "FRAUDS, CON ARTISTS, LIARS" etc. Was your outburst a diversionary tactic, or, what seems more likely, were you projecting your own guilt on others? There is nothing "fraudulent" or in any way dishonest about asking you to clarify direct contradictions in your own public position.»

Nothing fraudulent? *Siscoe truncates my words in mid-sentence* in order to make it appear (as he and Salza repeatedly claim), that *I hold Opinion No. 2, and that it is I who contradict myself:*

«Finally, and for the record, I do indeed hold that hypothetically, losing the virtue of faith, the pope would lose office…»

What I plainly expressed in my words is that, the *very notion upon which Opinion No. 2 is founded, inexorably leads to an irresolvable logical opposition, and therefore the major premise of Opinion No. 2 involves itself in a contradiction.* Here is what I actually wrote:

"Finally, and for the record, I do indeed hold that hypothetically [as a purely abstract hypothesis without any practical applicability], losing the virtue of faith, the pope would lose office, but due to Christ's efficacious prayer for the unfailing faith of the Pontiff, it is impossible for the pope's faith to fail. [*Therefore a pope cannot become a formal heretic.*] Salza attempts to make my opinion appear eccentric and bizarre, but I have more than adequately demonstrated, with copious quotations from the original Latin texts of St. Robert Bellarmine and other authors, that my position on this point is exactly that of the Holy Doctor [i.e. that without faith as the necessary disposition to conserve the form of the Pontificate in the person of the pope, he would straightaway cease to be pope]; and that the pope cannot become a formal heretic (Opinion No. 1)], which is today, and was for most of the 20th Century, the *opinio communior*".

It is to no avail that Siscoe quotes Bellarmine:

«Bellarmine: "It is certain, whatever one or another might think, a secret heretic, if he might be a Bishop, **or even the Supreme Pontiff**, does not lose jurisdiction, nor dignity, or the name of the head in the Church, **until either he <u>separates himself publicly from the Church</u> (i.e., openly leaves the Church), or being convicted of heresy, is separated against his will**" (Bellarmine, On the Church Militant, ch X).»

This is only *half of Bellarmine's position*. Bellarmine speaks of the *hypothetical* case of a secret heretic pope *as a practical hypothesis*, but does not admit that such a case is really possible (as I have amply documented). Bellarmine argues that the preservation of the form of the Pontificate in the person of the pope requires *faith "simpliciter"* as the *necessary disposition;* and therefore without this necessary disposition, *"he would straightaway cease to be pope"*; thus, considered *per se* as a purely *abstract hypothesis without any practical applicability*, Bellarmine concludes that a heretic pope would simply cease to be pope. I have provided the philosophical and theological basis for this proposition and its demonstration. Since its certitude ultimately hinges on Papal Infallibility, Bellarmine was not able to avail himself of such a demonstration, because (as I have explained), the dogma of Papal Infallibility had not yet been defined. Nevertheless, he argued that without faith, as a *purely abstract hypothesis*, the pope would cease to be pope *simpliciter*; while also arguing that *as a practical hypothesis with hypothetical applicability to a real situation* (if that were possible) the secret heretic pope would remain pope until convicted of heresy *because he would still be a visible member of the Church*. In stating this opinion, Bellarmine does not contradict his position on Opinion No. 5, according to which a manifest heretic would cease to be pope straightaway without first being judged and convicted. One notices the careful wording Bellarmine employs, saying the secret heretic, *"does not lose jurisdiction, nor dignity, or the name of the head in the Church*, until either he separates himself publicly from the Church [by an act of manifest heresy], *or being convicted of heresy, is separated against his will"*[544]. By being convicted of heresy, the heresy is made manifest, and by means of the convition, the secret heretic becomes a manifest heretic. Here Bellarmine

---

[544] «*Certum est autem, quidquid unus, aut alter senserit, occultum haereticum, si Episcopus, aut etiam summus Pontifex esset, non ammitere jurisdictionem, nec dignitatem, aut nomen capitis in Ecclesia, donec aut ipse se ab Ecclesia publice separet, aut convictus haereseos invitus separetur.*»

is following a doctrinal/canonical tradition that goes back to the early Decretists, which logically and correctly reasoned that as a public heretic, the pope would lose office *ipso jure* without trial, whereas an occult heretic would have to be tried and convicted in order to be proven guilty and thus considered to have lost office. Since the pope is the supreme judge possessing universal jurisdiction, he could not be subjected to a trial; and therefore, the procedure would have to be similar to a trial, in the manner of those medieval canonists who reasoned that an *accusatio* could be brought against a pope to be tried for occult heresy; who, because of his heresy would already be considered an *uncertain pope*, i.e., a *papa dubius,* and thus at least could be presumed to be *minor quolibet catholico*; whereas a public heretic could be dealt with by an *exceptio*, thereby entirely eliminating the need for a trial or an inquest. In either case, once the heresy is made manifest, the heretic would necessarily fall from office and be judged, removed and punished; *but the loss of office could not now be considered as the result of a trial and deposition by the judgment of the Church, but by the fact of the heresy being made manifest he would be judged to have fallen from office and would then be removed; and thus be judged and removed by men; and in this manner "he is separated against his will"*. This is why Bellarmine says that in the case of a secret heretic, he would not cease to be pope unless his heresy would be discovered, and he would then be judged by men to have fallen from office; whereas in the case of a manifest heretic, he would lose office *ipso facto* by professing himself a heretic and thereby pronouncing upon himself the judgment of self-condemnation: It would be by means similar to the judicial process of a trial that the heresy would be made manifest in the case of an occult heretic whose heresy has been discovered, and upon being proven, the now manifest heretic would thereby lose office *ipso jure*. Since no individual and no body (neither the bishops nor the cardinals as Bellarmine argues in his refutation of Opinion No. 4), and therefore not even a general council may judge a pope, one grasps why Bellamine says the occult heretic pope must be "judged by men", but not "judged by the Church", since there exists no jurisdiction in the Church to subject a pope to trial and pass judgment on him. Once a deliberative inquest, which would exercise no jurisdiction over the pope to subject him to a trial and judgment for the crime of heresy, but would only exercise jurisdiction to ascertain the vacancy of the papal office by means of verifying that the certain fact of *defection from the faith* had taken place, the judgment of the Church would be pronounced, as Gregory XVI explained *only against the person who was before adorned with the papal dignity* (ma soltanto contro la persona, che era prima ornata di papal dignità), but who *had fallen from office by himself* (per se decaduto dal pontificato). In this manner, the Church would not be exercising jurisdiction over the pope, but would render a judgment which does pertain to ecclesiastical jurisdiction; namely, *the authority to judge that the see is vacant*. At this point, with the formerly occult but now manifest heretic falling from office by himself *ipso facto* by his formal heresy having been made manifest, the papal see could be declared vacant, and the former pope could then be judged and punished by the Church, as Bellarmine explains. Hence, it cannot be maintained that according to Bellarmine, an occult heretic pope would have to be juridically convicted of the crime of heresy in order for him to fall from office; while a manifest heretic would fall automatically without any judgment of the Church, since in both cases, there would be no juridical deposition and no judgment of the Church pronounced on a reigning pontiff before the fall from office, but the heretic pope would be "shown to be already judged", and therefore, Bellarmine says he would need only to be "removed" as one who is already *depositus*, rather than "be deposed" by the Church, as would be a pope who is *deponendus*.

The reason why such a trial, or more accurately such an *inquest* can be conducted in the manner above described in such a case when there is *prima facie* evidence sufficient to establish probable cause of guilt of a suspected pope accused of occult heresy, or in the case of a *papa dubius* whose material heresy is publicly known, is firstly because the Church possesses by divine law the right to know, and therefore the right to judge whether or not a man is their visible head and supreme judge and legislator to whom they must be subject; and secondly, because in matters of faith, it is manifestly a divinely revealed truth of the universal magisterium that one is strictly bound to profess the faith without any mental reservation when the demand is reasonably made concerning the faith. When there exists positive doubt about the faith of the pope, his subjects have the right in strict justice to demand and receive a clear answer from him on the point in question. Thus, without any jurisdiction over the pope, an *inquest* would have to be conducted by those *who would have the jurisdiction to determine and judge if the see is vacant, and to juridically declare it to be so were it to become manifestly evident that the pope*, **(or the man believed to be pope, i.e. the papa putativus)** *has defected from the faith and lost any office he may have held ipso jure*. That jurisdiction lies preeminently within the competence of the Cardinals of the Roman Church; i.e. within the competence of those members of the Sacred College who are themselves not suspected heretics or manifest heretics themselves; since it is a cardinal – the Cardinal *Camerlengo* who officially declares the see to be vacant when he pronounces officially that "*the pope is truly dead*", and above all, because the responsibilities for detemining and dealing with the vacancy of the See of Rome and electing a new pontiff pertain particularly to the Cardinals of the Roman Church. It is for this reason, therefore, that Ballerini says in the first place it is the "cardinals", and then the "Roman clergy", or a "Roman synod"⁵⁴⁵ that would conduct the inquest; and this would be done first by means of *warnings*. Hence, the need for presenting the *dubia*, and then by a solemn and public *correction* (not the canonical admonitions of a superior). By this means, they would thereby determine whether the pope is innocent and still the legitimate pope occupying the chair (*sede plena*), or whether he has "*hardened in his heresy*", and thus, "*in some manner to have abdicated the Pontificate*" (*sede vacante*). In this manner, they would not be exercising any power over a pope, but merely determining whether the papal *cathedra* is occupied or vacant; and in the event of the latter, they would declare it juridically. Hence, says Ballerini, "his sentence which he brought upon himself, would have to be publicly pronounced, made known to the whole Church, that he by his own will departed, making known to be severed from the body of the Church, and in some manner to have abdicated the Pontificate".

The manifestation of pertinacity in heresy can be manifested by explicitly affirming the heretical proposition after the correction, or by **refusing to answer**, either by silence or evasive, non-responsive equivocations which amount to silence. The rule of tacit admission is rooted in an ancient principle of law: "Silence gives consent." In a 1967 article it is explained,

> "So runs an ancient maxim of common law, and from that maxim flows a widely applied legal principle: the rule of tacit admission. On the theory that an innocent man would loudly deny a serious charge, the rule holds that a suspect silent in the face of an accusation has tacitly admitted the crime. And such silence can later be introduced at his trial as an indicator of guilt."⁵⁴⁶

In an article entitled, *Admission by Silence Law and Legal Definition*, U.S. Legal explains,

---

⁵⁴⁵ "Cardinales, qui ipsi a consiliis adstant; poterit Romanus Clerus; Romana etiam synodus."

⁵⁴⁶ *Time*, May 5 1967.

«Admission by silence means the failure by a party, in whose presence, hearing, or observation of an act or declaration is made, to assert that such act or declaration is untrue. Admission by silence is based upon the principle that when the act or declaration is such as naturally to call for action or comment if not true, the party against whom such act or declaration is made must assert it as untrue if it is proper and possible for him/her to do so.

In order to take an admission as admission by silence it must appear:

(1) that the party heard and understood the act or declaration;

(2) that the party was at a liberty to make a denial of such act or declaration;

(3) that the act or declaration was in respect to some matter affecting the party's rights, to which s/he had interest, and which naturally calls for an answer;

(4) that the facts were within the party's knowledge; and

(5) that the inference to be drawn from the party's silence would be material to the issue.

In People v. Cihak, 169 Ill. App. 3d 606 (Ill. App. Ct. 1988), the court observed that "to qualify as an admission by silence or an implied admission, it is essential that the accused heard the incriminating statement and that it was made under circumstances which allowed an opportunity for the accused to reply, and where a man similarly situated would ordinarily have denied the accusation".»

Admission by Silence is also a principle of divine law. Which will be applied by the supreme Judge on the last day at the General Judgment:

«^{11} intravit autem rex ut videret discumbentes et vidit ibi hominem non vestitum veste nuptiali

^{12} et ait illi amice quomodo huc intrasti non habens vestem nuptialem at ille obmutuit.» (Matthæus 22, 11-12)[547]

Thus, it can be seen that only as a purely abstract hypothesis, a secret heretic would automatically cease to be pope, having lost the necessary disposition to conserve within himself the form of the Pontificate; while as a practical hypothesis, if it were really possible for a pope to become an occult heretic, *he would necessarily retain the papal name and dignity until discovered and proven guilty of heresy*. This last consideration *sufficiently refutes Opinion No. 2*, if the case of an occult heretic were to be considered

---

[547] «And the king went in to see the guests: and he saw there a man who had not on a wedding garment. And he saith to him: Friend, how camest thou in hither not having a wedding garment? But he was silent.»

hypothetically as a real possiblity. Both Bellarmine and I adhere to this position, *which does not end in a contradiction,* which, therefore, is not a contradiction in Bellarmine's thinking, (nor in my thinking as Salza & Siscoe mendaciously state), but, as I have explained earlier in this work, *this contradiction is intrinsically inherent to the explication of the notion of an occult heretic pope, rendering logically impossible the major premise of Opinion No. 2; namely, that a pope can actually be an occult heretic.* Furthermore, there is no logical contradiction in this position, as Siscoe claims (appealing to the principle of non-contradiction), because **Siscoe forgets that the principle is only applicable to that which is contradicted simultaneously**, *in the same sense* **and** *in the same respect.* Opinion No. 2 is false, because it is impossible for a secret heretic pope to lose office due to the consequent defection of the Church the loss of office would cause; but the contrary is also impossible, because, as Bellarmine, and finally, I have demonstrated theologically, it is intrinsically impossible for any formal heretic to be a valid pope, which is what Paul IV taught by strict implication in *Cum ex apostolatus officio,* and therefore, he did not even consider such a thing as worthy of mention in the document. The *only logically possible solution to the dilemma of Opinion No. 2 is Opinion No.1, which categorically rejects the possibility that the pope can be a heretic, and thereby resolves the dilemma of the irreconcilable contradiction into which the premise of Opinion No. 2 leads.* Opinion No. 1 is Bellarmine's and my own, as well as the fifth opinion considered as a hypothesis. *Salza & Siscoe most stupidly claim that I hold to Opinion No. 2.* They cannot be so stupid as that. Their argument in this matter, as in so many others, is a deliberate *fraud.*

Robert J. Siscoe: "Fr. Kramer cannot get around the fact that **he simultaneously holds two contradictory positions, which is irrational, being contrary to the principle of non contradiction."**
Elsewhere I wrote:

> «In my work on *Faith, Heresy and Loss of Office,* I have elaborated and commeted on the Five Opinions on the deposition of a heretic pope that emerged from the writings of theologians over the centuries. The doctrine I present is clear enough; but instead of presenting objectively its content and commenting honestly on it, Siscoe has again embarked on his habitual devious path of deception by means of distortion > misrepresentation > falsification; creating a grotesque caricature of my argument for the purpose of refuting the caricature of his own making. So a few words are in order to debunk the fraudulent reply he is preparing, and in which he says he will refute the contradiction which he says he will attribute to me.»

Siscoe produces a selective *partial* quotation:

> «Fr. Kramer: I also wrote, "in the case of a secret heretic, the heretic has not pronounced judgment against himself, thereby ceasing by his own judgment against himself to be pope, as does the manifest heretic; **and does not cease to be a visible member of the Church..."**»

Then, [...], he continues:

> «I would also note that you just said a pope who is a secret heretic has not ceased "by his own judgment against himself to be Pope;" yet, you have also said, repeatedly, that a pope who is a secret heretic **does** automatically ceases to be pope, since he lacks the virtue of faith. No need to comment on how a pope who is a secret heretic **does not** cease to be pope, and how, at the same time, **he does...**»

By means of selectively producing truncated segments of my words and dishonestly commenting on them, Siscoe attempts to deceive his readers into thinking that it is *my position* that is contradictory: *that a secret heretic would both cease and not cease to be pope.* Siscoe craftily spins this absurdity, and then attributes it to me. Fraud is clearly what he is best at.

As I said before, it is *not my position*, but is the absurd outcome to which Opinion No. 2 logically leads. According to that opinion (No. 2), a heretic pope would cease automatically to be pope upon falling into heresy, *because he would cease (according to the holders of that opinion) to be a member of the Church*. However, Bellarmine explains that by external union only, the secret heretic pope would still be a member of the Church[548], and therefore, the basis of Opinion No. 2 is a false premise that Bellarmine easily refutes; ***ergo:*** *The heretic pope would not cease to be pope in the manner asserted by the argument advanced by the theologians holding to Opinion No. 2.*

However, there is an additional problem with Opinion No 2: As I explained, Bellarmine teaches that faith is the necessary disposition to preserve the form of the Pontificate in the person of the pope. So in reality, according to Bellarmine (i.e. according to the explicit doctrine set forth in his writings, which I quoted in his original Latin), the pope

---

[548] Not only does Bellarmine hold this opinion that occult heretics are members of the Church, but in Chapter 10 of *De Ecclesia Militante*, he conclusively demonstrates that occult heretics remain in the Church as dead and withered members, united to the Church by external union only.

would, *hypothetically* cease to be pope if he were to become a formal heretic; but, (he says), it is impossible for the pope to become a formal heretic, given the fact that Christ Our Lord prayed that the Pontiff's faith not fail.

Pastor Æternus teaches *explicitly* that the Lord's prayer was for the *Roman Pontiff*, that *his faith may not fail.* His faith does not fail if he errs in ignorance and falls into *material heresy*, because material heresy does not destroy the formal cause of faith, and therefore, the virtue of faith remains operative in his soul; and that faith, which cannot be extinguished in the Roman Pontiff, is the necessary disposition to conserve the form of the pontificate in the person of the pope so that he may infallibly define in matters of faith and confirm his brethren. However, even if by some absurd miracle a faithless heretic pope were to only externally define the faith infallibly, while not assenting to it interiorly; that would not change the fact that *his faith* would have actually failed at the moment he became a formal heretic; and therefore, Christ's prayer that the Pontiff's faith not fail would have been in vain; and it would have been superfluous as well – serving no purpose, since the pope would be able to exercise the charism by some other means than by the dispositive habit of unfailing faith. But it was precisely in order that the pontiff may be disposed to confirm the faith of the whole Church that Christ prayed that *his faith* not fail. *Pastor Æternus* asserts this teaching as a premise for its definition of Papal Infallibility. It does not define that the pope cannot personally become a heretic, because; as Gasser explained, *it was the intention of the Council only to define the point of the infallibility of the pope's definitions, and **not** to define on the question of papal heresy*. So, although the Council did not define on this latter point, it follows by strict logical implication, that since the Council taught that the efficacious prayer of Christ to His Father that Peter's faith not fail was also for Peter's successors, and therefore like Peter, *their faith cannot fail*, and *by way of strict logical consequence*, they cannot fail in their faith and fall into formal heresy. Since this point was not defined, it is not *de fide*, but since it is **strictly implied by the Council's teaching**, it is at the very least, *proxima fidei*.⁵⁴⁹ The Salza/Siscoe belief that a pope can become a formal heretic is, therefore, *proximate to heresy*.

---

⁵⁴⁹ "*Proximate to Faith*. This frequently used not is applied to a doctrine that by almost unanimous consent is held to be revealed but is not yet expressly proposed as such by the infallible magisterium. That 'God sincerely wills the

Having already been demonstrated to be in heresy on two points, Siscoe becomes indignant about his opinion on the question at hand to be classified as *hæresi proxima*; so he attempts to refute the charge by first resorting to a red herring argument: «This argument is a perfect example of what one finds constantly in Sedevacantist writings: private interpretation of doctrine (backed up by nothing), followed by accusations of heresy (or 'proximate to heresy') for contradicting what they think the doctrine means.» First of all, I am not aware of such an argument being found in any sedevacantist writings, (which I do not ordinarily read); but that is a matter of no importance. If some sedevacantists do argue the point in this manner, that fact would not prove the opinion wrong, but would merely illustrate the fact that some sedevacantists are more competent in theology than Robert Siscoe. Siscoe resorts to the same tactic further on, when he says, «Fr. Kramer gives us his private interpretation of what 'the unfailing faith of Peter' means, which, coincidentally, is the same private interpretation as a certain Sedevacantist apologist». Siscoe then lies (as I will prove), saying, I did not «provided a single authoritative source to back up» what he dismissively refers to as my «private interpretation». (I quoted Bellarmine and Lang.) His obvious motive, as will be seen, is to falsely make it appear that my opinion is merely a gratuitously stated assertion. The truculent Siscoe then says, «I'll break down Fr. Kramer's argument, leading to his false accusation, one step at a time.» What he means by "break down" is that he will 'spin' my argument by means of his habitual and chronic distortions in order to twist my meaning into something else that he can refute. The paragraph he quotes consists of only twelve lines of straightforward exposition which is easily understood as is, so it is hardly in need of being 'broken down' in order to be understood. Siscoe continues, «He then admits that Vatican I did not define whether or not a Pope could lose his personal faith – i.e., become a formal heretic. That is also correct. What this proves is that the Council did not define 'the unfailing faith of Peter' as meaning a pope cannot lose his personal faith.» Our "learned" commentator is becoming repetitive at this point, since he just quoted the passage in which I say precisely that the Council did not define this point, but he repeats exactly the same thing, namely, that what it proves is that the Council did no define this point!

So, where is all this obfuscation leading? Right here:

---

salvation of all adults' is said to be such a doctrine. This note does not command absolute assent." [*New Catholic Encyclopedia*, "Notes, Theological".

«Finally, based on the unproven assumption of what the phrase means, Fr. Kramer claims that because Vatican I taught that the efficacious prayer of Christ to His Father (that Peter's faith fail not) applies by extension to Peter's successors, 'it follows by strict logical implication' that a Pope 'cannot... fall into formal heresy'.»

Siscoe's convoluted verbal peregrination finally approaches the dubious point he fecklessly intends to demonstrate: «what Fr. Kramer did not mention is that Bishop Gasser, who was charged with providing to the council Fathers the official interpretation of the document, referred to the opinion that a Pope could not lose the faith (i.e., Bellarmine's Opinion #1) as an "extreme opinion".» He continues, «But this would have made no sense if the opinion (that a Pope cannot fall into formal heresy) really "followed by a strict logical implication" from what the council taught, as Kramer gratuitously claims. *(sic)*» (Since when is basing my position on the argument of a Doctor of the Church a "gratuitous claim"?) Now this is what Siscoe is getting at:

«Rather than being an extreme opinion, it would have been qualified as theologically certain. And this is precisely why Fr. Kramer said denying it was proximate to heresy. What this obviously shows is that Bishop Gasser did not believe that "the unfailing faith of Peter" meant that a Pope could not become a formal heretic. To the contrary, Bishop Gasser and the council Fathers recognized that a Pope could fall into formal heresy without compromising Christ's promise of infallibility, which was not only the common opinion at the time of Bellarmine, but also during the First Vatican Council, as indicated by the fact that Gasser referred to the contrary opinion as "extreme".»

This passage is replete with non sequiturs and false premises: 1) it assumes that an "extreme" opinion is uncertain or even improbable; 2) it does *not* show «that Bishop Gasser did not believe that "the unfailing faith of Peter" meant that a Pope could not become a formal heretic», but it merely shows that Bishop Gasser intended to make it clear that the Council did not intend to define on this point; 3) nor does it show that «the council Fathers recognized that a Pope could fall into formal heresy without compromising Christ's promise of infallibility, which was not only the common opinion at the time of Bellarmine, but also during the First Vatican Council, as indicated by the fact that Gasser referred to the contrary opinion as "extreme"» – but it does show again *only* that the Council fathers did not intend to define on this point of doctrine.

Siscoe's erroneous inference that the Council fathers "recognized that a Pope could fall into formal heresy without compromising Christ's promise of infallibility," is a *non sequitur* founded primarily on the false premise that the Council interpreted Bellarmine's First Opinion to be "extreme". The false premise is itself a *non sequitur* drawn from the premises contained in Siscoe's statement, «Bishop Gasser, who was charged with providing to the council Fathers the official interpretation of the document, referred to the opinion that a Pope could not lose the faith as an "extreme opinion".» The fact that the *Gasser Relatio* did provide a non-authentic and semi-official version of the Holy See's interpretation of the definition on Papal Infallibility contained in *Pastor Æternus*, in no way implies that every statement Gasser made in the *Relatio* officially interprets the mind of the Church magisterially expressed in that Dogmatic Constitution. Only that in the *Gasser Relatio* which relates properly to the interpretation of the dogmatic definition of infallibility constitutes the interpretation of that definition according to the mind of the Council. The Council issued no definition on the question of papal heresy, nor did it issue a judgment Bellarmine's opinion on that question, declaring it to be "extreme". Gasser's characterization of Bellarmine's opinion as "extreme" does not represent the mind of the Council, but it merely expresses his own fallible opinion. Not only did Gasser express his own fallible opinions in the document, but at least one of those opinions in his *Relatio* was not only fallible, but was in fact erroneous. In the text of the *Relatio*, one reads,

> «(03) Note well. It is asked in what sense the infallibility of the Roman Pontiff is "absolute." I reply and openly admit: in no sense is pontifical infallibility absolute, because absolute infallibility belongs to God alone, who is the first and essential truth and who is never able to deceive or be deceived.»

The statement is false. His premises are indeed correct, but the conclusion does not follow logically from the premises. Gasser's premises are stated:

> All other infallibility, as communicated for a specific purpose, has its limits and its conditions under which it is considered to be present. The same is valid in reference to the infallibility of the Roman Pontiff. For this infallibility is bound by certain limits and conditions. What those conditions

may be should be deduced not "a priori" but from the very promise or manifestation of the will of Christ. Now what follows from the promise of Christ, made to Peter and his successors, as far as these conditions are concerned? He promised Peter the gift of inerrancy in Peter's relation to the Universal Church: "You are Peter, and on this rock I will build my Church, and the gates of hell shall not prevail against it…" (Mt. 16:18). "Feed my lambs, feed my sheep" (Jn. 21:13-17). Peter, placed outside this relation to the universal Church, does not enjoy in his successors this charism of truth which comes from that certain promise of Christ.

Now, while it is true that, "Peter, placed *outside this relation to the universal Church*, does not enjoy in his successors this charism of truth which comes from that certain promise of Christ;" it is also true that Peter placed *inside that relation to the universal Church* enjoys that charism of truth *absolutely*. What the pope defines on faith and morals *ex cathedra* is absolutely infallible. Cardinal Manning explains:

«1. First, that what depends on no other is altogether independent. 2. Secondly, that what is circumscribed by no condition is absolute. 3. Thirdly, that what is by God committed to one alone, depends on God alone. But perhaps it will be said that all this relates not to infallibility, but to the power of jurisdiction only. To this I answer: 1. That if the primacy be personal, all its prerogatives are personal. 2. That the doctrinal authority of the Pontiff is a part of his jurisdiction, and is therefore personal. 3. That infallibility is, as the Definition expressly declares, a supernatural grace, or charisma, attached to the primacy, in order to its proper exercise. Infallibility is a quality of the doctrinal jurisdiction of the Pontiff in faith and morals. And such also is the doctrine of Ballerini, who lays down the following propositions: "Unity with the Roman faith is absolutely necessary, and therefore the prerogative of **absolute infallibility** is to be ascribed to it, and a coercive power to constrain to unity of faith, in like manner, absolute; as also the infallibility and coercive power of the Catholic Church itself, which is bound to adhere to the faith of Rome, is absolute."»* [550],[551]

Thus it is that when defining *ex cathedra* on matters of faith and morals, the Roman Pontiff enjoys the prerogative of *absolute infallibility*.

---

[550] «* Ballerini *de Vi et Rat. Primatus*: Unitas cum Romana fide absolute necessaria est, ac proinde infallibilatis prærogativa absoluta illi est tribuenda, et vis coactiva ad fidei unitatem pariter absoluta: sicuti absoluta est item infallibilitas et vis coactiva ipsius Ecclesias Catholicæ, quae Romanæ fidei adhærere oportet. Appendix De infall. Pont. Prop. vii.»

[551] Manning, *The Vatican Council and its Definitions*, p. 103.

Gasser's opinion on this point, that "in no sense is pontifical infallibility absolute," was not correct.

Siscoe's error is also rooted in his own fundamentalistic understanding of the term "extreme" (and in his uncritically rigid fundamentalist understanding of theological notes[552]) which construes the meaning of the term to exclude the possibility that the extreme opinion could also be theologically certain[553], or nearly theologically certain. However, the certitude of a theological opinion does not depend on whether or not it is said to be "extreme", but on its directly hinging on a revealed truth. Furthermore, to be *hæresi proxima*, a proposition need not be opposed to a doctrine that is *theologically certain*, but it suffices that it would be "proximate to heresy when its opposition to a revealed and defined dogma is not certain, *or chiefly when the truth it contradicts, though commonly accepted as revealed, has yet never been the object of a definition (proxima fidei)*"[554] Opinion No. 1 is founded on the words of Christ Himself who prayed that the Pontiff's faith not fail. Pope Innocent III and St. Robert Bellarmine based their teaching that the pope cannot become a heretic on the foundation of that scripture passage. Since Vatican I taught on the basis of that passage that the grace is given to the pope lest his fail, precisely so that he may be able to define infallibly; the First Opinion, namely, that the pope cannot fall into formal heresy, has become

---

[552] The Salza/Siscoe oversimplified and fundamentalistic interpretation/application of theological notes, which they employ to dogmatize their own private opinions will be dealt with in a separate section.

[553] "*Theologically Certain.* This is another very common but not very satisfactory note. For it is sometimes applied only to strict theological conclusions, sometimes also to Catholic doctrine, sometimes even more widely to any common and certain doctrine of theologians. Hence 'theologically certain' propositions must be carefully examined to determine just what this qualification means in each case [...] In its strictest sense a proposition is called 'theologically certain' if it is a certain theological conclusion from one premise that is revealed and from another that is not revealed but is naturally certain. Thus the proposition that Christ is capable of laughter is called theologically certain because it is deduced from a revealed premise (Christ is man), and from a naturally certain premise (every man is capable of laughter)." [*New Catholic Encyclopedia*, Notes, Theological]

[554] *Catholic Encyclopedia*, Theological Censures.

"commonly taught as the most probable", as Don Curzio attests[555]. Fr Gleize states (in his above cited article) on the question, "Can a pope fall into heresy?": "In fact, the negative answer to this question is the **common opinion** of theologians of the modern era." This sufficiently establishes the doctrine of the First Opinion as *proximate to faith*, and its denial as *hæresi proxima*. However, in order to deceive their readers into believing that their contrary opinion represents the mind of the Church, and seduce them into thinking the opposite opinion is the common opinion, Salza & Siscoe falsely state on page 191 of their screed: "It is the common opinion among theologians that a Pope can fall into personal heresy (internally), and even public and notorious heresy (externally)." Salza & Siscoe then attempt to convince their readers that they sin if they disagree with what they falsely assert is common opinion. On page 274, they declare: *"departing from the 'common opinion' of the theologians is, at minimum, an act of imprudence and possibly a mortal sin."* This is absurd. If that were true, then St. Thomas Aquinas would have sinned against prudence for believing against the common opinion, that the rational soul is the substantial form of the human body. It was St. Thomas' opinion that was later infallibly defined to be the true belief. Unfortunately, the deception doesn't stop there – they go on to make the false and very misleading statement: "Cartechini explains that opinions held in common by all theologians are *theologically certain*, the denial of which constitutes, usually, *a mortal sin* of temerity." Fr. Sisto Cartechini said no such thing. This matter will be dealt with in its proper place in this work; in Part V on Salza's and Siscoe's Fraud and Sophistry. It will suffice to point out here the distinction between the notes of *commune*, and *commune et certum*; and that to be considered a mortal sin of temerity, it would not suffice that the denied *common opinion* be a mere matter of opinion on an open question, i.e., a mere *common opinion of theologians,* but rather than merely held as an *opinion*, it would have to be *common and certain* as a **point of doctrine taught** by theologians. The doctrine denied would have to be *common and certain*, and thus, *certain*, either in the strict sense of *theologically certain*, which would be, as the *New Catholic Encyclopedia* explains, "a certain theological conclusion from one premise that is revealed and from another that is not revealed but is

---

[555] "la *prima opinione* o meglio l'antecedente, che è quella insegnata comunemente come la più probabile dalla maggior parte dei teologi e dei Dottori"

naturally certain"[556] (which would strictly require an internal assent); or less certain, such as *Catholic Doctrine*:

> "whatever the supreme magisterium wishes to teach expressly, without proposing it for belief, such as the chief ideas of encyclicals, propositions contrary to those that have been condemned, what is contained in the chapters of general councils without being certainly defined or what is easily deduced from these chapters, doctrinal decrees of the Roman pontiff or of Roman congregations if these have been approved and confirmed by the pope"[557].

These latter require a religious assent, but since these pronouncements are not infallible, it is commonly taught that the obligation for assent is not absolute[558]; so that the assent may be suspended when there is sufficient positive doubt about the truth of such a doctrine. Hence, the Salza/Siscoe proposition, "that opinions held in common by all theologians are theologically certain, the denial of which constitutes, usually, *a mortal sin* of temerity" is plainly false, and is contrary to Catholic Moral Theology.

To say that an opinion is "extreme" means only that the opinion stands at one extreme of the spectrum of opinions, such as Opinion No. 2 and Opinion No. 3. According to the second, even a secret heretic pope would automatically lose office for heresy, and the third stands at

---

[556] *New Catholic Encyclopedia*, Notes, Theological

[557] *Ibid.*

[558] "Non-infallible acts of the Magisterium of the Roman Pontiff do not demand an absolute and definitive subjection... the obligation to adhere to them could begin to cease in the case (to be rarely found) when a man capable of judging the question, after a very diligent and painstaking analysis of all the reasons, arrived at the conviction that error was introduced into the decision." Franciscus Diekamp, *Theologiae Dogmaticae Manuale*, Vol. I, p. 72; "Since the referred to religious assent is not based upon a metaphysical certainty, but only upon a moral and ample one, it does not exclude all fear of error. That is why, as soon as sufficient motives of doubt arise, the assent is prudently suspended." Christianus Pesch, *Praelectiones Dogmaticae*, Vol. I, p. 315; "Where the Church does not teach with infallible authority, the proposed doctrine is not of itself irreformable, that is why, if per accidens in an hypothesis (albeit very rarely); after the most careful examination, there seems to be very grave reasons against the proposed teaching, it would be licit without temerity to suspend internal assent..." Benedictus Henricus Merkelbach O.P., *Summa Theologiae Moralis*, Vol. I, p. 598.

the opposite extreme, holding that even a manifest heretic pope does not lose office and cannot be deposed. In the middle, between the two extremes were the fourth and fifth opinions. Similarly, the three opinions on the Conception of the Blessed Virgin Mary had at one extreme, the Protestant belief that the Blessed Virgin was conceived in sin like everyone else, and at the other extreme, that She was conceived from the first instant of Her Conception utterly Immaculate and without ever having any stain of original sin whatsoever on Her soul. The middle position was the Thomist opinion, according to which She was immediately cleansed from original sin at the first instant of Her Conception. It was not the moderate opinion, i.e. the Thomist opinion occupying the middle that was solemnly defined as a dogma of faith, but the extreme opinion of the Scotists that was dogmatically defined. Thus, it is absolutely a *non sequitur* to say, as Siscoe does, that Gasser's charachterization of the first opinion as "extreme" demonstrates that, "Bishop Gasser and the council Fathers recognized that a Pope could fall into formal heresy". Bellarmine himself admitted that in his day, his opinion on this point was against the more common opinion, yet he says it is "probable" and "easily defended", but is not entirely certain. Likewise, he explained that the doctrine of papal infallibility was the *opinio communissima*[559] among all Catholics, but the contrary opinion, namely, that the pope can be a heretic and teach heresy, if he defines without a general council, which was the opinion of Pope Adrian VI; was at that time, according to the Holy Doctor, not properly heretical, because the Church still tolerated it, but, he explained, it "appears to be entirely erroneous and *proximate to heresy*." Using the same criteria as the Doctor of the Church in judging Adrian VI's opinion to be proximate to heresy, I similarly conclude, as I explained above, that Siscoe's opinion on the point at issue, is *proximate to heresy*.

The teaching of Vatican I, therefore, vindicates and underscores Bellarmine's argument that the pope cannot become a formal heretic. I have provided the systematic philosophical and theological basis of Bellarmine's teaching on this point earlier in this work, which Siscoe blindly attacks as "disastrous". First, as I pointed out, Siscoe misrepresented Gasser on the Vatican Council's teaching. Siscoe also objected most stupidly by claiming that my quotations of St. Thomas,

---

[559] «*Pontificem, sive haereticus esse possit, sive non, non posse ullo modo definire aliquid haereticum a tota Ecclesia credendum: haec est comunissima opinio fere omnium Catholicorum.*»

have "nothing to do" with the question. I explained that since virtues are of the nature of **habit** and **disposition**, it is necessary to understand the role of dispositve habits in the operation of the powers of the soul, in order to understand why Bellarmine says that *faith is the necessary disposition for preserving the form of the pontificate in the person of the pope*; since it is only if the subject of Infallibility has the virtue of faith as the *dispositio animæ* to operate that charism, that his operation of the charism can be performed as a human act by means of the natural powers of the soul. Without faith as the dispositive habit to teach infallibly, *ex cathedra* pronouncements would not be human acts of the pope, but would be acts of God speaking directly through a human mouth in the same manner that God spoke through the mouth of the ass of Balaam.

Unswayed by clear and rational demonstration, Siscoe continues to blindly object that those passages of St. Thomas have nothing to do with infallibility, and that I quoted them in Latin in order to hide this from the readers and thereby deceive them. It is painfully evident, that Siscoe & Salza are incapable of understanding theological arguments that have a philosophical basis; and thus, cannot grasp the connection between St. Thomas' teaching on the operation of the powers of the soul and the necessary dispositions for those operations, and Bellarmine's doctrine that **faith is the necessary disposition** for a man to have the form of the Pontificate preserved in his person, because it enables him to perform a particular supernatural operation of the soul which is the exercise of the charism of Infallibility, which is essential to the papal *munus*. I even **bolded** the key phrases to make clear the logical nexus between the general doctrine of St Thomas on the operations of the soul and the role of dispositions, and its particular application to the doctrine of Bellarmine on *faith as a necessary disposition for the operation of the charism of Infallibility*. What I have explained is precisely why faith is the *necessary disposition*; and I explained exactly why Bellarmine, before Vatican I, could not qualify his opinion on this point as "certain", but only "probable". All of this was simply impenetrable to the obtuse fundamentalist minds of Salza & Siscoe. Predictably, Siscoe offers no rational objection, but attempts to entirely distort my theologically clear and systematic argumentation; and attack it with scurrilous objections based on deceptively fallacious interpretations of Church teaching, **as I have amply demonstrated.** (Siscoe's treatment of the doctrine of *minor quolibet catholico* is also a prime example of the fundamentalist's incapacity to grasp a synthetic application of a principle, but more on that later.)

Siscoe responded saying, "I'll respond with one final e-mail later next week and bring this to a close." We've heard this before from Salza & Siscoe, but they eventually rant on an on, demonstrating their own theological ineptitude. Indeed, he did, "bring this to a close", but in a manner that he was too blind to even suspect. I made short shrift of his response (as will be shown below).

On my explication of Bellarmine's doctrine of faith as a necessary disposition to preserve the form of the pontificate in the person of the pope, Siscoe then repeats his hysterical objection, "You then cite a quotation from St. Thomas that has absolutely nothing to do with the issue at hand, and you cite it in Latin (when it would have been just as easy to quote it in English), thereby preventing the average lay reader, whom you are deceiving, from realizing it." Apparently Siscoe is incapable of understanding how the philosophical doctrine on the operation of the powers of the soul in general is validly applied as the basis of the particular operation of a power of the soul in the case of exercising the charism of Infallibility. There is a logical nexus, but he is too obtuse to grasp it. Siscoe then replies,

> "I understand it perfectly and it has absolutely nothing to do with infallibility, since there is no 'logical nexus' between the power and act of the soul and the 'exercise of the charism of infallibility'. **You would know this if you thought of <u>the basic distinction</u> that I keep alluding to, but which I am not going to tell you now.** You can find it addressed in our book and in the writings of traditional theologians."

Siscoe refuses to grasp that since, in the exercise of the powers of the soul, dispositive habits are required for the performance of certain operations, therefore, *virtues* are required as dispositve habits, in order to perform certain optimal operations of those powers: "Whence also it is stated (Metaph. v, text. 25) in the definition of habit, that it is a disposition whereby that which is disposed, is well or ill disposed either in regard to itself, that is to its nature, or in regard to something else, that is to the end."[560] Hence, virtues are *dispositive habits* that are necessary for the performance of optimal operations of the soul:

---

[560] «Unde habitus non solum importat ordinem ad ipsam naturam rei, sed etiam consequenter ad operationem, inquantum est finis naturae, vel perducens ad finem. Unde et in V Metaphys. dicitur in definitione habitus, quod est dispositio secundum quam bene vel male disponitur dispositum aut secundum

"Virtue denotes a certain perfection of a power. Now a thing's perfection is considered chiefly in regard to its end. But the end of power is act. Wherefore power is said to be perfect, according as it is determinate to its act. But the rational powers, which are proper to man, are not determinate to one particular action, but are inclined indifferently to many: and they are determinate to acts by means of habits, as is clear from what we have said above (I-II:49:4). Therefore human virtues are habits."[561]

Virtue is therefore the *"dispositio animæ"* by which ordered operations are accomplished: *"Facit autem virtus operationem ordinatam. Et ideo ipsa virtrus est quædam dispoitio ordinata in anima."* (I – II Q. 55 a. 3) If faith were not required as a necessary disposition for the pontiff to infallibly profess the faith and thereby confirm the faith of his brethren, then Christ would not have prayed that Peter's faith not fail, since faith would not be needed for Peter to perform that operation; but it was precisely in order that Peter be disposed to infallibly profess the faith, that Christ prayed that his faith not fail. Siscoe then declares that I did not provide "a single authoritative source to back up" my argument, (which he dismisses as merely *my* "private interpretation") and that I "just assume that 'the unfailing faith of Peter' means that a pope cannot lose the virtue of faith". No single authoritative source to back up my *"private interpretation" of what the unfailing faith of Peter means?* I do not provide *"a single authoritative source"*? **Siscoe is lying: 1) I quoted Bellarmine** – "Therein it is gathered correctly that the Pope by his own nature can fall into heresy, but not when we posit the singular assistance of God which Christ asked for him by his prayer." **2) I quoted Dr. Albert Lang** (*Fundamentaltheologie*, Band II *Der Auftrag der Kirche*, München, 1962, p. 80), where he states that the grace of unfailing faith was not a personal privilege granted to the Apostle, but was a singular grace given to Peter

---

se, idest secundum suam naturam, aut ad aliud, idest in ordine ad finem.» *Summa Theol.* I – II Q. 49, a. 3.

[561] «Respondeo dicendum quod virtus nominat quandam potentiae perfectionem. Uniuscuiusque autem perfectio praecipue consideratur in ordine ad suum finem. Finis autem potentiae actus est. Unde potentia dicitur esse perfecta, secundum quod determinatur ad suum actum. [...] Potentiae autem rationales, quae sunt propriae hominis, non sunt determinatae ad unum, sed se habent indeterminate ad multa, determinantur autem ad actus per habitus, sicut ex supradictis patet. Et ideo virtutes humanae habitus sunt.» *Summa Theol.* I – II, Q. 55 a. 1

to enable him to fulfil his official duty of exercising the charism of Infallibility, and thereby confirm the faith of his brethren; and that Christ's prayer was an efficacious prayer, and thus accordingly, to Peter, to whom was given the task of leading the Church through all dangers, was also given the assurance that his faith would not fail. I quoted others as well. Thus, the unfailing virtue of faith of the Pontiff is a dispositive habit which pertains essentially to the Petrine office in order that he be equiped to confirm the faith of the Church by means of the exercise of the charism of Infallibility.

So, what is this esoteric "basic distinction" that Siscoe only alludes to but refuses to reveal, which supposedly proves that there is no logical connection between the doctrine on the operation of the powers of the soul and the exercise of a particular power of the soul, to wit, the power to infallibly define in matters of faith? Siscoe does provide an answer:

> «What, then does "the unfailing Faith of Peter" mean? I could cite multiple authorities (from before and after Vatican I) who explain the meaning of the phrase, but I will limit myself to the explanation of John of St. Thomas [...]:
> *The authority of the papacy is not founded upon the personal faith of any individual, inasmuch as any one person can express it according to his own understanding; rather, it is founded upon the common faith of the whole Church. The fact that the Pope cannot fail in this faith means that, even if he were personally a heretic, yet insofar as he teaches ex cathedra he cannot teach anything contrary to the faith. It is in this faith, therefore— which is the faith of the papacy, and not of the person, and which was the faith of Peter and his confession—in this alone the papacy is founded, and not in the personal faith even of the very person of the Pope.»*

Papal infallibility indeed is not *founded* on the personal faith of an individual man, but on the supernatural power added to the pope's personal faith so that **he** can teach the faith infallibly; and hence, the exercise of that supernatural power requires the *virtue of faith* as its necessary dispositive habit existing in the soul of the individual man. On the basis of a defective medieval doctrine of infallibility, John of St. Thomas bases his theory of the infallible authority of the pope on the infallibility of *the common faith of the whole Church*. From this, Siscoe concludes, "As we see, "the unfailing faith of Peter" means that a Pope cannot err when he defines a doctrine, *ex cathedra*". **Non sequitur!** *If only the common faith of the Church cannot fail, but the pope's faith can fail, then there would be no need for the pope to confirm the faith of the whole Church by means of infallible definitions.* No! The unfailing faith of Peter means that *the pope's* *faith cannot fail*, and since his faith *cannot fail*, he is able to confirm the faith of the *Church by defining doctrine infallibly*. Papal Infallibility is not "founded upon the common faith of the whole Church," so that, "It is in this faith, therefore—which is the faith of the papacy, and not of the person, and which was the faith of Peter and his confession—in this alone the papacy is founded, and not in the personal faith even of the very person of the Pope." If that were true, then the charism of Infallibility could logically only be understood as a collective charism exercised by the pope together with the all the bishops of the universal Church. Papal Infallibility is founded on Christ's promise to *Peter* of the singular gift that *his faith and that of his successors will not fail*; in order that by the exercise of the authority of the Petrine Office, the Pontiff, by means of that singular gift, confirms the faith of the Church so that the common faith of the Church cannot fail.

The very notion of the infallible authority of the pope being founded on the infallibility of *the common faith of the whole Church*, is rooted in a Conciliaristic conception of infallibility that would restrict its exercise to a collective act of an ecumenical council, or of the universal and ordinary magisterium. Cardinal Manning cites the passage of St. Vincent Ferrer:

> «Vincentius Ferré says, "The exposition of certain Paris (doctors) is of no avail, who affirm that Christ only promised that the faith should not fail of the Church founded upon Peter; and not that it should not fail in the successors of Peter taken apart from (seorsum) the Church." He adds that our Lord said, "I have prayed for thee, Peter; sufficiently showing that the infallibility was not promised to the Church as apart from (seorsum) the head, but promised to the head, that from him it should be derived to the Church." †[562]»[563]

Manning then quotes Dominicus Marchese[564], «Marchese, before quoted, repeats the same words, "The infallibility in faith which (our

---

[562] «† "Nec valet expositio aliquorum Parisiensium affirmantium hic Christum tantum promisisse fidem non defecturam Ecclesiæ fundatæ super Petrum, non vero promisisse non defecturam in successoribus Petri seorsum ab Ecclesia sumptis. Christus dicens, ego autem rogavi pro te Petre, satis designat hanc infallibilitatem non promissam Ecclesiæ ut seorsum a capite, sed promissam capiti, ut ex illo derivetur ad Ecclesiam." — Ferre, *De Fide*, qusest. xii. apud Rocaberti, tom. xx. p. 388.»

[563] Cardinal Manning, *The Vatican Council and its Definitions*, p. 105.

[564] Dominicus Maria Marchese, O.P. (2 Mar 1633 – May 1692), Bishop of Pozzuoli.

Lord) promised, not to the Church apart from (seorsum) the head, but to the head, that from him it should be derived to the Church."*565»566 As I have amply demonstrated, for the pope to define infallibly *by himself* ex cathedra, the habit of faith existing in the soul as a *dispositio animæ* would be required to dispose him to exercise the charism *by himself*. The *common faith of the whole Church* by itself cannot function as a *dispositio animæ* in the soul of the pope. In fact, the *common faith of the whole Church* by itself, apart from the source of its infallibility, which is the Faith of Peter manifested in the exercise of the singular charism of *papal infallibility*, cannot dispose the bishops to collectively define infallibly. Such a collective exercise of the Church's infallibility is only possible when exercised in conjunction with the infallible exercise of the Petrine *munus docendi*.

If Peter's faith were to be understood to be the common faith of the whole Church represented in Peter, but not the personal faith individually of Peter and his successors, then Christ's prayer (Luke 22: 31-32) would not have been for Peter singularly, that his faith not fail, but it would have been for the whole Church, that the faith of the whole Church not fail; but it was precisely for Peter's faith not to fail that Christ prayed, so that Peter could confirm the faith of the Church. In *liber iv caput iii* of *De Romano Pontifice* (the chapter on Papal Infallibility), St. Robert Bellarmine thoroughly refutes the argument that in praying for Peter to be given the grace of unfailing faith, the faith of Peter is merely representative of the faith of the whole Church. The argument, Bellarmine explains, is founded on one of three interpretations of the Lord's promise in Luke 22, «*Simon, Simon,* sic enim habetur in Græco, *ecce Satanas expetivit vos ut cribraret sicut triticum, ego autem rogavi pro te, ut non deficiat Fides tua, et tu aliquando conversus confirma fratres tuos.*»567 The interpretation in question, Bellarmine explains, is that given by certain

---

565 «* "Satis designat infallibilitatem in fide quam promisit, non Ecclesiæ seorsum a Capite sed Capiti ut ex illo derivetur ad Ecclesiam." — Marchese, *de capite Visib. Eccles.* disput. iii. dub. 2; apud Rocaberti, tom. ix. p. 719.»

566 Cardinal Manning, *The Vatican Council and its Definitions*, p. 106.

567 «*Simon, Simon,* for thus it is given in Greek, *behold Satan has desired to have you* [plural, i.e. "all of you"] *to sift you* [plural] *as wheat, but I have prayed for thee* [singular] *that thy faith not fail, and thou once converted confirm thy brethren.*» — *De Romano Pontifice* IV, iii. The complete verse: «31 ειπεν δε ο κυριος σιμων σιμων ιδου ο σατανας εξητησατο υμας του σινιασαι ως τον σιτον 32 εγω δε εδεηθην περι σου ινα μη εκλειπη η πιστις σου και συ ποτε επιστρεψας στηριξον τους αδελφους σου.»

Parisians whom he cited earlier who claimed that in this passage, the Lord prayed for the universal Church, or for Peter, as the one who bears the image of the whole Church (*sive pro Petro, ut totius Ecclesiæ figuram gerebat*); and this He obtained so that the faith of the Catholic Church should never fail. Bellarmine then makes the critical distinction that if this interpretation is to be understood as meaning that the prayer was immediately for the head of the Church, and consequently for the whole body, which is represented by the head, it would be true. But that is not how they understood it, but they would have it that the prayer was solely for the Church – «which interpretation is false.»

Bellarmine demonstrates from the words of Our Lord Jesus Christ that in the Gospel, the Lord's prayer was not merely for the faith of the universal Church represented by Peter, so that the faith of the whole Church would not fail (*quod Dominus hic oraverit pro Ecclesia universali, sive pro Petro; ut totius figuram gerebat*); but the Lord prayed for one person only (*quia Dominus unam tantum personam designavit*) – and he points out that Jesus began the discourse in the plural: *Satan expetivit **vos** ut cribraret*) [σατανας εξητησατο **υμας** του σινιασαι]; and then He quickly changed his form of speech to the singular: *Ego autem rogavi pro **te*** [εγω δε εδεηθην περι **σου**] – and then Bellarmine pointedly asks, why did He not say *pro vobis* in the plural as He had done at the beginning? "Certainly," Bellarmine observes, "If He were speaking of the whole Church, it would have been much more correct for Him to say, *rogavi pro vobis*." But Christ, (Bellarmine explains), prayed singularly for *Peter* – thus he prayed not only for Peter's perseverance, but for a grace to be given to Peter that is to be translated to the usefulness of others – so that this grace being obtained at the time for Peter pertains also to his successors; *because the Church always stands in need to be confirmed by one whose faith cannot fail*:

> «*Confirma fratres tuos;* non igitur pro sola Petri perseverantia Dominus rogavit, sed pro aliquo dono Petro communicando in aliorum utilitatem… donum hoc loco Petro impetratum, etiam ad successores pertinet: nam Christus oravit pro Petro in utilitatem Ecclesiæ: Ecclesia autem semper indiget aliquo a quo confirmetur, cujus Fides deficere non possit.»

If Peter's faith is understood to mean the faith of the whole Church, there would be no need for the pope's faith not to fail, or for the pope to confirm the faith of his brethren; since Christ's infallibly effective prayer would have been not for Peter's faith individually, but for the faith of the whole Church not to fail. In that case then, it would not be the pope who would need to confirm the faith of the Church, but it would be the faith of the whole Church which would need to confirm the very fallible faith of the pope, in order to prevent the pope's faith from failing; and thus to prevent him from defining false dogmas. Peter would not be confirming the faith of his brethren, but the brethren would be confirming the faith of Peter. And if Peter's faith is the common faith of the whole Church, then it would be *the common faith of the whole Church which would confirm the common faith of the whole Church* (a patent absurdity); and there would be *no need for Peter's individual faith not to fail for the faith of the Church to be confirmed, since the faith of the whole Church would be confirmed without Peter's successor needing to exercise the singular charism of Infallibility, since that chaism would exclusively reside in the collectivity of the whole Church*. But Peter's profession of faith was not the product of the common faith of the disciples, but was *his* profession, and *that profession of the divinity of Christ and His divine Sonship was the result of the revelation made to Peter directly and personally by the Father: "Blessed art thou, Simon Bar-Jona: because flesh and blood hath not revealed it to thee, but my Father who is in heaven."* (Mt. 16: 17) **It is for this reason, namely, that Peter, having received a personal revelation from God made a singular profession of his personal faith in Christ's divinity, that he was blessed with the singular grace of unfailing personal faith for himself and for his successors, which is the necessary disposition for the operation of the charism of Infallibility, and for the preservation of the form of the pontificate in the person of the pope.** Thus it is that the common faith of the Church is infallible because the faith of Peter, which confirms the faith of the whole Church, cannot fail; and consequently, the faith of Peter is not the faith of the Church; but the faith of the Church is the faith of Peter, *which cannot fail* – or as Suárez put it: «*Fides Petri catholica fuit, et deficere non potest; sed fides Ecclesiæ Romanæ est fides Petri; ergo fides Ecclesiæ Romanæ est fides catholica a qua numquam illa sedes potest deficere.*»[568]

Faith would be utterly unnecessary for a Pontiff to profess the faith infallibly in such a manner as would a faithless pope exercising the charism of Infallibility by speaking like the ass of Balaam; and therefore the grace of unfailing faith, which was promised by Christ to the Pontiff precisely for the purpose of enabling him to confirm the faith of his brethren, would have been given by Christ to serve no purpose, and would be utterly superfluous if the *confirmator fratrum* could exercise the charism of Infallibility with no faith at all; but since Christ gave to Peter

---

[568] *Defensio Fidei Catholicae Adversus Anglicanae Sectae Errores*, cap. v, n. vii.

and his successors the gift of unfailing faith precisely for the purpose of infallibly confirming the faith of the brethren, faith is seen, therefore, to be the absolutely necessary disposition for the exercise of the charism of Infallibility, and hence, pertains essentially to the form of the Supreme Pontificate, and is therefore the necessary disposition for the form of the Pontificate to be conserved in the person of the Pontiff, and remain united to him. I have explained this point at length, quoting authoritative sources. The virtue of faith is the *necessary disposition* for the exercise of the charism of Infallibility, and for that reason, Christ prayed that the Pontiff's faith not fail:

> «*Nam Pontifex non solum non debet, nec potest hæresim prædicare, sed etiam debet veritatem semper docere, & sine dubio id faciet, cum Dominus illi jusserit confirmare fratres suos, & propterea addiderit, Rogavi pro te, ut non deficiat fides tua, idest, ut saltem non deficiat in throno tuo prædicatio veræ Fidei:* **at quomodo, quæso, confirmabit fratres in Fide, & veram Fidem semper prædicabit Pontifex hæreticus?** *Potest quidem Deus ex corde hæretico extorquere veræ Fidei confessionem, sicut verba posuit quondam in ore asinæ Balaam: at violentum erit, & non secundum morem providentiæ Dei suaviter disponentis omnia.*» (S. Robertus Bellarminus)

The last response I heard from Siscoe which was passed on to me:

> «A traditional priest and author, who is probably the best theologian I know, refuted Fr. Kramer's central argument in a private e-mail to me. I sent him my own refutation of Fr Kramer's error to review. He responded by agreeing entirely with everything I wrote, and then added another refutation of his own that I had not thought of.»

Siscoe says that an anonymous priest refuted my "central argument"! Who is this anonymous priest, and where is the direct refutation of my "central argument"? What, according to this anonymous priest, is alleged to be my "central argument"? If Siscoe really believed that he has the refutation of my "central argument", then why does he guard it like a state secret? Siscoe does not say what (according to him) is my "central argument"; and the anonymous priest also allegedly "agrees" with Siscoe's unstated "refutation" of my unspecified "central argument"; and all this clownery which says **absolutely nothing** proves that my unspecified "central argument" is an *error*!

Siscoe, has said **nothing** – yet he expects people to believe on blind faith that his **unstated argument** refutes my **unspecified "central**

argument". Siscoe is plainly hysterical. What I have written on the Five Opinions is in agreement with the unanimous consensus of expert scholars. My central thesis is that of St. Robert Bellarmine, namely, that manifest heretics cease entirely by themselves to be members of the Church, and therefore lose office *ex natura hæresis*; and from which premise it necessarily follows that if a pope could be a heretic, then a manifest heretic pope *sine alia vi externa* would cease by himself to be pope, a Christian, and a member of the Church.

ON OPINION NO. THREE:

A HERETIC POPE CAN BE JUDGED TO HAVE FALLEN FROM OFFICE:
1) A MANIFEST HERETIC FALLS FROM OFFICE BY HIS PUBLIC ACT OF DEFECTION;
2) A SECRET HERETIC IS JUDGED TO HAVE FALLEN FROM OFFICE ONCE THE HERESY IS PROVEN AND MADE MANIFEST

Bellarmine presents the Third Opinion as the opposite extreme (to the extreme opinion that not only a manifest heretic pope would lose office by the very act of manifest heresy [Opinion No. 5], but **even an occult heretic** would lose office and could be judged [Opinion No. 2]); according to which, "The third opinion is on another extreme, that the Pope is not and cannot be deposed either by secret or manifest heresy." ("Papam neque per hæresim occultam, neque per manifestam, ***esse depositum*** aut ***deponi posse***".) I have explained in the previous section that Bellarmine rejects the third opinion not on the basis that a pope would be *deponendus*, i.e., that he can be judged and deposed by the Church (*deponi posse*) for heresy (Opinion No. 4), but because he can be judged to have fallen from office *ipso facto* **by himself** and therefore to simply "be deposed" (*esse depositum*) by his own actions (*deponi posse*) (Opinion No. 5).

The basis for Bellarmine's opinion which refutes Opinion No. 3, is set forth in his refutation of Opinion No. 4, and in his explication of the Fifth Opinion: that a manifest heretic ceases to be pope, because he ceases to be a member of the Church by the very act of manifest heresy, which is an act of manifest defection from the Catholic faith, which, by its very nature and thus intrinsic to the act of public heresy, severs a member from the body of the Church, and as a direct consequence of that defection, results automatically in the *ipso facto* loss of office. Bellarmine cites the unanimous teaching of the Fathers in support of his position, and particularly St. Jerome, saying "Jerome comments on the same place, saying that other sinners, through a judgment of excommunication are excluded from the Church; heretics, however, leave by themselves and are cut from the body of Christ". Ballerini follows Bellarmine on this point exactly, and quotes St. Jerome verbatim:

> «Perspicua hac in re est S. Hieronimi ratio in laudata Pauli verba, *Propterea a semetipso dicitur esse damnatus, quia fornicator, adulter, homicida, et cetera vitia per sacerdotes ex Ecclesia propelluntur: hæretici autem in semetipsis sententiam ferunt, suo arbitrio de Ecclesia recedentes: quæ recessio propriæ conscientiæ videtur esse damnatio.*»

Both Bellarmine and Ballerini were certainly aware that their position on this point was firmly supported by the teaching of St. Pius V in the Roman Catechism: "Heretics and schismatics are excluded from the Church, because they have defected (desciverunt) from her and belong to her only as deserters belong to the army from which they have deserted." Therefore, Bellarmine declares: "this is indeed very certain. A non-Christian cannot in any way be Pope, as Cajetan affirms in the same book, and the reason is because he cannot be the head of that which he is not a member, and he is not a member of the Church who is not a Christian. But a manifest heretic is not a Christian, as St. Cyprian and many other Fathers clearly teach. Therefore, a manifest heretic cannot be Pope." Thus, according to Bellarmine, if a pope were to fall into manifest heresy, by the very nature of his act of defection, he would by himself (*per se*), sever himself from the body of the Church and bring about his immediate fall from office, which Ballerini describes as an act of abdication (*ipso facto sua voluntate primatu & pontificatu exauctoratus*; and *abdicasse quodammodo Pontificatum*). This opinion was summed up by Gregory XVI, who wrote (on the case of Pedro de Luna), "So then he could be considered, as noted by Ballerini, to have been a public schismatic and heretic, and consequently to have fallen from papacy by himself, even if he had been validly elevated to it."[569]

---

[569] «Ond'è che poteasi, come osserva il Ballerini, considerarlo quale pubblico scismatico e eretico, ed in conseguenza **per se decaduto dal pontificato**, se anche ad esso fosse stato validamente innalzato.» (*Il trionfo della santa sede e della chiesa contro gli assatti dei novatori*, p. 47)

In his own words Bellarmine explains, "The foundation of this [fifth] opinion is that a manifest heretic, is in no way a member of the Church; that is, neither in spirit nor in body, or by internal union nor external." A manifest heretic pope would cease to be pope, because by the very act of defection from the faith, he would cease to be a member of the Church; and this is so because heresy, in its nature is an act of defection from the faith, which *suapte natura* and not by authority of the Church, severs the heretic from the body of the Church. On this solid doctrinal foundation Bellarmine concludes:

> "Therefore, the true opinion is the fifth, according to which the Pope who is manifestly a heretic ceases by himself to be Pope and head, in the same way as he ceases to be a Christian and a member of the body of the Church; and for this reason he can be judged and punished by the Church. This is the opinion of all the ancient Fathers, who teach that manifest heretics immediately lose all jurisdiction."

And, "Thenceforth, the Holy Fathers teach in unison, that not only are heretics outside the Church, but they even lack all Ecclesiastical jurisdiction and dignity ipso facto." And further, "those Fathers, when they say that heretics lose jurisdiction, do not allege any human laws which maybe did not exist then on this matter; rather, they argued from the nature of heresy."

Bellarmine is clear and explicit on this general point: that the separation from the body of the Church, as well as loss of office and all jurisdiction, are accomplished by the very act of heresy, *ex natura hæresis,* and not by the judgment of the Church, or as a penalty for an ecclesiastical delict. This *sententia* is *de fide* regarding firstly the separation from the Church, in virtue of 1) the unanimity of the Fathers, 2) the teaching of the universal magisterium set forth in the Roman Catechism, and, 3) the teaching of Pius XII in *Mystici Corporis*; and secondly, it is *de fide* regarding the loss of office and jurisdiction, because of 1) the unanimity of the Fathers on this point which Bellarmine amply demonstrates in his refutation of Opinion No. 4, and 2) the canonical doctrine of the Church proposed by the papal *ordinary magisterium* in Canon 188. 4°; which, therefore, qualifies it as a doctrine pertaining to the *universal and ordinary magisterium*. Thus, it is not a mere question of law, but of definitive magisterial doctrine that heretics and schismatics are separated from the Church by their own actions *suapte natura*, apart from any ecclesiastical law or judgment; and that the consequent loss of office and jurisdiction is not the result of any penal sanction or any judgment pronounced by the Church, but is the direct effect of the act of defection from the Church, *sine alia vi externa*; which therefore, **not by any human law**, takes place *ex natura hæresis* or *ex natura schismatis*.

The Sixteenth, Seventeenth, and Eighteenth Century exponents of Opinion No. 4, (which holds that a manifest heretic pope must either be deposed by the Church, or at least be juridically judgerd by the Church before the loss of office takes place), can perhaps be excused for having held this errant legalistic opinion, but there is no longer any excusing circumstance to justify adherence to it now. The doctrine of Bellarmine and Ballerini on this point was advocated by Pope Gregory XVI, and adopted by the Apostolic See at the First Vatican Council; and was then formally incorporated into the 1917 Code of Canon Law as the doctrinal basis for the *ipso jure* loss of office provision in Canon 188. 4°, and in the 1983 Code (Canon 194 §2). Since the loss of office and jurisdiction takes place not as a penalty for the ecclesiastical crime of heresy, **but is the natural consequence which necessarily follows from the *fact* of public defection into formal heresy** (which also happens to be a canonical delict) **ex natura hæresis**, apart from any human law, it is an "*ipso jure*" provision applicable to "*quælibet officia*" (can. 188 4°), for which reason *there can be* **no exception for a pope**.

Clearly, the mind of the Church on the question of loss of office for defection from the faith into heresy has been magisterially expressed as a tacit renunciation from office, which brings about the automatic removal from office *ex natura hæresis*, as Bellarmine taught. Loss of office due to defection from the faith is not a divine punishment for the *canonical delict* of heresy resulting from a judgment expressed as a *declaratory sentence* by Church authority; nor is it *penal deprivation of office* which would have to be pronounced as a judicial sentence of Church authority by a tribunal exercising *jurisdiction* over an individual to convict him of a crime; and in the case of a pope, pronouncing a *penal sentence* on a reigning Pontiff; but it is a *tacit resignation from office* by which the office is lost *ipso facto* as a natural consequence of the act of manifest heresy *per se*, which is then enforced by a declaratory sentence so that the loss of office can be officially recognized, the heretic removed, and the vacancy filled. *"Therefore, the true opinion is the fifth, according to which the Pope who is manifestly a heretic ceases by himself to be Pope and head, in the same way as he ceases to be a Christian and a member of the body of the Church; and for this reason he can be judged and punished by the Church."*

The distinction made by Bellarmine and Ballerini between a manifestly heretical pope to be judged as having fallen from office **by himself** and therefore to simply "be deposed" (*esse depositum*) by his own actions (Opinion No. 5), as opposed to one who is to be tried and deposed (*deponendus*), i.e. deprived of office either by a juridical pronouncement, or merely *ipso facto* deposed upon a juridical declaration, as a punishment for a penal canonical delict of heresy (Opinion No. 4), has either been studiously ignored by Salza and Siscoe, or else they have simply been obliviously unaware of it staring them in the face in Book II Chapter XXX of *De Romano Pontifice*.[570] Whether their oversight is due to deliberate sophistry or oblivious incompetence, in either case, they have interpreted St. Robert Bellarmine's rejection of Opinion No. 3 to be an endorsement of the opinion that the Church has the authority to judge a reigning pontiff for heresy, and ministerially bring about his deposition from office (Opinion No. 4). In view of all that has been stated above, the heterodoxy of that opinion is patent.

The virtually unanimous opinion of modern theologians since the First Vatican Council is that a manifest heretic pope is not *deponendus*, but *depositus*. If the pope were to say, "There is no Blessed Trinity; God is not Triune"; that is manifest formal heresy. He would clearly not be pope, nor would he even be a member of the Church, regardless of whether or not he had ever been a valid pope; but certainly, in either case, he *would not be* a valid pope if he were to profess a heresy so manifest as this. Clearly then, such a pope would be a manifest heretic who therefore, by his manifest heresy, would have severed himself from the body of the Church, ceased to be pope and a member of the Church; and therefore, having cast himself outside of the Church, he would no longer be capable of holding office inside the Church. He would therefore lose rank, and, as a consequence thereof, would thus become

---

[570] It appears more likely that they have studiously avoided the distinction; since, they quoted a passage of Cardinal Journet on page 277 of their screed that makes the distinction: "Some, such as Bellarmine and Suarez, considered that such a Pope, withdrawing himself from the Church, was ipso facto deposed, papa haereticus est depositus. (...) Others, such as Cajetan, and Johnof St. Thomas, whose analysis seems to me more penetrating, have considered that even after a manifest sin 114 of heresy the Pope is not yet deposed, but should be deposed by the Church, papa haereticus non est depositus, sed deponendus." However, the authors pass over it in silence as a matter of little or no importance.

minor quolibet catholico, and would then be able to be judged and punished by the Church, as Bellarmine explains.

But what if he were to profess a new heresy not yet condemned – something clearly against a doctrine of divine faith and the ordinary magisterium that has not yet been solemnly defined; or a doctrine not immediately and directly opposed to the letter of a solemn definition, but opposed to the unanimous opinion of theologians on the proper meaning of a defined dogma? If his heresy would be against a manifest dogma of divine faith as it is and has been unanimously, universally, and perpetually *professed* and understood by Catholics, which is manifestly contained by strict logical implication in a solemnly defined or universally professed article of faith; then, as was in the case of Arius[571], he could be licitly rejected by Catholics as a heretic and shunned as an infidel even on a point that had not yet been explicitly defined by the extraordinary magisterium; because such an *error against divine faith* on a point that is theologically certain and therefore *de fide divina*, and which is at the same time *strictly implied in a defined article of faith*, is essentially no different from, and is virtually identical to a defined article of faith; and would actually pertain to the universal and ordinary magisterium. Since the full and equal divinity of Jesus Christ as the Son of the Eternal Father, was seen to be so clearly taught in scripture, and was universally *professed* in even the most primitive *credal formulæ* of the Church; the Bishop of Alexandria, St. Alexander, saw fit to condemn his error, and excommunicate Arius for heresy even before the Council of Ephesus,

---

[571] The *Catholic* Encyclopedia relates that Arius, "was made presbyter […] in 313, and had the charge of a well-known district in Alexandria called Baucalis. This entitled Arius to expound the Scriptures officially, and he exercised much influence when, in 318, his quarrel with Bishop Alexander broke out over the fundamental truth of Our Lord's divine Sonship and substance. While many Syrian prelates followed the innovator, he was condemned at Alexandria in 321 by his diocesan [bishop] in a synod of nearly one hundred Egyptian and Libyan bishops. Deprived and excommunicated, the heresiarch fled to Palestine. He addressed a thoroughly unsound statement of principles to Eusebius of Nicomedia, who yet became his lifelong champion and who had won the esteem of Constantine by his worldly accomplishments. […] In 321 was held the council that first condemned Arius, then parish priest of the section of Alexandria known as Baucalis. After his condemnation Arius withdrew to Palestine, where he secured the powerful support of Eusebius of Caesarea." Thus he was rightly condemned as a heretic on a point that the Church had not yet solemnly defined.

infallibly professed against the Arian heresy with an explicit formulation. What is mainly the basis for justifying such a judgment of heresy on a doctrine not yet explicitly condemned by the magisterium but contrary to the faith of the Church, is expressed by St. Robert Bellarmine in his letter to Fr. Paolo Foscarini:

> "Nor may it be answered that this is not a matter of faith, for if it is not a matter of faith from the point of view of the subject matter, it is on the part of the ones who have spoken. It would be just as heretical to deny that Abraham had two sons and Jacob twelve, as it would be to deny the virgin birth of Christ, for both are declared by the Holy Ghost through the mouths of the prophets and apostles."

However, if it is not morally certain that the pope *scienter* rejects defined dogma, or a manifest dogma universally professed by the Church, he could not be considered to be a heretic in the strict sense of one who knowingly rejects a manifest or defined dogma professed by the whole Church; since, without a clear-cut case of heresy, as heresy is canonically defined; a pope, no matter how egregious his deviation from the doctrine of the faith, cannot be removed. A council would certainly lack jurisdiction to judge in such a case, so its judgment would be *tamquam non existens*. The materially erring pope, who has not clearly professed manifestly formal heresy, must be presumed to remain validly in office; and for so long as he remains certainly a valid pope, he would retain his jurisdiction as the supreme judge, and his power to define infallibly. But if a pope were to profess material heresy in such a manner that would make him vehemently suspect of heresy[572] — aided and

---

[572] Can. 2315 – *Suspectus de haeresi*, qui monitus causam suspicionis non removeat, actibus legitimis prohibeatur, et clericus praeterea, repetita inutiliter monitione, suspendatur a divinis; quod si intra sex menses a contracta poena completos suspectus de haeresi sese non emendaverit, habeatur tanquam haereticus, haereticorum poenis obnoxius. Can. 2316 – Qui quoquo modo haeresis propagationem sponte et scienter iuvat, aut qui communicat in divinis cum haereticis contra praescriptum can. 1258, *suspectus de haeresi est*.
«Can. 2315 – The Code declares the following persons as suspect of heresy: 1. The propagators of heresy and those who participate with non-Catholics *in divinis* (Can.2316); [...] As may be seen from this list, each species of suspicion here enumerated may be removed in a different way: by formal retraction, by withdrawing the condition and complying with Catholic principles, or by protesting against what was done or received, [...] Can. 2316 This crime is singled out as a species for itself, and the penalty is taken partly from older

abetted by a cowardly hierarchy that refuses to fraternally admonish and correct him; then in such an eventuality, he would become a *papa dubius*, a "doubtful pope", and the harm to souls and the damage to the Church resulting from the situation would be a direct consequence of the negligence of the upper hierarchy of the Church, and not the private judgment of the abandoned faithful, who would be left to fend for

---

sources and partly from the Bull *"Apostolicae Sedis.*1*"* Two distinct cases are contained in our canon, and the penalty is the same as for those suspected of heresy.

1. Whosoever *spontaneously and knowingly assists in any way in the propagation of heresy, is himself suspected of heresy.* Under this heading fall, according to *"Apostolicae Sedis,"* all those who believe the errors of heretics, or who receive, protect, and defend heretics. There is little doubt2 that our text includes all these, provided, of course, they act of their own accord and knowingly. Hence

   a) *Credentes* are such as externally profess the errors of heretics, e.g., by asserting that Luther or Dollinger were correct in their views, even though they may not know the particular errors of these leaders.

   b) *Receptores* are those who receive and shelter heretics, especially with the intention of hiding them from the ecclesiastical authorities.

   c) *Fautores* are such as favor heretics because of their heresy, by omitting to denounce them when required or demanded by their office, or by giving support to non-Catholic propaganda, This latter way of propagating heresy is followed by public and private persons who write for heretics, praise their methods and objects, recommend their work and give it material support, always provided that the heresy itself is the object of their mental and material favors.

   d) *Defensores* means those who defend heretics for the sake of heresy, orally, in writing, or by acts of defence proper. All such persons are suspected of heresy if they act of their own accord and knowingly. *Sponte* is opposed to compulsion and fear, and therefore implies full deliberation and a free will not hindered by any extrinsic or intrinsic impediment, such as fear of losing an office, or one's reputation, or customers. *Scienter* is opposed to ignorance, the object of which here is heresy, and means that these promotors or propagators of heresy must be aware that they are helping *heresy as such*. Besides, as *propagationem* seems to imply an effective propaganda, it may be said that these *fautores*, etc., must produce an effect. However, this is rarely wanting if the support is a material one.

2. Those *who communicate with heretics in divinis* are themselves suspect of heresy. Here we refer to can.1258, where the necessary explanation has been given.

3. These and all others suspected of heresy incur the penalty stated in can.2315» [Fr. Charles Augustine, *Op. cit.*, Volume VIII, pp. 284 – 289]

themselves only with their own conscience to judge. The definitions of such a *doubtful pope* would be of *doubtful validity*, and would therefore not qualify as having the note of *infallibility* (Can. 749 § 3). If a pope were to profess a heresy in such a manner that would make him *vehemently* or *violently* suspect of heresy, and if he were to persist in his heresy even after correction, then it would be morally certain that he has fallen from office. If, however, he were to directly, immediately, and contradictorily assert his own judgment against a *de fide* dogma about which he could not be ignorant, or if he were to remain incorrigible even after correction on a dogma about which he may have been ignorant, he would by the fact of his pertinacity, manifest his tacit resignation from office and cease to be pope.

If, on the other hand, the pope were to merely oppose the common opinion of theologians, he would be able to settle the question by means of an *ex cathedra* definition, or in the manner that Alexander III judged against the prevailing opinion of theologians on the question of the human nature of Christ. The Church interprets the meaning of its own dogmatic pronouncements; and the pope is the supreme interpreter and judge. If the theologians say the pope is in heresy, he can judge that they are in heresy. If an illegitimately assembled council judges the pope to be in heresy, and pertinacious; he can judge that they are in heresy – and he can define *ex cathedra* that his opinion is **dogma**. But if material heresy were such as to make him a doubtful pope, it would be difficult, and in some cases nearly impossible for anyone to judge whether the pope's definition is infallible dogma or the perverse pronouncement of a heretic. The result would be that the Church would be effectively deprived of the magisterial function of the *confirmator fratrum*. If the pope could be judged by his inferiors before he falls from office, then he is not the supreme judge. If they judge him a heretic while he is still in office, he, as the supreme judge, can overturn their judgment and define the contrary, and declare them heretics, since it is infallibly defined that the pope is the final judge in all cases. If the final authority does not rest in the reigning pontiff, then there can be no final judgment of a supreme tribunal; because a council, according to the divine constitution of the Church, is defined to be subordinate to the authority and subject to the jurisdiction of the Roman Pontiff. Hence, it is manifest that the opinion that says one who is certainly reigning as pope can be judged for heresy while still in office, is false and heretical. The pope can be judged only in the qualified sense that if he would be plainly seen to be pertinacious in manifestly heresy, he would cease to be pope and could therefore be judged, and thus, he would be *shown to be already judged*.

If the judgment of the Church were required to depose a sitting pope for heresy and remove him from office (*deponendus*), and if it were not the pope's own manifest judgment against himself which would cause him to fall by himself from office (*depositus*), then, since only the pope possesses the jurisdiction as the supreme judge to judge or define on whether or not the proposition he professes is heretical, it would ultimately be for him, as the supreme judge, to judge himself, since, for so long as he is pope, *he is the final and infallible judge in doctrine*; so there exists no tribunal on earth that can judge the pope for so long as he remains in office as pope. If the pope's subordinates would declare the pope to be in heresy, he could *infallibly define* that they are in heresy; or he could infallibly judge that they are right; and retract his heresy; but if the pope would solemnly define his doctrine to be *de fide*, then his judgment is *infallible*, and theirs is *heresy*. Therefore, for so long as the pope remains in office, it is patent, as St. Robert Bellarmine says (essentially repeating the dictum of Pope St. Gregory VII): "The pope cannot be judged". Thus it is patent that no one, not even a council, may judge the pope *juridically* for the crime of heresy or declare him *vitandus*; but only if he plainly and indisputably defects from the faith of the Church into manifest heresy, only then can he *be shown to be already judged*, i.e. as one who has already fallen by himself from the pontificate.

ON OPINION NO. FOUR:

A MANIFEST HERETIC POPE CANNOT BE JUDGED AND DEPOSED BY THE CHURCH (*DEPONENDUS*)

St. Robert Bellarmine, in his doctrine on the question of the deposition of a manifestly heretical pope, with a tightly woven logic, gives systematic expression to the teaching of Pope Innocent III set forth in his *Sermons*; 1) on the point that the Roman Pontiff may be judged by no one, except for heresy, in which case he cannot be judged as pope and deposed *by the Church* (*deponendus*), but, 2) he can only be shown to have already been judged – to have fallen from the Pontificate *by himself* (*depositus*). Thus, the Church would exercise no power over an actually reigning pontiff if it were to judge that the man who was pope, but is still physically occupying the *cathedra*, had actually fallen from the pontificate by his heresy. the Church would only determine that the occupant of the throne, being a heretic, and thereby having fallen from the pontificate *ipso facto*, is no longer the pope; and would therefore declare the See to be vacant, and proceed to the election of a new pope. It is in this qualified sense that Bellarmine speaks of the manner in which a heretical pope can be "deposed".

The *Catholic Encyclopedia* notes that, "No canonical provisions exist regulating the authority of the College of Cardinals sede Romanâ impeditâ, i.e. in case the pope became insane, **or personally a heretic**, in such cases it would be necessary to consult the dictates of right reason and the teachings of history." The teachings of history demonstrate that there is no such case in history in which a pope manifestly defected into formal heresy; and therefore it is not surprising that there do not exist any canonical provisions for such a case. Bellarmine himself stated that there has never been such a case, and (as quoted earlier) Archbishop John Purcell, who was present at the First Vatican Council, related that,

> «The question was also raised by a Cardinal, "What is to be done with the Pope if he becomes a heretic?" It was answered that **there has never been such a case**; the Council of Bishops could depose him for heresy, **for from the moment he becomes a heretic he is not the head or even a member of the Church** [...] **and he would cease to be Pope, being deposed by God Himself.**»

It is manifestly evident that the relator's reply to the Cardinal did not refer to an internal heretic, since he further stated, «If the Pope, for instance, were to *say* that the belief in God is false, [...] or if he were to deny the rest of the creed, 'I believe in Christ,' etc. [...] If he denies any dogma of the Church held by every true believer, he is no more Pope than either you or I".»

What is particularly worthy of note, is that the reply to the Cardinal on the question of a pope who becomes a heretic, was given as a pure hypothesis, and was not considered as a serious possibility, as is evident from the relator's words, "**The supposition is injurious to the Holy Father in the very idea, but** serves to show you the fullness with which the subject has been considered and the **ample thought given to every possibility**." At the First Vatican Council, (as Pope Pius XI stated in the earlier cited passage of *Providentissimus Deus*) "the Fathers of the [1870] Vatican Council employed his [Bellarmine's] writings and opinions to the greatest possible extent" – and indeed, as is evident from what is related by Archbishop Purcell, at the Council, the Apostolic See adopted as its own policy his position on the question of a heretical pope, namely, his position on Opinion No. 1; as well as hypothetically adopting his position on Opinion No. 5. Thus, as a matter of stated policy, the opinion of Bellarmine, Ballerini, de Liguori, and Gregory XVI was the adopted position of the Holy See under Pius IX at the First Vatican Council, to wit: that a pope who becomes a manifest heretic, 1) "ceases by himself to be Pope and head, in the same way as he ceases to be a Christian and a member of the body of the Church; and for this reason he can be judged and punished by the Church" [Bellarmine][573], 2) that "by his public pertinacity... he declares himself to be a heretic, i.e. to have withdrawn from the Catholic faith and the Church by his own will, so that no declaration or sentence from anyone would be necessary," [574] "that he by his own will departed", and is "severed from the body of the Church, and has in some manner abdicated the Pontificate"[575] – i.e. that he "*ipso facto* by his own will *abdicated* the primacy and the pontificate",[576] [Ballerini]; 3) "For the rest, if God should permit that a Pope should become a notorious and contumacious heretic, he would cease to be Pope, and the pontificate would be vacant" [St. Alphonsus de Liguori][577]; 4) that he "would be considered as a public schismatic and heretic, and in consequence, and to have fallen by himself from the pontificate, ***if he had been validly elevated to it***"[578], and therefore, "the deposition is

---

[573] «papam haereticum manifestum per se desinere esse papam et caput, sicut per se desinit esse christianus et membrum corporis Ecclesiae; quare ab, Ecclesia posse eum judicari et puniri.»

[574] «hac sua publica pertinacia... semetipsum palam declarat haereticum, hoc est a fide catholica, & ab Ecclesia voluntate propria recessisse, ita ut ad eum praecidendum a corpore Eccleaiae nulla cujusquam declaratio aut sententia necessaria sit.»

[575] «ne aliis perniciem afferret, in publicum proferenda esset ejus hæresis, & contumacia, ut omnes similiter ab eo caverent, sicque sententia, quam in se ipsum tulit, toti Ecclesiæ proposita, **eum sua voluntate recessisse, & ab Ecclesiæ corpore declararet avulsum, atque abdicasse quodammodo Pontificatum.**»

[576] «ipso facto sua voluntate primatu & pontificatu exauctoratus.»

[577] "Del resto, si Dio permettesse che un papa fosse notoriamente eretico e contumace, egli cesserebbe d'essere papa, e vacherebbe il pontificato." (*Verità della Fede*, part 3, ch. 8, no. 10. In: *Opere dommatiche di S. Alfonso de Liguori*, Torino, G. Marietti, 1848, p. 720; *Opere di S. Alfonso Maria de Liguori*, v. 8)

[578] «considerarlo quale pubblico scismatico e eretico, ed in conseguenza ***per se decaduto dal pontificato***, se anche ad esso fosse stato validamente inalzato.»

not a prescription against… the current representation of the Church in the Pope recognized as such, but only against the person, who was before adorned with papal dignity."[579] [Gregory XVI]).

Ballerini applied this doctrine specifically to the case of Pedro de Luna (Benedict XIII), who, "if one believes him to have been a true pontiff, by his own will ipso facto abdicated the primacy and the pontificate, [and] rightly and legitimately was able to be deposed by the Council as a schismatic and heretic".[580] What is of the greatest importance to note is that the Council did not actually depose Benedict, but, as Ballerini explains, "by what means the divine providence employed the synod of Constance to end the most tenacious schism, so that that synod did not need to exercise any power of jurisdiction by its authority to depose any true, albeit unknown, actual Pontiff."[581] Thus, Ballerini concludes, the Council did not declare that it had "deposed" him, but simply declared him to "be deposed" (*depositum declaruit potius quam deposuit*); and Gregory XVI likewise, "So then he could be considered, as noted by Ballerini, to have been a public schismatic and heretic, and consequently to have fallen from the pontificate by himself, even if he had been validly elevated to it."[582]

Ballerini expounded on Bellarmine's doctrine on this point with great precision, explaining how a heretic pope would fall from the pontificate at the moment he manifests his pertinacity in heresy, and any action taken against him before that point is a work of charity – fraternal correction; but once he manifests that he is a heretic, he severs himself automatically from the body of the Church, falls from the Pontificate

---

[579] «non è la deposizione una prescrizione… contro l'attuale rappresentanza della Chiesa nel Papa per tale riconosciuto, ma soltanto contro la persona, che era prima ornata di papal dignità.»

[580] «Benedictus XIII, (si verum Pontificem fuisse existimes) ipso facto sua voluntate primatu & pontificatu exauctoratus, rite ac legitime deponi potuit a Concilio tamquam schismaticus & haereticus; quod non congrueret Joanni XXIII, in sententia contra hunc edita declaratum non legitur.»

[581] «Vides interim, quibus modis divina providentia usa est ad abolendum per Constantiensem synodum pertinacissimam schisma, ut ne opus esset eamdem synodum quiquam juris exercere ad deponendum sua auctoritate quempiam verum, licet ignotum, actualem Pontificem.»

[582] «Ond'è che poteasi, come osserva il Ballerini, considerarlo quale pubblico scismatico e eretico, ed in conseguenza per se decaduto dal pontificato, se anche ad esso fosse stato validamente inalzato.» (*Il trionfo della Santa Sede e della Chiesa contro gli assatti dei novatori*, p. 47)

and ceases to be pope; and then, any judgment pronounced against him would be pronounced on one who already is no longer pope, and no longer superior to a council:

(Text highlighted in yellow has either been cut out or left out by Salza and Siscoe, and the faulty translation has been carefully crafted to falsify the authentic text of Ballerini, and to change his meaning, in order to make Ballerini as well as Bellarmine appear to be of the same opinion as Suárez.)

Latin text: (Pietro Ballerini, *De Potestate Ecclesiastica. Summor. Pont. Et Conc. Gen. Cap. IX § II. pp. 128-9*)

«**Cur vero** in præsentissimo omniumque gravissimo periculo fidei, quod ex Pontifice hæresim privato licet judicio propugnante impendens, **diuturniores moras non pateretur, remedium ex generalis synodi non ita facili convocatione expectandum credatur**? Nonne etiam inferiores quicumque in tanto fidei discrimine superiorem suum correctione fraterna commonere queunt, in faciem eidem resistere, atque revincere; &, si opus sit, redarguere ac ad resipiscentiam urgere? Poterunt id Cardinales, qui ipsi a consiliis adstant; poterit Romanus Clerus; Romana etiam synodus, si expedire judicetur, congregata poterit. Quemcumque vel privatum respiciunt illa Pauli ad Titum: *Hæreticum hominem post unam & alteram correctionem devita, sciens quia subversus est, qui ejusmodi est, & delinquit, cum sit proprio judicio condemnatus.* Qui nimirum semel & bis correptus non resiscipit, sed pertinax est in sententia dogmati manifesto aut definito contraria; hac sua publica pertinacia, cum ab hæresi proprie dicta, quæ pertinaciam requitur, excusari nulla ratione potest; tum vero semetipsum palam declarant hæreticum, hoc est a fide catholica, & ab Ecclesia voluntate propria recississe, ita ut ad eum præcidendum a corpore Ecclesiæ nulla cujusquam declaratione aut sententia necessaria sit. **Perspicua hac in re est S. Hieronymi ratio in laudata Pauli verba.** *Propterea a semetipso dicitur esse damnatus, quia fornicator, adulter, homicida, & cetera vitia per Sacerdotes ex Ecclesia propelluntur: hæretici autem in semetipsos sententiam ferunt, suo arbitrio de Ecclesia recedentes: quæ recessio propriæ conscientiæ videtur esse damnatio.* Pontifex ergo, qui post tam solemnem et publicam Cardinalium, Romani Cleri, vel etiam synodi monitionem se se obfirmatum præferret in hæresi, & de Ecclesia palam recessisset, juxta præceptum Pauli esset vitandus; & ne aliis perniciem afferret, in publicum proferenda esset ejus hæresis, & contumacia, ut omnes similiter ab eo caverent, sicque sententia, quam in se ipsum tulit, toti Ecclesiæ proposita, eum sua voluntate recessisse, & ab Ecclesiæ corpore declararet avulsum, atque abdicasse quodammodo Pontificatum, **quo nemo fruitur, nec frui potest, qui non sit in Ecclesia. Vides igitur in casu hæresis, cui Pontifex in privato sensu adhæreret,** promptum & efficax remedium absque generalis synodi convocatione: qua in hypothesi quidquid contra ipsum ageretur ante declaratam ejus contumaciam & hæresim, ut ad sanum consilium adduceretur, caritatis, non jurisdictionis officium esset: postea vero manifestato ejus recessu ab Ecclesia, si quæ sententia a concilio in eumdem ferretur, in eum ferretur, qui Pontifex amplius non esset, neque superior concilio. Sed hæc (3) hypothesis nullo facto comprobatur; siquidem nullus vel privatus error cuipiam Pontifici adscriptus contra ullum dogma evidens aut definitum hactenus inventus est, aut futurus putatur. Quid igitur in mera hypothesi laboremus pluribus.»[583]

My literal translation:

«**But why is it to be believed, that the remedy is to be expected from the not so easily done convocation of a general synod**, when a most present and gravest of all dangers for the faith, which, impending from a Pontiff espousing heresy even in his private judgment, **would not be able to be endured through lengthy delays**? In such a crisis for the faith, cannot even inferiors warn their superior by fraternal correction, resist him to the face, and subdue; and, if need be, refute and drive him to the recovery of his good sense? The Cardinals, who are there to advise him, will be able to do it; the Roman Clergy will be able to; even a Roman synod, if it is judged to be expedient, having been convened, will be able to. For any person, even a private person, the words of Saint Paul to Titus hold: *"A man that is a heretic, after the first and second admonition avoid: knowing that he that is such a one, is subverted, and sinneth, being condemned by his own judgment."* (Tit. 3, 10-11). He forsooth, who having been once or twice corrected, does not repent, but remains obstinate in a belief contrary to a manifest or defined dogma; by this his public pertinacity which for no reason can be excused, since pertinacity properly pertains to heresy, he declares himself to be a heretic, i.e. to have withdrawn from the Catholic faith and the Church by his own will, so that no declaration or sentence from anyone would be necessary. **Conspicuous in this matter is the explanation of St. Jerome on the commended words of Paul.** *Therefore, by himself [the heretic] is said to be condemned, because the fornicator, adulterer, murderer, and those guilty of other misdeeds are driven out from the Church by the Priests: but heretics deliver the sentence upon themselves, departing*

---

[583] https://books.google.ie/books?id=saaqPWkUgKEC&pg=PA151&lpg=PA151&dq=Una+cum+vindiciis+auctoritatis+pontificiae+contra+opus+Justini+Febroni&source=bl&ots=HNlPiupSCa&sig=_ZvBpEY_djDCtKQ5MDJ-3dI0VkA&hl=en&sa=X&redir_esc=y#v=onepage&q&f=false.

from the Church by their own will: this departure is seen to be the condemnation by their own conscience. Therefore a Pontiff, who after such a solemn and public admonition from the Cardinals, Roman Clergy, or even a synod would maintain himself hardened in heresy, and have openly departed from the Church, according to the precept of Paul he would have to be avoided; and lest the ruin be brought to the rest, his heresy and contumacy, and thus his sentence which he brought upon himself, would have to be publicly pronounced, made known to the whole Church, that he by his own will departed, making known to be severed from the body of the Church, and in some manner to have abdicated the Pontificate, which no one holds or can hold, who is not in the Church. One sees in the case of heresy to which a **Pontiff adhered in a private manner, an efficacious remedy without the convocation of a general synod: in which hypothesis whatever action that would be taken against him before the declaration of his contumacy and heresy, in order to bring him back to reason, would be a duty of charity and not of jurisdiction: but afterward, with his departure from the Church having been manifested, if a sentence were to be pronounced upon him by a council, it would be pronounced on him who would no longer be the Pontiff, nor superior to the council. But this (3) hypothesis is not established by any fact, since no private error ascribed to any Pontiff against any evident or defined dogma has been found, or is believed will be. Why then belabour further a mere hypothesis?**»

The Salza and Siscoe version in True or False Pope:

"Is it not true that, confronted with such a danger to the faith [a Pope teaching heresy], any subject can, by fraternal correction, warn their superior, resist him to his face, refute him and, if necessary, summon him and press him to repent? The Cardinals, who are his counselors, can do this; or the Roman Clergy, or the Roman Synod, if, being met, they judge this opportune. For any person, even a private person, the words of Saint Paul to Titus hold: 'Avoid the heretic, after a first and second correction, knowing that such a man is perverted and sins, since he is condemned by his own judgment' (Tit. 3, 10-11). For the person, who, admonished once or twice, does not repent, but continues pertinacious in an opinion contrary to a manifest or defined dogma – not being able, on account of this public pertinacity to be excused, by any means, of heresy properly so called, which requires pertinacity – this person declares himself openly a heretic. He reveals that by his own will he has turned away from the Catholic Faith and the Church, in such a way that now no declaration or sentence of anyone whatsoever is necessary to cut him from the body of the Church. Therefore the Pontiff who after such a solemn and public warning by the Cardinals, by the Roman Clergy or even by the Synod, would remain himself hardened in heresy and openly turn himself away from the Church, would have to be avoided, according to the precept of Saint Paul. So that he might not cause damage to the rest, he would have to have his heresy and contumacy publicly proclaimed, so that all might be able to be equally on guard in relation to him. Thus, the sentence which he had pronounced against himself would be made known to all the Church, making clear that by his own will he had turned away and separated himself from the body of the Church, and that in a certain way he had abdicated the Pontificate..." (TOFP? pp. 245-6)

With such pre-eminent theologians as Pietro Ballerini and St. Alphonsus de Liguori in the 18th Century, and Bartolomeo Cappellari (Gregory XVI) in the late 18th and early 19th Century, decisively adopting Bellarmine's doctrine of automatic papal loss of office for manifest heresy (Opinion No. 5) as their own, the death knell for the legalistically flawed and conciliaristically tainted theology, formulated in Opinion No. 4 mainly by 16th and 17th Century Counter-Reformation theologians, was already sounding. Bellarmine's teaching, that the Pope is the supreme judge who cannot be judged, echoes the ancient teaching of the Apostolic Fathers that the Church of Rome is preeminent, and the teaching of St. Gelasius that the Roman Church and the See of Rome absolutely cannot be judged by anyone. It is already asserted emphatically by Innocent III, confirmed by the Fifth Lateran Council (which defined the pope's absolute authority over a council) as well as the Council of Trent (which confirmed the status of the Roman Pontiff as the supreme judge), and is infallibly taught by the first Vatican Council. Therefore, it was inevitable that the Church would eventually incorporate Bellarmine's doctrine on the injudicability of the Roman Pontiff in the 1917 and 1983 Code of Canon Law, which declares that that the "First See is judged by no one". (*Prima sedes a nemine judicatur.*)[584] His doctrine that the loss of any ecclesiastical office whatsoever takes place automatically for public defection from the faith into heresy was enshrined in the provision for tacit renunciation of office. So, while the Church has not solemnly defined whether or not it is possible for a pope to fall into heresy, she has already taught infallibly that the pope cannot be judged, and that all offices are automatically lost by public heresy; and therefore, if a pope were to fall into manifest heresy, he would

---

[584] This doctrine expressed in these terms, *apostolica sedes a nemine iudicatur*, dates back to the 4th Century pontificate of Pope St. Damasus.

automatically lose office, and the Church could then only judge him after he would have fallen from office by himself as a consequence of defection from the faith. This doctrine was advocated by St Robert Bellarmine at a time when the more common opinion was the doctrine of Mitigated Conciliarism, i.e., that a heretic pope would remain in office until he would be judged to be a heretic by the Church. Bellarmine explicated and applied the teaching of the Fathers, Doctors, popes and councils to prove that a manifest heretic pope would cease by himself to be pope, *ipso facto*, upon falling into heresy, thereby refuting the more prevalent opinion of the day, which was based on an interpretation tainted by Conciliarism and rooted in the spurious *Canon Si papa*, which had been erroneously attributed to St. Boniface.

BELLARMINE'S ARGUMENT

Bellarmine states the Fourth Opinion, which, in its most classical formulation, is that of Cajetan: "that a manifestly heretical Pope is not ipso facto deposed (non esse ipso facto depositum); but can and must to be deposed by the Church (sed posse, ac debere deponi ab ecclesia)." The distinction made by Bellarmine, as I have demonstrated above, is between a pope who simply "is deposed" (*depositus*) by pronouncing the judgment of heresy against himself by manifesting his obstinacy in heresy, thereby separating himself from the Church, ceasing to be a Christian, a member of the Church, and its head; and one who "can and must be deposed by the Church" (*deponendus*). The clear distinction between the two consists in the difference between a pope who "**ceases by himself** to be Pope and head, just as he ceases in himself to be a Christian and member of the body of the Church: **whereby**, he can [then] be judged and punished by the Church" – "***quare*** ab Ecclesia posse eum judicari et puniri" (***per se depositus***), (as Bellarmine explains in Opinion No. 5), and one who "is not ipso facto deposed"; i.e., does not cease by himself to be pope as a direct consequence of his own judgment pronounced against himself; but who remains in office as pope until he is judged, and must be judged by a juridical act of Church authority before he ceases to be pope (***ab ecclesia deponendus***) – in Bellarmine's own words, *sed posse, ac debere deponi ab ecclesia*. Thus, it is patent that according to Bellarmine, what essentially distinguishes Opinion No. 4 from Opinion No. 5 is that according to No. 5, the heretic loses office and ceases to be pope **"by himself"** *("per se")*, **without any external agent (*"sine alia vi externa"*); and therefore,**

"ipso facto", since heretics are condemned by their own self-pronounced judgment upon themselves *(sunt enim proprio judicio condemnati)*⁵⁸⁵, **and for that reason he can then be judged by the Church**, whereas according to Opinion No. 4, **he must be judged by the Church in order to lose office, and he remains in office until he is judged by the Church.** According to this basic distinction which Bellarmine makes between Opinion No. 4 and Opinion No. 5: *all* the variant opinions on this point which require the judgment of the Church as a necessary condition for the loss of office, for the very reason that they require the judgment of the Church in order for the loss of office to take place, fall under the heading of Opinion No. 4. Thus, not only Cajetan, John of St. Thomas, Bordoni, Billuart, Laymann – but *all* others without exception, ***including Suárez***, who hold or who have held this opinion (that the judgment of the Church is required for the loss of office to take place) are of Opinion No. 4. ⁵⁸⁶ "Now in my judgment," says Bellarmine, "such an opinion cannot be defended."

He argues thus: "[T]hat a manifest heretic would be ipso facto deposed" (quod hæreticus manifestus ipso facto sit ***depositus***); and this, he says "is proven from authority and reason." "The Authority," he elaborates, "is of St. Paul, who commands Titus, that after two censures, that is, after he appears manifestly pertinacious, a heretic is to be shunned: and he understands this before excommunication and sentence of a judge," i.e. ***before he is judged***. Thus Bellarmine explains that before the sentence of *excommunicatus vitandus* and even before being judged guilty of the crime, a heretic is to be avoided "after he appears manifestly pertinacious" – but one cannot avoid a pope, because ***one who remains pope cannot be shunned***: "Jerome comments on the

---

⁵⁸⁵ "Yet heretics are outside the Church, even before excommunication, and deprived of all jurisdiction, for they are condemned by their own judgment, as the Apostle teaches to Titus; that is, they are cut from the body of the Church without excommunication, as Jerome expresses it."

⁵⁸⁶ This point is simply lost on Salza and Siscoe, who in all their writings insist that Suárez was of Opinion No. 5 (!), and that Suárez and Bellarmine were of the same opinion on this point. By means of this sophistry they then mendaciously assert that the great theologians of the Counter-Reformation period were of the unanimous opinion that the loss of office does not take place until the pope has been judged by the Church, and that this opinion, even in the more recent centuries after the Counter-Reformation, after Vatican I, and even up to the present era has continuously been the common opinion of theologians!

same place, saying that other sinners, through a judgment of excommunication are excluded from the Church; heretics, however, leave by themselves and are cut from the body of Christ, but a Pope who remains the Pope cannot be shunned. How will we shun our Head? How will we recede from a member to whom we are joined?" Bellarmine provides the solution to the problem in the same sentence, "heretics, however, leave by themselves and are cut from the body of Christ". Therefore, a heretic can be shunned because heretics cease to be members of the Church. "Now in regard to reason this is indeed very certain. A non-Christian cannot in any way be Pope, as Cajetan affirms in the same book, and the reason is because he cannot be the head of that which he is not a member, and he is not a member of the Church who is not a Christian. But a manifest heretic is not a Christian, as St. Cyprian and many other Fathers clearly teach. Therefore, a manifest heretic cannot be Pope." And thus he argues, that it is proven from reason that a manifestly heretical pope is *ipso facto* deposed before judgment or excommunication. A pope who becomes a manifest heretic simply is no longer pope because he has ceased by himself to be pope, so a pope who would be a manifest heretic would not need to be deposed by the Church, because he would already have ceased by himself to be pope and a member of the Church;

ON OPINION NO. FIVE:

A MANIFEST HERETIC POPE CAN BE JUDGED TO HAVE ALREADY FALLEN FROM OFFICE BY HIS ACT OF MANIFEST HERESY (*DEPOSITUS*)

hence: "the fifth true opinion, is that a Pope who is a manifest heretic, ceases by himself to be Pope and head, just as he ceases in himself to be a Christian and member of the body of the Church: whereby, he can be judged and punished by the Church." "This is the opinion," he continues, "of all the ancient Fathers, who teach that manifest heretics straightaway lose all jurisdiction". Thus he concludes, "The foundation of this opinion is that a manifest heretic, is in no way a member of the Church; that is, neither in spirit nor in body, or by internal union nor external."

It is of the most critical importance to bear in mind that from the clear and undeniable context of his words, St. Robert Bellarmine plainly speaks of "manifest heresy" in the most proper sense of the word "manifest", meaning that the heresy is manifest in virtue of the formal heresy being a patent and obvious fact, in a similar manner as as there would be notoriety of fact of a crime in penal law; i.e., by the plainly evident *dolus* of the fact itself, and not notorious in virtue of a judicial or declaratory sentence. This is obvious in view of the simple fact that Bellarmine argues against the pope ever being judged by the bishops or the cardinals, and declares simply that "the pope cannor be judged". If any official judgment at all were to be required for a pope to lose office for 'manifest' or 'notorious' heresy, he could never lose office because he could not be judged for so long as he remains in office. Thus if Opinion No. 5 required a judgment of the Church to precede the loss of office, the loss of office would never be able to take place. Thus, the deposition process of the fifth opinion would never be able to arrive at its conclusion, and woud therefore only reach the same outcome and effectively conclude in the same manner as Opinion No. 3. It is for this reason that Bellarmine says the manifest heretic would cease to be pope ***by himself***, and for which reason he could then be judged and punished by the Church.

Fr. Gleize comments, "The opinion of St. Robert Bellarmine (1542-1621), which is found in *De romano pontifice*, Book 2, chapter 30, and which is followed by Cardinal Billot (1846-1931) (*Traité de l'Église du Christ*, question 14, thesis 29, Part 2, nos. 942-946), is purely theoretical, because his real thesis is that the pope will never fall into heresy. Assuming nevertheless that, per impossibile, the pope happened to fall into public heresy, he would *ipso facto* lose the pontificate." For Billot it is indeed purely theoretical, but for Bellarmine it was not considerd impossible, but only highly improbable. Fr Gleize continues, "As Bellarmine explains clearly, the basis for this thesis is that a notorious heretic as such is no longer a member of the Church. Now, the pope necessarily must be part of the society of which he is the head. This is why the heretical pope, no longer being a member of the Church, ceases to be her visible head." The problem with this explanation is that nowhere does Bellarmine make any mention whatsoever of the term, 'notorious heretic', but he says, "a Pope who is a **manifest heretic**, ceases in himself to be Pope and head, just as he ceases in himself to be a Christian and member of the body of the Church". Fr. Gleize then asks, "As of what moment can one say that the heresy is notorious, in the case of the pope?" And from there, he comments, "At the very most, it could happen that only a few *periti* [experts] in the Church were endowed with the necessary theological intelligence to assess the whole situation; the others (in other words almost the totality of the Church) would not be capable of understanding the whole import of the crisis, even though their virtue of faith sufficed for their personal conduct." This leads him to the conclusion that, "The Church's historic Canon Law (CIC 1917, canons 2264 & 2314) allows, for persons other than the pope, an intermediary situation in which, if the heresy has not been manifested sufficiently, all acts of jurisdiction in the external forum would remain valid albeit illicit. By analogy, a pope who is formally but not yet notoriously heretical could for some time remain at the head of the Church." This is essentially the fatally flawed argument of Billuart, which will be dealt with presently, just as soon as I finish with Fr. Gleize's comments. His entire argument against Bellarmine's position hinges on the use of the word *notorious* (employed by Fr. Gleize according to its strict canonical meaning in penal law) – a word which Bellarmine never used in his argument in favour of Opinion No. 5, and which is quite different in meaning from the word "manifest", which Bellarmine uses, and which conforms to the 1917 Code's definition of "public" rather than "nororious", and therefore any argument attempting to interpret Bellarmine's doctrine based on the question of determining the degree of canonical notoriety required for a pope to fall from office for manifest heresy is logically inapplicable. What suffices for the automatic *ipso jure* loss of office to take place is that the canonical criteria for *public* defection from the Catholic faith be met, i.e. that the formal heresy be public and manifestly evident, but the defection need not be *notorious*. The problem of what, "if the heresy has not been manifested sufficiently", does not arise in the case of *manifest heresy*, because if it has not been manifested sufficiently, it is not **manifest heresy**. However, even if only a few periti were determine that the pope is indeed a formal heretic, that would suffice for loss of office: The Very Rev. H. A.Ayrinhac comments on Canon 2197, of the 1917 code: "Public defection from the faith, by formal heresy or apostasy [...] must be public, that is, generally known **or liable to become so before long**."[587] Since mere *material* heresy is neither pertinacious nor is it necessarily gravely imputable, it does not

---

[587] "A formal act is not required for the defection in canon 194; the only requirement is that it be public (known or likely to become known).[114] Neither is it required that the officeholder join another religion, although this could be an objective indication of defection. [[114] Socha, in *Münster Com, 194/2—3;* Urrutia, n. 925, confuses this with "notorious".]" – (John P. Beal, New Commentary on the Code of Canon Law pp. 226-7)

suffice to effect a tacit renunciation or removal due to defection from the faith, since it is precisely because the material heretic who does not formally defect from the Church retains the formal cause of faith, and thus still has the Catholic faith, and therefore material heresy cannot be said to constitute a defection from the faith. Hence, public defection from the faith can only be considered to have taken place if the matter of heresy, and its pertinacity, which is the *form* of heresy, are manifest. For the formal heresy to be manifest, it must only be *public*, but not *notorious*. Therefore, it would first be necessary that the conditions for an *act* to be considered *public* be fulfilled, as set forth in Canon 2197 1° of the 1917 Code; but for the act to be *public*, it would not be necessary for those conditions to be present which would be required for the heresy to be deemed **notorious** by *notoriety of fact*, as enumerated in 2197 3°. Regarding the publicity of the *pertinacity* of the act, the pertinacity would need to be *public* as stated in no. 1 of the canon; but additionally, for the *pertinacity* to be public, it would also be necessary that it fulfill the conditions for *notoriety of fact*, regarding the *imputability* of the act set forth in no. 3 of the same Canon: "*3° Notorium notorietate facti, si... in talibus adiunctis commissum, ut nulla tergiversatione celari nulloque iuris suffragio excusari possit*". Thus, as the above quoted commentary of the Pontifical Canon Law Faculty of Salamanca explains, it would need to have been committed under such circumstances that by no subterfuge can it be concealed, nor by any understanding of the law can it be excused.[588] The same commentary on page 785, in its fairly lengthy comment on the canon under consideration, explains the sense in which the act must be publicly known, in essentially the same, but in a more detailed and precise manner, as Ayrinhac and Beal explain it; namely, that it must be "generally known *or liable to become so before long*" (Ayrinhac); or "known or *likely to become known*" (Beal).

The case of Pedro de Luna sufficiently settles the question. Hence, the problem that, "it could happen that only a few *periti* [experts] in the Church were endowed with the necessary theological intelligence to assess the whole situation", while, "the others (in other words almost the totality of the Church) would not be capable of understanding the whole import of the crisis", would in reality not be a problem at all. The fact that the vast majority of Catholics, being uneducated, were unaware of

---

[588] "Para que haya *notoriedad de hecho* se requiren dos condiciones: *a)* ... *b)* **que haya sido cometido en las circumstancias que indica el canon**." Miguelez – Alonso – Cabreros; *Op. cit.* p. 785.

and possibly would not have grasped the fact that de Luna's pronouncement was not only *wrong*, but in fact constituted an objective and manifestly heretical act of public defection from the faith, had no bearing whatsoever on the ruling of the Council, which declared that he had already lost all office and all ecclesiastical dignity *ipso jure* for his formal act of manifest heresy and schism even before the Council ruled on the case. That ruling was the basis of Bellarmine's and Ballerini's doctrine on loss of office for manifest heresy, which eventually became enshrined in the Codes of Canon Law of the Church regarding loss of ecclesiastical office for public defection from the faith.

COMMENTARY

It is manifestly evident that in the clearly stated context where he speaks of warnings, that Bellarmine is not stating or implying that there is any need for *canonical admonitions* for a pope to lose office. It was the exponents of Opinion No. 4 who maintained that canonical admonitions are necessary for a pope to be deposed for heresy. Canonical admonitions are proper only to a superior, and are administered by a superior as the initial phase of a penal process[ii]. Bellarmine qualifies the sense of the term as he means it to be understood with the words, "that after two censures, that is, **after he appears manifestly pertinacious**", thereby making it clear that the warnings are not part of a juridical procedure, but only serve the purpose of fraternal correction in order to determine whether or not the pope in question **"ceases by himself to be pope"** by his heresy, **ipso facto**, and not by the ministerial instrumentality of any judgment at the conclusion of an official procedure, whereby the Church authorities would render a judgment on the supreme judge and ruler, and as a consequence of which the heretic Pontiff would only then fall from the Pontificate upon such judgment passed on him by his subjects and inferiors. Ballerini, a follower of Bellarmine's opinion, understood perfectly that Bellarmine was not speaking of *canonical admonitions* being necessary in this context when he commented (in the above cited passage), "In such a crisis for the faith, cannot even **inferiors** warn their superior by **fraternal correction** [?]"; and, "For any person, even a private person, the words of Saint Paul to Titus hold" – and he demonstrates that he understood well that Bellarmine's reason for the Pontiff's subjects to administer the warnings would not be an official act of ecclesiastical authority, but "a duty of charity and not of jurisdiction", for the purpose only of discerning whether or not there is pertinacity, in order to determine whether or not the individual in question is properly a heretic who has fallen from the Pontificate: "having been once or twice corrected, does not repent, but remains obstinate in a belief contrary to a manifest or defined dogma; by this his public pertinacity which for no reason can be excused, since pertinacity properly pertains to heresy, he declares himself to be a heretic".

Since Bellarmine speaks properly of an *ipso facto* **loss of office, which is essentially a tacit renunciation of office** due to **defection from the faith into heresy**, the warnings are not strictly necessary as they normally would be in a *penal* canonical process of *deprivation of office*[589], by which ecclesiastical authority establishes the fact of pertinacity and *inflicts the penalty*, but are only of a relative and practical necessity to determine whether the Pontiff has only erred in ignorance or negligence without pertinacity, *or if he has obstinately and consciously hardened in heresy, thereby ceasing by himself to be pope.* (papam hæreticum manifestum *per se desinere esse papam*) Thus, in such a case when the heresy of a pope is expressed in such a manner that the pertinacity is manifested *sponte sua* (as was the case of Pedro de Luna "Benedict XIII"[590]) against a manifestly evident dogma,

---

[589] Canonical admonitions are not always necessary: *"Neither is it always demanded in the external forum that there be a warning and a reprimand as described above for somebody to be punished as heretical and pertinacious, and such a requirement is by no means always admitted in practice by the Holy Office" (De Lugo, disp. XX, sect. IV, n. 157-158.* De Lugo elaborates further in his continuation of the passage: *"For if it could be established in some other way, given that the doctrine is well known, given the kind of person involved and given the other circumstances, that the accused could not have been unaware that his thesis was opposed to the Church, he would be considered as a heretic from this fact [...] The reason for this is clear because the exterior warning can serve only to ensure that someone who has erred understands the opposition which exists between his error and the teaching of the Church. If he knew the subject through books and conciliar definitions much better than he could know it by the declarations of someone admonishing him then there would be no reason to insist on a further warning for him to become pertinacious against the Church."*

[590] "Now such harassment she, the Church received from Benedict, who obstinately with the fact attacked the article unam, sancatm? He fulminated these most terrible anathemas against the Council, and against adherents to other Pontiffs, and made the more precipitous attacks in order to keep himself on the illegitimately occupied throne; claiming that the Church of Jesus Christ

or a defined dogma, explicitly professed by all Christians; and especially if it be one of the principal dogmas, known even to the most ignorant Catholics, or known to all men as a matter of Natural Law, then it is patent that in such a case, no warnings would be necessary, being that warnings would be superfluous under those given circumstances; and therefore, the fall from office for manifest heresy would be plainly evident as a ***judgment against himself***, as Bellarmine argues in his refutation of Opinion No. 4, and therefore would be a ***tacit renunciation of office***. This is exactly how Ballerini, a follower of Bellarmine's Fifth Opinion, understood this opinion: that the Pope, "in some manner" would "have abdicated the Pontificate".

Now it might be argued that such a loss of office is a matter of law, and that the provisions for tacit renunciation set forth in the 1917 Code of Canon Law are not found in the New Code of 1983; however, the provisions for loss of office due to defection from the faith, which is in its very nature, a tacit but real renunciation; which is to say, not merely implicit, and not a penalty, remain in the 1983 Code in the third section on **Loss of Office** under **Removal**, which the Code explicitly distinguishes from the penalty of **Privation of Office**, dealt with in the fourth section.[591] Loss of office takes place by, 1) Renunciation, 2) Transfer, 3) Removal, and 4) Privation. The Code is explicit: Only loss of office by privation is a penalty[592], and is dealt with separately in the section of the Code that deals with penal law, whereas the first three sections on loss of office, under which is included *Removal*, are set forth in the second chapter (On the Loss of Ecclesiastical Office) of Title IX

---

to have perished in all other parts of the world, and that it was restricted only in Paniscola, as he said to the legates of the Council: 'That is not a Church, but in Paniscola, I say, is the true Church… This is Noah's Ark'. So then be could be considered, as noted by Ballerini, to have been a public schismatic and heretic, and consequently to have fallen from papacy by himself, even if he had been validly elevated to it." (Gregorio XVI: *Il trionfo della santa sede e della chiesa contro gli assatti dei novatori*, p. 47)

[591] **Can. 192** — Ab officio quis amovetur sive decreto ab auctoritate competenti legitime edito, servatis quidem iuribus forte ex contractu quaesitis, sive ipso iure ad normam can. 194

Can. 194 — § 1. Ipso iure ab ecclesiastico amovetur: 2° qui a fide catholica aut a communione Ecclesiae publice defecerit;

[592] **Can. 196** — § 1. Privatio ab officio, in poenam scilicet delicti, ad normam iuris tantummodo fieri potest. § 2. Privatio effectum sortitur secundum praescripta canonum de iure poenali.

on ecclesiastical offices (De Officiis Ecclesiasticis). Nevertheless, Salza and Siscoe adamantly continue to maintain that loss of office by tacit renunciation (*amotione*) is a "severe vindictive penalty" which must be inflicted *sententia ferenda*.[593] However, not only is the Code explicit on this point, but it is manifestly patent in the very nature of the acts that result in "removal", that such loss of office is not of the nature of a penalty – acts such as attempting to marry, losing the clerical state, and defection from the faith or from communion with the Church, are intrinsically incompatible with the essential requirements for holding of ecclesiastical office, which can only be validly held by a **Catholic cleric in major orders**, and therefore, for such acts which are incompatible with the clerical state, the law statutes a removal from office, which is not penal in nature. Thus it is, as is patently clear from the wording of the canon, that the loss of ecclesiastical office takes place *ipso facto*, by the very act of defection into heresy, and does not require that a judgment be pronounced by Church authority as Salza and Siscoe claim[594]. Removal from office by means of loss of office due to tacit renunciation applies to all offices, including the papacy: The Very Rev. H. A. Ayrinhac taught, in his General Legislation in the New Code of Canon Law, on *Loss of Ecclesiastical Offices,* that such loss of office (Canons 185-191) "applies to all offices, the lowest and the highest, not excepting the Supreme Pontificate." (p. 346)

Elsewhere I explained (to Salza/Siscoe cheerleader Paul Folbrecht), «As I have documented […], Salza & Siscoe have desperately argued against these magisterial teachings of the

---

[593] "The sin of heresy alone, which has not been judged and declared by the Church, does not result in the loss of ecclesiastical office for a cleric. The loss of office for a cleric is a vindictive penalty, and there is a process in Church law which must precede vindictive penalties" (TOFP p. 260)

[594] Salza and Siscoe deceptively interpret Section 2 of Canon 194 (§ 2. Amotio, de qua in nn. 2 et 3, urgeri tantum potest, si de eadem auctoritatis competentis declaratione constet.), to make it appear that the loss of office does not take place until it has been declared by the competent ecclesiastical authority. The canon states explicitly (§ 1) that the loss of office takes place by the operation of the law itself (*ipso jure*), and therefore **automatically**; and § 2 states that the loss of office, which as a fact took place *ipso jure*, "can be enforced only if it is established by the declaration of a competent authority." Thus, § 2 only specifies that the *post factum* **enforcement** of the loss of office (that has already taken place *ipso jure*) can only be carried out after having been confirmed by declaration of Church authority.

Church, *de fidei* and *proxima fidei, blindly* adhering to the positions of John of St. Thomas, which 1) clearly oppose the teaching of Pius XII in *Mystici Corporis*; and, 2) oppose the teaching enshrined in the Codes of Canon Law (1917 & 1983). The unequivocally clear Canon 194 states tersely, "*Can. 194 — § 1. Ipso iure ab officio ecclesiastico amovetur: [...] 2° qui a fide catholica aut a communione Ecclesiæ publice defecerit*". Thus, one who publicly defects from the faith *is removed "ipso jure".* The loss of office happens by itself, AUTOMATICALLY, i.e. *"ipso jure"*, in exactly the manner set forth by Sess. 37 of the Council of Constance in the case of Pedro de Luna: *The defector immediately ceases to hold office, "by the law itself".* "*Can. 194 — § 2. Amotio, de qua in nn. 2 et 3, urgeri tantum potest, si de eadem auctoritatis competentis declaratione constet.*" ("§2. The removal mentioned in nn. 2 and 3 can be enforced only if it is established by the declaration of a competent authority.") The actual FACT of the loss of office takes place by itself – *automatically*, "BY THE LAW ITSELF", as the canon states, i.e. before any judgment is pronounced. Its juridical *enforcement* only takes place upon an *official declaration* by competent authority. *This is in total conformity with the ruling of the Council of Constance.*

Salza & Siscoe then deftly alter the clear meaning of the canon by quoting a commentary revised by the *Conciliar* canonist, Beal[595], which explains *not according to the teaching of the Church and the letter of the law,* according to which the *fact of the loss of office* does not depend on the authority's declaration; but incorrectly *alters that meaning* by stating nonsensically, "*the fact on which the loss of office is based* does not depend on the authority's declaration"; and "the officeholder remains in office", *even after he has lost office ipso jure* (!), "until the declaration or removal has been communicated to the officeholder in writing."[596] On the basis of this twisted interpretation of Canon 194, Salza 7 Siscoe elaborate: "Thus, according to the Code currently in effect, the removal from office must be established by a declaration from the competent authorities. The declaration makes the loss *effective.* It is similar to the loss of office, *by law,* for a bishop who reaches the age of seventy-five. He retains the office until the resignation is accepted. For a cleric who *publicly defects from the*

---

[595] Beal, John; Coriden, James; Green, Thomas, *A New Commentary on the Code of Canon Law* (New York: Paulist Press, 2000), p. 227.

[596] True or False Pope: Canon 194: http://www.trueorfalsepope.com/p/canon-194.html?m=1.

faith, he will remain in office and all of the acts of his office will remain valid, until the Church declares him removed."[597]

No! The blatant fraud of these statements is plainly manifested in their silliness and absurdity: How can an officeholder "remain in office" if he has already lost his office *ipso jure*? Indeed, a bishop who resigns retains his office until his resignation is accepted; but a cleric who has lost his office *ipso jure* has already *ceased to occupy the office*, and therefore he cannot at the same continue to occupy the office until the Church declares him removed. The statement is patently contradictory, and therefore absurd. Likewise, to say that "the *fact* on which the loss of office is based does not depend on the authority's declaration", is the same as saying, "The fact of the defection, on which loss of office is based, does not depend on the authority's declaration" – thereby falsely and deceptively implying that the actual *ipso jure* loss of office does depend on the authority's declaration. This is plainly fraudulent, because the canon clearly states that the loss of office itself, (and not the fact on which it was based), being an *ipso jure* loss of office, does not depend on any declaration of ecclesiastical authority. As I stated earlier, the text of the canon is plainly clear and unambiguous. Its meaning is luminously unequivocal, and is straightforwardly explained in the earlier quoted commentary of the Canon Law faculty of Navarre: "In the 2nd and 3rd cases, the act of the ecclesiastical authority is declarative, and it is necessary, not to provoke the vacating of the right of the office, but so that the removal can legally be demanded (also for the purposes of 1381 § 2), and consequently the conferral of the office to a new officeholder can be carried out (cfr. C. 154)."[598] The officeholder does not actually remain in office after the *ipso jure* loss of office and all *ordinary jurisdiction*; but, *in accordance with the canonical tradition of the Church, g*oing back to *Ad evitanda scandala* of Martin V (1418), *even after the ipso jure loss of office, he exercises supplied jurisdiction until the juridical declaration has been communicated. So it is that Salza & Siscoe, assisted by the Conciliar commentary on Canon Law, which they say is "highly acclaimed", but which is actually thoroughly contaminated with Conciliar-Modernist taint (as Fr. Gruner and I noticed years ago), alter the authentic meaning of the canon on loss of office.*

Furthermore, as Bellarmine demonstrates from the teaching of the Fathers in his exposition on Opinion No. 4, loss of office due to heresy

---

[597] *True or False Pope?*, p. 288.
[598] UNIVERSIDAD DE NAVARRA, FACULTAD DE DERECHO CANÓNICO; *Op. cit., p. 176.*

and schism is ultimately not a question of law: it is not the effect of any human law but, "Patres illi", Bellarmine explains, "cum dicunt hæreticos ammitere jurisdictionem, non allegant ulla jura humana, quæ etiam forte tunc nulla extabant de hac re, sed argumentantur *ex natura hæresis*."[599] In a desperate and futile attempt to refute the argument of Bellarmine on this point, [which they do not attribute to Bellarmine, but to the Sedevacantists], Salza & Siscoe adduce the argument of Billuart, based on the ruling of Martin V in 1418 during the Council of Constance. (*Ad evitanda scandala*) On this point, Bellarmine makes the very telling observation in the continuation of the just cited passage: "Moreover, the Council of Constance does not speak except on the **excommunicates**, that is, **on these who lose jurisdiction through a judgment of the Church**." In the previous sentence, Bellarmine established the unanimity of the Fathers, quoting an impressive array of Fathers, saying, "the Holy Fathers teach in unison, that not only are heretics outside the Church, but they even lack all Ecclesiastical jurisdiction and dignity ipso facto."

Salza and Siscoe quote Billuart[600] (who quotes Martin V's *Ad evitanda scandala*) in a futile attempt to refute Bellarmine and the unanimous teaching of the Fathers:

I say that manifest heretics, unless they are denounced by name, or themselves depart from the Church, retain their jurisdiction and validly absolve. This is proved by the Bull of Martin V, Ad evitanda scandala, [which reads thus]:

> "To avoid the scandals and the many perils that can befall timorous consciences, we mercifully grant to the faithful of Christ, by the force of this decree (tenore praesentium), that henceforth no one will be obliged, under the pretext of any sentence or ecclesiastical censure generally promulgated by law or by man, to avoid the communion of any person, in the administration or reception of the Sacraments, or in any other matters sacred or profane, or to eschew the person, or to observe any ecclesiastical interdict, unless a sentence or censure of this kind shall have been published by a judge, and denounced specially and expressly, whether against a person,

---

[599] "For those Fathers, when they say that heretics lose jurisdiction, do not allege any human laws which maybe did not exist then on this matter; rather, they argued from the nature of heresy."

[600] True or False Pope: Summa S. Thomae of Charles Rene Billuart, O.P. – http://www.trueorfalsepope.com/p/thefollowing-excerpt-from-charles-rene.html?m=1

or a college, or university, or church, or a certain place or territory. Neither the Apostolic Constitutions, nor any other laws remain in force to the contrary."

Then [the Bull] lists, as the only exception, those who are notorious for having inflicted violence on the clergy. From these lines, we argue that the Church is granting permission to the faithful to receive the sacraments from heretics who have not yet been expressly denounced by name; and, therefore, that she allows the latter to **retain their jurisdiction** for the valid administration of the sacraments, since otherwise the concession granted to the faithful would mean nothing.

Our argument is confirmed by the current praxis of the entire Church; for no one today... avoids his pastor, even for the reception of the sacraments, as long as he is allowed to remain in his benefice, even if the man is, in the judgment of all or at least of the majority, a manifest Jansenist, and rebellious against the definitions of the Church; and so on with the rest.

Billuart's error consists in his failure to make a critical distinction between those who lose their jurisdiction as a result of excommunication, and those who lose it *ex natura hæresis*, as a consequence of defecting from the faith and the Church, and thereby losing office and jurisdiction. Bellarmine points out that the decree only applies to excommunicates. Conlon, in the earlier cited article, observes: «As was previously noted Pope Martin V's Constitution "Ad Evitanda Scandala" of 1418 introduced the distinction between the tolerati and vitandi. Though it may sound redundant, these laws regarding **excommunicates**, applies to all **excommunicates, even heretics**. This is self-evident from the fact that the Church made no exceptions in regard to heretics when promulgating these laws concerning communication with excommunicates.» He quotes Suárez, «This new law established by the Council of Constance also extends to heretics and the words of Extrav.[Ad evitanda] prove this, which are both general and add an exception to confirm the rule towards everybody else.»[601] He then makes the very crucial point that the heretics to be considered *vitandi* must be **excommunicates**, and have been **declared** such: «Cardinal De Lugo, another eminent Catholic theologian, also affirms that *the strict obligation to avoid a heretic depends on whether the Church has declared*

---

[601] Suarez, Francisco, S.J. De Fide: Disputatio XXI, Sectio 3.1621

them, by name, as an **excommunicate** *that is to be avoided.*»[602] He quotes *The Irish Ecclesiastical Record* of 1886:

> «...according to the unanimous teaching of theologians the Constitution Ad evitanda includes heretics (excipiendis exceptis) equally with all other excommunicates in its provisions of toleration, so that, ex vi illius Constitutionis, as full communication with all heretics in quibuscumque divinis as with the rest of the excommunicates is granted to the faithful. Theologians make practically no distinction whatever on this point. (Livius, p.38)»

Conlon then quotes De Lugo again, mentioning the extremely important point that under certain circumstances, sacraments may be received from such excommunicates, even heretics: «Cardinal De Lugo further teaches, in the same previously mentioned work of his, that communication with undeclared heretics is, in certain cases, also permitted in sacred matters».[603]

The reason why Billuart's failure to distinguish between those who lose their jurisdiction as a result of excommunication, and those who lose it *ex natura hæresis*, is of such great consequence, is that the ordinary and habitual jurisdiction of the officeholder is lost upon loss of office due to tacit resignation; but the excommunicates were provided with supplied jurisdiction in virtue of *Ad evitanda scandala*, and by the

---

[602] "The first opinion teaches, as often as it is evident that someone is a heretic, the very fact makes communication with him forbidden. Thus, Soto 4. Dist.25. Quast.1 art.1 & 3. & dist. 20. Quast.1. art.5. conclus. 2. The common opinion, however, denies this, in as much as they are not legally declared a heretic, & denounced; because the Council of Constance granted all the faithful in general, as to permit communication with all the excommunicated, except those denounced by name, & those notorious for striking a cleric, with no given exception of heretics: therefore, there is no reason by which that permission does not extend to communicate with them [heretics]. Thus teach Toetus, Ugolinus, Suarez, Azor, & others, whom I have reported, & followed by Thomas Sanchez lib.2. in Decal. cap.9. n. 3 Hurtado in prasenti, disp.76&4. & others in common, which I've always embraced in other places." (De Lugo, *Tractatus de Virtute Fidei Divinae*: Disputatio XXII, Sectio.1. 1646)

[603] "So as these heretics are not declared excommunicates or notoriously guilty of striking a cleric, there is no reason why we should be prevented from receiving the sacraments from them because of their excommunication, although on other grounds this may often be illicit unless necessity excuse as I have explained in the said places." (*Tractatus de Virtute Fidei Divinae*: *Disputatio* XXII, *Sectio*.1. 1646)

subsequent legislation that later replaced its provisions. In the *Catholic Encyclopedia*, it is explained:

> «We may now proceed to enumerate the immediate effects of excommunication. They are summed up in the two well known verses: *Res sacræ, ritus, communio, crypta, potestas, prædia sacra, forum, civilia jura vetantur*, i.e. loss of the sacraments, public services and prayers of the Church, ecclesiastical burial, jurisdiction, benefices, canonical rights, and social intercourse. *Potestas* signifies ecclesiastical jurisdiction...»

The *Encyclopedia* then explains why the habitual and ordinary faculties and jurisdiction that are lost by *excommunicati tolerati* are replaced with *supplied jurisdiction and faculties* in virtue of the law itself:

> «It is easy to understand that the Church cannot leave her jurisdiction in the hands of those whom she excludes from her society. In principle, therefore, excommunication entails the loss of jurisdiction both in *foro externo* and in *foro interno* and renders null all acts accomplished without the necessary jurisdiction. However, for the general good of society, the Church maintains jurisdiction, despite occult excommunication, and supplies it for acts performed by the *tolerati*. But as the *vitandi* are known to be such, this merciful remedy cannot be applied to them except in certain cases of extreme necessity, when jurisdiction is said to be "supplied" by the Church.»

Thus, Billuart erroneously deduced that "heretics *retain their jurisdiction*", whereas all jurisdiction is lost by heretics, *ex natura hæresis*; but since heretics incur excommunication *latæ sententiæ*, jurisdiction was supplied by the decree *Ad evitanda scandala*.

Billuart's failure to distinguish between **retaining jurisdiction** and **receiving supplied jurisdiction** in virtue of the law itself led him into error on the question of loss of jurisdiction of a heretic pope. Salza and Siscoe quote Billuart further:

> "the law and praxis of the Church require that a heretic be denounced before he loses his jurisdiction, not for his own benefit, but for the benefit and tranquility of the faithful. But the Church does not require a denunciation for someone to be considered a public sinner, or to be repelled from Communion, because the welfare and tranquility of the faithful do not require that. Also, it is not the business of the faithful to pass judgment on the jurisdiction of their ministers, and often it is impossible for them to do so; but this pertains to the superiors who grant the ministers their

jurisdiction. It pertains to the ministers, however, to pass judgment on those who receive the sacraments. ..."

And,

"The pope... does not have his jurisdiction from the Church, but from Christ. Nowhere has it been declared that Christ would continue to give jurisdiction to a manifestly heretical Pope, since his heresy could become known to the Church, and the Church could provide another pastor for herself. Nevertheless, the more common opinion (sententia communior)[604] holds that Christ, by a special dispensation, for the common good and tranquility of the Church, will continue to give jurisdiction even to a manifestly heretical pope, until he has been declared a manifest heretic by the Church."

Billuart's argues that since heretics retain jurisdiction "for the benefit and tranquility of the faithful", therefore similarly, "Christ, by a special dispensation, for the common good and tranquility of the Church, will continue to give jurisdiction even to a manifestly heretical pope, until he has been declared a manifest heretic by the Church." Bellarmine's words crush Billuart's thesis: "I say this avails to nothing. For those Fathers, when they say that heretics lose jurisdiction, do not allege any human laws which maybe did not exist then on this matter; rather, they argued **from the nature of heresy**." Hence, there can be no exception by way of a "special dispensation" from a loss of jurisdiction that results from the very nature of heresy. Heretics do not retain their jurisdiction: Jurisdiction is supplied to *latæ sententiæ* excommunicated heretics who not only lose all habitual jurisdiction, by their excommunication, but lose it *ex natura hæresis*. Billuart correctly notes that "The pope... does not have his jurisdiction from the Church, but from Christ", but the pope would cease to be a member of the Church and lose all jurisdiction from Christ if he fell into manifest heresy; and since the pope cannot incur excommunication for so long as he remains pope, he could not receive supplied jurisdiction from such legislation as *Ad evitanda scandala* unless he were to fall from the Pontificate by tacit renunciation of office. Only then would he become *minor quolibet catholico* and accordingly incur excommunication *latæ sententiæ*, and straightaway receive supplied jurisdiction until his loss of office could be enforced by a declaratory sentence – but he would already have ceased to be pope.

---

[604] It was the *sententia communior* in Billuart's day, but is no longer.

So, what has been Salza's response to my critical analysis of St. Robert Bellarmine's doctrine concerning the deposition of a heretical pope?

John F. Salza declares:

"There are so many errors, omissions and question-begging in this analysis," Salza begins, "it is difficult to believe that Fr. Kramer has done any real study of St. Bellarmine." ... "Fr. Kramer advances the Sedevacantist interpretation of Bellarmine to a tee: a manifest heretic falls from office, and this determination is made by private judgment, without the judgment of the Church." ... "Fr. Kramer is an amateur. He fails to read the Fifth Opinion in light of Bellarmine's rejection of the Second Opinion" ... "Fr. Kramer has simply vomited up the same old arguments of the Sedevacantists, that a manifest heretic is no longer Pope" ... "Fr. Kramer," Salza continues, "clearly does not understand the deeper, theological nuances of dispositive and efficient cause as regards a heretical Pope, addressed by John of St. Thomas, who affirms the opinion of both the Dominicans and the Jesuits that the Church is the dispositive cause of the loss of office, and Christ the efficient cause." Salza concludes: "Fr. Kramer's analysis is one of the more shallow and superficial interpretations of Bellarmine that we have seen".[605]

SALZA & SISCOE ON THE FIVE OPINIONS

In their oversized screed, Salza & Siscoe explain, "The well-read Brazilian scholar Arnaldo Xavier da Silveira, in his book 'La Nouvelle Messe de Paul VI: Qu'en penser,' and Fr. Dominique Boulet, of the Society of St. Pius X, categorized various authors according to the five opinions laid out by Bellarmine."[606] The reason why they limit themselves to these two authors, and leave out the eminent theologian/canonists I have quoted will become apparent presently. The tax lawyer and his businessman sidekick then continue:

«The Five Opinions, and the categorization of those holding the various opinions by these two authors, are as follows:

---

[605] Message to Five Recipients, 8 September 2016, 13:42.
[606] *True or False Pope?*, p. 268

- First Opinion: The Pope can never fall into heresy (e.g., Bellarmine, Billot).
- Second Opinion: The Pope loses his office ipso facto for occult heresy (e.g., Torquemada). This opinion "has been completely abandoned by the theologians."
- Third Opinion: The Pope never loses his office for manifest heresy (Bouix).
- Fourth Opinion: "The manifestly heretical Pope is not ipso facto deposed, but can and must be deposed by the Church." (e.g., Cajetan, Suarez91)
- Fifth Opinion: "The Pope who is manifestly a heretic ceases by himself to be Pope and head... and for this reason he can be judged and punished by the Church." (e.g., Bellarmine, Billot).»

Concerning the First Opinion, one notices on their list the conspicuous absence of the names of eminent theologians who held that opinion: Francisco Suárez, Melchior Cano, Domingo Soto, John of St. Thomas, Juan de Torquemada, Joachim Salaverri, A. Maria Vellico, Charles Journet, and Cajetan. This is no accident. Salza & Siscoe want their readers to think that Opinion No. One is held only by a miniscule minority of theologians; because they fraudulently claim that the contrary opinion, namely, that a pope can become a formal heretic, is the *common opinion*. As has been proven above, the *opinio communissima* is the contrary opinion to theirs, i.e. the First Opinion. In their faulty analysis of Bellarmine's exposition on the Second Opinion, Salza & Siscoe conclude with a *non sequitur* that Bellarmine's doctrine holds that even a manifest heretic pope would not lose office unless he is first judged by the Church. As I have demonstrated, Bellarmine says nothing of the kind, but only that an occult heretic pope would first have to be convicted of heresy before losing office; and that the opposite is true regarding a manifest heretic, who would automatically cease by himself to be pope *ipso facto*, without first being judged. Their characterization of the Third Opinion, "The Pope never loses his office for manifest heresy (Bouix)", is worded in such a manner that it leaves out the critical distinction made by Bellarmine, Ballerini, and Billot: that of *depositus* and *deponendus*. In his description of the Third Opinion, Bellarmine (as does Ballerini) makes that crucial distinction: "The third opinion is on another extreme, that the Pope is not deposed (*esse depositum*) and cannot be deposed (*deponi posse*) either by secret or manifest heresy." Salza & Siscoe leave this distinction out because they will falsely explain that according to Bellarmine, a manifestly heretical pope is not deposed *ipso facto* but must be judged by the Church; but in his refutation of the Fourth Opinion, Bellarmine argues against the thesis that "a manifestly heretical pope is not ipso facto *depositus*, but can and must be deposed by the Church"[607], because, it is his teaching (quoted above) that "the pope cannot be judged", and therefore, he argues that the pope may not be deposed by the bishops or the cardinals. They quote Bellarmine, who says, "Firstly, because, that a heretical Pope can be judged is expressly held in the Canon, Si Papa, dist. 40, and with Innocent." However, by leaving out the critical distinction between *depositus* and *deponendus*, they facilitate their own fraudulent interpretation of Bellarmine, saying that contrary to what they stupidly claim is the "sedevacantist interpretation" of Bellarmine: "the Doctor explicitly rejects the Sedevacantist thesis by teaching that heretical bishops must be deposed by the Church", and, "Bellarmine himself defended the opinion that a heretical Pope can be judged by a council, which eviscerates the Sedevacantist argument altogether, and further proves they have not understood Bellarmine's position." Indeed, Bellarmine held correctly that the penal deprivation from office, i.e. deposition of a bishop (or any cleric), can only be done by *ecclesiastical superiors*, and therefore he argued that neither the bishops nor the cardinals had the power to judge and depose a pope; but that *loss of office* takes place *ipso facto* for heresy, and not by any human law, but *ex natura hæresis*. So it is clear that Salza & Siscoe left out all mention of that distinction precisely in order to obscure the qualified sense according to which Bellarmine says, "that a heretical Pope can be judged", while upholding the principle of the absolute injudicability of the pope; and thus he explains in his exposition of the Fourth and Fifth Opinion, that the bishops cannot judge and depose a pope because, "for one to be deposed from the pontificate against his will is without a doubt a penalty; therefore, the Church deposing a Pope against his will, without a doubt punishes him; but to punish is for a superior and a judge"; and the cardinals cannot depose a pope, because, "when Cardinals create the Pontiff, they exercise their authority not over the Pontiff, because he does not yet exist; but over the matter, that is, over the person whom they dispose in a certain measure through election, that he might receive the form of the pontificate from God; but if they depose the Pope, they

---

[607] «Papam haæreticum manifestum, non esse ipso facto depositum: sed posse, ac debere deponi ab Ecclesia»

necessarily exercise authority over the composite, that is, over the person provided with pontifical dignity, which is to say, over the Pontiff." He then concludes that since it is precisely for the reason that the pope cannot be judged by the bishops or the cardinals that a pope cannot be deposed (*deponi posse*) by the Church; that "therefore", the Fifth Opinion is the true opinion: *"Est ergo opinio quinta vera"*— and according to that opinion, the manifest heretic "ceases *by himself* to be Pope and head, just as he ceases *by himself* to be a Christian and member of the body of the Church: for which reason, he can be judged and punished by the Church."

Their explanation of Bellarmine's Fourth Opinion, that, "The manifestly heretical Pope is not ipso facto deposed, but can and must be deposed by the Church", is expressed in such a manner that it can only be interpreted to mean that a manifestly heretical pope can and must be juridically deposed for heresy, but not that he can be deposed by the Church in such a manner that he would immediately fall from office *ipso facto* upon his having been juridically judged by the Church for the crime of heresy; because according to them, this latter opinion would be the Fifth Opinion! However, Bellarmine, in his refutation of the Fourth Opinion categorically excludes that a pope can be deposed by the bishops or the cardinals, because deposition is for a superior or judge. Thus accordingly, he explains, "For, if the Church deposes a Pope against his will, certainly it is over the Pope." [608] And having explained in *lib. iv. cap. vii* that, "the pope cannot be judged", he explains in *lib. ii cap. xxx* that "the Church deposing a Pope against his will, without a doubt punishes him; but to punish is for a superior and a judge."[609] Therefore what Salza & Siscoe claim is Bellarmine's Fifth Opinion cannot be understood to be the "fifth and true opinion" of Bellarmine, but is in fact the Fourth Opinion which he rejects. Hence, the more accurate description of the Fourth Opinion is that given by the eminent canonist/theologians of the Pontifical Gregorian University I quoted earlier: 1) Wernz-Vidal: «The fourth opinion, with Suarez, Cajetan and others, contends that a Pope is not automatically deposed even for manifest heresy, but that he can and must be deposed by at least a declaratory sentence of the crime, "Which opinion in my judgment is indefensible" as Bellarmine teaches.» Likewise, 2) Moynihan: «Those in

---

[608] «Nam si Ecclesia invitum Papam deponit, certe est supra Papam.»

[609] «Ecclesia invitum Papam deponens, sine dubio ipsum punit; at punier est superioris et judicis.»

favor of the fourth opinion say that should a pope publicly profess a heretical doctrine he would not be automatically deposed, but his deposition could be brought about by a declaratory sentence.» What these eminent scholars are pointing out is that the Fourth Opinion requires the judgment of the Church for the manifest heretic pope to fall from office, as opposed to the Fifth Opinion, according to which the manifest heretic pope would fall from office automatically, without the judgment of the Church: «a Pope who fell into public heresy would cease by that very fact to be a member of the Church [...] it must be firmly stated that a heretical Roman Pontiff would by that very fact forfeit his power. Although a declaratory sentence of the crime which is not to be rejected in so far as it is merely declaratory would be such, that the heretical Pope would not be judged, but would rather be shown to have been judged.» (Wernz-Vidal). And Moynihan:

> «The fifth and last opinion Wernz-Vidal regard as *communior*. According to this view, a pope notoriously preaching a heretical doctrine would be automatically excommunicated and deprived of the papacy. The principal argument for this last opinion is based upon the fact that a pope who by his heresy is no longer a member of the Church, is *a fortiori* no longer the Head of the Church. Hence this opinion would admit of a declaratory sentence, but it would have to be one that was merely declaratory and nothing more."»

Incredibly, in their Fairyland interpretation of the Fourth and Fifth Opinions, the amateur armchair theologians, Salza & Siscoe, judge that the eminent scholars of the pontifical universities are wrong. The two pompous comedians declare, "We note that the treatises of all four theologians are highly complex. It is therefore understandable that Suarez could have mistakenly been included as holding the Fourth Opinion. In fact, **Wernz-Vidal also mistakenly placed Suarez in the same camp as Cajetan**."[610] (!) Da Silveria and Boulet simply follow the sound and unanimous interpretations of the eminent theologian/canonists, as Salza & Siscoe note, «Silveira and Boulet presumably include Suarez as holding the Fourth Opinion because Suárez says: "I affirm: if he were a heretic and incorrigible, **the Pope would cease to be Pope just when a sentence was passed against him for his crime**, by the legitimate jurisdiction of the Church."» Suárez understood perfectly well that there is no judgment of the Church unless there is at least a sentence juridically passed by those who possess the

---

[610] *True or False Pope?*, p. 278, Footnote 117.

jurisdiction to pronounce that sentence. This point is entirely lost on Salza & Siscoe, who, as we have seen, hold that even a merely declaratory sentence, which according to them is not a juridical act, is not necessary; but all that is needed for there to be a public judgment of the Church, is that the Church establish the crime; but the establishment of the crime in the manner described by Salza & Siscoe is manifestly not a public judgment of the Church. This is, in fact, how they interpret Bellarmine's explanation of the Fifth Opinion: "Pope loses his office ipso facto after crime established", but the need a declaratory sentence for Bellarmine is (according to them) "probable". [611] Salza & Siscoe seem to be incapable of grasping that the very notion of a public judgment of the Church establishing the crime without at least a declaratory sentence pronounced by a competent tribunal is *self-contradictory*. Thus, (they say), "The Church declares that the Pope has lost his office due to heresy. This merely confirms that the loss of office has already taken place." (That is, by the mere fact that the crime has been established without any sentence being pronounced.)[612] However, according to Bellarmine, (and according to all the eminent theologian/canonists), the Fifth Opinion does not involve any judgment of the Church establishing the crime as a condition for the loss of office to take place, but the public commission of manifest heresy by itself establishes the *fact* of defection into heresy, apart from any considerstion of *crime* or penal law; and thus, it directly causes the loss of office, for which reason it suffices *by itself* for the loss of office to take place "*sine alia vi externa*", (which is why Bellarmine says the manifest heretic ceases to be pope "*by himself*"); whereas, according to the Fourth Opinion, the loss of office does not take place without the juridical judgment of the Church.

This point is entirely lost upon the simplistic fundamentalist minds of Salza & Siscoe who say, "The problem, which we have not seen addressed before, is that the Silveira/Boulet classification of Suarez as sharing the opinion of Cajetan (listed as the Fourth Opinion) is not correct."[613] Suárez and Cajetan definitely agreed that the loss of office cannot take place without the juridical judgment of the heretic pope for the crime of heresy. This is Opinion No. 4, refuted by Bellarmine. However, Salza & Siscoe explain, "Suarez did not agree with Cajetan, but instead held that a heretical Pope loses his office ipso facto (being

---

[611] *Ibid.* p. 683.
[612] *Ibid.* p. 358.
[613] *Ibid.* p. 269.

deposed immediately by Christ), which is the Fifth Opinion."⁶¹⁴ No. While it is true that Suárez did not agree with Cajetan's opinion, Suárez does not say "that a heretical Pope loses his office ipso facto (being deposed immediately by Christ)," (Opinion No. 5); but, he says, "Against this opinion I say... in no case, even of heresy, is the Pontiff deprived of his dignity and power immediately by God, without the foregoing judgment and sentence of men."⁶¹⁵ And the judgment, says Suárez, must be made with an act of jurisdiction: "I say: If the pope were a heretic and incorrigible, he would cease to be pope just as soon as a declaratory sentence would be pronounced upon him by the legitimate jurisdiction of the Church."⁶¹⁶ (Opinion No. 4) Salza & Siscoe falsely and deceptively argue that that the **uninamous opinion** is that a heretic pope does not lose office until he is judged by the Church. The evidence proving the contrary has already been presented earlier in this work. The virtually unanimous opinion of canonists and theologians who admit at least the hypothesis of a heretical pope, since the time of Wernz, holds that a manifest heretic pope would be automatically deprived of the papacy without any judgment pronounced by the Church.

According to Salza & Siscoe, the eminent scholars are all wrong in their interpretation of Opinion No. 5, "by interpreting the ipso facto loss of office to be similar to an 'ipso facto' latae sententiæ excommunication, which occurs automatically (or ipso facto), when one commits an offense that carries the penalty, without requiring an antecedent judgment by the Church. But this is not at all what Bellarmine and Suarez meant by the ipso facto loss of office. What they meant is that the ipso facto loss of office occurs after the Church judges the Pope to be a heretic and before any additional juridical sentence or excommunication (which differs from Cajetan's opinion). In other words, after the Church establishes 'the fact' that the Pope is a manifest heretic, he, according to

---

⁶¹⁴ *Ibid.*

⁶¹⁵ Suarez, *Op. cit.*, p. 318: «Contra hanc sententiam dico secundo: in nullo casu, etiam hæresis, privatur Pontifex sua dignitate et potestate immediate ab ipso Deo, absque hominum præeunte judicio et sententia.»

⁶¹⁶ Suarez, *Op. cit., De Fide Theologica. Disputatio X. De Summo Pontifice, Sect. VI.* p. 317: «Dico tertio: si Papa sit hæreticus et incorrigibilis, cum primum per legitimam Ecclesiæ jurisdictionem sententia declaratoria criminis in eum profertur, desinit esse Papa.»

this opinion, is deemed to lose his office ipso facto ('by the fact')." [617] Incredibly, in support of their belief that the fifth opinion holds that the Church must judge a manifestly heretical pope before he can lose office, they cite this segment of text of Bellarmine's refutation of Opinion No. 4:

> «The fourth opinion is that of Cajetan, for whom (de auctor. papae et con., cap. 20 et 21) the manifestly heretical Pope is not "ipso facto" deposed, but can and must be deposed by the Church. To my judgment, this opinion cannot be defended. For, in the first place, it is proven with arguments from authority and from reason that the manifest heretic is "ipso facto" deposed. The argument from authority is based on St. Paul (Titus, c. 3), who orders that the heretic be avoided after two warnings, that is, after showing himself to be manifestly obstinate — which means before any excommunication or judicial sentence. (...)»
>
> «Therefore, the true opinion is the fifth, according to which the Pope who is manifestly a heretic ceases by himself to be Pope and head, in the same way as he ceases to be a Christian and a member of the body of the Church; and for this reason he can be judged and punished by the Church. This is the opinion of all the ancient Fathers, who teach that manifest heretics immediately lose all jurisdiction...»

In the cited text, Bellarmine makes absolutely no mention of any need for the Church to juridically "establish the crime" or "judge"; but on the contrary, he says only "that the manifest heretic is ipso facto deposed...after showing himself to be manifestly obstinate". They go on to explain what they think Bellarmine means: "What Bellarmine means is that the ipso facto loss of office occurs when the Church judges him to be a heretic, and before the vitandus declaration. This is evident from the fact that he is attempting to refute Cajetan's opinion, which maintains that the fall is not ipso facto after he is judged by the Church, but only follows the juridical sentence of the vitandus declaration (which, again, directly separates the Church from the Pope, not the Pope from the Church). The reason Kramer and the Sedes have misunderstood Bellarmine is because they have misunderstood Cajetan's opinion, and therefore did not know what Bellarmine was trying to refute." This interpretation is manifestly nonsensical in view of the fact that that in refuting Cajetan, Bellarmine says nothing about the thesis "which

---

[617] True or False Pope: WHY FR. KRAMER AND THE SEDEVACANTISTS MISUNDERSTAND BELLARMINE – http://www.trueorfalsepope.com/p/whyfr.html.

maintains that the fall is not ipso facto after he is judged by the Church, but only follows the juridical sentence of the vitandus declaration", but *he argues expressly that the manifest heretic pope simply cannot be deposed by the Church*, and says it is proven that the manifest heretic pope is *ipso facto* deposed[618]; and, as I have explained at length, he demonstrates why **neither the bishops nor the cardinals can depose a pope**; and "**Therefore**, the true opinion is the fifth, according to which the Pope who is manifestly a heretic **ceases by himself** to be Pope and head**, in the same way as he ceases to be a Christian and a member of the body of the Church**; and **for this reason** he **can be judged and punished by the Church**." As on so many other points, Salza & Siscoe have completely inverted the teaching of Bellarmine, as they have also done with the teachings of the popes, Doctors, and Fathers of the Church.

CONCLUSION OF PART THREE

"a nemine est iudicandus, nisi deprehendatur a Fide devius"

In his earlier cited *Fundamentaltheologie*, Albert Lang points out that in the time of the Apostolic Fathers, "the primacy did not appear so strongly in the early days of the Church", but he also points out that "the traditional testimonies are sufficient to prove for the first three centuries both the practical exercise of primacy by Rome and also a factual and theoretical recognition by the universal Church."[619] St. Irenæus of Lyon

---

[618] «Nam *in primis*, quod hæreticus manifestus *ipso facto* sit depositus, probatur auctoritate & ratione.»

[619] Lang, *Op. cit.*, Band II, *Der Auftrag der Kirche, II. Hauptstück*, München, 1962, pp. 139-140: «Läßt sich aber der Jurisdiktionsprimat Roms auch schon in den ersten christlichen Jahrhunderten aufweisen? Es ist verständlich, daß in der ersten Zeit der Kirche der Primat noch nicht so stark in Erscheinung treten konnte, weil überall die Apostolische Tradition noch nachwirkte, und weil wegen der geringeren Ausdehnung der Kirche die Notwendigkeit zum Eingreifen für die oberste Leitung der Kirche noch weniger gegeben war. Auch muß man bedenken, daß die Quellen aus der ersten christlichen Zeit noch recht spärlich fließen und daß den Fragen der kirchlichen Organisation gegenüber den inhältlich bedeutsamen dogmatischen Fragen anfangs wenig Beachtung geschenkt wurde. Trotzdem reichen die überkommenen Zeugnisse voll aus, auch für die ersten drei Jahrhunderte sowohl die *praktische Ausübung* des Primats durch Rom vie auch eine *faktische* und *theoretische Anerkennung* durch die

asserted the Church's doctrine on the universal authority of the magisterium of the Church of Rome, but in the early centuries there existed no developed formulation of legal principles clearly outlining the papal prerogatives and powers. Pope St. Damasus I was the first to refer to the See of Rome as the *Sedes Apostolica*. Pope St. Zozimus in *Quamvis Patrum* teaches that the authority of the Fathers attributes such authority to the Apostolic See, that no one would dare to dispute its judgment which is set forth in canons, regulations, and ecclesiastical laws.[620] Pope St. Gelasius, (as noted earlier) set forth the canons which declared the See of Rome to be the judge over the whole Church, which is judged by none, and against whose judgment there can be no appeal. During the pontificate of Leo I the *plenitudo potestatis* is first spoken of; and primacy of Rome was forcefully stated at Chalcedon and accepted by the

---

Gesamtkirche zu erweisen. Die Bischöfe von Rom haben für sich eine Vorrangstelle beansprukt und sich für die Erhaltung der Einheit im Glauben und der sittlichen Ordnung verantwortlich gefühlt. Sie haben praktisch den Primat ausgeübt, wenn sie sich auch nicht ausdrüklich darauf berufen haben. [...]1. Den Anlaß des Schreibens bildeten Zwistikeiten, die in Korinth ausgebrochen waren, weil ein Teil der Gemeinde einige der kirchlichen Vorsteher ablehnte. Die römische Kirche fühlte sich verpflichtet, in diesen Zwist einer der ältesten apostolischen Gemeinden einzugreifen, ohne von der Gemeinde von Korinth zu einem Schiedsspruch oder einer Vermittlung eingrladen worden zu sein. Sie tat es aus eigener *Machtvollkommenheit* und *Verantwortlichkeit* zu einer Zeit, als der Apostel Johsnnes und die unmittelbaren Schüler der heiligen Paulus noch lebten. Sie tat es mit *wahrhafter Autorität und Jurisdiktion*.»

[620] «(n 1) Quamvis Patrum traditio Apostolicae Sedi auctoritatem tantam tnbuerit, ut de eius iudicio disceptare nullus auderet, idque per canones semper regulasque servaverit et currens adhuc suis legibus ecclesiastica disciplina Petri nomini, a quo ipsa quoque descendit, reverentiam quam debet exsolvat: ...

«(3) cum ergo tantae auctoritatis et Petrus caput sit et sequentia omnium maiorum statuta firmaverint, ut iam humanis divinisque legibus disciplinisque omnibus finiretur Romanam Ecclesiam, cuius locum regeret (al.: firmetur Romana Ecclesia, cuius locum Nos regere), ipsius quoque potestatem nominis obtinere: ...

«(4) tamen, cum Nobis tantum esset auctoritatis, ut nullus de Nostra possit retractare sententia, nihil egimus, quod non ad vestram notitiam Nostris ultro litteris referremus, dantes hoc fraternitati et in commune consulentes, non quia quid deberet fieri nesciremus aut faceremus aliquid, quod contra utilitatem Ecclesiae veniens displiceret, sed pariter vobiscum voluimus habere tractatum de illo (Caelestio accusato).» [St. Zozimun 21 March 418 *"Quamvis Patrum"*]

Patriarch of Constantinople. Pope Innocent III set forth and theologically elaborated the doctrine of the primacy in terms of the *plenitudo potestatis* in his letter to the Patriarch John of Constantinople.[621] *Lætentur Cæli*[622] (Florence) then defines the papal primacy over the whole

---

[621] «Apostolicae Sedis primatus, quem non homo, sed Deus, immo verius Deus homo constituit, multis quidem et evangelicis et apostolicis testimoniis comprobatur, a quibus postmodum constitutiones canonicae processerunt, concorditer asserentes sacrosanctam Ecclesiam in beato Petro Apostolorum principe consecratam quasi magistram et matrem ceteris praeeminere. Hic enim... audire promeruit: 'Tu es Petrus... tibi dabo claves regni caelorum' (Mt 16, 18 s). Nam licet primum et praecipuum Ecclesiae fundamentum sit unigenitus Dei Filius Jesus Christus, iuxta quod dicit Apostolus 'Quia fundamentum positum est, praeter quod aliud poni non potest, quod est Christus Jesus' (1 Cor 3, 11), secundum tamen et secundarium Ecclesiae fundamentum est Petrus, etsi non tempore primus, auctoritate tamen praecipuus inter ceteros, de quibus Paulus Apostolus inquit: 'Iam non estis hospites et advenae, sed estis cives sanctorum et domestici Dei, superaedificati supra fundamentum Apostolorum et Prophetarum' (Eph 2, 20). ... Huius etiam primatum Veritas per se ipsam expressit, cum inquit ad eum: 'Tu vocaberis Cephas' (Io 1, 42): quod etsi 'Petrus' interpretetur, 'caput' tamen exponitur, ut sicut caput inter cetera membra corporis, velut in quo viget plenitudo sensuum, obtinet principatum, sic et Petrus inter Apostolos et successores ipsius inter universos Ecclesiarum praelatos praerogativa praecellerent dignitatis, vocatis sic ceteris in partem sollicitudinis, ut nihil eis de potestatis plenitudine deperiret. Huic Dominus oves suas pascendas vocabulo tertio repetito commisit, ut alienus a grege dominico censeatur, qui eum etiam in successoribus suis noluerit habere pastorem. Non enim inter has et illas oves distinxit, sed simpliciter inquit: 'Pasce oves meas' (Jo 21, 17), ut omnes omnino intelligantur ei esse commissae. ... (Explicando allegorice Jo 21, 7:) Cum enim mare mundum designet (juxta Ps 103, 25), per hoc, quod Petrus se misit in mare, privilegium expressit pontificii singularis, per quod universum orbem susceperat gubernandum, ceteris Apostolis ut vehiculo navis contentis, cum nulli eorum universus fuerit orbis commissus, sed singulis singulae provinciae vel Ecclesiae potius deputatae. (Simile argumentum allegoricum deducitur ex Mt 14, 28 ss:) Per hoc quod Petrus super aquas maris incessit, super universos populos se potestatem accepisse monstravit.» *[Innocent III, Ep. 'Apostolicae Sedis primatus' ad (Iohannem) patriarcham C'polit., 12 novembre 1199]*

[622] (Ordo sedium patriarch.; primatus Rom.) «Item diffinimus, sanctam Apostolicam Sedem, et Romanum Pontificem, in universum orbem tenere primatum, et ipsum Pontificem Romanum successorem esse beati Petri principis Apostolorum et verum Christi vicarium, totiusque Ecclesiae caput et omnium Christianorum patrem ac doctorem exsistere; et ipsi in beato Petro

world and the "full power" of the Roman Pontiff for "ruling and governing the Church". But in spite of that "full power", there has always been the belief in the Church that if the pope were to fall into heresy he can be judged for heresy, "or rather," as Innocent III qualifies it, he "can be shown to be already judged." Hinschius points out the early example of such a case at the sixth general Council (Third Council of Constantinople), where the posthumous condemnation for heresy of Pope Honorius I was confirmed by Pope Leo II, and several popes subsequently upheld the admissibility of such a judgment.[623] Nevertheless, he was never proven to have been a formal heretic, and he was not judged by his inferiors during his lifetime, nor was he deposed. In a passage I quoted in Part I of this work, Hinschius pointed out that there has been a series of Catholic writers, and in particular St. Robert Bellarmine, who find no exception in such a case to the rule that the pope is judged by no one, because the pope who falls into heresy would thereby sever himself from the Church and forfeit the Pontificate by himself in such a manner that the Church would not be able to impose a deposition, but would only be able to establish the loss of the papal dignity that has already taken place; and that this line of thought is already found in Pope Innocent III's Sermo IV. In consecrat. pontiff.[624]

---

pascendi, regendi ac gubernandi universalem Ecclesiam a Domino nostro Jesu Christo plenam potestatem traditam esse; quemadmodum etiam in gestis oecumenicorum Conciliorum et in sacris canonibus continetur.» (*"Laetentur Caeli"* 6 July 1439)

[623] «Freilich ist eine derartige Verurtheilung wegen Ketzerei schon früh vorgekommen, indem die sechste allgemeine, von Leo II. Bestätigte Synode von Konstantinopel (680) den Papst Honorius I. (625 — 638) nach seinem Tode wegen Ketzerei anathematisirte. Später haben mehrere Päpste die Statthaftigkeit eines Urtheils über den Papst in dem gedachten Fall anerkannt, und demnach kann an der Geltung jenes Satzes nicht gezweifelt werden». (Hinschius, *Op. cit.*, p. 307.)

[624] «Eine Reihe katholischer Schriftsteller wollen aber darin keine Ausnahme von der gedachten Regel finden, weil der in Ketzerei verfallene Papst sich dadurch selbst von der Kirche ausscheide, damit weiter den Pontifikat verwirke und also das Konzil keine Deposition mehr verhängen könne, sondern nur die Thatsache des erfolgten Verlustes der Päpstlichen Würde zu konstatiren habe. [3] (Dieser Gedanke tritt schon bei Innocenz III. auf (im Sermo IV. In consecrat. pontiff. opp. Colon. 1575. 1. 197): «Potest (pontifex) ab hominibus iudicari vel potius iudicatus ostendi, si videlicet evanescat in haeresim, quoniam qui non credit, iam iudicatus est») Vgl. ferner Bellarmin, christ. Fidei controv. gen. III. De Romano pontifice II. 30. (ed. Ingolstadt. 1605. 1083): «Est ergo

It is certainly not surprising that Innocent III taught that if a pope would "wither away into heresy", he would automatically cease to be pope; and it is no mystery from whom he learned that doctrine. The Encyclopedia of the Middle Ages (under Uguccio) relates, "Uguccio (Hugh of Pisa) studied theology and probably canon law at Bologna, before teaching there; among his pupils was the future Pope Innocent III." The Catholic Encyclopedia adds, "Among his pupils was Lothario de' Conti, afterwards Innocent III, who held him in high esteem as is shown by the important cases which the pontiff submitted to him, traces of which still remain in the "Corpus Juris" (c. Coram, 34, X, I, 29). Two letters addressed by Innocent III to Huguccio were inserted in the Decretals of Gregory IX (c. Quanto, 7, X, IV, 19; c. In quadam, 8, X,III,41). Besides a book, "Liber derivationum", dealing with etymologies, he wrote a "Summa" on the "Decretum" of Gratian, concluded according to some in 1187, according to others after 1190, the most extensive and perhaps the most authoritative commentary of that time." It was in his *Summa* that, "Huguccio argued, in a widely known opinion, that a pope who fell into heresy automatically lost his see, without the necessity of a formal judgment.[4]"[625] Thus, we find the doctrine, (which Salza and Siscoe claim is an invention of the Sedevacantists), that a pope who would become a heretic, would lose office automatically; being taught in Bologna in the 12th Century by the most eminent canonist of that century, Huguccio of Pisa, whose student, Lothair de Conti, as Pope Innocent III taught that same doctrine in his sermons. St. Robert Bellarmine and Don Pietro Ballerini theologically elaborated that doctrine, which was eventually adopted as the position of the Holy See at the First Vatican Council. The doctrine that all who publicly defect from the faith into heresy or apostasy lose ecclesiastical office automatically was then incorporated into the 1917 and 1983 Codes of Canon Law. It is on this solid doctrinal basis that the inescapable conclusion rests, namely, that the only doctrinally orthodox opinions

---

opinio quinta vera, papa haereticum manifestum per se desinere esse christianus et membrum corporis ecclesiae, quare ab ecclesia posse eum iudicari et puniri. Haec est sententia omnium veterum patrum qui docent haereticos manifestos mox amittere omnem jurisdictionem»; Fagnan. comm. Ad c. 4. X. de elect. I. 6. n. 70 ff; Fragosi, regimen reipubl. Christianae lib. II. c. I. §. 2. n. 21 (Lugduni. 1648. 2, 11); Kober, Deposition. S. 585.

[625] Wikipedia provides the reference: "4. See the text from Huguccio's Summa printed in Appendix 1 of Brian Tierney, Foundations of the Conciliar Theory, Cambridge: Cambridge University Press, 1955)."

that are possible today on the question of a manifestly heretical pope are Opinion No. 1, and Opinion No. 5 considered as a hypothesis.

I have already pointed out in Section II of this Part, the fatal defect in the opinion that it is even possible for a pope to become a heretic, given the divine promise to Peter and his successors of unfailing faith. The opinion, explained by Cardinal Stickler in the article I quoted seems to have originated from the early Decretists of the French school, and as then more systematically elaborated by Huguccio, and was taken up in modified form by Ostiense and others. *The New Catholic Encyclopedia* (under Conciliarism) explains,

> «Huguccio also considered the question of how the possibility of a pope erring in faith, which he admitted, could be reconciled with the ancient doctrine that the true faith would always live on in the Roman Church. His answer was based on a distinction between the local Roman Church and the universal Roman Church. "The Roman Church is said to have never erred in faith… but I say that the whole Catholic Church which has never erred in toto is called the Roman Church." And again, "Wherever there are good faithful men there is the Roman Church." This distinction between the proneness to error of a pope and the indefectibility of the whole Church became a most important element in later conciliar theories.»

The defect of Huguccio's notion of the "Roman Church" is so patent, that it needs only to be pointed out without further elucidation, except to say; that the sense which Huguccio gives to the term is entirely alien to the sense according to which it was used in the canons of St. Gelasius, which is its proper sense, and is the way it has always been generally understood since the doctrinal pre-eminence of the Roman Church was first explained by St. Irenæus. It suffices to point out Cardinal Manning's observation stated in 1871, "But Ballerini has declared that whatsoever is ascribed to the Roman See, Cathedra, or Church is to be ascribed to the Person of the Roman Pontiff only."[626] The reason why so many of the medieval canonists formulated such errant theories on their understanding of the infallibility of the "Roman Church" is ultimately that there was at that time an inadequate understanding of the doctrine of Papal Infallibility. "Not only," explains Moynihan, "was there no adequate formulation in the twelfth century of the distinction between a pope's private opinions and his public teaching

---

[626] Cardinal Manning, *The Vatican Council and its Definitions*, p. 104.

as Head of the Church, but quite obviously the doctrine of papal infallibility had not yet systematically been developed."[627]

The Encyclopedia continues,

> «Huguccio's views were repeated with various modifications by the canonists of the early 13th century. Some taught that a pope could be condemned only for heresy, not for notorious crimes in general. Others held that he could be deposed for professing a new heresy and not for only adhering to an old one. All agreed that a doctrinal definition of a general council, that is of pope and bishops acting together, possessed a higher authority than the bare word of a pope alone. A few accepted the more radical view that a decision of the fathers of a council acting in concert against the pope should be preferred to the pope's decision. Sometimes the language employed was ambiguous, and perhaps deliberately so. The Glossa Ordinaria to the Decretum of Joannes Teutonicus, a work used as a standard text in canon law schools throughout the Middle Ages, declared simply, "Where a matter of faith is involved a council is greater than a pope."»

"This assertion," comments Moynihan, "that a pope-in-council, as it were, is superior to a pope acting alone is consonant with twelfth century thinking." The doctrine of Johannes Teutonicus, written around 1217, was a yet more radical formulation of conciliar supremacy. "It was pointed out," says Moynihan,

> "... that the doctrine of conciliar supremacy had been asserted in unambiguous terms by the author of the Summa De iure canonico tractaturus toward the close of the twelfth century, and more clearly still by the English canonist Alanus at the beginning of the thirteenth. [...] The nucleus of the conciliar doctrine consisted in the belief that a general council could sit in judgment on a pope and depose him, and that decisions of a general council were preferable to those of a pope – at least at least as far as articles of faith were concerned."[628]

It is precisely this idea, "*where a matter of faith is involved a council is greater than a pope*," which is the basis of the Conciliarist Argument, which is Opinion No. 4. *It is the foundation of the argument which holds that a council can canonically admonish a pope, and if he remains obstinate in heresy, can then pronounce judgment upon him so that he then falls from office*; and according to some, a

---

[627] Moynihan, *Op. cit.*, p. 67
[628] *Ibid.* p. 123

council would even need to pronounce a vitandus sentence upon the heretic pope for him to fall from office – a sentence which presumes the power to excommunicate the heretic Pontiff, because as explained earlier, **only an excommunicatus can be pronounced "*vitandus*"**.

St. Robert Bellarmine, in the following segment of *De Romano Ponifice* (Book II Chapter XXX) on Opinion No. 4 (precisely and accurately translated by Ryan Grant) destroyed this argument that a pope can be judged by the Church, by explaining that neither the bishops nor the cardinals have any power over a pope, (and to pronounce official judgment **on** a pope is to exercise *power of jurisdiction* **over** a pope):

Next, what Cajetan says in the second place, that a heretical Pope who is truly Pope can be deposed by the Church, and from its authority seems no less false than the first. For, if the Church deposes a Pope against his will, certainly it is over the Pope. Yet the same Cajetan defends the opposite in the very same treatise. But he answers; the Church, in the very matter, when it deposes the Pope, does not have authority over the Pope, but only on that union of the person with the pontificate. As the Church can join the pontificate to such a person, and still it is not said on that account to be above the Pontiff; so it can separate the pontificate from such a person in the case of heresy, and still it will not be said to be above the Pope.

On the other hand, from the very fact that the Pope deposes bishops, they deduce that the Pope is above all bishops, and still the Pope deposing a bishop does not destroy the Episcopacy; but only separates it from that person. Secondly, for one to be deposed from the pontificate against his will is without a doubt a penalty; therefore, the Church deposing a Pope against his will, without a doubt punishes him; but to punish is for a superior and a judge. Thirdly, because according to Cajetan and the other Thomists, in reality they are the same, the whole and the parts are taken up together. Therefore, he who has so great an authority over the parts taken up together, such that he can also separate them, also has it over the whole, which arises from those parts.

Furthermore, the example of Cajetan does not avail on electors, who have the power of applying the pontificate to a certain person, and still does not have power over the Pope. For while a thing is made, the action is exercised over the matter of the thing that is going to be, not over a composite which does not yet exist, but while a thing is destroyed, the action is exercised over a composite; as is certain from natural things. Therefore, when Cardinals create the Pontiff, they exercise their authority not over the Pontiff, because he does not yet exist; but over the matter, that is, over the person whom they dispose in a certain measure through election, that he might receive the form of the pontificate from God; but if they depose the Pope, they necessarily exercise authority over the composite, that is, over the person provided with pontifical dignity, which is to say, over the Pontiff.

The belief that a reigning Pontiff, by way of exception, can be juridically judged for heresy by his inferiors, has neither a basis in scripture nor in the doctrinal tradition of the Church. It was a ***theory*** of ***law*** developed by ***canonists***, based on the spurious *Canon Si papa,* and on a defective notion of papal infallibility. It gained momentum under the influence of ***Conciliarism***, and later became the more common opinion of theologians during the Counter-Reformation period. Its remote origin was the spurious *Canon Si papa*, which was not written by St. Boniface, but was authored by Cardinal Humbert in the 11th Century, as both Vacca (cited above) and Moynihan[629] explain. Its demise was the result of the influence of the doctrine of St. Robert Bellarmine on the theologians of the Eighteenth and Nineteenth Centuries. By the late 19th Century the opinion was already entirely abandoned, and only in its mitigated form, which admits only of a declaratory sentence after a merely deliberative examination of the case, had survived among a very few theologians even until then. Among those who admit the possibility of a pope becoming a heretic, it is now a unanimous majority who endorse Opinion No. 5 which holds that a manifest heretic pope falls automatically from office *ipso facto* before any judgment is made by the Chuch. With the absolute injudicability of the Romn Pontiff established by Vatican I, and with the principle, *"Prima Sedes a nemine judicatur"* incorporated into the Code of Canon Law as a universal statute, and unanimously interpreted by canonists in such a manner that no exception can be considered admissible, Opinion No. 4 in its classical formulation, which advocated either a juridical deposition of a reigning heretic pope or a juridical judgment of heresy on the pope followed by an *ipso facto* fall from office, and which had been promoted by so many canonists and theologians of the Counter-Reformation period and for about a century thereafter in the Dominican school, experienced its demise already in the 19th Century, having been universally abandoned by theologians. Since the late 19th Century **it has been the *common opinion* that a heretic falls from office *automatically*, BEFORE any judgment is passed; and the *post factum* declaration would only give formal juridical recognition to the *fact*. Sydney F. Smith S.J. wrote in 1895 (and published in book form in 1896):**

---

[629] Moynihan; *Ibid.*, pp. 29 – 33.

"[I]t has been **generally held** that, **given the possibility of a personally heretical Pope, he would *ipso facto* cease to be Pope by ceasing to be a member of the Church.** The Church in that case, as represented by the Cardinals or otherwise, could **on due information of the *fact*** pass a **declaratory sentence** on one who being no longer Pope was no longer its superior, and **then take measures to remove him from the see in which he had become an intruder.**"[630]

In spite of the antiquity and unequivocal nature of the principle that *the first See is judged by no one*, it is contrasted by the historical fact of depositions of popes, and a tradition of some canonists which held that a pope could be judged by a general council. On this point of the injudicability of the Roman Pontiff, Hinschius makes a poignant observation and asks, "But with this theory [the injudicability of the pope] there stands in contrast the undeniable fact several times during the course of the earlier centuries, depositions of popes had taken place, which brings up the question whether these depositions were only blameworthy violations of a principle of law indisputably held in the Catholic Church from the beginning, or was it not rather that this principle became fixed only later in the course of its development?" [631] His answer to the question is emphatic and unequivocal: "A detached consideration without presuppositions of the particular occurrences that enter into the question would appear to justify the latter conception. During the time of the Roman Empire and throughout the greater part of the Middle Ages, in which the opposition between the Pontificate and the Episcopacy was not yet the driving factor of the development, rather the bishops for the most part, and only in part joined with the secular power, we encounter only cases, where the secular rulers, took part in the depositions at councils, while toward the end of the Middle Ages, as the downtrodden Episcopacy, by means of the earlier conception, raised its head and sought to decrease the papal prerogatives, bringing

---

[630] Sydney F. Smith S.J., *Dr. Littledale's Theory of the Disappearance of the Papacy*, Catholic Truth Society, London, 1896.

[631] "Aber mit dieser Theorie steht die unleugbare Thatsache in Widerspruch, dass mehrfach im Verlauf der früheren Jahrhunderterte Absetzungen von Päpsten erfolgt sint, und es fragt sich daher, ob diese Depositionen bloss verwerfliche Verletztungen eines von Anfang an in der katolischen Kirche unbestritten feststehenden Rechtssatzes waren oder ob sich nicht vielmehr dieser letztere erst im Laufe der Entwicklung fixiert hat." (Op. cit., p. 297)

practically into effect the claimed supremacy over the popes by means of depositions."[632]

Don Curzio Nitoglia quotes Fr. Salvatore Vacca, who elaborates on this point of the two conflicting canonical traditions that were simultaneously present in the Church:

> "Gratian, in order to establish the principle of the injudicability of the pope, as opposed to the previous canonical tradition [...] left the principle *Prima Sedes a nemine judicatur* unshaken. However, he partially transcribed the *Fragmentum A* (174-178) of Umberto di Silva Candida. He thus gathered into his Decretum the two conflicting juridical traditions which were present together in the Church: the first, maintained by the Symmachian Apocrypha [Pope St. Symmachus (498 – 514) put under the judgment of the particular council known as the Synod ad Palmaria in the atrium of St. Peter's Basilica in the Vatican by the Emperor Theodoric in 501. During the course of the controversy, numerous polemical writings were drafted, among them the *Symmachian Apocrypha*, put together by the supporters of Pope Symmachus, which stated the axiom *Summa Sedes a nemine iudicatur* Ed] affirms that *the Pope cannot be judged by anyone*; the second holds, that *in the case of heresy the Pope can be caught on heresy*. So, this conception was passed down until the 12th Century [...]."[633]

---

[632] "Eine unbefangene, voraussetzungslose Betrachtung der einzelnen, in Frage kommenden Begebnisse wird die letztgedachte Auffassung als berechtigt erscheinen lassen. In der Römischen Kaiserzeit und den grössten Theil des Mittelalters hindurch, in welchem der Gegensatz zwischen dem Pontifikat und Episkopat noch nicht der hauptsächliche treibende Faktor der Entwicklung gewesen ist, vielmehr die Bischöfe sich höchstens und nur zum Theil der weltlichen Macht angeschlossen haben, begegnen uns daher nur Fälle, wo die weltlichen Herscher allerdings unter Hinzutritt von Kirchensammlungen dergleichen Absetzungen vornahmen, während gerade gegen Ende des Mittelalters, als der durch die frühere Verfassungsgestaltungen zurückgedrängt Episkopat sein Haupt erhoben und die päpstlichen Rechte zu vermindern suchte, dieser beanspruchte Oberhoheit über die Päpste auch durch Depositionen der letzteren praktisch zur Geltung brachte."

[633] Ora «Graziano, per fondare il principio sulla ingiudicabilità del Papa, a differenza della tradizione canonistica precedente [...] ha lasciato inconcusso il principio *Prima Sedes a nemine iudicatur*. Tuttavia, ha trascritto parzialmente il *Fragmentum A* (174-178) di Umberto di Silva Candida. Egli raccoglie così nel suo Decreto le due tradizioni giuridiche contrastanti, che sono state compresenti nella Chiesa: la prima, sostenuta dagli apocrifi simmachiani [papa san Simmaco (498-514) sottoposto al giudizio del concilio particolare detto palmare nell'atrio della basilica di San Pietro in Vaticano dall'imperatore

So, even long after the principle *Apostolica sedes a nemine judicatur* had established the absolute injudicability of the pope, and had become firmly entrenched in the canonical tradition of the Church, the "earlier conception" was still resorted to by the Episcopacy, not only to counterbalance the supreme authority of the pope, but even to challenge papal supremacy and exert supremacy over the pope. The *New Catholic Encyclopedia* elaborates:

The circumstances in which a pope's pronouncements could be regarded as infallible had been neither defined nor much discussed. It was generally accepted that a pope could err in faith and it seemed intolerable that the whole Church should be thrown into confusion as a result. There was ***a need then to find norms that might set proper limits to the powers even of a pope***. In seeking such norms the canonists turned to the general councils of the past and it became commonplace around 1200 to assert that the pope was bound by the canons of councils "in matters touching the faith and the general state of the Church."

> This raised the problem of how to deal with a pope who offended against such canons. The most eminent canonist of the age, Huguccio, discussed the problem at length. He concluded that a pope who publicly professed his adherence to a known heresy could be deposed by the Church and, further, that a pope who contumaciously persisted in notorious crime could likewise be deposed since "to scandalize the Church is like committing heresy."

Pope Innocent III affirmed in his ordinary magisterium that the Roman Pontiff cannot be judged by men for any crime, but if he were to fall into heresy, he could be "shown to be already judged". Enrico da Susa, known as "l'Ostiense", came after Innocent III, and accordingly, «believed that while the pope should follow positive law he was not bound by it. Thus the pope could not be tried for any crime, except that of heresy, in which case "the pope could be subject to the 'ecclesia' (the

---

Teodorico nel 501. Nel corso della controversia furono stilati numerosi scritti polemici, fra cui gli *apocrifi simmachiani*, redatti dai sostenitori di papa Simmaco, che emanò l'assioma *Summa Sedes a nemine iudicatur* ndr], afferma che *il Papa non può essere giudicato da nessuno*; la seconda ritiene che, *in caso di eresia, il Papa può essere ripreso*. Dunque questa concezione si è tramandata sino al secolo XII. [...].» (S. Vacca, *Prima Sedes a nemine iudicatur*, cit., p. 253-254).

Church)." For any other violation of law the pope could be judged by no one save God.»[634]

The fact that the pope could be tried at all for heresy was premised on the principle that as a heretic, he would have ceased to be pope and become *minor quolibet catholico*; but whether the heresy would be considered as the basis for an *accusatio,* necessitating a trial, or an *exceptio,* whereby case could be decided administratively, thereby avoiding the necessity of a trial, remained unresolved in Blessed Henry's doctrine.[635] There was no unanimity among canonists of the 13th Century. Moynihan observes,

> "Pope Innocent III (1198-1216) had forcefully proclaimed the doctrine of papal monarchy, and that doctrine had gained considerable support among several Decretalists writers such as Tancreed and Bernard of Parma. Since an *exceptio* in cases of heresy would not involve a trial strictly speaking, but only a declaration that a pope, because of his heresy, had never been validly elected, it is understandable that a papal monarchist like Bernard would have favored such a view. Hostiensis was of the opinion that acusation of heresy as well as exceptions could be brought against the pope, and Innocent IV, while admitting both, favored accusations."[636]

As the passage from Cardinal Stickler which I quoted in the previous section, explains, «In the case of an obstinate and public profession of certain heresy, since it is condemned by the Church, the Pope becomes "minor quolibet catholico" (a common phrase of canonists) and ceases to be pope (...).» Although not solemnly defined, this doctrine is clearly the doctrine of the Catholic Church in respect to **all** offices in the Church, being incorporated into both the 1917 and 1983 Code of Canon Law, in the canons on Tacit Loss of Office (1917), and Removal (1983). Therefore, if it were possible for a pope to become a formal heretic, he could be deposed only in the qualified sense that he could be shown to be already judged – judged to have already fallen from office. Hence, any

---

[634] Wikipedia – (In: Kenneth Pennington, *Popes, Canonists and Texts, 1150-1550.*)

[635] Moynihan, *Op. cit.* p.116: "In his *Commentarium,* Hostiensis stated that the only *exceptio.* which could be brought against the pope was that of heresy, but he seemed to admit that opposition to heretical pope could take the form of an *accusatio.*" He quotes the text of *Commentaria in Decretalium libros,* «... (Electio papae) de nullo crimine excipi possit nisi de haeresi, de qua etiam consecratus accusari posset, xl. *dist. Si papa* (D. XL, c. 6) ...» (p. 115 footnote 13)

[636] *Ibid.*, p. 116

opinion or theory which postulates any exception to the principle, *Prima Sedes a nemine judicatur*, and accordingly therefore, that a pope can be judged by the Church for heresy before he falls from office on the basis of a Conciliarist application of the principle *cunctos ipse iudicaturus a nemine est iudicandus, nisi deprehendatur a fide devius*, is contrary to the Catholic faith.

This is manifestly evident in view of the fact that not only did St. Robert Bellarmine demonstrate that the Fathers teach unanimously that heretics cease to be members of the Church automatically by their heresy (as St. Pius V teaches in the Roman Catechism, and Pius XII in *Mystici Corporis*), and by the very nature of heresy *(ex natura hæresis)* lose office and all jurisdiction; but ultimately because the primacy of jurisdiction of the Roman Pontiff defined by Vatican I is the *plenitudo potestatis* taught by Innocent III, the *potestas absoluta* taught by Ostiense,[637] and the *plena potestas* defined at Florence; to which essentially pertains the power of the **supreme judge** (as constantly taught by the Church and in the decrees of the Council of Trent and in *Pastor Æternus*), whose judgment may be questioned by no one *(Quamvis Patrum, Pastor Æternus, etc.)*, and who absolutely cannot be judged by anyone.[638]

Thus Opinion No. 5, understood as a hypothesis, unlike Opinions nos. 3 & 4, rests on the firm basis of magisterial doctrine that heresy by itself, according to its nature, and not by any human law, separates the manifest heretic from the body of the Church; and on the basis of this doctrine, it was thus judged by Bellarmine to be the true opinion: «Therefore, the true opinion is the fifth, according to which the Pope who is manifestly a heretic ceases by himself to be Pope and head, in the

---

[637] "Gli storici moderni hanno individuato due campi nei quali E. ha contribuito in modo rilevante al pensiero giuridico: si tratta delle dottrine sull'autorità papale e su quella episcopale. Fu il primo ad applicare il termine "potestas absoluta" al papa. Pur nell'esaltazione del potere papale si avvalse della teoria collegiale per sostenere il diritto dei vescovi e dei cardinali a partecipare al governo della Chiesa. La sua dottrina è un complesso tessuto di pensiero autoritario e di pensiero costituzionale in cui entrambe le tendenze raggiungono un equilibrio." – ENRICO da Susa, detto l'Ostiense [Dizionario Biografico degli Italiani – Volume 42 (1993) di **Kenneth Pennington**]

[638] «c. 16 (Gelasius I. a. 493) C. IX. qu. 3: *'Ipsi sunt canones qui appellationes totius ecclesiae ad huius sedis examen voluere deferri. Ab ipsa vero nusquam prorsus appellari debere sanxerunt ac per hoc illam de tota ecclesia iudicare, ipsam ad nullius commeare iudicium nec de eius unquam praeceperunt iudicio iudicari'*; c. 17 (idem a. 498) ead.: *"Cuncta per mundum novit ecclesia, quod sacrosancta Romana ecclesia fas de omnibus habet iudicandi neque cuiquam de eius liceat iudicare iudicio.»* (Hinschius, Op. cit. p. 297)

same way as he ceases to be a Christian and a member of the body of the Church; and for this reason he can be judged and punished by the Church. This is the opinion of all the ancient Fathers, who teach that manifest heretics immediately lose all jurisdiction.» This opinion also reconciles the otherwise irresolvable opposition between the universally accepted doctrine of the *Canon si papa*, which states that a pope may not be judged except for heresy; and the infallible teaching that *the pope may be judged by no one* (which was also upheld by Gratian), since the judgment to be rendered against the fallen Pontiff would not be pronounced on one who would still be the pope, head and supreme judge, but on a pope who would already have become *minor quolibet catholico*; or in the words of Gregory XVI, one who would have already "fallen from the pontificate"; and who would therefore, in the words of Innocent III, be "shown to be already judged."[639]

Unswayed by the iron logic of theological demonstration, Siscoe, unfathomably obdurate in his obstinate pertinacity, resorts to patently absurd argumentation:

> «The article of yours from which these quote (sic) were taken is FULL of errors from start to finish. You even seek to interpret Bellarmine in light of the *minor quilobet catholico* argument, when Bellarmine explicitly rejects itt (sic). You would know that if you took the time to study the origins of that theory, which you clearly haven't. But you will be able to read a very detailed explanation of it in the upcoming second edition of True or False Pope?.»

---

[639] "In tantum enim fides mihi necessaria est ut cum de cæteris peccatis solum Deum judicem habeam, propter solum peccatum quod in fide committitur possem ab Ecclesia judicari. Nam **qui non credit, iam iudicatus est**. (Joh.3 18)" (*Sermo II De Diversis*); and: "Servus enim, secundum Apostolum, «suo domino stat aut cadit (Rom. xiv).» Propter quod idem Apostolus ait; «Tu quis es, qui judicas alienum servum?» (Ibid.) Unde cum Romanus pontifex non habeat alium dominum nisi Deum, quantumlibet evanescat, quis potest eum foras mittere, aut pedibus conculcare? Cum illi dicatur: «Collige causam tuam in sinum tuum?» Verum non frustra sibi blandiatur de potestate, neque de sublimitate vel honore temere glorietur; quia quanto minus judicatur ab homine, tanto magis judicatur a Deo. Minus dico; *quia potest ab hominibus judicari,* **vel potius judicatus ostendi**, si videlicet evanescat in hæresim; quoniam «qui non credit, jam judicatus est» (*Joan*. iii). In hoc siquidem casu debet intelligi de illo, *quod si sal evanuerit, ad nihilum valet ultra, nisi ut, mittatur foras, et conculcetur ab homninibus.*" (*Sermo IV De Diversis*)

One wonders why Siscoe is so afraid to state even briefly his "detailed explanation" of what he calls the "theory" of *minor quolibet catholico*. The fact that he refers to the simple notion of *minor quolibet catholico* – a generally valid principle of Canon Law, as a "theory" betrays his abysmal ignorance of the subject matter. As a principle, it is still applied in canonical rulings that remain valid to the present day. One such example of its valid application in Canon Law is the Holy Office ruling of 20 August 1671 on the extraordinary minister of baptism. The canon sets forth the order of precedence to be observed in determining who must be the extraordinary minister of the sacrament: Can. 742 § 2 *"Si tamen adsit sacerdos, diacono præferatur, diaconus subdiacono, clericus laico et vir feminæ, nisi pudoris gratia deceat feminam potius quam virum baptizare, vel nisi femina noverit melius formam et modum baptizandi."* Thus, a priest is to be preferred to a deacon, a deacon to a subdeacon, a cleric to a layman, a man rather than a woman, etc. The earlier cited Pontifical Canon Law Faculty of Salamanca commentary on the 1917 Code of Canon Law, notes the 1671 ruling of the Holy Office which applies the principle of *minor quolibet catholico* to this order of precedence in the choosing of an extraordinary minister. The ruling, the comment explains, is to be applied *"inter catholicos"*[640]; so that a Catholic layman is to be preferred to a heretical or schismatic cleric. Thus, a non-Catholic is allowed to perform the baptism only if there is no Catholic available to administer the sacrament; since a non-Catholic cleric is outranked by *any Catholic male or female* – the underlying principle being that the non-Catholic is *minor quolibet catholico*. Since this ruling pertains to the administration of sacraments, it remains in force up to the present day according to the prescription of Canon 2 of the 1983 Code: *"leges liturgicæ hucusque vigentes vim suam retinent, nisi earum aliqua Codicis canonibus sit contraria"*.

It is absurd on its face for anyone to say that St. Robert Bellarmine rejected this universally recognized principle; so what is it then, that according to Siscoe, Bellarmine "explicitly rejected"? Siscoe elaborates,

> «I have two older books that discuss the origins and history of the *minor quolibet catholico* theory in detail, and I have the original treatise from the person who came up with it. [...] I also have the complete treatise in the original Latin. I understand the theory. I know who came up with it, why he did so, and what canons he tried to reconcile by creating it. I know the

---

[640] "**742** El canon establece la preferencia *entre catolicos*. El seglar católico debe preferirse a un clérigo hereje o cismático (S. Of., 20 de agosto de 1671)." Miguelez – Alonso – Cabreros; *Op. cit.* p. 292.

problems associated with it, and I also know that none of the recent Popes would can be considered "less than any Catholoc" (sic) (*minor quolibet catholico*), since certain specific conditions are required, which none of them met – not even Francis. Finally, by understanding the theory, I also know that Bellarmine did not hold it, since he **positively affirmed** what those who held the theory denied, **and, in fact, what the theory itself was specifically created to avoid affirming.**»

Siscoe, in spite of his attempt to keep it as a closely guarded secret, gives it away in his statement, "Finally, by understanding the theory, I also know that Bellarmine did not hold it, since he **positively affirmed** what those who held the theory denied, **and, in fact, what the theory itself was specifically created to avoid affirming.**"

It is clear that Siscoe is again resorting to verbal sleight of hand when he attempts to equate the principle of *minor quolibet catholico* with the theory of one man (among many) who employed it in his doctrine on papal loss of office for heresy. What is comical in a pathetic way is how Siscoe is afraid to mention the titles or authors of the books, and the name of the man to whom he attributes the creation of the "theory". In all probability he is referring to Huguccio of Pisa, but that is really a matter of little importance. So, what is it that Bellarmine supposedly affirmed, that Huguccio and the early Decretists of the French school specifically avoided affirming? The canonists who applied the principle *minor quolibet catholico* to a heretic pope did so in order to not violate the principle of papal immunity from judgment. Their doctrine held that the heretic pope would have already ceased to be pope *ipso jure* because of his heresy; and therefore, he could be declared deposed without having to subject the reigning pontiff to trial and judgment, which would violate the doctrine of papal immunity. It is precisely this doctrine of the early Decretists which is the origin of Opinion No. 5, which Bellarmine calls the "fifth and true opinion". Based on their fundamentalistic oversimplification of Bellarmine's refutation of Opinion No. 2, Salza & Siscoe falsely claim that Bellarmine "positively affirmed" that the heretic pope must be judged by the Church in order to lose office; whereas in reality, as I have already demonstrated with a systematic analysis of Bellarmine's refutation of Opinion No. 2, and with the verbatim passage of the Holy Doctor, in which he positively excluded that the pope can ever be judged by anyone, that only if by his manifest heresy he were to cease by himself to be pope, a Christian, and a member of the Church, could he then be judged and punished by the Church. Since the occult heretic is not manifestly a heretic, there would exist the need for the charge of heresy to be examined, and it would have to be proven before the suspected heretic pope could could be *judged* to have fallen from office, as Bellarmine explains in *De Ecclesia Militante, Cap. X.*

What has been the most recent reply of Salza & Siscoe to my utter demolition of their arguments? They have totally ignored my arguments, and instead have simply repeated their old arguments essentially unchanged; apparently hoping that their readers will not even be aware that they have been discredited and refuted. Salza and Siscoe are utterly obstinate and incorrigible in their errors. Salza submitted a two-part article to the *Catholic Family News* for publication. I read his not yet published article. Salza argues like a lunatic: he repeats his argument over and over again, ignoring its refutation, as if totally oblivious to the fact that his arguments have been demolished. So, while there are many more errors in the Salza/Siscoe *magnum opus* on the question of how a heretic pope would lose office, one needs to draw a line under their madness, and so I conclude with the same words which Ballerini wrote when ending his discussion on this point: *Quid igitur in mera hypothesi laboremus pluribus?*

PART FOUR

THE DEPOSITION OF A POPE FOR HERESY

Of the Five Opinions on this question, No. One and No. 3 stand at the opposite extremes, neither allowing for the deposition of a pope for heresy: No. One, because it does not admit the possibility that a pope can become a heretic, and, No. 3., because it holds that even if the pope were to be a manifest and notorious heretic, he could not be removed; neither could he be deposed nor declared to have fallen from the Pontificate. Opinion No. 3 remains today among those theologically semi-literate writers who claim that only a future pope or council can declare with authority that a manifestly hertical pope was indeed a heretic and therfore was not a legitimate pope. Opinion No. One is the most common today, while No. 3 has rightly been universally abandoned by theologians; since, as both Bellarmine and Cajetan maintain correctly, a heretic is not a Christian, and therefore, Bellarmine judges, a heretic, being a non-Christian, simply cannot be pope. Since such a one would be visibly severed from the body of the Church, as *Mystici Corporis* teaches, he would no longer be a member of the Church, and therefore no longer its head. Opinion No. 2 is also an abandoned theory due to its problematic nature which I explained earlier. Opinion No. 4, which holds that a heretic pope can be deposed by a juridical sentence passed by a synod or universal council, was refuted by St. Robert Bellarmine, who explained its deficiencies and thus concluded the fifth Opinion to be the true one, according to which the manifest heretic pope would fall from office automatically by his own actions, by which he departs from the Church, ceases to be a member of the Church, and falls by himself from the Pontificate; and then can be judged and punished by the Church.

Fr. Gleize explains in his above cited article,

> "The common opinion of Medieval theologians is that a heretical pope in the external (and not just internal) forum must and can be deposed by a human authority, since there is (they claimed) here on earth a power above his. This authority is superior to the pope by way of exception, in the case of heresy. This could be the authority of the college of cardinals or possibly of an Ecumenical Council."

In the Counter-Reformation period and for roughly a century afterward, this opinion, listed by Bellarmine as the Fourth Opinion, was mainly represented by Cajetan, Suárez, John of St.Thomas, Laymann, Billuart, and Bañez, and was the more common opinion of the period.

While Opinion No. 4 was the more common opinion in the 17th Century and at least part of the 18th Century, its theological deficiencies became obvious after the rigorous critique of it was made by St. Robert Bellarmine, who exposed its fatal flaws and argued in favour of the Fifth Opinion. As I explained earlier, the two points on which Opinion No. 4 falls are, 1) that a pope, while still in office can be judged; and 2) that a pope who is a manifest heretic (i.e. manifestly guilty of formal heresy), remains in office as a member of the Church until he is deposed, or at least judged guilty of heresy by the Church. Since Vatican I (*Pastor Æternus*), the question of whether a pope can ever be judged while in office is forever closed; and likewise, since *Mystici Corporis* and the 1917 *Codex Juris Canonici*, the question whether a manifest heretic is a defector from the faith, who is cut off from the body of the Church by the act of his own defection and not by the authority of the Church, and thus **ceases by himself to be a member of the Church**; and as a consequence of the defection, falls from office *ipso facto,* is also closed and settled forever by the universal and ordinary magisterium of the Church. John Salza and Robert Siscoe have attempted to resurrect this defunct fourth opinion which has been universally abandoned, and can now be seen to be theologically erroneous and heretical; but in attempting to resurrect the defunct theory, they have succeeded only in exhuming a corpse. The arguments of all the adherents of opinion No. 4 suffer the fatal defect of appealing to the spurious *Canon Si papa* of Gratian's Decretum as the basis and justification for their opinion that the Church possesses the power to judge a reigning pope for heresy by way of exception. On this point, Don Nitoglia observes that *according to this opinion,*

> "The Church or an imperfect council does not act juridically **on the pope**, who is superior to the Church, but, in the hypothetical case of heresy, only dissolves the conjunction of the accidental form (of being pope) from the physical person or second matter canonically elected: Jorge Bergoglio. However, the two doctors [Cajetan and John of St. Thomas] base themselves on the Decretals of Gratian (pars I, dist. 40, canon 6 'Si Papa')

which has been demonstrated to be spurious, *and today, no canonist accepts it any more as a proof of authority.*"[641]

Yet, the very notion of the exception, *"nisi deprehendatur a Fide devius"*, is founded on this spurious canon, and is therefore without basis.

While this opinion in some of its variations *claims* not to properly depose the pope by an act of jurisdiction, yet in order to be a judgment of the Church, and not a private judgment of churchmen, the authors who advocate this opinion insist that the act of judgment must be a juridical act by which the pope is judged to be a heretic. However, such an act by its very nature requires jurisdiction: **"The very idea of the trial of a person supposes that the court conducting the trial has jurisdiction over the person**, but the Pope has no superior, wherefore **no court has power to subject him to judicial trial**."[642] Hence, Bellarmine says, *"For, if the Church deposes a Pope against his will, certainly it is over the Pope"*[643], and therefore, *"Being supreme head of the Church, he cannot be judged by any other ecclesiastical power"*[644]. This opinion of Bellarmine is therefore clearly seen to be dogmatized by the First Vatican Council[645], which solemnly taught and

---

[641] «la Chiesa o il Concilio imperfetto non interviene con un giudizio giuridico sul Papa in atto, il quale è superiore alla Chiesa, ma dissolve, in caso di eresia puramente ipotetica, solamente la congiunzione della forma accidentale (l'essere Papa) dalla persona fisica o materia seconda eletta canonicamente: Jorge Bergoglio. Tuttavia i due Dottori [Cajetan and John of St. Thomas] si rifanno al Decreto di Gratiano (pars I, dist. 40, canon 6 "Si Papa"), **che è stato dimostrato spurio *ed oggi nessun canonista prende più come un argomento d'autorità*.**»

[642] Rev. Stanislaus Woywod, A Practical Commentary on the Code of Canon Law, revised by Rev. Callistus Smith New York, 1952, n. 1549, p. 225.

[643] *De Romano Pontifice*, Lib. II Cap. XXX

[644] *De Romano Pontifice*, Lib. II Cap. XXVI

[645] Et quoniam **divino** Apostolici primatus **iure** Romanus Pontifex **universae Ecclesiae praeest**, docemus etiam et declaramus, eum esse **iudicem supremum fidelium** (Pii PP. VI Breve, *Super soliditate* d. 28 Nov. 1786), *et in omnibus causis ad examen ecclesiasticum spectantibus* ad **ipsius posse iudicium recurri** (Concil. Oecum. Lugdun. II); Sedis vero Apostolicae, **cuius auctoritate maior non est,** *iudicium a nemine fore retractandum, neque cuiquam de eius licere iudicare iudicio* (Ep. Nicolai 1 ad Michaelem Imporatorem). **Quare a recto veritatis tramite aberrant, qui affirmant, licere ab iudiciis Romanorum Pontificum ad oecumenicum**

declared that the Roman Pontiff *"divino jure,* presides over the universal Church as the supreme judge over the all the faithful", "and **all cases pertaining to ecclesiastical scrutiny are referable to him";** and **"whose judgment may be refused by no one, nor is it licit for anyone to judge his judgment"** – and hence, the stake through the heart of the Conciliarist Opinion No. 4 of Cajetan, Suárez, John of St. Thomas, Billuart, Laymann, *et al.*: ***"Quare a recto veritatis tramite aberrant, qui affirmant, licere ab iudiciis Romanorum Pontificum ad oecumenicum Concilium tamquam ad auctoritatem Romano Pontifice superiorem appellare."*** The proponents of Opinion No. 4 protest that the exceptional judgment on a heretic pope by a council would either not constitute an exercise of jurisdiction over the pope, nor exercise a superior power over the pope; but according to its very nature, such a judgment presumes an authority to judge the pope; and without such an authority, the judgment would be a mere nullity. Hence, whether its advocates wish to admit it or not, they who subscribe to Opinion No. Four heretically ascribe to the Church a power to judge the pope which directly opposes the dogma of the pope's universal primacy of jurisdiction.

Thus, the thesis that a pope can be judged juridically by the Church with a *sentence* that is not an *act of jurisdiction*, can be seen to be absurd on its face; since in order to act on the conjunction between the man and the office so as to effect a separation of the two, *a competent juridical sentence* must be pronounced on the ***person*** *of the Pontiff,* **who is the supreme head and judge, and who is subject to the judgment of no one.** Since such an act is made without jurisdiction, it is bereft of all juridical force; and therefore, there is no rational basis – *no sufficient reason to suppose that Christ would comply with that act of rebellious insubordination and depose the heretic pope ipso facto upon the pronouncement of a judgment of heresy on the pope, or after a vitandus sentence would have been pronounced (and which can only be pronounced on the excommunicated by those who possess the jurisdiction to excommunicate).*

In this part of the present work (IV), I will present a critical commentary of Opinion No. 4, as proposed by Suárez and John of St. Thomas; and expose the sophistry employed by Salza and Siscoe to defend, what is at this at this point, already an extinct opinion, but first, Cajetan:

Concilium tamquam ad auctoritatem Romano Pontifice superiorem appellare.

CAJETAN

In his above cited article, Fr. Gleize accurately sums up the position of Cajetan, which I simply quote, and for which no commentary is necessary:

> «Cajetan (1469-1534), in chapters 20-21 of his 1511 treatise, *De Comparatione auctoritatis papae et concilii*, holds that there is an authority that can undo the investiture, in other words, cause the existence of the pontifical authority and the pope's possession of it to cease. But Cajetan tries to differentiate his view from that of the theologians of the previous period by maintaining in principle that on earth there can be no authority superior to the pope, not even in the case of heresy. Indeed, the authority that is required to cause the investiture to cease would be exercised not on the pope but on the connection that exists between the person of the pope and the papacy.
>
> Cajetan's thesis is adopted by Domenico Báñez (1528-1604) (Commentary on the *Summa theologiae* II-II, q. 1, art. 10, conclusio 2, folios 194-196 of the 1587 Venice edition) and by John of Saint Thomas (1589-1644) (*Cursus theologicus*, 5:258-264: De fide, commenting on II-II, q. 1, art. 10, disputatio 2, art. 3, §§17-29). More recently, Cardinal Charles Journet (1891-1975) considered the argument "penetrating" (*The Church of the Incarnate Word*, vol. 1, Excursus 4). It is made up of two aspects.
>
> First, in *De comparatione*, chap. 20, §§280 and 281, Cajetan states an authentic principle: the solution to the problem raised must be rooted in the sources of revelation. Now, divine law is content to say that, if the pope becomes heretical, the Church must avoid him. In fact, we can cite at least six passages of Scripture in which God commands His people not to relate to a formal, public heretic.
>
> Passages cited by Cajetan in §280 include Num 16:26: "Depart from...these wicked men"; Gal 1:8: "Let him be anathema," in other words, separate yourselves from him; 2 Thess 3:6: "Withdraw yourselves from [him]"; and 2 Jn 10: "Receive him not into the house nor say to him: God speed you." The most eloquent passage (which Cajetan moreover cites constantly rather than the five others) is the one from the Epistle of Saint Paul to Titus 3:10: "*Hominem haereticum post unam et secundam correptionem devita.*" ["A man that is a heretic, after the first and second admonition, avoid."] Consequently, divine revelation teaches us no more and no less than this: the Church must avoid any dealings with the heretical pope.»

Fr. Gleize then comments on Cajetan's doctrine:

«Cajetan then proceeds to justify his own theory. He says that there is only one means of avoiding having anything to do with the heretical pope, in keeping with the requirement of divinely revealed law. This means the exercise of a ministerial power that is not a power of jurisdiction strictly speaking, the use of which implies no superiority over the pope. Indeed, this power is none other than the very power that the Church uses to establish the pope in his ministry: its precise object is not the person of the man who receives the papacy, nor the papacy (in other words the pope as such), but the connection between the two, in other words the relation that exists between the person who receives the papacy and the papacy itself (see *De comparatione*, chapter 20, §§282-297).

This power can be exercised in two directions: both to undo the connection as well as to make it. To illustrate this idea, Cajetan turns to an example. The generation or the corruption of a man is caused by an agent that has power over the union between a matter and a form, inasmuch as it disposes the matter, without thereby having power over the form. Similarly, the Church has the power to give the papacy to the person who receives it or to take it away from the one who loses it, inasmuch as she disposes this person, without thereby having power over the papacy.»

Fr. Gleize then points out what he considers the fatal flaw in Cajetan's doctrine:

«Cajetan's explanation suffers from a weakness that it without a doubt fatal to it. For it begs the question, supposing that the authentic meaning of Titus 3:10 (and of other similar passages in Scripture) is the sense required in order to be able to prove the alleged interpretation. Now this supposition is purely gratuitous. St. Paul says that it is necessary to avoid a notorious heretic, no more and no less.»

Fr. Gleize then concludes:

«On the basis of that, nothing proves that a notoriously heretical pope is dismissed from his office, because nothing says that the situation of someone who must be avoided by the faithful is incompatible with the title of the papacy.»

Bellarmine's answer to this objection is that St. Paul orders that the heretic is to be avoided, which he would not order if the heretic were still in the Church; since it is the duty of a pastor to look after those who belong to his flock; which he could not do if he were to be avoided.[646] In his refutation of Cajetan (see quotation below) he argues that even Cajetan admits that a non-Christian cannot be pope, and that a manifest heretic is not a Christian, and therefore not a member of the Church, as the Fathers teach; and not being a member of the Church, the heretic cannot be its head. Therefore, a manifest heretic cannot be Pope. Since the heretic would already be outside the Church even before the *vitandus* order, he would already have ceased to be pope, because one who is not a member of the Church cannot be its head. Thus, the "situation of one who must be avoided" because of heresy is the situation of one who is not a member of the Church, and therefore not its head. It is precisely on this point that the theories of Cajetan and John of St. Thomas fail, since the *vitandus* order would not dispose the pope to fall from office, because it can only be made after the fall from office would already have taken place, for the reason that already, *ex natura hæresis*, "the Pope who is manifestly a heretic ceases by himself to be Pope and head, in the same way as he ceases to be a Christian and a member of the body of the Church." (*De Romano Pontifice, lib. ii cap. xxx*) Thus Bellarmine proves that in the case of manifest heresy, the situation of someone who must be avoided by the faithful is indeed incompatible with the title of the papacy.

Now, here is Salza's summation on Cajetan's teaching:

«3. Cajetan's opinion, which was defended by John of St. Thomas, is that a Pope, who has been judged and declared a heretic by the Church, is then deposed by a separate act of the Church. This separate act is a vitandus declaration which commands that the faithful avoid the Pope who has been declared a heretic by the Church. Cajetan bases his teaching on Divine law, which commands that a heretic, after the first and second warning, must be avoided.»

«Therefore, if the Church warns the Pope twice that he is holding a heretical doctrine, and if he does not recant his heresy, the Church can declare him a heretic and then, according to Divine law, legally command the faithful that he must be avoided. Now, because a Pope who must be avoided can no longer function as the head of the Church, this vitandus declaration renders his authority impotent. It is at this point, according to

---

[646] "apostolus episcopi praecipit, ut haereticum vitet, quod certe non juberet, si esset intra Ecclesiam. Debet enim pastor non vitare, sed curare eos, qui ad suum gregem pertinent." *De Ecclesia Militante*, Cap. IV. p. 76.

Cajetan (and John of St. Thomas), that God Himself authoritatively deposes the Pope by severing the bond that units the man to the office.»

This opinion was refuted by Bellarmine in his presentation on the Fourth Opinion. As has been shown above from the verbatim text of Bellarmine's argument against the Fourth Opinion, the foundation of Bellarmine's argument is quite simply the principle of absolute injudicability of a pope while in office; because, as Don Curzio succinctly explains, that according to Bellarmine's teaching, when the cardinals elect the pope, or designate a person upon whom Christ confers the papal authority, they do not exercise a true and proper juridical selection of the Roman Pontiff, who *does not yet exist in* act, but they exercise upon the physical person of the pope *in potentia*; who, if he accepts the canonical election, receives the Pontificate *in actu*, otherwise he would not pass from being a pope in potentiality to an actual pope; and Bellarmine's conclusion is that the cardinals or the bishops cannot juridically depose the pope because they would be exercising jurisdiction over the pope, and not merely on a person who potentially could become pope, but an actual pope who would be superior to all human and ecclesiastical powers, including the cardinals and the bishops.[647] Hence, Salza's commentary on what Salza & Siscoe refer to on their website as Bellarmine's "attempted refutation" of Cajetan's position can be plainly seen to be utterly errant, and without any rational basis whatsoever:

«What Bellarmine means is that the ipso facto loss of office occurs when the Church judges him to be a heretic, and before the vitandus declaration. This is evident from the fact that he is attempting to refute Cajetan's

---

[647] «Anche S. Roberto Bellarmino (*De Romano Pontifice*, lib. II, cap. 30, Milano, Battezzati, 1857, pp. 418-420) [...] insegna che, quando i Cardinali eleggono il Papa o designano una persona alla quale Gesù conferisce l'autorità papale, non esercitano una vera e propria scelta giuridica sul Pontefice romano, che *ancora non esiste in atto*, ma la esercitano *sulla persona fisica del Papa in potenza* o materiale, che, se dice di accettare l'elezione canonica, riceve da Dio il Pontificato in atto [...] altrimenti non passa dalla potenza all'atto... Il Bellarmino ne conclude che i Cardinali o i Vescovi non possono "deporre" giuridicamente il Papa in concreto o in atto poiché allora eserciterebbero una certa giurisdizione sul Papa in atto o formale trovandosi davanti non solo una semplice persona umana che in potenza potrebbe diventare Papa, ma un Papa in atto o una persona umana eletta, che, avendo accettato l'elezione, è Papa formalmente e quindi è superiore ad ogni potere umano ed ecclesiale, anche ai Vescovi e ai Cardinali.»

opinion, which maintains that the fall is not ipso facto after he is judged by the Church, but only follows the juridical sentence of the vitandus declaration (which, again, directly separates the Church from the Pope, not the Pope from the Church). The reason Kramer and the Sedes have misunderstood Bellarmine is because they have misunderstood Cajetan's opinion, and therefore did not know what Bellarmine was trying to refute.»

The Salza/Siscoe critique of my exposition crosses the boundary of the real world and enters the irrational realm of Fairyland:

«Notwithstanding all of his self-proclaimed erudition, Kramer does not understand Bellarmine's position. And his misunderstanding means he actually disagrees with Bellarmine. The reason is due to a misinterpretation of what Bellarmine wrote in the Fourth and Fifth opinions.»

So, then Salza & Siscoe quote Bellarmine's summation of Cajetan's position:

«The fourth opinion is that of Cajetan, for whom (de auctor. papae et con., cap. 20 et 21) the manifestly heretical Pope is not "ipso facto" deposed, but can and must be deposed by the Church. To my judgment, this opinion cannot be defended. For, in the first place, it is proven with arguments from authority and from reason that the manifest heretic is "ipso facto" deposed. The argument from authority is based on St. Paul (Titus, c. 3), who orders that the heretic be avoided after two warnings, that is, after showing himself to be manifestly obstinate — which means before any excommunication or judicial sentence. (…) Therefore, the true opinion is the fifth, according to which the Pope who is manifestly a heretic ceases by himself to be Pope and head, in the same way as he ceases to be a Christian and a member of the body of the Church; and for this reason he can be judged and punished by the Church. This is the opinion of all the ancient Fathers, who teach that manifest heretics immediately lose all jurisdiction…»

The first thing to be noticed is that Bellarmine plainly states that in his judgment, the opinion which holds that the manifestly heretical pope is not *ipso facto* deposed, but must be deposed by the Church, "cannot be defended". The argument from authority, presented by Bellarmine (and quoted by Salza & Siscoe) is based on the authority of scripture, which says that after the heretic has shown himself to be manifestly obstinate, he must be avoided, "before any excommunication or sentence of a judge". Note that Bellarmine does *not* say, "the manifest heretic is to be avoided **before** a *vitandus declaration*, but **after** having been judged to be pertinacious"; but rather, he, upon *having manifested his pertinacity*, is to be avoided before any judgment at all: **"before any excommunication or sentence of a judge".** Now, 'before any sentence of a judge' means that once the heretic has manifested his pertinacity, he is to be avoided straightaway, before any judgment is pronounced, whether it be a penal, judicial sentence, or a merely declaratory sentence, or a judgment expressed as *vitandus* declaration. What is most conspicuous is the ellipsis in parentheses "(…)" which leaves out the text in which Bellarmine explains that since the heretic must be avoided *before any judgment is pronounced* proves that the heretic is already outside the Church and no longer its head: heretics "are severed from the body of Christ, **but a Pope who remains the Pope cannot be shunned.** How will we shun our Head? How will we recede from a member to whom we are joined?" Bellarmine does not say that the heretic falls from the Pontificate once he has been *judged* incorrigible but **before** a *vitandus* declaration; but rather he states quite the contrary: that the heretic pope simply falls from office *ipso facto "after he appears manifestly pertinacious"*, because "heretics […] **leave by themselves and are severed from the body of Christ**".

«but a Pope who remains the Pope cannot be shunned»

I quoted earlier the passage where Bordoni explains that,

> "the members do not judge their head, from which they have the influx, whence it is understood that the members are destroyed with the head being destroyed, and not conversely; and the members must follow the head and not the head to follow the members, *cap.* I. *dift.* 12. But a council consists of its members, whose head is the pope as is proven *q. 5* **therefore he cannot be deposed by a council.**"

Cardinal Manning explains why this is so:

1. It is *de fide*, or matter of faith, that the head of the Church, as such, can never be separated, either from the *Ecclesia docens*, or the *Ecclesia discens*; that is, either from the Episcopate or from the faithful.

To suppose this, would be to deny the perpetual indwelling office of the Holy Ghost in the Church, by which the mystical body is knit together; the head to the Body, the Body to the head, the members to each other; and to "dissolve Jesus,"* that is, to destroy the perfect symmetry and organization which the Apostle describes as the body of Christ; and St. Augustine speaks of as "one man, head and body, Christ and the Church a perfect man."† On this unity all the properties and endowments of the Church depend; indefectibility, unity, infallibility. As the Church can never be separated from its invisible Head, so never from its visible head.

2. Secondly, it is matter of faith that the *Ecclesia docens* or the Episcopate, to which, together with Peter, and as it were, in one person with him, the assistance of the Holy Ghost was promised, can never be dissolved; but it would be dissolved if it were separated from its head. Such separation, would destroy the infallibility of the Church itself. The *Ecclesia docens* would cease to exist; but this is impossible, and without heresy cannot be supposed.
3.

* St. John iv. 3, "Omnis spiritus qui solvit Jesum," &c.

† "Unus homo caput et corpus, unus homo Christus et Ecclesia vir perfectus."— S. Augustin. *In Psalm xviii.* tom. iv. p. 85, 86, ed. Ben. Paris, 1681.[648]

Thus it is, that if a council, with a judgment that is not *ex sese* infallible, were to judge the pope to be a heretic, and basing itself on that judgment, would then pronounce and bind the faithful of the universal Church with a *vitandus* order against the pope, effectively separating the Church from the pope or the pope from the Church, the infallibility of the *Ecclesia docens* would be destroyed, since the source of the Church's infallibility is the *absolute infallibility* of its head, and separated from its head, upon whose *absolute infallibility* the infallibility of the episcopacy depends, the Church cannot not teach or judge matters of doctrine infallibly. Manning explains, "1. First, that what depends on no other is altogether independent. 2. Secondly, that what is circumscribed by no condition is absolute." The pope's infallibility is a charism conferred on the pope directly by God, which is exercisd by the pope alone and independently from the bishops. Functioning within its specified parameters, the exercise of papal infallibility is not subject to by any limiting conditions, and is therefore, in this sense, **absolute**, insofar as what the pope infallibly defines is *absolutely certain to be free from error*, and is *absolutely binding in conscience on absolutely every member of the universal Church.*

The unity of the one faith of the Church would be destroyed if a council would be able judge a pope on a question of doctrine. I quoted earlier the words of Pope Gregory XVI, who explained that according

---

[648] Manning, *The Vatican Council and its Definitions*, pp. 112-113.

to St. Thomas, the Pontiff, "is the supreme judge of disputes, to whom belongs the solemn edition of the symbol, that is, the norm of our belief, and concludes: 1. ° That it is the Pope: 2. ° distinct, and separate from all the other bishops, having to Indeed be held by these, *inconcussa fide*, what he determines as the dogma of faith". Pope Gregory then says St. Thomas proves it "***from the unity of faith*** which is to be professed throughout the Church, **which unity would be lacking, if the Pope were not the supreme judge of the disputes**, and the only promulgator of the dogmatic definitions". Such judgments pertain by divine law to the jurisdiction of the pope *alone*. Cardinal Manning quotes Pope Clement VI:

> «Lastly, Clement VI, in the fourteenth century, proposed to the Armenians certain interrogations, of which the fourth is as follows: "Hast thou believed, and dost thou still believe, that the Roman Pontiff *alone* can, by an authentic determination to which we must inviolably adhere, put an end to doubts which arise concerning the Catholic faith; and that whatsoever he, by the authority of the keys delivered to him by Christ, determines to be true, is true and Catholic; and what he determines to be false and heretical is to be so esteemed?"[649] *»[650]

If a council rather than the pope were to attempt to exercise the authority to decide a dispute in a matter of faith against or without the pope, it would usurp the supreme jurisdiction which belongs to the pope alone by divine law; with the result that **the unity of faith would be lacking if the Pope were not the supreme judge of the disputes.**

Such a judgment against the pope would also destroy the governance of the Church divinely constituted under the one head by inverting the order of that governance, placing the members over the head. Cardinal Manning explains,

> «Ballerini says, that the jurisdiction of St. Peter, by reason of the primacy, was "singular and personal" to himself. The same right he affirms to belong

---

[649] «* "Si credidisti et adhuc credis solum Romanum Pontificem, dubiis emergentibus circa fldem catholicam posse per determinationem authenticam cui sit inviolabiliter adhærendum, finem imponere et esse verum et Catholicum quidquid ipse auctoritate clavium sibi traditarum a Christo determinat esse verum; et quod determinat esse falsum et hæreticum sit censendum." — Baronius, tom. xxv. ad arm. 1351, p. 529. Lucca, 1750.»

[650] Manning, *The Vatican Council and its Definitions*, p. 108.

also to the Roman Pontiffs, St. Peter's sucessors."[651] This doctrine he explains diffusely. "This primacy of chief jurisdiction, not of mere order, in St. Peter and the Roman Pontiffs his successors, is personal, that is, attached to their person; and therefore a supreme personal right, which is communicated to no other, is contained in the primacy."»

From this it follows,

«That infallibility is, as the Definition expressly declares, a supernatural grace, or charisma, attached to the primacy, in order to its proper exercise. Infallibility is a quality of the doctrinal jurisdiction of the Pontiff in faith and morals. And such also is the doctrine of Ballerini, who lays down the following propositions: "Unity with the Roman faith is absolutely necessary, and therefore the prerogative of absolute infallibility is to be ascribed to it, and a coercive power to constrain to unity of faith, in like manner, absolute; as also the infallibility and coercive power of the Catholic Church itself, which is bound to adhere to the faith of Rome, is absolute."*»[652]

The coercive power to constrain and bind the whole Church in law and doctrine pertains personally and exclusively to the Roman Pontiff in virtue of his primacy. Hence, an attempt by any kind of synod or council of bishops, the Roman clergy, or the college of cardinals, to exercise a coercive power over the whole Church against the pope would directly oppose the primacy of the pope; and therefore, the proposition that the Church would have the power to depose a pope either directly by a superior jurisdiction, or to depose him by exercising a power to dispositively disjoin him from the papacy by separating the Church from the pope, or the pope from the Church, is heretical.

Next, by means of the ellipsis Salza & Siscoe also leave out Bellarmine's strongest argument – his argument from reason:

---

[651] *Ibid.* p. 100 — «"Jurisdictio et prærogativæ quæ eidem sedi ab antiquis asseruntur ratione primatus ejusdem Petri ac successorum singulares et personales judicandæ sunt." — Ballerini, *de Vi et Ratione Primatus*, cap. iii. sect. 5, p. 14. Rome, 1849.»

[652] *Ibid.* pp. 100, 103 — «Ballerini *de Vi et Rat. Primatus*: Unitas cum Romana fide absolute necessaria est, ac proinde infallibilitatis prærogativa absoluta illi est tribuenda, et vis coactiva ad fidei unitatem pariter absoluta: sicuti absoluta est item infallibilitas et vis coactiva ipsius Ecclesias Catholicæ, quae Romanæ fidei adhærere oportet. Appendix De infall. Pont. Prop. vii.»

«Now in regard to reason this is indeed very certain. A non-Christian cannot in any way be Pope, as Cajetan affirms in the same book, and the reason is because he cannot be the head of that which he is not a member, and he is not a member of the Church who is not a Christian. But a manifest heretic is not a Christian, as St. Cyprian and many other Fathers clearly teach.»

Bellarmine explains further, «the Holy Fathers teach in unison, that not only are heretics outside the Church, but they even lack all Ecclesiastical jurisdiction and dignity ipso facto. Cyprian says: "We say that all heretics and schismatics have not power and right."» He then points out that the Fathers teach in unison that heretics do not lose office by means of judgment according to any human law, but they lose all jurisdiction and ecclesiastical dignity *ex natura hæresis*. Thus, St. Robert demonstrates irrefutably that a manifestly heretical pope would **by himself** (*"per se"*) cease to be pope *ipso facto*, and *"sine alia vi externa"*; hence, **without any judgment by the Church**, because, **"Being supreme head of the Church, he cannot be judged by any other ecclesiastical power"**.[653]

The failure of Salza & Siscoe to understand Bellarmine's refutation of the Fourth Opinion is rootd in their misinterpretation of Bellarmine's exposition on the Second and Third Opinions:

«Now, let's compare Kramer's interpretation of Bellarmine's Fifth Opinion to what Bellarmine himself wrote in the Second and Third Opinions:

Kramer: "While he holds office, the pope can be judged by no one."

Bellarimine: "That a heretical Pope can be judged is expressly held in the Canon, Si Papa, dist. 40, and with Innocent. ... heresy, the only reason where it is lawful for inferiors [the Church] to judge superiors [the pope]. (…) in the case of heresy, a Roman Pontiff can be judged."

Kramer: "the loss of office which takes place ipso facto and without any judgment or declaration."

Bellarmine: "For Jurisdiction is certainly given to the Pontiff by God, but with the agreement of men [those who elect him], as is obvious; because this man, who beforehand was not Pope, has from men that he would begin to be Pope, therefore, he is not removed by God unless it is through men. But a secret heretic cannot be judged by men..."»

---

[653] *De Romano Pontifice*, Book 2, Ch. 26.

As I explained above, Salza & Siscoe have totally failed to grasp the significance of the distinction in Bellarmine's doctrine between *depositus* and *deponendus*, which he made in his commentary on the Third Opinion; and according to which a manifestly heretical pope would not be able to be deposed (*deponi posse*) by the Church, but would already "by himself" (*per se*), *ipso facto* "be deposed" (*esse depositus*), by means of his manifest heresy. Likewise, as I explained above, they have failed to take into account Bellarmine's distinction between the procedures he prescribes to be followed in the case of one accused as an occult heretic pope in his rejection of the Second Opinion in *De Ecclesia Militante Cap. X*, and that to be followed in the case a manifestly heretical pope in *De Romano Pontifice lib. ii. cap. xxx*. According to Bellarmine, in the case of the occult heretic, the accusation must first be proven, so that his heresy becomes manifest, and he can be judged to have fallen from office before he can be removed; whereas in the case of the manifest heretic pope, he is condemned and falls from the Pontificate entirely by his own judgment, and therefore, **having fallen from office**, can be judged and punished by the Church.

SUÁREZ

1) *"Therefore when the Church would depose a Pope, she would not do it as a superior, but by the consent of Christ the Lord she would juridically declare him to be a heretic, and thus unworthy of the pontifical dignity; and then ipso facto he would be immediately deposed by Christ, and being deposed he would remain deposed, and could be punished."*[654]

To *juridically* pronounce judgment on a person, as has been shown, is properly the act of a superior which requires *jurisdiction*. If the Church would not act as superior to the pope, it would need to refrain from such an act of pronouncing judgment on him that is strictly proper to a superior, and for which it lacks jurisdiction. Bellarmine and Ballerini solved this dilemma by explaining and demonstrating that a manifest heretic, (in accordance with the Church's teaching on defection from the

---

[654] Suarez, *Op. cit.*, p. 318: «quando ergo Ecclesia Papam hæreticum deponeret, non ipsa tanquam superior id præstaret, sed ex consensione Christi Domini juridice declararet eum hæreticum esse, atque adeo prorsus indignum Pontificis dignitate; tuncque ipso facto immediate a Christo deponeretur, depositusque maneret inferior, ac posset puniri.»

faith and loss of office), first ceases to be a Christian and a member of the Church, ceases to be pope by falling from office *by himself*; and *therefore* can then be judged and punished by the Church. As explained earlier, it is the magisterial teaching and canonical position of the Church that those who publicly defect from the faith into heresy lose office automatically, i.e. *ipso jure* and *without any declaration*; and then the Church declares and enforces the loss of office *post factum*.

> 2) *"What stands in the way is that if even an external heretic, but occult, can still be a true pope, then for the same reason he could still be pope, even if his delict becomes known, as long as no sentence is pronounced upon him, accordingly because no one falls under a penalty, unless ipso facto or by a sentence; and also because greater troubles would follow; we would most assuredly fall into doubt as to how great must be the infamy, for it to be judged that he would fall from his dignity; schisms would result; and everything would be made perplexing, especially if after having become infamous, he would by force or by other means retain possession of the see, and exercise many acts of his office."*[655]

An external but occult heretic would still be a member of the Church, unlike the manifest heretic who by his defection from the faith would cease to be a member of the Church; and would lose office as a result of *removal*, which is *not* a penalty, but is the *natural and canonical consequence of defection from the faith*. As far as the *greater troubles that would follow*, the problem that, *"we would most assuredly fall into doubt as to how great must be the infamy, for it to be judged that he would fall from his dignity,"* has already been resolved by the canons of the 1917 Code of Canon Law, as has been pointed out earlier in this work. Furthermore, **those problems (as great as they might be) would be as nothing compared to the *universal ruin* that would result if the hierarchy would continue to tolerate and be subject to a manifest heretic Pontiff** – *"quod esset miserrima*

---

[655] «Sed obstat, quia si hæreticus etiam exterior, occultus tamen, adhuc potest esse verus Papa, eadem ratione poterit, esto delictum fiat notum, quandiu de illo non pronunciatur sententia; tum quia nullus incidit in pœnam, nisi vel ipso facto, vel per sententiam; tum etiam quia sic majora incommoda sequerentur; incideremus nimirum in dubium quanta deberet esse infamia, ut a dignitate cadere censeretur; sequerentur ergo schismata, et perplexa omnia redderentur, præcipue si, post infamiam, per vim vel modo alio retineret seddis possessionem, pluresque actus sui muneris exerceret.» — Suarez, *Op. cit.*, p. 316-317.

conditio Ecclesiæ, si lupum manifeste grassantem, pro pastore agnoscere cogeretur." (Bellarminus)

> 3) *"Against this opinion I say secondly: in no case, even of heresy, is the Pontiff deprived of his dignity and power immediately by God, without the foregoing judgment and sentence of men. Such is the common opinion today: Cajetan, de Auctoritate Papæ, c. 18 et 19; Soto, 4, d. 22, quæst. 2, art. 2; Cano, 4 de Locis, c. ult., ad 12; Corduba, lib. 4, q. 11."*[656]

Such was the more common opinion at *that time*, but is no more, having been refuted by Bellarmine and Ballerini, whose doctrine was then endorsed by Pope Gregory XVI, and has since become the unanimous opinion of all canonists who admit at least the hypothetical possibility of a pope becoming a public heretic. I repeat, as explained above, it is **now** the explicit magisterial teaching and canonical position of the Church that those who publicly defect from the faith into heresy lose **whatsoever offices** (*quælibet officia*) *ipso facto*, i.e. automatically: *ipso jure*, and *sine ulla declaratione*. It was **not** the clear magisterial teaching, nor was it yet set forth in Canon Law in Suárez's day. After Opinion No One, Opinion No. 5, at least as a hypothesis, is now the more common opinion, while Opinion no. 4 is not proposed by any serious theologian today[657] – it is dead.

> 4) *"And below, treating of penalties for heretics, we will explain and show generally that no one is deprived by divine law of ecclesiastical dignity and jurisdiction for the offense of heresy; now we will briefly give the reason a priori, since it is a most grave penalty, in order that it be incurred ipso facto, it would need to be expressly stated in divine law, however, no such law is to be found stating it for heretics in general, or especially for bishops, or most especially for a pope, nor is there any certain tradition for it."*[658]

---

[656] Suarez, *Op. cit.*, p. 316.

[657] The *gallicanizing* Cardinal Journet was the last.

[658] «Et infra agentes de pœnis hæreticorum alios referemus, ac generaliter ostendemus jure divino non privari quempiam dignitate et jurisdictione ecclesiastica propter culpam hæresis; nuc breviter ratio a priori redditur, quia cum ea sit gravissima pœna, ut ipso facto incurratur, oportet jure divino expressam esse; nullum autem jus tale invenitur, quod vel generaliter id statuat de hæreticis, aut specialiter de episcopis, aut specialissime de Papa; nec item certa traditio de eo habetur» — Suarez, *Op. cit.*, p. 316.

Here, as explained earlier in this work, Suárez makes the mistake of treating loss of office as if it were a penalty for a transgression against a judicial precept of positive law, which it is not, whereas on the contrary, it pertains to natural law, and as such is not to be found among any of the judicial precepts of positive law, whether divine or human. Bellarmine already proved the contrary opinion by demonstrating in his refutation of Opinion No. 4 that it is unanimously held by the Fathers; namely, that manifest heretics lose office automatically by themselves *ex natura hæresis*, because they cease by themselves to be members of the Church, and not as a punishment for having transgressed a precept of positive law.[659] The provision for tacit resignation of office in the 1917 Code of Canon Law, being founded on the unanimous teaching of the Fathers, forever lays this objection to rest.

5) *"... nor can the Pontiff fall ipso facto from his dignity by any human law, since it would be issued by an inferior, such as a council, or an equal, namely a predecessor pope; and neither of these has coercive force, to be able to punish a pope who is equal, or a superior."*[660]

It is not only a matter of divine law, as Bellarmine proved, but also has since been enacted into ecclesiastical law, as has already been explained above. Suárez makes the error of thinking in terms of a law that would bring about an *ipso facto* loss of office as a *punishment*, whereas in Canon Law, it is not a punishment, but the natural consequence of defecting from the faith into heresy, which the Church acknowledges by placing this provision in the administrative section of her canons.

6) *"You will say there can be a law interpretative of divine law. This however is contrived, because no such divine law has been brought forth; and so far none*

---

[659] «Therefore, the true opinion is the fifth, according to which the Pope who is manifestly a heretic ceases by himself to be Pope and head, in the same way as he ceases to be a Christian and a member of the body of the Church; and for this reason he can be judged and punished by the Church. This is the opinion of all the ancient Fathers, who teach that manifest heretics immediately lose all jurisdiction." And, "Thenceforth, the Holy Fathers teach in unison, that not only are heretics outside the Church, but they even lack all Ecclesiastical jurisdiction and dignity ipso facto." And further, "those Fathers, when they say that heretics lose jurisdiction, do not allege any human laws which maybe did not exist then on this matter; rather, they argued from the nature of heresy.»

[660] *Ibid.*

has yet been issued by councils or Pontiffs which would interpret that divine law. This is confirmed because such a law would be ruinous to the Church, therefore it is not at all to be believed that it was instituted by Christ; and the antecedent is proven, because if the pope were an occult heretic, he would fall ipso jure from his dignity, and all of his acts would be invalid.'[661]

Since the codification of Canon Law in the 20th Century, there is precisely that *"law interpretative of divine law"* – the canons on tacit renunciation of office and removal. Suárez imagines that *"such a law would be ruinous to the Church"*; but unfortunately, he did not imagine how much more greatly a heretic pope would endanger the Church and threaten it with universal ruin if he were to remain in office until the Church officials would finally get their act together and judge the heretical miscreant. The problem would not even arise if the pope were an occult heretic, and did nothing to disturb the general state of the Church, or against the teaching of the Church that would raise suspicions about his personal orthodoxy. If he were to manifest his heresy publicly by his words and actions, then it would no longer be a question of a merely occult heretic, but of *manifest heresy*.

7) *"Secondly it is strongly confirmed, for if it would happen that the pope were to become even an external heretic, but occult, who would then afterward come to his senses and repent, he would emerge entirely perplexed; for if he were to fall from his dignity, he would have to yield the pontificate, which is a very grave matter, and almost against nature, being tantamount to betraying himself; but he would not be able to retain the episcopate, because it would be intrinsically evil. Whence even the authors who are of the contrary opinion admit that in such a case he could retain the episcopate, and be a true Pope, which is the common opinion of canonists, in accordance with the Gloss, c. Nunc autem, d. 21.'*[662]

---

[661] «Dices posse haberi legem interpretativam juris divini. Est tamen hoc commentitium, quia nullum tale præfertur jns diviuum; præterra nulla hactenus a Conciliis vel Pontiticibus lata lex est, quæ id jus divinum interpretetur. Confirmatur, quia ejuscemodi jus perniciosum esset Ecclesiæ; minime ergo credendum est fuisse a Christo institutum; probaturantecedens, quia si Papa hæreticus occultus esset, et ipso jure a dignitate caderet, omnia ab eo facta irrita forent.» — *Ibid.*

[662] «Confirmatur secundo urgentissime, quia si accideret Papam hæreticum fieri etiam exteriorem, sed occultum, qui postea resipisceret ac vere pœniteret, omnino evaderet perplexus; nam si per hæresim cecidit a dignitate, debet

This argument is a most valid objection against Opinion No. 2, but is patently inapplicable to Opinion No. 5, which is a matter of manifest heresy, which constitutes an act of tacit abdication – not implicit but (as explained earlier) a true but tacit act of abdication.

> 8) *"Finally, faith is not altogether necessary in order that a man be capable of spiritual and ecclesiastical jurisdiction, and he would be able to exercise true acts requiring such jurisdiction; therefore, etc. The antecedent is quite clear, since in extreme necessity a heretical priest can absolve, as is taught in the material on penance and censures; which is not done without jurisdiction. [...] From which the foundation of the contrary opinion collapses; for as faith is not the necessary fundament for the power of orders, which in its own way is more excellent, likewise neither for jurisdiction; and to these arguments I believe no author will say with even a shadow of probability that by interior heresy alone the papal dignity is lost, although it is certain that faith is lost."*[663]

However, while *"faith is not altogether necessary in order that a man be capable of spiritual and ecclesiastical jurisdiction, and he would be able to exercise true acts requiring such jurisdiction"*; nevertheless. (as explained earlier): faith is absolutely necessary for a man to exercise the charism of Infallibility and perform the function of *confirmator fratrum*, and therefore, without faith, the necessary disposition for the preservation of the form of the Pontificate in the person of the pope would be absent, and the heretic

---

omnino pontificatu cedere, quod est gravissimum, et fere contra jus naturæ, se nimirum prodere; retinere autem episcopatum non posset, quia intrinsece malum esset. Unde ipsi etiam contrariæ sententiæ auctores fatentur, in eo casu posse retinere episcopatum, atque esse revera Papam, quæ est commuuis sententia Canonistarum, cum Glossa, c. *Nunc autem*, d. 21.» — Suarez, *Op. cit.*, p. 317.

[663] «Tandem fides non est omnimode necessaria, ut homo sit capax spiritualis et ecclesiasticæ jurisdictionis, possitque exercere veros actus talem jurisdictionem exigentes; ergo, etc. Antecedens patet manifeste, quippe in extrema necessitate sacerdos hæreticus potest absolvere, ut in materia de pœnitentia et censuris docetur, quod non fit sine jurisdictione. [...] Ex quo fundamentum contrariæ sententiæ ruit; sicut enim fides non est fundamentum necessarium ad potestatem ordinis, cum suo modo præstantior est, ita neque jurisdictionis; ad hæc nullus, ut credo, auctor dicet, cum probabilitatis umbra, per solam interiorem hæresim amitti dignitatem papalem, quamvis sit certum amitti fidem.» — *Ibid.*

would necessarily fall from the Pontificate as Bellarmine explained.[664] However, it is impossible for a pope to become a heretic, as Bellarmine explained, *"the Pope by his own nature can fall into heresy, but not when we posit the singular assistance of God which Christ asked for him by his prayer."*[665] Thus, Bellarmine's argument does not support Opinion No. 2, but rather underscores the validity of Opinion No. One. Finally, while it is true that the argument, *"for as faith is not the necessary fundament for the power of orders, which in its own way is more excellent, likewise neither for jurisdiction"* is valid regarding the retaining of jurisdiction of the occult heretic, and the exercise of supplied jurisdiction by the public heretic; it is not applicable to the *loss of office* and *ordinary jurisdiction* in case of public defection from the faith into heresy, which entails an *ipso facto* loss of office and of *ordinary jurisdiction*, due to withdrawal from communion and cessation of membership in the Church.

> 9) *"The Church cannot validly exercise any act of jurisdiction over the Pope, nor does she confer any power on him by electing him, but designates the person upon whom Christ by himself confers the power; therefore, when the Church would depose a heretical Pope, she would not do it as a superior, but by the consent of Christ the Lord she would juridically declare him to be a heretic, and thus entirely unworthy of the papal dignity; and then ipso facto he would be immediately deposed by Christ, and being deposed, he would remain inferior, and could be punished."*[666]

The Church, *"would juridically declare him to be a heretic"*, according to Suárez, but to **juridically declare him to be a heretic**, is to pronounce a judgment over **him**; and to do this, they who judge must possess jurisdiction over him and act as a superior, otherwise the judgment is simply not a juridical judgment at all, lacking the nature of a judgment,

---

[664] "ista dispositione sublata per contrariam quae est haeresis, mox papa desinit esse; neque enim potest forma conservari sine necessariis dispositionibus." — *De Romano Pontifice, Lib. II, Cap. XXX.*

[665] *De Romano Pontifice, Lib. IV, Cap. VII.*

[666] «Ecclesia nullum actum jurisdictionis exercere valet in Papam, neque confert illi potestatem eligendo, sed personam designat cui Christus per se confert potestatem; quando ergo Ecclesia Papam hæreticum deponeret, non ipsa tanquam superior id præetaret, sed ex consensione Christi Domini juridice declararet eum hæreticum esse, atque adeo prorsus indignum Pontificis dignitate; tuncque ipso facto immediate a Christo deponeretur, depositusque maneret inferior, ac posset puniri.» — Suarez, *Op. cit.* p. 318.

and therefore is not being *juridical*, it would lack all authority. The claim that the judgment would be pronounced, *"by the consent of Christ the Lord"*, is a premise that is utterly lacking any foundation (except for the spurious *Canon Si papa*) – it is a mere conjecture; as is, therefore, also the conclusion, *"and then ipso facto he would be immediately deposed by Christ"*. The argument that the Church does not *"does she confer any power on him by electing him, but designates the person upon whom Christ by himself confers the power [...] therefore, when she would depose a heretical Pope, she would not do it as a superior"*, is a fallacious argument which is essentially the argument of Cajetan which Bellarmine refuted: **"For while a thing is made, the action is exercised over the matter of the thing that is going to be, not over a composite which does not yet exist, but while a thing is destroyed, the action is exercised over a composite; as is certain from natural things."** A *juridical* act of deposition involves an act of judgment over the composite (as Bellarmine explains), which is essentially distinct in its nature from the ministerial act which (says Suárez) *"designates the person upon whom Christ by himself confers the power"*. Bellarmine explains the distinction, which is, that:

> "when Cardinals create the Pontiff, they exercise their authority not over the Pontiff, because he does not yet exist; but over the matter, that is, over the person whom they dispose in a certain measure through election, that he might receive the form of the pontificate from God; but if they depose the Pope, they necessarily exercise authority over the composite, that is, over the person provided with pontifical dignity, which is to say, over the Pontiff."

According to Suárez, the heretic pope would be deposed immediately by Christ "ipso facto" — *"by that very fact"*, i.e. by that very fact that the **CHURCH**, *"would juridically declare him to be a heretic"*. Thus, *"ipso facto he would be immediately deposed by Christ"*; which is clearly an act of **deposition** which falls under Opinion No. 4, and **NOT**, (as *Salza and Siscoe fraudulently claim*), the opinion of Bellarmine (and Ballerini), namely, Opinion No. 5; according to which, the **fact by which the heretic pope ceases to be pope ipso facto is HIS OWN JUDGMENT pronounced against himself**, and thereby ceases to be pope *"by himself" (per se)* — *"sine alia vi externa"*. For Suárez (Opinion No. 4), the "fact" by which he is deposed *ipso facto* for heresy by Christ is the *declared judgment of heresy by the Church*; whereas for Bellarmine (Opinion No.5), the "fact" by which he ceases to be pope by himself (*per se*) is *his own judgment declared against*

himself, **since heretics are judged by their own condemnation** *(sunt enim proprio judicio condemnati).*[667] As mentioned above, on the opinion of an *ipso facto* loss of office *by the act of heresy itself,* Suárez declares, "Against this opinion I say secondly: in no case, even of heresy, is the Pontiff deprived of his dignity and power immediately by God, without the foregoing judgment and sentence of men."[668] On the same page he then contradicts himself saying on the one hand that when *the Church deposes* the heretic pope, she does so with the consent of Christ *juridically declaring him to be a heretic*; but then he says that *ipso facto* he would be deposed *immediately by Christ*: «*when the Church would depose a heretical Pope, she would not do it as a superior, but by the consent of Christ the Lord she would juridically declare him to be a heretic, and thus entirely unworthy of the papal dignity; and then ipso facto he would be immediately deposed by Christ*» So, according to Suárez, the Church deposes the pope by juridically declaring him personally to be a heretic with a juridical act that by its nature requires the jurisdiction of a superior, but the Church does not act as a superior when it deposes the pope juridically, because after judging him juridically as a superior on the unfounded presumption of Christ's consent, he is then presumed to be deposed immediately by Christ!

> 10) "*... a heretical Pope is not a member of the Church, with respect to the substance and form by which the members of the Church are constituted, but he is the head with respect to his office and inflow; which is no wonder, because he is not the first and primary head, conveying by his own strength, but as if instrumental, and vicarious of the first head, which is able to give the spiritual inflow to the members, even through a head of bronze; since by proportional reckoning it sometimes baptizes, sometimes even absolves, as has been said."*[669]

---

[667] "Yet heretics are outside the Church, even before excommunication, and deprived of all jurisdiction, for they are condemned by their own judgment, as the Apostle teaches to Titus; that is, they are cut from the body of the Church without excommunication, as Jerome expresses it." *De Romano Pontifice,* Lib. II, Cap. XXX.

[668] Suarez, *Op. cit.*, p. 318: «Contra hanc sententiam dico secundo: in nullo casu, etiam hæresis, privatur Pontifex sua dignitate et potestate immediate ab ipso Deo, absque hominum præeunte judicio et sententia.»

[669] «[Ad tertiam confirmationem unico verbo respondetur,] Papam hæreticum non esse membrum Ecclesiæ, quoad substantiam et formam qua constituuntur membra Ecclesiæ, esse tamen caput quoad officium et influxum; quod non est mirandum, quia non est primum et præcipuum caput sua virtute influens, sed quasi instrumentale, et vicarium primi capitis, quod potens est

If the heretical pope is not a member of the Church (and a manifest heretic is not a member), then he cannot be the head, since the head is a member. So, if he *is not a member of the Church, with respect to the substance and form by which the members of the Church are constituted*, then he is not the head either; and therefore is an incapable subject to hold the office from which comes the instrumental power to infallibly convey the spiritual inflow to the members. Furthermore, the pope is not a bronze statue, but a man endowed with a free will, and therefore, respecting the nature He created, God cannot force a heretic pope *against nature* to confirm the faith of the bishops if the heretic is opposed to their faith and unwilling to confirm it – hence, Bellarmine rightly rejects this idea saying, "this will be a great violence, and not in keeping with the providence of God that sweetly disposes all things."

> 11) *"Thirdly I say: if the Pope is heretical and incorrigible, as soon as a declaratory sentence of the crime is pronounced upon him, he ceases to be Pope. It is the common opinion of the Doctors, taken from the first letter of Clement I, where it is said Peter taught that a heretical Pope is to be deposed. Now this is the foundation, that it would be gravely harmful to the Church to have such a pastor, nor could she come to her own assistance in such a grave peril; and additionally it would be contrary to the dignity of the Church to remain subject to a heretical Pontiff, nor could she drive him away, for such as are the priests, so are the people to be evaluated."*[670]

This opinion has already been sufficiently dealt with and refuted. Ballerini explains why no declaratory sentence is needed in order that the heretic cease to be pope. To the statement that, "*It is the common opinion*

---

influxum spiritualem membris tribuere, vel per caput æneum; proportionali enim ratione per hæreticos interdum baptizat, interdum etiam absolvit, ut dictum est.» — *Ibid.* p. 317.

[670] «Dico tertio: si Papa sit hæreticus et incorrigibilis, cum primum per legitimam Ecclesiæ jurisdictionem sententia declaratoria criminis in eum profertur, desinit esse Papa. Est communis Doctorum; colligitur ex Clemonte I, epistola prima, ubi ait Petrum docuisse hæreticum Papam esse deponendum. Fundamentum autem hoc est, quia gravissimum foret nocumentum Ecelesiæ talem habere pastorem, nec posse sibi subvenire in tam gravi periculo; præterea contra dignitatem Ecclesiae facit subditam manere hæretico Pontifici, neque posse illum a se depellere; nam qualis est princeps et sacerdos, talis solet existimari populus» — *Ibid.*

of the Doctors, taken from the first letter of Clement I, where it is said Peter taught that a heretical Pope is to be deposed," Michael Davies answers:

> On this subject Suarez's credibility is open to serious question, for his contemporary St. Robert Bellarmine, who was thoroughly familiar with the whole of patristic literature, assures us in his own consideration of this subject [*De Romano Pontifice*] that "the Fathers are *unanimous* in teaching, not only that heretics are outside the Church, but also that they are *'ipso facto'* deprived of all jurisdiction and ecclesiastical rank." Certainly the single instance adduced by Suarez in support of his statement shortly after the words quoted above does nothing to weaken St. Robert's assurance, for Suarez's claim that some Fathers differed from the view he rightly attributes to SS. Cyprian, Ambrose, Augustine, etc., is, he says, gathered from the first epistle of Clement I [...] which says, according to Suarez, that St. Peter taught that a heretical pope is *to be deposed* (rather than *automatically deposed*). And yet the fact is that St. Clement *nowhere* represents St. Peter as having said anything of the kind, as readers can confirm by reference to any of the translations of this epistle available in good libraries. The nearest Clement approaches to the subject is his statement that "our Apostles" i.e. SS. Peter and Paul, "knew that there would be contention concerning the name of the episcopacy" and consequently left instructions "in what manner, when they [bishops and deacons] should die, other approved men should succeed them in their ministry (Chapter 44)." It is of little consequence whether Suarez was trusting an unreliable secondary source, or a corrupt primary text, or whether he has just made a mistake, what cannot be denied is that his position is based on a misrepresentation of the teaching of the Fathers.[671]

> 12) *"Concerning this conclusion there are some things to be explained. First, by whom is to be delivered this sort of sentence. Some say it is to be handed down by the Cardinals; and indeed the Church could commit this case to them, especially if it were to be so established as it has been done with the election; but until now we do not read this judgment to have been committed to them; and therefore it is to be said that it pertains to all the bishops of the Church; for since they are the ordinary pastors and pillars of the Church, it is to be believed that this matter pertains to them, and since by divine law there is no greater reason for these ones rather than those, and about this nothing is established in human law, it would necessarily be said to be up to all of them, and so to a general Council, and thus the common opinion has it."*[672]

---

[671] Michael Davies, *An Evaluation*, p. 174.
[672] «Circa hanc vero conclusionem sunt nonulla explicanda. Primo, a quo ferri debeat hujusmodi sententia. Quidam enim dicunt a Cardinalibus ferendam;

This opinion has been amply refuted by Bellarmine and Ballerini in the texts I quoted earlier.

> 13) *"Whence is it established that by divine law the Pontiff is immediately deposed upon the sentence being passed? I answer first that I have already brought forth the testimony of Clement from the mouth of Peter; secondly, the sacred Scriptures which command that heretics be avoided sufficiently indicate this; thirdly, it is had from the common consensus of the Church and the Pontiffs; fourth, natural reason teaches it, since it is not to be believed Christ abandoned the Church without any remedy in such a danger, but the remedy I have adduced seems to be most adapted to the case we are disputing."*[673]

There is no such testimony of St. Clement of any such words from the mouth of St. Peter. The scriptural passages that command us to avoid heretics can just as easily be observed if the heretic fell from office automatically; there is nothing in the scriptural passages in question that would necessitate that a sentence be passed (which would be impossible) before the heretic would cease to be pope, in order that the scriptural injunction be observed, since a manifest heretic can and must be avoided even before a sentence is pronounced, and a declaratory sentence can just as easily be pronounced (and in fact could only be validly pronounced) *after* the *ipso facto* loss of office; nor is it proven from reason, first, because the passing of such a sentence on the Pope while still in office violates divine law, and secondly, from reason itself we know that one who is not a member cannot be the head – the Church cannot cut off the head which has severed itself from the body by its own public act of severing. Therefore, the *"remedy for so great a peril"* that Christ gave to the Church, was not the power to depose a heretic pope, but to bestow upon the pope the grace of an unfailing faith, which prevents the pope from ever becoming a formal heretic; and if it be possible for a pope to

---

et potuisset quidem Ecclesia hanc causam iilis committere, præcipue si ex consensu vel ordinatione summorum Pontificum ita esset statutum, sicut de electione factum est; sed non legimus hactenus judicium hoc illis esse commissum; ideoque dicendum per se pertinere ad omnes Ecclesiæ Episcopos; nam cum illi sint ordinarii pastores et columnæ Ecclesiæ, ad illos credendum hujusmodi causam interesse, et cum ex jure divino non sit major ratio de his quam de illis, atque jure humano nihil de hoc sit statutum, necessario dicendum spectare ad omnes, atque adeo ad generale Concilium, et ita communis sententia Doctorum habet.» — Suarez, *Op. cit.* p. 318.

[673] *Ibid.*

fall into manifest heresy, there would still be the remedy that the pertinacious act of public heresy would directly bring about the heretic's *ipso facto* fall from the Pontificate, so that there could then follow upon the fact of his fall from office, a declaration of his removal from office and of the **vacancy of the Apostolic See**, which would occur immediately upon the pope's public defection from the faith into manifest heresy; which the Church, through the remaining Catholic members of the Sacred College of Cardinals, would need only declare after the fact of the defection.

Fr. Gleize summarizes the doctrine of Suárez:

> «Francisco Suarez (1548-1617), in his *De Fide*, disputatio 10 *De Summo Pontifice*, section 6, §§3-13. *Opera omnia*, 12:316-318, states, like Cajetan, that the pope does not lose his pontificate by reason of his heresy itself, whether it be occult or even notorious. He then presents what in his opinion is the common explanation of the theologians. A publicly and incorrigibly heretical (*i.e.* pertinacious) pope loses the pontificate when the Church declares his crime. This declaration constitutes a legitimate act of jurisdiction, but it is not a jurisdiction that exercises a superior power over the pope. In this case the Church is represented not by the cardinals but by the Ecumenical Council: the latter can be convoked by someone other than the pope since it does not meet to define faith and morals.
>
> Suarez then explains the essential point of his thesis: he refuses to say that in this exceptional case the Church possesses a true power of jurisdiction over the pope. The Church does nothing but declare in the name of Christ the pope's heresy, which amounts to declaring that the pope has become unworthy of the papacy. And by means of this declaration of the Church, Christ immediately takes the papacy back from the pope.
>
> In a third logical moment, the pope who has fallen from his office becomes inferior to the Church and she can punish him. The thesis therefore is based entirely on one truth. This truth is that the previous declaration of the Church that notes the pope's heresy is the necessary and sufficient condition for Christ to withdraw the papacy from the pope. And Suarez proves this truth by saying that it is spelled out in the divine law of revelation. In support of this, Suarez also cites Titus 3:10 along with a passage from the First Epistle of St. Clement of Rome which allegedly says that *"Petrum docuisse haereticum papam esse deponendum."*»

Fr. Gleize then comments:

> «'Suarez' explanation (see Part 6a) is original. In fact it can be likened neither to Cajetan's nor to St. Robert Bellarmine's. For Cajetan, the Church alone causes the pope's dethronement; for Saint Robert Bellarmine it is

Christ alone. *[P.K. — Actually, for Bellarmine it is the pope alone who abandons the office "per se" by severing himself from the body of the Church.]* For Suarez it is Christ and the Church at the same time. We should note in passing that this way of viewing the problem is characteristic of his eclecticism. Suarez has a lot of erudition but little genius. He does not synthesize. He always has trouble deciding among opposing authorities, and his tendency is to reconcile them is a sort of middle-of-the-road solution. In acting this way, he weakens the principles: this, incidentally, is the main reason why Father Reginald Garrigou-Lagrange disapproves of Suarez. For example in *De Christo salvatore*, pp. 108-109, Fr. Garrigou-Lagrange writes:

"In this question, Suarez, as is often the case with his eclecticism, refutes Scotus by relying on Saint Thomas and Saint Thomas by relying on Scotus. But this intermediate position is very difficult to hold, and it is not at all easy to preserve its equilibrium or stability, and this is why it is not uncommon for Suarez, when he sets forth his theses, to waver or oscillate between Saint Thomas and Scotus without finding a firm position."»

JOHN OF ST. THOMAS

Thesis of John of St. Thomas:

"It cannot be held that the Pope, by the very fact of being a heretic, would cease to be pope antecedently to [before] a declaration of the Church. (...) What is truly a matter of debate is whether the Pope, after he is declared by the Church to be a heretic, is deposed ipso facto by Christ the Lord, or if the Church ought to depose him. In any case, as long as the Church has not issued a juridical declaration, he must always be considered the Pope." (Cursus Theologicus, Tome 6. Questions 1-7 on Faith. Disputation 8., Article 2)[674]

John of St. Thomas on the Deposition of a Heretical Pope[675]

"De Auctoritate Summi Pontificis" Disputatio III, Articulus II XVII De Depositione Papae & Seq.

---

[674] (Quoted by Salza & Siscoe)
[675] Translated by Fr. François Chazal, with some of my own minor edits of the English.

KEY TEXTS AND COMMENTARY

1) *"It cannot be held that the Pope, by the very fact of being a heretic, would cease to be pope antecedently to a declaration of the Church."*

He argues:

> *"The pope does not cease to be the pope before any ecclesial trial sentence by the fact itself of heresy, and before he is proposed as to be avoided. Neither is Jerome, when he says that the heretic walks out per se from the Body of Christ, excluding him from the judgment of the Church, especially in a thing so grave as the deposition of a pope, but she judges the quality of the crime that excludes from the Church without any over added censure, as long as it is declared by the Church."*

I respond saying that according to the unanimous consensus of the Fathers, ecclesiastical office is lost *ex natura hæresis*,[676] by the very fact of public defection, and is lost *"sine ulla declaratione"*[677] by that act of defection from the faith into formal heresy, as has been demonstrated and explained. As has been amply demonstrated, it pertains to the nature of heresy, that according to the doctrine of the Catholic faith, the public heretic, *without any other qualifying circumstances such as formally rejecting the Church*, ceases to be a member of the Church and loses office *ipso facto*, by the public act of formal heresy. To the objection, *"Neither is Jerome, when he says that the heretic walks out per se from the Body of Christ, excluding him from the judgment of the Church"*, **I reply:** The words of St. Jerome are self-explanatory, explicitly stating that the heretic *condemns himself*, because *other sinners are expelled from the Church by the priests*, but *heretics pronounce the sentence upon themselves*: *"Propterea* **a semetipso dicitur esse damnatus**, *quia fornicator, adulter, homicida, et cetera vitia per sacerdotes ex Ecclesia propelluntur:* **hæretici autem in semetipsis sententiam ferunt**, *suo arbitrio de Ecclesia recedentes: quæ recessio propriæ conscientiæ videtur esse damnatio."*

John of St. Thomas destroys the distinction between heretics, who, Jerome says, *"condemn themselves"* by *"withdrawing"* from the Church; and other sinners who are *"driven out by the priests"*; since, if the official judgment of the Church were to be involved in the process of that withdrawal and separation, then the heretics also would be driven out of the Church by the priests, **and they would therefore not walk out by**

---

[676] Bellarmine, *De Romano Pontifice*, Lib. II Cap. XXX
[677] Canon 188. 4°.

themselves; nor would they have, **"*miserably separated themselves from union with the Church*"** *(a Corporis compage semetipsos misere separarunt)*, as Pius XII teaches in *Mystici Corporis* and thereby distinguish themselves in any way from other sinners who are cut off by Church authority, **"*ob gravissima admissa a legitima auctoritate seiuncti sunt*"**. St. Jerome made this distinction, the Roman Catechism made this distinction[678], St. Robert Bellarmine made this distinction, but John of St. Thomas just didn't quite get it. Finally, Pope Pius XII explained this distinction again, even more explicitly, saying that ***it pertains to the very nature of schism, heresy, and apostasy*, that by them one is cut off from the body of the Church by them (*suapte natura*), and NOT by any ecclesiastical censure or judgment**, which is to say, unlike any other sin *(omne admissum)* which, "even if a grave misdeed" *(etsi grave scelus)*, does **NOT** separate one from the Church *by its very nature*, but by **ecclesiastical censure**, i.e. by the *"legitimate authority of the Church" (ob gravissima admissa a legitima auctoritate seiuncti sunt)*[679] – and ***they***, as St. Pius V teaches in the Roman Catechism, who are cut off from the Church by legitimate authority, are the **"*excommunicati*"**.

So finally, as far as the assertion of John of St. Thomas, that the Church, *"judges the quality of the crime that excludes from the Church without any over added censure, as long as it is declared by the Church"*, is concerned: ***if there is any judgment by the Church at all* (upon which no additional censure need be added), *then heretics would not have "miserably separated themselves" (Mystici Corporis) from the Church by their own defection from the Church, by heresy "suapte natura", as Pius XII teaches; but they would be severed from the Church by something else which does not pertain to the nature of heresy, to wit, an ecclesiastical judgment, i.e. "by the legitimate authority"***

---

[678] "Ex quo fit ut tria tantummodo hominum genera ab ea excludantur: primo infideles, deinde **haeretici et schismatici**, postremo **excommunicati**. Ethnici quidem, quod in Ecclesia numquam fuerunt, neque eam umquam cognoverunt, nec ullius sacramenti participes in populi christiani societate facti sunt. **Haeretici vero atque schismatici, quia ab Ecclesia desciverunt**, neque enim illi magis ad Ecclesiam spectant quam transfugae ad exercitum pertineant a quo defecerunt; non negandum tamen quin in Ecclesiae potestate sint, ut qui ab ea in iudicium vocentur, puniantur et anathemate damnentur. **Postremo etiam excommunicati, quod Ecclesiae iudicio ab ea exclusi ad illius communionem** non pertineant donec resipiscant."

[679] *Siquidem non omne admissum, etsi grave scelus, eiusmodi est ut — sicut schisma, vel haeresis, vel apostasia faciunt — suapte natura hominem ab Ecclesiae Corpore separet.*

(*Mystici Corporis*), which would place them not among those who according to the Roman Catechism have *defected* (*desciverunt*) *by themselves*, but among those excluded *by legitimate authority*, i.e., the *excommunicati*, who have been expelled by the sentence of Church authority. Thus it is that this doctrine of John of St. Thomas which received its *coup de grâce* from *Mystici Corporis*, destroys this essential distinction which pertains to the very essence of a *de fide* doctrine of the Church. John Salza and Robert Siscoe, failing to see the gaping hole made by the stake which Pius XII drove through the heart of this heretical doctrine, have exhumed and attempted to revive the corpse of this errant doctrine, which, in the light of *Mystici Corporis*, the unanimity of the Fathers, and the constant teaching of the universal magisterium of the Church set forth in the Roman Catechism, and the unanimous teaching of theologians in the modern era, can be plainly seen to be heretical.

> 2) *"Despite being separated per se from the Church, quo ad nos, [as far as we are concerned], such a separation is not understood to take place without such declaration. And in the same way do we reply to the argument that says that the non Christian who neither per se, nor quo ad nos is a Christian, cannot be the pope, for in himself he has ceased to be a Christian because he has lost the faith. But for us [quo ad nos] he is not yet declared infidel or heretic, no matter how much he may be manifest [heretic] according to private judgment. He is still a member of the Church for us [quo ad nos], and consequently its head."*

This question has been settled, and is now closed. **I have demonstrated beyond all shadow of doubt that the Church teaching is: 1) that those who publicly defect from the faith by manifest formal heresy, are separated from the Church *by the very nature of heresy*, and therefore sever themselves from the body of the Church *ipso jure* and cease to be members of it; as opposed to all others who are cut off from membership by the legitimate authority of the Church, i.e., by means of excommunication (*de fide* teaching of the universal & ordinary magisterium); and, 2) those who publicly defect from the faith by an act of formal heresy, by that very act automatically lose office and all ecclesiastical dignity (*de fide* teaching of the universal & ordinary magisterium).** As a strict logical consequence of these *de fide* premises, it follows necessarily and is thus *theologice certum* with an equal degree of certitude that a manifestly heretical pope would cease by himself to be a member of the Church, and therefore would cease entirely by himself to be pope, in the manner explained by Bellarmine, Ballerini, and Gregory XVI.

Bellarmine understood the doctrine on loss of office for manifest heresy exactly in the manner set forth in Session 37 of Constance before him, as did Ballerini after him. **Bellarmine demonstrated that the ancient Fathers teach in unison that the loss of office takes place automatically, *ex natura hæresis*, and not by any human law (and therefore entirely independent of any judgment by the Church). Thus, automatic loss of office for public heresy *before any judgment by the Church* is a a point of *magisterial doctrine,* which was *applied by the Ecumenical Council of Constance in the case of Pedro de Luna;* and secondly, this *doctrine* is acknowledged in the canonical tradition of the Church, and is incorporated into the Code of Canon Law (Can. 194).**

The Very Rev. H.A. Ayrinhac comments on Canon 2197, that public defection from the faith means: "Public defection from the faith, by formal heresy or apostasy, with or without affiliation with another religious society. The offense must be public, that is, generally known or liable to become so before long." The *New Commentary on the Code of Canon Law* explains, "A formal act of leaving the Church is not required for the defection in canon 194; the only requirement is that the heresy must be public (known or likely to become known).[114] Neither is it required that the officeholder join another religion, although this could be an objective indication of defection. [[114] Socha, in *Münster Com, 194/2-3;* Urrutia, n. 925, confuses this with "notorious".]"[680] This is all that is required for loss of office to take place according to the law and teaching of the Church as it is understood by the magisterium: **the external act of defection from the faith** that is public or liable to become public, before any judgment, and without any judgment pronounced by the Church. Thus, *quo ad nos,* the public heretic whose heresy may not be

---

[680] John P. Beal, *New Commentary on the Code of Canon Law* pp. 226-7. It is to be noted that by "formal act", the author does not refer to an act of formal heresy, but to a defector's formal declaration of defection from the Church, as set forth in *Prot. 10279/2006* of the Pontifial Council For Legislative Texts, *ACTUS FORMALIS DEFECTIONIS AB ECCLESIA CATHOLICA*, 13 March 2006.

known to all may be erroneously considered by some, or even by many, to still retain his office; nevertheless, since he has ceased *per se* to be a member of the Church by manifest formal heresy, he will have already **in fact** fallen from office automatically *ipso jure* (Can. 194 § 1), and that loss of office would only need to be declared by the Church in order to be **enforced** (Canon 194 § 2), but is not required as a condition for the actual loss office to take place.

> 3) *"Therefore the judgment of the Church is required by which he is declared as a non-Christian, to be avoided, and then he ceases to be a pope to us [quo ad nos] and before then he did not desist, even per se, because all he was doing was valid per se."*

Ex supradictis it can plainly be seen that the proposition is demonstrated to be false: the heretic loses office *per se*; and anything he does that is juridically valid would only be valid in virtue of supplied faculties granted to excommunicates *ipso jure*; since even the heretic pope would immediately incur a *latæ sententiæ* excommunication upon falling from office and ceasing to be pope.

Since the proposition, *"It cannot be held that the Pope, by the very fact of being a heretic, would cease to be pope antecedently to a declaration of the Church"*, is demonstrated to be false, the proposition that logically hinges upon it, *"What is truly a matter of debate is whether the Pope, after he is declared by the Church to be a heretic, is deposed ipso facto by Christ the Lord, or if the Church ought to depose him. In any case, as long as the Church has not issued a juridical declaration, he must always be considered the Pope"*, is therefore patently and necessarily false.

Likewise, the objection that, *"The first point of Cajetan is manifest from the above and cannot be attacked legitimately by Bellarmine. Its truth is obvious: either because the pope no matter how much he is truly and publicly a heretic, if he is ready to be corrected, cannot be deposed"*, fails to take into consideration the fact that Bellarmine explicitly taught that a pope who is manifestly *pertinacious* in heresy, "ceases by himself to be pope"; and as noted earlier, a pope who is not pertinacious in heresy, but errs out of ignorance, would remain in office as pope. Bellarmine made it explicitly clear that when he spoke of a pope who is a manifest heretic, he spoke of one who is manifestly an obstinate formal heretic.

> 4) *"Secondly it is objected that the Church has no power over the conjunction between the pontiff and the person, unless she has power on the pontificate*

itself, and the pope does nothing more, when he deposes a bishop, than destroying his link with the episcopate, for he does not destroy the episcopate itself. Therefore if the Church has power in the conjunction of the pontificate with the person, consequently it can or has power over the pontificate and the person of the pope. What confirms it is that the pope is deposed unwillingly; and therefore is punished by such a deposition. To punish is the act of a superior and a judge; therefore the Church that deposes, or punishes by the punishment of deposition has a superiority over the person of the pope. Lastly he who has power over both parts or over their conjunction, has power over the whole simpliciter; just like the one who generates a man has power simpliciter over the whole man himself. Therefore if the Church has power over the conjunction of the pontificate with the person, she has power over the pope simpliciter, something that Cajetan denies."

John of St. Thomas then answers this objection:

- *"It is answered that the pope deposes a bishop in a different way than the Church deposes a pope. For the pontiff deprives him as one deprives a subordinate and someone subjected to him and having a power subordinate and dependent that can be limited and constrained. Hence whereas it takes the episcopate from the person and does not destroy the episcopate, nevertheless he removes it by the superiority that he has over that person, concerning also the power subordinated to himself by the person of which he removes it from the person, and not just the person from it [the power].* **The Church takes away the pontificate not out of a superiority to the power itself, but a ministerial and dispositive power by which it can induce a disposition incompatible with the pontificate as we said."**

- *"To confirm this we answer that* **the pope can be disposed against his will ministerially and dispositively by the Church**, *authoritatively by Christ the Lord, hence, properly speaking, he is punished by Christ, not by the Church."*

- *"And to the last point we say that* **the one who has power in the conjunction of the parts has power in the whole simpliciter, but not if this is done ministerially only and dispositively over such a conjunction.***"*

The opinion that the Church can depose a heretical pope is premised on the argument that, **"The Church takes away the pontificate not** *out of a superiority to the power* [over the conjunction] *itself, but a ministerial and dispositive power by which it can induce a disposition incompatible with the pontificate"*, and is founded on the principle that, *"The Church has a right to separate itself from a heretical pope in virtue of divine right, and as a result can take all the means necessary for such a separation."* The defect of this argument is, **1)** its failure to recognize that it is according to the nature of heresy, that a manifest heretic **separates himself from the Church**, by pronouncing the sentence of condemnation upon himself and falls from office **by himself**, and therefore, **no deposition is even possible**, and thus, all that would be needed is a simple declaration of loss of office by competent ecclesiastical authority (Canon 194 § 2); **2)** and, (as Bellarmine said) *"if they depose the Pope, they necessarily exercise authority over the composite"*, which is to say, over the pope. However so much as one may claim that the Church would only act ministerially and dispositively by inducing *a "disposition incompatible with the pontificate"*, the pronouncing of a sentence of heresy on the pope and declaring him deposed would not be a ministerial and dispositive act, but would be an exercise of power over the pope. **Therefore, regardless of whether it be claimed that power would be exercised *simpliciter*, or if it would be alleged to be exercised *ministerially* and *dispositively*, in either case, as Bellarmine says, "if they depose the Pope, they necessarily exercise authority over the composite",** *and that is a power that neither the bishops as a whole nor the cardinals possess, as Bellarmine proved in his refutation of Opinion No. 4, and the First Vatican Council confirmed;* and 3) the foundation of the belief that the Church possesses the power to dissolve the conjunction between the Pontiff and the Pontificate is the spurious *Canon Si papa*, and has no basis in either sacred scripture or sacred tradition. **HENCE:** The following propositions are seen to be false:

- *"we see that this power to deal with the causes of the pontiffs, and what belongs to their deposition, do not pertain to the cardinals. It remains in the deposition of the Church, whose authority is represented by a general council"*
- *The necessary means is that per se that such a crime be evidenced juridically, and it cannot be evidenced juridically unless a competent judgment is formed, and such a competent judgment cannot be in such a grave matter except by a general council, because it is dealing about the universal head of the Church,*

which make it the object of the judgment of the universal Church, which is a general council.

- "this council can be convoked by the authority of the Church, which is over the bishops or their biggest portion."
- "Hence the pope cannot annul or recuse such council, because he is a part, and the Church can convoke it by divine right for that purpose, because she has the right to separate herself from heretics."
- "Concerning the second point, namely by whose authority the declaration and deposition is to be made, there is dissent among theologians, and it does not appear by whom such a deposition is to be made, because it is an act of **judgment**, and **jurisdiction**, which can be exercised by **no one over the pope.**"

John of St. Thomas was correct on one point in this matter, namely, *"it does not appear by whom such a deposition is to be made"*, **since such a deposition can be made by no one**: He explicitly teaches that a **"general council"** can **depose a pope**, by an **"act of judgment"** and **"jurisdiction"**, **which directly opposes the doctrine of the Fifth Lateran Council:** "[I]t is clearly established that the Roman Pontiff alone, possessing as it were authority over all Councils, has full right and power of proclaiming Councils, or transferring and dissolving them, not only according to the testimony of Sacred Scripture, from the words of the holy Fathers and even of other Roman Pontiffs, of our predecessors, and from the decrees of the holy canons…"[681]**, as well as the solemn dogma of the universal primacy of jurisdiction defined by the First Vatican Council – *"Quare a recto veritatis tramite aberrant, qui affirmant, licere ab iudiciis Romanorum Pontificum ad oecumenicum Concilium tamquam ad auctoritatem Romano Pontifice superiorem appellare."***

ANY JUDGMENT WHATSOEVER PRONOUNCED BY A COUNCIL ON A REIGNING PONTIFF DIRECTLY OPPOSES THE INJUDICABILITY OF THE POPE, AND THE AUTHORITY TO DISSOLVE ALL COUNCILS INHERENT IN THE SUPREME AND UNIVERSAL PRIMACY OF JURISDICTION OF THE ROMAN PONTIFF.

---

[681] *Denzinger 740*, Fifth Lateran Council (Session XI) Dec. 19, 1516

CONCLUSION

In view of what has been stated and elaborated above, the observation of Fr. Gleize can be seen to be entirely correct on this point:

«The opinion of the medieval theologians (cf. no. 3), which acknowledges that the Church has a power to depose the pope if necessary, contradicts the divine constitution of the Church: Cajetan recognizes that this thesis mentioned in an objection was (at least in his era) the common opinion. But it does not hold up, because since the pope is above the Church by divine right, if there is an exceptional case in which the Church has power over him, this case must be explicitly foreseen and stated as such in the sources of revelation. Now, "when we consider the exceptional case of heresy, divine law does not foresee that the pope should be subject to the Church" (see *De comparatione*, chapter 20, §280). This is why the explanation set forth by these theologians should be rejected: it contradicts the explicit teaching of revelation.»

Fr. Gleize then quotes Cardinal Billot to show that Cajetan's solution does not solve the problem, explaining,

«that Cajetan's explanation in reality does not avoid saying that the Church is above the pope. Cardinal Billot saw this clearly in his *Traité de l'Église du Christ*, question 14, thesis 29, part 2, pp. 605-606, nos. 940-941:

Let no one say that the deposal could still be understood not as the direct withdrawal of the papacy (since this power is given directly by God and subordinates all other power in the Church to itself), but rather as a simple change of subject, inasmuch as one would withdraw from the pope the legitimacy that acquired his election for him. In fact...far from being the contrary corresponding to the election, this change of person is dependent on another order, for it corresponds to an act of jurisdiction and to the exercise of a power. This is why the objection's conclusion does not follow: just because the person of the pope can be designated by men, this does not mean that the latter have the legitimate power to dismiss the person of the pope from the papacy. ... The Church, or an ecclesiastical assembly, cannot perform any act upon the person of the pope, except for the election. And therefore, once the election is canonically terminated, the Church has nothing more to do until a new election takes place, which can occur only after the see becomes vacant.

And, further, Billot observes the following:

Cajetan takes a lot of trouble without managing to show how it would be possible to keep these three principles together: a pope who has fallen into heresy is not thereby deposed by virtue of divine law nor by virtue of human law; the pope who remains pope has no superior on earth; if the pope loses the faith, the Church has the power to depose him all the same. But one may reply that, if the pope who has fallen into heresy remains pope and can be deposed by the Church, one or the other of these two consequences must necessarily be admitted: either the fact of deposing the pope does not require the one who deposes him to have power over him, or else the pope while remaining pope is really subject on earth to a superior power, at least in a particular situation. Moreover, as soon as we open the door to a deposal, there is no longer any reason to restrict it (by the very nature of things or by virtue of a positive law) to deposal solely in the case of heresy. For then we have already destroyed the principles that make the deposal impossible in general, and nothing remains but a voluntaristic rule, accompanied by an arbitrarily defined exceptional case.»

Clearly there can be no exception to the principle of papal injudicability. It has no basis in divine revelation, and is contrary to the divine constitution of the Church as defined in *Pastor Æternus* and in many other documenrs of the Supreme Magisterium. Opinion No. 4 in all its variations requires a judgment of the Church — a juridical act in the external forum, namely, a *sentence of guilt* to be pronounced *upon the heretic pope* as a condition for him to fall from office. Such a judgment on the pope, of its very nature requires jurisdiction over the *person* of the pope — a jurisdiction over the supreme judge of all cases — a jurisdiction which does not exist in the Church. A jurisdiction which is only presumed as a mere postulation arising from "an arbitrarily defined exceptional case." The very notion of any kind of jurisdiction whatsoever over the person whose universal primacy of jurisdiction constitutes him by divine law as having full and absolute jurisdiction over the whole world[682] is a self-contradictory notion; yet, without jurisdiction, the judgment would be nothing but a mere opinion pronounced without authority or force of law. Furthermore, a jurisdiction ovewr the pope would be required not only to directly depose a pope; but would equally be required for the Church to judge him guilty of heresy with a valid juridical act, in order to validly order him with a juridical act to be

---

[682] «Hoc consensu praestito... illico electus est verus Papa, atque actu **plenam absolutamque iurisdictionem supra totum orbem** acquirit et exercere potest» [Constitutio Apostolica «*Vacantis Apostolicæ Sedis*» Pius XII, 8 December 1945.

avoided by the faithful of the universal Church, and thereby ministerially dispose him to fall from the pontificate. The proposition, therefore, that anyone in the Church, even an imperfect ecumenical council, may legitimately judge the pope while still in office for heresy, is plainly seen to be heretical. He could only be judged to have already fallen from office, if indeed it is possible for a pope to fall into heresy. That being said, if it were possible for a pope to fall openly into heresy that is, into manifest, formal heresy, the very fact of his heresy would prove beyond doubt that he simply is not the pope of the Catholic Church; and therefore, his removal would not violate the principle of papal injudicability.

Although Bellarmine refuted the Third Opinion by proving that a manifestly heretical pope would in fact not be a pope at all, he did not say that the Church would have the authority to remove a heretical pope who is suspect of heresy but not certainly heretical. In the case of a manifest heretic, no further justification would be needed for the removal beyond the patent fact that the manifest heretic, by the very fact of his inexcusable heresy, would simply not be pope, but an intruder usurping the papal throne. However, the question of a suspected heretical pope who is apparently not invincibly ignorant of his heresy, but not manifestly pertinacious either; or a pope who is vehemently suspect, or bordering on, but not certainly violently suspect of heresy on the basis of credible evidence, presents great difficulties, which might not even be possible to resolve. In order to remain in power, a heretic could even feign orthodoxy in the manner that the heretic, Alfred Loisy feigned orthodoxy – and then later boasted how he had deceived the Archbishop of Paris. So, there would not only be the difficulty of determining in some cases, whether the pope's beliefs are actually heretical or merely erroneous, (as would be the case of a heresy not yet formally condemned, but apparently at variance in some manner against some point of defind or manifest dogma); but even if he were to visivbly appear to accept correction, it could never really be morally certain that the heretic would be sincerely accepting correction, or if he would just be following the deceitful example of Loisy, merely in order to preserve his temporal status. Hence, except for a clear-cut case of manifestly formal heresy that is at least morally certain by way of a clear-cut *violent suspicion of heresy* based on certain *indicia*, it would really be impossible to determine if a materially heretical pope is guilty of formal heresy or not. Thus, the observation made in the earlier cited Canon Law Society of America's *New Commentary on he Code of Canon Law* needs to be seriously considered: "The anomaly about these severe consequences (loss of ecclesiastical office, etc.) is that some of the most serious of them are 'automatic or self-imposed' (*ipso jure, ipso facto, latæ sententiæ*), while the alleged offenses are often quite complex, nuanced, and vigorously disputed, except in the extremely rare event that the persons themselves admit to being in heresy, apostasy, or schism. In other words, this system of sanctions for the serious doctrinal deviaions does not work." (p. 915) Since the *fact* of public defection into heresy is the necessary condition for the statutory *ipso jure* loss of office to occur, the mere presumption of guilt in penal law does not suffice to effect the loss of office prescribed in the administrative section of the Code, because the defection from the faith is not made manifest by a mere presumption of guilt, but can only be truly *manifest* if the fact itself is plainly obvious.

The problem of papal heresy is a hypothesis without any satisfactory solution for all contexts. Fr Gleize remarks on Bellarmine's opinion. "This opinion is therefore a probable approach to a solution in a certain context, but it could not be applied to every context. As we explained earlier, this way of solving the theoretical problem is not a universal principle of responding in practice to it." Since it is only a hypothesis, as Don Curzio says, a mere hypothesis at most possible, but by no means theologically certain, (una pura ipotesi possibile o al massimo probabile, ma mai teologicamente certa); to hold as theologically certain the hypothesis of papal heresy and the consequent loss of office, (ritenere teologicamente certa l'ipotesi dell'eresia del Papa e la conseguente perdita del Pontificato), would constitute an undue leap of logic from the possible or probable to the certain, (un passaggio indebito dal possibile/probabile al certo). We are left with one certitude on this question: If it is beyond reasonable dispute that a man is undeniably a manifest heretic, then, whether he is believed to have fallen from the Pontificate, or to never validy assumed the Pontificate; his manifest heresy would prove beyond all shadow of doubt that whichever the case may be, he *is* not the pope.

Although the Counter-Reformation canonists were understandably phobic about the impetus such a doctrine as that of automatic loss of the papal office for heresy without the judgment of the Church might give occasion to the abusive application of the Protestant principle of Private Judgment against the Papacy, the ancient age-old principle of law (*Ab abusu ad usum non valet consequentia*) remains ever valid, that an abuse is no argument against legitimate use; and therefore, *Abusus non tollit usum*: the abuse of a right does not nullify the right to its legitimate exercise. Their understandable concern for the possibility and even the likelihood that private individuals could seize upon the right to judge privately as a matter of conscience, and abuse it in the manner that it was abused by Luther to pronounce the pope a heretic, led them to adopt the opposite extreme, equally harmful and heterodox, according to which even a manifestly heretical pope remains in office and retains jurisdiction until the Church, by a juridical act pronounces judgment on him; and that private individuals may not avail themselves of their God-given right and last means of defense against the ravenous wolf, to form an opinion to acknowledge the defection and loss of office resulting from even the most manifest and patent public rejection of the Catholic faith by a heretic pope; and as a consequence to be compelled to remain subject to him, and be in communion with the public enemy of the Church for months, years or even decades, until the Church, by some miracle of providence, can finally be able to pronounce a judgment which effectively results in the heretic's removal.

The word "manifest" means, "clear or obvious to the eye or mind". If not only the matter of heresy is clearly manifest, but the conscious and wilful profession of "a doctrine that immediately, directly, and contradictorily opposes the truths revealed by God and authentically set forth as such by the Church,"[683] is patently obvious to the mind, then the person who professes it may be judged by others to be a heretic, even without a juridical pronouncement of the Church, since no one needs any official declaration to be made in order to form a judgment of opinion on a matter that by its very nature is already "clear or obvious to the eye or mind". The proposition that one is not a manifest heretic until an ecclesiastical judge pronounces that one is a manifest heretic is absurd on its face, since by the very fact that the heresy is manifest, it is already "clear or obvious to the eye or mind" before any judgment is pronounced; yet this is precisely the silliness that John Salza and Robert Siscoe maintain in their rabid legalism. However, it is clearly the doctrine of the Catholic faith that if a person is a manifest heretic, then it is manifest that heresy has *suapte natura* severed that one from the body of the Church, and if he is a holder of ecclesiastical office, he has *ipso jure* automatically lost office and all habitual or ordinary jurisdiction *ex natura hæresis*, before any sentence is pronounced by the Church. Since the loss of office for public defction from the faith was prescribed in the 1917 Code to take place *ipso facto* and "without any declaration", and it remains

---

[683] Albert Michel, *Dictionnarire de théologie catholique*, VI, ii.

that way in the 1983 Code; it is absurd for anyone to claim that the faithful must wait for a declaration from Church authorities before judging in conscience on an *ipso jure* loss of office that takes place "without any declaration"; and that until a judgment be pronounced by competent authority, they need to and must remain subject to a heretic pope and to a vast portion of the hierarchy who have visibly expelled themselves from the body of the Church; while those pastors who remain faithful, and who are competent to judge, are either too blind or too frightened to speak.

It is plainly evident that the Counter-Reformation theologians and canonists who subscribed to Opinion No. 4 theorized a hypothetical scenario of a pope who falls into manifest heresy, in which the rest of the hierarchy, or at least the vast majority of it would still be orthodox in their faith, and who would administer correction to an errant Pontiff; and, if he were to remain obstinate in heresy, pronounce a juridical judgment upon him, and thereby effect his loss of office. However, when a sizable portion of the hierarchy is already in heresy, and the vast majority is to some degree infected by the heresy, one can easily understand how such a manifestly heretical "pope" would be tolerated and even fully accepted as a legitimate pope by the great majority of bishops and cardinals who themselves appear also to be heretics. In his *Dialogue Against the Luciferians*, St. Jerome remarked, "The whole world groaned and was astonished to find itself Arian." In Chapter 4 of his *Commonitory*, St. Vincent of Lérins speaks of the time, "when the Arian poison had infected not an insignificant portion of the Church but almost the whole world, **so that a sort of blindness had fallen upon almost all the bishops of the Latin tongue**, circumvented partly by force partly by fraud, **and was preventing them from seeing what was most expedient to be done in the midst of so much confusion**".

It is plainly evident that in our own time, **a sort of blindness has fallen upon almost all the bishops of the Latin Church**. With a prophetic insight, more than 1,500 years ago St. Vincent of Lérins described the present condition of the Church today: "if some novel contagion seek to infect not merely an insignificant portion of the Church, but the whole". Under such circumstances, the clergy and faithful cannot reasonably be expected to suspend judgment on manifest heresy and remain subject to a ravenous wolf and destroyer of souls until the Church pronounces officially – *quod esset miserrima conditio Ecclesiæ, si lupum manifeste grassantem, pro pastore agnoscere cogeretur. (Bellarminus)*

PART FIVE

FRAUD & SOPHISTRY

THE PSEUDO-SCOLARSHIP OF
JOHN SALZA & ROBERT SISCOE

From the **True or false Pope?** Website:

«Kramer: "A complete refutation of the errors and heresies of Salza & Siscoe will soon follow."»

«Siscoe: We can't wait. But if Kramer is going to provide a completely refutation of the "errors and heresies of Salza & Siscoe" he better at least quote us directly before "refuting" what he claims we hold [...] **So, when Kramer issues his '"refutation of the errors and heresies of Salza & Siscoe" make sure he quotes us directly.**»

SECTION ONE

In any disciplined pursuit of knowledge by which one intends to conduct an enquiry and engage in dialogue, and thereby arrive at the truth, an honest objectivity is required; and in order for such an enquiry to be objective, it is absolutely necessary that it be carried out in a dispassionate and impartial manner, which therefore demands, (in the words of Hinschius), "detached consideration without presuppositions". What is utterly absent in the writings of John Salza and Robert Siscoe is precisely that – "detached consideration without presuppositions". In their book, True or False Pope, and in their many articles and internet posts, Salza and Siscoe manifest, in a very undisguised manner, that they have no intention to approach theological questions in a detached and objective manner, and arrive at the truth without presuppositions; but in order to persuade their readers to accept their strongly held and preconceived personal opinions, they perpetually resort to "subtly deceptive reasoning or argumentation... that seems plausible on a superficial level but is actually unsound, or reasoning that is used to deceive."[684] I place the phrase in quotation marks, because it is a

---

[684] Christopher A. Ferrara in *Fatima Perespectives;* http://archive.fatima.org/perspectives/fe/perspective941.asp.

dictionary definition – the definition of the word, "sophistry". Yes, it is by ***sophistry*** that Salza and Siscoe cold-bloodedly twist facts, doctrines and opinions like pretzels, in order to make them fit into the heterodox framework of their legalistic Fundamentalism; and to vilify anyone who dares attempt to fraternally correct them.

SOPHISTRY – this is the great defect in their writings and the great flaw in their character, which can be seen to run systemically throughout all their writings – the great blemish which stains their work like the mark of Cain, and exposes their superficial erudition and apparent scholarship as something counterfeit and untrustworthy. Some readers may at first uncritically object to such a condemnatory judgment which I pronounce against these hitherto undeservingly respected authors, but the deliberate mendacity they have employed in their writings, on the one hand to twist and bend Catholic doctrine according to their own errant convictions, and on the other to defame anyone who has the courage to oppose them, has been plainly exposed for what it is: **FRAUD.** Their deceptive falsification of the lengthy quotation of Pietro Ballerini, which I exposed in Part III of this work, is a prime example of the fraud these men undertake to persuade their readers to accept their errant opinions by means of deception. There are many more examples of such fraud in their writings. I will enumerate and expose some of them, but not all, for their number is legion. I will begin in this section by presenting some of the more striking examples of their fraudulent scholarship, which clearly and indisputably destroys their credibility as Catholic authors.

SALZA & SISCOE FABRICATE A FRAUDULENT QUOTATION OF POPE ALEXANDER III

On page 265 of their *magnum opus*, Salza & Siscoe write:

> Again, the reason this point is significant is because, since the loss of office occurs immediately by an act of God, and not as a direct consequence of the crime, Christ can continue to give jurisdiction even to a notoriously heretical Pope as long as he is being recognized by the Church as its head. It is possible for Christ to sustain a heretical Pope in office because the relationship between heresy and jurisdiction is not one of total metaphysical incompatibility, and Christ will do so because He will not secretly depose a Pope while he is being tolerated by the Church and publicly recognized as its head. This is confirmed by the teaching of Pope Alexander III (d. 1181) who said "a heretic retains his jurisdiction as long as he is tolerated by the Church; he loses it at the time he is reprobated by Her."

Salza & Siscoe have quoted a non-existent papal teaching. There exists no such papal teaching of Alexander III, but what Salza & Siscoe present ostensibly as a direct quotation of a pope's magisterial teaching, is a passage of a 20th Century author who paraphrases an opinion written in a book attributed to Cardinal Orlando (Rolando) Bandinelli, who later became Pope Alexander III. Salza and Siscoe have fabricated a bogus papal teaching out of a private opinion and inverted its meaning. At this juncture, one may reasonably speculate how it came about that Salza & Siscoe were able to concoct this bogus papal teaching, since they certainly did not read the Latin work attributed to Cardinal Bandinelli. In his article, *Deposing a Heretical Pope*, Robert J. Siscoe quotes a 20th Century author by the name of Peter Huizing S.J., author of several works on Canon Law, who was born in 1911. Siscoe & Salza therefore, have at least a modicum of familiarity with this author. It just so happens, that Huizing wrote those exact words that Salza & Siscoe put into quotation marks, and attribute them not to their author, Peter Huizing S.J., but to Pope Alexander III!

Huizing was addressing a particular point on a bishop's loss of jurisdiction for heresy when he penned the words that Salza & Siscoe place into the mouth of Pope Alexander III. Huizing explains,

> "«The decretists undoubtedly admitted that a heretic was «ipso facto» cut off from the Church as an excommunicated person. Some expressly state that even if there were no positive legislation of the Church on the point, the separation arose from the Natural Law." One can recall that it was St. Robert Bellarmine who quoted the unanimous teachings of the Fathers on this point, and concluded that such a loss of office does not result from any human law but *ex natura hæresis,* i.e. by the very nature of heresy. Huizing continues, "If he were excommunicate then he also lost his jurisdiction immediately, for an excommunicate cannot sit in judgment on the faithful. Gratian himself treats this matter. In C. 24 q. I, he deals with the question of whether a heretical bishop still has the power to excommunicate his subjects. The answer is relatively simple if the heresy which he maintains has already been condemned [...] An action against the heretic is unnecessary, the excommunication which has once and for all been settled takes effect. The heretical bishop is therefore excommunicated and has lost his power to condemn his subjects. This is therefore a clear case of excommunication latæ sententiæ".»

Huizing then asks a question on a related point: "But what is the position of the bishop who «ex corde suo» has thought out a new heresy?

Gratian decides that as soon as he begins to proclaim a heresy he loses the power to excommunicate." Gratian's opinion was already the common opinion in his day, but there was a negligible one or two who held the opposing opinion. Roland Bandinelli was of that negligible minority, so Huizing wrote, "Roland offers another solution. According to him a heretic retains his jurisdiction as long as he is tolerated by the Church; he loses it at the time when he is reprobated by Her." These words of Huizing are exactly the words which Salza & Siscoe declare to be the verbatim words of a papal teaching of Alexander III: "a heretic retains his jurisdiction as long as he is tolerated by the Church; he loses it at the time he is reprobated by Her." Where did they find the quotation which they fraudulently declare to be a papal teaching? Their own footnote provides the answer: "Summa, in C. 24, q. 1. p. 100. Peter Huizing, The Earliest Development of Excommunication latae sententiae, Studia Gratiana 3 (1955), p. 286."

When I first exposed their fraudulent fabrication of a papal teaching, Siscoe replied, «No "fake quote" was cooked up. Just because the citation was made before Alexander was elected Pope, does not mean it is "fake." Nor was it in any way inappropriate to attribute it to him under his papal name.» **This is an outright lie,** because the quotation is indeed fake: It is **not a quotation of Alexander's words** before he became pope; but is a **quotation of the words of Peter Huizing S.J.**, which Salza & Siscoe fraudulently attribute to Pope Alexander III, in an attempt to invert the meaning of Alexander's opinion, and make that inverted meaning appear to be a papal teaching. In an e-mail reply to me Siscoe then brazenly attempts to justify his fraud and "prove" that they did not concoct a fake quotation by reaffirming the lie that they were merely quoting Cardinal Bandinelli's work published before he became pope:

> The famous work on Canonizations, *De Servorum Dei Beatificatione et Beatorum Canonizatione* was written by of Cardinal Prospero Lambertini, **before** he was elected Pope and took the name Benedict XIV. Nevertheless, this work is commonly referenced as a work of Pope Benedict XIV himself. This can be seen in the Original Catholic Encyclopedia (1913) entry on Canonizations, as well as many other places. In fact, when *De Servorum Dei Beatificatione et Beatorum Canonizatione* was translated into English in 1850 (London, Thomas Richardson and Son), **the author was officially listed as Pope Benedict XIV**. So, just as it was not "fake" to attribute the book

on canonizations to Benedict XIV, neither is it "fake" to attribute the quotation to which you are referring to Pope Alexander. Nice try, though.[685]

It is most certainly not just *fake,* but a most deliberate **fraud** for Salza & Siscoe to not only attribute a quotation of Peter Huizing S.J. to Pope Alexander III, but to quote Huizing totally out of context in order to invert the meaning of Huizing's paraphrase of Bandinelli's text in order to make it appear that Bandinelli was saying the opposite from what he actually taught; and to make it appear that their twisted and inverted interpretation of what Alexander wrote before he became pope is a magisterial papal teaching. That Salza & Siscoe deliberately intend to create the appearance that their own false doctrine is a papal teaching is patently evident in all their writings which cite the fraudulent quotation. In his *Remnant* article, **Heresy Does Not Automatically Sever One from the Church**, Salza writes:

> The legal separation from the Church is actualized when the Church's authorities externally *recognize* the separation (by publicly judging that the subject is a heretic or has openly left the Church). In the case of the Pope, note that it is Christ Himself Who severs the bond between the heretical Pope and the papacy (since the Church has no authority over the Pope)... It is possible for Christ to sustain a heretical Pope in office because the relationship between heresy and jurisdiction is not one of total metaphysical incompatibility... This is confirmed by the teaching of Pope Alexander III (d. 1181) who said "a heretic retains his jurisdiction as long as he is tolerated by the Church; he loses it at the time he is reprobated by Her.[686]

As has been amply demonstrated in this work, it would be absolutely impossible for Christ to sustain a manifestly heretical pope in office because the relation between a public heretic and the Church is of one who has been visibly severed from membership in the Church *suapte natura* by the act of public heresy, and therefore, according to Canon Law, as a public heretic he loses office *ipso facto* without any declaration. Alexander III's opinion is clearly in conformity with this doctrine regarding loss of jurisdiction by any bishop who would profess an already condemned heresy. Nevertheless, Salza & Siscoe clearly and

---

[685] *Re: Faith Heresy & Loss of Office,* 22 June 2017 15:59.
[686] https://remnantnewspaper.com/web/index.php/fetzen-fliegen/item/3232-note-to-sedevacantists-heresy-does-not-automatically-sever-one-from-the-church.

beyond all doubt have deliberately, obstinately, and with conscious premeditation, attempted to make it appear that the opposite is true. Accordingly, Salza concludes his article with the *explicit heretical assertion* which directly opposes the definitive teaching of the Church's universal magisterium: "Thus, heresy, by its nature, severs one's spiritual bond with the Church, but not his legal bond, until it is recognized as such by the Church's authorities." *Sententia hæretica.* Pius XII teaches in conformity with the Church's perpetual doctrinal tradition and in unison with the ancient Fathers, that public heretics are not severed from the Body of the Church by their being judged heretics *by legitimate authority*, but they *separate themselves*, because heresy *suapte natura* visibly separates one from membership in the Body.

SALZA & SISCOE FRAUDULENTLY ALTER THE TEXT OF BALLERINI AND INVERT ITS MEANING

As I have demonstrated above, Salza & Siscoe are verbal con artists who resorted not only to fraudulently fabricating a papal quotation, but also to falsifying a quotation of Ballerini; and thereby blatantly altering the clear meaning of Ballerini's text to fraudulently invert its meaning make it appear to be in agreement with their own errant opinion. What is their errant opinion? In his e-mail message to me, Siscoe declares, "Heresy, of its nature, does not result in the loss of ecclesiastical office". Again, "The point is this: The sin of heresy, *of its nature*, severs a person from the Church (*quoad se*), **but it does not cause the loss of ecclesiastical office, and if you think it does, that is the root of your error.**" In these statements, Siscoe errs on two points: 1) One visibly separates himself from the Church by a manifestly formal act of heresy, he by that act leaves the Church, and thus has "miserably separated" himself from the **Body** of the Churh, as *Mystici Corporis* teaches; and 2) As has been explained above, Bellarmine demonstrates with the verbatim texts of the Fathers, that it is the unanimous teaching of the Fathers that by the act of manifest heresy, heretics lose jurisdiction and all ecclesiastical dignity not by any human law, but *ex natura hæresis*.

Siscoe, however, remains adamantly entrenched in his heretical opinion, and inverts the teaching of Ballerini in order to enlist Ballerini in support of his and Salza's heresy: "We did not falsify the teaching of Ballarini. In the book, we state over and over again that the pope will not lose his jurisdiction until the Church establishes the crime (that is the phrase we use). The Church "establishes the crime" by judging that the doctrine he professes is qualified as heretical (not a lesser error), and then issuing one or more ecclesiastical warnings. If the pope remains hardened in heresy in the face of these warnings, he publicly **reveals his pertinacity and thereby manifests his heresy** (since heresy requires pertinacity). This is an indirect judgment of the Pope which reveals that "he is already judged" (by God). All of this precedes the loss of papal jurisdiction for an heretical Pope. That is how we explain it in the book, and it is exactly how Ballerini explains it." Against Siscoe's inverted interpretation of Ballerini, Pope Gregory XVI, who explicitly endorsed Ballerini's teaching and adopted it as his own, explains that the judgment would not be made on the "Pope recognized as such, ***but only against the person, who was before adorned with papal dignity***".[687]

Nowhere does Ballerini say that the Church must *"establish the crime"*, but on the contrary, that the heretic pope, "[H]aving been once or twice corrected, does not repent, but remains obstinate in a belief contrary to a manifest or defined dogma; ***by this his public pertinacity*** which for no reason can be excused, since pertinacity properly pertains to heresy, **he declares himself to be a heretic**, i.e. ***to have withdrawn from the Catholic faith and the Church by his own will, so that no declaration or sentence from anyone would be necessary***." Then Ballerini quotes St. Jerome's comment on St. Paul, (the text which Salza & Siscoe removed from the quotation), *"by himself [the heretic] is said to be condemned, because the fornicator, adulterer, murderer, and those guilty of other misdeeds are driven out from the Church by the Priests: but heretics deliver the sentence upon themselves, departing from the Church by their own will: this departure is seen to be the condemnation by their own conscience."* Thus, by the "sentence which he brought upon himself" for remaining "obstinate in a belief contrary to a manifest or defined dogma", he would have ***"by his own will departed", "and in some manner to have abdicated the Pontificate"***, so that "whatever action that would be taken against him before the declaration of his contumacy and heresy, in order to bring him back to reason, would be a duty of charity and not of jurisdiction: **but afterward, with his departure from the Church having been manifested, if a sentence were to be pronounced upon him by a council, it would be pronounced on him who would no longer be the Pontiff, nor superior to the council.**" (Salza & Siscoe also left out this yellow highlighted text.)

---

[687] Gregorio XVI, *Op. cit.*, p. 270.

The Salza/Siscoe interpretation of Ballerini is fraught with crude errors and irresolvable contradictions: 1) "The Church 'establishes the crime' by judging that <u>the doctrine</u> he professes is qualified as heretical" **[The Church does not establish a crime by judging a doctrine to be heretical. Judging a doctrine to be heretical is *per se* a magisterial function; such as when a list of condemned propositions is promulgated. It is an act of teaching authority, and is not penal in nature. Even when examining the writings of a suspected heretic, the mere judgment that a proposition of the suspect is heretical does not establish that a crime has taken place, but only when a tribunal judges that the proposition has been professed with pertinacity, does the Church establish a crime. Thus, a crime is established by a public judgment of the Church when a *tribunal* in possession of *proper jurisdiction over a subject* determines that *this* man who is subject to the jurisdiction of the court has professed heresy, and has done so with pertinacity, and then pronounces him guilty of the *crime of heresy* by means of a penal or declaratory sentence. Only then can it be said that a crime has been established by a "public judgment of the Church". The pope, by his universal primacy of jurisdiction is the supreme judge and final judge of appeal in *all cases* according to the solemn definition in *Pastor Æternus*, and superior to every other jurisdiction, and is subject to no other jurisdiction on earth. No one may judge the pope guilty of the crime of heresy or any other crime.]** 2) "then issuing one or more ecclesiastical warnings" **[Ecclesiastical warnings are by their very nature juridical acts of jurisdiction by a superior in a penal process over his subject. *Thus, it is impossible for the Church to juridically establish the crime of a pope.* Ballerini avoids this dilemma by avoiding ecclesiastical warnings in the procedure he prescribes, and speaks only of fraternal correction – charitable warnings:** "a duty of charity and not of jurisdiction".**]** The Salza/Siscoe proposition, "If the pope remains hardened in heresy in the face of these warnings, he publicly **reveals his pertinacity and thereby manifests his heresy**", is followed by the *non sequitur*: (3) "This is an <u>indirect</u> judgment of the Pope which reveals that 'he is already judged' (by God)." **Nonsense! This is not a judgment of the Church at all – neither direct nor indirect. The cardinals, or a synod listening to a heretic abdicate by pronouncing a judgment upon himself does not constitute a judgment of the Church. As mentioned earlier, for there to be a judgment of the Church, there must be a *juridical act* of judgment – either a penal sentence or a declaratory sentence of heresy pronounced on the guilty party; and t*o pronounce a pope guilty of the crime of heresy would not be an indirect judgment*. Ballerini quotes St. Jerome: the heretic is *"condemned by his own judgment"*. **This is part of the passage that Salza & Siscoe excised from their translation of the Ballerini text**. Thus, Ballerini continues, "by this his public pertinacity which for no reason can be excused, since pertinacity properly pertains to heresy, **he declares himself to be a heretic**, i.e. to have **withdrawn from the Catholic faith and the Church by his own will**, so that **no declaration or sentence from anyone would be necessary**"; and thus he would have "**openly departed from the Church**, [...] and thus **his sentence which he brought upon himself**, would have to be publicly pronounced, made known to the whole Church, that **he by his own will departed**, making known to be severed from the body of the Church, and **in some manner to have abdicated the Pontificate**". No juridical act or ecclesiastical judgment of any kind precedes the heretic pope's fall from office: "whatever action that would be taken against him before the declaration of his contumacy and heresy, in order to bring him back to reason, **would be a duty of charity and not of jurisdiction**: but **afterward, with his departure from the Church having been manifested**, [i.e. manifested by his own act of pertinacity] *if a sentence were to be pronounced upon him by a council*, **it would be pronounced on him who would no longer be the Pontiff**". Thus Ballerini explains explicitly and unequivocally that the official judgment of the Church would take place after the *ipso facto* fall from office, to wit, the *declaratory sentence* by the Church of the "sentence which he brought upon himself, would have to be publicly pronounced [...] **on him who would no longer be the Pontiff**". So, while Ballerini says the judgment would be pronounced "**on him who would no longer be the Pontiff**", Siscoe totally inverts his doctrine, and concludes: "***All of this precedes the loss of papal jurisdiction for an heretical Pope***. That is how we explain it in the book, and it is exactly how Ballerini explains it."

SALZA & SISCOE FRAUDULENTLY FABRICATE
A TEACHING OF POPE ADRIAN VI

On page 194 of their screed, Salza & Siscoe write, "Bellarmine also believed that a Pope could not actually fall into personal heresy, even though Popes Innocent III and **Adrian VI expressly taught the contrary**." First of all, it is an error to claim that Innocent III "expressly taught" that a pope could actually become a heretic, since it has been clearly demonstrated that Innocent, (like Bellarmine) treated the question of a heretical pope as a hypothesis, and he clearly leaned toward the opinion later adopted by Pighius and Bellarmine. The erroneous interpretation of Innocent III on this point is a result of taking the quotation of Innocent out of context, and considering it in isolation from that context. I have already shown the actual context of his words, and what is their proper interpretation in Part II of this work. Cardinal Adriaan Florisz Boeijens (a.k.a. Adrien Florent or Adrianus Florentius) wrote in his work, *Quæstiones in IV. Sententiarum, art. 3,* (reprinted in 1522 in Rome while he was pope):

> "*Ad secundum principale de facto Gregorii, dico primo quod si per Ecclesiam Romanam intelligatur caput ejus, puta Pontifex,* **Certum est quod possit errare, etiam in his, quæ tangent fidem, hæresim per suam determinationem aut Decretalem asserendo**; *plures enim fuere Pontifices Romani hæretici. Item et novissime fertur de* **Joanne XXII, quod publice docuit, declaravit, et ab omnibus teneri mandavit, quod animas purgatæ ante finale judicium non habent stolam, quæ est clara et facialis visio Dei.*"

This text is the theological opinion of a Cardinal, which he expressed in his book. As Pope, **Adrian VI never magisterially taught the propositions, *1)* "***Certum est quod possit errare, etiam in his, quæ tangent fidem, hæresim per suam determinationem aut Decretalem asserendo"; 2) "plures enim fuere Pontifices Romani hæretici",* or *3) "quod publice docuit, declaravit, et ab omnibus teneri mandavit, quod animas purgatæ ante finale judicium non habent stolam, quæ est clara et facialis visio Dei."* St. Robert Bellarmine, understanding the clear meaning of the terms, "per suam detemationem aut Decretalem asserendo" in proposition **no. 1** to denote *papal definitions*, and declared the proposition to be *proximate to heresy*. As I mentioned in Part III, since *Pastor Æternus*, the proposition in now plainly seen to be heretical. Proposition **no. 2** is simply false (or at least cannot be proven, as Bellarmine says), as has been explained in Part III, and there is no reputable theologian in the world who holds this opinion; and **no. 3** is simply erroneous: John XXII never *declared and commanded to be held by all that the souls of the departed that had already completed purgation do not enjoy the beatific vision.* These three propositions of Cardinal Adrianus Florentius are all, without exception, erroneous, but they are only the personal opinion of the man who became Pope Adrian VI, who never taught them magisterially as pope. For Salza & Siscoe to flatly characterize what was merely Adrian's erroneous personal opinion as something that *"Adrian VI expressly taught"*, is false and misleading, and to do so knowingly as Salza and Siscoe undoubtedly have done, constitutes a **fraud.**

THE APOCRYPHAL "COUNCIL OF SINUESSA" AND THE SUPPOSED "FALL" OF POPE ST. MARCELLINUS

On page 341 of their *magnum opus*, Salza & Siscoe state, "Another council that is often mentioned is the Council of Sinuesso (sic), which was convened by the bishops to oversee the matter of Pope Marcellinus (d. 304), who had offered incense to idols." In support of this assertion, they quote a **Ninth Century** letter of Pope Nicholas: "In the reign of the sovereigns Diocletian and Maximian, Marcellinus, the Bishop of Rome, who afterwards became an illustrious martyr, was so persecuted by the pagans that he entered one of their temples and there offered incense." The problem with the Salza/Siscoe assertion is that, 1) there was never any council at Sinuessa, 2) there is no credible evidence that Pope St. Marcellinus ever offered incense to idols, and 3) it is considered certain that he did not die a martyr, but died of natural causes. The *Catholic Encyclopedia* has this to say about St. Marcellinus and the apocryphal "Council of Sinuessa":

> Marcellinus died in the second year of the persecution and, in all probability, a natural death. No trustworthy sources of the fourth or fifth century mention him as a martyr. His name does not occur either in the list of martyrs or the bishops in the Roman "Chronograph" of the year 354. Neither is he mentioned in the "Martyrologium Hieronymianum". The "Marcellinus episcopus" on 4 Oct. in "Codex Bernensis" (ed. De Rossi-Duchesne, 129) is probably not identical with the pope. In mentioning Marcellinus, Eusebius uses an obscure expression; he merely says: "the persecution also affected him" (*'òn kaì a'utòn kateílephon 'o diogmòs Church History* VII.32). From this one must obviously conclude that the pope did not suffer martyrdom, otherwise Eusebius would have distinctly stated it. There were even later reports in circulation that accused him of having given up the sacred books after the first edict, or even of having offered incense to the gods, to protect himself from the persecution. But the sources in which this reproach is clearly stated are very questionable.
> The Donatist Bishop Petilianus of Constantine in Africa asserted, in the letter he wrote in 400 and 410, that Marcellinus and the Roman

priests Melchiades, Marcellus, and Sylvester (his three successors) had given up the sacred books, and had offered incense. But he could not adduce any proof. In the Acts of confiscation of the church buildings at Rome, which at the great Carthaginian conference between Catholics and Donatists, were brought forward by the latter, only two Roman deacons, Straton and Cassius, were named as traitors. St. Augustine, in his replies to Petilianus, disputes the truth of the latter's report (*Against Petilian* 2.202: "De quibus et nos solum respondemus: aut non probatis et ad neminem pertinet, aut probatis et ad nos non pertinet"; "De unico baptismo contra Petilianum", cap. xvi: "Ipse scelestos et sacrilegos fuisse dicit; ego innocentes fuisse respondeo"). One can only conclude from Petilianus's accusation that such rumours against Marcellinus and Roman priests were circulated in Africa; but that they could not be proved, otherwise St. Augustine would not have been able to assert the innocence of the accused so decidedly, or safely to have referred to the matter at the Carthaginian conference. But even in Rome similar stories were told of Marcellinus in certain circles, so that in two later legendary reports a formal apostasy was attributed to this pope, of course followed by repentance and penance. The biography of Marcellinus in the "Liber Pontificalis", which probably alludes to a lost "passio" of his, relates that he was led to the sacrifice that he might scatter incense, which he did. But after a few days he was seized with remorse, and was condemned to death by Diocletian with three other Christians, and beheaded. It is clear that this report attempts to combine a rumour that the pope had offered incense to the gods, with the fact that, in other circles he was regarded as a martyr and his tomb venerated.

According to Vol. IV of *The Lives or the Fathers, Martyrs and Other Principal Saints* by the Rev. Alban Butler, (1864 Edition),

> "He succeeded St. Caius in the bishopric of Rome, in 296, about the time that Diocletian set himself up for a deity and impiously claimed divine honours. Theodoret says that in those stormy times of persecution Marcellinus acquired great glory. He sat in St. Peter's chair eight years, three months, and twenty-five days, dying in 304, a year after the cruel persecution broke out, in which he gained much honour. He has been styled a martyr, though his blood was not shed in the cause of religion, as appears from the Liberian Calendar, which places him among those popes that were not put to death for the faith."

In *A New History of Ecclesiastical Writers.*, we read in the section, "Of the pretended COUNCIL of Sinuessa":

This Council of *Sinuessa* would be the Fifth Council held in this Century, if the Acts which bear the Name of this Council were Genuine: But it is notoriously known among all Learned Men, that they are suppositions, and the Story on which they are grounded is a Fable which has no foundation in Antiquity. It is suppos'd in those Acts, That this Council was assembled t the beginning of the fourth Century, on the occasion of the Fall of the Pope *Marcellinus*, who had sacrificed to Idols; that it was held at *Sinussa* in a Grotto; that there were 300 Bishops present at it; That the Pope *Marcellinus* having confess'd his Fault condemn'd himself, and that the Bishops durst not depose him, till he had pronounced Sentence upon himself. None of these things have any probability: For, First, This History is not founded upon the Testimony of any ancient Author: Secondly, St. *Austin* in his Book against *Petilian*, Ch. 16. Defends the Innocence of *Marcellinus* against this *Donatist*, who accus'd him of having sacrificed to Idols; and therefore to maintain the Acts of the Council of *Sinuessa*, is to take part with the *Donatists* against the Church. 'Tis more probable that they were forg'd by the *Donatists* to support the Accusation which they had made against this Holy Bishop without Foundation. Thirdly, What probability is there that 300 Bishops could be assembled in the time of the most violent Persecution that ever the Church suffer'd, [...][688]

The author's comment about giving credence to the phony "Council of Sinuessa" most aptly are applicable to John F. Salza & Robert J. Siscoe: ***"to maintain the Acts of the Council of Sinussa, is to take part with the Donatists against the Church"***. What is absolutely certain is that the fictional "Council of Sinuessa", which Salza & Siscoe treat as a historical fact, *never happened*, as Fr. Moynihan explains in Chapter One of his above cited work: "a group of spurious documents known as the *Symmachian forgeries* were fabricated and circulated, in which apochryphal incidents were written into the lives of earlier popes [...] These apochrypha were principally contained in four documents: the *Gesta Marcellini* (or the False Synod of Sinuessa), the *Constitutum Silvestri*, the *Gesta Liberii*, and the *Gesta de Xysti purgatione*."[689]

SALZA & SISCOE FRAUDULENTLY DOGMATIZE "COMMON OPINION"

---

[688] Louis Ellies du Pin, *A New History of Ecclesiastical Writers,* Vol. 1, London, 1693, p. 241.
[689] Moynihan; *Op. cit.*, p. 3.

On page 274 of their screed, the fundamentalists, Salza & Siscoe declare that, *"**departing from the 'common opinion' of the theologians is, at minimum, an act of imprudence** and possibly a mortal sin.107"*. On the same page they attempt to justify their fundamentalistic belief that it is always a sin of imprudence to disagree with a common opinion by fraudulently citing the doctrine of Cartechini: "**Cartechini explains that opinions held in common by all theologians are *theologically certain*, the denial of which constitutes, usually, *a mortal sin* of temerity.**" The assertion is a fraudulent misrepresentation, since *theologically certain doctrines* are not mere matters of *opinion* on open questions. A common opinion on an open question remains a matter of opinion, and is therefore not *theologically certain*. Accordingly, it is to be noted that **Cartechini adds the qualification that the unanimous doctrine must also be *derived from divine faith* in order for it to be considered *theologically certain*. The fundamentalists, Salza & Siscoe *omitted all mention of this crucial qualification*.** Don Alfredo Morselli rightly includes the additional qualification that what is to be considered *theologice certum* must be deduced from a revealed *sententia*, and from another which is certain from another source (i.e. such as from reason or a historical fact). This is entirely consistent with the teaching of Cartechini.

Cartechini carefully distinguishes between what is of *divine faith*, what is *theologically certain*, and what is *proximate to faith*. I will quote Harold E. Ernst's article which appeared in the reputable theological journal, *Theological Studies*, and thereby avoid being accused by Salza & Siscoe of misinterpreting Cartechini. In his article, Ernst quotes Cartechini, who says, "Divine faith, as it is revealed, is essentially not different from divine and Catholic faith, but only... extrinsically as far as one is clearly proposed by God, the other by God and by the Church."[690] Cartechini further elaborates,

> "One who denies a matter clearly contained either in Scripture or in Tradition as revealed, commits a mortal sin against divine faith, but is not a heretic because he or she does not sever himself or herself from an opinion expressly proposed by the Church. Some call this erroneous in faith: erroneous, if you attend to that which is properly error: for error, if it is taken up in a strict sense, is not only something false, but a falsehood which

---

[690] HAROLD E. ERNST, *THE THEOLOGICAL NOTES AND THE INTERPRETATION OF DOCTRINE*, Theological Studies 63 (2002), p. 816.

is opposed to something clearly true, or certain, that which is commonly known among all as certain."[691]

Ernst then concludes, "Thus in order to incur the censure error in fide, one must affirm something contrary to a proposition that is clearly and certainly held by the Catholic faithful as a revealed truth."[692]

"Proxima fidei, the fourth category, is the theological note applied to propositions somewhat less certainly held than those designated de fide divina. These are opinions that, while also not expressly proposed by the magisterium, are almost unanimously regarded as revealed, such as the doctrine of the satisfaction of Christ. 'In other words: they are propositions which, although not entirely certain, nevertheless probably, and as it seems to many, are of the faith.' This note does not require absolute, but theological assent, and its corresponding censure is errori proxima. The fifth category is theologice certum, applied to theological conclusions deduced from one revealed proposition and another proposition that is certain in reason, such as the conclusion that the existence of God is rationally demonstrable."[693]

Among the categories that Cartechini considers "less important", Ernst explains,

"Category seven includes the notes commune et certum, certum, and moraliter certum. An individual proposition is designated commune if it is held by all the theological schools, while certum is applied in contradistinction to theologice certum to indicate that the conclusion is less immediately or less clearly deduced from a revealed truth. The denial of a proposition of this kind, such as that the sacraments are causes of grace, would be assigned the censure temeraria."[694]

While there is a general agreement among authors on the most important theologicsl notes, they are not all in total agreement on every point.[695] There exist various opinions, so no single author's opinion on

---

[691] *Ibid.*
[692] *Ibid.*
[693] *Ibid.* p. 817.
[694] *Ibid.*
[695] «(1) *Hæretica* (heretical), *erronea* (erroneous), *hæresi proxima* (next to heresy), *errori proxima* (next to error), *temeratia* (rash), etc.
A proposition is branded heretical when it goes directly and immediately against a revealed or defined dogma, or dogma *de fide*; erroneous when it

a point that is not unanimous, can be uncritically held up as a rigid and authoritative magisterial standard of orthodoxy to which all are bound, in the manner that Salza & Siscoe employ the teaching of Fr. Cartechini, which they also manage to distort considerably.

From the above brief exposition of Cartechini's teaching on theological notes, it is clear that Salza & Siscoe state a falsehood in their proposition, "Cartechini explains that opinions held in common by all theologians are theologically certain". Furthermore, their assertion, that to depart from a common opinion is "usually, a mortal sin of temerity", is likewise false; since Cartechini is careful to distinguish between that

> contradicts only a certain (*certa*) theological conclusion or truth clearly deduced from two premises, one an article of faith, the other naturally certain. Even though a statement be not obviously a heresy or an error it may yet come near to either. It is styled next, proximate to heresy when its opposition to a revealed and defined dogma is not certain, or chiefly when the truth it contradicts, though commonly accepted as revealed, has yet never been the object of a definition (*proxima fidei*). The censure next, or proximate to error, whose meaning may be determined by analogy to the foregoing, is of less frequent use than that of rashness or temerity, which means opposition to sound common opinion (*communis*), and this either for paltry reasons or no reasons at all. A still finer shade of meaning attaches to such censures as *sapiens hæresim, errorem* (smacking of heresy or error), *suspecta de hæresi, errore* (suspected of heresy or error). Propositions thus noted may be correct in themselves, but owing to various circumstances of time, place, and persons, are prudently taken to present a signification which is either heretical or erroneous. To this group also belong some special stigmata with reference to determined topics, e.g. the preambles of faith (*infidelis, aversiva a fide*), ethical principles (*improbabilis, non tuta*), history (*antiquata, nova*) and Holy Scripture (*verbo Dei contraria*), etc.
>
> (2) *Ambigua* (ambiguous), *captiosa* (captious), *male sonans* (evil-sounding), *piarum aurium offensive* (offensive to pious ears), etc.
>
> A proposition is ambiguous when it is worded so as to present two or more senses, one of which is objectionable; captious when acceptable words are made to express objectionable thoughts; evil-sounding when improper words are used to express otherwise acceptable truths; offensive when verbal expression is such as rightly to shock the Catholic sense and delicacy of faith.
>
> (3) *Subsannativa religionis* (derisive of religion), *decolorativa canodris ecclesiæ* (defacing the beauty of the Church), *subversiva hierarchiæ* (subversive of the hierarchy), *eversiva regnorum* (destructive of governments), *scandelosa, perniciosa, periculosa in moribus* (scandalous, pernicious, dangerous to morals), *blasphema, idolatra, superstisiosa, magica* (blasphemous, leading to idolatry, superstition, sorcery), *arrogans, acerba* (arrogant, harsh), etc.» [*Catholic Encyclopedia* – "Theological Censures"]

which is merely *commune*, and that which is *commune et certum*; and only the denial of the latter "would be assigned the censure temeraria." Thus, Salza & Siscoe, contrary to the theologians they quote, treat common opinions almost as if they were dogmas, although they admit elsewhere in their book that that common opinions are sometimes modified and even abandoned.

Cardinal Manning gives examples of common opinions that have been modified and even abandoned in his Letter to the Duke of Norfolk:

> Another instance of a similar kind is suggested by the general acceptance in the Latin Church, since the time of St. Augustine, of the doctrine of absolute predestination, as instanced in the teaching of other great saints besides him, such as St. Fulgentius, St. Prosper, St. Gregory, St. Thomas, and St. Buonaventure. Yet in the last centuries a great explanation and modification of this doctrine has been effected by the efforts of the Jesuit School, which have issued in the reception of a distinction between predestination to grace and predestination to glory; and a consequent admission of the principle that, though our own works do not avail for bringing us under the action of grace here, that does not hinder their availing, when we are in a state of grace, for our attainment of eternal glory hereafter. Two saints of late centuries, St. Francis de Sales and St. Alfonso, seemed to have professed this less rigid opinion, which is now the more common doctrine of the day. {337}
>
> Another instance is supplied by the Papal decisions concerning Usury. Pope Clement V, in the Council of Vienne, declares, "If any one shall have fallen into the error of pertinaciously presuming to affirm that usury is no sin, we determine that he is to be punished as a heretic." However, in the year 1831 the Sacred *Pœnitentiaria* answered an inquiry on the subject, to the effect that the Holy See suspended its decision on the point, and that a confessor who allowed of usury was not to be disturbed, "non esse inquietandum." Here again a double aspect seems to have been realized of the idea intended by the word *usury*.

The most notable example of the Church's reversal of its approval of a common opinion, and the dogmatization of the contrary opinion is that of the doctrine of the substantial unity of body and soul in man. Wikipedia explains, "On 18 January 1277, Pope John XXI instructed Bishop Tempier to investigate the complaints of the theologians. 'Not only did Tempier investigate but in only three weeks, on his own authority, he issued a condemnation of 219 propositions drawn from many sources, including, apparently, the works of Thomas Aquinas, some of whose ideas found their way onto the list.'"[696] The *Stanford Encyclopedia of Philosophy* mentions that, "Other propositions may well have been derived from the teaching of theologians, such as Thomas Aquinas. In particular, John Wippel has argued (against Roland Hissette) that Aquinas' teaching was also implied in Tempier's condemnation and that some of the positions were taken from his writings." This would clearly appear to be the case when one considers some of those propositions:

- «42A.1 That God cannot multiply individuals of the same species without matter.»
- «43A. That God could not make several intelligences of the same species because intelligences do not have matter.»
- «110A. That forms are not divided except through matter. – This is erroneous unless one is speaking of forms educed from the potency of matter.»

The *Catholic Encyclopedia* relates:

"the same year Robert Kilwardby, a Dominican, Archbishop of Canterbury, in conjunction with some doctors of Oxford, condemned those same propositions and moreover attacked St. Thomas's doctrine of the unity of the substantial form in man."

The *Encyclopedia* relates further:

St. Thomas was solemnly vindicated when the Council of Vienna [i.e. Vienne] (1311-12) defined, against Peter John Olivi, that the rational soul is the substantial form of the human body (on this definition see Zigliara, 'De mente Conc. Vicnn.', Rome, 1878). The canonization of St. Thomas by John XXII, in 1323, was a death-blow to his detractors. In 1324 Stephen de Bourret, Bishop of Paris, revoked the censure pronounced by his predecessor, declaring that "that blessed confessor and excellent doctor, Thomas Aquinas, had never believed, taught, or written anything contrary to the Faith or good morals."

---

[696] https://en.m.wikipedia.org/wiki/Condemnations_of_1210%E2%80%931277.

The Council defined the dotrine of St. Thomas, which had been contrary to the common opinion, and which had been condemned by the Archbishop of Canterbury:

> Moreover, with the approval of the said council, we reject as erroneous and contrary to the truth of the catholic faith every doctrine or proposition rashly asserting that the substance of the rational or intellectual soul is not of itself and essentially the form of the human body, or casting doubt on this matter. In order that all may know the truth of the faith in its purity and all error may be excluded, we define that anyone who presumes henceforth to assert defend or hold stubbornly that the rational or intellectual soul is not the form of the human body of itself and essentially, is to be considered a heretic.

The above is not such an isolated example as one may at first think. Fr. Gaetano Maria di Bergamo Cappucino explained in his *Reflections on the Probable Opinion*:

> It is said to be common that Opinion, which claims to be able to lawfully follow the least likely opinion. I want to grant it, that it is common to many: but why? That Opinion was also common, that the Savior was one of the previous Prophets; and yet it was false, because it was of Men, who opted for the mad glimmerings of human intelligence. By observing, on which foundations, this Opinion is made, which makes the least Probable lawful; and finding nothing else, what reasons, or purely human little reasonings, for which the Probable is based on the Probable, and the Equivocal on the Equivocal, and the uncertain on the uncertain, the stupor will cease, as to how the Common opinion, is at the same time false: *Tamdiu enim sermo communis est, quamdiu humana intelligentia ambiguitas explicatur.* In the Probabilities of our Moral Theology, *Quis nesciat*, says Lattanzio (b), *plus esse momenti in paucioribus doctis, quam in pluribus imperitis?* How many condemned opinions before they were condemned, were said to be common? How many opinions are there among the Moralists, considered to be common, which are also lax, but never *secundum Pietatem*? How many times are said to be the common opinion, both the one, and the other of two that are contrary to each other? How many times among modern authors it is written: *Certum est apud omnes: est communissima Opinio*: and yet this, which is said to be certain, will be false; and that opinion, which is called most common, will be the most false? Of this Opinion, *Est licitum Religious calumniatorem occidere, quando alius modus se defendendi not suppetit*: which was condemned by the Supreme Pontifece Alexander VII. num. 17, was described by Caramuele, to be *omnium communis, cujus contraria neque sit*

Probabilis (c). So much suffices to instill caution, and not to trust everything, that is said, to be common opinion.[697]

The condemned proposition, *"Est licitum Religioso clumniatorem occidere, quando alius modus se defendendi non suppetit"*, (It is licit for a religious to kill a calumniator when there exists no other means to defend oneself), was said by Caramuel to be *"omnium communis, cujus contraria neque sit Probabilis"* (common of all whose contrary is not even probable); yet that *"unanimous opinion"* was finally condemned by Caramuel's[698] personal friend, Pope Alexander VII. It is also no wonder that St. Alphonsus de Liguori bestowed on him the dubious title, "The Chief of the Laxists". Thus Fr. Gaetano Maria concludes, "So much suffices to instill caution, and not to trust in everything that is said to be *common opinion*." So much also

---

[697] *RIFLESSIONI SOPRA L'OPINIONE PROBABILE Per I Casi della Coscienza nella Teologia Morale*; Fr. Gaetano Maria di Bergamo Cappucino, volume secondo, Brescia, 1739, p. 338: «Si dice esser comune quella Opinione, che tiene di potersi lecitamente seguire l'Opinione meno Probabile. Voglio concederlo, che sia commune a molti: ma e per questo? Era commune anche quella Opinione, che il Salvatore fosse uno de' precedenti Profeti; e tuttavia era falsa, perchè era di Uomini, che opinavano ai folli barlumi dell'intelligenza umana. S'osservi, sopra quali fondamenti siasi fabbricata questa Opinione, che fa lecito il meno Probabile; e trovandosi non altro, che ragioni, o ragiocelle puramente umane, per le quali il Probabile si fonda sopra il Probabile, e l'Equivoco sopra l'Equivoco, e l'incerto sopra l'incerto, cesserà lo stupor, come sia l'Opinione commune, ed insieme anche falsa: *Tamdiu enim sermo communis est, quamdiu humana intelligentia ambiguitas explicatur*. Nelle Probabilità della nostra Morale, *Quis nesciat*, dice Lattanzio (*b*), *plus esse momenti in paucioribus doctis, quam in pluribus imperitis?* Quante Opinioni dannate pri[m]a che si dannassero, erano dette comuni? Quante Opinioni vi sono tra I Moralisti, riputate comuni, che pure sono lasse, non mai *secundum Pietatem*? Quante volte si chiama Opinione commune l'una, e l'altra delle due contrarie? Quante volte ne' Moderni si trova scritto: *Certum est apud omnes: est communissima Opinio*: e pure ciò, che si chiama certo, sara falso; e quella opinion, che si chiama comunissima, sara falsissima? Di questa Opinione, che *Est licitum Religioso calumniatorem occidere, quando alius modus se defendendi non suppetit*: dannata dal Sommo Pontifece Alesandro VII. num. 17 lasciò scritto il Caramuele, che era *omnium communis, cujus contraria neque sit Probabilis (c)*. Tanto basta ad insinuare la Cautela, e non fidarsi di tutto, ciò, che si dice, *Opinione commune*.»

[698] Juan Caramuel von Lobkowicz (1606-1682) refered to as the "Scourge of Heretics", and one of the most vastly learned and encyclopedic intellectuals, styled *"supreme doctor of the whole Catholic world"*; and the "Last Scholastic Polymath", was the Bishop of Vigevano (Lombardy), and personal friend of Pope Alexander VII.

suffices to dispense with the nonsensical proposition that, "departing from the 'common opinion' of the theologians is, at minimum, an act of imprudence"; and that "opinions held in common by all theologians are *theologically certain*".

Salza & Siscoe falsely state:
1. «It is the common opinion among theologians that a Pope can fall into personal heresy (internally), and even public and notorious heresy (externally).» (p. 191)
2. «The common opinion that a Pope can become a heretic is taught in the consecration sermon of Pope Innocent III, who in 1198» (p. 191)
3. «it is certainly within the realm of possibility for a Pope to lose the faith internally, and he can without a doubt profess error externally. [...] To insist on the contrary [...] is to extend infallibility beyond its narrowly defined limits. [...] It is to reject the teaching of Popes Innocent III and Adrian VI as well as the 'common opinion' of the Church's theologians [...] It is to deny the historical cases of Popes Honorius and John XXII.» (p. 227)
4. «Billuart teaches that: 'Christ by a particular providence, for the common good and the tranquility of the Church, continues to give jurisdiction to an even manifestly heretical pontiff until such time as he should be declared a manifest heretic by the Church.' This **common opinion** was also confirmed by John of St. Thomas, who said a Pope who is manifestly heretical, according to private judgment, remains Pope until he is declared such by the Church».
5. «As further evidence that Bellarmine (d. 1621) and Suarez (d. 1617) held the same opinion regarding crime versus punishment, we note that the two lived at the same time, yet ***both held that their position represented the common opinion of the Fathers and Doctors of the Church***. [...] For example, after teaching that a heretical Pope ceases to be Pope upon a declaratory sentence of the Church, Suarez says, ***'This is the common opinion among the doctors.'*** However, when Bellarmine says a heretical Pope ceases to be Pope automatically, he says, ***'This is the teaching of all the ancient Fathers who teach that manifest heretics immediately lose all jurisdiction.'*** [...] How can they both say that their seemingly contradictory opinions represented the common teaching of the Fathers and Doctors of the Church?» (p. 273)

Number One is simply an outright falsehood as has already been shown above. Number Two has also been shown to be false. Number Three states multiple falsehoods: 1) "To insist on the contrary [...] is to extend infallibility beyond its narrowly defined limits", is false, because the doctrine that the pope is infallible in his definitions, and the opinion that the pope cannot be a formal heretic are simply statements on two different questions; 2) "It is to reject the teaching of Popes Innocent III and Adrian VI as well as the 'common opinion' of the Church's theologians", is false, because Innocent III did not teach that a pope can become a heretic; Adrian VI only expressed his private opinion that a pope can become a heretic; and as already mentioned, it is not a common opinion of the Church's theologians that a pope can become a heretic. Number Four is false, because it is not the common opinion, but the opinion that "a Pope who is manifestly heretical, according to private judgment, remains Pope until he is declared such by the Church"; far from being common, has been universally abandoned. Number Five is false: Suárez refers to the "doctors" i.e. the 'common opinion' of his Counter-Reformation contemporaries, that the fall from office follows judgment of the crime by the Church; Bellarmine refers to the "*ancient* Fathers" whom, he explains, taught the opposite, i.e. that heretics lose office automatically not for a crime against any human law, but *ex natura hæresis*. Therefore, in answer to their question, "How can they both say that their seemingly contradictory opinions represented the common teaching of the Fathers and Doctors of the Church?" I simply respond: Salza & Siscoe employ verbal sleight of hand: Bellarmine's and Suárez's opinions are indeed contradictory, but they do *not* "both say that their seemingly contradictory opinions represented the common teaching of the Fathers and Doctors of the Church".

SALZA & SISCOE FRAUDULENTLY ALTER MY MEANING AND FALSIFY MY WORDS

On 21 January, I wrote to Siscoe:

> Your ignorant rants have descended to the level of lunacy: The external act of heresy is in its nature a sin, but is not in its nature a crime. The sinfulness of heresy pertains to the specific nature of the act, regardless of the circumstance of whether the sin is committed with an internal or external act. Such a circumstance does not alter the specific nature of the sin, which is the same for both the internal and the external sin. The specific nature of heresy (as I pointed out in my book) is identically defined in Moral Theology as a sin, and in Canon Law as a crime (i.e. the pertinacious denial or doubt of a revealed truth which must be believed with divine and Catholic faith)*. Thus, the nature of heresy is the same for the internal sin, the external sin, and the crime. The internal sin of heresy differs from the crime of heresy not in an essential difference in the [specific] nature of the act, but

according to the circumstance of it being an internal act, and according to its formal aspect considered as a violation of divine law. The external sin of heresy differs from the crime of heresy, neither according to its nature, nor according to any circumstance of the act; but only according to the formal aspect of the act considered as a sin (i.e as a violation of divine law) as distinguished from its formal aspect considered as a crime (i.e. as a violation of ecclesiastical law). The intrinsic nature of the act, considered under both formal aspects remains the same. The thing that distinguishes the external sin of heresy from the crime of heresy is not the specific nature of the act (which is identical in both), but the circumstance extrinsic to its nature, namely, the fact that the legislator enacted a law [or added a penalty] that made that external sin a crime. Your incredibly ignorant statement that, "The sin of heresy can be distinguished [*in its specific nature*] from the crime solely according to the circumstances of whether or not the sin was committed internally" is patently and absurdly false, since the external sin of heresy is by definition identical to the external act defined in law as the crime of heresy; and both are therefore indistinguishable in their nature. The external sin of heresy is not in its nature a crime; and therefore, it was not a crime before penal legislation made it a crime; and it would not be a crime today if there were no law enacted against it, thereby making it a crime. The external sin of heresy is identical in nature to the crime of heresy, and therefore the crime of heresy can only be distinguished from the external sin of heresy not according to its nature, but according to its formal aspect of its being considered as a violation of ecclesiastical positive law. However, whether considered according to its formal aspect of being a criminal violation of Church law; or a sin against Divine law; the specific nature of the act of heresy, as defined in Canon Law and Moral Theology, is identical in both cases. The difference between the specific nature of a crime as such (as defined in Canon Law), and the specific nature of a sin as such (as defined in Moral Theology), is a difference of circumstance and formal aspect of an act; but the intrinsic nature of the criminal act is identical to the intrinsic nature of the sinful act if the act is of the same species. The nature of sin, considered under the formal aspect of sin, is of a violation of divine law; whereas the nature of crime, considered under the formal aspect of crime, is of an external violation of ecclesiastical or human positive law; but the objective nature intrinsic to the act is the same for both the sin and the crime of the same species. The sinful act does not differ in nature from the criminal act, and therefore the sin and the crime of the same species are distinguishable solely according to the circumstances of the act and the differing formal aspect under which they are considered, but not according to the [specific] nature of the act which is identical in both. You would understand all of this if you had a proper, formal education in Moral Theology and Canon Law, but you obviously lack a proper education in these academic disciplines; yet you ignorantly pontificate on Canon Law and

Theology, presenting yourself as if you were one who is academically qualified to expound on matters pertaining to these disciplines, but you only succeed in manifesting your utter incompetence and your profound ignorance of the subject matter.

* "Can. 751 — Dicitur hæresis, pertinax, post receptum baptismum, alicuius veritatis divina et catholica credendæ denegatio, aut de eadem pertinax dubitatio; apostasia, fidei christianæ ex toto repudiatio".

"Hæresis est error intellectus, et pertinax contra Fidem, in eo qui Fidem suscepit. ... Unde patet, ad Hæresim, ut et Apostasiam, duo requiri, 1. Judicium erroneum, quod est ejus quasi materiale. 2. Pertinaciam; quæ est quasi formale. Porro pertinaciter errare non est hic acriter, et mordicus suum errorem tueri; sed est eum retinere, postquam contrarium est sufficienter propositum: sive quando scit contrarium teneri a reliqua universali Christi in terris Ecclesia, cui suum iudicium præferat" – St. Alphonsus M. De Liguori, Lib. II. Tract. I. De præcepto Fidei. Dubium III.

Fr. Paul Kramer B.Ph., S.T.B., M. Div., S.T.L. (Cand.) 》

On 22 January I wrote:

《Salza & Siscoe also make the incredibly stupid assertion that, "The external act of heresy is, by its nature, a crime." This statement is absurd on its face, because if that were true, then the external act of heresy would be a crime even if there were no law (!) – but a crime is defined as an external violation of a LAW [i.e. an *ecclesiastical* law]. Siscoe errantly explains further that, "there's a difference between the definition of the sin of heresy, and the definition the crime of heresy: there is a difference between the nature of the respective acts". Now that's about as insanely ignorant as one can get, since both the sin (in Moral Theology) and the crime (in Canon Law) are identically defined as "the pertinacious denial or doubt of a revealed truth which must be believed with divine and Catholic faith". I have already explained this point fully and quoted the authoritative sources in my latest reply to Siscoe. Salza & Siscoe have manifested their utter incompetence in Theology and Canon Law by nonsensically asserting that the external act of heresy is in its nature a crime (!). Every theologian and canonist on earth knows that the act of heresy, both internal and external, in its nature is a sin; and that only the law [i.e. an ecclesiastical law], (which is extrinsic to the nature of the act whether internal or external, and does not enter into the definition of the external act) makes the external sin a crime. The circumstance of being an "external violation of a law" [i.e. of an *ecclesiastical* law] defines the nature of a crime; but it does not enter into the definition of the act of heresy, which is the same definition, specifying the same nature for both the internal and external SIN of heresy. The circumstance of being an "external violation of a law" is merely an accidental circumstance that does not pertain to the nature of the external act of heresy. That is why it is the sin of heresy, committed as a public act, which separates one from the body Church *suapte natura* and not the crime, since a crime separates one from the Church not by its nature, but "by legitimate authority" [i.e. excommunication], as Pius XII explains in *Mystici Corporis*. Similarly, the sin of public defection from the faith by formal heresy effects the *ipso jure*, i.e. automatic loss of any office whatsoever, without any official judgment; as is plainly set forth in the relevant canons, and clearly explained in the commentaries on Canon Law written by the Faculties of Canon Law of the PONTIFICIA UNIVERSIDAD ECLESIÁSTICA DE SALAMANCA and the UNIVERSIDAD DE NAVARRA, which I quoted in my manuscript.»

Siscoe's reply desperately resorts to extremely dishonest verbal trickery, saying:

«Fr. Kramer: The intrinsic nature of the act, considered under both formal aspects remains the same. The thing that distinguishes the external sin of heresy from the crime of heresy is not the specific nature of the act (which is identical in both), but the circumstance extrinsic to its nature, namely, the fact that the legislator enacted a law that made that external sin a crime. Your incredibly ignorant statement that, "The sin of heresy can be distinguished from the crime solely according to the circumstances of whether or not the sin was committed internally" is patently and absurdly false.

Siscoe, But Father, I was quoting you verbatim. The "ignorant statement" that you condemned as "patently and absurdly false," is your own. You'll see the entire quotation in part II. Now, since you can't even get your own argument straight, condemning as "patently and absurdly false" today, what you yourself explicitly taught yesterday, it is clearly a waste of time to continue this discussion.»

This is the same kind of malicious sophistry Siscoe resorted to when he dishonestly attempted to make it appear that I had contradicted myself on the question of Opinion No. 2, regarding the deposition of an occult heretic pope. I exposed Siscoe's fraud on that point in my manuscript, and I will presently expose his latest fraud here:

«The statement, "The sin of heresy can be distinguished [*in its specific nature*] from the crime [*in its specific nature*] solely according to the circumstances of whether or not the sin was committed internally" is indeed "patently and absurdly false", ***if in its plainly stated context the*** *proposition is expressly intended to posit a distinction of specific nature between the nature of the sin and the nature of the criminal act; i.e. that there is a difference in specific nature of the act between the sin of heresy and the crime of heresy, [which in fact is not distinguished by specific nature, but is only distinguished by the sin of heresy belonging to the genus of internal acts, and the crime of heresy to the genus of external acts].* [That is exactly what Siscoe attempted to prove, namely, that the *sin of heresy*, and the *external act of the crime of heresy*, are of *two different specific natures; i.e., sins of different species.*] However, in the context that I made the statement, it did not refer to a distinction in *specific* nature, but to the distinction of the circumstance which distinguishes their *generic nature* which [alone] distinguishes the sin from the crime, *which are acts of the same specific nature of heresy*. **Now it is manifestly evident that the external act of heresy, whether occult or public, is a criminal act; and the only thing that distinguishes the materially criminal act from the merely sinful act is the circumstance that the internal sin is not a crime – what disgtinguishes the external criminal act from the merely sinful internal act is not a difference in specific nature.** Hence, it is thus plainly evident that Robert Siscoe's statement, "Now, since you can't even get your own argument straight, condemning as 'patently and absurdly false' today, what you yourself explicitly taught yesterday, it is clearly a waste of time to continue this discussion", is a skilfully crafted, deliberate lie; written for the purpose of defending his heresy which asserts that only the delict of heresy, but not the public sin as such, *suapte natura* separates one from the body of the Church; and similarly that only the notorious *crime* of heresy, but not the mere *sin* of public defection into heresy *ipso jure* results necessarily in the automatic loss of office (as is clearly explained in the passages I quoted in the commentaries of the Canon Law faculties of Navarra and Salamanca) – and they still heretically insist that even in the latter case, a juridical pronouncement is required for the actual loss of office to take place.»

So this is how Siscoe attempts to end the discussion, with lying sophistry expressed with the deliberate intention to deceive. Even **after** I explained this point on 22 January, Salza & Siscoe stated the same premeditated and very deliberate lie in Part II of their Formal Reply:

«Fr. Kramer Explicitly Condemns His Very Own Words! Now, since Fr. Kramer's new argument is clearly contrary to what he wrote a mere 18 months ago *(sic)*, and because Fr. Kramer always denies contradicting himself when the contradiction is pointed out *(sic)*, we decided to respond to the e-mail in which he sent out the above argument, by quoting his own words, without telling him the words were his own. How did he respond?

Did he recognize his own writing style, as we suspected would happen, or perhaps see the truth in his former position when it was presented to him as he himself formulated it? Nope. Instead, he responded by declaring his own previous teaching to be "incredibly ignorant" and "patently and absurdly false.»

As I pointed out, in the context in which Siscoe made the statement, the abusive taking of my words out of their proper context to assert an erroneous distinction of *specific* nature between the internal sin of heresy and the crime of heresy is indeed *"incredibly ignorant" and "patently and absurdly false."* It was *his* proposition (which I condemned), which made use of my words to assert something I have never asserted; to wit, a proposition which erroneously and most ignorantly posits a difference between the *specific nature* of the *sin* of heresy and the *specific* nature of the *crime* of heresy, **thereby nonsensically making internal heresy and external heresy two different species of sin**. It was **not** *my own previous teaching*, which asserted the *same specific nature* and *only* an *accidental distinction of qualitative circumstance pertaining to the generic nature, and not of specific nature*, that I condemned. Siscoe's proposition and mine use the same words to express something entirely different, since each proposition addresses a different formal aspect of the same matter. Thus it can be clearly seen that Siscoe's statements, 1) "Fr. Kramer Explicitly Condemns His Very Own Words!"; and, 2) "Fr. Kramer's new argument is clearly contrary to what he wrote a mere 18 months ago", are deliberately crafted lies.

The entire argument that Salza & Siscoe present in their Formal Reply, which attempts to prove that I have changed my position, is based on fraudulently altered quotations of my words by which they deceitfully attempt to make me appear to deny what I actually affirm. Here is a typical example of their fraudulent alteration of my words:

«Fr. Kramer: "Salza's error...[is this]: 'Separation from the Soul of the Church is intrinsic to the nature of the internal act of heresy, and separation from the Body of the Church is intrinsic to the nature of the external act of [notoriously] heresy, even if external heresy were not a crime in canon law.'»

They deleted my words which specify Salza's error, "[*the internal sin and the external sin are not of the same nature*]"; and changed my meaning by adding in their place the words, "[is this]", ("Salza's error... [is this] ...") From this falsified quotation, one would easily be led to the conclusion that I reject the quoted proposition as as an error; which in fact, I have consistently upheld as true, and amply demonstrated it to be true in this work. **What I actually condemned and clearly explained to be Salza's error is the doctrine that, according to the proper interpretation of *Mystici Corporis*, the internal sin and the external sin are not of the same *specific* nature**; and accordingly:

> «Salza's error (***the internal sin and the external sin are not of the same nature***): "Separation from the Soul of the Church is intrinsic to the [*specific*] nature of the internal act of heresy, and separation from the Body of the Church is intrinsic to the [*specific*] nature of the external act of heresy, even if external heresy were not a crime in canon law."»

ROBERT J SISCOE'S CLUMSY ATTEMPT TO COVER UP HIS GRAVE ERRORS AGAINST THE CHURCH

In his *Remnant* article of March 3 2017, *Robert Siscoe Responds to Fr. Kramer Concerning the Case of Celestine III*, Siscoe replies to my earlier, unedited reply to his original article on Pope Celestine III, which had been posted on some sedevacantist websites. In doing so, Siscoe avoided replying to the point I made in my more complete treatment of the topic, namely, **that the ruling of Celestine III had never been incorporated into Canon Law**, as Siscoe still erroneously and obstinately maintains. After studying the matter more carefully, I posted an amplified and amended version of my reply to his very grave errors, which I also sent by e-mail to Robert Siscoe. The *Remnant* refused to post my comments, which I had submitted to them for publication on their website, and which I also posted on Twitter and Facebook. Siscoe has no excuse for knowingly propagating serious errors against the Church. Siscoe continues to falsely claim that "the error of Pope Celestine was later included in the Decretals of Pope Gregory IX".

Here is the full text of what I wrote in response to Siscoe:

> I have read the relevant Latin texts of Celestine III, and of Innocent III. They were ruling on two different cases. Celestine III ruled that the husband who defected from the faith out of hatred for his wife, thereby forfeited his matrimonial rights, so that the wife was not bound to return to her first husband, but was free to enter the monastic life, even with the husband opposed; and that the husband could marry the former infidel wife (the second wife), converted to the Catholic faith, only after the death of the first wife. Innocent III ruled on a case referred to him by Bishop Hugo of Ferrara, that the wife of a man who defected into heresy could not remarry. Two entirely different cases. Celestine did not rule that the woman could

divorce and remarry, but only that she was not bound to return to the first husband, and was free to enter religious life, even against the opposition of her husband, who had forfeited his matrimonial rights. Celestine did make the error of basing his correct ruling on an erroneous interpretation of the Pauline Privilege, and thus condoned the woman's second marriage – however, his error was not expressed in a magisterial teaching, but was only an erroneous opinion on a point not yet settled by the magisterium, expressed in a legal case, upon which he correctly ruled that the woman was no longer bound to return to the first husband. He expressed an erroneous opinion that the woman's second marriage was legitimate, but that was not his RULING, but only an erroneous basis for a CORRECT RULING that the woman was free to enter religion against the will of her first husband. Siscoe's claim that, "The case eventually reached Pope Celestine III (d. 1198), who considered the matter and judged that the woman should remain in her second adulterous union, rather than returning to her true husband", is utterly false. Likewise, Siscoe's claim that Celestine TAUGHT the error in his magisterium [1] is false, and likewise, his claim that Gregory IX incorporated into Canon Law [2] a ruling allowing divorce and remarriage is absurdly nonsensical, and only demonstrates how utterly incompetent he is in Canon Law and Theology. Celestine's use of the expression *"non videtur nobis"* clearly indicates his intention to state an opinion, and not to impart a teaching.

[1] "The erroneous judgment of Pope Celestine highlights the limitations of papal infallibility by showing that a true Pope can, as part of his teaching office (Magisterium), render a judgment that contradicts divine revelation and confirms a person in objective mortal sin."

[2] "Celestine's Error Incorporated into Canon Law": "The limitations of Papal Infallibility is further highlighted by the fact that the error of Pope Celestine was later included in the Decretals of Pope Gregory IX (known as Quinque Libri Decretalium), which was the first collection of Canon Law promulgated by a Pope for the universal Church." And, "this non-infallible papal judgment confirmed a woman in the objective state of adultery."

Siscoe's claim that Celestine's error was "incorporated into Canon Law" is absolutely false. That ruling of Celestine III, in which the erroneous opinion was expressed was excluded from the Decretals by order of Gregory IX. A detailed and precise presentation on this matter is made by Fr. Anthony Cekada.[699] Fr. Cekada quotes eminent authorities in his presentation on this point, the first, Pietro Card. Gasparri, who wrote saying, there is "neither a trace nor a vestige" of Celestine's decree in the Decretals of Gregory IX. He goes on to explain

---

[699] http://novusordowatch.org/tag/pope-celestine-iii/.

that it is found in the *Second Compilation*, a private collection of John of Wales (1210), which, Amleto Cicognani explains, "did not obtain public authority" – but was drawn upon by St. Raymond of Penafort in his compilation. Cardinal Louis Billot (*De Ecclesiæ Sacramentis I v. 2 p. 441*) says: "it never became law", and, "Gregory IX expressly commanded that it be excluded... from the authentic collecton of canons made by St. Raymond" Thus, Celestine's decree pertains to the "*partes decisæ*", which, as Cicognani pointed out, "have no legal force" That portion of text which was excluded pertains to the "partes decisæ", which were never officially incorporated into the Corpus of Canon Law. In the Richter-Friedberg edition of the Decretals (DECRETALIUM COLLECTIONES – EDITIO LIPSIENSIS SECUNDA), those "excluded parts" were re-inserted into the text by the editors, and indicated by italics, as the editors explain on page XLV: "Ut vero quæ inserui a Gregoriano textu discerni possent, illa italicis quos vocant typis exprimenda curavi."

Although I disagree with Fr. Cekada on the issue of Sedevacantism, and some of his theological opinions; on this question he is entirely correct. The page of Gregory IX's Decretals, quoting Celestine III's ruling:

http://www.columbia.edu/cu/lweb/digital/collections/cul/texts/1 dpd_6029936_002/pages/ldpd_60299 36_002_00000336.html?toggle=image&menu=maximize&top=199 px&left=70px[700]

---

[700] Innocent III's ruling: "Quanto te magis novimus in canonico iure peritum, tanto fraternitatem tuam amplius in Domino commendamus, quod in dubiis quaestionum articulis ad sedem apostolicam recurris, quae disponente Domino cunctorum fidelium mater est et magistra, ut opinio, quam in eis quondam habueras, dum alios canonici iuris peritiam edoceres, vel corrigatur per sedem apostolicam vel probetur. Sane tua nobis fraternitas suis literis intimavit, quod, altero coniugum ad haeresim transeunte, qui relinquitur ad secunda vota desiderat convolare et filios procreare, quod, utrum possit fieri de iure, per tuas nos duxisti literas consulendos. Nos igitur consultationi tuae de communi fratrum nostrorum consilio respondentes, distinguimus, licet quidam praedecessor noster sensisse aliter videatur, an ex duobus infidelibus alter ad fidem catholicam convertatur, vel ex duobus fidelibus alter labatur in haeresim, vel decidat in gentilitatis errorem. Si enim alter infidelium coniugum ad fidem catholicam convertatur, altero vel nullo modo, vel saltem non sine blasphemia divini nominis, vel ut eum pertrahat ad mortale peccatum, ei

cohabitare volente: qui relinquitur, ad secunda, si voluerit, vota transibit. Et in hoc casu intelligimus quod ait Apostolus: 'Si infidelis discedit, discedat. Frater enim vel soror non est servituti subiectus in huiusmodi,' et canonem etiam, in quo dicitur, quod 'contumelia creatoris solvit ius matrimonii circa eum, qui relinquitur.' Si vero alter fidelium coniugum vel labatur in haeresim, vel transeat ad gentilitatis errorem, non credimus, quod in hoc casu is, qui relinquitur, vivente altero possit ad secundas nuptias convolare, licet in hoc casu maior appareat contumelia creatoris. Nam etsi matrimonium verum quidem inter infideles exsistat, non tamen est ratum. Inter fideles autem verum quidem et ratum exsistit, quia sacramentum fidei, quod semel est admissum, nunquam amittitur; sed ratum efficit coniugii sacramentum, ut ipsum in coniungibus illo durante perduret. Nec obstat, quod a quibusdam forsan obiicitur, quod fidelis relictus non debeat iure suo sine culpa privari, quum in multis casibus hoc contingat, ut si alter coniugum incidatur. Per hanc autem responsionem quorundam malitiae obviatur, qui in odium coniugum, vel quando sibi invicem displicerent, si eas possent in tali casu dimittere, simularent haeresim, ut ab ipsa nubentibus coniugibus resilirent. Per hanc ipsam responsionem illa solvitur quaestio, qua quaeritur, utrum ad eum, qui [vel] ab haeresi vel infidelitate revertitur, is, qui permansit in fide, redire cogatur. [Dat. Lat. Kal. Maii 1199.]

http://www.kingscollege.net/gbrodie/Timeline%201199%20Quanto%20te.html

Pope Innocent III: On the Bond of Marriage and the Pauline Privilege [From the letter "Quanto te magis" to Hugo, Bishop of Ferrara, May 1, 1199]

405 Your brotherhood has announced that with one of the spouses passing over to heresy the one who is left desires to rush into second vows and to procreate children, and you have thought that we ought to be consulted through your letter as to whether this can be done under the law. We, therefore, responding to your inquiry regarding the common advice of our brothers make a distinction, although indeed our predecessor seems to have thought otherwise, whether of two unbelievers one is converted to the Catholic Faith, or of two believers one lapses into heresy or falls into the error of paganism. For if one of the unbelieving spouses is converted to the Catholic faith, while the other either is by no means willing to live with him or at least not without blaspheming the divine name or so as to drag him into mortal sin, the one who is left, if he wishes, will pass over to second vows. And in this case we understand what the Apostle says: "If the unbeliever depart, let him depart: for the brother or sister is not subject to servitude in (cases) of this kind" [1 Cor. 7:15]. And likewise (we understand) the canon in which it is said that "insult to the Creator dissolves the law of marriage for him who is left." [from Isaac406 But if one of the believing spouses either slip into heresy or lapse into the error of paganism, we do not believe that in this case he who is left, as long as the other is living, can enter into a second marriage; although in

In his clumsy attempt to cover up his own errors, Siscoe resorts to a considerable amount of mendacity and sophistry in order to make it appear, "that Fr. Kramer's objection is entirely without merit." Siscoe claims, "Fr. Kramer simply chose two of the five judgments and claimed they alone constituted his 'ruling.'" This is simply false: What I did was to comment on the essential point of Celestine's ruling that is relevant to Siscoe's erroneous assertions. Nowhere did I make any claim about anything that "alone constituted his ruling". Siscoe interprets the ruling: "This is the primary answer given and it is absolutely clear. Pope Celestine considered the matter and judged that the woman could remain in her second [adulterous] union". No. That is *not* the primary answer. **The primary answer is that the woman is not bound to return to the first husband, because he had forfeited his matrimonial rights.** Pope Celestine ruled that the first husband had **forfeited his matrimonial rights, and that she was free to enter the monastic life.** According to Siscoe, "strictly speaking, the question was not whether a woman could divorce and remarry, but whether a sacramental marriage bond would be dissolved by heresy, and if the abandoned spouse would be permitted to remarry." In fact, strictly speaking, **the question was whether the woman was bound to return to her (first) husband, or**

---

this case a greater insult to the Creator is evident. Although indeed true matrimony exists between unbelievers, yet it is not ratified; between believers, however, a true and ratified marriage exists, because the sacrament of faith, which once was admitted, is never lost, but makes the sacrament of marriage ratified so that it itself lasts between married persons as long as the sacrament of faith endures.

Summary: 1) Quanto te affirms that true marriage does exist among unbelievers, (notwithstanding the fact that they do not regard marriage as indissoluble.)

2) Quanto te affirms that a marriage between believers is "ratified" because of the "sacrament of faith." A ratified marriage remains even if one of the partners should renounce their faith.

3) The Pauline Privilege is affirmed and the grounds permitting the convert to remarry are expanded to include not only a) convert who have been deserted by the unbelieving spouse, (as per Paul) but also, b) a convert who would be subjected to blasphemy by an unbelieving spouse who remains, or, c) a convert who would be led into mortal sin by a spouse who remains. How the unbeliever's blasphemy or drawing to mortal sin amounted to the forfeiture of the unbelievers marriage and how these acts were to be proved were not determined by these decretals. The implication of course was significant: a valid, consummated marriage between Christian and unbeliever was dissoluble.

if she was free to enter the monastic life. The question was not whether or not the woman was permitted to remarry — she had already remarried with the permission of the local church, and therefore, she would not have been petitioning again for something that had already been granted to her. On the contrary, it would logically have been more likely that the first husband who asked for the ruling, and Pope Celestine ruled that the woman was not bound to return to him, who had forfeited his matrimonial rights. The question was not "whether a matrimonial bond would be dissolved by heresy", as Siscoe claims, but *whether the woman was bound to return to the first husband.* Regardless of whether or not the bond had been considered to be dissolved, *the matter of the ruling was that she was not bound to return to her first husband, who had forfeited his matrimonial rights.* In making that ruling, Celestine expressed the opinion that the woman had been free to remarry, *but that was not the matter of the ruling; because regardless of whether the bond (i.e. the 'vinculum') would have been dissolved or not, the husband had forfeited his matrimonial rights (ius matrimonii).*

Siscoe claims that his "explanation also demonstrates how mistaken Fr. Kramer was to claim that Pope Celestine and Pope Innocent were ruling on two different cases. No, they were ruling on the same case (or, more properly, the same general question) — i.e., whether 'the affront to the Creator dissolved the matrimonial bond,' and, consequently, whether the abandoned spouse could licitly remarry. Celestine simply provided four additional answers to questions that related to the specific case on which he was ruling. And we should again note that when Pope Innocent provided his answer to the question that was proposed to him, he stated that his predecessor (Celestine) 'thought otherwise,' which further confirms that they were addressing the same issue, not different issues, as Fr. Kramer claims."

I reply saying that Celestine and Innocent were ruling on two different cases, and two different questions: Celestine ruled on whether or not a woman who had already remarried was bound to return to her first husband who had abandoned her and apostatized. He ruled that she was not bound to return to him, but was free to enter monastic life. The ruling was not, as Siscoe claims, on "whether 'the affront to the Creator dissolved the matrimonial bond,' and, consequently, whether the abandoned spouse could licitly remarry", although in issuing his ruling, *he expressed the opinion that the woman had been free to remarry.* Innocent ruled on a case in which a spouse who had not remarried, but "*with one of the spouses passing over to heresy the one who is left desires to rush into second vows and to procreate children*". He ruled that the spouse in question could not remarry. Two different cases, with two different rulings on two different questions.[701] Bordoni summed up the matter by explaining that Innocent III and Celestine established contrary positions on the proposition that with one spouse going into heresy, the other could contract a second marriage; but Celestine did not define anything as certain, but merely expressed an opinion, as Innocent expressly acknowledged; while Innocent defined on that question, ruling that the conjugal bond is not dissolved if one of the Catholic spouses falls into heresy.[702]

SALZA & SISCOE DECLARE ON THE AUTHORITY OF THEIR OWN PRIVATE JUDGMENT THAT THOSE WHO BELIEVE THE APOSTOLIC SEE IS VACANT ARE IN HERESY

Salza & Siscoe claim that, "The Sedevacantist thesis begins by affirming that there is no Pope, [...] ends in a rejection of the Church itself." (15) This proposition depends ultimately on the uncertain and

---

[701] The silliness of Siscoe's arguments comes to the fore in his question, "we should point out that answer #1 only says the wife could enter religious life against the wishes of her first husband [...], yet is silent about whether she could do so against the wishes of her second (and current) husband. Does this omission not seem odd?" Siscoe desperately makes suppositions in order to give basis to his idle speculation that Celestine was probably ruling that the woman would be free to enter religious life *only after the death of the second husband*. (!) There is absolutely no basis whatever to suppose that this was Celestine's meaning, because, if the woman were to be in need of obtaining the consent of the second husband, it would have been mentioned in the ruling that she is not free to enter religious life without the consent of the second husband while the second husband is still living. There was obviously not even a question of her needing the consent of the second husband, and that is the obvious reason for Celestine's "silence" on the non-question.

[702] Bordoni, *Sacrum Tribunal Iudicum*, cap. v. pp. 131-132: «Quarto, lnnocentius lll. & Celeſtinus contraria ſtatuerunt circa cam propoſitionem, vno coniugum tranſeunte ad hxreſim, alter poteſt tranſire ad ſecundas nuptias, *ex cap. Quanto de diuortijs*. [...] Coeleſtinus nihil certi definiuit, ſed illius tantum erat opinionis, vt expreſsè lnnocentius *cap. Quanto 7. de diuort.* Sed quid definiuit Innocentius ſuper ea quæſtione in dicto cap.7. de *diuortijs*? Vinculum coniugale non diſſolui, ſi vnus coníugum fidelium incidat in haereſim.»

magisterially unestablished premise that a vacancy cannot exceed even a brief duration of only a few years, and on the plainly false premise that the visibility of the Church cannot be obscured. On the basis of this first very uncertain premise, and the false second premise, they then further postulate a *non sequitur* conclusion, "The second error, which follows almost immediately, is that **the entire Church** *over which the post-Vatican II Popes have reigned* **is a false Church**." (15) (emphasis mine) Salza & Siscoe create a false paradigm by means of a fundamentalistic oversimplification that asserts a monolithic "post-Vatican II Church", and fails to make the critical distinction that, like the Church infected by Arianism, as well as the Church infected by Protestantism, and the Church infected by Gallicanism, Jansenism, etc., there are at present **two Churches**, *with one visibly existing as a cancer in the other* – one Catholic, and the other a heretical parasite. As Mgr. Tissier de Mallerais explains, the "Conciliar Church" is a false, counterfeit "church" created by Freemasonry which exists as a cancer within the Church. It is a parasite growing within the body of the Catholic Church. The fact that the false church is at present enjoying a higher degree of visibility – a visibility by far greater than the obscured visibility of what remains of the Catholic Church at the present time, does not logically involve a negation of the existence and visibility of the true Church, which remains with all its marks and attributes, but whose visibility has been temporarily reduced in this exceptional time. Hence, the denial that "the permanent qualities (the attributes and the marks) that constitute and identify the true Church" exist in the heretical 'Conciliar Church', does not logically result in a denial that they still exist in the Catholic Church; nor does it result in an inability to "point to a Church that does possess them".

> «While most Sedevacantists claim to believe in the Catholic Church, and in the permanent qualities (the attributes and the marks) that constitute and identify the true Church, their refusal or inability to see them in the crucified Church of our day results in a practical denial of their existence (which results in a practical or explicit denial of several articles of Faith). Because the Sedevacantists cannot see these enduring qualities in the post-Vatican II Church (which they claim is a false Church), and further cannot point to a Church that does possess them, they end by reducing the meaning of "Church" to the Protestant concept of a scattered body of "true believers" (rather than a visible institution) the unavoidable consequence of their stated position is that "the gates of hell"1 have indeed prevailed against the visible Church founded by Christ. (15 -16)»

Salza & Siscoe then quote snippets of *Pastor Æternus*. I produce here the passages in their proper context:

> «*Dominus Christus Iesus in perpetuam salutem ac perenne bonum Ecclesiæ instituit, id eodem auctore in Ecclesia, quæ fundata super petram ad finem sæculorum usque firma stabit, iugiter durare necesse est.*»
>
> «*Petrus, Apostolorum princeps et caput, fideique columna et Ecclesiæ catholicæ fundamentum, a Domino nostro Iesu Christo, Salvatore humani generis ac Redemptore, claves regni accepit: qui ad hoc usque tempus et semper in suis successoribus, episcopis sanctæ Romanæ Sedis, ab ipso fundatæ, eiusque consecratæ sanguine, vivit et præsidet et iudicium exercet (Cf. Ephesini Concilii Act. III).*»

Salza & Siscoe comment on this dogmatic teaching: «This means the Church will always be able to elect a new Pope to fill the chair of St. Peter after the death or resignation of the former Pope (of course, having a perpetual office does no good unless the Church is able to fill the office with a successor).» (19) and further, «Now, because Sedevacantists claim we have not had a successor of St. Peter for the past six decades (or longer), some will attempt to limit the council's teaching to affirming that the office of Peter will continue until the end of time (i.e., that the primacy didn't die out when Peter died), but not that there will be "perpetual successors in the Primacy.» (19)

What Salza & Siscoe fail to mention, is that even asserting a decades long interregnum does not necessarily deny the perpetuity of successors. If the succession were to end, then it would not be a perpetual succession. However, a prolonged hiatus does not in its nature produce an ending of the succession, as would be the case of such an eventuality such as that affirmed by the medieval "Franciscan Spirituals", followers of the Franciscan friar, Gerardo di Borgo di San Donnino; a "Joachimite", i.e. a disciple of Gioachino da Fiore; who postulated a scenario in which there would begin the age of the Holy Ghost in the year 1260, with the Church transformed in such a manner that there would no longer be a governing hierarchy under the pope, but under the *Order of the Just*, a new order of spiritual men under the guidance of the Holy Ghost.] **HENCE, it does not logically follow that,** «**the Sedevacantist thesis is not tenable and, in fact, *leads directly to heresy*»** [and] «**Sedevacantism, ... is not only a rejection of the recent Popes, but also a rejection of the visible Church founded by Christ, over which the recent Popes have reigned.**»

They quote Fr. E. Sylvester Berry: «Fr. Berry explains that "the primacy with all its powers and privileges is transmitted to the successors of St. Peter, who form an unbroken line of supreme pastors to rule the Church in its continued existence." A little later, he adds: "the Church must ever have a custodian, a supreme law-giver and judge, if she is to continue as Christ founded her."» (Berry, The Church of Christ, (Eugene, Oregon 2009, pp. 196-197) [703] And Van Noort:

> «Msgr. Van Noort teaches the same as Fr. Berry. He wrote: "it is a fact beyond question that the Church can never fail to have a successor to Peter…" (*Christ's Church*, Westminster, Maryland, 1961, p. 153). Commenting further on the same point, he wrote: "Since Christ decreed that Peter should have a never-ending line of successors in the primacy, there must always have been and there must still be someone in the Church who wields his primacy."»[704]

And then they comment:

> «Needless to say, this poses an insurmountable problem for Sedevacantists who claim that the Church has been unable to elect a Pope for generations. While it is true (as the Vatican Council Fathers were obviously aware) that there is a temporary vacancy during an interregnum (following the death of one Pope and the election of another), the Church has never failed to provide a successor to St. Peter.» (21-22)

The quotations that Salza & Siscoe cite do not support that argument. Neither of the theologians they quote even attempt to specify with any precision just how long a vacancy might be able to last without violating the divine constitution of the Church. How long the Apostolic See might be able to remain vacant during an interregnum is an *open question* that can only be settled definitively by the magisterium of the Church, and not by the lay *Vigilante Inquisition* of John Salza and Robert Siscoe, which anathematizes any opinion that happens to disagree with their own.

For a long time it was debated who might have been the legitimate pope during the Great Western Schism. Fr. Edmond O'Reilly SJ, one of the more prominent theologians at the time of the First Vatican Council, thought it probable that "John XXIII" was the valid pope. Pietro Ballerini, one of the most eminent theologians of the previous century

---

[703] TOFP p. 21
[704] *Ibid.*

(in the above cited work) commented on the situation of the papacy during that time, saying that the most he could conjecture was that Gregory XII was "probably" the legitimate pope at the time that the Council of Constance began (*Gregorium enim XII., qui probabilius erat verus et legitimus Papa*").[705] Since then, Pius XII confirmed the papal pedigree of Gregory XII, and the Holy See since then has recognized the legitimacy of the pontificate of Gregory XII. O'Reilly maintained that the See was definitely occupied, but that it was not certain by whom: "There was, I say, at every given time *a* Pope, really invested with the dignity of Vicar of Christ and Head of the Church, whatever opinions might exist among many as to his genuineness".[706] However, Ballerini did admit the extremely unlikely hypothesis that the See might have been vacant during the entire period, but did not himself follow that opinion on the basis that it was *"absonum"* and seemingly impossible[707] – nevertheless, he did not reject it as heretical, nor did he reject it in principle; but as he explains, he did not consider such a lengthy vacancy possible under the particular circumstances (i.e. that the election of all the claimants during that entire period could have been invalid) that were present during the Great Western Schism. O'Reilly was even more explicit in not excluding **"that an interregnum covering the whole period would have been impossible or inconsistent with the promises of Christ, for this is by no means manifest", but only that,** "as a matter of fact, there was not such an interregnum."[708]

Until the magisterium authoritatively settles and closes the question, it cannot be conclusively maintained that the proposition, that *"the Church has been unable to elect a Pope for generations"*, necessarily "results in a practical denial of… [the] qualities (the attributes and the marks) that constitute and identify the true Church"; and "leads directly to heresy". That assertion remains a mere opinion – a conjecture that lacks any solid

---

[705] Ballerini, *Op. cit. Cap. IX, S. V,* p. 138.

[706] *The Relations of the Church to Society*, Edmond J. O'Reilly S.J., London, 1892, p. 283.

[707] "Quodsi illud efatum *Papa dubius, Papa nullus*, incrediile judicetur praesertim in diuturniori illo schismate, in quo dicere Ecclesiam per annos triginta et amplius, quibus idem schism duravit ab election Urbani VI. Usque ad electionem Martini V. caruisse semper vero Pontifice, omniumque electionem fuisse illegitimum, absonum videtur et fere etiam impossibile" (Ballerini, *Op. cit.* p. 131)

[708] Edmond J. O'Reilly S.J., *Op. cit.*, p. 283.

magisterial foundation. On this point as to what God might or might not permit, Fr. O'Reilly cautions:

> There had been anti-popes before from time to time, but never for such a continuance, nor even with such obscurity as to who was the rightful pontiff, nor ever with such a following. A General Council was the proper remedy, or rather the proper road to a remedy. Clearly the Church, when destitute of a Head, or of a certain unquestioned Head, has the right and the power to provide for herself, and determine on a course which seems fit to furnish her with a Supreme Pontiff, and the course maturely taken is to be considered as Divinely authorised. The Pope does not derive his jurisdiction from the Church; but the determination of the person who is to possess that jurisdiction coming from God, is effected by men, according to rules laid down by the supreme authority in the Church, that is, by existing Popes, and supplementary, where necessary, by a General Council, or even perhaps by the College of Cardinals. If it should happen that there are one or more doubtful Popes, whose pretensions are an obstacle to the government of the Church by one universally recognised Vicar of Christ on earth, a General Council can set aside the obstacle. A doubtful Pope may be really invested with the requisite power; but he has not practically in relation to the Church the same right as a certain Pope. He is not entitled to be acknowledged as Head of the Church, and may be legitimately compelled to desist from his claim.
>
> The great schism of the West suggests to me a reflection which I take the liberty of expressing here. If this schism had not occurred, the hypothesis of such a thing happening would appear to many chimerical. They would say it could not be; God would not permit the Church to come into so unhappy a situation. Heresies might spring up and spread and last painfully long, through the fault and to the perdition of their authors and abettors, to the great distress too of the faithful, increased by actual persecution in many places where the heretics were dominant. But that the true Church should remain between thirty and forty years without a thoroughly ascertained Head, and representative of Christ on earth, this would not be. Yet it has been; and we have no guarantee that it will not be again, though we may fervently hope otherwise. What I would infer is, that we must not be too ready to pronounce on what God may permit. We know with absolute certainty that He will fulfill His promises; not allow anything to occur at variance with them; that He will sustain His Church and enable her to triumph over all enemies and difficulties; that He will give to each of the faithful those graces which are needed for each one's service of Him and attainment of salvation, as He did during the great schism we have been considering, and in all the sufferings and trials which the Church has passed through from the beginning. We may also trust He will do a great deal more

than what He has bound Himself to by His promises. We may look forward with a cheering probability to exemption for the future from some of the troubles and misfortunes that have befallen in the past. But we, or our successors in future generations of Christians, shall perhaps see stranger evils than have yet been experienced, even before the immediate approach of that great winding up of all things on earth that will precede the day of judgment. I am not setting up for a prophet, nor pretending to see unhappy wonders, of which I have no knowledge whatever. All I mean to convey is that contingencies regarding the Church, not excluded by the Divine promises, cannot be regarded as practically impossible, just because they would be terrible and distressing in a very high degree.[709]

Salza & Siscoe then resort to patently nonsensical arguments claiming that jurisdiction in the Church would cease if there would be a vacancy of the apostolic See for any considerable length of time. However, during the nearly four years of vacancy between the pontificates of St. Marcellinus, which ended with his death in 304, and of St. Marcellus (whose pontificate began in May or June 308), and the vacancy of nearly three years from November 1268 to September 1271 (which ended with the election of Bl. Gregory X), the Church carried on with its mission without a pope, and without any interruption of ordinary jurisdiction in the particular churches. Their argument (quoting Fr. Tranquillo on pp. 75 and 78) is plainly fallacious:

> «In a recent article published in the Courrier de Rome, Fr. Tranquillo explains that supplied jurisdiction presupposes habitual (ordinary) jurisdiction in the Church. Because all jurisdiction comes to the Church through the Pope, if there is no Pope, and if there are no more bishops who received jurisdiction from a valid Pope, "then jurisdiction delegated in extraordinary fashion [i.e., supplied jurisdiction] would also no longer exist... If ordinary jurisdiction were to disappear completely from the individuals living upon this earth... then jurisdiction delegated in extraordinary fashion would also no longer exist, **because it is delegated by someone**, in the terms of the law, and not by the 'Church,' as understood in the abstract."»

This is false. Supplied jurisdiction in all the canons that mention it, is granted *ipso jure*, i.e. "by the law itself"; hence, there is no need for some superior to delegate it. The most common example of this is the granting of faculties to confessors to absolve either by the delegation of the

---

[709] *Ibid.* p. 287.

competent authority, or **by the operation of the law itself**, as set forth in Canon 966 § 2: *Hac facultate donari potest sacerdos, sive **ipso iure** sive concessione **ab auctoritate competenti** facta ad normam can. 969.* If the pope dies, and a lengthy vacancy ensues, bishops & priests will be supplied with all the necessary faculties and jurisdiction by the law itself. It is precisely in order to remedy the situation in which there is no superior or no access to a superior; or when it is impossible or nearly impossible for subjects to know who the legitimate superior is, and hence, who is invested with the authority to delegate jurisdiction, that the law provides for supplied jurisdiction *ipso jure*. This was exactly the remedy prescribed by Martin V in *Ad Evitanda Scandala*, so that if ever again there should be a prolonged period in which it is not clear who the legitimate pope or bishop is, the law itself will provide the supplied jurisdiction. The provisions of *Ad Evitanda Scandala* have been abrogated, but, as noted in the *Catholic Encyclopedia*, they have been taken up in the succeeding legislation; and there remain to this day such provisions for supplied jurisdiction in all the sections Code of Canon Law that deal with cases of necessity and common error, etc. Even in earlier centuries, when canon law was still in a primitive state, and particular churches in geographically remote places (such as Ireland) were effectively cut of from communication with the Church of Rome for long periods of time; those churches continued to function, and exercised the *de facto* power of jurisdiction which Natural Law required that they be given *ipso jure* in accordance with Natural Equity, even when there was no pope available to them to grant them jurisdiction by express delegation, since the God of infinite justice cannot deny what is just; and with the power of orders together with the power of jurisdiction having been permanently bestowed on the Church by her divine Founder, it is therefore quite impossible that they could be lacking, or withheld by God during an exceptional time when the ordinary manner of the rule of law would break down and be interrupted due to such extraordinary circumstances as those foretold in Scripture for the End Times. I have already explained the matter sufficiently in my book, *The Suicide of Altering the Faith in the Liturgy*. Even in the time of the great tribulation, when the Church will be reduced in numbers and its visibility temporarily obscured, and the See of Rome may be vacant for some years as it has been for some years in past centuries; the Church will carry on with its mission, because it has received the attribute of indefecibility from its divine Founder, who is not subject to the mere letter of any human law. Thus, it is clear, that Salza & Siscoe are again indulging in their own homespun *voodoo theology* when they claim, "The Sedevacantist thesis begins by affirming that there is no Pope, [...] ends in a rejection of the Church itself." Just as Ballerini judged the thesis that would hold for a vacancy to have lasted nearly forty years during the Great Western Schism to be *absonum* and highly improbable – but not heterodox, and certainly not heretical; the same judgment can be made about the Sedevacantist thesis which claims that the Apostolic See has been vacant for sixty years. The question of the possible duration of a vacancy of the papal see has not been definitively settled by the ecclesiastical magisterium, and thus remains an **open question**. It does not lie within the non-existent jurisdiction of the Salza/Siscoe lay *vigilante inquisition* to pontificate a judgment on this question, in the manner they have presumed to do.

THE LATEST SALZA/SISCOE FRAUD

Salza accuses me of making a false accusation: «you continue to accuse us of holding that only the crime of heresy severs one from the Body [of the Church]» – yet Salza & Siscoe emphatically declare in their Formal Reply to the earlier draft of this volume, «heresy includes everything from the internal sin alone, to the public **crime** of notorious heresy – and only the latter [**i.e. the public *crime* of notorious heresy**] automatically severs a person from external union with the Church "without a declaration."» Again, they assert in their Formal Reply:

> «the sin of heresy, of its nature, severs a person from the Body of the Church dispositively, but not formally. The formal separation from the Body of the Church occurs when the juridical bond is severed by the public act (**crime**) of notorious heresy (notorious by fact), or when the **crime** has been judged and declared by the Church (notorious by law).»

Salza went on to say, «And, even more so, we will show how Kramer is a diabolical liar for accusing us of claiming that admissum in Mystici Corporis "STRICTLY means crime and not sin".» Salza again: «We never said it was based on "penal law" and always said it was the nature of the act.» ...

> «AND THAT MEANS SUCH HERESY DOESN'T NEED TO BE LISTED AS A CRIME IN CANON LAW TO SEVER ONE FROM THE BODY OF THE CHURCH (although it is listed as a crime). And yet that is what you falsely accuse us of holding.» I answered: «**If it is not "listed as a crime", it is not "an external violation of a law or precept"; and is**

therefore not a "crime", but only a *sin*, Salza. You wrote, "Again, Pope Pius XII is referring to the 'offense' or CRIME (not SIN) of heresy". No, Salza: Pius XII explains that a crime causes one to be severed from the body of the Church, not by the nature of the act, but *"by legitimate authority"*. The *sin* of heresy does so *suapte natura*.»

Here is what I wrote in my more complete reply:

«This is what YOU wrote, Salza: "Pope Pius XII is referring to the 'offense' or CRIME (not SIN) of heresy, which severs one from the Body of the Church, after the formal and material elements have been proven by the Church." Thus you perversely twist a clear papal moral teaching on the natural consequence of the *sin* of heresy into a nonsensical hair-splitting legal commentary on the canonical *crime* of heresy.»

After that, their next attempt to distance themselves from Salza's own published words, is to falsely claim that I depend on a secondary source for the quotation – a Sedevacantist author:

«So, where did Fr. Kramer get the idea that we "insist" admissum must be translated as crime? You guessed it. He got it from a Sedevacantist website, and he even admits the same. In fact, it came from the same article that caused him to entirely misunderstand what we meant by the word "alone" (as in "the sin of heresy alone does not sever a person from the Church").»

This is a desperate web of lies that Salza & Siscoe have weaved – **I copied the quotation from Salza's article posted on his own website.** I have not misrepresented Salza and Siscoe in any of my commentary on their pseudo-theology.

I went on to explain that their heretical interpretation of *Mystici Corporis* is what they use to justify their heretical proposition, "the sin of heresy alone does not sever one from the Church". Thus I replied to Salza:

«It is your explicitly stated position, (based on your errant legalism which you employ to heretically interpret *Mystici Corporis*), which holds that, "the nature of the crime of heresy requires no additional censure to sever one from the Body. But this does not nullify the necessity of the Church – who alone has the authority to judge whether a person is guilty of the crime of heresy – rendering a judgment, and most certainly in the case of a person who continues to present himself as a Catholic (as opposed to one who openly left the Church)." Again, Pius XII explicitly teaches that it is heresy itself, the sin, *by its own nature* (and not the *crime* by the authority of the Church) which separates the heretic from the body of the Church, as I pointed out in my manuscript, Salza, and therefore there can be no necessity for the Church to judge in order that one be separated from the body of the Church by heresy; because, (Pius XII explains) that the separation is effected by the heresy itself, *suapte natura*, and **not** "by legitimate authority" -- thus, **no judgment of the Church is involved in the separation of the heretic from the body of the Church.** You remain obstinate in your heresy on this point.»

Salza & Siscoe then attempt to extricate themselves by deceptively suggesting that I misquoted them, insinuating that their own words, "the sin of heresy alone does not sever one from the Church", were never written by them. Thus they claim: «To begin with, the "quotation" Fr. Kramer attributes to us, which he qualifies as heretical, is nowhere to be found in our book.» They quote me: «Fr. Kramer: "John Salza and Robert Siscoe are in heresy. Their entire doctrine on heresy and loss of office is based on their heretical proposition: 'the sin of heresy alone does not sever one from the Church'."» They distance themselves from their own words by saying they are not found in their book. However the words, «**The sin of heresy alone does NOT 'sever the person from the Body of the Church'** because sin is a matter of the internal forum»; and «the sin of heresy alone does not "automatically expel" one from the body of the Church», do appear in the above mentioned article written by John Salza[710], which remains posted on Salza's website at the present time as I write. On the basis of their heretical premise, they conclude in their book that: "The sin of heresy alone, which has not been judged and declared by the Church, does not result in the loss of ecclesiastical office for a cleric. The loss of office for a cleric is a vindictive penalty, and there is a process in Church law which must precede vindictive penalties"[711] The falsehoods contained in this statement have already been amply exposed and refuted earlier in this work.

It is their clearly stated position that even the sinful external act of manifest public heresy, (as distinguished from what they define as the crime of public and notorious heresy), does not of its own nature sever one from the body of the Church, but requires the judgment of the

---

[710] *John Salza Responds to Another Sedevacantist*
[711] *True or False Pope?*, p. 260.

Church to "establish the crime", before the heretic is separated from the body of the Church and loses office.[712]

Siscoe elaborates on the need for the Church to "establish the crime" before a heretic is severed from the body of the Church and lose office. Here are Siscoe's own words and my commentary:

> «Siscoe likewise remains entrenched in heresy: "I applied the Thomistic distinction of quoad se/quoad nos to show that, just because heresy of its nature severs a person from the Church (spiritually), does not mean heresy, of its nature, causes a person to cease being a member of the Church (legally). And I quoted the great John of St. Thomas who explained it exactly the way I did." Siscoe elaborates: "Did you even read John Salza's recent article that prompted this e-mail exchange? John and I both contributed to that article so it represents both of our opinions. We both affirm that the sin of heresy, of its nature, separates a person from the Church quoad se (of itself), but the sin of heresy, of its nature, does not result in a separation from the Church quoad nos (according to us), nor does it result in the loss of office. [...] As long as a person remains a member of the Church quoad nos – even if he committed the sin of heresy and has lost the faith – *he remains a legal member of the Church*; and if the person in question is a bishop or Pope, *he retains his office until the crime has been legally established by the proper authorities*." Then he quotes John of St. Thomas:
>
> "[J]ust as the Church, by designating the man, proposed him juridically to all as the elected Pope, so too, it is necessary that she depose him by declaring him a heretic and proposing him as vitandus (one to be avoided). Hence, we see from the practice of the Church that this is how it has been done; for, in the case of the deposition of a Pope, his cause was handled in a general Council before he was considered not to be Pope, as we have related above. **It is not true, then, that the Pope ceases to be Pope by the very fact [ipso facto] that he is a heretic, *even a public one*, before any sentence of the Church and before she proposes him to the faithful as one who is to be avoided.** Nor does Jerome exclude the judgment of the Church (especially in so grave a matter as the deposition of a Pope) when he says that a heretic departs from the body of Christ of his

---

[712] In Part II of their *Formal Reply*, Salza & Siscoe declare: "If the culprit's heresy is not deemed to be notorious by fact, however, he must be formally judged and declared a heretic by the Church (rendering him notorious by law) before he is legally separated from the Body of the Church." Directly opposing the doctrine of *Mystici Corporis*, Salza & Siscoe state categoricaslly that the public heretic's separation from the body of the Church only takes place *by legitimate authority*, and not by the public act of formal heresy itself *suapte naura*.

own accord; rather, he is judging the quality of the crime, which of its very nature excludes one from the Church—provided that the crime is declared by the Church—without the need for any superadded censure; for, although heresy separates one from the Church by its very nature, nevertheless, this separation is not thought to have been made, as far as we are concerned [quoad nos], without that declaration."

Siscoe then comments, "Before continuing, notice the point he makes about heresy, of its nature, severing a person from the Church without the need for any additional censure. This is how heresy, schism and apostasy differ from other mortal sins, which, of their nature, deprive a person from sanctifying grace, but do not separate them from the Church. It requires an additional censure for other sins to sever a person from the Church. For example, abortion severs a person from the Church, not by the nature of the sin, but due to the censure of excommunication that has been attached to it by the Church." Siscoe is simply saying that other sins require the additional censure of excommunication for one to be cut off from membership in the Church, but for heresy, schism and apostasy, excommunication is not necessary, but only the judgment of the Church by which one is declared a heretic.

He again quotes John of St. Thomas:

"Likewise, we respond to his reasoning in this way: one who is not a Christian, both in himself (quoad se) and in relation to us (quoad nos), cannot be Pope; however, if in himself he is not a Christian (because he has lost the faith) **but in relation to us has not yet been juridically declared as an infidel or heretic** (no matter how manifestly heretical he is according to private judgment), he is still a member of the Church as far as we are concerned (quoad nos); and consequently he is its head. **It is necessary, therefore, to have the judgment of the Church, by which he is proposed to us as someone who is not a Christian, and who is to be avoided**; and at that point he ceases to be Pope in relation to us (quoad nos); and we further conclude that he had not ceased to be Pope before [the declaration], even in himself, since all of his acts were valid in themselves."»

Thus, my reply to Salza on this point of "additional censure":

«It is very clear from these and other texts of yours, what you and Siscoe mean by the words, "no additional censure"; namely, that there is no need in addition to the judgment of heresy, the "additional censure of a vitandus declaration" or of the "additional censure of excommunication". Nevertheless, you engage in deliberate deception when you say, "And to respond to yet another of Fr. Kramer's straw man arguments, when we use the phrase 'additional censure' or 'further censure,' we do not mean a second censure in addition to some prior censure. As should be obvious to anyone of sound mind, when we say heresy, OF ITS NATURE, severs a person from the Church without an additional censure, we do not mean heresy DOES NOT sever a person from the Church, of its nature, but instead does so due to a preceding censure! How Kramer could have possibly thought that is what we meant is anyone's guess, but it is certainly not correct." How Kramer could have possibly thought that "additional censure" means *an excommunication in addition to a judgment of heresy by the Church* is obvious from your own words, Salza[713]; and therefore, what is obvious to anyone of sound mind is that *you are lying*.

You have gone to great length to obscure, obfuscate, and create a fog of confusion on this point, but your heretical doctrine is plainly expressed, and can easily grasped for what it is, once the fog of obfuscation you deliberately created has been cleared away from the explicit essential content of your words.

However, it doesn't stop there, Salza, but it becomes pathetically *comical*, when you & Siscoe insist on the one hand that *heresy publicly manifested* does not sever one from the body of the Church without the judgment of the Church; and then you go on to state the absurdity that *not even a declaratory sentence is required for such a "public judgment of the Church" to be made!* Your doctrine is a self-negating web of contradictions, Salza!

Salza, you wrote: *"Only public and notorious heresy separates one from the Body of the Church."* But what YOU erroneously explained to be "public and notorious heresy" is what you explicitly and wrongly equated with publicly renouncing the Church as the rule of faith: **"Publicly renouncing the Church as the rule of Faith (abandoning the profession of the faith) –** *by its nature* **– severs the juridical bonds. It is the** *nature* **of the act itself that does so without any extrinsic authority. And this can be the case even if the person is still united to the Soul of the Church, which proves that the nature of the sin of heresy does** *not* **sever the juridical, external bonds, like Fr. Kramer argues. It is rather the nature of notorious heresy that does so."** Thus, you, Salza, confuse *formal defection from the Church* with *formal heresy* properly understood as the *pertinacious denial or doubt of a revealed truth which must be believed with divine and Catholic faith.* Whether public, notorious, occult, or merely internal, the act of heresy, is defined as *the obstinate denial or doubt of an article of faith*, and **NOT** the public renunciation of the Church, as you, Salza, erroneously characterize notorious heresy.

---

[713] «As we explain in great detail in our book, Bellarmine and Suarez teach that the Pope will lose his office, ipso facto, once he is judged by the Church to be a heretic, without the additional juridical act of vitandus declaration.»

[I have also commented elsewhere on this point: «Furthermore, one does not become a member of the Church by means of a *legal* or *juridical bond*. The sacrament of faith (baptism) and the external profession of faith makes one a member of the Church. The Church merely recognizes that fact juridically. The Church teaches that when one defects from the faith by the public sin of heresy, both the internal [by the act of faith] and extetnal union [i.e. by the exernal profession of faith], by which the *bond of faith* was created, is destroyed; and one thereby ceases to be a member of the Church. Membership creates the juridical bond [but the juridical bond does not create membership]; but the juridical bond continues to some extent even after one ceases to be an actual, visible member. Thus, although already outside of the Church, the defector may still be punished, and be subject to further penalties, etc. So, Salza's claim that one does not cease to be a member of the Church until the "legal bond" is ended, is patently false. As I have already demonstrated, the doctrine and law of the Church have always recognized that the public profession of manifestly formal heresy terminates one's membership in the Church, and severs the juridical bond of membership *ipso jure*. [One does not need to be guilty of a criminal offense to terminate one's membership in the Church. It suffices that the bond of visible external union be severed *suapte natura* by the public sinful act of heresy itself, regardless of whether or not it incidentally happens also to be a crime in law.] When one defects from the Catholic faith, or formally defects from the Church; the juridical bond of membership (which Pius XII mentions in *Mystici Corporis* n. 70) is severed *ipso jure*, as the Council of Constance made explicitly clear in its ruling on Pedro de Luna.]

It has been amply demonstrated in my manuscript, quoting the most authoritative documents, and the relevant canons and the most authoritative commentaries on Canon Law, that the **public SIN of heresy constitutes an *ipso facto* defection from the faith and the Church, and effects an *ipso jure* loss of office, which take place before any *declaratory sentence* is pronounced. A formal act of explicit defection [from the Church] is not required for one to automatically cease to be a member of the Church and fall from office. I have already amply refuted this and related errors; but YOU, Salza simply ignore that fact and repeat your errors anew.**

You remain entrenched in the crude error that "sin is internal", and it is a matter of the internal forum. You have been repeatedly corrected on this point, Salza, but in your blind fundamentalism, you remain adamant in your fanatical adherence to this error that is contrary to what is explained in all works of Fundamental Moral Theology, which teach that a sin committed with an internal act is *internal*; and a sin committed with an external act, is an **external sin**. In Canon Law, **public external sin pertains to the external forum, Salza:** "915 Ad sacram communionem ne admitantur excommunicati et interdicti post irrogationem vel declarationem poenæ *aliique in manifesto gravi peccato obstinate perseverantes."* I already quoted the canons which declare the moral imputability of such sins to be presumed in law unless there is evidence to the contrary. It is so clownish of you to adamantly persist in professing a false doctrine even after it has been proven to you to be false.

Only a bold-faced liar like you, Salza, could say it is "Fr. Kramer's position, that the Pope is not the Pope." – as if there were not [at present] two claimants to the Petrine *munus* – yet YOU, Salza, have the sacrilegious audacity to publicly accuse *me* of being *dishonest*. (!) YOU guilefully say to Dr. Chnojnowski, "We know it troubles you greatly that the SSPX seminary published and endorsed our book" – but in reality, that is no big deal for anyone who understands what has happened to the SSPX. If it really troubles anyone greatly, the fact that the SSPX published it would certainly trouble the SSPX greatly, and would be a great embarrassment to them, since your book is manifestly based on the home-spun, half-baked "theology" of amateur "armchair theologians" who are woefully lacking formal education in theology.

You manifest that you have become plainly delusional when, even after I wrote a lengthy and critical examination of Bellarmine's original Latin texts, and exposed the crude and patently fallacious premises on which you base your ignorant exposition on Bellarmine's teaching, you still expect people to believe your words: "We wrote a book proving that Fr. Kramer's position is erroneous, that he does not understand Bellarmine's position".

You are **insane**, Salza – according to you, by implication, all the Catholic ecclesiastical authors are wrong for unanimously explaining Bellarmine's teaching to mean that a manifestly heretical pope would automatically cease to be a member of the Church and lose office straightaway by the very act of manifest formal heresy. I even quoted the eminent 19th Century jurist, Paul Hinschius, who explained that *a whole series of Catholic writers* have followed Bellarmine in this interpretation of the Fifth Opinion; yet you, in your manic state of mind, continue to obstinately claim that my interpretation of Bellarmine, which is identical with the unanimous interpretation of scholars, is rooted in an incomplete understanding of Bellarmine, and is based only on snippets of text read on the internet! Of course, you are deliberately lying, Salza, because I already pointed out to you well over a year ago that I first examined Bellarmine's Latin text of *De Romano Pontifice, Chapter 29 – 30* **more than 25 years ago**, at the express request of Fr. Gruner (who understood the text exactly as I do).»

APPENDIX TO PART FIVE

SALZA & SISCOE FRAUDULENTLY CONCOCT A CASE OF HERESY AGAINST FR. KRAMER

In the first of Salza & Siscoe's «REPLIES TO FR. PAUL KRAMER, **(FR. KRAMER CITES A FRAUDULENT "QUOTE" TO JUSTIFY HIS REJECTION TRADITIONAL CATHOLIC THEOLOGY),**», the pair of propagandists accuse me of "clandestine criticisms"! They were posted in a public forum for the whole world to see, but according to Salza and Siscoe, that is "clandestine". ... Then they resort to a baseless *ad hominem* slur: "«he seems to be quite anxious to provide his fans with the sensationalism and controversy"» ... and then the lie: **«it is clear that he did not actually read the book he has chosen to publicly criticize»** [FALSE: I never criticized the book before reading it.] ... "What this shows is that **Fr. Kramer simply pulled the quotation from an internet source** [FALSE]: I found the quotation in an SSPX flier in Manila ca. 1990] without checking the reference to see if it was authentic" [I made the mistake of trusting the scholarship of the SSPX priest who published the flier.] ... "Had Fr. Kramer read our book (which is he publicly criticizing) **[They repeat the lie that I publicly criticized their book before reading it.]**..." ... «The reason the "quote" is theologically erroneous is because if the Church were reduced to only a handful, it would violate the Church's perpetual mark of catholicity, as we will further discuss below.»

The spurious quotation erroneously attributed to St. Athanasius (which Salza & Siscoe insist, without proof, is the product of deliberate fraud), is in fact **neither heretical nor theologically erroneous**. I explained in my first reply on this point, that the statement would have to be in the *indicative mood* to be possibly judged heretical, but it is not: the statement is expressed in the *conditional mood* by means of an "if" clause. Now "the conditional mood (abbreviated cond) is a grammatical mood used to express a proposition whose validity is dependent on some condition". The "if" clearly expresses something **hypothetical**, depending on a condition that in this case will never be actually realized – just like the statement of Our Lord Jesus Christ, whose statement, "insomuch as to deceive even the elect", is conditioned with the words, "if possible". (ita ut in errorem inducantur si fieri potest etiam electi;

ωστε πλανησαι ει δυνατον και τους εκλεκτους) **The spurious Athanasius quotation does not say the Church *will* be reduced to a handful (indicative); but only conditionally states that even *if* that would happen, it would still be the true Church.** Salza & Siscoe continue to deliberately falsify the clear meaning of the phrase as a phony pretext to accuse me of manifest formal heresy, and on that fraudulent basis, they *hypocritically presume* to solemnly judge me to be outside the Church. I say *hypocritically*, because **it is they who profess that one who merely professes a heretical opinion is not outside the Church until he is judged by the Church, or explicitly rejects the authority of the magisterium of the Church, or joins another religion or sect**. Even after sending them my article explaining and upholding the authority of the ecclesiastical magisterium – i.e. the same article which in revised and amplified form appears as the first chapter of this book; Salza & Siscoe still falsely, obstinately, and with patent malice and deliberate mendacity insist that I have openly rejected the authority of the magisterium of the Church. In view of these considerations, it can be stated with certitude that their crime is manifest and quite obviously *notorious by fact*.

Furthermore, they pronounce judgment of heresy against me on the basis of their own application of the Protestant principle of Private Judgment. They cite the opinions of theologians (which they twist to fit into the framework their own fundamentalist theology) as the basis of their own private judgment of heresy against me **on a point which the magisterium has not defined**. How small the Church can be reduced to in the exceptional time of the great tribulation is an **open question and remains a matter of opinion** – and I have not ventured to express a precise opinion on this question; other than to say, in unison with many approved Catholic authors, (among them Joseph Ratzinger), that during the exceptional time of the great tribulation foretold by Christ in the Gospel, the Church will temporarily be greatly reduced in numbers. I have never said anything that even remotely resembles heresy.

The most radical opinion on this point is that of William of Ockham, who, as Ian Smith explains in his article, "If a time existed after Christ when because of universal heresy there were no genuine Catholics, then Christ's promise would be broken, and Ockham does not see that as possible. The faith could feasibly dwindle down to a single true individual, whilst everyone else is preaching heresy. But as long as one individual maintains the true faith, Christ's promise will not be broken."⁷¹⁴ While I do not share this opinion, which I personally consider heretical, the proposition was not condemned, and Ockham was never condemned as a heretic. The magisterium has not defined on this question; only Salza & Siscoe define on this point according to the Protestant principle of Private Judgment, which they justify by fraudulently applying to the question their own twisted interpretation of such theologians as Msgr. Gerardus Van Noort as will be shown below.

[As I explained in my reply, the spurious Athanasius quotation is not erroneous, any more than was Christ's pronouncement about the elect being deceived, since both are expressed as *pure hypotheses***. Nor is it heretical to hold that the Church will be reduced to a small number of members compared to the previously much larger number of members that existed before the time of general apostasy.]** ...

«Fr. Kramer: *"Salza thinks it is a heresy to hold that the Church will be reduced to a small number, and revert to the catacombs, and for a short time become invisible."* ... *"****Fr. Kramer errs by denying an essential mark of the Church.*** In expounding on the mark of catholicity, Van Noort explains that this mark requires that the Church consists "of a great number of people," "a great number of men from many different nations," and a "really large number of adherents." He further says that this "moral catholicity" is a "quality belonging to Christ's Church perpetually and necessarily." If the Church were reduced to only a handful of scattered believers, it would lose this mark of catholicity (universality), and therefore would no longer possess the four marks that the true Church must always possess. Furthermore, because the marks are those things which render the Church formally visible, the loss of a single one of them would result in the loss of her attribute of "visibility," which is also a perpetual quality of the true Church of Christ. Hence, Fr. ***Kramer's error, which he justifies by appealing to a fraudulent "quote," opens the door to many other errors.***»

[Salza gratuitously and falsely claims that the quote in question denies an essential mark of the Church. I have already demonstrated the fallacy of this claim. Furthermore, the quotation was not the basis of my doctrinal position, as I have already explained in my reply, so it is an outright falsehood and a mendacious misrepresentation for Salza to claim that I "appeal"

---

⁷¹⁴ https://philosophynow.org/issues/56/William_of_Ockham_Defending_the_Church_Condemning_the_Pope

to it in order to "justify" what he claims is an "error" – an "error" which (as I demonstrated in my reply) many approved Catholic authors have expressed, including ancient Fathers, as Cardinal Manning explained. Salza & Siscoe fraudulenty attribute to me the statement that the Church will be reduced to "a handful of scattered believers". Salza and Siscoe have also fundamentalistically radicalized and dogmatized in an unqualified manner the theological explications of Ott and Van Noort, which must be understood *in a properly qualified manner according to the nuances of the context in which they were expressed*. This defective hermeneutic, which attempts to dogmatize in an absolutely definitive manner, undefined doctrinal formulations of theologians, whose formulations, being undefined by the magisterium, still remain open to qualification, modification and revision; is one of the principal methods which Salza and Siscoe dishonestly employ throughout their writings, in order to make it appear that any opinion that dissents from their own, is either heretical, or at least contrary to the mind of the Church.]

> «This error of Fr. Kramer can be seen when he claims that the Church "will be reduced to a small number," and then claims that the Church will "revert to the catacombs" and become "invisible." Fr. Kramer fails to make the distinction between these two very different claims. The Church may indeed "revert to the catacombs" and become "invisible" to the outside world for a time (as it was during the first three centuries), but this does not mean that she will lose her attribute of visibility, or her mark of catholicity, which is precisely what would happen if it were reduced "to a small number" of faithful.»

This is nonsense. The *magisterium* has not defined on this point regarding how great must be the number of faithful to constitute "moral catholicity", nor has it defined on how small that number may be reduced to during the exceptional time of the persecution during the "great tribulation" foretold for the end times in scripture. Therefore, Salza & Siscoe have absolutely no right or authority to pontificate on these matters, on the basis of non-magisterial theological writings, as if, by some strange divine privilege, they possessed a private magisterium to speak in God's name. If the Church were in our time to be reduced to a condition similar to the condition it was in during the early centuries – such as the relatively small number of faithful as was the case during the persecution of the Apostolic period, it would be no less Catholic in our time than it was during the first persecution during the Apostolic period. Salza & Co., however, dogmatize their own private judgment by appealing to a non-dogmatic theological opinion, which they fail to qualify according to the nuance of its context:

> «... As Van Noort explained above, the mark of catholicity (i.e., universality) requires "moral catholicity" (i.e., large numbers of people) which is a perpetual quality of the true Church. The true Church is not simply a scattered group of "true believers," but a visible hierarchical society, consisting of a Pope, bishops and large numbers of faithful. ***Fr. Kramer errs by confusing the predictions of an underground Church during the end times, with a farcical reduction of the number of faithful to only a handful, and ends by denying the mark of catholicity.***»[715]

No, it is Salza & Siscoe who lie when they attribute to me the belief in a ***"reduction of the number of faithful to only a handful"***.

Salza & Siscoe have grossly misrepresented the doctrine of Msgr. Van Noort on the *moral catholicity* of the Church. In *De Ecclesia Christi, Art. IV De Ecclesiæ Catholicitate*, Van Noort explains the distinction between *absolute* and *moral* catholicity, and the diffusion of the Church's members throughout the world which is necessary for there to be that *moral catholicity*:

> "Catholicitas facti consistit in lata diffusione actuali per orbem; quæ si revera ad omnes et singulas gentes pertingit, vocatur catholicitas *absoluta;* si ad multas tantum gentes se extendit, dicitur catholicitas *moralis*. Jam ecclesiæ Christi necessarium est, ut post prima exordia *semper gaudeat diffusione moraliter universali et progressiva, donec tandem aliquando ad omnes omnino gentes perveniat*."[716]

---

[715] I never stated nor ever implied the Church would be reduced to a handful or that it would be reduced to a "scattered group" of "true believers", without a hierarchy. Salza's statement is a deliberate, fraudulent misrepresentation, which he manifested to be maliciously deliberate later in a subsequent post, when he totally disregarded my clarification on the matter, and again insisted that the quotation is heretical, in spite of the fact that I had already proven the contrary by pointing out to him the hypothetical nature of that quotation.

[716] N. 116 II. p. 126.

Salza & Siscoe quoted Van Noort on these points, but what they deliberately left out in their quotations of the passages of Van Noort's exposition are the texts in which Van Noort qualifies his statements on the diffusion and number of the faithful throughout the world:

> "*Ecclesia post prima exordia semper conspicua esse debet diffusione moraliter universali,* hoc scil. sensu, quod semper gremio suo comprehendere debet *ingentem numerum hominum de multitudine gentium.* [...] Jam qualitas, quæ absque ulla temporis limitatione exhibetur veluti character proprius ecclesiæ, ei semper convenire debet, **saltem aliquo gradu**. [...] Ex *verbis Christi et testimonio apostoli.* Christus absolute voluit, ut ecclesia inter omnes gentes diffunderetur et ad hunc effectum auxilium perenne promisit. Necesse igitur est, ut ecclesia huic suæ destinationi semper actu respondeat, **saltem aliqua mensura**."[717]

The passages in which he qualifies his statements with the words, **saltem aliquo gradu**, and, **saltem aliqua mensura**, are conspicuously absent in the Salza/Siscoe article. It is precisely by means of these qualifications that Msgr. Van Noort makes allowance for the massive reductions in numbers and geographical diffusion of the faithful throughout the world in times of schism and heresy, and especially during the defection at the time of the great apostasy towards the end of the world.[718] Concerning that great defection of the end time, Van Noort points out that it is *only the* **more common opinion** *of theologians* that rejects the hypothesis that the Church could be so overwhelmed by heresies that it would be restricted for a brief time to one region; and he says only that (in his opinion) it does not seem that the predictions of the Sacred Scriptures on the great defection at the end of the world are to be interpreted in this sense.[719] Thus, Msgr. Van Noort's exposition on the *moral catholicity* of the Church does not entirely rule out that the Church during the great tribulation of the end time could even possibly

---

[717] N. 117 2°. p. 128

[718] "*Diffusio moraliter universalis, quæ ecclesiæ semper competit, debet esse progressiva.* [...] (p. 130) Observa tamen, *continuitatem* progressivæ expansionis nimis urgendam non esse; nam loci citati non videntur excludere, quominus ecclesia aliquando notabiliter decrescere queat per schismata aut hæreses, (quarum ortum Scriptura prædixit) quin perdita *statim* resarciantur." (p. 129, 3°)

[719] "Nihilominus theologi communius rejiciunt hypothesim ecclesia ita hæresibus obrutæ, ut saltem pro brevi tempore ad unam regionem coarcteretur. Neque in hunc sensum interpretandæ videntur prædictiones Scripturæ de magna defectione in fine mundi." (p. 129, 3°)

result in the Church being largely, or even almost completely limited to one geographical area; and even makes complete allowance for the possibility, and even the overwhelming likelihood that the Church, during that great apostasy and persecution, *may result in the reduction of the number of the Church's members to a relatively* **small number** in comparison to the vastly greater number of members of the immediately preceeding period. This last proposition, for which Van Noort makes explicit allowance, coincides exactly with my own opinion on the question, but according to the fundamentalism of Salza & Siscoe, that opinion denies the Church's *note of catholicity*. Yet, in spite of the fact that my own exposition on this question, as I **repeatedly pointed out to them**, is plainly in full agreement with that expressed by many eminent theologians and approved ecclesiastical writers, Salza & Siscoe continue to obstinately assert that **when I give voice to that opinion**, it is, *according to them*, heretical: "Fr. Kramer not only denies the doctrine of moral catholicity but has embraced the heretical Protestant definition of the Church (i.e., "an invisible Church of true believers"). It is quite sad to see Fr. Kramer now publicly professing Protestant errors in the name of Catholicism."

Salza & Co. continue, «We also note that Fr. Kramer did not explain how "Salza's doctrine" is in contradiction with "the unanimous consent of the fathers." He simply made a baseless assertion that he backed up with nothing.» **[This is an outright lie to say I "backed [it] up with nothing": the quotation of Cardinal Manning on this point is self-explanatory; yet Salza misrepresents my position again by fraudulently attributing to me the opinion that the Church will be reduced to "very few members", (something which I have never claimed); and by twisting Manning's words, and gratuitously imposing his own personal interpretation on them, thereby falsifying Manning's meaning.]**

> «Again, the problem with Fr. Kramer's position is that **he conflates an underground Church (which the Fathers predicted during the end times) with a Church consisting of only few members (which is incompatible with the mark of catholicity).** Cardinal Manning, to whom Kramer fallaciously appeals, did not make this error. When Manning said the Church would be "invisible" for a time, he was explaining that the Church – the visible social unit with all four marks in tact – would not be visible to the secular world for a time while she went "underground"; not that the Church would lose her attribute of visibility, which is precisely what would happen if it were reduced to *very few members*. In other words, the

Cardinal was most certainly not arguing that the Church would lose her mark of catholicity, nor any of her other perpetual qualities that render her formally visible, even if forced underground.»

I also, and no less than Cardinal Manning, "was most certainly not arguing that the Church would lose her mark of catholicity, nor any of her other perpetual qualities that render her formally visible, even if forced underground." **I simply quoted verbatim Cardinal Manning's summation on the testimony of the Fathers concerning the early Church's beliefs concerning the great apostasy: I added nothing to alter or twist his meaning. Salza's lies again when he says,** "When Manning said the Church would be "invisible" for a time, he was explaining that the Church – the visible social unit with all four marks in tact – would not be visible to the secular world for a time while she went "underground"; not that the Church would lose her attribute of visibility," **is absolutely false. Manning made no such explanation – he simply stated the point without elaborating any further qualifications on the manner in which the Church would become invisible. Again, I never said the Church would be reduced to** *"a few members"* **– another of Salza's fraudulent misrepresentations that he repeats over and over again. Salza continues to repeat this lie endlessly, following the dictum of Voltaire:** *"Mentez, mentez, il en restera toujours quelque chose."*

Salza then continues his defamatory rant: «Fr. Kramer: "NO! The visible entity will be APOSTATE. The true Church will be a remnant in hiding. The Church will be briefly INVISIBLE, as the Fathers teach." Posted July 21, 2016 at 4.05am.» It is plainly evident that my meaning is that when the persecuted Church goes underground, the remaining highly *visible entity will be a counterfeit "church"*, which will be apostate in the same manner as the Church of England was the highly visible entity that remained when the Catholic Church was compelled to go underground in England. This thesis, as I have shown, has been proposed by many approved Catholic authors over the centuries. It is not the *Catholic Church* that will *become apostate*, which would constitute a defection. Salza deceptively and deliberately misrepresents the clear meaning of my words, in order to fraudulently make it appear that I am professing the heresy of saying that the *visible Catholic Church will become apostate* – which is clearly not my meaning, and is contrary to the literal signification of my words. On the basis of their fraudulent misrepresentation of my words, Salza & Siscoe then maliciously accuse me of a heresy:

«Salza/Siscoe: By claiming that the "visible entity" will *become* "apostate," *Fr. Kramer, in a single sentence, has just publicly denied the indefectibility of the Church*, which is another of the perpetual attributes of the true Church! [...]The problem with Fr. Kramer's opinion is that he divorces the "visible entity" (which he says will become "apostate") from the "remnant Church in hiding," which he says is the "true Church." Not so, Fr. Kramer. Christ's promises (e.g., "the gates of hell shall not prevail") apply to the visible Church itself and not to a "remnant" or "handful" of true believers, which is actually the Protestant definition of "indefectibility," as we demonstrate in Chapter 1 of True or False Pope?»

The falsehood and malice of the accusation in this paragraph is manifestly evident – it is yet another *fraudulent* **misrepresentation:** the idea that the «problem with Fr. Kramer's opinion is that he divorces the "visible entity" (which he says will *become* "apostate") from the "remnant Church in hiding," which he says *is* the "true Church,"» is founded on the false premise that attributes to me the opinion that the Church will be, or already has been reduced to a literal 'handful' of a 'few' scattered members without any ecclesiastical hierarchy; *something which Salza knows I have never said*, but which he and Siscoe *deliberately* assert and falsely allege that I have said, *deliberately* misrepresenting me so as to make it appear that I actually have said it, and actually hold that opinion. Salza and Siscoe have *deliberately and calumniously* misconstrued the meaning of my words in such a manner so as to *maliciously* make it appear that I heretically profess that the visible Catholic Church will "become apostate"; whereas in reality, **what I actually stated is that the Church will be reduced to a remnant, a fraction of its former number of members, which will have to go into hiding for a time during the persecution of the great tribulation, and will appear to have disappeared**, (as Cardinal Manning says), *from the face of the earth*, while the **remaining highly visible, material entity (i.e. the Vatican, Bishops' Conferences, diocesan curias, parishes etc.) will comprise the apostate, counterfeit "Church". Whereas I clearly distinguish between the Catholic Church, whose visibility will be (and to some extent already is) obscured, and the visible ENTITY, the material organization of the Vatican, the Bishops' Conferences, and most dioceses and parishes, which will become apostate under the occupation of the Masonic 'counter-church' – i.e. the counterfeit "Conciliar Church" which will formally defect;**

Salza & Siscoe falsify my clear meaning that the mass defection into apostasy by those who will exit the Church and become a formally distinct counter-church, to mean that the Catholic Church herself will defect! Their fallacious argument is founded on the erroneous premise that the Philo-Masonic "Conciliar Church" IS the Catholic Church; whereas the "Conciliar Church" is in fact nothing but a cancer within the body of the Church, just as Protestantism was a cancer within, until it was solemnly anathematized, cast out, and formally expelled from any apparent, and merely material and external union with the Catholic Church.

On the basis of their distortion and misrepresentation, the Salza/Siscoe sophistry then resorts to **an outright lie**: «Like the members of the Sedevacantist sect, who fail to see the marks and attributes of the true Church in the suffering Church of our times, Fr. Kramer denies that the marks and attributes will continue to exist in the underground Church during the end times.» **There are two lies in this sentence:** 1) "Like the members of the Sedevacantist sect, who fail to see the marks and attributes of the true Church in the suffering Church of our times" – (I have never denied the marks and attributes of the Church of our times, that is the fundamentalistic *non sequitur* conclusion of Salza & Siscoe), and 2) "Fr. Kramer denies that the marks and attributes will continue to exist in the underground Church during the end times" – (a brazenly stated lie based on the false premise which fraudulently asserts that I claim the Church will be reduced to a mere handful – an assertion which I have demonstrated to be totally false).

Although I have not misrepresented *them*, as Salza & Co. scurrilously claim whenever I refute their sophistry, here is a passage of theirs in which they clearly falsify my position:

> «Fr. Kramer also appeals to Cardinal Manning's statement that the Church would become "invisible" for a time. But as we explained in our original refutation, Cardinal Manning was obviously explaining that the "visible social unit" would be "invisible" to the secular world insofar as she would be driven underground; *not that she would become "apostate,"* **as Kramer argues (sic),** which would mean she would lose her mark of formal visibility *(sic)*. Clearly, Cardinal Manning did not say "visible entity will become apostate." Whether above ground or underground, the "visible entity" will never become "apostate," because she is indefectible and will always be formally visible.»

I have clearly distinguished between the mere *physical infrastructure and the human institutions* belonging to the Church, which I refer to as the *"visible entity"*, such as the Vatican, etc. – which will nearly all become apostate; and the ***morally and formally visible body*** **of the *Church*,** which Manning says will appear to have been *"swept from the face of the earth"*. Salza & Siscoe have falsified my meaning by negating the clear distinction I made.

Salza & Co. again resort to the same kind of subterfuge:

> «Fr. Kramer's Fallacious Appeal to Pope Leo XIII
>
> Finally, Fr. Kramer appeals to the private revelation attributed to Pope Leo XIII. This gives us yet another angle to expose Kramer's error. In the revelation, Pope Leo had a vision of Lucifer unchained and attacking the Church during a 100-year period. After this vision, Pope Leo wrote a prayer of exorcism, in which he reveals (as Kramer himself quotes from) that the Church will be infiltrated by her "crafty enemies" who will "set up the throne of their abominable impiety, so that the shepherd being struck, the sheep may disperse."
>
> Once again, Fr. Kramer fails to make a key distinction, here between "the visible entity becoming apostate" and "the visible entity being infiltrated." Because the "visible entity" (the true Church, the visible social unit founded by Christ) will always be formally visible, the "entity" can never become "apostate," no matter how many demons, or Freemasons, or Communists infiltrate her.»

The *visible entity* I refer to is *not* the Church. The sophistry of Salza & Siscoe collapses on this point, namely, that **the words of Pope Leo XIII**, *"In the Holy Place itself, where the See of Holy Peter and the Chair of Truth has been set up as the light of the world, they have raised the throne of their abominable impiety"*; actually refer to that *place*, the **Vatican**, where the *"**visible entity**"*, i.e. ***"the throne of their abominable impiety"*** will be *"raised up"* – the ***visible entity*** that will occupy ***the* Vatican**, *"where the See of Holy Peter and the Chair of Truth has been set up as the light of the world"*, which will be the headquarters of the apostate and counterfeit "Conciliar Church".

Thus, the Salza/Siscoe lie is exposed:

> «Fr. Kramer's Fallacious Appeal to Fr. Berry
>
> Fr. Kramer attempts to extricate himself from his heretical statement by appealing to Fr. Berry's The Church of Christ, a book with which we are very familiar (we quote from it many times in True or False Pope?). Unfortunately for Fr. Kramer, Fr. Berry does not say that the "visible

entity will become apostate." No Catholic who knows his faith would ever say such a thing. Rather, Fr. Berry says that Satan will set up a counter-church to mimic the true Church and lead souls away, which "might" even become "more universal" that the true Church, "at least for a time."

There is an obvious distinction between the "visible entity becoming apostate," and a counter-church being set up in opposition to that "visible entity." Nowhere does Fr. Berry say that the "visible entity" (translation; the TRUE Catholic Church) will become "apostate," and thus Kramer's appeal to Fr. Berry is fallacious. And even if Fr. Berry's opinion that this counter-church "might" have more members, "for a time," than the true Church, this would not mean the true Church becomes "apostate," as Fr. Kramer argues. The true Church, or "visible entity," will remain formally visible, constituted by a Pope and hierarchy, and many faithful, irrespective of how big or small the counter-church may be (and irrespective of whether or not the "visible Church" is forced underground).»

The deliberate fraud of this passage becomes manifest by pointing out what has really been obviously my clearly expressed meaning from the beginning, namely, that the *visible entity* I refer to *is NOT* the Catholic Church. *I plainly and explicitly distinguished between "Catholic Church" and that apostate "visible entity"* which will be the heretical counterfeit church: i.e. *the Conciliar Church and its materially visible components after it defects into formal apostasy* – which is exactly that counter-church which Fr. Berry says may, for a time, become even more universal and more visible than the true Catholic Church. Thus, in order to maliciously make me appear to be a heretic, Salza & Siscoe have resorted to the calumny of falsifying my meaning by inverting the signification of my term "visible entity" to mean exactly the opposite of what I have clearly expressed it to mean, so that they can then falsely accuse me of professing the defection of the indefectible Catholic Church.

Here is my first reply on this point, which Salza & Co. have attempted to refute with their characteristic mendacity:

REPLY TO JOHN SALZA PART III

"Scrutati sunt iniquitates; defecerunt scrutantes scrutinio" (Ps. 63)

Using the methods so chronically used by Masons, the former (?) Mason Salza and his partner Siscoe falsify my position by craftily misrepresenting it; and then they proceed to refute the caricature of their own making. Salza/Siscoe claim, "Fr. Kramer errs by confusing the predictions of an underground Church during the end times, with a farcical reduction of the number of faithful to only a handful, and ends by denying the mark of catholicity." This is a **bold-faced lie**: Nowhere have I ever stated such a thing.

Again, Salza/Siscoe state falsely, "[T]he problem with Fr. Kramer's position is that he conflates an underground Church (which the Fathers predicted during the end times) with a Church consisting of only few members". Following the perverse dictum of the Freemason Voltaire, ("Mentez, mentez, il en restera toujours quelque chose"), Salza/Siscoe brazenly repeat the lie, hoping that something of it will stick in the minds of their unfortunate readers. Again, I have not asserted the proposition that the universal Church will be reduced to only a mere handful of scattered members; but only that during the exceptional time foretold in sacred scripture and permitted by God, the Church will be greatly reduced, and scattered; as many approved and eminent authorities have explained.

Salza/Siscoe skilfully misrepresent my position by deftly interpreting a quotation expressed in the conditional mode, according to an indicative sense. Thus, their bogus interpretation of the (in fact spurious) words attributed to St. Athanasius, "Even if Catholics faithful to Tradition are reduced to a handful, they are the ones that are the true Church of Christ." These words do not state that the Church will in fact be literally reduced to a mere handful, but express in hypothetical mode that **if** such a thing **were** to happen, then that small group **would** still be the true Church of Christ. Hence, there is absolutely nothing heterodox about the quotation; but it is only the malicious spinning of it by Salza & Siscoe that makes it seem heretical. It is in fact no more heretical than the prophecy of Our Lord Jesus Christ who foretold that in the time of tribulation, "there shall arise false Christs and false prophets, and shall show great signs and wonders, insomuch as to deceive (if possible) even the elect." (Mt. 24:24)

If the elect were really to be deceived, then the defection of the Church would result, thereby nullifying the attribute of indefectibility promised by Christ Himself. However, the conditional qualifying "if" does not permit such an heretical interpretation of the verse to be made; and that same qualifying "if" in the spurious Athanasius quotation likewise rules out categorically that its meaning may be interpreted heretically to mean that the Church will indeed be reduced to a mere handful.

Furthermore, the spurious quotation is not the basis of my theological opinion on the exceptional circumstances that will befall the Church during the great tribulation foretold in scripture, by the ancient Fathers, and in the approved writings of many saints and theologians. I have already set forth what is the basis of my position in my brief article (and in previous posts and comments), "Re: My Reply to John Salza" -- which manifests the absurdity of the Salza/ Siscoe claim that, "By embracing the spurious quote, Fr. Kramer errs by denying an essential mark of the Church."

As I have shown, the quotation does not deny an essential mark of the Church, and the quotation is not the basis of my theological opinion. St. Thomas Aquinas wrote against the errors of the Greeks, supporting his position with spurious quotations of the Fathers. The fact that many of the passages he cited were later shown to be spurious did not diminish the orthodoxy of his opuscule, *Contra Errores Græcorum* – and neither does the fact that the Athanasius quotation is in fact spurious diminish in the least the orthodoxy of my theological position on the tribulation the Church will undergo in the time of tribulation.

I did not say that the Church will be reduced to a handful. What I did say is that the Church will be greatly reduced, and driven into the catacombs in the manner described by Cardinal Edward Manning. Salza & Siscoe engage in the verbal manipulation of relative terms like "large" and "small", in the deliberate attempt to misrepresent me in a heretical manner. In the great tribulation in which it can be foreseen that a great portion of humanity will perish, and a huge number of Catholics will apostatize, one can safely conclude, without violating the principle of "moral catholicity" that the total number of Catholics will be significantly reduced to a small number in comparison to what it was before.

The manner in which it will be reduced to in visibility and in numbers is described by Cardinal Manning:

> "The apostasy of the city of Rome from the vicar of Christ and its destruction by Antichrist may be thoughts very new to many Catholics, that I think it well to recite the text of theologians of greatest repute. First Malvenda, who writes expressly on the subject, states as the opinion of Ribera, Gaspar Melus, Biegas, Suarez, Bellarmine and Bosius that Rome shall apostatize from the Faith, drive away the Vicar of Christ and return to its ancient Paganism. ... Then the Church shall be scattered, driven into the wilderness, and shall be for a time, as it was in the beginning, invisible; hidden in catacombs, in dens, in mountains, in lurking places; for a time it

shall be swept, as it were from the face of the earth. Such is the universal testimony of the Fathers of the early Church." — Henry Edward Cardinal Manning, *The Present Crisis of the Holy See*, 1861, London: Burns and Lambert, pp. 88-90)

There exists only one word that adequately describes the method of argumentation of Salza & Siscoe in their misrepresentation of my theological arguments, and their falsification and inversion of Catholic teaching; and that word is *fraud*.

Their silly claim that I have made a "procedural error" is a falsehood. I did not have access to the Latin text of the St. Athanasius letter, so I had to make do with three versions of the passage in question in modern languages that I was able to find. All the translations were identical, and had the identical reference. The page numbers in the reference in English, Spanish and French were "p. 411-412". Somewhere along the line of transmission, a typographical error occurred, which Salza & Co. gratuitously assume is a "procedural error".

It was only afterwards, when I had learned that the letter begins with the words, "Deus quidem vos consoletur", that I was able to locate sources containing the letter, and verify the fact that the passage in question is indeed spurious. However, Salza & Siscoe state falsely that, "Fr. Kramer simply pulled the quotation from an internet source without checking the reference to see if it was authentic". In fact, long before the internet became available to the general public, I had to rely on the word of the SSPX in one of their publications concerning the passage in question, since I did not have an adequate library at my disposal to verify the authenticity of the passage.

The much more grave error of Salza & Siscoe is their claim that, "Fr. Kramer errs by confusing the predictions of an underground Church during the end times, with a farcical reduction of the number of faithful to only a handful, and ends by denying the mark of catholicity." As I have already stated, I have never said that the number of faithful will actually be reduced to a handful — this claim is a malicious invention of Salza & Siscoe.

What I have said is that the Church will be reduced to a small number during the great persecution foretold in the book of the Apocalypse; and not only does this opinion not deny the dogma of the indefectibility of the Church by destroying its catholicity or its visibility, but is in fact the doctrine of scripture as interpreted by the ancient Fathers, and is therefore at the very least *proxima fidei*.

In the above cited work of Cardinal Manning, it is stated that, "The writers of the Church tell us that in the latter days the City of Rome will probably become apostate from the Church and the Vicar of Jesus Christ; and that Rome will again be punished, for he will depart from it, and the judgment of God will fall on the place from which he once ruled over the nations of the world." (p. 87) Fr.E. Sylvester Berry, in his work on The Apocalypse of St. John says, "After the destruction of Rome in the days of Antichrist, it shall forever remain a heap of ruins and the haunt of filthy animals; "that great city shall be found no more at all." (p. 193)

At the beginning of Chapter XX, Fr. Berry explains, "[P]ractically all interpreters who accept these conclusions (that Antichrist must be a definite individual and…that he has not yet made his appearance in the world) take the reign of Antichrist as a prelude to the last judgment end the end of the world. Then contrary to the plain sense of Holy Scripture, they place the universal reign of Christ before the reign of Antichrist." (p. 189)

"A careful reading of the Apocalypse," Fr. Berry explains, "shows clearly that Antichrist will appear long centuries before the last judgment and the end of the world. In fact his reign will be but the final attempt of Satan to prevent the universal reign of Christ in the world." (p. 189-90) This opinion of Fr. Berry is supported by the prophecy of St. John Eudes (which I read about 25 years ago), who foretold that the triumph of the Heart of Mary will be a triumph over the Antichrist. I mention this here only in order to dispel the false interpretations that conclude that the great tribulation of the time of Antichrist cannot happen in the very near future; and also to provide a general context for the events that are foretold in scripture and by ecclesiastical writers, when the Church will be persecuted to near extinction, but will, by divine intervention, rise in triumph from her apparent defeat.

In this context one can place the future events spoken of by Cardinal Manning, who wrote, "And therefore the writers of the Church tell us that the City of Rome has no prerogative except only that the Vicar of Christ is there; and if it become unfaithful, the same judgments which fell on Jerusalem, hallowed though it was by the presence of the Son of God, of the Master, and not the disciple only, shall fall likewise upon Rome." (p. 88) Manning cites multiple authorities, including St. Robert Bellarmine: "In the time of Antichrist, Rome shall be desolated and burnt, as we shall learn from the sixteenth verse of the seventeenth chapter of the Apocalypse." (p. 89)

Manning continues, "Finally, Cornelius à Lapide sums up what may be said to be the common interpretation of theologians... 'These things are to be understood of the city of Rome, not that which is, nor that which was, but that which shall be at the end of the world... For from Christian it shall again become heathen. It shall cast out the Christian Pontiff, and the faithful who adhere to him. It shall persecute and slay them...'" (p. 90)

Thus we have the context of Cardinal Manning's words quoted earlier:

> "The apostasy of the city of Rome from the vicar of Christ and its destruction by Antichrist may be thoughts very new to many Catholics, that I think it well to recite the text of theologians of greatest repute. First Malvenda, who writes expressly on the subject, states as the opinion of Ribera, Gaspar Melus, Biegas, Suarez, Bellarmine and Bosius that Rome shall apostatize from the Faith, drive away the Vicar of Christ and return to its ancient paganism. ... Then the Church shall be scattered, driven into the wilderness, and shall be for a time, as it was in the beginning, invisible; hidden in catacombs, in dens, in mountains, in lurking places; for a time it shall be swept, as it were from the face of the earth. Such is the universal testimony of the Fathers of the early Church."

"Such is the universal testimony of the Fathers," says Manning, the Church "will be as it was in in the beginning" -- "invisible, hidden... swept, as it were from the face of the earth"; and this is "the universal testimony of the Fathers"; but according to Salza & Siscoe, this is an opinion that denies the essential mark of the catholicity of the Church.

In the great commentary of Cornelius à Lapide, explanation is given of the meaning of the words spoken by Christ in the 12th chapter of the Gospel of St. Luke, where the Lord describes His Church as a "pusillus grex", a "little flock". And the first reason given why the Lord refers to the Church as a "little flock" is: "PUSILLUS GREX, id est parvus, Primo, quia tum pauci erant fideles" — at the beginning the number of faithful was small; and also is small in comparison with the great number of the infidels and the wicked (pusillus est grex fidelium si comparatur cum maxima multitudine infidelium, & impiorum); and he cites the opinion of Bede, according to whom the flock is small in comparison to the number of reprobates (ad comparationem majoris numeri reproborum).

The Church will be comprised of a small number of faithful especially during the persecution of Antichrist for all the reasons given above, because, as ecclesiastical writers explain, that during that exceptional persecution, by the disposition of the divine will, the Church will revert for a time to the state it was in during the early persecutions. This is explained by Cardinal Manning not as merely his own personal opinion, but, as he says in his own words, "In treating of this subject, I shall not venture upon any conjectures of my own, but shall deliver simply what I find either in the Fathers of the Church, or in such theologians as the Church has recognised, namely, Bellarmine, Lessius, Malvenda, Viegas, Suarez, Ribera, and others".

"The history of the Church," says Cardinal Manning, "and the history of our Lord on earth, run as it were in parallel. For three-and-thirty years the Son of God incarnate was in the world, and no man could lay hand upon Him. No man could take Him, because His "hour was not yet come." There was an hour foreordained when the Son of God would be delivered into the hand of sinners. He foreknew it; He foretold it."

"In like manner with His Church. Until the hour is come when the barrier shall, by the Divine will, be taken out of the way, no one has power to lay a hand upon it. The gates of hell may war against it; they may strive and wrestle, as they struggle now with the Vicar of our Lord; but no one has the power to move Him one step, until the hour shall come when the Son of God shall permit, for a time, the powers of evil to prevail. That He will permit it for a time stands in the book of prophecy. When the hindrance is taken away, the man of sin will be revealed; then will come the persecution of three years and a half, short, but terrible, during which the Church of God will return into its state of suffering, as in the beginning; and the imperishable Church of God, by its inextinguishable life derived from the pierced side of Jesus, which for three hundred years lived on through blood, will live on still through the fires of the times of Antichrist." (pp. 55-56)

"THE CHURCH OF GOD WILL RETURN INTO ITS STATE OF SUFFERING, AS IN THE BEGINNING" – when it was a "*pusillus grex*" (Luke 12:32); a "little flock", small in number.

Cardinal Louis Edouard Pie, a contemporary of Cardinal Manning, wrote, "The Church, though still a visible society, will be increasingly reduced to individual and domestic proportions."…"Surrounded on all sides, as the other centuries have made her great, so the last will strive to crush her. And finally the Church on earth will undergo a true defeat:… 'and it was given unto him [the Antichrist] to make war with the saints and to overcome them.'" (Apocalypse 13:7)

Hillaire Belloc, honoured by Pius XI with the title, "Defender of the Faith", expresses the same opinion, (which Salza & Siscoe claim to be heretical), namely, that the Church during the great tribulation will be severely reduced in numbers. In *The Great Heresies*, (which I read multiple times and of which I have multiple copies, including an original edition), Belloc says, "The Church will not disappear, for the Church is not made of mortal stuff; it is the only institution among men not subject to the universal law of mortality. Therefore we say, that the Church may not be wiped out, but that it may be reduced to a small band almost forgotten amid the vast numbers of its opponents and their contempt of the defeated thing."

This conviction, which Salza & Siscoe say is heretical, has been voiced also by the future Pope Benedict XVI in a radio address on Hessischer Rundfunk in Germany in 1969:

> "It [the Church] will become small and will have to start pretty much all over again. It will no longer have use of the structures it built in its years of prosperity. The reduction in the number of faithful will lead to it losing an important part of its social privileges."

Salza & Siscoe take issue with my entirely orthodox comment that, "The visible entity will be **apostate**. The true Church will be a remnant in hiding. The Church will be briefly **invisible**, as the Fathers teach." According to their grotesquely distorted and fundamentalistic notion of the Church, that which has been clearly foretold in scripture and expounded by the Fathers and by ecclesiastical writers through the ages of Catholicism, constitutes a denial of the indefectibility visibility of the Church. However, as we have seen in the preceding segment of this article, it is Salza & Siscoe who deny Catholic doctrine by maintaining that the Church will not be reduced to a small number during the reign of Antichrist; and similarly, the diminution of the Church's visibility correlative to its reduction in numbers as a logical corollary of that reduction of numbers.

Salza & Siscoe also, in a desperate attempt to make me appear heretical, fraudulently misrepresent my words by claiming that the "visible entity" I refer to is the Catholic Church. Since I clearly distinguished between the persecuted Church that will be greatly reduced in numbers and visibility, and which will revert to the catacombs ("The true Church will be a remnant in hiding"), and the "visible entity" which will be the highly visible apostate entity ("The visible entity will be

apostate"), it is plainly evident that the "visible entity" that I say will become "apostate" is something entirely different from the Catholic Church – but Salza & Siscoe deliberately falsify my meaning in order to make me appear to be a heretic.

Likewise, they gratuitously and absurdly accuse me of professing the Protestant doctrine of an "invisible church", which would be a **totally invisible** scattered number of believers unknown to each other, without hierarchy, without priesthood, without any visible characteristics. Since I explicitly stated that the persecuted Church will revert to its condition of the early persecution of Roman times, it is manifestly evident that I do not profess the Protestant heresy of an invisible church. My words were patently clear in their meaning. Salza & Siscoe deliberately falsify my meaning in order to make it appear heretical. Thus, the attempt to make me appear to be a heretic is the work of deliberate deception by Salza & Siscoe.

Cardinal Manning expounds meticulously and at some length, citing the writings of the Fathers and other eminent authorities, that Rome will apostatize, and a counterfeit entity will rise in Rome, where the Vicar of Christ formerly reigned — a pagan counterfeit entity will rise in its place. The Holy Sacrifice of the Mass will cease, and counterfeit pagan worship will take its place.

Fr. E. Sylvester Berry, D.D., in *The Church of Christ, An Apologetic and Dogmatic Treatise*, explains, "The prophecies of the Apocalypse show that Satan will imitate the Church of Christ to deceive mankind; he will set up a church of Satan in opposition to the Church of Christ. Antichrist will assume the role of Messias; his prophet will act the part of Pope, and there will be imitations of the Sacraments of the Church." (p. 119) Since the scriptures themselves foretell that the reign of Antichrist will be universal, the false worship of the apostate entity will be globally imposed. (Apoc. 13:7-8) Thus, Fr. Berry says, "there seems to be no reason why a false Church might not become universal, even more universal than the true one, at least for a time." (p.155)

Even after the cessation of the Holy Sacrifice, when the Church, reduced to a small number and nearly everywhere in hiding, will appear to have been swept from the face of the earth; even then, the essential marks of catholicity, and the essential attribute of indefectibility and its corresponding visibility will remain intact, although diminished for a time. In, *The Divine Plan of The Church*, by the Rev. John MacLaughlin, (Burns & Oates, London, 1901. Chapter VI, on indefectibility. Pp. 93-94.), we read:

We concede, moreover, that there may have been occasions in the past (and such intervals may occur in the future) when, through the opposition of anti-popes and a variety of untoward circumstances, it was difficult for individuals for the moment to tell where the right source of authoritative teaching was to be found.

This, however, does not change the state of the case in the least; the one true Church was in the world somewhere all the same, and in full possession of all her essential prerogatives, although, for the passing hour – from transient causes – she may not have been easily discernible to the less observant.

Just as there have been times when some dense fog or mist made it impossible for the ordinary observer to tell the exact spot the sun occupied in the sky, although everybody knew that he was there somewhere; knew, too, that he would in due course make the exact location of his presence visible to all, and that, as soon as the mist lifted, his rays would come straight to the earth again, and every one would see that he was identically the same luminous orb that had shone before.

Thus the accusation made by Salza & Siscoe, that "By claiming that the 'visible entity' will become 'apostate,' Fr. Kramer, in a single sentence, has just publicly denied the indefectibility of the Church", is plainly seen not only to be false, but contrary to the plain teaching of scripture as understood according to the mind of the Church.

> *"And it was given unto him to make war with the saints, and to overcome them. And power was given him over every tribe, and people, and tongue, and nation. And all that dwell upon the earth adored him, whose names are not written in the book of life of the Lamb, which was slain from the beginning of the world."* (Apoc. 13: 7)

The fraud which is the basis of the calumnious verdict of heresy which the Salza/Siscoe lay vigilante tribunal solemnly pronounces against me consists not only in their false assertion I say the Church will be reduced to a handful, but more importantly, it is their basing of their judgment of heresy on their understanding of a doctrine that has not been defined by the Church. How great must be the number of Catholics in the world for the Church to be truly catholic (universal)? How small can that number be reduced to, and to what degree can the visibility of the Church be diminished during the exceptional time of the Great Tribulation foretold by Christ and the Apostles? **The Church has not dogmatically defined on these points**, so Salza and Siscoe have absolutely no basis to justify their hypocritical accusation of heresy against me. They base their judgments on the expressions of opinions of the authors of theological works, and they treat these opinions as if they were solemn dogmatic definitions that are definitive, *ex sese* infallible and irreformable, and not subject to qualification or revision. Their hypocrisy is patent due to the fact that Archbishop Lefebvre, Fr. Gregor Hesse S.T.D.[720], Christopher A. Ferrara, Mgr. Tissier de Mallerais, and many other Catholic authors (some of whom I have quoted), have expressed the same opinions as I have expressed, which Salza & Co. declare to be heretical when I pronounce them; while they remains silent on the others expressing the same opinions, and even recognizes them as orthodox in their doctrine. When I pointed out this glaring double standard employed by Salza & Co. in their private Vigilante-Inquisition condemnation of me as a heretic, **their reply was to accuse me of trying to create division in the traditional movement!** I need not say that such behavior is manifestly tantamount to an admission of guilt on their part.

Salza and Siscoe declare me to be a heretic, because I declare the Conciliar Church to be a heretical entity. Salza & Co. explicitly declare the Conciliar Church to be the Catholic Church, and adamantly insist that those who refuse to be in communion with the Conciliar Church

---

[720] Salza & Co. fraudulently quote Fr. Gregor Hesse against me on the point of defection from the faith and the Church. In order to deceive their readers into believing that Fr. Hesse was of the same opinion as Salza/Siscoe, who maintain that heretics are not severed from the Church without a judgment from Church authority, they quote Dr. Hesse's words which explain that "there is no formal schism unless it is declared schism". Salza & Siscoe oafishly interpret the theologian's words to mean that there is no schism unless the Church authority declares it! Long before the days of YouTube, by which Salza & Siscoe access the words of Fr. Gregory, I lived in Rome and earned my degrees at the same Pontifical University where he earned his theological degrees. We spent many evenings together in Rome discussing Philosophy, Theology, and ecclesiastical issues. We met many times afterward in Canada, USA, Vienna, Rome, Los Angeles, Belize, etc. – we were the closest of friends from 1975 to 2006. (We first met on the assembly line at the Mercedes-Benz factory in Germany while working at our summer jobs in 1975) No one on earth knows the theological mind of Fr. Gregor Hesse as well as I do. It was I who suggested and convinced him to write his doctoral thesis on the Theology of Chesterton. What Fr. Gregor was saying (and any academically qualified theologian knows this), is that for someone to be a schismatic, that one must declare himself to be separated, either by words or actions, and **not the other way around.**

are outside of the Church. They say my position that the Conciliar Church is not the Catholic Church is a heresy that denies the indefectibility of the Church. They claim that in order to remain in communion with the Church, it is necessary to be in communion with the Conciliar hierarchy, and be subject to the Conciliar pope (no matter how manifestly heretical he may be). Fr. Gregor Hesse, in his homily in Woonsocket RI, in 1997 declared the Conciliar Church to be, "that counterfeit church out there". There are still living other witnesses who vividly remember those words in that sermon. Archbishop Lefebvre was, to my knowledge, the first one to point out the essential difference between the "Conciliar Church" and the Catholic Church. The bishop he consecrated, Mgr. Bernard Tissier de Mallerais, in his article, *Is There A Conciliar Church*,[721] theologically elaborates the essential differences between the Conciliar Church and the Catholic Church. In defining the Conciliar Church, Mgr. Tissier sets forth the material cause, efficient cause, final cause, and formal cause that constitute the Conciliar church as a an entity distinct and different from the Catholic Church – "two Churches that have the same heads and most of the same members", a "counterfeit Church", "although we can reduce the belonging to it of most of its members to a simple material belonging, from the simple fact that most of the members follow the movement by conformity, without knowing or sharing the goals of the Conciliar Church". He quotes the author, Julio Meinvielle, who describes the Conciliar Church as a "Church of publicity magnified in propaganda, with bishops, priests, and theologians publicised, perhaps won over to the enemy and changing from the Catholic Church to the gnostic Church, (as against) the other, Church of silence, with Pope faithful to Jesus Christ in its teaching and with some priests, bishops and faithful who are attached to it, scattered like the *pusillus grex* over all the earth."

Mgr. Tissier further explains that, "Formally considered the conciliar church is a sect which occupies the Catholic Church"; and "the establishment of the Conciliar Church is the fruit of a plan plotted by Freemasonry". Mgr. Tissier quotes Archbishop Lefebvre, "Which Church are we talking about? Are we talking about the Catholic Church, or another Church, a Counter Church, a counterfeit of the Catholic Church?" – "The Church of today is only the true Church in the measure that it continues exclusively, and makes itself one with exclusively the

---

[721] L'Église conciliare existe-t-elle? – http://www.dominicainsavrille.fr/leglise-conciliaire-existe-t-elle/.

Church of yesterday and of all time." Mgr Tissier finally asks, "And besides this vulgar conciliar Church, what remains of the Catholic Church? We respond that, even reduced to a modest number, the sane faithful and perhaps only one faithful bishop, as perhaps will be according to Father Emmanuel, the Church at the end of time, the Catholic Church remains the Catholic Church." While I have never maintained that the Church will be reduced to such dire circumstances as hypothesized by Mgr. Tissier, It needs to be borne in mind that the magisterium of the Church has not defined on this point; and therefore, Salza & Siscoe act with criminal malice to declare me to be a heretic for professing such a doctrine as that, *which in fact I have never professed*; and they manifest their premeditated hypocrisy and malice in declaring me to be a heretic for allegedly professing this doctrine which they know perfectly well that I do not profess, while feigning reverence and respect for Mgr. Tissier who does profess it, *merely as a hypothetical possibility* – and they yet have the sacrilegious and demonic audacity to declare the calumny that it is I, and not they, who am without personal integrity.

Salza & Siscoe deliberately and knowingly fabricated a bogus case of heresy against me, being fully conscious that their maliciously concocted case of heresy against me is fraudulent and false. They committed this crime not because they sincerely believe me to be in heresy, but simply out of the base motive which is their vindictive desire to retaliate against me, for having exposed their heresy. The proof of this consists in their glaring failure to cite any credible *indicia* of heresy against me. **Never have they been able to cite a single proposition of mine which asserts some doctrine against any defined teaching of the Church.** As I have demonstrated in this *Appendix*, Salza & Siscoe fabricate a false *indicium* by interpreting a doctrinally orthodox hypothetical proposition which says one thing expressed in the *conditional mood*, and interpret it as if it were an *assertion* of something quite different pronounced in the *indicitave mood*. This kind of fraud can only be the consciously fabricated product of a perverse and malicious intention to deceive and to defame. All of their alleged *indicia* of heresy they hurl against me can likewise be seen to be malicious artifices of sophistry, by which they spin out logically incoherent heretical conclusions which they attempt to draw out of my words, but which do not logically follow from any of my statements. There is no need for me to elaborate further on this point, except to say: "*Alienati sunt peccatores a vulva, erraverunt ab utero, locuti sunt falsa*" (Ps. 57:4). I publicly corrected them, so they were forced to modify their position, and thus in their *Formal Reply* they resorted to the usual sort of malevolent innuendo they chronically employ: «If Fr. Kramer falls into the same error [as the Sedevacantists]… (assuming he hasn't already), and publicly declares that *he* is not a member of the Church headed by Pope Francis and the bishops in union with him, no "pronounced judgment of the Church" will be required in his case either.» Their response to theological argumentation is always calumny, sometimes overtly stated, otherwise by way of pointed innuendo. Here are some examples:

1. «It has become painfully evident that *Fr. Paul Kramer is getting his theology on a heretical Pope exclusively from Sedevacantist websites.* He is surely not getting it from St. Robert Bellarmine, even though that is the impression he wants to give his flock.»
2. «It is sad to see what has become of Fr. Paul Leonard Kramer and the depths to which he has now sunk in his mad campaign to discredit us, and publicly promote the errors of Sedevacantism that he once himself rejected.»
3. «Kramer has sinned against the Faith – according to John of St. Thomas, Kramer is a public heretic.»
4. «Fr. Kramer errs by denying an essential mark of the Church. This error of Fr. Kramer can be seen when he claims that the Church "will be reduced to a small number," and then claims that the Church will "revert to the catacombs" and become "invisible." It is quite sad to see Fr. Kramer now publicly professing Protestant errors in the name of Catholicism.»
5. «Fr. Kramer actually says the sin of heresy is also the crime of heresy, and he evidently thinks he is the judge of both!»
6. «Perhaps Fr. Kramer now embraces Dignitatis Humanae's erroneous teaching that man has a "natural right" to form his judgments, irrespective of the teachings of the Church.»
7. «Fr. Kramer argues Private Judgment prevails over the public judgment of the Church.»
8. «Fr. Kramer is in a diabolical rage over a book that he has not read, and adamantly refuses to read it. That is not rational.» [Robert Siscoe] N.B. In this last outburst, Siscoe is referring to the Salza/Siscoe magnum opus, *True or False Pope?* In their *Formal Reply* to my refutation of the principal errors asserted in their book, Salza & Siscoe do not offer any serious response to my arguments, but instead launch into an *ad hominem* tirade – and in spite of my copious citations of verbatim passages from their book, they still attempt to foist their canard on the public by insinuating that I

have never read their book by declaring: "Kramer Defends His Decision To Criticize a Book He Hasn't Read".

I am not a sedevacantist. I have never belonged to the sedevacantist school. According to my judgment, Pope Benedict XVI remains the true and legitimate Roman Pontiff. That matter will be discussed in the second volume of this work. Unlike Salza & Siscoe, I do not presume to declare all sedevacantists excommunicated as heretics. All they can allege is that I profess what they, but not the Church, define as, "sedevacantist errors"; and according to the Salza/Siscoe lay tribunal, I was therefore judged by them to be in heresy; and on the basis of their Private Judgment, they presumed declare me outside the Church.

There exists a multitude of examples of deliberately crafted falsification of my words and my meaning throughout every article they have written aginst me; but to expose them all would require a volume at least twice the size of this one. I therefore leave the reader with one final observation on the greatest Salza/Siscoe fraud of all on the question of whether or not a heretical pope can be deposed by the Church. John Salza and Robert Siscoe claim that their 700 page book, *True Or False Pope?,* faithfully explains the mind of the Church on this question. I have quoted their book giving the verbatim passages, so they cannot possibly say honestly that I am misrepresenting them, as they constantly claim. Salza & Siscoe reject the First Opinion – they state their opinion that a pope can indeed become a formal heretic. They reject the Second Opinion which holds that even a secret heretic would automatically fall from the pontifical office. They reject the Third Opinion – they profess that a heretical pope can be deposed. They reject the Fifth Opinion (which they dismiss as a Sedevacantist opinion), according to which a manifestly heretical pope would fall from office *ipso facto,* entirely by himself, *sine alia vi externa,* such as a judgment of heresy pronounced by the Church. That leaves the Fourth Opinion. Opinion No. Four holds that a manifestly heretical pope does not fall from office *ipso facto,* but must be deposed by the Church. The classical representatives of this opinion were all opposed to the heresy of Conciliarism, and attempted to formulate their respective doctrines in such a manner that would avoid making a Council superior to a pope.

In the eleventh chapter of their bulky screed, they begin the chapter saying, "we will examine the issue of how a heretical Pope is deposed. … We will employ the distinctions necessary to navigate through the minefield of possible errors that touch upon the matter, while carefully avoiding the heresy of Conciliarism." They correctly state that,

"Conciliarism is a heresy that holds that a council is superior to the Pope." (p. 331) They falsely state that they have

"demonstrated from the writings of Bellarmine, Suarez, Francis de Sales, John of St. Thomas and others that the *Church* (not individual Catholics) must *prove* (not presume) the Pope is guilty of the crime of heresy through a formal finding of fact before a reigning Pope loses his office for heresy."

They have done no such thing. The Church teaches that one who is manifestly a formal heretic loses office *ipso jure*; and if the heresy is not manifest, then the heresy of the *suspected heretic* must be proven. The very idea that formal heresy that is manifest needs to be proven "through a formal finding of fact" is absurd on its face, since heresy which is manifestly evident is already manifestly proven by the evidence which is manifest. That which is manifest is immediately evident, and therefore certain and proven. That which is not certain is doubtful, and needs to be proven.

"This finding of fact," say Salza & Siscoe, "includes ecclesiastical warnings (as a matter of charity, not jurisdiction), which is based upon St. Paul's instruction in his Epistle to Titus, 3:10." Ecclesiastical warnings are by definition acts of authority by one having jurisdiction over a subject. The notion of ecclesiastical warnings that are "a matter of charity, not jurisdiction" is a contradiction in terms. Furthermore, as Fr. Bordoni explains, when pertinacity is manifest, it is manifest that the heretic knows his opinion is heretical, and thus it is in vain that warnings be given to one who already knows he is in heresy. Warnings are necessary for *suspected heretics*, but not for heretics who have already manifested pertinacity without warnings. Next, «If the Pope remains obstinate following these public warnings, he publicly manifests his pertinacity and "judges himself," thereby demonstrating to all that he is, in fact, a heretic.» On this point they are correct: if a pope *suspected of heresy* remains obstinate after warnings, he manifests his pertinacity, and demonstrates to all that he has *publicly defected from the faith*. That is all that is necessary for the loss of office of a heretic pope whose heresy was not *manifest*, but only *suspected* until it became manifest after unheeded warnings. In such a case, the cardinals need only issue a declaration that the pope has in some manner abdicated by defecting from the Catholic faith. There exists absolutely no need, neither according to doctrine nor according to law, for *establishing a crime* according to penal law and procedures; nor to render a judgment that the pope is guilty of the *crime of heresy* for him to lose office, if his pertinicaty is already manifestly evident. The Church declares the loss of office on the basis of the *fact* of public defection alone.

Salza & Siscoe apparently declare themselves to hold the Fourth Opinion:

> "After the Church establishes that the Pope is guilty of the crime of heresy, she renders a judgment of the same… What is *unanimous*, however, is that *the Church* must establish that the Pope is guilty of the crime of heresy before a Pope will lose his jurisdiction. … The Church's formal judgment of the crime is a *condition* necessary for a sitting Pope to be deprived of the pontificate for heresy."

Formal judgment of a crime can only be pronounced by a judge or by a tribunal of judges exercising power over one who is subject to their jurisdiction. The objection that in deposing a pope, a council, a synod, or the cardinals, would not directly exercise power over a pope has been shown to be fallacious. I have quoted Bellarmine, who explained that such an act of deposition requires an exercise of power over the pope: "For, if the Church deposes a Pope against his will, certainly it is over the Pope." (Nam si Ecclesia invitum Papam deponit, certe est *supra Papam*.) I have quoted Cardinal Billot who explained against Cajetan why it cannot be legitimately objected, "that the deposal could still be understood not as the direct withdrawal of the papacy"; and the reason he gives is that of Bellarmine, and of Bordoni after him: Such a deposal, says Billot, "corresponds to an act of jurisdiction and to the exercise of a power. This is why the objection's conclusion does not follow: just because the person of the pope can be designated by men, this does not mean that the latter have the legitimate power to dismiss the person of the pope from the papacy." Such a power, Bellarmine explains, requires the jurisdiction of a superior: "for one to be deposed from the pontificate against his will is without a doubt a penalty; therefore, the Church deposing a Pope against his will, without a doubt punishes him; but to punish is for a superior and a judge". This *sententia* is echoed by Wernz & Vidal and is unanimously taught by canonists: "*For every judicial sentence of privation supposes a superior jurisdiction over him against whom the sentence is laid.*" It therefore necessarily follows, as Cardinal Billot explained, "The Church, or an ecclesiastical assembly, cannot perform any act upon the person of the pope, except for the election. And therefore, once the election is canonically terminated, the Church has nothing more to do until a new election takes place, which can occur only after the see becomes vacant." The Salza/Siscoe doctrine flies in the face of all this doctrine – they have the heretical temerity to declare, "The Church's formal judgment of the crime is a *condition* necessary for a sitting Pope to be **deprived of the pontificate** for heresy." It has been demonstrated in this volume that the opposite is true; namely, that it pertains to faith that only after the see has become vacant that the Church can declare with a formal judgment that (if possible) the pope has fallen from office by an act of tacit resignation for having defected from the Catholic faith by formal heresy.

What logically follows from their own premises is that the Salza & Siscoe doctrine does not even fall into the category of the Fourth Opinion as it formulated by Cajetan and John of St. Thomas, but is an expression of the older Conciliarist theory, according to which the Church possesses the power, and by way of exception, the *jurisdiction* to **deprive** *a pope of his office for the crime of heresy*. This opinion is based on the perceived authority supposedly granted to a council by the spurious *Canon si papa*, which had been erroneously attributed to the "Apostle of Germany", St. Boniface, Bishop and Martyr, a Benedictine monk of Exeter; but which Salza & Siscoe ignorantly state, "is attributed to Pope Boniface" (p. 333). It has been amply demonstrated that according to Church teaching, the public sin (not necessarily *notorious*, but only *public* as defined in canon law) of manifest formal heresy constitutes the fact of defection from the Catholic faith which directly results in the automatic loss of whatever offices a cleric may have held. The legitimate authority merely declares the fact juridically *post factum*. No power over the defector is exercise that would effect the loss of office in making such a declaratory sentence. The *Code of Canon Law* explicitly distinguishes between loss of office which takes place *ipso jure*, and is simply declared *post factum*; and *penal deprivation of office which is* **inflicted by a superior** *according to the prescriptions of penal law*.[722] It is stated precisely according to Salza & Siscoe: "The sin of heresy alone, which has not been judged and declared by the Church, does not result in the loss of ecclesiastical office for a cleric. **The loss of office for a cleric is a vindictive penalty**… This also means that **the loss of office for a cleric must be imposed (*ferendae sententiae*) by Church authority**". According to the Church's canonical doctrine, such an act

---

[722] "**Can. 196** — § 1. Privatio ab officio, in poenam scilicet delicti, ad normam iuris tantummodo fieri potest. § 2. Privatio effectum sortitur secundum praescripta canonum de iure poenali…"

of *penal deprivation of office* can only be accomplished by a *superior exercising the power of jurisdiction over a subject*. All of the classical exponents of the Fourth Opinion studiously avoided postulating in their logically incoherent theories a jurisdiction that would involve the exercise of direct power over a pope by his inferiors by inflicting a vindictive penalty on the pontiff. It is precisely on this point that they formulated their logically incoherent notions with which they attempted to explain how the Church could depose a pope with a jurisdictional act, but without acting as a superior exercising power of jurisdiction over the pope. Bordoni understood and exposed the logical inconsistencies of these theories, so he held to the opinion that by way of exception, the proper jurisdiction of a superior is granted to a council in the case of papal heresy. The more radical formulation of the Salza/Siscoe doctrine on the deposition of a heretical pope goes far beyond the mitigated Conciliarism of the Counter-Reformation theologians who espoused the Fourth Opinion, and it postulates for a heretic pope, a loss of office by means of a **penal deprivation** of office – "**a vindictive penalty… imposed (*ferendae sententiae*) by Church authority**." Salza & Siscoe convict themselves with their own confession of heresy: "The Church's **formal judgment of the crime is a *condition* necessary for a sitting Pope to be deprived of the pontificate for heresy.**" (*True Or False Pope?*, p. 332) Such a formulation of doctrine professes an authority in the Church that can exercise a power of jurisdiction over the pope in order to **penally deprive** him of his office by means of a **vindictive penalty**. The dogmatic definition of the primacy, as formulated in *Pastor Æternus* established with infallible certitude that such a theory is heretical, and therefore inadmissible. Salza & Siscoe are condemned by their own words: "Conciliarism is a heresy that holds that a council is superior to the Pope." (p. 332) After I pointed out to them that *loss of office* due to defection from the faith is not a vindictive penalty nor a penalty at all, but is an administrative measure that takes place automatically, and without any declaration; Salza & Siscoe, after taking "two steps forward" by asserting their heresies, took "one step back" by equivocating; and **without retracting their error** or substantially modifying their opinion, they simply *created a fog of equivocation* by attempting to interpret canon 194 according to the prescriptions of the penal canons; and then they quoted the opinion in Beal's commentary on that same canon, who wrote not specifically on the hypothesis of papal heresy, but expressed his opinion within the context of the general framework of the application of the canon's prescription by a superior exercising jurisdiction over a subject:

"*the officeholder remains in office until the declaration or removal has been communicated to the officeholder in writing.*"

Without the explicit abjuration of their heresy, the *indicium* of heresy remains, with the result that there is no purgation of their heresy. Rather than retract their errors, Salza & Siscoe engage in the tactic of equivocation by stating, out of both sides of their mouths with their two-pronged tongues, contradictory positions on the same point – merely verbally and apparently contradictory positions which are logically reducible to one and the same heretical proposition, namely, that **the Church possesses the authority to judge the pope for heresy**. Salza & Siscoe remain obstinate in professing principles from which it necessarily follows that the "Church", i.e. the pope's inferiors in the hierarchy, by way of exception, possess the *jurisdiction* to depose the reigning pontiff by means of a vindictive penalty of deprivation of office if they judge him guilty of the delict of heresy; and that heretics do not automatically fall from office by publicly defecting into manifest formal heresy; while at the same time they claim to reject that position as an expression of *Conciliarism*, and accordingly opt for the equally heretical doctrine of *Mitigated Conciliarism*, categorically declared in Chapter 10, p. 295 of their book, *True or False Pope?*: '**the Church alone possesses the authority to judge the crime of papal heresy.**"

«**Yes, that is correct. […] heresy does not directly cause a Pope to fall from the pontificate.**»

(Salza & Siscoe in their *Gloria TV Interview*)

"After the **Church establishes that the Pope is guilty of the crime of heresy, she renders a judgment** of the same (and, as we will see, this is to be done during an *"imperfect" ecumenical council*)." – *True or False Pope?* p. 331

"**The Church must render a judgment before the pope loses his office.**"

Robert J. Siscoe — Article in *The Remnant* (Nov. 18, 2014)

A *judgment of a Council* pronouncing the Pope guilty of a crime is a judgment pronounced on *him who is the Pope*. It requires the power of jurisdiction to be exercised over *the person of Pope*; and *not* over the *conjunction* that unites the person to the Papacy. Such a judgment to be validly made with authority, would only be possible if it would be pronounced over the man who *was* the Pope, but who has already fallen from the Papacy *by himself* and *lost rank*.

EPILOGUE

The purpose, i.e. the *formal intention* of this volume has been to explain the Church's doctrine on faith, heresy and loss of ecclesiastical office, in order to lay the groundwork for Volume Two, which will examine the question of the validity or nullity Jorge Bergoglio's claim on the papacy. Fr. Nicholas Gruner had asked me to write on the Bergoglio question before I ever expressed any disagreement with the opinions of John Salza and Robert Siscoe. This work is no more intended merely to be a formal rebuttal of the heresies of Salza & Siscoe any more than were Conan Doyle's Sherlock Holmes stories principally intended to merely narrate the detective's confrontations with the wicked Moriarty. There is a greater depth and scope to this work which has led to the inevitable personal confrontation with the exponents of heresy who masquerade as traditional Catholics. Under the nominally Catholic outer wrappings of their works, there is found within the putrid mess of heresy which reeks of the Sect that has infiltrated the Church, even to the point of occupying the key positions in the Vatican.

It was the late Mons. Mario Marini, Secretary of the Pontifical Commission «*Ecclesia Dei*», a personal friend of thirty-five years, who told me in October 2008, only months before his death, "We are under Masonic occupation." When I was in Rome in the spring of 1996, he said to me, "Our hands are tied. We can do nothing. The Masons occupy the key positions." On 13 March 2013 at a pub in Cork City, Ireland, a group of Masons sat watching the image of the balcony of St. Peter's Basilica on the TV screen waiting to see who would emerge onto the balcony as the new pope. When Jorge Mario Bergoglio appeared on the balcony in papal attire, and flashed the *Master Mason's Sign of Recognition* in front of a world-wide TV audience, one of the Masons in that group in the pub stood up, and with his voice raised in excitement, declared, "Look, it's one of ours at the top!" Jorge Bergoglio, publicly praised by Freemasonry, intruded onto the papal throne, and for six years has presided over the *demolition of Catholicism*. It is no accident that he has done so, and it can be no mere coincidence that the agenda of Freemasonry, which is the *demolition of Catholicism*, and the *transformation of the Church so it can be merged with other religions*, is precisely the agenda that Bergoglio has been carrying out for the last six years. That agenda is explained and documented in Fr. Manfred Adler's book, *Die*

Antichristliche Revolution der Freimaurerei. That will be discussed in Volume Two.

The Bergoglio problem and where it's leading to is the proper topic of this three-volume work. In their Narcissism, Salza & Siscoe think this book is about them. So far, they have responded to my arguments and documentation with personal denigration, fraudulent misrepresentation, and strident vitriol; yet it is they who scream that I am the "father of lies" who has misrepresented them! It is therefore highly likely that Salza & Siscoe will reply to this volume with yet more idle and empty verbiage. Thus far, their response to me has been quintessentially Masonic in its character and methods, to the extent that I have been led even to question the sincerity of the conversion from Freemasonry of the former 32° Scottish Rite Freemason, John Salza. While it is far from certain that Salza has remained in the sect of Masonry, it is plainly evident that if he has indeed left Masonry as he claims, then even so, the demons of Masonry have not left him. And so, with fanatical zeal, Salza & Siscoe defend the indefensible, defending the bogus claim on the papacy of the destroyer of souls, who relentlessly pursues the agenda of ecclesiastical Masonry, which is to replace the Light of Christ with *Darkness Visible*.[723] That they so fanatically uphold the legitimacy of the standard-bearer of that sectarian darkness, only underscores the actual relevance of the Divine Savior's words, "If then the light that is in thee be darkness, how great is that darkness." (Matt. 6:23)

Fr. Paul Kramer, 13 March, 2019 Mallow, Ireland

SOME OF THE SOLEMN ANATHEMAS PRONOUNCED AGAINST ME VIA E-MAIL BY THE SUPREME SALZA-SISCOE INQUISITIONAL VIGILANTE TRIBUNAL

18/10/2016
Kramer,

Here's what you don't understand: You have publicly defected from the faith **by leaving the Church. <u>You are now a public heretic. Period.</u>** You are no longer a **Catholic** priest (since you are no longer a

---

[723] *Darkness Visible* is a 1952 Christian appraisal of Freemasonry, written by Anglican cleric, Walton Hannah.

member of the Catholic Church). Not only have you left the Church, but you now declare it to be a false Church (just like other ex-Catholics). All throughout our book, we make the distinction between a Catholic who merely professes a heretical doctrine and someone, such as yourself, who has openly left the Church. [...]

Your false understanding of the Concilair Church is what has led you into your heresy. [...]

If you want help seeing your errors, let me know and I will help you. That is true charity on my part. WWIII is probably very close and your particular judgment could happen much sooner than you think. You don't want to go to your judgement as a public enemy of the Church, **which is what you are at the moment.** Hopefully you will humble yourself, repent of all your public crimes against the Faith, and beg God for the light to see your grave errors. I'll keep prayer that you do so.

14 10 2016

You lost your faith in the Church during its Passion, just as those of weak faith lost their faith in Christ during His. Due to your heretical ecclesiology, you are now a sworn enemy of the Church, and that is how you will be treated.

14 10 2016

No, it is you who are a public enemy of the Church. If you believe yourself justified in publicly vilifying a bishop [*i.e. Jorge Bergoglio*] that you believe is an enemy of the Church, how are we wrong for vilifying a priest who we believe is a public enemy of the Church? And you are, objectively speaking, a public enemy of the Church since you declare the true Church to be a false Church.

13 10 2016

Kramer,

You are a neophyte. If you read our book you would feel like a complete fool. And I noticed that you quoted the notorious Modernist Yves Congar and the Novus Ordo apologist, Steve Ray as your "authorities". Is that the best you could come up with? Probably so since you get your information from the internet. Who will you quote next? Hans Kung and Mark Shea?

From: John Salza — Subject: Re: Faith Heresy & Loss of Office — Sent: Friday, June 23, 2017 — 8:14

Exactly like the Sedevacantists, you continue your amateur approach by screaming that the loss of office is "ipso facto," "ipso jure," "automatic," and "per se," when a Pope "manifests that he knowingly rejects a truth of the faith that must be believed de fide." Sigh…We already know that this is what those in your sect believe. You are not telling us anything more than the Sedevacantists have been saying for 40 years.

The error of your position (among many others) is that you don't know if Pope Francis has "knowingly" rejected a dogma; you only presume it, based on his words and actions. But your presumption is insufficient, as all the theologians teach. This is why Cardinal Billot and the rest of the Church's real theologians teach exactly the opposite of you – that pertinacity is established only if the Pope were to renounce the Church as the RULE of faith by PUBLIC PROFESSION. You explicitly reject this unanimous opinion of the theologians.

You say heresy is established "by a public external act," but Cardinal Billot says heresy is NOT established "by those who indeed manifest their heresy by external signs." Again, he also requires a renunciation of the Magisterium as the RULE of faith by PUBLIC PROFESSION. You stand alone in disagreeing with Billot. You reject Billot's teaching by saying "it is not necessary that such a one explicitly reject the Church as the rule of faith," even though Cardinal Billot says "heresy by its nature REQUIRES departure from the RULE of the ecclesiastical magisterium."

We can't wait for your book to be finished. … We may even write a book contra your book, so make sure you actually address the issues that you have embarrassingly avoided in this exchange.

From: John Salza — Subject: Re: Faith Heresy & Loss of Office — Date: 23/06/2017 00:12

Your methodology and position is so foreign to Catholic teaching it is frightening. You repeatedly throw around quotes of speculative theology that say a manifest heretic loses his office ipso facto, and further claim that no judgment from authority is necessary, and yet you never address precisely how the guilt of manifest heresy is determined. Yet, your position is obvious – it is determined by your personal judgment of a person's words and actions, even if your judgment is contrary to the judgment of the Catholic Church. Utter and complete absurdity. This much is obvious to anyone with the sensus Catholicus. But let's further pinpoint your theological error. Like Fr. Cekada, you carefully avoid defining what you mean by "public formal heresy" because you don't want to be pinned down. But it is evident that by "public formal heretic" (or "manifest heretic") you mean a person who has manifested heresy by public, external actions, which then lead others, like yourself, to conclude that the person is not a Catholic and hence cannot hold office in the Church. If you disagree, then provide your definition. The error of your position is that such a person, who has manifested his heresy by public actions (and may even be a formal heretic in the internal forum), will only be considered an occult heretic unless his pertinacity is also public. "Public formal heresy" requires "public pertinacity." This is your key error, because pertinacity will considered public only if the person publicly renounced the Church as the infallible RULE of faith – either by publicly defecting from the Catholic religion, or publicly admitting that he knowingly and wilfully rejects a dogma of Faith. Pope Francis has done neither, and your private judgment – which is contrary to the public judgment of the Catholic Church – does not change that fact. Your crafty ambiguity and deceptive explanations never require that pertinacity be public, and that means that your use of "public formal heresy" is actually referring to "occult formal heresy," not "public formal heresy." This is the common teaching of all the theologians, including the great Thomist Cardinal Billot, who teaches that a public heretic is not a person who professes heresy externally by words and actions, but rather one who publicly renounces the RULE of the Church's Magisterium (again, which Pope Francis has not done). To be sure, you disagree with Cardinal Billot. You continually throw around the terms "manifest heretic" and "public formal heretic," but you don't ever define them. Nevertheless, your use of the terms differs from the meaning given to them by all the classical theologians, as we prove in our book. For example, in his classic book De Ecclesia Christi (1927):

"The notion of heresy, however, includes another element: departure from the social magisterium, which was divinely constituted to be the authoritative organ for the proposal of revealed truth in Christian society." […] "Now, heresy by its nature requires departure from the RULE of the ecclesiastical magisterium." […] "Heretics are divided into occult and notorious. Occult heretics are, in the first place, those who by a purely internal act disbelieve dogmas of faith proposed by the Church, and after that, those who do indeed manifest their heresy by external signs, but not by a public profession [i.e., departure from the

Magisterium as the rule of faith]. Among them, you will easily understand that many men of our times fall into the latter category—those, namely, who either doubt or positively disbelieve matters of faith, and do not disguise the state of their mind in the private affairs of life, but who have never expressly renounced the faith of the Church, and, when they are asked categorically about their religion, declare of their own accord that they are Catholics."

And the final nail in your coffin:

"…only the notorious are excluded [from the Church], and not the occult—among whom we must also number (as it seems to us) those who, sinning against the faith even externally, have never departed from the RULE of the Church's magisterium by a public profession."

So, you see Fr. Kramer, one can sin against the Faith externally, and manifest one's heresy externally, but he will not be considered a "public formal heretic" unless he openly leaves the Church by "departing from the RULE of the Church's Magisterium by PUBLIC PROFESSION" – something that you expressly deny. Because Pope Francis has not "publicly professedthat he is "departing from the rule of the Church's Magisterium," he is not a "public formal heretic."

You can no longer hide behind your ambiguous and undefined "public formal heretic" terminology, no matter how much fancy Latin you want to throw at us. We now know that a "public formal heretic" is one who has renounced the RULE of the Church's Magisterium by PUBLIC PROFESSION, WHICH POPE FRANCIS HAS NOT DONE. (If you want to see the Billot quotes in Latin, we will provide them to you. But that won't help you.)

From: John Salza — Date: 21/06/2017 23:32 — Subject: Re: Faith Heresy & Loss of Office

For a Pope to publicly defect from the Church, he would have to publicly renounce the Magisterium as the infallible rule of faith (and choose another rule, i.e., joining another religion). None of the conciliar Popes have done this, and thus they have not publicly defected from the Church according to the Church's judgment. Their material heresies, false worship and even public sins against the Faith do not constitute public defection from the Church. Indeed, the conciliar Popes may have spiritually severed themselves from the Church by the sin of heresy (which happens by the very nature of heresy), but they are not legally severed from the Church until the Church either (1) declares them guilty of heresy, or (2) they publicly defect from the Church (and note well that the 1983 Code of Canon law requires a canonical warning and a declaration by the Church externally recognizing the public defection has taken place). If the conciliar Popes are not legally severed from the Church, they retain their offices in the Church.

From: John Salza — Date:14/09/2016 — 03:22

You say: Red Herring Argument: The point at issue is not about warnings, but about the loss of office without any declaration or sentence by the Church -- the public heretic ceases to be pope and member of the Church BY HIMSELF (as Bellarmine says), "without any "declaration or sentence" (as Ballerini says).

JS: Your response proves that <u>you don't even understand our position</u>. WE DO NOT HOLD THAT A DECLARATORY SENTENCE IS REQUIRED FOR LOSS OF OFFICE! And yet you *continually* accuse us of this falsehood! Thus, it is you who uses straw men arguments and red-herrings, and you do so either out of profound ignorance or malice, God knows. You confuse the public judgment of pertinacity with a declaratory sentence of the crime, which shows you don't know the material. As I said in the last email, whether a declaratory sentence is required after the Church establishes the fact of public pertinacity is irrelevant. You are not making even the most basic, elementary distinctions. You are not capable of discussing the finer points of this theology because you don't even know the basics.

You say: When the pope falls into manifest heresy, he leaves the Church by himself and leaves the office he occupied in the Church and goes out.

JS: This is more petitio principii. Who establishes the FACT that "the Pope fell into manifest heresy" in the first place? People like you with no authority, who simply presumes it based on external words and actions (and whose judgment is contrary to what the Cardinals and bishops believe)? Your argument is the same as the Sedevacantists. You want to run to second base before you get to first base. Your argument regarding Francis is NO DIFFERENT than theirs regarding the other Popes.

You say: Warnings only verify the defection from the Church and loss of office that has already taken place.

JS: You can't be serious. "Warnings only verify the defection from the Church and loss of office"? Again, Fr. Kramer, are you serious? With all due respect, you cannot be this ignorant. Ballerini clearly says that the warnings PRECEDE the loss of office, since it's by VIRTUE of the warnings that pertinacity is ESTABLISHED (not before), by which the Pope THEN loses the office, the FACT (existence) of the heresy having been established by the Church.

From: John Salza — Date:13/09/2016 22:04 — Subject: Re: Salza's Colossal Blunder

The opinion of "the second Thomas" binds no one? The same can be said for any theologian you choose to erroneously interpret. None of them are "binding." Does your dismissal of JST [*i.e. John of St. Thomas*] mean you haven't read him and his treatment of dispositive vs. efficient cause, or that you reject his teaching? Have you even heard of it before I explained it to you? I doubt it.

You want to rely on Ballerini? Excellent. So do we, since his position is our position and refutes yours. Ballerini (who was an adherent of Bellarmine, unlike yourself) says that pertinacity is established publicly by the Church through ecclesiastical warnings. You conveniently omitted the entire teaching from Ballerini, and that is because Ballerini expressly REFUTES your position that, in the case of the "Pontiff," public pertinacity is not established by the Church (this is false). You operate just like a Sedevacantist.

TABLE OF CONTENTS

INTRODUCTION 5
JORGE BERGOGLIO IS THE SPARHEAD OF THE GREAT APOSTASY
  FORETOLD IN THE SECRET OF FATIMA 50
BERGOGLIO IS THE LEADER OF THE REVOLT 76
BERGOGLIO IS A FAITHLESS APOSTATE 78
"POPE" FRANCIS HAS OFFICIALLY APPROVED OF HOLY COMMUNION
  FOR PEOPLE LIVING IN ADULTERY 81
BERGOGLIO'S REFORM 90
JORGE BERGOGLIO'S RELIGION – FREEMASONIC NATURALISM 101
BERGOGLIO DENIES THE FIRST PRINCIPLE OF CHRISTIANITY – THE
  NECESSITY OF FAITH FOR JUSTIFICATION & SALVATION 102
JORGE BERGOGLIO IS THE SPARHEAD OF THE GREAT APOSTASY 105
PROLEGOMENON TO VOLUME ONE 126
DEFECTION FROM THE FAITH & THE CHURCH: FAITH, HERESY, AND
  LOSS OF OFFICE – AN EXPOSÉ OF THE HERESY OF JOHN SALZA &
  ROBERT SISCOE - PART ONE 205
SECTION ONE - FAITH, HERESY & LOSS OF OFFICE 205
SECTION TWO - HERETICS 345
PART TWO - THE FIRST PAPAL TEACHING ON A HERETIC POPE'S LOSS
  OF OFFICE 369
PART THREE - THE FIVE OPINIONS ON A HERETICAL POPE 388
SECTION ONE - THE FIVE OPINIONS 388
SECTION TWO COMMENTARY ON THE FIVE OPINIONS 392
SECTION THREE - ST. ROBERT BELLARMINE'S TREATMENT OF THE
  FIVE OPINIONS 441
PRELIMINARY REMARKS 441
ON OPINION NO. ONE: THE POPE CANNOT BE A FORMAL HERETIC .. 442
ON OPINION NO. TWO: THE POPE WHO IS VISIBLY ELEVATED TO THE
  PONTIFICATE BY MEN CANNOT BE INVISIBLY DEPOSED BY GOD .. 445
ON OPINION NO. THREE: A HERETIC POPE CAN BE JUDGED TO HAVE
  FALLEN FROM OFFICE: 1) A MANIFEST HERETIC FALLS FROM OFFICE
  BY HIS PUBLIC ACT OF DEFECTION; 2) A SECRET HERETIC IS JUDGED
  TO HAVE FALLEN FROM OFFICE ONCE THE HERESY IS PROVEN AND
  MADE MANIFEST 477
ON OPINION NO. FOUR: A MANIFEST HERETIC POPE CANNOT BE
  JUDGED AND DEPOSED BY THE CHURCH (*DEPONENDUS*) 486
BELLARMINE'S ARGUMENT 494
ON OPINION NO. FIVE: A MANIFEST HERETIC POPE CAN BE JUDGED
  TO HAVE ALREADY FALLEN FROM OFFICE BY HIS ACT OF MANIFEST
  HERESY (*DEPOSITUS*) 496
COMMENTARY 500
SALZA & SISCOE ON THE FIVE OPINIONS 511
CONCLUSION OF PART THREE 519

PART FOUR - THE DEPOSITION OF A POPE FOR HERESY	537
CAJETAN	541
SUÁREZ	551
JOHN OF ST. THOMAS	564
KEY TEXTS AND COMMENTARY	565
CONCLUSION	573
PART FIVE - FRAUD & SOPHISTRY THE PSEUDO-SCOLARSHIP OF JOHN SALZA & ROBERT SISCOE	579
SECTION ONE	579
SALZA & SISCOE FABRICATE A FRAUDULENT QUOTATION OF POPE ALEXANDER III	580
SALZA & SISCOE FRAUDULENTLY ALTER THE TEXT OF BALLERINI AND INVERT ITS MEANING	584
SALZA & SISCOE FRAUDULENTLY FABRICATE A TEACHING OF POPE ADRIAN VI	587
THE APOCRYPHAL "COUNCIL OF SINUESSA" AND THE SUPPOSED "FALL" OF POPE ST. MARCELLINUS	589
SALZA & SISCOE FRAUDULENTLY DOGMATIZE "COMMON OPINION"	591
SALZA & SISCOE FRAUDULENTLY ALTER MY MEANING AND FALSIFY MY WORDS	600
ROBERT J SISCOE'S CLUMSY ATTEMPT TO COVER UP HIS GRAVE ERRORS AGAINST THE CHURCH	606
SALZA & SISCOE DECLARE ON THE AUTHORITY OF THEIR OWN PRIVATE JUDGMENT THAT THOSE WHO BELIEVE THE APOSTOLIC SEE IS VACANT ARE IN HERESY	612
THE LATEST SALZA/SISCOE FRAUD	620
APPENDIX TO PART FIVE	628
SALZA & SISCOE FRAUDULENTLY CONCOCT A CASE OF HERESY AGAINST FR. KRAMER	628
REPLY TO JOHN SALZA PART III	639
EPILOGUE	659
SOME OF THE SOLEMN ANATHEMAS PRONOUNCED AGAINST ME VIA E-MAIL BY THE SUPREME SALZA-SISCOE INQUISITIONAL VIGILANTE TRIBUNAL	660

i The Ordinary and Universal Magisterium

A. Tanquerey, *A Manual of Dogmatic Theology*, transl. by Rev. Msgr. John J. Byrnes, Desclee, New York, 1959, pp. 176-182. All emphasis in the original.

Tract V, The Sources Of Revelation, Tradition, The Organs of Tradition.

B The Ordinary and Universal Magisterium of the Church.1

The *ordinary and universal* magisterium is that which is carried on daily through the continuous preaching of the Church among all peoples. It includes:

1. The preaching and proclamations of the Corporate Body of Bishops,
2. universal custom or practice associated with dogma,
3. the consensus or agreement of the Fathers and of the Theologians,
4. the common or general understanding of the faithful. 2

1. The Morally *Unanimous Preaching* (Teaching) of the Bishops

290 Bishops teach the flock entrusted and subject to them by means of catechisms, by synodal directives, mandates, and in public sermons. If it is evident from these documents that some doctrine is being set forth universally as an object of faith, then nothing else is required for this doctrine to be accepted de fide. Bishops spread throughout the world, but with the Roman Pontiff forming one Corporate Body, are infallible when declaring a teaching on faith or morals.

2. Practice of the Church Associated with Dogma

291 Among the customs and practices which have been closely joined to dogma we mention especially the public rites used in the solemn celebration of the sacrifice, or in the administration of the sacraments; also the formulas of prayers and various feasts or offices instituted by the Church; or sacred practices which have been associated with doctrine.

For a practice of the Church to become a criterion of faith there are two requirements:

a. that the practice be necessarily connected with the dogmatic truth; for in imposing a practice or custom, the Church by that very fact orders that dogmas connected with this practice must be adhered to;

b. that a custom of this kind be universal or approved at least tacitly by infallible authority; for only the *universal* Church enjoys infallibility. Therefore, a custom or practice of one particular Church produces only a probable argument for revealed truth. The *Roman Liturgy*, approved in a special manner by the Supreme Pontiffs, cannot contain errors in dogma. Historical mistakes can creep in, and, as a matter of fact, they have slipped into the legends in the Breviary, as the best critics admit. But this fact is easily understood because the special lessons of the Second Nocturns were written at a time when apocryphal works were being spread abroad. Nevertheless, these lessons should not be despised because many points contained in them are true and are suitable for fostering piety and goodness.

3. The Agreement of the Fathers and of the Theologians

a. The Authority of the Fathers

292 1. Who are the Fathers? The Fathers are those men, distinguished for their sanctity and their doctrine, who in the first centuries made the Church renowned by their writings, and who received full approbation from the Church, at least in an implicit manner. In order to recognize these men, we should look for four marks or signs: renowned and orthodox teaching, holiness of life, antiquity, and the approbation of the Church. Among the ecclesiastical writers some have been adorned with the title, Doctor of the Church, because they have surpassed others with their superior knowledge. Of these eight are the major Doctors of the Church, the others are called the minor Doctors.

293 2. Rules concerning the Authority of the Fathers.

a. Introductory notes. In order to make a study of the teaching of the Fathers, we must pay attention to the laws of historical criticism. We may consider the Fathers either as private doctors or as witnesses to the Church or to the faith.

1) They are regarded as private doctors when they reason and present their arguments in the manner of the philosophers, when they make use of analogies or comparisons, or propose their own opinion in such a way that they do not exclude the contrary opinion.

2) They speak as witnesses to the Church when they teach that a doctrine has been revealed, or has been accepted by the universal Church, or that a doctrine must be so held that it cannot be denied without the loss of faith or cannot be called into doubt. Similarly they speak as witnesses to the faith when they assert that a contrary opinion is heretical or opposed to the word of God.

If they speak as private doctors, their authority is only as great as is their knowledge or as is the force of their arguments; but if they speak as witnesses for the Church, they manifest not their own mind, but the faith of the infallible Church.

b. Rules to be followed:

1) The morally unanimous agreement of the Fathers declaring that a doctrine is de fide is a certain argument of divine Tradition. Three conditions are necessary that an argument be considered certain: that it relate to a doctrine pertaining to faith or morals; that the testimony be free of doubt, that it be firm and that the Fathers declare positively that the doctrine is a doctrine of the Church; that the agreement of the Fathers be not mathematically but morally unanimous. For in this way the faith or belief of the universal Church can be certainly known. With these conditions posited, it can be said that the Fathers record the teaching of the universal Church. But the Church is infallible in teaching Christ's doctrine.

Further, in order that an argument may be regarded as completely certain, *the moral unanimity of the Fathers of one age is required* and is sufficient.3 The Church at all times is indefectible and so in no age can it be guilty of error.

2) The *testimony of one Father or of many Fathers in matters of faith and of morals is a probable argument,* the force of which increases as the number and authority of the Fathers increase.

3) *When the Fathers disagree, then their authority offers no firm argument*; rather it proves that the matter on hand has not been explicitly defined; for if a matter had been clearly defined, then the Fathers could not have defended the contrary opinion without being condemned by the Church as heretics. If the disagreement is manifest, we must confess that certain Fathers have erred: for as individuals they are fallible. But if their words are doubtful, they must be explained by referring to subject matter which is clearer. In every case their words must be treated with respect; we must not attribute error to them because they have had no knowledge of the more explicit definitions of a following age.

b. The Authority of Theologians

294 After the Patristic age Theologians arranged in logical order the doctrines contained in Scripture and in Tradition and they explained these doctrines with the help of philosophical reasoning. These theologians can be considered as witnesses to the faith or as private doctors. They should not be esteemed lightly no matter what the Protestants, Modernists or other adversaries alleged against them.

In regard to their authority the following rules should he admitted:

1. When theologians unanimously teach that something is not only true but also that it must be accepted in Catholic faith, such consensus on their part presents a certain argument;

2. If all proclaim some doctrine in regard to faith and morals as true or certain, it is rash to reject this doctrine;

3. If there is a division of opinion among the different schools, even if the theologians of one school hold their opinion as certain or as very close to faith, no obligation exists of accepting such an opinion.

4. The Common Understanding of the Faithful

295 Revealed doctrine can be discovered not only among the Pastors and other leaders who teach with the Pastors, but also among the faithful who with a common or general understanding profess a unanimous faith.

In order that this common understanding be a criterion of revelation, it must be:

a. certain and clear,
b. unanimous,
c. concerned with important matters of faith and of morals.

The fact that the general agreement of the faithful is then a criterion of revelation is proved:

a. From the *indefectibility of the Church*. We have already stated that the Church cannot fail. But the Church would be failing in essentials if she were a society of erring souls. Therefore.

b. From the *Fathers*. For example, St. Augustine, in refuting the Pelagians, proved the existence of original sin in little children and the need, therefore, of baptism for these, from the common understanding of the faithful. This he regarded as a very strong argument of faith.

296 Other pertinent notes on this subject are these:

a. This infallibility in believing is often-times called passive infallibility; it depends on active infallibility (in teaching) which should always direct it.

b. We should avoid the error of those who think that the *Church teaching* merely confirms the opinions of the *Church learning*.4 For the *Church teaching* must pass judgment on these opinions, approve them or condemn them, and in this way direct the faith of her subjects and turn them from error.

c. Therefore, the faithful in the Church are in no way the teachers, they do not define authoritatively, but they give their belief. The Teachers impart and define the truth which all believe. But God is able to employ the faithful to promote some devotion, for example, the devotion to the Sacred Heart of Jesus; but even in such an instance all proceeds under the authority of the Bishops — they alone are the authoritative judges and proclaimers of the faith.

Notes:
1. VACANT, *La magistére ordinaire de l'Église et ses organes*.
2. We should note that the words: *Fathers, theologians*, and the *faithful* refer to the *Church Hearing*, not to the *Church Teaching*.
3. In this case the argument has force only for Catholics who admit the infallibility of the Church; but when the Fathers of different times and from different places agree on some dogma, then we have an apologetical argument for non-Catholics since it is evident from this argument that our faith is the same as the faith of the Apostles.
4. In the decree Lamentabili proposition 6a is condemned "The *Church learning* and the *Church teaching* collaborate in such a way in defining truths that it remains for the *Church teaching* only to sanction the Opinions of the Church learning". D.B., 2006.

[ii] Christopher Conlon quotes multiple authorities in his excellent article, *On the Admonitions of Titus 3:10: An analysis of Catholic history, laws, and teachings which illustrate the true nature of the "admonitions" referenced in Titus 3:10:"A man that is a heretic after, the first and second admonition avoid"* (pp. 4 -7)

«These admonitions or correptions must be given to such as err, by our spiritual governors and pastors, to whom if they yield not, Christian men must avoid them. (Rheims New Testament, p.549)

According to the original annotations of the Rheims NT, in St. Paul's Epistle to Titus, "he instructeth him, and in him all Bishops" (p.545), affirming that the purpose of the Epistle to Titus is to instruct the Church hierarchy. Then, in the specific annotation for Titus 3:10, it is explained that the admonitions mentioned therein are given by our "spiritual governors and pastors". If, after these admonitions, the heretic does not yield to our spiritual governors and pastors, then the faithful must avoid the heretic. Though a layman might attempt to admonish or instruct a heretic in some way, the Rheims New Testament annotation shows that the admonitions that could effectively result in having to avoid, or shun, a heretic are those that come from the authorities in the Church. The layman's admonition is obviously not the same as the admonitions of Church officials mentioned in Titus 3:10. Those admonitions of a layman, therefore, have no bearing on the instruction of Titus 3:10and who ought to be avoided. Though there may be other reasons to avoid a heretic, the instruction of Titus 3:10 does not oblige the faithful to avoid anyone if only a laymen has admonished them, since the passage is referring to authoritative, or official, admonitions. These official admonitions in Titus 3:10 are, in other words, canonical admonitions.

Canonical Admonitions

The only article of the Catholic Encyclopedia with the word "admonition" in the title, the 1907 article, Canonical Admonitions, defines these as, "A preliminary means used by the Church towards a suspected person, as a preventive of harm or a remedy of evil" (Burtsell). According to this article, an Instruction directed by Pope Leo XIII states that, "Among the preservative measures are chiefly to be reckoned the spiritual retreat, admonitions, and injunctions." This Instruction also says, "the canonical admonitions may be made in a paternal and private manner (even by letter or by an intermediary person), or in legal form, but always in such a way that proof of their having been made shall remain on record." It is then explained that these admonitions are founded, "after an investigation to be made by one having due authority, with the result of establishing a reasonable basis for the suspicion." The first admonition is a paternal admonition, by which "the prelate either personally or through a confidential delegate informs the suspected person of what has been said about him, without mentioning the source of information, and without threat, but urges amendment." If the paternal admonition, and other measures, are ineffective; then a legal admonition is resorted to, and this is, "to a great extent akin to the summons to judgment."

Canon 2143 of the 1917 Code of Canon Law prescribes the way in which admonitions are to be administered.

Admonitions, if necessary, may be made orally or in writing. If they are administered orally, this must be done by the Ordinary in the presence of the chancellor, or some other of-ficial of the diocesan court, or two witnesses. If by letter, the latter should be registered and receipted by the post office...

(Augustine, p.405. 1921)

That the admonitions mentioned in Titus 3:10 are canonical admonitions is obvious from the fact that, as was previously shown, St. Paul's Epistle to Titus, including the instruction in verse 3:10, was addressed to him in his capacity as a Church official. The 1910 Catholic Encyclopedia article on heresy also explains that this instruction to Titus was an early piece of legislation in regards to the way the Church dealt with and excommunicated heretics. The spirit which animates the dealings of the Church with heresy and heretics is one of extreme severity. St. Paul writes to Titus: "A man that is a heretic, after the first and second admonition, avoid: knowing that he, that is such a one, is subverted, and sinneth, being condemned by his own judgment" (Titus 3:10-11). This early piece of legislation reproduces the still earlier teaching of Christ: 'And if he will not hear the church, let him be to thee as the heathen and the publican' (Matthew 18:17); it also inspires all subsequent anti-heretical legislation. The sentence on the obstinate heretic is invariably excommunication. He is separated from the company of the faithful, delivered up 'to Satan for the destruction of the flesh, that the spirit may be saved in the day of our Lord Jesus Christ' (1 Corinthians 5:5).

(Wilhelm)

Affirming what the 1910 Catholic Encyclopedia article said above and further showing that the admonitions in Titus 3:10 are what would be called canonical admonitions, the 1932 book,The Delict of Heresy, by Rev. MacKenzie, states that St. Paul's order to Titus in this verse indicates part of a "more or less formal process of trial."

Paul's orders to Titus have already been quoted, requiring that there be a first and second warning, and then avoidance of the heretic. He also wrote to Timothy decreeing that there must be two witnesses before certain punishments be inflicted, and this text has been thought to indicate a more or less formal process of trial even in these earliest days of ecclesiastical organization.

(MacKenzie, p.4. 1932)

The following quotes also illustrate that the Church officials are those that determine, by their admonitions, who is to be avoided.

"A fortiori, therefore, must the faithful have been obliged to shun the company of those whom the Apostles found necessary to separate from the communion of the faithful."

(Excommunication. Francis Hyland, J.C.L., p.36. 1928)

"Those who voluntarily separate themselves from the Church are (a) heretics, i.e., those who profess a doctrine declared as heretical by the Church, and infidels, who entirely reject the Church's teaching. Fore whosoever publicly departs form the unity of the faith thereby ceases both inwardly and outwardly to belong to the Church. Therefore St. Paul admonishes the pastors of the Church: "A man that is a heretic after the first or second admonition, avoid" (Tit. iii. 10). If such a man still belonged to the fold the Apostle would not admonish the pastors to shun him."

(Handbook of the Christian Religion. Wilmers, Wilhelm, S.J., p.381. 1891)

"The heretic, St. Paul instructs Titus, shall be admonished a first and a second time of the grave character of his offense; if he will not heed, he must be avoided by Christians as a man in evident bad faith, who stands self-condemned... a heretic was a person who deliberately taught a doctrine he knew to be false, in contradiction of the infallible teaching of the Church. Heretics were consequently cut off from all association with the faithful, who must hold no relations with them so long as they obstinately refuse to heed the official remonstrances of the Church authorities."

(The American Catholic Quarterly Review, vol.24. "Church and State in the Fourth Century." Rev. Maurice M. Hassett, pp.301-302. 1909)

"The external enforcement of laws against heretics as heretics, always involves some judicial process. This process may have various stages, marked by the judicial sentences imposed: a declaratory sentence that excommunication has been incurred by a delict of heresy; a sentence of juridical infamy; deprivation of offices, benefices, etc.; deposition and degradation. The issuance of any of these sentences (save the declaratory sentence), requires canonical warnings and trials, with full observance of the criminal code in all details of the process." (The Delict of Heresy. Rev. Eric MacKenzie, A.M., S.T.L., J.C.L., p.98. 1932)

"And in matters spiritual, a bishop, by virtue of his office, is an inquisitor of the same kind. It is his duty, laid down in the plainest language of Holy Writ, to watch over those who are entrusted to his charge; and where he sees any going astray, to "reprove," to "rebuke sharply," and "with all authority," and if necessary, "after the first and second admonition to reject," that is, to cut off from the society of the church, or in other words, to excommunicate (2 Tim. iv, 2. Titus i, 13. ii, 15. iii, 10). This, I say, is contained in the very idea of a bishop, or overseer "of God's flock. He is bound to maintain the integrity of the faith, and to keep his people from being corrupted by teachers of false doctrines; and he has authority given him for this special purpose."

(The Catholic Missionary, "The Inquisition." Andrew Kim (first Korean-born Catholic priest), Martyred, p.5. 1853)

"Moreover, so far from wishing to tolerate such persons in the Church, St. Paul warns the faithful to avoid them (Romans 16:17), calls upon those who are set over Churches to cast out the recalcitrant heretic, as one who is "subverted and self-condemned" (Titus 3:10-11), and, in a particular instance, tells St. Timothy that he has "delivered" two such heretics "to Satan" — that is, cast them out of the Church — "that they may learn not to blaspheme" (1 Timothy 1:20)."

(The Catholic Encyclopedia. "Union of Christendom". Sydney Smith, S.J. 1912)

"Moreover, we determine to subject to excommunication believers who receive, defend or support heretics... If however, he is a cleric, let him be deposed from every office and benefice, so that the greater the fault the greater the punishment. If any refuse to avoid such persons after they have been pointed out by the Church [postquam ab ecclesia denotati fuerint], let them be punished with the sentence of excommunication until they make suitable satisfaction. Clerics should not, of course, give the sacraments of the Church to such pestilent persons nor give them a Christian burial..."

(Fourth Lateran Council, Constitution 3, On Heretics. Pope Innocent III. 1215)

The admonitions that Titus is instructed to give are clearly official admonitions, or those that come from a Church authority; and they relate to the Church's official process of excommunicating and separating heretics from the faithful. This fact is also drawn from the works of St. Thomas Aquinas.» (The author then presents the exposition of St. Thomas.)